12/21

Churchill's Shadow

Churchill's Shadow

The Life and Afterlife of Winston Churchill

GEOFFREY WHEATCROFT

W. W. NORTON & COMPANY
Independent Publishers Since 1923

For information about permission to reproduce selections from this book, write to
Permissions, W. W. Norton & Company, Inc., 500 Fifth Avenue, New York, NY 10110

For information about special discounts for bulk purchases, please contact
W. W. Norton Special Sales at specialsales@wwnorton.com or 800-233-4830

Manufacturing by Lakeside Book Company

Library of Congress Cataloging-in-Publication Data

Names: Wheatcroft, Geoffrey, author.
Title: Churchill's shadow : the life and afterlife of
Winston Churchill / Geoffrey Wheatcroft.
Description: First American edition. | New York : W. W. Norton & Company, 2021. |
Originally published: Churchill's shadow : an astonishing life and a dangerous
legacy. Great Britain : Bodley Head, 2021. | Includes bibliographical references
and index. Identifiers: LCCN 2021037032 | ISBN 9781324002765 (hardcover) |
ISBN 9781324002772 (epub)
Subjects: LCSH: Churchill, Winston, 1874–1965. | Prime ministers—
Great Britain—Biography. | Great Britain—Politics and government—20th century. |
Churchill, Winston, 1874–1965—Influence.
Classification: LCC DA566.9.C5 W44 2021 | DDC 941.084092 [B]—dc23
LC record available at https://lccn.loc.gov/2021037032

W. W. Norton & Company, Inc., 500 Fifth Avenue, New York, N.Y. 10110
www.wwnorton.com

W. W. Norton & Company Ltd., 15 Carlisle Street, London W1D 3BS

1 2 3 4 5 6 7 8 9 0

To the memory of my father, Stephen Wheatcroft, Sub-Lieutenant Royal Naval Volunteer Reserve, Fleet Air Arm pilot in HMS Indomitable *1943–45;*

and of his brother, Albert Wheatcroft, Flight Sergeant, Royal Air Force Volunteer Reserve, 455 Squadron Coastal Command, killed 24 May 1943;

and of my mother, Joy Reed Wheatcroft, personnel manager, Hoover munitions factory 1943–45;

and of her brothers, Geoffrey Reed, Lieutenant Royal Engineers, Prisoner of War in North Africa, April 1941, and Robert Reed, Lance-Sergeant, Royal Artillery 7 Commando, Prisoner of War in Crete, May 1941;

and of my wife's father, Frank Muir, Aircraftman First Class, Royal Air Force 1940–45;

and of his wife, Polly McIrvine Muir, Wren, Women's Royal Volunteer Service 1943–45;

and of her sister, Sister Isabella IBVM, ambulance driver in London, 1940;

and of her brother, Brian McIrvine, Lieutenant, Seaforth Highlanders, Prisoner of War at St Valery, May 1940;

and of all who served in Churchill's war.

If we open a quarrel between the past and the present, we shall find that we have lost the future.

Winston Churchill, May 1940

Who controls the past controls the future; who controls the present controls the past.

George Orwell, *Nineteen-Eighty-Four*, 1949

The victor will never be asked if he told the truth.

Adolf Hitler, September 1939

Contents

Churchill's Shadow

6-II-'64.   Juliet Pannett.

Prologue: 'This little place'
House of Commons 1963

A hush fell as he entered the chamber in a wheelchair and took his seat, not on the Treasury Bench where he had sat as prime minister at an exalted moment in his country's history, but in another hallowed place below the gangway, from where he had once delivered his warnings about the threat from Adolf Hitler, and before that about the threat from Mohandas Gandhi. Sir Winston Churchill had sat in the House since the beginning of the century, but hadn't spoken for some years, was visibly frail, and may not have properly followed proceedings: by now more sacred talisman than elder statesman.

That day in the summer of 1963 was the one occasion when I ever saw Churchill plain and close at hand. I was a schoolboy absorbed by politics, and a friend's father, a Labour Member of Parliament, had given me a pass to the gallery of the House of Commons. For all that he was aged and infirm, I was glad to have seen him for myself, and to have seen him where I did. 'This little place,' Churchill had once said, 'is what makes the difference between us and Germany.' He was talking to another MP as they left the darkened chamber late one night in 1917, but he might have used the same words still more truly in 1940: 'This little room is the shrine of the world's liberties.' He left Parliament at last the year after I saw him, and died only months later, in January 1965 aged ninety, as if the last drop of political lifeblood had been drained from him when the initials 'MP' no longer stood after his name.

This book is an attempt to make sense of the man I saw that day long ago; to look hard at his reputation during his lifetime, and his influence since he died; to make a reckoning with his life and with his legacy, the long shadow he still casts; and to understand what he really meant to his contemporaries, and what he means to posterity. When I saw Churchill, no reminder was needed of how much he had loomed over our lives; what I couldn't have guessed then was how large he would still loom so long after his death – and yet how hard to grasp the reality of Churchill it would still be.

A few things should be said. 'Far too much has been and is being written about me,' Churchill sarcastically observed – and that was the best part of a hundred years ago, when he little guessed how much more, enormously more, would be written about him, not least by himself. Any writer might hesitate before adding to the huge corpus, or at least try humbly to explain himself if he does so. First of all, this book is not in any way a conventional biography. 'A shilling life will give you all the facts,' said Auden, and the official life of Churchill, begun by his errant son Randolph and completed by the late Sir Martin Gilbert, while costing a good deal more than a shilling, gives you many of the facts, though by no means all.

But then that's only part of the story. 'The posthumous life of Winston Churchill is one of the most remarkable phenomena of the post-Churchillian age and might serve as the subject for a book in itself,' the eminent American historian of modern England Peter Stansky wrote – as long ago as 1974, on the occasion of Churchill's centenary, less than ten years after his death! Nearly fifty years later, as we approach his sesquicentenary, Churchill's posthumous life has become a far more remarkable phenomenon. At one time I thought of writing a book to examine that afterlife, the scholarly and political debates over his reputation, his representation or misrepresentation in popular culture, 'Churchillism' in England, and the truly extraordinary growth of the Churchill cult in America. But I found it impossible to explain that without looking back at his life. Even then, to do so in a comparatively short compass might have a ring of Monty Python's 'summarise Proust' competition, but I emphasise that this is not a 'Life and Times'.

As far as possible I've tried to write as what Keynes called 'the historian of Opinion', seeing Churchill through the eyes of his contemporaries, and keeping in mind F.W. Maitland's rule: 'It is hard to think away out of our minds a history which has long lain in a remote past but which once lay in the future.' Events must be understood according not to how they turned out, but to how men at the time expected them to turn out: a principle which applies to Churchill's career more than most. And while I haven't tried to imitate the fashionable cinematic technique of non-linear narrative, since I'm not constrained by a month-by-month, year-by-year account, I've sometimes taken episodes out of sequence with flashbacks, and my lens has sometimes panned round a wider field, or zoomed in for close-ups of critical moments.

This has allowed me to dwell on certain passages or controversies in Churchill's career which have a particular resonance to this day: his imperial and racial attitudes; his belief in 'the English-speaking races' (later 'peoples') and their supposed unity, particularly in the form of an Anglo-American 'special relationship'; his strategical ambitions, obsessions and follies; his dealings with Ireland; his support for Zionism; his confused and conflicted attitude towards the bombing of cities and civilians; his complicated engagement with European integration and with what part, if any, the British should play in it; and, far from least, the legacy to this day of what he so dubiously called his 'wilderness years' and his critique of appeasement and the Munich agreement.

Part of the problem may be the sheer vastness of Churchill's life. He was born less than ten years after an American Civil War which would endlessly fascinate him, fought in a country he would visit for the first of many times at the age of twenty, and which would play a large part in his life, long before he was adopted there as a national hero and made an honorary citizen, in a ceremony which took place almost exactly on the centenary of Gettysburg. Or again, he was born four years after the Franco-Prussian war, whose sequel would dominate much of his life; he played a leading part in two more wars between Germany and France, but lived to see that 're-creation of the European family' based on a 'partnership between France and Germany' of which he had dreamed in 1946, if not quite the 'United States of Europe' he also advocated.

He rode in a cavalry charge in 1898; he lived to control atomic bombs. He celebrated his twenty-first birthday in 1895 while witnessing a patriotic rebellion in Cuba; he approached his eighty-eighth birthday as the world was nearly plunged into nuclear war over Cuba. He was elected to Parliament in the reign of Queen Victoria; he was prime minister to greet a new young queen fifty-one years later. He was appointed a Parliamentary Under-Secretary aged thirty-two in December 1905; he resigned as prime minister aged eighty in April 1955, the longest such ministerial span in British political history. The scope of his story is still hard to grasp.

Then again, this is not a hostile account, or not by intention, nor consciously 'revisionist' or contrarian, except to the extent that any history worth reading must in some way revise what has gone before, and maybe also that I have a contrary nature. 'Alternative' might be a better word for my approach. 'The English-speaking peoples seem to have a settled view of Churchill's glory which no amount of historical debate will now alter,' his admiring biographer Andrew Roberts has confidently asserted. But do they, or should they? There was no 'settled view' of him during most of his lifetime, and controversy follows him to this day, as numerous episodes in recent years have shown.

Over the past thirty years, since the heavy hand of the official biographer was lifted from Churchill's archive, there has been a great flowering of serious Churchillian studies, which has opened many new perspectives on his life and conduct, some of them far from flattering. It's significant that the best of those books have been on specific aspects of his career: Churchill and domestic politics, Churchill and Empire, Churchill and America, Churchill and Ireland, Churchill and Zionism, Churchill as war leader, Churchill and the Bengal famine, Churchill and his war cabinet, Churchill and the writing of *The Second World War*, Churchill as rhetorician, Churchill as writer, Churchill and Lloyd George, Churchill and Attlee, Churchill and Roosevelt, Churchill and Orwell, Churchill and his son, Churchill and his money, Churchill and his horses, Churchill and his cook. Even others have to be seen in his shadow, so that a biography of the great union leader who became a central figure in Churchill's wartime government and then a famous Foreign Secretary is called *Ernest Bevin: Labour's Churchill*. And yet with all those books, and even now, so long after his death, the political historian Vernon Bogdanor has said plausibly that the definitive biography of Churchill is still to seek.

A photograph taken in the south of France in 1937 shows Churchill standing between the seated figures of two of the few writers of the age even richer and more successful than himself, Somerset Maugham and H.G. Wells. And it was Wells who once said that an ideal biographer would be 'a conscientious enemy'. He meant that a hero-worshipper would be blinded by devotion to his subject, in a way that might even provoke adverse reaction in an uncommitted reader. That's indeed true of Churchill's own fiercely partisan biographies of his father Lord Randolph Churchill and his forebear the first Duke of

Marlborough, and even truer of Churchill's many biographers, or hagiographers. 'Speak of me as I am; nothing extenuate,' said Othello, and yet many hero-worshippers have extenuated lengthily and evasively, on everything from Churchill's racism to his drinking, to the extent that he may even have suffered more from worshippers than from detractors.

In November 1940, Churchill gave one his greatest and most moving speeches, if now too little remembered, his elegy for Neville Chamberlain, who had died of cancer only six months after he resigned as prime minister. It was a very difficult speech for Churchill, after his sustained criticism of Chamberlain's policy only two years earlier, but he handled this in masterly fashion, praising Chamberlain for his sincerity and his honourable hopes for peace, 'the most noble and benevolent instincts of the human heart'. After dictating the speech to his secretary, he said slyly, 'Of course, I could have done it the other way round.' But then that's true of almost any story, not least Churchill's own. 'Give me the facts, Ashley,' he once said to a research assistant with wilful naughtiness, 'and I will twist them the way I want to suit my argument.' I trust that I haven't twisted any facts, but I'm telling a story, and I could have 'done it the other way round'.

At the same time, with all his immense renown, Churchill remains in some ways a mystery. He was the most famous man of his century, but one of the most elusive. We seem to know everything about him, and nothing. We know his quips and quirks, we know about his cigars and his champagne, his dragon dressing gown, his silk underwear, his velvet siren suits and his innumerable hats, his paintings, his pigs and his budgerigars. But do we know his inner essence? Books have been written about the meaning of Hitler,* but what was the meaning of Churchill – or the reality?

'You know Winston has become a legend,' Churchill's wife said to his doctor in 1957, and many years later Umberto Eco was amused by a poll which found that more than a fifth of British children thought that 'Winston Churchill' was a fictional character. But Clementine spoke more truly than she knew, and those children weren't entirely wrong. A *legenda* was originally the life of a saint, and one later definition of 'legend' is 'an inauthentic story handed down by tradition

---

* *Anmerkungen zu Hitler* by Sebastian Haffner, 1978, translated as *The Meaning of Hitler*, 1979.

and popularly regarded as historical'; not a bad description of the Churchill the world knows. He's part of our mental furniture, but in the same way that a fictional character is: part-Prince Hal and part-Falstaff, part-Sydney Carton and part-Mr Pickwick, part-Ben Ritchie-Hook and part-Ivor Claire. He has become a fabulous personage, like King Arthur or Robin Hood, who stands outside formal historical narrative and eludes it. When Sir Nicholas Soames was a little boy he went into his grandfather's bedroom and asked, 'Grandpa, is it true that you're the greatest man alive?' to be told, 'Yes it is. Now bugger off.' In a sense he has been saying that to all of us ever since, daring us to challenge the verdict.

'Such is the admiration for him, especially in the United States,' Wm. Roger Louis of the University of Texas and the late Robert Blake of Oxford, observed in 1993, 'that it sometimes seems difficult to separate the legendary figure from the man.' They might have added that by now the mythologising has gone beyond a point where such separation can be easily effected. The line at the end of *The Man Who Shot Liberty Valence* – 'When the legend becomes fact, print the legend' – has been the guiding principle for depictions of Churchill in popular culture. If you go to a movie called *Lincoln,* it will be sentimental and reverential in the Spielberg manner, but will stick quite close to historical truth; if you go to a movie called *Churchill,* or *Darkest Hour,* it will be a travesty or fantasy unrelated to reality, and no one minds. And the myth-making – the transformation of flesh and blood into legendary 'Churchill' – was begun by himself. He was acclaimed as a new Caesar, a man who not only made history but wrote it; one might say rather that he remade history and rewrote it. His books are more than merely partisan, and sometimes frankly deceptive; they were all part of his wilful creation of a personal romance, or legend, and in the end more than that.

'What I've hoped to do,' said Joe Wright, the director of *Darkest Hour,* 'is reclaim the man from the icon,' in which case he conspicuously failed. 'Icon' or 'iconic' have become tiresome vogue words, along with 'totem' and 'totemic', but they really do apply to Churchill. He has long since been a totem, like the poles that the indigenous Haida and Tlingit peoples of the American north-west worshipped; and at the time of the invasion of Iraq, he was well-nigh borne aloft, like the icons or sacred images once held up before the Tsar's army as they marched to war, and too often to death and defeat.

But then, icons or portraits of Churchill – photographs, paintings, sculptures, cartoons, posters, even figurines and Toby jugs – had made his appearance familiar from a very early age, and even now they're everywhere. A portrait photograph as a tiny boy shows him looking girlish, with long ringlets and a lace collar in the manner of the age. Then he was clad in a sailor suit, and went on to wear a dark coat and straw hat at Harrow as well as the uniform of the school Rifle Corps. At nineteen a formal portrait photograph has him wearing the magnificent full-dress uniform of the 4th Hussars (and wearing as well the 'sneer of cold command'), before he's seen on horseback in tropical khaki.

Entering the political fray, he could be addressing an election crowd from the top of a van in Manchester in 1908, or clad in astrakhan-lined greatcoat and tall silk hat beside the Guardsmen and armed policemen at the siege of Sidney Street in 1911. Even then he was still often in uniform; sometimes with a Privy Councillor's feathered hat, sometimes the tunic of the Royal Oxfordshire Hussars with whom he continued to train each summer while he was a Cabinet minister. By 1915 we see him in the trenches, wearing infantryman's khaki under a long shiny waterproof coat, and a French *poilu*'s helmet – always the distinguishing touch – which he alone of British officers on the Western Front had borrowed. To make the point, he was photographed in December 1915 wearing that helmet alongside General Fayolle, Commander of the French 333rd Corps.

In the next war, when he was the only prime minister, in a line which included the Duke of Wellington, ever to wear uniform while in office, he would sometimes be clad in the pale blue of an honorary Royal Air Force commodore, or the dark blue of the honorary colonel of the 4th Hussars, or the nautical rig he wore when meeting President Roosevelt at Placentia Bay in 1941, which was not, as one American popular historian had it, 'the mess jacket of the Royal Yacht Squadron', to which he never belonged, but the apparel of an Elder Brother of Trinity House.* Some images pleased him more than others. He delighted in one 1940 photograph of him at his cheekiest, fondling a

---

* This admirable long-established institution administers lighthouses and other navigational aids, and its Brethren are persons of eminence; Churchill once explained to a French visitor, 'Je suis un Frère Aîné de la Trinité,' and was congratulated on this high connection.

tommy gun while he grins through his clenched cigar. In another image from that summer he appeared gazing resolutely ahead, a flight of aircraft above him, captioned with his words 'Let Us Go Forward Together', on a famous poster which would have a later career all of its own. But the 1941 portrait photograph by Karsh of Ottawa which now adorns the five pound note seems sententious, the jaw jutting a little too deliberately, the defiant glare a touch too blatant.

At a moment during the Great War when his fortunes had fallen very low, Churchill took up painting as a consoling recreation, but well before then others had painted him. He was painted in Dublin at the age of four and then around 1900, when he was still in his mid-twenties, Edwin Ward pictured him pensive at his desk, while the caricaturist 'Spy' caught him in a way that seems truer to life, legs asplay and hands on hips, with a faintly sarcastic smile on his lips. Sir John Lavery painted him in 1916 in that *poilu*'s helmet, but Lavery had also painted him just before this, as had Sir William Orpen, both catching him in melancholy mood at the moment his political career seemed finished. A portrait commission for the National Liberal Club was the first to be suppressed, or removed from display, when Churchill deserted Asquith. Ten years later he was painted by Walter Sickert, and ten years after that Sir William Nicholson painted an informal conversation piece of the Churchills taking tea at Chartwell. At the height of his fame, portraits were commissioned by the Carlton Club and by the House of Commons. The latter was the most famous, or notorious, of all – Graham Sutherland's portrait given to Churchill on his eightieth birthday, which Clementine hated so much that she later destroyed it.

Then there were the sculptures. His head was twice sculpted in 1942, by his cousin Clare Sheridan – a remarkable if ill-starred woman, who had briefly been infatuated with Bolshevism, and was certainly the only artist to portray Churchill as well as Lenin and Trotsky, as she had done while visiting Russia after the revolution – and by Sir William Dick Read, whose bust, now in the Imperial War Museum, has Churchill wearing his defiant scowl. Most famous is the 1946 bust by Jacob Epstein, different casts of which have stood on and off in the White House and have been the subject of endless controversy. Besides the large statue in Parliament Square, which was daubed by demonstrators in the summer of 2020, there are many others. At his old house of Chartwell, Churchill squats beside Clementine, above the caption 'Married Love'; a replica of this statue can be found in a shopping plaza in Kansas City. That's almost rivalled as kitsch by a double statue on the pavement at the bottom of Bond Street, where he and Roosevelt sit on a bench chaffing and laughing together. And he also now gazes over Jerusalem, and for no obvious reason over New Orleans beside the Riverfront Hilton.

If the world was conscious of Churchill's appearance, that was his doing, or at least his wish. From an early age, as he admitted himself, he wanted to be conspicuous in the front line, skirmishing on horseback on the Afghan frontier, or provoking his opponents in Parliament, but always recognisable. In an essay on political cartoons, he said that 'One of the most necessary features of public man's equipment is some distinctive mark which everyone learns to look for and recognise. Disraeli's forelock, Mr Gladstone's collars, Lord Randolph Churchill's moustache, Mr Baldwin's pipe – these "properties" are of the greatest value. I have never indulged in any of them, so to fill the need cartoonists have invented the legend of my hats.'

But he did 'indulge a prop', or more than one. A sarcastic observer said in 1940 that he was much the same as other politicians 'except that his hats are supposed to be funny', and they were certainly numerous and distinctive, from the *poilu*'s helmet to the nautical cap to the curious hat he took to wearing in London between the wars, a cross between a top hat and a bowler.* And another prop was his cigar. Having confirmed the habit of smoking Havanas while visiting Cuba, he was smoking ten a day as a young politician (which meant that he spent on cigars alone more than a labourer earned), and by his years of greatest fame he was never seen without one.

By then he was the cartoonists' delight, captured particularly well on many occasions by David Low of the *Evening Standard*, most famously just after the 1945 election, of 'Two Churchills': the grumpy, arms-folded 'Party Leader', despondent and sour after his rout at the polls, and then atop a plinth, 'The Leader of Humanity', looking much more cheerful and, of course, flourishing a cigar, as he tells the other, 'Cheer up! They will forget *you*, but they will remember *me* always.' Photographs, paintings and sculptures would be followed by movies and television, rather slowly at first but in the end a torrent. However good, or more often bad, they were, they were apt: Churchill loved

---

* Was it the '*Daily Mail* hat' which that newspaper tried not very successfully to promote?

performance, on stage and then on screen, and saw public life as a great drama, with himself of course in the lead.

That drama has itself been revised and distorted, and has transcended serious historical discussion. How many people who saw *Darkest Hour*, how many viewers of television dramas about Churchill, how many members of Churchill Societies, how many of those who buy popular biographies, have read, or are even aware of a book published in 1932 called *The Tragedy of Winston Churchill*? American devotees will lap up a book called *Churchill: A Study in Greatness*, but how many have read an excellent book published in 1970 called *Churchill: A Study in Failure*?

That book told the story of his career until 1939, and cast a sharp light on any idea of his inexorable 'destiny' to become a great leader. Had he been killed at Omdurman in 1898 he wouldn't even merit a footnote, and had he been killed on the Western Front in 1916 he would be known, like Haldane or McKenna, only to more serious students of early twentieth-century British political history. But if he had been killed by the van that knocked him down on Fifth Avenue in 1931, or even if he had died as late as the New Year of 1939, he would, as Paul Addison says, 'perhaps be remembered today as the most illustrious and interesting failure in twentieth-century British politics'. Certainly until his apotheosis he was more often seen as an 'interesting failure' than as the subject for a study in greatness.

One of his more entertaining books (although not his unaided work) was the collection of pen-portraits published in 1937 as *Great Contemporaries*. They include Bernard Shaw, and a question a critic once asked of Shaw might be applied to Churchill also: He was a great something, but a great what?

Was he a great politician? His own contemporaries rarely thought so, at least until his apotheosis. Was he a great democrat? His saying that democracy is the worst possible system apart from all the others has become one of the most hackneyed of all Churchillian saws, but we shall see that his attitude to democracy was complicated and compromised. Was he a great strategist? *The World Crisis*, his ostensible history of the Great War, is a lengthy defence of his own dubious record in that war, and almost an advertisement for his own strategic brilliance; it took another war in which he led his country to demonstrate how limited he was as a strategist, or even how little he properly understood modern war.

Was he then a great writer? This Nobel laureate was acclaimed as one in his time, and he wrote fluently, prolifically and readably, with a real gift of self-expression, while making himself what Evelyn Waugh called 'a master of sham-Augustan prose'. But after around 1930 any assessment of him as a writer has to begin by establishing what proportion of the books or journalism, appearing under his name was actually written by him. And even at his best and most personal, he was incapable of writing history with any degree of detachment.

But surely he was a great prophet? This is at the heart of his self-created legend, the lone voice in the wilderness before the war, who told an American audience in 1946, 'I saw it all coming and cried aloud to my own fellow-countrymen and to the world, but no one paid any attention,' while claiming that the war 'could have been prevented in my belief without the firing of a single shot'. On close examination these claims are at best highly speculative.

For all that, Churchill was without doubt a great survivor, and a wonderfully successful story-teller. And that is at the heart of this book. 'I had a good tale to tell,' he said, looking back at his speeches and broadcasts in the first months of the war, and his whole life was spent telling stories, unsuccessfully until 1940, compellingly thereafter. After victory five years later he was *In Command of History,* the title of David Reynolds's outstanding book about the writing of *The Second World War,* and he has largely remained in command ever since.

That helps to explain why his afterlife has been as remarkable as his own long life. It was scarcely surprising that he was *Time's* Man of the Year for 1940, or acclaimed five years later as 'The Leader of Humanity', or seemed by the time of his death the most famous person in the world, or was later dubbed 'Man of the Century'. Maybe it was inevitable that a poll in his own country in 2002 would consider him the Greatest Briton, and that he would later grace British banknotes. Less easy to foresee was the full degree to which, nearly six decades after his death, he would still dominate his country's consciousness, a country whose later history has been called a footnote to Churchill, or that he would be endlessly invoked by American politicians and publicists, while shrines and sectaries devoted to his memory would spring up, in England and all across America.

Whether this Churchillian obsession, or 'Churchillism', has been healthy or fruitful is another matter. Early in the last century the

Italian prime minister Giovanni Giolitti spoke revealingly of 'beautiful national legends' which sustain a country (and which he didn't want undermined by allowing inquisitive scholars into the archives). How Churchill created a beautiful national legend of his own, and became one himself, is a central part of our story. 'His life stopped in 1940,' says Hester in Terence Rattigan's play *Flare Path*, about her sodden, faithless lover, a former fighter pilot. 'He loved 1940, you know. There were some like that.' Winston Churchill was like that. Although it would be too much to say that his life stopped that year, he said that '1940 was the best', and it was the best for him, his personal finest hour which would sustain him – and beguile his country – ever after. He led the British nobly and heroically during one of the great crises of history, and has misled them ever since, sustaining the country with beguiling illusions of greatness, of standing unique and alone, while preventing the British from coming to terms with their true place in the world.

'Men run with great avidity to give their evidence in favour of what flatters their passions and national prejudices,' David Hume told Edward Gibbon. 'Churchillism' has been a prolonged exercise in flattering passions and prejudice, those of his own country but those of his mother's country also: before his apotheosis in 1940, Churchill had become a widely published, and very highly paid, journalist and author, in America as well as England, although that didn't mean that he was universally popular with those Americans, high or low, who were aware of him. He had rediscovered America during his visit in 1929, and increasingly came to see the Americans as cousins, friends and instinctive allies of the British, a view which was partly inspired by his own literary and financial career. The belief was quite false at the time he conceived it, and would feed many illusions before, during and after the World War.

Even after the United States had belatedly and involuntarily entered that war, and then after the final victory, considerable suspicion of Churchill persisted among some Americans. Books severely critical of his conduct were published by American authors who included, most painfully, the president's own son Elliott Roosevelt; Churchill's monumental six volumes of *The Second World War* were, among other things, an answer to those critics. But quite soon American attitudes towards Churchill changed. Once he had been ejected by the British electorate at the moment of victory, observers noticed that he might be more popular across the Atlantic than in his own country.

After John Kennedy was inaugurated in 1961, 'Churchillolatry' grew immeasurably. He was the first president to invoke Churchill's name – perhaps significantly, he was also the first president in nearly thirty years who had never worked with him – and it was at his bidding that Churchill was made an honorary American citizen. Almost every president since Kennedy has followed his reverential allusion to the great name, which was ever more insistently cited by American politicians and publicists, at least as often as the names of Washington or Franklin Roosevelt. Ronald Reagan mentioned Churchill in his first inaugural speech, kept a 1940 poster of him in the Situation Room at the White House, and filled his administration with votaries of the cult. Even that was surpassed by the endless Churchillian invocations of George Bush the Younger.

By now Churchill was on his way to becoming not only an honorary citizen but well-nigh an honorary president, an ethereal presence on Mount Rushmore. He was mysteriously assimilated by Americans as one of their own and, as Sir Michael Howard said, seen by them as an ultimate hero and oracle, 'surpassing any comparable American figure in his goodness and greatness'. This reached a crescendo as the 11 September outrage was followed by a campaign in Afghanistan, a country where Churchill once fought, and with the invasion of Iraq, a country he largely invented. Along with his name, 'Munich' and 'appeasement', which he had turned into curses, were all too often shouted by American politicians and journalists in empty and ignorant fashion.

And so my title has a double meaning: the darker side of his character and career, too often brushed over, and the long shadow which he has cast since his death. And if I make much of Churchill's failures and follies, that's partly because others have made too little of them since his rise to heroic status. Harsh words about him will be found in these pages, but the harshest come from his contemporaries. And if I've stressed the dislike and distrust he inspired through much of his life, that's with a purpose.

At the heart of any discussion is Churchill's apotheosis in 1940. Lord Randolph Churchill's description of Disraeli's career, 'Failure, failure, failure, partial success, renewed failure, ultimate and complete triumph,' could to some extent be applied to Lord Randolph's son.

Churchill's life until the age of sixty-five had certainly been a dramatic roller-coaster ride of highs and lows, or a game of Snakes and Ladders, with each ascent up a ladder followed by a precipitous fall, until that ultimate and complete triumph.

A more serious contention turns on that word 'destiny'. In a haunting passage, Churchill said that at the moment he was appointed prime minister 'I felt that I was walking with destiny, and all my life had been but preparation for that hour', hence the title of Andrew Roberts's biography, *Churchill: Walking With Destiny*, implying that because something happened it had to happen. By contrast, the title of Paul Addison's brilliant short biography *Churchill: the Unexpected Hero* rightly challenges any idea of inexorable 'destiny'. One may think that Churchill's accession to power in May 1940 was providential, as I do myself, but it was also astonishing, and in no way whatever pre-ordained.

My difficulty might be further explained by the responses of two celebrated English writers following Churchill's death in January 1965. Months later, A.J.P. Taylor published his very popular book *English History 1914–1945*, in which a biographical footnote on Churchill ended with the simple sentence, 'The saviour of his country.' But at the time of the funeral, Evelyn Waugh had told his friend Anne Fleming (widow of the writer Ian) that Churchill's death had left him unmoved: 'Always in the wrong, always surrounded by crooks, a most unsuccessful father.' My problem, that's to say, is that I think they were both right! Churchill *was* the saviour of his country. And he *was*, if not always, then far too often in the wrong. He was also a very poor judge of character who over the years surrounded himself with a crew whom indulgent biographers like to call buccaneers or adventurers, but for whom 'crooks' is scarcely too strong. As for 'unsuccessful father', that's all too tragically true, as the fates of three of Churchill's four children attest, all of them leading lives clouded by amorous and alcoholic turbulence or worse.

These difficulties were grasped by a great historian already mentioned. In 1940, Michael Howard was a schoolboy and three years later he was a subaltern in the Coldstream Guards, with whom he won the Military Cross at Salerno, before in the fullness of time he entered academic life, wrote an unsurpassed account of *The Franco-Prussian War* and several volumes on Churchill's war, became Regius Professor of Modern History at Oxford and professor at Yale, was knighted and, well before his death in 2019 on the day after his ninety-seventy birthday, was honoured as one of the two dozen holders of the Order of Merit. A half century after the Finest Hour, this grand old soldier and scholar put it briskly: 'The problem for the historian, is not, as so many Americans believe, '– and have been encouraged to believe by doting biographers –' why Churchill's advice was ignored for so long, but how it was that a man with so unpromising a background and so disastrous a track record could emerge in 1940 as the saviour of his country.'

That is the problem this book addresses. As Howard went on: 'His arrogance, his egocentricity, his flamboyance, his emotionalism, his unpredictability, his remorseless energy, not least his eccentric taste in friends and generous indulgence in drink made him an outsider to the British "establishment" from the moment he entered politics at the beginning of the century until the day in May 1940 when they turned to him in despair because there was no one else to whom they could turn.' And yet that acute assessment has quite escaped public consciousness.

So has something else. Churchill brilliantly created a legend of himself as the man who 'saw it all coming' before 1939. He taught the terrible lesson of 'Munich', which could be invoked as warning, and guide. And yet on every occasion when action has been informed by the fear of appeasement or the ghost of Munich, woeful failure has followed, from Korea to Suez to Vietnam to Iraq and much more besides. Some American politicians like to say that they address any problem with the question, 'What would Jesus do?', although a detached reading of the Gospels doesn't suggest that they are a sure guide to everyday political action. 'What would Winston do?' is no better. If Churchill was such an oracle of wisdom, why has his shadow fallen over so many disasters?

This is also inescapably a personal book, because of who and what and when and where I was and am. I'm an early boomer, born two days before Christmas 1945. My conception the previous March when my father was on leave from the Royal Navy was an expression of hope, a mood of optimism strengthened, while my mother was bearing me, by the victories over Germany and Japan, as well as, for my parents and so many others of their age, by that other great victory, of Attlee and Labour over Churchill and the Tories in the general election.

For those of us born after it, the war – and 'the war' for us always meant the one which ended in 1945 – was inescapable. So was Churchill, and not only because of his rather eerie return to Downing Street from 1951 to 1955. As my eminent contemporary Neil MacGregor has said, 'we all grew up not so much in the shadow of the Second World War, but in its presence ... from early childhood we lived with the consequences.' In a still more extreme case, my late friend and sparring partner Christopher Hitchens recalled his own childhood, when the war was 'the entire subject of conversation'.

Some memories of war were audible. When I was about twelve I was watching something on television in which an air-raid siren was heard. At that moment my mother came into the room, and I saw her shudder involuntarily, as anyone might who had known London during the Blitz. Some memories were visible. Every other house seemed to have its wartime souvenir, from 'liberated' army revolvers to the hermetically-sealed tins of fifty Senior Service cigarettes, untouched years after they had been intended for warships in tropical ports or the Fourteenth Army in Burma, and whose lid was pierced with a satisfying hiss. Or there was the Fleet Air Arm flying jacket which my father had brought home, and which I later wore inappropriately, and lost, on a nuclear disarmament march.

Much of rural and urban England was still an audit of war. Ordnance Survey maps were speckled with the ghostly outlines of former aerodromes, Fighter Command airfields from Essex to Hampshire from which the Battle of Britain had been fought, or the stations from Yorkshire to Suffolk whence Bomber Command had waged the most distinctive, and controversial, British campaign of the war, as well as American relics in East Anglia, like the spectral Eighth US Army Air Force base which Dean Jagger revisits in *Twelve O'Clock High*. London was pockmarked by bomb sites, and many back gardens still had the quickly-built 'Anderson' bomb shelters, in which our elders had huddled during the raids and where we children now played. Even today, as far away as a tranquil stretch of the River Frome in Somerset where I swim in summer, there stands a 1940 pillbox, part of the last of three concentric defensive lines built against a German invasion which never came.

As schoolboys we catalogued Eighth Army and Africa Korps uniforms, we made model Spitfires – topside painted in camouflage, underside duck-egg blue – and we consumed a heavy diet of war books and war movies, good and bad, *The Wooden Horse*, *The Cruel Sea*, *The Dam Busters*, *The Cockleshell Heroes*. In the cheaper boys' comics, plucky Tommies hit Jerry for six, while in the *Eagle*, a more sophisticated comic for the better class of boy, we read the adventures in space of Dan Dare, and MacDonald Hastings the 'Special Investigator', but also 'The Happy Warrior', an interminable cartoon-series telling Churchill's life story up to the glorious year of 1945. Like every family home, it seemed, ours had Churchill's *The Second World War* standing imposingly on the bookshelves. Those six volumes also sat in countless American homes, the readership for which it was in some ways intended, even if far more people may have bought it than read it through. Read or unread, its influence was very great, and far from benign.

When I was seven, Everest was climbed and the Queen was crowned, with schoolchildren throughout the land given a day's holiday for the Coronation. That year of 1953 was for Churchill an *annus mirabilis* such as few men had ever known, winning the Nobel Prize in Literature and being dubbed Sir Winston as a Knight of the Garter. I was nine when Churchill finally retired, nineteen when he died. It's said that everyone of my generation remembers what he or she was doing on 22 November 1963 when the shattering news came from Dallas (quite true in my case: I was rehearsing *Volpone*, the school play).

By contrast with the assassination of President Kennedy, Churchill's death was anything but a sudden shock. His physical constitution was very tough, and his heart kept beating as he turned ninety, but if the flesh was almost willing the spirit was weak, and he had for some time ceased to take any pleasure in life. As 1965 began, the world waited for news from his deathbed, and the inevitable end was foretold with varying degrees of tact in newspapers and broadcast news everywhere: '*L'agonie de Churchill*' said a French newspaper headline I remember seeing in a Soho newsagent's shortly before he died on 24 January. And we who watched his funeral six days later – hundreds of millions of us in scores of countries – surely still remember it. What we couldn't begin to know that day was how loudly it would still resonate half a century and more later.

A note on nomenclature. The Churchill family adopted the idiosyncratic, and confusing, habit of rotating Christian names. To clarify as best one can, more than two centuries after the first Sir Winston Churchill was born in 1620, Lord Randolph Churchill was born in 1849, the younger son of the seventh Duke of Marlborough and died in 1895, having married Jennie Jerome and fathered Sir Winston Churchill, who was born in 1874 and died in 1965, having married Clementine Hozier and fathered Randolph Churchill, who was born in 1911 and died in 1968, having married Pamela Digby and fathered Winston Churchill, who was born in 1940 and died in 2010, having married Minnie d'Erlanger and fathered Randolph Churchill, who was born in 1965, married Catherine Lancaster, and fathered John Winston Spencer Churchill who was born in 2007. The subject of this book was one of the rare public figures recognisable from early years simply by their forenames, and over the years he has been referred to as 'Winston' by everyone from his political contemporaries to successors like Margaret Thatcher to some authors. I've avoided this familiarity and called him 'Churchill'. 'Lord Randolph' means his father and 'Randolph' his son. 'Little Winston' was what his grandparents called Randolph's son, who became another Winston S. Churchill MP, and I've used that name, not out of mockery but to avoid ambiguity.

'I do not consider that names that have been familiar for generations in England should be altered to suit the whims of foreigners living in those parts,' Churchill wrote defiantly on 23 April 1945. 'Constantinople should never be ... Istanbul ... If we do not make a stand we shall in a few weeks be asked to call Leghorn Livorno, and the BBC will be pronouncing Paris Paree. Foreign names were made for Englishmen, not Englishmen for Foreign names. I date this minute from St George's Day.' This might seem like a losing battle – few now say Constantinople, or would know where Leghorn is – but I sympathise with Churchill and have followed his advice. After all, we don't yet talk about Chamberlain and the München agreement, or the Allied armies taking Napoli in 1943. Quite apart from the very dubious cases of saying 'Mumbai' and 'Myanmar' to gratify bigoted Hindu nationalists on the one hand and on the other a brutal military junta, it would be absurd to use those forms rather than 'Bombay' to describe where Churchill alighted in 1896 and 'Burma' where a campaign was fought in 1944, and I have stuck to the forms he used. That includes the name of his own country. 'The conclusion of the Great War raised England to the highest position she has yet attained,' Churchill wrote a hundred years ago. He did not say 'Britain', still less 'the UK', he said what everyone then said, a usage I've also followed: either 'England' or 'Great Britain' but not the solecistic and ambiguous 'Britain'.

'Whosoever, in writing a modern history,' Sir Walter Raleigh said, 'shall follow truth too near the heels it may haply strike out his teeth,' a point he illustrated rather too vividly when he wrote his *History of the World* and was then beheaded. And Lord Clarendon was concerned that his history of the Civil War would 'make mad work among friends and foes'. I've tried my best to follow truth near the heels, and wait to see what happens to my teeth, or what mad work is made. But all in all, if my years in the company of Winston Spencer Churchill were sometimes exhausting, they were also exhilarating. I hope that I have in some measure repaid my absorption with this endlessly fascinating man.

"CAN'T YE STAND LIKE MEN!"

1

'Jolly little wars'
Malakand 1897

'After today we begin to burn villages. Every one. And all who resist will be killed without quarter.' Churchill was twenty-two when he took part in a punitive expedition on the frontier of Afghanistan, near where British as well as American soldiers would be fighting more than a hundred years later. One of our first images of him is as a boy on horseback, much later re-enacted by Simon Ward in *Young Winston*, but most memorably evoked by himself. He rode all along the skirmish lines 'where everyone else was lying down in cover,' he wrote to a friend. The Pashtuns 'need a lesson, and there is no doubt we are a very cruel people'. Riding like this might be foolish but he liked to play for high stakes, 'and given an audience there is no act too daring or too noble. Without the gallery, things are different.'

It was 1897, the year of Queen Victoria's Diamond Jubilee. Ten years earlier a huge thanksgiving service in Westminster Abbey marking her Golden Jubilee was attended by rulers from across Europe and a gaudy assemblage of Indian princes, an affirmation of the majesty and might of the greatest empire the world had ever seen. There were celebrations throughout the land. In every village a free tea was given where squire and labourer, parson and innkeeper, all sat down together as equals for the first time, and maybe the last: this was the swansong of a rural England already on the point of economic collapse.

Then the fires were lit. 'From Clee to heaven the beacon burns': A.E. Houseman was topographically almost right, since it was on a peak of the Malvern Hills, not far from the Shropshire Lad's Clee Hill, that the first bonfire was lit, to signal the firing of lines of flame on every hilltop south towards Land's End and north to John O'Groats:

Look left, look right, the hills are bright,
The dales are light between,
Because 'tis fifty years to-night
That God has saved the Queen.

Over those fifty years that God had saved her since she inherited the throne in 1837 as a girl of eighteen, the queen's sway had grown wider and farther. It was the Emperor Charles V, at least as Schiller imagined him, who spoke of his empire 'on which the sun never sets', and that phrase was much used by Victorians, if not with universal approval: when the radical Ernest Jones heard someone speak of 'our glorious empire on which the sun never sets', he interjected, 'and on which the blood never dries.'

One little boy was enthralled by it all. 'P.S. Remember the Jubilee,' said one of many letters to his mother from 'Your loving son Winny' that summer, begging to be allowed out of his school in Brighton and taken to see the great event, although he was also 'looking forward to seeing Buffalo Bill, yourself, Jack [his brother], Everest [his nanny, and the most important woman in his life apart from his mother, if indeed apart from her], and home'. The twelve-year-old's pertinacity was rewarded when he came up to London for the festivities, quite unaware of the crisis engulfing the political career of his father.

Born in 1849 the younger son of the seventh Duke of Marlborough and educated at Eton and Oxford, Lord Randolph Churchill was elected to Parliament in February 1874 as Member for Woodstock, still in effect a family pocket borough. Weeks later, at the British Embassy in Paris he married Jennie Jerome, whom he had met the year before at a ball given by the Royal Yacht Squadron in Cowes. American heiresses weren't yet the adornment of English aristocratic life they would soon become,* and the Marlboroughs required some suasion, as well as Leonard Jerome's offer to settle £50,000 on his daughter, before the duke relented. At Blenheim on 30 November, Lady Randolph, as she now was, gave birth to a boy, christened Winston Leonard Spencer Churchill.

---

* Lord Randolph's nephew, Winston's cousin, the ninth Duke of Marlborough, known as 'Sunny' from his Sunderland title and very much not from his disposition, married not one but two Americans, Consuelo Vanderbilt and Gladys Deacon.

No sooner had his political career begun than Lord Randolph was embroiled in scandal. The Prince of Wales, Queen Victoria's affably indolent son, visited India in 1875 accompanied by a group of dissolute rich friends, among them Lord Aylesford. While they were away Aylesford learned that his wife had taken Lord Blanford, Lord Randolph's elder brother, as her lover, and he decided to divorce her. Throwing fuel on the fire, Lord Randolph let it be known that he possessed compromising letters from the Prince of Wales to Lady Aylesford. The prince was incandescent as Randolph and Jennie slipped across the Atlantic to avoid the wrath of Court and society. Or as their son much later coyly wrote, 'Engaging in his brother's quarrels with fierce and reckless partisanship, Lord Randolph incurred the deep displeasure of a great personage.' Winston himself would one day incur the deep displeasure of many personages, great and small, and his career was often marked by fierce and reckless partisanship.

To let tempers cool, Marlborough agreed to go to Dublin as Lord Lieutenant, with Lord Randolph as his unpaid private secretary. After the 1880 election, Gladstone became prime minister again and Lord Randolph was back at Westminster. He then embarked on a hectic campaign with the ill-disguised object of winning the Tory leadership, by what was then the outrageous means of appealing to the party outside Parliament. He was elected chairman of the National Union of Conservative Associations in 1883, he attacked the party leadership, and then, in an audacious gamble for high stakes, he resigned the chairmanship and was re-elected by acclamation. By May 1885 he had helped bring about the parliamentary defeat of Gladstone's government, and in Salisbury's short-lived first administration that followed he was made Secretary of State for India, aged thirty-six. Lord Randolph had already visited India, telling Parliament on his return that British supremacy was essential and would be doomed 'the moment we showed the faintest indications of relaxing our grasp', and in the mere seven months he held the office, he sent British forces on the road to Mandalay, while Upper Burma was annexed by the Crown. None of this was universally welcomed, and nor was Lord Randolph universally admired. His Cabinet colleague, the veteran Tory statesman Lord Derby, thought him 'thoroughly untrustworthy: scarcely a gentleman and probably more or less mad', words which would echo many years later.

For a generation to come, British politics would be dominated, and poisoned, by Irish conflicts, in which Lord Randolph and his son would play leading and often malign parts. Gladstone's private conversion to the principle of Irish self-rule became public, and was followed by an election which returned him to office, his introduction of a Home Rule Bill in Parliament in April 1886, and its defeat in the Commons in June when the Liberals split wide apart. Another election saw a Tory victory and Salisbury's return to the prime ministership. He made Lord Randolph his Chancellor of the Exchequer and Leader of the House of Commons, but not for long. Plunging recklessly into the Home Rule controversy, Lord Randolph visited Belfast. Whether or not he used the words often attributed to him, 'Ulster will fight and Ulster will be right', he certainly inflamed local passions. There was and would remain a case for the democratic rights of the Protestants of eastern Ulster, but the situation was potentially violent enough without Churchill's inflammatory grandstanding. Besides that, he angrily criticised the government's foreign policy in private letters, and in public speeches advocated reform, to the loud applause of a journalistic claque: by that autumn, the *St Stephen's Review* would describe him as 'the central figure in English politics'.

Then came another daring gamble for still higher stakes, and this time Lord Randolph lost. He wanted a reduction in military spending, which the war ministry opposed: a Cabinet dispute of a familiar kind usually resolved by compromise. On 20 December 1886, when Lord Randolph had gone to dine with the queen, he wrote to Salisbury from Windsor Castle – most improperly, and to the queen's great displeasure – threatening to resign. By now Lord Randolph had convinced himself that he was indispensable, and he thought that Salisbury would be obliged to make terms with him, but Salisbury called his bluff and accepted his resignation. He never held office again.

In his formal letter to the departing chancellor, the prime minister expressed his profound regret; speaking privately, Salisbury had complained that Lord Randolph had a 'wayward and headstrong disposition' and that he treated the Cabinet like 'an orchestra in which the first fiddle plays one tune and everybody else, including myself, wishes to play another'. When it was suggested that he might return, Salisbury said, 'Did you ever know of a man who, having got rid of a boil on his neck, wanted it back?' adding to another confidant, 'the qualities for which he is most conspicuous have not usually kept men for any length of time at the head of affairs.' As he grew up, Winston Churchill persuaded himself that his father's career afforded an inspiration; it should have offered a warning. Lord Randolph's contemporaries wondered whether he was a brilliant but thwarted statesman, or an impetuous adventurer and something of a mountebank, undone by his lack of judgement so that he threw away golden chances. These were the very apprehensions Winston's own contemporaries would so often feel about him: gifted but wayward and headstrong; energetic but overbearing and troublesome.

By 1890 Lord Randolph was a dying man, in the later stages of what was long thought to have been syphilis but may have been an obscure brain disease. Either way, his remaining years were horrible to contemplate: as Lord Rosebery chillingly wrote, 'He died by inches in public.' Excluded from power at home, he spent most of 1891 in South Africa trying to buy mining concessions while killing as many beautiful wild animals as he could, before he returned and tried to re-enter the political arena. But by the time he made his last Commons speech in June 1894 he was incoherent. He was taken on a last journey round the world, with Jennie and a doctor, but by the end of the year he was too ill to continue and was brought home as speedily as could be. He died on 24 January 1895, aged forty-five.

To understand a man, Napoleon said, you need to know how the world looked when he was twenty. Winston Churchill was twenty when his father died. Lord Randolph had lived to see his son grow up, and to be bitterly disappointed by him, a disappointment he never disguised. Both parents treated their son appallingly. They were both, in different but odious ways, wholly absorbed in themselves and their own lives, Lord Randolph with politics and finance, Jennie with luncheons and lovers. They rarely visited him at his schools or even wrote to him, leaving him to find what emotional support he could from his nanny, Mrs Everest; a neglect which had curious results.

He was a curious boy in any case. Churchill was clever but unacademic, with no gift for foreign tongues, either the Latin or Greek Classics which were then the staple of patrician education or modern languages, as he demonstrated in his later attempts at speaking French. But he could express himself – one schoolmaster was much impressed by a 1500-word essay on a coming war between England and Russia which he wrote at fourteen – and he had a very retentive memory. 'It was thought incongruous, that while I apparently stagnated in the lowest form,' he won a prize for reciting twelve hundred lines of Macaulay's 'Lays of Ancient Rome' 'without making a single mistake'.

A lifetime later, Churchill's capacity to quote reams of verse would impress some, and irritate others, including Franklin Roosevelt.

His literary style was also formed in another unmistakable way. In adult life Churchill rarely went to church or pretended to be a believing Christian. He engagingly said that, having been obliged at school to go to chapel twice a day, he had acquired a 'balance of observance', like a bank balance, and that thereafter he only needed to top it up from time to time by attending christenings, weddings and funerals. But by sitting in chapel for many hundreds of hours during his schooldays, he absorbed into his marrow two priceless English inheritances, which his speeches and writings would often echo, and which a later generation would barbarously discard: the King James Bible and the Book of Common Prayer.

Having hoped that his son would become a barrister, Lord Randolph sourly settled on the military academy at Sandhurst rather than the intellectual rigours of Oxford. Even then, Churchill failed the Sandhurst entrance twice before passing with marks which ruled out the infantry and the crack 60th Rifles, the regiment of Lord Randolph's choice for him. Winston was commissioned into the 4th Hussars, the cavalry accepting lower grades from their officers, though requiring more private money. Lord Randolph ended his years of unremittingly harsh criticism of all his son's failings with a contemptuous blast: 'if you cannot prevent yourself from leading the idle useless unprofitable life you have had during your schooldays & later months you will become a mere social wastrel, one of the hundreds of the public school failures.' This was at the very time when Sigmund Freud was formulating his theories of childhood repression and reaction. And yet, so far from Oedipal rejection, which Lord Randolph's neglect and contempt might have merited, Churchill was obsessively devoted to his father, and ever after passionately concerned to justify himself to the shade of the man whose death had ended 'all my dreams of comradeship with him, of entering Parliament at his side, and in his support. There remained for me only to pursue his aims and vindicate his memory.' There is the crucial word: *vindicate*.

In 1897 the Queen's Diamond Jubilee was less opulent and triumphant than its Golden precursor. A procession took the queen through London to St Paul's where her carriage halted while a brief service was held on the steps of Sir Christopher Wren's great cathedral. The sight of the queen remaining seated in her open carriage shocked one German princess – 'after 60 years Reign, to thank God in the Street!!!' – but by now the queen, in her seventy-ninth year and increasingly infirm, would have had difficulty walking up the cathedral steps. Lord Salisbury was prime minister again as he had been for the Golden Jubilee, after the Liberal interlude of 1892–5, which saw the heroic return of Gladstone, prime minister again for the fourth and last time at the age of eighty-two, introducing a second Home Rule Bill which was passed by the Commons but thrown out by the Lords. After this defeat Gladstone resigned and was succeeded by Lord Rosebery for his brief prime ministership of 1894–5 – 'a strangely-lighted episode' as Churchill later called it – before the Tories were back in office for another ten years.

But the mood was perceptibly turning. While the end of the century saw a new boastful vein of imperialism, personified by Joseph Chamberlain and Cecil Rhodes, more acute observers could sense that something had changed. Houseman's brand of pessimism gave way to Rudyard Kipling's, with its mixture of imperial bravado and acute apprehension. Despite having become the Bard of Empire, Kipling disliked any idea of an official position, turning down the office of Poet Laureate, as well as a knighthood more than once (quite apart from privately calling King Edward VII, as the Prince of Wales became, 'a bloated corpulent voluptuary'). And his contribution to the Diamond Jubilee was a great minatory poem. 'Recessional' spoke of 'Dominion over palm and pine', but it warned:

> If, drunk with sight of power, we loose
> Wild tongues that have not Thee in awe,
> Such boastings as the Gentiles use,
> Or lesser breeds without the Law* –
> Lord God of Hosts, be with us yet,
> Lest we forget – lest we forget!

---

* Writing about Kipling more than forty years later, George Orwell said that these lines were 'always good for a snigger in pansy-left circles', conjuring up the image of a white master kicking some dark-skinned lesser breed, but that this couldn't be Kipling's meaning. The poem warns against conquerors' hubris, not a temptation for most Asian or African peoples at the time. The boastful Gentiles are plainly the Germans in their first flush of imperial arrogance; since Kipling seems to be making a distinction with 'or', the lesser breeds might be the Italians.

Those profound words had no effect at all on Churchill. He relished dominion over palm and pine. He loved Sandhurst, he loved horses, he loved his regiment, he loved his country's greatness, he loved the Empire, he loved the colour and dash of battle even before he experienced it. Othello's 'Pride, pomp, and circumstance of glorious war!' was a phrase that might have been made for Churchill, not to say 'big wars that make ambition virtue'. To make ambition virtue for the time being, what he boastfully called 'jolly little wars against barbarous peoples' had to suffice, although the first war he witnessed, while comparatively little, was far from jolly.

In faraway Cuba José Martí led a patriotic rebellion against the Spanish rulers, a prelude to the Spanish–American War. By the autumn of 1895 Churchill had joined his regiment at its Hounslow depot, close to where Heathrow airport now stands. Eager for experience, he obtained leave to travel to the distant island, along with his first commission from a newspaper, the *Daily Graphic*, at the age of twenty, and paid his first visit to his mother's country when he stopped briefly at New York. Looking back in 1930, he wrote that 'The minds of this generation, exhausted, brutalised, mutilated and bored by War, may not understand the delicious yet tremulous sensations with which a young British officer bred in the long peace approached for the first time an actual theatre of operations.' He was quite right that most people felt very differently after the carnage of the Great War, but Churchill's 'delicious' account gives no hint of the savagery of these 'operations' in Cuba under General Valeriano Weyler to put down the rebellion, which prefigured the horrors of the coming century. At least 200,000 Cubans died, Martí among them, while Weyler herded civilians into what he called *reconcentrados*. In a few years' time during the Boer War the British would borrow the name 'concentration camp' for the same purpose, before it was later borrowed again, in cruel mockery, by Adolf Hitler.

Having marked his twenty-first birthday in Cuba and confirmed his taste for Havana cigars, Churchill returned by way of New York, reaching the *Etruria*, his homebound liner, with only five minutes to spare, the *New York Herald* reported. He told the *Herald* that General Campos, his Spanish host in Cuba, was a most distinguished man who had shown 'rare judgement and great humanity', a dubious verdict. What Churchill didn't discuss, although he was very well aware of, was another war which impended during his brief stay in New York.

At the end of 1895 a footling border dispute between Venezuela and British Guiana blew up into a crisis which very nearly led to armed conflict; at that very moment Churchill was in New York on his way home. With President Cleveland rattling his sabre, the *New York Times* sported the headline on 18 December, 'WANT TO FIGHT ENGLAND – Army and Navy Men Profess Great Eagerness to Go to War', while there was also loud talk of invading Canada. Even though it never took place and is now forgotten, this war that might have been casts a fascinating and ironical light on Churchill's later career.

By this time the phrase 'English-speaking races' was already current, with its strong overtones of Anglo-Saxon superiority. The scoundrelly Rhodes dreamed of bringing the United States back into the fold of the British Empire, while founding his scholarships at Oxford for 'Anglo-Saxons' in the form of 'white colonials', Americans and Germans. And Sir Arthur Conan Doyle, having built his fame with Sherlock Holmes, published in 1891 his mediaeval romance *The White Company*, which he dedicated 'To the hope of the future, the reunion of the English-speaking races.' A grave misunderstanding was in the making.

One of Churchill's biographical essays is on Joseph Chamberlain, the brilliant and sulphurous politician who had transformed Birmingham before entering Parliament 'to establish', in Churchill's words, 'quite new levels for the political and social status for the mass of the people'. Having broken with Gladstone over Home Rule in 1886, Chamberlain moved from Radicalism to Imperialism and served as Colonial Secretary under Lord Salisbury in the 1890s. He was closely implicated in the Jameson Raid, which Rhodes had helped instigate at the end of 1895 and which adumbrated the Boer war. Before that, Chamberlain had been sent to Washington by Salisbury to settle a dispute over Canadian fisheries. Both of his first wives had died young after giving birth to sons, and in America he met his third wife, Mary Endicott, daughter of President Grover Cleveland's Secretary of the Army. Thus it was that, apart from two twentieth-century British prime ministers who had American mothers,* thanks to the third Mrs Chamberlain, a foreign secretary and another prime minister – the half-brothers Austen and Neville Chamberlain – had an American stepmother.

---

* Churchill and Macmillan.

And it was Joe Chamberlain who said: 'I refuse to think or speak of the United States as a foreign nation.' Much later this would be turned by Churchill into a doctrine, the Anglo-American 'special relationship'. Alas, Chamberlain's sentiment, like Churchill's doctrine, was rarely reciprocated by Americans, then or since, and was based on a complete misprision, as well as a rewriting of history. What was 'special' about the relations between the two countries from the eighteenth to the twentieth century was mutual hostility and suspicion. Not only had the United States been born through armed rebellion against England, the two countries were at war again in 1812, when the redcoats burned the Capitol, and a British 'rocket's red glare' over besieged Baltimore inspired what would become the American national anthem.* During that century the two countries nearly went to war again at least three more times. As prime minister in the 1840s, Sir Robert Peel was acutely conscious of the American threat to Canada, and warned Parliament of possible war. This was the age of 'manifest destiny', which for many Americans meant their country's destiny to rule the whole of North America, including Canada. At the 1844 presidential election James Polk and the Democrats campaigned on a bellicose platform, demanding the territory which would become the Canadian province of British Columbia, the Pacific coast from Oregon north to the 54th parallel and the border with Russian America, now Alaska: hence the unwieldy slogan 'Fifty-four forty or fight!' When Polk was elected, he backed off and found an easier target to the south, embarking on the Mexican–American War of 1846.

Little more than fifteen years later the United States was again at war, the one war in their history in which American forces endured really heavy casualties and in which the country knew terrible suffering: the war they fought against each other. Not only did the Civil War divide England as well as America, a war between the two countries seemed close on more than one occasion. With the Confederacy demanding that London recognise its sovereignty and threatening to cut off cotton supplies, some English politicians, including Gladstone, soon to be prime minister, favoured recognition. Two Confederate commissioners were despatched to England in November 1861 aboard the *Trent*, a British mail packet, but were seized near Cuba by the USS

---

* Whose last words, '... and the land of the free', needed qualification. Maryland was a slave state at the time: the land was more free for some than others.

San Jacinto. 'Have these Yankees then gone completely crazy?' Friedrich Engels asked his friend Karl Marx. Taking 'political prisoners' in this way, Engels thought, was 'the clearest *casus belli* there can be. The fellows must be sheer fools to land themselves in war with England.' Some hotter heads in Washington wouldn't have minded that, and Lincoln had to tell his Secretary of State, 'One war at a time, I think, Mr Seward.' Even after the Civil War, animosity remained acute, thanks partly to the quarrel over the *Alabama,* a commerce raider built in England for the Confederacy.

Many years later Churchill would 'remember vividly' his return voyage from New York, 'looking at ships off the English coast and wondering which one would be our transport to Canada'. In the event the 4th Hussars weren't sent westwards to fight the United States Cavalry. The crisis was defused by Salisbury's wise restraint but, as Churchill said, 'the exuberant pride of Americans could not long be held in check,' and the Spanish–American war duly followed, to begin America's great age of empire. What he omitted to say was what others saw at the time: that whereas the English were dismayed at the prospect of war with the United States, in America, as Sir Robert Ensor wrote, 'a war with England was the most popular of all wars'.

Having returned to England, Churchill sailed with his regiment for India, and for the golden days and nights of Bangalore. *My Early Life*, his memoir published in 1930, conjures up the enchanted life of a young English officer in an Indian cantonment in the last years of Victoria's reign, a world so distant from the twenty-first century that it might be Classical Antiquity. Churchill shared a bungalow with two other officers, Reggie Barnes, who had been his companion in Cuba, and Hugo Baring. His salary of fourteen shillings a day, or around £250 annually, with £3 a month to keep two horses, was supplemented by an annual allowance from his mother of £500 a year (about ten times an English miner's income). With this he was able to retain three personal Indian servants, a butler, a dressing boy or valet, and a groom.

His day began as he was woken before dawn by 'a clammy hand adroitly lifting one's chin and applying a gleaming razor to a lathered and defenceless throat'. Then came parade at six, drill and manoeuvres, hot baths followed by breakfast, stables and orderly room until ten-thirty, and the bungalow again: 'long before eleven o'clock all white men were in shelter'. After a brief lunch at one-thirty they slept – or in Churchill's case read – until five, when they could devote themselves to 'the serious purpose of life ... in one word – Polo'. Usually Churchill played at least eight chukkas, 'and often more than ten or twelve', before they went sweating and exhausted to more hot baths, the mess, and 'the clinking of ice in well-filled glasses', dinner with the regimental band playing, 'smoking in the moonlight till half-past ten or eleven', and bed. That was his day, 'and not such a bad day either'. The glow of this happy memory stayed with him ever after, with less happy consequences.

A cavalry officer's unexacting life afforded Churchill the opportunity to catch up on the education he had missed at Harrow. He read Gibbon and Macaulay, and from them acquired a love of history, as well as that sham-Augustan style, he read Adam Smith and Darwin's *Origin of Species*, he read the *Annual Register*, a catalogue of political events, and he read *The Martyrdom of Man* by Winwood Reade. Now forgotten, this book was hugely influential in its day, a popularised cocktail of godless pessimism, Nietzsche, 'Dover Beach' and Kipling's 'If ...'. Although Churchill was never an 'intellectual', a word he would later use contemptuously, still less a scholar, his natural intelligence was formed by this ragbag of reading. And his belated education inspired a love of the story-telling which would play a central part in his life.

Later generations can still sympathise with some of what he absorbed, at least the Victorian belief in human betterment, but some now seem far darker. Churchill learned about the grandeur of the Roman Empire from Gibbon: 'If a man were called to fix the period in the history of the world, during which the condition of the human race was most happy and prosperous, he would, without hesitation, name that which elapsed from the death of Domitian to the accession of Commodus.' For Churchill, that Golden Age of the Antonines in the first century was equalled for happiness and prosperity by the golden age of Victoria, and the British Empire, whose progressive and enlightened character Macaulay extolled, rivalled the Roman Empire as a force for good. And yet Churchill's much later phrase about 'the august, unchallenged and tranquil glories of the Victorian Era' was distinctly rosy: there wasn't a single year of the Queen-Empress's very long and 'tranquil' reign when British soldiers weren't fighting and killing somewhere on earth.

More than that, Churchill learned from Reade that man was alone in the world and master of his fate, that life was constant conflict, and that, as Darwin had taught, the fittest survived. 'Social Darwinism' later became an opprobrious term, and any belief in racial superiority would be irredeemably tainted. But Charles Darwin was himself a social Darwinian. He envisaged that quite soon 'the civilised races of man will almost certainly exterminate, and replace, the savage races throughout the world', so that there would be a wider break 'between man and his nearest allies', a distance between 'the Caucasian, and some ape as low as a baboon, instead of as now between the negro or Australian and the gorilla.'

This was often elided into imperialism and 'Anglo-Saxonism'. A generation older than Churchill, Sir Charles Dilke was a rising Liberal politician who might have become prime minister but for a melodramatic divorce case. His 1868 book *Greater Britain* was very widely read for years to come with its gospel of 'England round the world', drawing from his lengthy travel conclusions, as a biographer has said, 'at once radical and racialist'. He believed that 'America offers the English race the moral directorship of the globe,' while writing with something near pride about the fate of the American Indians that 'the Anglo-Saxon is the only extirpating race on earth'. The young Churchill absorbed this idea of racial struggle. He sometimes spoke of the need to extirpate the Chinese, and he never lost a Darwinian contempt for non-European races.

Ten years after 'Winny' had begged to see the Golden Jubilee, the Diamond Jubilee of 1897 found him back in England once more, on leave but ready for a fight, verbal or physical. He had already begun to combine one career in the army with another in journalism, and yet another beckoned in politics. On 26 June 1897, just four days after Queen Victoria visited St Paul's, Churchill made his first political speech. This honour goes to Claverton Manor, a country house just outside Bath, now by fortuitous but felicitous coincidence the American Museum, where a fete was held by the Primrose League, that remarkable Conservative organisation of its age. Fifty years later Churchill would boast that his father's membership card was Number 1, and the Primrose League was indeed founded by Lord Randolph, not to say largely to promote his interests, although ostensibly in memory of that other half-mountebank, Disraeli. With much flummery – badges worn by 'knights' and 'dames' meeting in 'habitations' – its membership grew from 11,000 in 1885 to more than a million when

Churchill spoke at Claverton Manor to an astonishing two million in 1910, when the electorate was still no more than 7.7 million.

His speech was given at the height of the Season, when that still meant something, and when, as Churchill liked to say later with undisguised regret, Society meant even more: a tight-knit interrelated patriciate which had owned and ruled the country since the Glorious Revolution, which still dominated Parliament, and which shared the same amusements. Apart from the round of dinners and dances, he attended race meetings which were also social occasions, although it would be another half century before his son-in-law Christopher Soames kindled in Churchill a real enthusiasm for the Turf. And it was 'on the lawns of Goodwood in lovely weather' that he heard riveting news. He had thought of persuading a newspaper to let him cover conflicts brewing in the Balkans, but this was something much better.

As British rule in India expanded it had come to a halt in the north-west where it ran up against the mountainous kingdom of Afghanistan. On the far side lay Russia, expanding just as relentlessly, and Afghanistan was caught in the Great Game for mastery of central Asia. Neither power ever subdued the country, and the British had learned the hard way in 1839–42 and 1878–80 just what a thankless and fruitless task invading Afghanistan was, a lesson which they had quite forgotten by the twenty-first century. The first of those two Afghan Wars saw one of the worst disasters in imperial history, an entire expeditionary force to Kabul wiped out save the one survivor memorably portrayed in Lady Butler's painting 'Remnants of an Army'.

Nor did the next war subdue 'the wily Pathan', as the English then knew those who would later be called Pashtuns. One officer who had served in what was candidly described as the punitive expedition of 1880 was General Sir Bindon Blood (a name only the rashest author of imperial yarns would confer on a character), who was now given charge of another such expedition. Churchill already knew General Blood, and frantically secured an attachment to his force, along with a commission from the *Daily Telegraph* to write about it, before reaching India post haste to join the force on the North-West Frontier. 'War' might not be quite the word for an expedition whose purpose wasn't to conquer and occupy territory but to punish the tribesmen by burning their villages, destroying their crops, filling in their wells, and otherwise depriving them of food and water.

'Financially it is ruinous, morally it is wicked,' Churchill told his mother, 'but we can't pull up now.' The Pashtuns 'recognise superiority of race'. And anyway, 'it was all very exciting and for those who did not get killed or hurt, very jolly.' He wasn't one of those who got killed but, not for the last time in his life, Churchill might have been. He was brave, and foolish, and lucky. It could so easily have been the end of a young Englishman imagined in another of Kipling's verses – well known to British officers in India, as Churchill sardonically noted – the bitter little 'Arithmetic on the Frontier'.

> A scrimmage in a Border Station –
> A canter down some dark defile –
> Two thousand pounds of education
> Drops to a ten-rupee jezail* –
> The Crammer's boast, the Squadron's pride,
> Shot like a rabbit in a ride!

Having played to the gallery on his grey pony, he then looked for another audience by turning his reports into his first book, *The Story of the Malakand Field Force*. In the following year, enjoying a remarkable degree of tolerance from the military authorities as well as the string-pulling influence of his mother, although not the warm approval of all his brother officers, Churchill joined one more campaign, this time led by General Kitchener. Its purported aim was to suppress a rising in Sudan by an army of 'dervishes', the Islamic radicals of their day, led by the self-proclaimed Mahdi, a warrior preaching holy jihad in the name of the Prophet, although along with a crusade against jihad, and belated vengeance for the death of General Gordon in 1885, Salisbury was concerned to pre-empt French moves towards the upper Nile.

'I have a keen aboriginal desire to kill several of these odious dervishes,' Churchill wrote to his mother from Sudan, and so he did. On 2 September 1898, at the battle of Omdurman beside the Nile just north of Khartoum, Churchill charged with the 21st Lancers, and personally killed a number of 'odious dervishes' with his pistol, in what was less battle than slaughter, conducted on the very principle

---

* The approximate cost of educating a boy at a fashionable English boarding school for five years; something in excess of two hundred thousand pounds of education would be more like it today. A jezail was a cheap rifle.

Hilaire Belloc described in his verse satire *The Modern Traveller*, published that same year: 'Whatever happens we have got / The Maxim gun and they have not.' Kitchener had in fact no fewer than fifty-two Maxim machine guns ranged against dervishes armed with spears. Here was a different kind of arithmetic on the frontier: all of forty-seven British soldiers fell, while more than 10,000 Sudanese were killed in the hail of bullets. 'Talk of fun! Where will you beat this?' Churchill said, while also tersely recording that 'all Dervishes who did not immediately surrender were shot or bayoneted', including the wounded.

This campaign quickly produced another book, *The River War*, whose few sharp criticisms of Kitchener caused controversy. Churchill was still more trenchant on the faith for which those dervishes died. 'How dreadful are the curses which Mohammedanism lays on its votaries!' he wrote. 'Besides the fanatical frenzy' and 'this fearful fatalistic apathy,'

> improvident habits, slovenly systems of agriculture... exist wherever the followers of the Prophet rule or live. A degraded sensualism deprives this life of its grace and refinement; the next of its dignity and sanctity. The fact that in Mohammedan law every woman must belong to some man as his absolute property – either as a child, a wife, or a concubine – must delay the final extinction of slavery until the faith of Islam has ceased to be a great power among men... No stronger retrograde force exists in the world.

This was one more opinion which Churchill never changed.

Even before sailing east for the first time Churchill had told his mother that he looked upon going to 'the tedious land of India – where I shall be equally out of the pleasures of peace and the chances of war ... as a useless and unprofitable exile'. He hoped to find action in South Africa, where a few months would win him a couple of medals, and 'Thence hot foot to Egypt – to return with two more decorations in a year or two – and beat my sword into an iron despatch box,' meaning a political career. This wonderfully flagrant catalogue of ambition was fulfilled, although not in that order, and Churchill returned to India for one last time, and one last purpose.

'I can hardly describe the sustained intensity of purpose with which we threw ourselves into this audacious and colossal undertaking.' It might be Churchill in his later years, and at his ripest and most majestic, perhaps on the Normandy landings of 1944. He is in fact describing the Inter-Regimental Polo Tournament of 1899, held at Meerut, a 1400-mile railway journey from Bangalore. When he had first arrived in India Churchill had dislocated his left shoulder by falling as he disembarked at Bombay, and now the shoulder went again. In one more display of his courage and sheer tenacity, he played with that arm strapped to his side. He was still able to help the 4th Hussars beat the Royal Dragoons in the final, a glorious victory, followed by 'Prolonged rejoicings, intense inward satisfaction, and nocturnal festivities from which the use of wine was not excluded.'

After telling his mother that he wanted to win renown as a soldier before politics, he had made detailed plans for the year 1899: 'To return to India and win the Polo Tournament: to relieve my mother from paying my allowance: to write my new book ... and to look out for a chance of entering Parliament.' He even conceived a fancy for belatedly going to Oxford, until he realised that some knowledge of Classical languages would be required. Since 'I could not contemplate toiling at Greek irregular verbs after having commanded British regular troops', he abandoned the idea. But he resigned his commission, returned to England, and stood that summer as a Tory parliamentary candidate in a by-election at Oldham. He and his running-mate in the two-member constituency were both beaten, at which 'Everyone threw the blame on me. I have noticed that they nearly always do.'

Three wars had begun to launch Churchill's career; a fourth would make him famous. In the autumn of 1899 the war in South Africa, which he had only half-humorously predicted, would be the next step in his quest for fame and fortune as journalist, publicist and politician. The British had acquired a toehold at the Cape of Good Hope during the Napoleonic Wars, but until the second half of the nineteenth century it remained one of the most neglected of imperial outposts, and 'South Africa' was a geographical description rather than a country, a patchwork of surviving African kingdoms, two British colonies and two Boer republics, the South African Republic or Transvaal and the Orange Free State, ruled by a few score thousand farmers ('boer' is 'farmer' in Dutch) descended from Dutch and French settlers.

But South Africa had been utterly transformed by the discovery of diamonds at Kimberley in 1867 and then gold on the Witwatersrand in 1886, and it was gold that lay behind this strange, bitter conflict, a 'war of choice' if ever there was, as even Lord Salisbury acknowledged in private. In 1899 he was head of the greatest empire ever known, both Prime Minister and Foreign Secretary, but curiously detached from a war he didn't want. He told the queen in May that war would be unpopular with the British people and was 'very much to be deprecated'. At the end of August he told Lord Lansdowne that they had been forced to act on a ground prepared by Sir Alfred Milner, the scheming, clever, deplorable High Commissioner in South Africa, 'and his jingo supporters. And therefore I see before us the necessity for considerable military effort – and for people whom we despise and for territory which will bring no profit and no power to England.' This was quite close to what radical opponents of the war said: that it was fought to make the Rand safe for the Randlords, the immensely rich mine-owners, all at enormous cost to England, and deepest shame.

Within three days of the outbreak of war on 11 October, Churchill was sailing south aboard the *Dunottar Castle*. He was commissioned by the *Morning Post*, one day to become his most envenomed foe, on a lucrative contract of £250 a month and expenses, and he was fortified by a personal consignment of five dozen bottles of assorted drink from champagne to whisky. By the time he reached Cape Town, the war was going badly for the British, and would go worse before the year ended. Indeed the Boers might have won with wiser strategy. Once the Orange Free State threw in its hand with the Transvaal, the Boers had 50,000 horsemen in the field: not cavalrymen like Churchill's hussars but mounted infantry of outstanding quality, countrymen who had learned to ride a horse and fire a rifle from boyhood. To begin with they were more than a match for the plodding British, but the Boer commanders dissipated their forces by fruitlessly laying siege to Ladysmith, Kimberley and Mafeking. Had they masked and by-passed those towns and driven south as fast as possible, they might well have taken Cape Town before British reinforcements could arrive, and the future of South Africa would have been very different.

Soon after Churchill arrived at Durban he set off in an armoured train through Natal, but it was ambushed and he was taken prisoner. He was lucky to survive, and not just the skirmish when the Boers surrounded the train. On the North-West Frontier and at Omdurman, Churchill had played an unusual (and unpopular) role as a soldier who was also a reporter, but at least he was an officer holding the queen's commission. When the Boers captured him his position was much more ambiguous, and made no less so by his change of tune. He was legally a civilian, but he admitted that 'I had taken with me, Correspondent status notwithstanding, my Mauser pistol', though later he claimed to have lost his pistol before he was captured.

On 26 November he demanded to be released as a non-combatant, saying that 'I have consistently adhered to my character as a press representative, taking no part in the defence of the armoured train,' but then on 30 November, after he heard that there might be an exchange of prisoners, he asked to be classified as a 'military officer'. Through all this obfuscation it's clear that he was armed but in plain clothes when the attack began, in which case his captors would have been entitled, as he well knew, to treat him as a *franc tireur*: under the recognised custom of war, anyone captured in civilian dress but bearing arms could be shot out of hand, as had happened to numerous Frenchmen (and women) during the Franco-Prussian War in 1870–71, and would happen to plenty of German men (and boys) in north-western Europe in 1944–5.

But the Boers recognised his importance and were determined to keep him in captivity, even when he said on 8 December, 'If I am released I will give any *parole* that may be required not to serve against the Republican forces or to give any information affecting the military situation.' He was taken to Pretoria, the Transvaal capital, and held in prison, before he made a dramatic escape. This became part of the Churchill legend, and his own account of how he hid in a mineshaft before he crossed into Portuguese territory secreted among bales of wool in a railway truck is wonderfully vivid. And yet the ambiguities persisted. Did he leave behind two comrades with whom he had promised to make the escape, and did he in fact break the parole or promise he had given the Boers? At any rate, the story long pursued him: as late as 1912, when he was First Lord of the Admiralty, Churchill was still suing for libel over the 'broken parole' charge. From boyhood onwards no one had doubted Winston Churchill's energy and ambition; now for the first time, his honesty and honour were questioned.

For the moment, he returned to Durban a hero, before joining a column commanded by his friend Ian Hamilton, who would one day play a much unhappier part in Churchill's career. While turning out a stream of newspaper reports which became another two books, both appearing in 1900, *London to Ladysmith Via Pretoria*, and *Ian Hamilton's March*, he found the energy in the same year to write his only novel. *Savrola* is a swashbuckling if not quite bodice-ripping adventure novel, and his only attempt at fiction; he later endearingly, and understandably, said that, 'I have consistently urged my friends to abstain from reading it.' It still made a tally of five published books to his name by the age of twenty-six.

In the autumn of 1900 Salisbury sought to take advantage of apparent victory by calling what became known as the 'khaki* election' to exploit patriotic enthusiasm, a trick Lloyd George successfully repeated in 1918 but Churchill conspicuously failed to repeat in 1945. Churchill returned home and stood again for Parliament at Oldham, and this time he managed to win the seat. When the election took place, over several weeks, as was then customary, from 28 September to 24 October, few guessed that the war would last for another year and a half; a bitter guerrilla campaign needlessly prolonged by the British, who used means – the burning of farms and the internment of Boer civilians in self-proclaimed concentration camps, where many women and children died – which earned lasting obloquy. As it was, the election was another triumph for the Tories, and for Salisbury. It was his last hurrah: his powers already fading, he handed over the Foreign Office to Lord Lansdowne, and then, in July 1902, the premiership to his nephew A.J. Balfour, before dying a year later.

Although the new Parliament met for a brief autumn session, the new Member for Oldham was absent. Oldham was one of the first constituencies to declare, and Churchill set off forthwith to give a lantern-slide lecture about South Africa, at the St James's Hall in London, and then throughout the provinces, earning himself £3782 in all. His lecture was called 'The War As I Saw It'. That was not only just right, or all too true, it was a title which would have served accurately enough for his two later histories of the much greater wars which began in 1914 and 1939. He then left England until the new year for a lucrative north American lecture tour. At the Waldorf-Astoria in New York he was introduced by Mark Twain, with undisguised irony: 'Mr Churchill by his father is an Englishman, by his mother he is an American, no doubt a blend that makes him the perfect man.' A myth later arose that Twain had called Churchill the 'hero of five

---

* From the Urdu word for 'dust-coloured', khaki is the drab brown which the British Army, finally abandoning its red coats on active service in all climes, had now adopted for wartime uniform.

wars, author of six books and future prime minister of England', a vainglorious phrase which was actually coined by Major James B. Pond, Churchill's tour manager. What Twain said was very different.

One more memorable if uncomfortable political poem by Kipling had been published the year the Boer War began, but 'The White Man's Burden' was about another war, and addressed to another nation; as is too often forgotten, its subtitle is 'The United States and the Philippine Islands'. While congratulating the Americans, Kipling adjured them to accept their imperial mission, when they would be dealing with 'Your new-caught, sullen peoples, / Half devil and half child.' And he warned that, by taking up that white man's burden, the American would 'reap his old reward':

> The blame of those ye better,
> The hate of those ye guard –
> The cry of hosts ye humour
> (Ah, slowly!) towards the light:–
> 'Why brought ye us from bondage,
> 'Our loved Egyptian night?'

In sharp contradiction to Kipling, Mark Twain had no wish to succeed the British in any imperial role. He abhorred what his country had done to the people of the Philippines as much as what the British had done to the Boers, and so he finished introducing his English guest with the playfully reproachful words: 'We are kin. And now that we are kin in sin, there is nothing more to be desired.'

'The only thing that worries me in life is money,' Churchill had told his brother Jack in 1898. 'We shall finish up stone broke.' But as 1901 began, his prospects brightened. 'I am very proud of the fact that there is not one person in a million who at my age could have earned £10,000 without any capital in less than two years.' He would need it, and making money would remain one of his central preoccupations for decades to come. He was trying to make more money lecturing in Winnipeg on 22 January 1901, when he heard the long-expected news of the death of Queen Victoria, at the age of eighty-one after a reign of more than sixty-three years, the longest in English or British history, until Elizabeth II overtook her in September 2015. A new reign began with the new century, and for Churchill a new life.

MY AFRICAN JOURNEY

BY THE RT. HON.
WINSTON SPENCER CHURCHILL
M.P.

2

'The transatlantic type of demagogue'
Blenheim 1908

In London there is a square named after a battle, with Nelson, the victor of Trafalgar, standing high above it, and a railway station named after another, Waterloo.* But there is only one great country house named after a battle. It was at Blenheim Palace, his ancestral home, where Churchill said that he had taken the two most important decisions in his life: to be born in 1874, and to get married. Having been turned down by three women already, he met Clementine Hozier and proposed marriage while they were staying at Blenheim in 1908. And yet Blenheim and the man for whom it was built, the first Duke of Marlborough, really played a much larger part in his life, and his constant struggle for reputation and vindication.

But to begin at the beginning. Sir Winston Churchill was born in 1620. His father, John Churchill of Wootton Glanville in Dorset, had married Sarah, the daughter of Sir Henry Winston of Standish in Gloucestershire, thereby ensuring that Sir Henry's surname would one day become the most famous forename in the world. It was never used outside the family until Sir Winston's descendant and namesake made it universally recognisable, was known as 'Winston' to friend, foe and stranger, and had his name conferred admiringly on men as various as Denis Winston Healey, John Winston Howard and John Winston Lennon. The first Sir Winston was a country gentleman and a minor public official; like his father, he fought on the royalist side in the Civil War, and he then became a Member of Parliament after the Restoration of 1660, was knighted, and died in 1688. Far more significantly, he fathered three remarkable sons and a daughter. Arabella Churchill became the mistress of the Duke of York and bore

---

* Paris makes a defiant point with a station named for another battle, the Gare d'Austerlitz, as well as a metro station for one more, Stalingrad.

him several children, while one of her brothers became an admiral and the other a general. But it was the third brother who achieved European renown.

Born in 1650, John Churchill rose to greatness as soldier, courtier and turncoat. In 1685 the Roman Catholic Duke of York succeeded his brother King Charles II to become James II, but not for long. Lord Churchill, as John now was, joined the group of Whig nobles who deserted their rightful king, and saw the Protestant William of Orange, James's nephew, and son-in-law through his marriage to James's daughter Mary, installed in his place. Those who made it called this the Glorious Revolution, claiming that they had saved England from popery and absolutism and preserved the Protestant religion and constitutional government, although they also made themselves much richer and more powerful in the process. The Churchills now joined the ruling elite. In the new century, serving Queen Anne, James's other daughter, who came to the throne in 1702, John Churchill achieved the highest fame, and the highest rank in the peerage as Duke of Marlborough, as well as Freiherr of Mindelheim and Prince of the Holy Roman Empire. These titles were won by his prowess as the greatest military commander of his age, leading the armies of the Grand Alliance – England, Prussia, Savoy and the Dutch Republic – in the War of Spanish Succession against the overmighty Louis XIV of France. Every English schoolboy once knew 'BROM', the mnemonic for Marlborough's quartet of victories from 1704 to 1709, Blenheim, Ramillies, Oudenarde and Malplaquet.

All this excited the brilliant scorn of the greatest English popular historian of Victoria's reign. One of the books Churchill had read in Bangalore was *The History of England*, that masterpiece of historical imagination and English prose by Thomas Babington Macaulay, with its brilliant and brutal portrait of Marlborough as an unscrupulous, avaricious scoundrel. Vindicating his father's memory would be one task Churchill set himself; vindicating his earlier ancestor's would be another – and above all vindicating himself. One day Winston Churchill too would be called a deserter, abandoning not king but party, and not once but twice, which gave a sharper edge to his angry defence of his fickle forebear. And with his perennial taste for conflating of past and present, he would use the sonorous name of *The Grand Alliance* as the title of one of his volumes about another war, describing how a combination undreamt of by Marlborough, between Great

Britain, Soviet Russia and the United States, defeated another and more terrible domination of Europe.

When a magnificent palace near Woodstock in Oxfordshire was offered as the state's reward to the duke for his famous victory, the duchess had wanted Sir Christopher Wren, greatest of English architects, to design it, but the duke chose on a whim Sir John Vanbrugh, a fashionable playwright and amateur architect who had worked with the wonderfully original Nicholas Hawksmoor. It was Hawksmoor who completed Blenheim after Vanbrugh fell out with the Marlboroughs, but it doesn't match the delicate beauty of Easton Neston, Hawksmoor's gem in Northamptonshire, or the awesome grandeur of his mausoleum at Castle Howard in Yorkshire. And as Alexander Pope observed at the time, Blenheim has always felt more monument than home:

> Thanks, Sir, cry'd I, 'tis very fine.
> But where d'ye sleep, or where d'ye dine?
> I find by all you have been telling,
> That 'tis a house, but not a dwelling.

With his formidable wife Sarah, Marlborough had several children. Their favourite son and best hope, also John, went to King's College, Cambridge, where he died of smallpox at seventeen, with his grief-stricken parents at his bedside. No other sons survived. What happened to the family and the titles after Duke John died in 1722 had a ring of what one of Oscar Wilde's characters says: 'You should read the *Peerage*. It's the best thing in fiction the English have done.' When the duke's daughter Henrietta married the Earl of Godolphin she became a countess, but now, thanks to an elaborate legal provision, she also became Duchess of Marlborough in her own right: hence the oddity that there was a first and a third Duke of Marlborough, but no second. Henrietta had a son who predeceased her without issue, leaving her younger sister Anne, who had married Lord Spencer. He became Earl of Sunderland, and their son became third Duke of Marlborough.

For several generations the family name of the dukes remained Spencer, until quietly changed to Spencer-Churchill as a reminder of past glories, despite the absence of any direct descent in the male line from the victor of Blenheim. Altogether Winston Churchill's family chronicle was replete with the story-telling, rewritten history and invented tradition which would be prominent in his own political and literary career. A younger brother of the third duke was himself ennobled, as first Earl Spencer. Apart from the fifth earl, who sat in Gladstone's last Cabinet, the Spencers then minded their own business until 1981, when Lady Diana Spencer, daughter of the eighth earl, married the Prince of Wales in St Paul's Cathedral. And so Prince William of Wales, next heir to the throne, who was made Duke of Cambridge at his marriage in 2011, is one more descendant of the victor of Blenheim.

Through most of the Hanoverian and Victorian years the dukes of Marlborough were notable for their obscurity, or worse. The third, fourth and fifth dukes were 'profligate even by the standards of the late eighteenth and early nineteenth centuries', and if life is getting and spending, as Wordsworth said, then the Marlboroughs were much better at spending than at getting. Compared with grandees like the Dukes of Devonshire and Bedford, who'd been in the game longer, the Marlboroughs didn't have so much land anyway, even before the seventh duke sold a large part of his estates in Wiltshire and Shropshire. Then he sold more land in Buckinghamshire to Baron Ferdinand de Rothschild for £220,000, the family jewels for 35,000 guineas, and the great Sunderland library for £56,581, a sale so legally fraught that it required an Act of Parliament. Finally, after the eighth duke succeeded in1883, another great collection, the Old Master paintings at Blenheim, was disposed of for £350,000.

Briefly a Cabinet minister under Lord Derby and then Disraeli, the seventh duke had married a daughter of the Marquess of Londonderry, which would have important consequences for his grandson Winston. As well as six daughters, he had two sons, the Marquess of Blandford, who became eighth duke, and Lord Randolph Churchill. Neither brother was long lived: the eighth duke died in 1892 and was succeeded by his son, Churchill's first cousin 'Sunny', who married Consuelo Vanderbilt. She had a son in 1897, who would succeed his father in 1934, but for the five years between the eighth duke's death and that boy's birth, Winston Churchill was heir presumptive to the dukedom. If Sunny had died without begetting an heir, Churchill would have become Duke of Marlborough, and would never have sat in the House of Commons, let alone become prime minister.

As it was, he entered the Commons, where he would sit for more than sixty years. In early 1901, Churchill returned to London and took the oath as a Member of Parliament for the first time of many, before he made his maiden speech on 18 February. It contained a chivalrous aside – 'and if I were a Boer, I hope I should be fighting in the field' – which chivalrous words caused deep Tory resentment. That awful ignoble campaign still wore on, with more and more women and children dying in the camps. What the Liberal leader Sir Henry Campbell-Bannerman bravely condemned as 'methods of barbarism' persisted only thanks to the wretchedly narrow-minded High Commissioner, Sir Alfred Milner, who had helped engineer the war in the first place and now insisted that there should be no amnesty for 'Cape rebels' – Boers in the Cape Colony who were technically British subjects but who had understandably sided with their fellow Afrikaners.

Now Commander-in-Chief in South Africa, Kitchener wrote in March to St John Brodrick, the Secretary for War, that Milner's views 'may be strictly just, but they are to my mind vindictive,' and that to prolong the war 'seems to me absurd and wrong'. Churchill agreed. 'This miserable war, unfortunate and ill-omened in its beginning, inglorious in its course, cruel and hideous in its conclusion,' he called it in a letter to Milner himself. 'I have hated these latter stages with their barbarous features.' The Boers 'must be helped to rebuild their farms; the gold mines must do that. What more fitting function for the wealth of South African soil (better build farms in South Africa than palaces in Park Lane!*).' This change, from the happy warrior to the young MP who could now say, 'I hate and abominate all this expenditure on military armaments,' was one of his first transformations.

A series of great issues had riven British politics in Lord Randolph's lifetime and since, splitting parties within as well as distinguishing them without. Irish Home Rule was the only question which really separated Winston from the Liberals, or so he had told his mother, just as it had brought together the Tories and the Liberal opponents of Home Rule, now conveniently designated as Unionists. The Boer War caused another rift within the Liberal Party between the imperialists of the Liberal League who supported the war and the faction dubbed (not quite fairly) 'pro-Boers' who opposed the war, none more prominent than the Welsh firebrand David Lloyd George. Some of

---

* A number of the Randlords had acquired houses in Park Lane or elsewhere in Mayfair.

the most bitter political battles in the first years of the new century were sectarian, with the Dissenters, Methodists, Congregationalists and others, who were so strong in the Liberal Party, fighting for the disestablishment of the Episcopalian Church in Wales and for an end to Anglican control of education. That left Churchill cold, as did all religious questions.

But the other inescapable question was Free Trade against Protection, where he remained a passionate Free Trader. In 1903, Chamberlain raised the banner of 'tariff reform', Protection by any other name, and he was clearly determined to impose this on the Tories, at risk of splitting the party as he had split the Liberals over Home Rule. Once Balfour succeeded as prime minister, Churchill's relationship with his own party deteriorated rapidly, as became actually visible. Political drama in the House of Commons has always been heightened by its history and physical shape. Its original home was St Stephen's Chapel in the mediaeval Palace of Westminster, and so MPs don't debate in a semicircle of seats like the House of Representatives or the French Assembly (whose seating from the time of the Revolution gave us the potent if often misleading political metaphor of Left and Right) but facing each other across the floor as in the original chapel stalls.

As Churchill's criticisms of the government became sharper, they were more and more resented until, one day when he was speaking in the Commons, Balfour, on the Treasury Bench, stood up and walked out, followed by many other Tory MPs. The Unionist whip was then withdrawn from the Member for Oldham, and on 31 May 1904 Churchill 'crossed the floor': he entered the Chamber, walked towards the Speaker's Chair, bowed, and then turned right instead of left to sit on the Opposition benches, from which he would savagely attack the party he had just deserted. For the Tories he was now 'the Blenheim rat', and it did look as though he was leaving a sinking ship. Shipping water from the Chamberlain explosion, Balfour's ministry listed and lurched until December 1905, when he resigned, daring Sir Henry Campbell-Bannerman, the Liberal leader, to take office in his place. This was a long-standing tactical gambit, as in 1873 when Gladstone resigned, but Disraeli had seen a trap and declined to take over. This time Campbell-Bannerman accepted the challenge. He formed a new ministry and asked for a dissolution of Parliament, followed by an election in the new year. It was a Liberal landslide, and a new dawn, with a government of new men for a new age. Churchill's reward for changing parties came straight away, when he was made Parliamentary Under-Secretary for the Colonies. The position was all the more important since the new Secretary of State, Churchill's chief, was Lord Elgin sitting in the Upper House, and so Churchill was responsible for colonial questions in the Commons.

Abandoning the Tories meant that Churchill had to leave Oldham and find a Liberal seat. North-East Manchester had already been proffered to him, and he now gladly accepted, with one unforeseen but most important consequence. His new constituency had a large Jewish population: not a majority, as some historians have suggested, but substantial. That suited Churchill, who had been brought up to share his father's philosemitism, a contrast indeed to many Englishmen of his age and class like his cousin the Duke of Marlborough, who would respond to a hostile review of Churchill's life of Lord Randolph in the *Daily Telegraph* by saying that he wanted 'to administer a good and sound trouncing to that dirty little Hebrew' Harry Levy-Lawson, the owner of the paper. Churchill had inherited his father's friendship with the Rothschilds, and as a young man spent so much time with them and other rich Jewish acquaintances like Baron de Forrest that his son Randolph would write many years later with heavy-handed humour that 'During this period he was sometimes invited into Gentile society.'

Already Churchill had won the golden opinions of the *Jewish Chronicle*. After the assassination of Tsar Alexander II in 1881, Jews living in the Russian empire had been tormented by a wave of persecution, with another recrudescence only recently, most notoriously seen in the savage Kishinev pogrom of 1903. This had stimulated a great migration of Jews to the west, mostly across the Atlantic but some to England, and in response the Balfour government had introduced an Aliens Bill to staunch immigration. Churchill had opposed the Bill, and now spoke at a meeting in Manchester to protest against the pogroms. It led to a fateful meeting, a new friendship, and a theme that would echo through his life, making Churchill a Jewish hero who would still be honoured from Jerusalem to New York in the twenty-first century.

Another speaker that evening was Chaim Weizmann, whose day job was as a research chemist at Manchester University, but whose emotional energy was directed towards the Zionist movement he

would one day lead and the creation of a Jewish state whose first
president he would be. Born three days before Churchill, though in
a White Russian shtetl rather than a palace, Weizmann was a dreamer,
a luftmensch, or even a fantasist: he told Dorothy Rothschild, an
English supporter, that he had helped defend the Jewish quarter in
Kishinev during the pogrom, when he was undoubtedly in Geneva at
the time. But then Churchill was a luftmensch himself, and the sheer
romantic dream of 'restoring' the Jews spoke powerfully to him. He
was captivated by the cause of Zionism, and from the beginning, he
emphatically saw Zionism as a colonial enterprise which would benefit
his own country and its imperial mission. As early as 1908 he thought
that 'the establishment of a strong, free Jewish state astride the bridge
between Europe and Africa, flanking the land roads to the East, would
not only be an immense advantage to the British Empire, but a notable
step towards the harmonious disposition of the world among its
peoples,' one dream which conspicuously did not come true.

The election coincided with publication of Churchill's two-volume
biography of his father. His improbable but remarkably effective
literary agent was Frank Harris,* who secured a breathtaking advance
of £8000, more than the prime minister's salary. In many ways it's an
accomplished and enjoyable book, for all its absurdities: his son claimed
that Lord Randolph had struggled as hard as Disraeli to make his way
in politics, with 'No smooth path of patronage', as if there were any
comparison between the outlandish grandson of Jewish immigrants
and the son of a duke.

What interest the book retains lies in its method and its purpose,
and what it says about the son as much as the father. Unusually among
European languages, English has distinct words for 'story' and 'history'
rather than the same word for both: '*Was für eine Geschichte!*' means
'What a story!' rather than 'an excellent history book', and *une histoire*
can be tittle-tattle in the street as well as a work of historical scholarship. For Winston Churchill, there was never any distinction. History
meant telling a story, a drama which was often melodrama, with
heroes and villains, all thrown into relief by his gift for language. And
he always wrote as a partisan and advocate, with a case to make, on
behalf of his subject, though on behalf of himself as well. As Peter

---

* Now mostly remembered for his lewd memoirs, but in his day an outstanding
magazine editor, as well as a general literary factotum.

Clarke has noted, that first biography managed to be not only 'an explicit defence of Lord Randolph's career in loyally sticking with the Conservative Party in the 1880s but also as an implicit apologia for Winston's action in abandoning it twenty years later'.

More disturbing were the distortions and omissions, beyond the call of filial duty. Even serious biographies weren't then expected to carry an apparatus of notes and references, and so the reader was left dependent on the writer's good faith. Churchill had been granted privileged access to documentary sources, at Blenheim and elsewhere, and he used them very capriciously. One reviewer who had known and worked with Lord Randolph rightly said that Winston had played down his father's lack of principle and knack of changing positions. In his own far more scholarly and detached biography,* Roy Foster has shown how Churchill would distort the effect of documents by cutting passages without suggesting any omission.

One alarming example can stand for others: selective quotation of a letter from Lord Dufferin, the Lord Lieutenant of Ireland, implies that he supported Lord Randolph's position, when 'in fact, the original reads in a directly contrary sense'. Lord Randolph's letters are polished and embellished to improve them, inconvenient facts are ignored, and all in all, 'a great weight of minor alterations and major emphases combined to produce a portrait in the painting of which Churchill not only discovered his father, but refashioned him in his own image'. The harshest verdict on the biography came from the White House. 'I dislike the father and dislike the son,' said President Theodore Roosevelt. Both Randolph and Winston possessed 'such levity, lack of sobriety, lack of permanent principle, and an inordinate thirst for that cheap form of admiration which is given to notoriety, as to make them poor public servants', thought 'TR', and Winston's book was 'A clever, forceful, rather cheap and vulgar life of that clever, forceful, rather cheap and vulgar egoist.'

In England the reception was warmer than that, and seemed to enhance Churchill's standing in his new office, which now afforded another friendship. Jan Smuts, Boer general, scholar and thinker, at least by repute, came to London to negotiate the restoration of responsible government to the Transvaal. That is to say for its white inhabitants: this condition had been implicit in the Treaty of Vereeniging

---

* *Lord Randolph Churchill: A Political Life*, R.F. Foster (Oxford 1981).

which had finally ended the Boer War in 1902. Despite some hypocritical mutterings from the British, all non-whites – those known as
'Coloured' or mixed-race as well as Africans – were excluded from
the Transvaal franchise. Not that this disturbed Churchill, who thought
that 'The African aboriginal, for whom civilisation has no charms',
shouldn't be expected to vote, and who viewed the Boers or Afrikaners
fondly, not only then but still fifty years later when they were creating
the system they called apartheid.

One more meeting decidedly did not lead to a friendship. In
November 1906 Mohandas Gandhi came to London. He had lived
there earlier as a law student before returning to India, and then went
to South Africa where he worked as a lawyer on behalf of the Indian
community, as well as serving as an ambulance attendant in the Boer
War in which he ardently supported the British Empire. The community he served had been brought to Natal as indentured or semi-servile
plantation workers, as Indians had been to so many parts of the
empire, from Trinidad to Mauritius to Fiji, and they were detested by
Boers like Smuts, who hoped to wipe out the 'Asiatic cancer'. Gandhi
and H.O. Ally, a Muslim colleague, had come to London from Natal
to plead for their fellow Indians, threatened with gross discrimination.
They saw Lord Elgin, and then his junior minister. 'We met Mr
Winston Churchill,' Gandhi recorded, who 'spoke nicely' and patted
Ally on the back, though he offered no practical help. The meeting
seems to have made no impression at all on Churchill. He never met
Gandhi again, but the two would play a large part in each other's
lives.

In 1907, Parliament went into recess for the autumn and early
winter, and Churchill took the opportunity to leave the country from
September until the following January. Not only was the political
calendar then much more leisurely, the distinction between public and
private life was much looser. Before Churchill sailed for Egypt and
then east Africa, recently acquired by the British, and today the republics of Kenya and Uganda, Elgin had innocently supposed this was 'a
purely sporting and private expedition', but Churchill liked to mix
business with pleasure. He wrote well-paid accounts of his outing for
newspapers, and then published My African Journey; a most interesting
book, and a most telling one.

To modern eyes, the most distasteful thing about the first edition
may be its cover. In pictorial embossing on shiny red cloth, Churchill

stands, grinning broadly, large-bore rifle in hand, beside the body of a handsome elephant he has just shot. It was one of twenty-three kinds of animal he had killed in ten days, he boasted. As to the human inhabitants, although his view of Africans was always condescending, and sometimes brutal, he sometimes showed paternalist benevolence. Earlier in 1907, Churchill had learned about a massacre of Kisi tribesmen in the British colony he was shortly to visit, and had protested: 'Surely it cannot be necessary to go on killing these defenceless people on such an enormous scale,' and he was shocked by reports from Natal of the 'disgusting butchery of the natives'. And yet he insisted that the obviously backward and inferior Africans needed to be taught the merits of hard work, by compulsion if need be, by the superior race of Englishmen. There was no country on earth 'where the conditions were more favourable than in Uganda to a practical experiment in State Socialism ... A class of rulers is provided by an outside power as remote from, and in all that constitutes fitness to direct, as superior to the Baganda as Mr Wells's Martians would have been to us.'* What Churchill would have made of an American president with a Kenyan father a hundred years after his African journey scarcely bears thinking about.

Even his benevolence must be qualified. In 1906 he had attended the annual manoeuvres of the German army and met Kaiser Wilhelm II. Many years later Churchill recalled that occasion, when the Kaiser had talked 'in great animation and at some length' about 'the native revolt in German South-West Africa'. The reader wouldn't know from Churchill's casual tone that this 'revolt' in what is now Namibia had been a near-genocidal massacre of the Herero people by German troops, enthusiastically supported by the Governor-General, Heinrich Ernst Goering, father of a more famous son. Churchill would later wax eloquent about the horrors of 'Prussianism' in Europe; he minded less what Prussia did to Africans.

For all his self-confidence when he dealt with imperial and foreign affairs, the rarely remarked fact is that Churchill was never really a well-travelled man. In the 1860s, Dilke had visited north America, New Zealand, Australia, India and Egypt and in the 1880s Churchill's

---

* In H.G. Wells's 1898 science fiction novel *The War of the Worlds*, southern England is invaded by Martians.

future cabinet colleague George Nathaniel Curzon had prepared himself for his mission as an 'Asiatic statesman' with an astonishing series of journeys, through Russia and central Asia, at length through Persia, then to the Far East and, most intrepidly, through the Pamir mountains into Afghanistan. Curzon was strongly committed to his country's imperial mission, and he took this task seriously. When he was viceroy of India from 1899 to 1905 he became deeply interested in Indian culture and civilisation, in a way that Churchill never was for a moment, and he was later praised by Nehru for his work in conserving the architectural glories of the country (more than the Indians themselves have sometimes done since independence). A subsequent viceroy, who played a crucial part at the climactic moment of Churchill's life, travelled further still: in 1904, Edward Wood, one day to be Lord Halifax, and his friend Ludovic Heathcoat-Amory undertook a tour to South Africa, India, Australia and New Zealand. Even Lord Randolph had travelled round the world towards his sad end.

By contrast, after his victory on the polo field in 1899, Winston Churchill never set foot in India again. He never revisited South Africa after 1900, or east Africa after 1907. Although he would later travel to Morocco for recreation, as well as to meet a later President Roosevelt, and Egypt by way of duty, as Colonial Secretary and then wartime prime minister, he never visited any of the British territories in west Africa, or anywhere else south of the Sahara. He never once travelled further east of India, not to the British territories of Burma, which his father had acquired, to Malaya or Hong Kong, nor to Singapore whose name would one day lie in his heart as Calais did in Queen Mary's, still less to China or Japan. And the champion of 'the English-speaking peoples' never visited Australia or New Zealand.

For that matter, after he returned from his lecture tour in 1901, it was the best part of three decades before he crossed the Atlantic again, and then only to the United States and Canada. Apart from two sojourns in Cuba, when he was twenty-one and seventy-one, Latin America was unknown to him. He visited Europe often enough, but mostly for leisure and pleasure. Writing affectionately about King Alfonso XIII, king of Spain from his birth in 1886 until his deposition in 1931, Churchill mentions their first meeting in the spring of 1914, when 'I had come to Madrid to play polo', a carefree enough recreation for the man responsible for the greatest navy in the world just as the greatest war in history approached.

This insularity mattered less at a time when Churchill was anyway turning towards domestic politics. In early 1908, Campbell-Bannerman learned that he had terminal cancer. He resigned on 5 April and died just over two weeks later. The sybaritic King Edward was amusing himself at Biarritz and, with little sense of constitutional propriety ('an inconvenient and dangerous departure from precedent', *The Times* called it), summoned Asquith thither to kiss hands on his appointment as prime minister on 8 April. On that day, Asquith wrote from the Hôtel du Palais to 'My dear Winston', offering him the post of President of the Board of Trade with a seat in the Cabinet and a hope that his salary might be increased: there was then an invidious distinction among Cabinet ministers, with the grander secretaryships of state paying £5000 a year but lesser offices only £2000. Churchill jumped at the chance of promotion, and threw himself into his new role of social reformer with his usual gusto.

By now the political weather was changing. In the nineteenth century, 'classical liberalism' had meant a small state, a pacific foreign policy, and *laissez-faire* in domestic politics. Industry was left to its own devices, and the citizenry, rich and poor, were left to fend for themselves. When the state did begin to look after the hungry and weak, it had more often been Conservatives than Liberals who took the lead. Otto von Bismarck, the most astute reactionary of his time, had introduced public welfare in his new Reich to dish the Social Democrats, and it was Disraeli's Tory government of 1874 to 1880 which had, said one union leader, done more for the working class in six years than had the Liberals in a generation.

But the new century brought a 'New Liberalism', which saw social improvement as something which the state should deliberately direct. The President of the Board of Trade took this up with the zeal of a convert, proposing a minimum wage, creating labour exchanges to find work for the unemployed, suppressing 'sweat shops' – small garment factories where men, and often women, many of them immigrants, worked very long hours for very low wages – and then helping Lloyd George, who had been promoted as Chancellor of the Exchequer, to introduce National Insurance and an old age pension. Only one woman had been emotionally central to him as a child, not his mother but his nanny Mrs Everest, or 'Woomany' as he called her, a nickname which might have interested Freud. He described her fondly, without mentioning that when his younger brother Jack, who played little part in his life, was thirteen, Mrs Everest had been abruptly dismissed. 'When I think of the fate of poor old women' like her, Churchill wrote many years later, 'so many of whom have no one to look after them and nothing to live on at the end of their lives, I am glad to have had a hand in all that structure of pensions and insurance which no other country can rival.'

An excellent convention which lasted until after the Great War and was only ended when politicians decided that it suited the interests of the electorate rather than themselves meant that an MP newly appointed to the Cabinet had to resign his parliamentary seat and stand for re-election. At the ensuing Manchester by-election, Churchill was defeated by a Tory, William Joynson-Hicks.* 'We have all been yearning for this to happen,' crowed the *Daily Telegraph*, with which Churchill would one day be closely linked: 'Winston Churchill is out, Out, OUT.' Another seat was quickly found and he was parachuted into Dundee, with which he had no connection at all, a largely impoverished working-class city which was, like so much of Scotland then, solidly Liberal. He easily defeated three others, among them Edwin Scrymgeour standing as Prohibitionist, who won barely a tenth of Churchill's votes.

As Churchill entered the Cabinet aged thirty-three, a thoughtful journalist called him 'the most interesting problem of personal speculation in English politics', words which would apply for most of his career, and even after his death. No one who speculated for a moment could doubt that his ambition was to become prime minister, and sooner rather than later. But how seriously did others take him? In his new role Churchill was 'full of the poor, whom he has just discovered', as one colleague sardonically put it. The mild sarcasm wasn't unfair, and the scepticism about him which those words suggest was widely shared.

In his rapid ascent, Churchill had acquired plenty of enemies, and harsh critics. 'I refuse to be shut up in a soup kitchen with Mrs Beatrice Webb', Churchill said about his work at the Board of Trade,

---

* The much-mocked Joynson-Hicks or 'Jix' was also an abstainer, a solicitor, an antisemitic reactionary, an early advocate in 1916 of the terror bombing of German cities, and from 1924 a Cabinet colleague of Churchill's, when as Home Secretary he exercised his obsessive puritanism by trying to stem 'the flood of filth coming across the Channel' in the form of books such as *Ulysses*.

but she might not have wished to be cooped up with him. That imperious lady and her husband Sidney were lampooned by H.G. Wells in *The New Machiavelli*, although in truth a couple who could spend their honeymoon attending the Trade Unions Congress in Glasgow were beyond satire. They would help impose on the Labour Party the Fabian managerialism which was its dominant ethos for most of the twentieth century, and then much later they would find another secular salvation. The Webbs visited Russia just as Stalin's awful terror began in earnest, and in 1936 published an utterly credulous and admiring account of *Soviet Russia: A New Civilisation?*, which was republished without the question mark a year later as the purges grew more murderous still, and has been called, 'despite severe competition, the most preposterous book about Communist Russia ever written'.

In the summer of 1903, Beatrice Webb had met Churchill and found 'too unpleasant a flavour with his restless self-regarding personality and lack of moral or intellectual refinement'. She foresaw that he might go far 'unless he knocks himself to pieces like his father', although he was 'egotistical, bumptious, shallow-minded and reactionary, but with a certain personal magnetism, great pluck and some originality, not of intellect but of character. More of the American speculator than the English aristocrat.' In years to come Churchill would make a great show of his half-American parentage, but at this time his enemies had no more bitter term of abuse for him. With Mrs Webb on one side, the *National Review* weighed in from the other. Churchill had deserted his first party 'because promotion tarried', said that vituperative High Tory journal. 'He always plays up to the loudest gallery. He is the transatlantic type of demagogue ("Them's my sentiments and if they don't give satisfaction they can be changed"*). There has never yet been a man of this peculiar temperament in a position of responsibility and power in British politics, and it will be interesting to see how far a politician whom no one trusts will go in a country where character is supposed to count.'

After less than two years at the Board of Trade Churchill was promoted again to Home Secretary in February 1910, where his tenure was even briefer, before he became First Lord of the Admiralty in

---

* A line Groucho Marx later borrowed.

October 1911; he remained at the Admiralty for three and a half highly dramatic years. While international tension mounted, and brutal wars erupted in the Balkans prefiguring a far more terrible conflict, these prewar years were also a time of vibrant intellectual and artistic life, with cultivated London agog at the Post-Impressionist exhibition and the Ballets Russes. Not all of this touched Churchill. He loved the theatre if it wasn't too demanding, and he had, as Orwell later said, 'a real if not very discriminating feeling for literature'. But he had no ear for music and, although he took up painting as a form of therapy when his fortunes fell low during the Great War, his taste in art was no more discriminating; he showed little enthusiasm for the Post-Impressionists, and none at all for their Cubist successors.

Besides artistic innovation, those years saw increasing social turbulence. Industrial strife escalated towards a series of great strikes in 1912 and often tended towards violence, while the angry campaigners for the female suffrage used civil disobedience, or more. Churchill had half-heartedly supported votes for women but changed his mind, provoked by the women who disrupted his meetings. In October 1909, he was attacked with a horse whip at Temple Meads, the Great Western railway station in Bristol, by a militant named Theresa Garnett. At the same time a showdown over curbing the powers of the House of Lords became exceptionally bitter, while the Irish conflict reached the brink of civil war. Churchill was in the thick of it, on all fronts.

His ally was Lloyd George, who introduced his 'People's Budget' in 1909, raising money to pay for old age pensions and also for new battleships evidently needed as the Reich began building a huge new High Seas Fleet. In a wondrous phrase, the German Chancellor, Theobald von Bethmann-Hollweg, explained that this fleet was needed by Germany 'for the general purposes of her greatness', but the British not surprisingly saw it directed against themselves. The new taxes, on the highest incomes and on land values, were remarkably mild by later standards, but they sent the rich into paroxysms of rage, and the Lords threw out the budget, against all constitutional precedent. This could only be resolved by legislation to curb the Lords, but first by a general election.

In the event, there was not one election in 1910 but two, one in January and February and then one in December, after a pause from political hostilities when King Edward VII died in May and was succeeded by his son as King George V. The two elections produced almost identical results, dead heats between Liberals and Unionists, although the Tories won a plurality of the popular vote, as they did in every election in the first half of the twentieth century apart from 1906 and 1945. There was talk of a coalition government embracing both parties, an idea favoured notably by Lloyd George, who would indeed lead such a coalition government before long although in very different circumstances, but the Liberals continued in office as a minority government with the support of some eighty Irish and some forty Labour MPs.

As a price for Irish support, the Asquith government committed itself to Home Rule. But first the Lords' veto had to be ended, as it was in the summer of 1911 by the passage of the Parliament Bill, despite the hysterical opposition of Churchill's great friend (and best man) Lord Hugh Cecil and his fellow 'Hughligans'. Churchill described Cecil as the only true High Tory he had ever known, and Cecil sincerely believed that any weakening of the power of the Lords was a kind of sacrilege. He was fanatical in his opposition to the disestablishment of the Church of England in Wales, as well as to the law legalising marriage to a deceased wife's sister, which humane measure the lifelong celibate Cecil called 'an act of sexual vice'. Thanks to the capitulation of a group of peers led by Curzon, the Act passed in the Lords, and the path was now clear for Irish Home Rule, a question which had been in abeyance since 1893 when the Lords threw out Gladstone's second Home Rule Bill after the Commons had passed it.

During this phase of an intense reforming radicalism, Churchill cheerfully played tribune of the masses against his own class. As early as May 1904 he had said that the Independent Labour Party was less to be feared than 'the Independent Capitalist Party', which was 'preaching the gospel of Mammon, advocating the 10 per cent commandments – who raise every day the inspiring prayer "Give cash in our time, O Lord".' Now he extolled the improvements made by government intervention, roads, water, electricity, 'and all the while the landlord sits still ... he contributes nothing to the process from which his own enrichment is derived.' He denounced the Tories, his once and future home, as the 'party of great vested interests ... corruption at home, aggression abroad to cover it up ... sentiment by the bucketful, patriotism by the imperial pint; the open hand at the public exchequer, the open door at the public house; dear food for the millions, cheap labour for the millionaire'.

As to the House of Lords, where his grandfather had sat and his cousin now did, 'The old doddering peers are there, the cute financial magnates are there, the clever wirepullers are there, the big brewers with bulbous noses are there. All the enemies of progress are there: the weaklings, the sleek, smug, comfortable, selfish individuals.' When Curzon was rash enough to say that 'all civilisation has been the work of aristocracies', Churchill retorted, 'The upkeep of aristocracies has been the hard work of all civilisations.' And he took the side in the Cabinet of those who wanted money spent on domestic reform rather than battleships, praising the German system of public welfare and ridiculing the idea of a war with Germany. There might be 'snapping and snarling' in the jingo press, he said in 1908, but 'these two great peoples have nothing to fight about, have no prize to fight for, and have no place to fight in,' one of the earliest cases of his knack for prophecy more confident than prescient.

All this caused both astonishment and rage. 'The big thing that has happened in the past two years is that Lloyd George and Churchill have practically taken the limelight, not merely from their own colleagues, but from the Labour Party,' a perplexed Beatrice Webb wrote in November 1910. 'They stand out as the most advanced politicians.' But King Edward had thought Churchill 'Almost more of a cad in office than he was in opposition', while Lord Knollys, the king's private secretary, said that, however Churchill's conduct might be explained, 'Of course it cannot be from conviction or principle. The very idea of his having either is enough to make anyone laugh.' Or as the line going round London clubland had it, 'Lloyd George was born a cad and never forgot it. Winston Churchill was born a gentleman and never remembered it.'

Such sneers underestimated Churchill's real if intermittent compassion, and his sense of justice. At the Home Office he had no need to discover the lot of the prisoners for whom he was now responsible. He said himself that his time in Boer hands had given him the keenest sympathy for all prisoners, and his brief tenure led Orwell many years later to acclaim him as the most humane Home Secretary in memory. There was surely enough scope for humanity. In May 1897, just after his release from prison, Oscar Wilde had published the noblest thing he ever wrote, a letter in the Liberal *Daily Chronicle*. 'The cruelty that is practiced by day and night on children in English prisons is incredible,' Wilde wrote, and that cruelty had barely lessened by 1910: Churchill was dismayed to learn of an eleven-year-old boy who had stolen a piece of fish worth a few pence and was sentenced to be birched and held in a reformatory for seven years.

But Churchill's spell at the Home Office also saw him embroiled in another fierce controversy, when a mining strike at Tonypandy in south Wales in November 1910 turned violent, verging on a small pogrom as Jewish-owned shops were looted. Churchill ordered police and additional troops to the town, but recalled some of the troops en route, since it was his intention only to maintain order and avoid bloodshed. For the most part avoided it was, and yet it was all too characteristic of Churchill the stormy petrel that this became in the telling a story of his brutish hostility to the working class. 'Tonypandy' was held against him not only then but as late as 2019, when John McDonnell, a prominent if ignorant Labour politician, called him a 'villain' because of Tonypandy.

Then in January 1911 three Russian anarchists were holed up in a house in Sidney Street in the East End, where policemen, reinforced by soldiers of the Scots Guards quartered nearby at the Tower of London, tried to flush them out, before the house caught fire and burned down, consuming the terrorists. One unforgettable image is the photograph of the rifle-toting soldiers and policemen with, alongside them, the Home Secretary in silk tall hat and long astrakhan-collared greatcoat. This prompted Balfour's barb in the Commons: 'He was, I understand, in military phrase, in what is known as the zone of fire – he and a photographer were both risking valuable lives. I understand what the photographer was doing, but what was the right honourable Gentleman doing?' This was 'a not altogether unjust reflection', Churchill wrote with a grin years later, and the answer was simple enough: he was there looking for action, and fame, and a story he could tell.

Whether or not Churchill was the political chameleon his enemies alleged, he was certainly a political jackdaw. One year he picked up military economy, Free Trade the next, then public welfare. And then came another enthusiasm, disturbing enough at the time, far more so in hindsight. 'Eugenics' was the dark side of progressive collectivism.

The Boer War had seen large-scale popular recruitment for the first time, from stockbrokers in the City to boys from the slums, but many of the urban poor who tried to join up were rejected because of their wretched physical condition, with rotten teeth and scrawny bodies enfeebled by malnutrition and rickets, and the governing classes were thrown into a panic about 'national deterioration'.

Some of them now saw an urgent need not only for improving the condition of the poor but for scientific breeding to eliminate the 'socially unfit'. Those most obsessed by this supposed decline of the racial stock were not reactionaries but progressives: the Webbs, Wells, Bernard Shaw and other Fabian socialists, dismayed by the influx of what Sidney Webb called inferior Irish and Jewish immigrants. In this guise, Churchill was a true progressive of his time, as he warned against 'the multiplication of the Feeble-Minded'. This was 'a very terrible danger to the race', he told Asquith in December 1910, and he advocated a policy of compulsory sterilisation to purify that 'race', with 100,000 to start with. Thirty years later Churchill would imperishably say that, were the Third Reich to triumph, the whole world, 'will sink into the abyss of a new Dark Age, made more sinister, and perhaps more protracted, by the lights of perverted science'. Here was one awful historical irony: the perverted science of National Socialism, beginning with sterilisation and proceeding to extermination, was what Churchill himself had once favoured, taken to a hideous conclusion.

While domestic politics were turbulent enough, a succession of international crises threatened war. English politicians, not least Sir Edward Grey, the Foreign Secretary, were baffled by the erratic, impulsive and often reckless conduct of the Kaiser. William Tyrrell was Grey's private secretary, and as exasperated as his chief by Wilhelm's unpredictable and garrulous meddling. Altogether, Tyrrell said drily, the Kaiser was, 'in fact, the Winston of Germany'. Others would have agreed. At the Home Office as at the Board of Trade, the Winston of England's conduct could infuriate those he worked with. 'Churchill is ill-mannered, boastful, unprincipled, without any redeeming qualities except his amazing ability and industry,' his Cabinet colleague Charles Hobhouse wrote in 1912. And his zeal exasperated those who tried to serve him. 'Once a week or oftener Mr Churchill came to the office bringing with him some adventurous or impossible projects,' recalled Sir Edward Troup, the Permanent

Secretary at the Home Office, 'but after half an hour's discussion something was evolved which was still adventurous but not impossible.' Churchill left the Home Office in October 1911; within four years his career would seem to have been finished by something very adventurous, but impossible.

Jllustriertes Wochenblatt   für Humor und Satire

Nr. 48   BERLIN

42. JAHRGANG   28. NOVEMBER 1913

Englisches Variété.

Was wird denn nun bei Churchills Schleiertanz herauskommen? — Der nackte Egoist!

3

'A tragic figure of failure & folly'
Gallipoli 1915

With only the faintest breeze ruffling the cypresses and lavender bushes, V Beach Cemetery lies very still, just above Cape Helles at the tip of the Gallipoli peninsula. Rows of neat headstones give names and regiments, 1st Royal Dublin Fusiliers, 2nd Hampshire Regiment, 2nd South Wales Borderers; at top left a cross, varied by a Star of David for one private from the Manchester Regiment; a pious or exalted inscription at the foot: 'Their Glory Shall Not Be Blotted Out' or the like. But every headstone in this long line of graves begins with the haunting words 'Believed to be buried in this cemetery ...', meaning that the bodies were recovered after the war and beyond certain identification. When the last Allied soldiers were evacuated from Gallipoli in early 1916, more than 34,000 British dead were left behind, as well as nearly 10,000 from Australia and almost 3000 from New Zealand, nearly 10,000 French and French colonial troops who are often forgotten, and some 1400 Indians who always are. They weren't the only casualties of the most controversial campaign of the Great War. Left behind also were Churchill's reputation and career. How had it come to this?

His personal involvement dated from October 1911, when he became First Lord of the Admiralty. Over the following years, a European war sometimes seemed possible, and a civil war in Ireland seemed likelier. As usual, Churchill was on the side of intransigent resistance although, as usual also, he could change his position with bewildering speed. When 1911 had begun, it found him for the moment a voice of calm and compromise. The Liberals remained in office after the two ambiguous elections held in 1910. In the new year, Churchill wrote to Asquith congratulating him, but saying that 'I hope we may be able to pursue *une politique d'apaisement*', by which he meant conciliating the Tory Unionists, little guessing how toxic that word *apaisement* – 'appeasement' – would one day become, thanks to him.

Behind this geniality, Churchill was increasingly disillusioned by Asquith's weakness and personal decline, partly for a reason notable in view of Churchill's own later reputation, an all-too-visible love of wine and brandy. 'On Thursday night the PM was vy bad: & I squirmed with embarrassment,' Churchill wrote to Clementine in April 1911 after one long evening in Parliament. 'He could hardly speak: & many people noticed his condition ... [He] trusts me with everything after dinner. Up till that time he is at his best – but thereafter! It is an awful pity & only the persistent freemasonry of the House of Commons prevents a scandal. I like the old boy and admire both his intellect and his character. But what risks to run.' Although Churchill was himself never a strict water-drinker, it was significant that he could be so shocked by intemperance, at that time.

By August, the Parliament Act opened the way for Home Rule, but by then even that drama was played out in the shadow of international conflict, and it was under that shadow that Churchill went to the Admiralty in October. He soon made himself deeply disliked by many naval officers by his energetic reforming and general meddling, although this was largely to his credit. He wanted to improve the conditions of ordinary seamen, and to increase their pay for the first time since the early days of Victoria's reign, and at the other end he created a naval staff. 'I knew thoroughly the current state of our naval affairs,' he claimed with justice, and he boasted later that he had ensured that the Fleet was ready for war, although it was also charged against him that he made that war more likely.

He took besides two related decisions whose consequences reverberated a hundred years later, when England had long since ceased to be a great naval power. One was to change the fuel of the Royal Navy's warships from coal to oil. This was technically the right choice, since oil was more efficient than coal, but while Great Britain sat on enormous deposits of coal and mined more than enough for home and abroad – in 1912, half of all coal in the world dug for export left the adjacent ports of Cardiff and Barry in South Wales – it had no oil, until it was discovered under the North Sea shortly after Churchill's death. Hence Churchill's other decision, to provide the navy with a reliable supply, by acquiring a controlling interest in Anglo-Persian Oil. This was done in peremptory fashion and with no heed for the inhabitants of Persia, later called Iran. Churchill would visit Persia as prime minister, for a most unusual meeting at Teheran in 1943 and then, ten years after that, his government would play a darker part in Persian affairs.

As if the sea weren't enough, Churchill was exhilarated by a new realm in the air. Only a few years after the Wright brothers had first taken off in North Carolina, he learned to fly. 'A lonely impulse of delight / Drove to this tumult in the cloud': Churchill may never have fought in those clouds, but he shared the exhilaration of Yeats's Irish airman, even when he was nearly killed and Clementine begged him to stop. In 1909 Louis Blériot had caused great excitement and won a £1000 prize from the *Daily Mail* when he flew across the Channel for the first time. Exciting, but ominous, and few then saw what it meant. Neither the hidebound admirals nor their reforming First Lord guessed that the great new Dreadnought battleships now being built would be obsolescent within a generation when they became highly vulnerable to attack from the air. A still more baleful turn came when Italy launched a cynical and brutal attack in 1911 to seize Tripolitania and Cyrenaica on the southern shore of the Mediterranean, ostensibly Ottoman vassals, and this squalid war saw for the first time ever aircraft dropping bombs, on combatants and non-combatants alike. Ill omens indeed for England: as Hitler later observed, there were no islands in the modern world.

For all of Churchill's boisterous self-confidence, national pride had been badly shaken by two simultaneous events: Captain Robert Scott's failure to reach the South Pole ahead of his Norwegian rival and his death in March 1912 attempting to return, and then, in the same month, the sinking of the *Titanic*, the largest liner afloat, on her maiden voyage (Scott's death was merely surmised until the bodies were found in November). Both supposedly provide heartening stories of British courage and chivalry, to make Churchill 'proud of our race and its traditions'. Captain Lawrence Oates, too weak to continue without help and burdening the rest of Scott's party, went out into the blizzard. 'It was the act of a brave man and an English gentleman,' said Scott, but the fact was that they had been beaten by Roald Amundsen's better-equipped and better-organised team, a parable of English gentlemanly amateurism.

As to the *Titanic*, in Imperial Rome, 'the swells and potentates would have gone off with their concubines,' said Churchill, 'and the rest could go to hell,' a decadence which explained the fall of the Roman Empire. The superior ethical code of imperial England meant that its rulers would accept sacrifice with honour, he claimed, which he saw exemplified by the *Titanic* story. This was more Churchillian wish-fulfilment. In reality, almost all the children in first and second class in the ship were saved, but only one in three children in third class, men in first class were twice as likely to be saved as those in third class, and Churchill conveniently forgot J. Bruce Ismay, the chairman of the White Star Line, Sir Cosmo and Lady Duff-Gordon, and a number of other swells and potentates who contrived to escape early from the stricken ship.

One effect of the *Titanic* disaster was to emphasise the importance of the new medium of wireless telegraphy or radio, and thus the value of the Marconi company, which had just been granted a lucrative contract by the government. It transpired that three senior members of the government, Lloyd George, Sir Rufus Isaacs and the Master of Elibank (Alexander Murray), respectively Chancellor, Attorney General and Chief Whip, had been speculating in shares in the distinct but related American Marconi Company, and in Isaacs's case had given highly disingenuous answers about these dealings in the Commons. This might have ended their careers, but they were saved by the determination of Asquith, and also of Churchill, who stuck by Lloyd George with a loyalty he wrongly thought would be repaid.

Despite the outward intensity of political strife, there was a curious artificiality about it. In May 1911, Churchill formed the Other Club, where political opponents who showered each other with public abuse could meet privately in convivial friendship, having ordained that 'Nothing in the rules or intercourse of the Club shall interfere with the rancour or asperity of party politics.' His boon companion was F.E. Smith, the brilliant barrister and vitriolic Tory who had encouraged every extreme cause, and whose *boutades* are now inevitably listed on the website of the International Churchill Society.* 'FE' became Churchill's closest friend until he drank himself to a premature death.

*

---

* Frederick Edwin Smith, 1872–1930, subsequently Earl of Birkenhead and Lord Chancellor, famous for his legal learning and insolent wit. To one judge who said, 'Having heard your submission, Mr Smith, I am none the wiser,' he replied, 'No m'lord, but much better informed.' Years later, when a pompous judge, perplexed about the correct sentencing policy in what was then called a case of unnatural vice, asked the Lord Chancellor, 'What do you give a man who allows himself to be buggered?' Birkenhead answered, 'Oh, thirty shillings, two pounds, whatever you have on you.'

As Berlin continued to build its great fleet, and to bluster and bully from Morocco to the Balkans, Churchill began to apprehend 'the coming war with Germany', as he called it as early as October 1910. 'Winston talks about nothing but the Sea and the Navy and the wonderful things he is going to do,' recorded his Naval Secretary, and he certainly saw a good deal of the sea. The First Lord had his own yacht, the *Enchantress*, in which Churchill spent as many as eight months of the first three years he held the office. Sometimes pleasure was mixed with business, and colleagues and friends were invited to cruise aboard the *Enchantress*, or 'Holidays at Govt. expense' as General Sir Henry Wilson sourly said. But more often she was used by Churchill to visit dockyards and ports around the British coast, and the Mediterranean.

His new position was a problem in another way, because of his reputation and his background. From the time that he was the khaki candidate par excellence in 1900, and then moved towards the front ranks of British politics, Churchill had been a most singular figure, not because of his ducal origins, but because of his military career. In Berlin, Bismarck had addressed the Reichstag wearing his reserve officer's uniform; in Paris, General Boulanger had tried to take power as 'a man on a horse'; in the United States, over the four decades from the death of Lincoln until 1904, every Republican presidential candidate but one had served as an officer of the Union army in the Civil War – and the 1904 election was won by Theodore Roosevelt, the Rough Rider of Cuba. This was the age when a Bulgar general could say, 'we have become the most militaristic state in the world' as boast rather than lament, and when uniforms were continually seen in every capital city.

Except London: as Orwell later observed, England was unique as a Great Power where officers of the regular army wore civilian plain clothes off duty. When Churchill entered the House of Commons there were plenty of old colonels and rear-admirals on its benches, but they sat as another form of public duty after they had hung up their uniforms, and certainly with no expectation at all of ministerial office. In contrast to those other countries, between December 1834 when the Duke of Wellington resigned and May 1940 when Churchill was appointed, no British prime minister had previously been a soldier* or fought in a battle. England may have exported violence to her

---

* Unless one counts Sir Robert Peel's occasional service in the Staffordshire Yeomanry.

empire, but she was, in Europe, without question the most pacific of the Great Powers, depending more than any other on peace for her trade, and also the only Power which could not possibly gain any territory in Europe by war. The English were deeply suspicious of militarism and military rulers; Wellington's own argument in favour of retaining the corrupt old system of purchase of commissions was that, by avoiding the military 'career open to the talents', the dangers of Bonapartism would also be avoided. Later events in much of Europe seemed to confirm Wellington's point.

And Churchill's military background was far from politically irrelevant, along with his bloodthirsty accounts of fighting and killing 'savages'. He was conscious of this, and in reaction had been ostentatiously hostile to militarism during his early political career. In his first parliamentary speech, he had borrowed a phrase from the elder von Moltke, who had observed in 1890 (using 'cabinet' to mean oligarchic government) that the age of 'cabinet wars' had passed and we now had 'wars of peoples'; or as Churchill said, 'Democracy is more vindictive than Cabinets. The wars of peoples will be more terrible than those of kings.' Penetrating words, and he had no idea just how horribly true they would prove over the next fifty years.

In 1904 he had joined a party which, more than ever after the Boer War, was deeply pacifistic, and sympathetic to Germany, at least until 3 August 1914. For some years Churchill played the good Liberal by opposing any increase in military and naval spending. But even so there were still many like the Labour politician J.R. Clynes who thought that 'Churchill was, and will always remain, a soldier in mufti,' or the Liberal journalist A.G. Gardiner, editor of the *Daily News*, who wrote, 'Remember, he is a soldier first, last and always. He will write his name big in our future. Let us take care he does not write in blood.'

And while he protested that he was more than just a soldier, Churchill recognised in himself an obsession with war, along with a contradictory fear of that obsession. 'Much as war attracts me,' he had written to Clementine from the German army manoeuvres in 1909, '& fascinates my mind with its tremendous situations – I feel more deeply every year ... what vile & wicked folly and barbarism it is.' Then again he wrote from the field day of the Oxfordshire Hussars, in which he continued to serve as a part-time soldier while he was a

Cabinet minister, 'I have much confidence in my judgement when I see things clearly, but on nothing do I seem to feel the truth more than in tactical combinations ... I am sure I have the root of the matter in me.' Soon enough it would seem that he was indeed writing his name big in blood, but that his belief that he had 'the root' of military matters was unfounded.

Voices prophesying war in Europe were almost drowned by the roar from across the Irish Sea. The Third Home Rule Bill was introduced in 1912, passed in the Commons, was inevitably rejected by the Lords, but thanks to the curbing of the Lords' veto could now become law anyway after two years. The Tories at first opposed Home Rule in any form at all. When Lord Randolph had spoken of 'playing the Orange card' it was an apt metaphor. One card wins a four-card trick at the bridge table, and his – and subsequently the Tories' – object was to play the Ulster card as a trump to keep all four Irish provinces in the Union. In time, even the Irish Unionists, and their English Tory allies, came grudgingly to recognise the impossibility of holding the south and west of Ireland, with their large Catholic-nationalist majority, under a Parliament they rejected. And so inexorably the Irish question became the Ulster question. Irish Nationalists and their English Liberal allies were just as slow to recognise the impossibility of forcing nearly a million Protestant Unionists against their will under a Dublin government they dreaded.

But Ulster defiance couldn't be ignored. The languid Balfour had been ejected from the Tory leadership and replaced by Andrew Bonar Law. Born in Canada the son of a Presbyterian minister from Coleraine in the far north of Ulster, Bonar Law was the only British party leader ever to have felt a deep personal involvement in the Ulster cause, and he was a much harsher personality than Balfour. The bitterness of the conflict was brought home to Churchill very directly in February 1912 when he paid a quixotic visit to Belfast to explain the necessity of Home Rule, as a step on the path 'to the unity of the English speaking races'. To give the event an ironical twist, in Cabinet, only days before the visit, Churchill and Lloyd George had proposed the exclusion of Ulster from the coming Bill, but were outnumbered.

Unaware of that, the Ulstermen were enraged. 'There may be bloodshed – I think there will,' one of them warned. 'The only way it can be avoided is by Mr Churchill staying away. His presence in that platform is an insult to loyal Ireland,' especially insulting, some thought, to the memory of Lord Randolph and 'Ulster will fight.' Churchill did not stay away, and there very nearly was bloodshed. In a defiant speech in Belfast, he tried to turn around his father's words: 'It is in a different sense that I accept and repeat Lord Randolph Churchill's words. "Ulster will fight and Ulster will be right". Let Ulster fight for the dignity and honour of Ireland. Let her fight for the reconciliation of races and for the forgiveness of ancient wrongs,' which must count among the most sadly optimistic words even Churchill ever uttered.

After the meeting, the motor car in which Churchill was being driven was almost overturned by an Orange mob. Clementine had bravely accompanied her husband, and this frightening episode may have precipitated a miscarriage she suffered soon afterwards. Within months the temperature had risen still further. Bonar Law recklessly said, 'I can imagine no length of resistance to which Ulster will go, which I shall not be ready to support, and in which they will not be supported by the overwhelming majority of the British people.' He repeated it in July at a great public meeting at Churchill's birthplace, so that, rubbing salt in Churchill's wounds, this incitement to civil war became known as the 'Blenheim pledge'.

As he plunged into these bitter controversies, Churchill had a problem. A critical distinction has been made between instinctive and reflective writers, and this applies more widely, even to politics. Churchill was pre-eminently instinctive. He didn't ponder questions long and hard, as Lord Salisbury had done, and had little or no interest in political theory. And for all his gifts of language, he was far from persuasive in argument. He had the partisanship of the barrister his father had wanted him to be, without the forensic skill or dialectical acuity. Throughout his life he took assertion for demonstration, and rhetoric for logic, and he was prone to making what English judges call bad points, arguments that aren't so much untrue, or true but irrelevant, as unintended 'own goals'. In his life of his father, Churchill defended Lord Randolph's demagogic opposition to Home Rule: 'A generation may arise in England who will question the policy of creating subsidiary legislatures as little as we question the propriety of Catholic Emancipation and who will study the fierce disputes of 1886 with the superior manner of a modern professor examining the controversies of the early Church. But that will not prove the men of 1886 wrong or foolish in speech or action.' Many years later, in November 1940, Churchill would say something similar: 'In one phase men seem to have been right, in another they seem to have been wrong. Then again, a few years later, when the perspective of time has lengthened, all stands in a different setting.'

This might seem plausible, since of course such perspectives do change. And yet Churchill could scarcely have chosen a worse example than Ireland. *'Ein Tag zuviel ist dreissig Jahr zu wenig'*: never has Franz Grillparzer's line been more apt. If Catholic Emancipation had been granted in 1800, accompanying the Act of Union, as Pitt would have done had not George III thwarted him, it wouldn't have made the English and Irish one people, but it would have transformed Irish sentiment. As it was, emancipation wasn't passed until 1829, by which time Grillparzer's 'a day too many is thirty years too few' was tragically illustrated. And so again with Home Rule, passed not in 1886 as Gladstone had hoped but more than thirty years later. Another royal George saw what this meant. 'What fools we were not to have accepted Gladstone's Home Rule Bill,' that sensible man George V told Ramsay MacDonald, his prime minister, in 1931. 'The Empire would not have had the Irish Free State giving us so much trouble and pulling us to pieces.'

Over the years, Churchill's record on Ireland was remarkable only for complete inconsistency and downright perversity. After Lord Randolph's 'Ulster will fight' in 1896, he had written to his mother from India in 1897 that his opinions 'excite the pious horror of the mess', and that 'Were it not for Home Rule – to which I will never consent – I would enter Parliament as a Liberal.' Churchill repeated this opposition when he joined the Liberals in 1904, and he defended his father in 1906. After his conversion to Home Rule in 1912 he suggested that the Ulster question could be answered by 'Home Rule all round', including 'subsidiary legislatures' echoing the seven kingdoms of Anglo-Saxon England (hence the derisive nickname for this scheme, 'Winston's Heptarchy'), but in the winter of 1913 he threatened to resign from Asquith's government if force were used against Ulster: 'You understand that if a shot is fired I shall go out.' By March 1914 he was himself preaching force against the Ulster Unionists with the deplorable words, 'There are worse things than bloodshed, even on an extended scale,' accompanied by the threat to send the fleet to Belfast to overawe the populace.

By this last point the government was dealing – or failing to deal – with the so-called 'Curragh mutiny', outrageous insubordination by army officers sympathetic to Ulster, clandestinely and treasonably encouraged at the highest level by the disgraceful Sir Henry Wilson, Director of Military Operations, later assassinated by Irish terrorists. Churchill could have played a moderating role, but moderation never came easily to him, and from now on he would be remembered with hatred by Unionists as the author of a planned 'Ulster pogrom'. The phrase was luridly exaggerated, but scarcely more so than Churchill's own shocking words about bloodshed.

A crisis which took the United Kingdom to the brink of civil war could not go unnoticed in Berlin, although no one there or anywhere else foresaw how a random event in Sarajevo would lead to catastrophe. The Serb cause had long been popular among Russians – when Anna Karenina meets her sad end, her heartbroken lover, Vronsky, with nothing left to live for, goes off to fight for the Serbs – and also with some Englishmen. But English opinion had been repelled when nationalist fanatics brutally murdered King Alexander of Serbia in 1903, and the assassination of the Archduke Franz Ferdinand on 28 June 1914 caused further revulsion. In 1930, the Serbs commemorated the place where Gavrilo Princip had done his fateful deed; or, as Churchill wrote, 'a monument erected in recent years by his fellow-countrymen records his infamy and their own'. At the time, Asquith thought that Serbia was 'a wild little state for which nobody has a good word', and the American ambassador in Berlin reported that no one thought the assassination 'would have any effect on the world'. And yet within weeks a series of diplomatic and military powder-trains across Europe had been ignited and had exploded into the greatest war in history.

Whatever its origins, it exhilarated one man. As the July crisis deepened, as the likelihood of war grew daily, and as the enormity of what impended became clearer, Asquith and Grey were despondent and even tearful, but not Churchill. The government was still trying to sort out the intractable question of whether Ulster should be excluded from Home Rule, or how much of it. On the afternoon of 24 July 1914, in Churchill's vivid description, the Cabinet 'toiled around the muddy byways of Fermanagh and Tyrone', when Grey interrupted with a note he had just received, the brutal ultimatum sent by Vienna to Serbia which made war almost inevitable. At that moment, 'the parishes of Fermanagh and Tyrone faded back into the mists and squalls of Ireland, and a strange light began immediately, but by perceptible gradations, to fall and glow upon the map of Europe.'

There was a strange light inside Churchill also. He wrote to Clementine on 28 July that 'everything tends towards catastrophe and collapse. I am interested, geared-up and happy. Is it not horrible to be built like that? ... I pray to God to forgive me for such fearful moods of levity.' Those preparations had been encouraged by him, and he now mobilised the Fleet without the authority of the Cabinet. Or as the Australian historian Douglas Newton says in one of the most detailed accounts of the weeks before and after the war began, 'Churchill succumbed to a temptation to frogmarch events.'

On 3 August, German troops invaded Belgium, causing a revolution in English sentiment, most of all among the Liberals and radicals who had for so long sympathised with Germany, and the London government presented an ultimatum to Berlin demanding withdrawal. On the following evening, Lloyd George and Asquith sat silently in the Cabinet room, when Churchill bounced in to say that he had signalled to every ship in the Navy to say that war had been begun. 'Winston, who has got on all his war-paint, is longing for a sea-fight,' Asquith wrote to his beloved confidante Venetia Stanley. 'Radiant, his face bright, his manner keen,' Lloyd George reported. 'You could see he was a really happy man. I wondered if this was the state of mind to be in at the opening of such a fearful war as this.' Churchill had always had a strong sense of personal destiny: 'Why have I always been kept safe within a hair's breadth of death, except to do something like this?' Now he felt that more than ever that, even if war was folly and barbarism, it was his fulfilment – and opportunity.

In its early advance through Belgium, the German army had almost cut off Antwerp, where a small British garrison had joined the defence. Some of them were Royal Marines, and some were men of the Royal Naval Division, the First Lord's brainchild and pet, the first of the so many 'special forces' he would nurture: sailors surplus to requirement at sea, as well as new volunteers, who were now turned into infantrymen, although 'scantily equipped and almost wholly untrained for land war'. Churchill dashed to Antwerp in a Rolls-Royce, and on

3 October sent an urgent telegram to Asquith asking authority to take charge in person with 'full powers of a commander of a detached force in the field'. As Asquith sardonically said, 'W is an ex-lieutenant of hussars, and would if the proposal had been accepted have been in command of 2 distinguished Major Generals, not to mention Brigadiers, Colonels & c.' When 'W's' telegram was read out to his colleagues, the Cabinet Room was swept by 'Homeric laughter', Asquith wrote, and Lord Stamfordham, the King's private secretary, expressed a general view when he said that 'our friend must be quite off his head'.

Soon the forlorn hope had been abandoned and Antwerp cut off. For those left behind there was no way out except into the neutral Netherlands, where a number of Marines did make their way, to be interned for the rest of the war. 'Our friend' also managed to escape, but sourly lamented that 'Antwerp was a bitter blow to me and some aspects of it have given a handle to my enemies.' In truth the whole episode suggested that Churchill's strategic judgement was grossly flawed, or even that he had a screw loose. Maurice Festing was a Marine officer at Antwerp, and left an angry record of the fiasco. After this episode, he wrote, anyone would have thought that 'a limit would have been placed upon Mr Winston Churchill's appetite for daredevil pranks and sensational attempts at strokes of genius. Not many months elapsed, however, before he was busy again – this time at the Dardanelles.'

Before then Churchill did have one highly gratifying sea-fight. Admiral Graf von Spee's distant squadron of cruisers in the Far East, including his flagship the *Scharnhorst* as well as the *Gneisenau*, wrought much damage as it crossed the Pacific eastwards and then destroyed a British squadron off the coast of Chile. But on 8 December von Spee was caught by the Royal Navy near the Falkland Islands. Four German ships were sunk and many lives lost, including von Spee and his two sons, in a victory Churchill described with relish. A week later, there was a different kind of naval engagement, and one more portent. German warships raided the coast of Yorkshire, shelling the seaside resorts of Bridlington, Whitby and Scarborough and killing more than a hundred civilians, a handful of children among them. Churchill bitterly denounced the German navy: 'the stigma of the baby killers of Scarborough will brand its officers and men while sailors sail the sea.' Those words would one day come to haunt him.

By Christmas, with the armies on the Western Front bogged down in a stalemate of mud and blood, Churchill was nevertheless thrilled to a degree that alarmed others and even himself occasionally. 'I would not be out of this glorious, delicious war for anything the world can give me,' he told Margot Asquith in the new year. But he was also dismayed by the course of events. He showed acute insight by grasping that the conditions of this new industrial war meant 'that neither side will have the strength to penetrate the other's line in the Western theatre', and by 29 December he wondered, 'Are there not other alternatives than sending our armies to chew barbed wire in Flanders?'

To be sure, no one at all had intended – or foreseen – that outcome. In August, the Kaiser had told his troops marching through Berlin that they would be home 'before the autumn leaves fall', and young Englishmen had joined up in high spirits lest the war should 'be over by Christmas'. A year later 'the Winston of Germany' was taken to see the desolate horror of the Western Front, and said morosely, 'Ich habe es nicht gewollt.' But then that – 'I didn't want this' – could have been said by every leader of all the Powers fighting. Churchill might claim great prescience for writing at that first Christmas of the war, when it was far from over, 'that the position of both armies is not likely to undergo any decisive change – although no doubt several hundred thousand men will be spent to satisfy the military mind on that point.' That would prove all too true. But what was his alternative?

His restless mind looked for one, more than ever convinced of his innate grasp of military affairs and his unfulfilled capacity for handling large forces. It was said of Lady Mary Wortley Montagu, the eighteenth-century traveller and eccentric, that she had a great deal of taste, most of it bad, and it could be said of Churchill that he had a great many military ideas, most of them likewise bad. The trouble with military notions is that they can only be tested by trial and – as all too often in Churchill's case – by costly error. There were flashes of real brilliance. Churchill was one of the first to envisage a 'land ship', soon called a 'tank', a codeword meant to conceal its nature, before the name stuck, and he encouraged the development of this new weapon. But too often his ideas were eccentric in conception and disastrous in execution, never more so than at the new year of 1915. Churchill had a tempestuous relationship with Admiral Lord Fisher, the First Sea Lord, another brilliant but erratic man. The two first toyed with hare-brained plans for expeditions to Sleswick or the Baltic, with Churchill advocating at one moment that Sylt should be taken, at the next Borkum, as though capturing either island would serve any purpose.

Then another destination beckoned at the far end of Europe. Shortly after the war began, Churchill had ordered the seizure of two battle-ships being built in British shipyards for Turkey. This high-handed action may have helped push the Porte into a declaration of war on the Austro-German side, which was followed by the escape, to Churchill's great embarrassment, of two German warships from the Adriatic to Constantinople. He now began to dream of an attack in the distant Aegean and a gateway to Constantinople and the Black Sea. Nor was he alone. There was a belief widely held in London that capturing Constantinople and the Straits would open a vital supply route to Russia, even though the British and French had no supplies to send, and also, albeit for no discernible reason, that knocking out Turkey would immeasurably help the Allies and maybe win the war.

By his own account, Churchill had been brought up in the Tory Turkophile tradition, but he now harangued his colleagues, 'Surely we do not intend to leave this inefficient and out-of-date nation which has long misruled one of the most fertile countries in the world still in possession!' This was one more about-turn for Churchill, rejecting not only his father's sympathies but the cardinal British policy for generations past that Turkey, albeit 'the sick man of Europe', should be kept on life-support lest Russia supplant her and achieve her long-held ambition of gaining control of the Straits.

Initially Churchill favoured an attack by sea, 'forcing the Straits'. A glance at a map shows the difficulty. From Antiquity until modern times, the Straits, which link the Black Sea with the Aegean while separating Europe from Asia Minor, have been one of the most impor-tant waterways on earth, the outlet for commerce which came down the Dnieper and Don as well as from the great port of Odessa once it sprang up in the eighteenth century, and, just as much, down the Danube, the lifeline of central Europe. Narrow at the eastern end, the Bosphorus on which Constantinople stands, the Straits broaden into the Sea of Marmara, and then close again at the western end, the Dardanelles, or Hellespont.

This is less than a mile wide at its narrowest: Leander swam nightly across to be with his beloved Hero, a feat emulated by Byron

(characteristically adding that Leander 'swam for Love, as I for Glory').
Strongly armed Turkish forts stood on both sides – Seddulbahir Fort
still stands imposingly on the north coast – and the waters were heavily
mined. Only four years earlier, Churchill had said, 'It is no longer
possible to force the Dardanelles, and nobody should expose a modern
fleet to such peril.' Now he falsely claimed that the admirals supported
such a plan, although they were in fact sceptical, and soon seen to be
rightly so when three elderly battleships were sunk in the 'forcing'
attempt.

Instead, plans were made for an 'amphibious' operation, the first
of so many that Churchill would foster. The Gallipoli peninsula, the
south-eastern extremity of Europe, is a sixty-mile finger of land
stretching west into the Aegean from Constantinople to its tip at Cape
Helles. It was there on 25 April that British and imperial troops landed,
commanded by General Sir Ian Hamilton, Churchill's old friend from
the Boer War. Another landing some miles to the north became known
as Anzac Cove, named for the Australian and New Zealand Army
Corps, and went awry from the moment when the boats laden with
soldiers drifted a mile northwards, to a still less hospitable beach facing
steep cliffs.

In the battle orders for the landing, the ostensible objective to be
taken on the first day was beyond the peak of Achi Baba, more than
five miles inland from Cape Helles; by nightfall, even the most
successful landing forces had fought no more than a few hundred
yards ashore; they would never reach Achi Baba. Over weeks and
months to come they struggled to advance further, as it became clear
that both the difficulty of the terrain and the fighting quality of the
enemy had been grossly underestimated. The Ottoman armies had
given a poor showing in the savage Balkan Wars which preceded the
Great War, but now, organised by Otto Liman von Sanders, a German
general, and led by a young Turkish officer, Lieutenant-Colonel
Mustafa Kemal, the Turks fought fiercely.

And so along with the Tommies in Flanders, British, Australian
and French troops chewed barbed wire in Gallipoli, to Churchill's
intense frustration, not lessened when Hamilton proved too courteous
and easy-going to be an effective commander in a tight spot. In August,
and in defiance of the old military maxim 'Never reinforce failure',
there was another landing still further to the north, at Suvla Bay.
Soldiers fought their way to 'Chocolate Hill' and 'Dublin Castle',

names soon familiar to English newspaper readers, but no further, leaving another cluster of sad and touching cemeteries at Azmar, Green Hill and Hill 60.

Even before the landings, Asquith was politically weakened, and Churchill increasingly isolated. One Liberal MP warned Asquith of the difficulties he faced 'brought about by the actions of Mr Churchill', and many other Liberals shared Asquith's own belief that 'Winston is "intriguing hard" to remove some of his colleagues', unaware that it was he who might be removed. In late May the crisis broke and brought to an end the last Liberal government in British history, ending also Churchill's tenure at the Admiralty. The Tories were now brought into a coalition and insisted on his removal as a first condition. Asquith had little choice, and no very obvious regrets, saying that 'Winston is far the most disliked man in my cabinet by his colleagues.'

And not only by them. Asquith sometimes stayed at Walmer Castle near Deal, the residence of the Lord Warden of the Cinque Ports. This ancient office was later held by Churchill, but at the time by Lord Beauchamp, who lent it to Asquith as a retreat. Two of his luncheon guests there one day were Churchill and Henry James, of whose identity Churchill seemed unaware as he talked ceaselessly and overbearingly. 'It has been a very interesting and encouraging experience to meet that young man,' the great novelist delicately, and inimitably, phrased his farewells to the Asquiths. 'It has brought home to me – very forcibly, very vividly – the limitations by which men of genius obtain their ascendancy over mankind.'

Even if Asquith himself was still 'really fond of him', he told Venetia Stanley, 'I regard his future with many misgivings ... He will never get to the top in English politics, with all his wonderful gifts; to speak with the tongues of men & angels, and to spend laborious days & nights in administration, is no good, if a man does not inspire trust.' Churchill was demoted to the empty post of Chancellor of the Duchy of Lancaster, while he was derided by *Punch* as 'Mr Winston Churchill, the greatest of our quick-change political artists,' and his removal was universally welcomed in the navy, not least by that old salt, George V. The formation of the new government was most desirable, since 'Only by that means can we get rid of Churchill from Admiralty,' the king told the queen. 'He is the real danger' and 'has become impossible'.

When Churchill pleaded to be allowed to go out and inspect the battlefield for himself, the vengeful Tories denied him even that honour, and he never did visit Gallipoli in all his life. After a prolonged Cabinet debate, and an official inquiry, it was decided in the autumn to withdraw the forces. The evacuation was carried out in January 1916 'amid general ignorant rejoicing', in Churchill's bitter words, but at any rate, and by ironic contrast with the landings, with high efficiency. Very heavy casualties had been foreseen by gloomy senior officers; in the event, there wasn't a single fatality during the evacuation, unless one counts more than 500 unfortunate mules shot by the departing British.

Although Churchill hadn't been the only sponsor of the doomed Gallipoli enterprise, he had played a leading role, and not even an honest one at times. In any case, the old saying goes that success has many parents but failure is an orphan, and Gallipoli had become a one-parent child. Speaking in the Commons on 2 November, Asquith mocked the idea that 'some undefined personality of great authority and overmastering will' had been responsible for the conception and conduct of the campaign, and accepted his own responsibility, at which Churchill, sitting beside him, 'bowed his head in apparent acknowledgement of the exoneration', *The Times* recorded. But nothing could disguise Churchill's bitterness ten days later, when he finally accepted the inevitable and resigned. 'My dear Winston,' Asquith had begun his letter offering a Cabinet post more than seven years before; 'My dear Asquith,' Churchill's resignation letter icily began. He 'could not accept a position of general responsibility for war policy without any effective share in its guidance and control', Churchill wrote, before saying defiantly that 'time will vindicate' – that word again! – 'my administration of the Admiralty'.

This episode highlighted all Churchill's greatest weaknesses, both strategic and political, 'as un-understanding as he is of personalities'. That was the exceptionally acute phrase of Maurice Bonham Carter, known as Bongie, Asquith's private secretary, soon to be his son-in-law when he married Violet, and it was just right: profound un-understanding of others persisted throughout Churchill's life. Hindered by that obtusity, he had discovered the extreme vulnerability of his own position, and the harsh reality of politics. The truth was painfully simple: he had too many enemies, too few friends, and almost no popular support. Lloyd George said that there is no friendship at the top, and he certainly followed that maxim himself. Churchill had loyally stood by him when the

Marconi scandal threatened to destroy him; now Lloyd George abandoned Churchill, by letting him take all the blame for Gallipoli.

Not that Churchill helped himself. At no time did admitting error ever come easily to him. He did later allow that 'I ought, for instance never to have gone to Antwerp,' but he never conceded that Gallipoli was a mistake. His ostensible history of the Great War, *The World Crisis*, defends the enterprise at great length, and in 1934 he still insisted quite absurdly that 'The main strength of the Turkish Army was broken on the Gallipoli Peninsula by British and Australasian forces.' He wrote with disdain about the subsequent British war against Turkey, deriding the campaign successfully fought from Egypt through Palestine by saying 'We began our attack from her finger-tips upwards' when the British could have landed further north, or, best of all, 'a renewed thrust at Gallipoli, the heart,' which would have destroyed Turkey. Or so he claimed, against all possible reason and experience.

Even now he has defenders. Nearly a hundred years later Gallipoli was described in the *New Yorker* as 'an end run around the stalemate on the Western Front' to give 'a clear shot at the soft underbelly of Germany. It was a brilliant and daring strategy.' The best answer to that is to do something Churchill never did: visit Gallipoli, and see in broad daylight how misbegotten and doomed the enterprise was from the start. A visitor observes the daunting beaches where troops quite untrained for such landings had struggled to get ashore and then fight inland, while looming above them were the heights of Achi Baba whence Kemal's gunners, anything but 'broken', had directed their fire.

And even supposing that the landings had been entirely successful, what was then meant to happen? A hundred years later, to drive from V Beach to Constantinople takes several tedious hours along a road littered with dead dogs. How much more gruelling would a long eastward march have been across terrain well suited to defence? As to 'end run' or 'soft underbelly' (an unhappy phrase to use when writing about Churchill), what difference would knocking Turkey out ever have made? Any idea of attacking the Central Powers from this most remote extremity of Europe was fantastical. Constantinople is further from Berlin than Kansas City from Washington, and it was a bizarre idea that an army might easily advance across the Balkans, which are anything but geographically 'soft'. A.J.P. Taylor pronounced the right verdict on Gallipoli: 'The campaign could have succeeded only if it had been fought somewhere else.'

Whatever it did to Churchill, Gallipoli saw the birth of a nation, or rather two. By no remote consequence of the campaign, Mustafa Kemal would become Kemal Ataturk, while the rump of the Ottoman Empire became a Turkish national state under his leadership. And Australia would change also. The headstone of one Australian infantryman bears the words, chosen by his parents, 'When day break, duty done for King and Country,' but that was not how later generations of Australians would feel. 'From a place you've never heard of, comes a story you'll never forget' was the quaint slogan advertising the 1981 Australian movie *Gallipoli*, which helped launch Mel Gibson's career, but every Australian has heard of it. A young reporter called Keith Murdoch sent despatches from Gallipoli describing the incompetence of the high command and implanting a legend: young Australians had been needlessly sacrificed by British generals who regarded them contemptuously as inferior colonials, although those generals were just as careless with the lives of working-class Englishmen. Murdoch's Anglophobia would be inherited by his son Rupert, while Australians would sanctify 'Anzac Day' on 25 April as their Independence Day.

In his resignation speech in the Commons, at once defiant, bitter and foolish, Churchill fatefully said that he had recommended the expedition 'to the War Council, and to the French Government, not as a certainty, but as a legitimate war gamble, with stakes that we could afford to lose for a prize of inestimable value – a prize which, in the opinion of the highest experts, there was a fair reasonable chance of our winning, a prize which at that time could be won by no other means.' A reckless gambler was precisely what his critics had always thought him, but to boast of gambling with men's lives explains why, when his speech ended and he left the chamber, as *The Times* recorded, 'there was hardly a Member of Parliament present who was not cheering' at his departure.

Licking his wounds, Churchill attempted an unlikely and quixotic form of redemption. 'I am an officer, and I place myself unreservedly at the disposal of the Military authorities,' his resignation letter stridently proclaimed; 'my regiment is in France'. He did go to France, on 18 November. His later essays 'With the Grenadiers' and 'Plugstreet' are misleading. He only briefly served with the Grenadier Guards, before taking command of the 6th battalion of the Royal Scots Fusiliers, enlisting as his second-in-command Archibald Sinclair, a young laird and future politician he had befriended. Although Churchill was a conscientious and popular commanding officer, his claim that, 'Having been trained professionally for about five years as a soldier, and having prior to the Great War seen as much actual fighting as almost any of the colonels and Generals in the British Army, I had certain credentials which were accepted in military circles,' should be taken with a pinch of salt. Anything he had learned in distant colonial conflicts was totally irrelevant on the Western Front, and 'military circles' were far from regarding him as a man with better credentials.

He served in the front line for rather more than three months, but when his battalion was amalgamated with another in April 1916, it afforded a respectable opportunity to return home. 'Colonel Churchill is being found out,' the *Spectator* sourly wrote. 'The charm, once universal, no longer works, or works only occasionally and on a limited number of those exposed to it ... To watch this fevered, this agonised struggle to regain the political fortune which the arch-gambler threw away by his own acts is to witness one of the tragedies of life.' A still crueller enemy said that 'The Arch-Mountebank' had taken off his uniform 'the moment it becomes unpleasantly stiff with trench-mud'.

That said more about the hatred he inspired than about him. Winston Churchill could be accused of many things, but not cowardice. He was often in range of German guns, and close to exploding shells. At any time when he was in the trenches he might have been caught by one of those shells, or by a sniper's bullet like the one that killed William Gladstone, a young Liberal MP and grandson of the prime minister, on his first day at the front. Churchill couldn't possibly have preordained that his months in the trenches would fall during a comparative lull, between the bloody battle of Loos in the autumn of 1915 and the appalling slaughter of the following summer. Had he still been at the front on 1 July when the Somme offensive began, Churchill would quite likely have been added to the thirty British officers of the rank of lieutenant-colonel or above who were killed that terrible day, and to the no less remarkable total of twenty-three sitting MPs who were killed in action during the war.

Some patriotic slogans of the age were bombastic and false, but 'Equality of sacrifice' was not; indeed, it was barely equality, since junior officers were three times more likely to be killed than privates. In the new coalition government, the Liberal Asquith was Prime Minister, Bonar Law, the Tory leader, was Colonial Secretary, and effectively second-in-command, while Arthur Henderson, leader of the smaller Labour Party, was Education Minister. Asquith's son Raymond was killed on the Somme serving with the Grenadiers, a brilliant spirit, and at thirty-seven already a successful barrister, while Henderson also lost a son, and Bonar Law lost two. In sharp contrast with those who would invoke Churchill's name in the twenty-first century, there was then a governing class prepared not only to wage wars, but to fight and die in them.

On his return to Westminster, Churchill threw himself into the political fray once more, not least by way of defending his own record, and criticising the mistakes of others as he saw them. Some high dramas at the time would much affect him. Ireland had seemed quiescent since the war began, when John Redmond, the admirable and brave leader of the Irish Party, told Parliament that Ireland would support the war. The Home Rule Bill had been passed but suspended for the duration of hostilities, with the question of Ulster unresolved. The Ulster Volunteer Force, the armed militia raised to resist Home Rule, and supported by Bonar Law and 'FE', was accepted wholesale into the Army, to become the 36th Ulster Division. Working-class Protestant boys from Belfast, Antrim and Enniskillen enlisted together, trained together and sailed for France together, before at last they went into action together. And on the Somme they died together, many thousands of them, when the 36th Division was cut down.

Less than seven weeks before that battle, on Easter Monday 24 April, a small group called the Irish Republican Brotherhood, led by James Connolly, Patrick Pearse and Eamon de Valera, staged an armed insurrection in Dublin, until it was put down by the Army, and the leaders shot, apart from the Cuban-American de Valera. Until the rising these zealots had little popular support in Ireland, but their blood sacrifice worked, and Churchill's saying that grass grows over the battlefield but never over the scaffold was again proved true. The constitutional Irish party of Redmond was eclipsed by the ultras of Sinn Fein. It also ensured that Ireland would be partitioned for any foreseeable future, and perhaps forever.

There was one other indirect consequence. An obscure British mission to Russia was arranged, to include Kitchener, the victor of Omdurman who was now War Secretary, and Lloyd George, who had become Munitions Minister when the coalition was formed. But Asquith's authority was failing, and he needed Lloyd George to help deal with the Irish crisis. As a result, Lloyd George wasn't aboard HMS

Hampshire when she left Scapa Flow on 5 June to sail around the North Cape to Archangel. Hours after sailing she struck a mine and sank, with Kitchener and almost all hands. Whatever they did for Ireland, Connolly and Pearse saved Lloyd George's life.

That Easter saw another disaster far away. When Turkey entered the war in October 1914, the British, and the Government of India which administered the Raj, were anxious to safeguard the oil wells of Basra at the head of the Persian Gulf, loosely part of the Ottoman Empire, as well as those Persian oilfields nearby to the east which Churchill had acquired; as an *arrière-pensée* London wanted to forestall any Russian advance towards the Gulf. A substantial force of partly British but mostly Indian troops was sent to Basra but, thanks to what wasn't yet called mission creep, this turned into a full-scale military expedition marching north. The humiliating outcome on 29 April 1916 saw General Townshend's army surrender at Kut-al-Amara, a hundred miles south-west of Baghdad.

On the last day and night of May 1916, the Grand Fleet of the Royal Navy fought its only large engagement of the war – not to say that Jutland was the only major battle ever fought between two great fleets of modern battleships. The German High Seas Fleet came out from its ports to lure the British; the two sides met and fought; they both withdrew. Since three British battlecruisers were lost to one German, and 6094 British sailors killed to 2551 Germans, there was only so much consolation that the British, and the former First Lord, could take, but Churchill was privately asked to help prepare an optimistic official account. Later Churchill had harsh words for Admiral Sir John Jellicoe, commanding the Grand Fleet, and more detached naval historians have tended to agree that Jellicoe made mistakes and missed opportunities which might have given him a decisive victory. On the other hand, while Jellicoe may have been too cautious, it was, as Churchill admitted, the caution of 'the only man who could have lost the war in an afternoon'. Besides that, after the battle the German fleet retired to its ports and didn't emerge again, while the Germans turned instead to unrestricted submarine warfare, thereby provoking the United States to enter the war.

Within weeks, an inconclusive outcome at Jutland was dwarfed by calamity in France. After the indelible horror of 1 July, when the Battle of the Somme began and more than 20,000 British soldiers were killed in one day, the army fought on blindly, taking small patches of ground, while official claims were embellished to the point of mendacity. Churchill saw through this. Writing after the war, he used savage irony about the official version which still presented the Somme as a victory: 'It needs some hardihood for Colonel Borraston to write ... [that] "the events of July ... bore out the conclusions of the British higher command and amply justified the tactical methods employed".' But he was privately little less harsh at the time. A month to the day after the disastrous offensive began, Churchill composed for limited private circulation a scathing critique of the battle, and, by implication, of Haig.

'We know that the whole front against us is firmly held,' Churchill wrote. The Germans were defending 'on the cheap'. Any element of all-important surprise 'was wholly lacking ... In *personnel* the results of the operation have been disastrous, in *terrain* they have been absolutely barren.' All in all, 'the British offensive *per se* has been a great failure.' He then repeated a milder version of his critique in secret sessions of the Commons. And yet, however obviously true this now seems, it did Churchill no good at all at the time. Another war was being fought, between soldiers and civilians, 'brass hats' and 'frocks' (from the frock coats, which were, as it happened, worn much less often in London during the war). Since the Tories had made it an article of faith that Haig and the other generals knew what they were doing, and that it was essential to support them, the main effect of Churchill's critique was to increase the Tories' loathing of him. He remained almost an outcast in the eyes not only of his political opponents but of his supposed friends: Lloyd George could only say that Gallipoli had been 'the Nemesis of the man who has fought for this war for years.'

When Asquith offered Churchill his first Cabinet post in April 1908, his star had shone brightly. Eight years later it had fallen so fast and far that in August 1916 Asquith could tell his friend Sheila Henley that Churchill was 'malignant, & clumsy to boot, without a friend or follower in the world (except perhaps F.E. & I suppose Clementine).' He was 'a tragic figure of failure & folly.'

4

'Peppery, pugnacious, proud'
Cairo 1921

By December 1916, discontent with Asquith's inert conduct of the war allowed Lloyd George to outplay him and replace him as prime minister, with the support of the press magnates, notably Lord Northcliffe, and Max Aitken, who would be rewarded the following year by being made Lord Beaverbrook. Lloyd George wanted to bring Churchill back into government, partly because he needed his dynamism, partly perhaps from a flicker of guilt (to the limited extent that Lloyd George ever felt that) after abandoning him, and partly on the principle later expressed with Texan bluntness by Lyndon Johnson: with a certain kind of man, you'd rather have him 'on the inside pissing out than on the outside pissing in'. When Lloyd George made just that point (in Welsh Baptist rather than Texan) to Bonar Law – would it not be better to have Churchill with us than against us? – Bonar Law replied, 'I would rather have him against us every time.'

Now the dissonance was louder than ever between Churchill's indomitable self-belief and the sheer dislike and distrust he inspired. By his early forties he had acquired two reputations: as a reckless, unstable adventurer, and as an unprincipled, self-seeking opportunist. These are the more striking because they would seem to be mutually exclusive, but they help explain why, for a man of his fame and his gifts, Churchill enjoyed so little political support. His Tory foes at this time conceded his courage, energy and brilliance, Lloyd George much later wrote, 'But they asked why, in spite of all that, although he had many admirers, he had fewer followers than any prominent man in Britain? ... Churchill had never attracted, and he had certainly never retained, the affection of any section, province or town.' And the answer was not far to seek: Lloyd George thought, 'His mind was a powerful machine, but there lay hidden in its material or its make-up some obscure defect which prevented it from always running true.'

Given Churchill's tendency to think in terms of 'race', it's ironical that there were some, including Asquith, who wondered whether that erratic temperament came from 'Mexican' or indigenous American blood on his mother's side, but Asquith's wife Margot saw more clearly. That silly, snobbish, but clever woman liked Churchill, but apart from thinking that his 'vanity is septic', she mused about 'what gives Winston his pre-eminence … It is certainly not his mind. I said long ago, and with truth, Winston has a noisy mind. Certainly not his judgement: he is constantly v wrong indeed … of course it is his courage and his colour, his amazing mixture of industry and enterprise … Poor Winston! His political position is nil.'

All the same, and through all his setbacks, Churchill never lost his reverence for constitutional parliamentary government. He briefed Alexander MacCallum Scott, a backbench Liberal MP, who had written a sympathetic biography of Churchill in 1905, when he was only thirty. Scott recorded a moment he had shared with Churchill in March 1917: 'As we were leaving the House late tonight, he called me into the Chamber to take a last look round. All was darkness except a ring of faint light all around under the gallery. We could dimly see the table, but walls and roof were invisible. "Look at it," he said. "This little place is what makes the difference between us and Germany. It is in virtue of this that we shall muddle through to success & for lack of this Germany's brilliant efficiency leads her to final disaster. This little room is the shrine of the world's liberties."' Those were fine words, especially at a time when that 'little room' wasn't listening to Churchill.

He did return to government in July 1917, but before then the course of the war had changed dramatically. The February revolution in Russia overthrew the Tsar. A new democratic government was still committed to the war, but halfheartedly, and the Russian people were even less enthusiastic. If Russia fell out of the war, the German army on the Western Front could be hugely reinforced from the east; but if the Entente was going to lose one ally, another arrived. When the European war broke out in 1914, President Woodrow Wilson had been in the White House for only seventeen months, which had been wholly preoccupied with domestic reform, and neither he nor most Americans wanted to enter the distant conflict. A few Anglophile New England Republicans, like Wilson's great antagonist Senator Henry Cabot Lodge from Massachusetts, favoured joining the British side, but they were in a small minority.

'In England particularly,' Churchill would later obtusely write, 'where laws and language seemed to make a bridge of mutual comprehension between the two nations', no one could understand why American entry into the war took so long. He claimed without evidence that Wilson underestimated American feeling in favour of the Allies, and that what Wilson did by entering the war in April 1917 could have been done in May 1915. 'And if done then what abridgement of the slaughter; what sparing of the agony; what ruin, what catastrophes would have been prevented; in how many million homes would an empty chair be occupied today; how different would be the shattered world in which victors and vanquished alike are condemned to live!'

This completely misunderstood American politics, and the Americans. The country had been peopled by migrants escaping from Europe and its conflicts, notably from military conscription. Not only did most Americans want to keep out of the war when it began, good contemporary judges reckoned that, had the United States been obliged to take sides then, more Americans would have preferred to fight against the Anglo-French-Russian Entente than for it. Millions of Irish Americans had no wish to fight for the King of England, millions of Jewish Americans had no wish to fight as allies of the Tsar whose oppression they had fled, and tens of millions of German Americans had no wish to fight against their ancestral homeland.

Even Wilson himself worried when the fighting began that he might have to go to war against England. He identified with James Madison, the only other Princeton man to have reached the White House, and memories of the British blockade which lay behind the 1812 war made him think that another blockade – an essential part of British strategy against Germany now as it had once been against France – might be the cause of war again. By 'May 1915', Churchill intended the sinking of the *Lusitania*, a liner carrying munitions as well as passengers; 1198 out of 1959 passengers and crew aboard the ship drowned, and the dead included 128 Americans. A persistent conspiracy theory holds that Churchill somehow deliberately directed the ship into the path of the U-boats to provoke an America reaction. In plain terms that is false, but Churchill did most incautiously write to Walter Runciman, the President of the Board of Trade, that 'it is most important to attract neutral shipping to our shores, in the hope especially of embroiling the United States with Germany ... We want the traffic – the more the better; and if some of it gets into trouble, better still,' which was by any standards heartlessly cynical enough.

Although many Americans were shocked by the *Lusitania*, there was still a very strong anti-war movement. 'He kept us out of the war' was the slogan on which Wilson was re-elected in 1916, and he might still have kept them out but for arrogant German folly. By proclaiming openly a campaign of unrestricted submarine warfare, and by secretly (but not secretly enough) urging Mexico to attack its northern neighbour, Germany finally provoked Wilson in April 1917 to proclaim that a state of war existed. In those distant days when Congress had not yet supinely surrendered its fundamental constitutional right to declare war, Wilson's request was debated at length on Capitol Hill before a declaration of war was passed on 6 April, though far from unanimously, eighty-two to six in the Senate, 373 to fifty in the House.

Ten days after the American declaration of war the brief, disastrous French offensive began, known by the name of General Robert Nivelle. In one more fruitless assault, the French army was finally pushed to the limit of endurance and beyond, and was swept by mutiny. Unlike the Somme, this offensive was soon broken off, and Nivelle was dismissed, to be replaced by Philippe Pétain. He restored order with a mixture of iron fist and light hand: scores of mutineers were shot, but conditions were improved, and there was an implicit promise of no more offensives for the moment. In secret sessions of the Commons, Churchill repeated his criticisms of allied strategy, with its endless hopeless 'pushes', and proposed that the British should in effect do the same as the French: stand to, embark on no more ruinous offensives, and wait until 'the American millions' arrived. This might have sounded like good advice, but it was a mark of how low Churchill's standing was that the Conservative Chief Whip told Lloyd George that Churchill's criticisms were 'futile'.

After the Dardanelles report in March partially cleared Churchill, Lloyd George felt he could at last bring him back into the government as Minister of Munitions, despite a motion signed by more than 100 Tory MPs deploring the appointment, and a blast from George Younger, the Tory Chairman, warning Lloyd George of 'his unfortunate record ... and his grave responsibility for two of the greatest disasters in the War'. Taking office again necessitated a by-election. Churchill was easily returned at Dundee, which was enjoying an uncovenanted temporary boom thanks to the horrors of trench warfare: the jute city's mills were producing six million sandbags a month for the Western Front.

As Churchill threw himself into his new job with his usual zest, he watched with dismay while Haig began another offensive on 31 July, this time in Flanders, officially the third battle of Ypres, although ever after known by the name of one village: in Churchill's words, this was 'the ghastly crime of Passchendaele'. Haig ignored weather forecasts correctly predicting the wettest summer on record, and for three months British soldiers fought through a sea of mud. In a grim reprise of the Somme, barely any ground was taken while huge casualties mounted.

By returning when he did, Churchill was in office at the time of several more fateful events whose sequels would play a large part in his life. The bombing of London by German airships and aircraft, trivial by later standards and killing about 1000 people in all, had produced an hysterical demand for reprisals, whipped up by demagogues like Pemberton Billing, who entered Parliament at a by-election as the self-proclaimed 'first air Member'. Churchill's friend Smuts, the old Boer general now improbably transmuted into a British national hero and a member of the War Cabinet, was commissioned to report on air policy. He became infatuated with the doctrine of 'air power', and his report of October 1917 recommended the creation of an independent Royal Air Force. Its declared purpose was to bomb enemy territory rather than to co-operate with the army and navy, with the plain implication that this would mean destroying cities, and their inhabitants. Churchill was an early convert to this new doctrine. In a Cabinet paper he recommended dropping 'not five tons but five hundred tons of bombs each night on the cities and manufacturing establishments' in Germany.

Then on 2 November, after much backstairs intrigue, a short letter from Balfour, now Foreign Secretary, to Lord Rothschild, stated that the government viewed 'with favour the establishment of a national home for the Jewish people in Palestine'. This Balfour Declaration divided opinion within the government as well as without, and across party lines. Churchill was an enthusiast already and Balfour was genuinely converted to the Zionist cause. So was Lloyd George, who claimed that 'the world owes much to the little five-foot-five nations' – the Welsh, the Greeks, the Jews – and recalled that when he was a boy in a humble Baptist home in Carnarvonshire he had known more about the ancient kings of Israel than the kings and queens of England.

But the Declaration was bitterly opposed by another Liberal. Edwin Montagu was the only Jewish member of the Cabinet and, like many assimilated Jews at the time, was appalled by the very idea of Zionism and a Jewish state, which seemed to brand him an alien in his own country. It was also opposed by a Tory. Curzon reminded his colleagues that the British Empire was 'the greatest Mahometan power on earth', and was dismayed at the effect the Declaration would have on those hundreds of millions of Muslim subjects of the Crown. He presciently asked how it was proposed 'to get rid of the existing majority of Mussulman inhabitants and introduce the Jews in their place', and he foresaw that the Arabs would not be happy 'either to be expropriated for Jewish immigrants or to act merely as hewers of wood and drawers of water'. As to the Jews themselves, Curzon told Montagu, 'I cannot conceive a worse bondage to which to relegate an advanced and intellectual community than to exile in Palestine.' Churchill was also conscious of the many 'Mahometan' subjects of the empire, but disdainful of them, and he was completely indifferent to the wishes or interests of the Palestinian Arabs.

Even his sympathy for the Jews was about to be tempered, by events in Russia. A week after the Balfour Declaration, and just before Haig at last decided to call a halt to the carnage in Flanders, Alexander Kerensky's democratic government was overthrown by a putsch: the October Revolution by the old Russian calendar. The Bolsheviks or Communists who seized power were adherents of Karl Marx and proclaimed his doctrine of historical inevitability, but there was nothing whatever inevitable about this event. In Vladimir Nabokov's marvellous phrase, the October Revolution was 'that trite *deus ex machina*', and it quite confuted Marx's prophetic schema, according to which proletarian revolution ought to have taken place already, in the west, where capitalism was in its most advanced or decadent stage, rather than in a backward country where industrial capitalism was in its infancy. While Lenin and Trotsky set about destroying their opponents, they prepared to make a peace of surrender with Germany inspired by what Lenin called 'revolutionary defeatism'. Churchill watched these events in Russia with horror, and they would affect him deeply.

After a bleak midwinter and a lull in the fighting, the German army launched a final great offensive on 21 March 1918. The British were caught by surprise, their line was broken, and they were driven back fifty miles. Not only were aircraft now playing a leading role on the Western Front, ministers and generals could cross from England to France by air, although Churchill was the only one who liked to take the controls himself. At Lloyd George's request, he flew to France to see Clemenceau, now prime minister, and the French generals, adumbrating the flights he would make there at a still greater crisis in 1940. The United States had been at war for almost a year, during which the British had suffered hundreds of thousands of casualties, but no American soldiers were yet serving in the front line, and only a few hundred had died, mostly in training accidents.

While the line was just held, the German attack was renewed, but failed to achieve a decisive victory and petered out. Wilson and General John Pershing were prevailed upon to join in the desperate fight, and by the summer American troops were in action at last, Marines as well as soldiers, and the Under Secretary of the Navy came to Europe to inspect them. In London Franklin Delano Roosevelt was bidden to a banquet at Gray's Inn, where the guests included the Minister of Munitions. This first meeting between Roosevelt and Churchill was unpropitious. Over the years, many people, political allies as well as foes, were repelled by Churchill's arrogant manner, and what Hobhouse had thought in 1912 Roosevelt thought six years later. He didn't forget the haughty and offhand Englishman, whereas Roosevelt made no impression at all on Churchill, who entirely forgot about the meeting, to his subsequent embarrassment.

On 8 August, the British at last launched a counter-attack, breaking through at Amiens. 'The Black Day of the German Army', as Ludendorff called it, began the Hundred Days' Battle, one of the greatest victories in military history, although the British have characteristically forgotten it and remember only the calamities of the Somme and Passchendaele. Churchill's relations with Lloyd George were superficially cordial again, but that concealed mutual suspicion and resentment. Churchill would say backhandedly that 'there is no doubt he was much better as No 1 than anybody else,' but that Lloyd George had been 'always wrong. He encouraged the Nivelle offensive which ended in disaster. He discouraged the final offensive in 1918 which ended in success. He gave way about the prolongation of

Passchendaele against true conviction.' How far this was a true account of Lloyd George's conduct may be disputed, but there's also no doubt that Churchill thought that he himself would have been much better as 'No 1'.

Before October the German generals knew they had lost, but found a way to avoid admitting it. Wilson had picked up the foolish phrase 'peace without victory' from the intellectual liberals of the *New Republic*, his favourite magazine, and the German generals made use of this. After two years in which Germany had effectively been ruled by the army High Command, Ludendorff guilefully and cynically made way for a civilian government under the Social Democrat Friedrich Ebert, who could end the war, and take the blame. After this final cowardly dereliction by the generals, an armistice was negotiated: not a formal surrender but a *Waffenstillstand* or ceasefire. Its terms should have made clear that Germany had accepted defeat, and Ludendorff for the moment wanted to fight on, but Germany was in turmoil, with factories riven by strikes, with the sailors of the Imperial Navy mutinying rather than put out to sea for a final, suicidal battle, and with the ruling elite gripped by fear of revolution. The implications of these events weren't easy to see at 'the eleventh hour of the eleventh day of the eleventh month', when the Armistice took effect on 11 November amid hysterical celebrations in London, but this was the cause of much subsequent woe.

'The conclusion of the Great War raised England to the highest position she has yet attained,' Churchill wrote. 'For the fourth time in four successive centuries she had headed and sustained the resistance of Europe to a military tyranny.' This was grandiloquent enough, but characteristic wishful thinking. Great Britain had not 'headed' the Entente any more than had France, and France had paid a far heavier price. Some three-quarters of a million soldiers from the British Isles had died, but France had lost almost twice as many men from a smaller population.

If Churchill had looked harder, he would have seen that England's 'highest position' was very tenuous. Apart from her dead sons, the balance of events had swung heavily against her. Not least, his country was hugely in debt. By 1917, the British were paying most of the cost of the war not only for themselves but for their allies: half of Belgian and Serbian, two-thirds of French and Russian, and all of Italian war expenditure was funded by London. In return, London depended more and more on the money loaned by Washington and Wall Street, in particular the great bank of J.P. Morgan, and victory found the British in the excruciating position of having to repay the immense debts they owed, with little hope of recovering the debts owed them, or in the Russian case no hope at all.

A peace conference was convened in Paris, and Wilson arrived, to be greeted as a great redeemer. In a manner reminiscent of Ferdinand Alf, the editor of the *Evening Pulpit* in Trollope's *The Way We Live Now*, the president now combined 'an air of wonderful omniscience ... with an ignorance hardly surpassed by its arrogance' as he disposed of nations and conflicts in Europe about which he knew almost nothing: he had never before visited Europe, and would never once visit central and eastern Europe, whose maps he so drastically redrew. Lloyd George had called an election a week before Christmas, on 18 December: this was the first British general election to be held on a single day. He was still leading a coalition, a fortuitous creation of a war which had disrupted the party system. Some Liberals were approved government candidates and others were not, deepening the rupture between the Lloyd George and Asquith fractions. One practical consequence of the war was the 1918 Representation of the People Act, which might be called the Fourth Reform Bill. All men over twenty-one were enfranchised, and women over thirty,* although Churchill had been in the parliamentary minority which, during the passage of the Act, voted to the end against giving women the vote.

This second khaki election was even more successful than the first, a landslide for the Coalition, with Asquith's Liberal faction reduced to a rump, although Labour hugely increased its vote, and Sinn Fein swept Ireland outside Ulster. As ever Churchill was ready with unsolicited advice. He wrote to Lloyd George on 26 December about reconstructing the ministry: 'there is a point about Jews wh[ich] occurs to me – you must not have too many of them.' He was thinking of Montagu, Rufus Isaacs, now Lord Reading – 'a close old friend at yr side', said Churchill in a sly allusion to the Marconi scandal in which Lloyd George and Isaacs had been embroiled – and 'the Infant Samuel', the sobriquet, recalling Sir Joshua Reynolds's painting of that name,

---

* The reason for this discrepancy was the concern, which like so many demographic forecasts proved false, that women would greatly outnumber men, so many of whom had just been killed.

by which Herbert Samuel's colleagues knew him. 'Three Jews among only 7 Liberal cabinet ministers might I fear give rise to comment,' Churchill suggested. In the event, Montagu remained at the India Office, and Reading remained Lord Chief Justice, his appointment to which office in 1913 had certainly given rise to comment, in the form of Kipling's savage pasquinade 'Gehazi'. Samuel remained out of office until his appointment as first High Commissioner for Palestine in 1920, which gave rise to even more comment from overt or covert antisemites.

Although he hoped to return to the Admiralty, Churchill was instead given the combined ministry of war and air. Here he threw himself with his usual energy into managing demobilisation, and the fraught question of which men should be released first from the enormous force of five million to which the British Army had swollen. Bitter resentment, to the point of mutiny, was caused when men with guaranteed jobs, or jobs in specialised occupations, were released early, while men who had volunteered at the outbreak of war were still in uniform. Churchill at his most impressive quickly grasped and imposed the simple and equitable principle of 'first in, first out'.

And yet that was now almost a minor concern for him compared with his horror of Soviet communism. His loathing found expression in nightmare imagery, 'the foul baboonery of Bolshevism', 'a plague bacillus', a 'cancer', a 'horrible form of mental and moral disease'. He was appalled by the prospects of Communist revolution in Germany, which made him much more conciliatory towards the Germans: 'Kill the Bolshie, kiss the Hun,' he urged, even if neither slogan could easily be made to work in practice. A British force had been sent to Murmansk in March 1918 to guard supplies, and to encourage Russian forces who might still want to fight Germany. But Churchill tried to persuade the government actively to join the White armies now fighting a bitter civil war against the Bolsheviks. There was little enthusiasm for more fighting from his own colleagues, and even less from the populace. Lloyd George had enough problems on his hands, and he cynically thought that Churchill's 'ducal blood ran cold' at the fate of the Russian nobility. Ernest Bevin was already a prominent union leader before he later rose to greater heights. He hated the Bolshevik terror, but deplored intervention, because 'we have no right to determine their government'. Some Allied troops did fight the Reds but they made little difference, while the Left added

Churchill's zeal for strangling the Bolshevik state at birth to the charge sheet against him.

Posterity may judge Churchill less harshly. If he thought that Russian Communism represented an awful regression into barbarism, he was quite right. Generations of starry-eyed enthusiasts in the West would be enchanted by the Soviet myth, and then disenchanted because they had learned what 'we never knew', when in fact everything could be known from the start. There was, after all, no mystery. 'Everyone who violates the labour discipline in any enterprise and in any business,' Lenin said, 'should be discovered, tried and punished without mercy.' His telegram of 11 August 1918 was to the point: 'The insurrection of five kulak districts should be pitilessly suppressed.... Hang (and make sure that the hanging takes place in full view of the people) no fewer than one hundred known landlords, rich men, bloodsuckers.' Trotsky was just as bloodthirsty when he commanded the Red Army, and not only towards the enemy: on his orders, large numbers of soldiers who had shown insufficient fighting spirit were shot, *pour encourager les autres*. Churchill's first instinct wasn't so wrong, even if the Muse of History had kept a few ironies up her sleeve.

With the Conference in Paris under way, Churchill lamented the rage against Germany which had been its domestic background. 'It was not from the majesty of the battlefield nor the solemnity of the council chamber,' he truly observed, 'but from the scrimmage of the hustings, that the British Plenipotentiaries proceeded to the Peace Conference.' British politicians had to negotiate amid cacophonous cries to 'hang the Kaiser' and 'squeeze Germany until the pips squeak': just that 'vindictive democracy' Churchill had once foreseen. When the Versailles Treaty was published in July 1919, it horrified the Germans, and even some among the Allies. Wilson, Smuts and Lloyd George had private misgivings, which Churchill shared. He thought that the economic clauses in the Treaty and the reparations Germany was obliged to pay were 'malignant and silly to an extent that made them obviously futile'.

This was the theme of the young economist Maynard Keynes in his philippic *The Economic Consequences of the Peace*, which began a myth which has never died. In reality, the real disaster wasn't the way the war had begun or who was responsible, but how it had ended; not the claim that Germany had started the war, but the Germans' belief that they hadn't lost it, a belief encouraged by both German generals and politicians. When returning troops marched through

Berlin in December, they were told, by Ebert of all people, the Social Democratic leader, 'No army has overcome you.' With that belief implanted, when the Treaty was published it was easy for demagogues to offer an answer. If the army had been '*im Feld unbesiegt*', undefeated in battle, it must have been betrayed by the 'November criminals', the treacherous politicians who had taken over, and then betrayed Germany, and then 'stabbed in the back' by civilians, and Jews. Thus was the seed planted that would bring forth a frightful blossom.

Any clemency Churchill felt towards 'the Hun' wasn't matched in domestic politics. The old Welsh radical Lloyd George had moved rightwards, and now hoped for a reordering of politics, in which his Coalition Liberals would merge with the Conservatives in an anti-socialist centre party, a plan warmly supported by Churchill. His savage tongue now turned against the democratic Left at home. Labour was 'quite unfitted for the responsibility of government', Churchill claimed in January 1920, and went on to say in 1923, that 'The enthronement in office of a Socialist Government will be a serious national misfortune such as has usually befallen great states only on the morrow of defeat in war.'

One word was toxic, associated with the ugly vogue for eugenics that Churchill had so strongly shared, and its disdain for 'unfit' or inferior racial stock. The *Nation*, a weekly voice of traditional Radicalism, reacted ferociously: 'The man who has made the most criminal misjudgement that has been made since the day when the Kaiser invaded Belgium, who has sent British soldiers to their deaths in a cause as hopeless as it was inhuman, who has added to the burdens that were crushing the life out of Europe, who has kept his place solely because of the prestige of his class, has the patrician insolence to talk of the incompetence of the Labour Party.' A similar point was made humorously by the cartoonist David Low when he drew 'Winston's bag': Churchill stood flourishing a shotgun, rather as he had on the cover of *My African Journey*, with an array of dead cats at his feet labelled 'Antwerp Blunder', 'Gallipoli Mistake', 'Russian Bungle' and others.

But if the Left loathed Churchill, his position among his colleagues was little more secure. Although both Lloyd George and Churchill were still ostensibly Liberals, the Liberal Party was in disarray, and Lloyd George was in reality 'a prime minister without a party'. He was distrusted by many of the Tories who dominated his government, and who distrusted Churchill if anything more. Stanley Baldwin was the prosperous owner of a family iron foundry, who had succeeded his father as Member for Bewdley in 1908, and had early shown his enlightened disposition as one of only twelve Conservative MPs who voted for the Old Age Pensions Act. He had risen steadily and was appointed to Churchill's old post of President of the Board of Trade in 1921, having donated a large part of his private fortune to the Treasury to help write off war debt, an example not widely followed among the rich. He would be both genial colleague and wily opponent to Churchill for more than fifteen years, during which Churchill consistently underestimated, and was outplayed by, a man whom Lloyd George, from chastening experience, called 'the most formidable antagonist whom I ever encountered'.

In 1952 G.M. Young published an authorised, though distinctly lukewarm, biography of Baldwin. An unused draft expressed the private feelings not only of Baldwin but of many others in those lurid years after the Great War: 'The Inner Ring, the Camarilla, Lloyd George, Churchill, Birkenhead and Beaverbrook, bent on nothing but the pursuit of power, were degrading public life and bringing Parliament into public contempt.' The reign of Edward VII and the first part of the reign of George V was indeed the most corrupt period in English political history since the eighteenth century, and Lloyd George has been called the first prime minister since Walpole to leave office flagrantly richer than he entered it.* Much the same distaste was voiced in America. The Boer War had wrought a great change, H.L. Mencken wrote in 1922, ironically echoing Beatrice Webb and the *National Review* with their contempt for Churchill, the 'trans-Atlantic demagogue': 'The English gentleman began to disappear from public life,' Mencken thought, 'and in his place appeared a rabble-rousing bounder obviously almost identical with the American politician – the Lloyd George, Chamberlain, F.E. Smith, Isaacs – Reading, Churchill, Bottomley,† Northcliffe type ... there was a shift of the social and political centre of gravity to a lower plane.'

---

* Though not the last, as Tony Blair reminds us.
† Horatio Bottomley was a boisterous fraudsman, who made and lost fortunes through shady stock-promotion and his jingoistic magazine *John Bull*, preaching hatred of the 'Germ-Huns'. Elected to Parliament, he beat the wartime recruiting drum to his considerable enrichment, but was finally imprisoned for fraud in 1922. A visitor who found him in his cell stitching mail bags and asked, 'Sewing, Bottomley?' was answered, 'No, reaping.'

Of all the camarilla, the most pernicious was Beaverbrook. He was for far too long treated as a cheeky adventurer, a provocative outsider or something of a card, not least by his friends and dependents ostensibly on the Left. They later included Aneurin Bevan, Michael Foot and A.J.P. Taylor, whose reputation as a serious historian is forever sullied by his sycophantic fawning on Beaverbrook, in a worthless biography and elsewhere. Like his friend Bonar Law, Max Aitken was the son of a Presbyterian minister in New Brunswick. By the age of twenty-four he was running the Royal Securities Corporation in Halifax, Nova Scotia, the first bond-selling company in Canada, and he became a youthful master of company flotations and mergers, by way of over-valuation of stocks, market manipulation, insider trading, shady deals, fraudulent audits and huge personal commissions.

He was a sterling millionaire at thirty, but had a 'dreadful' financial reputation in Canada, and so took his ill-gotten gains to London, one step ahead of the law. Aitken then bought his way into British politics and press with astonishing speed. By the age of thirty-two he had acquired the *Daily Express*, entered Parliament thanks to a large donation to the Tory party, and been knighted. He was a baronet at thirty-six and a peer at thirty-eight, despite the strong objections of King George. Beaverbrook had a certain impish charm and appearance, although G. M. Young thought that he looked 'like a doctor who has been struck off the roll for performing an illegal operation'. Altogether, Beaverbrook was truly wicked, a puppet-master and wire-puller, a flatterer, a seducer and a corrupter, a bully, a liar and a crook, a thorough-going scoundrel, whose influence on journalistic and public life was wholly malign, far from least his influence on Churchill.

In 1919, F.E. Smith had been elevated from Attorney General to Lord Chancellor as Lord Birkenhead. He was dangerous, avaricious, erratic and ultimately doomed: drink caught up with him as it never quite did with Churchill. During the war, Smith visited the United States and Canada on behalf of the government, and Clementine later heard from a Canadian journalist that 'at every public dinner he was drunk, that every speech he made was tactless, patronising & in bad taste'. Although his years as Lord Chancellor saw Birkenhead's brilliant legal mind at its best, in the reform of the law of real property, his inebriety on the Woolsack did little to enhance the dignity of the office. Clementine's judgement of character was far better than her husband's. She always viewed Birkenhead and Beaverbrook with suspicion and some dislike, thinking Birkenhead a dangerous influence who encouraged her husband and then her son to drink and gamble, or more than they would have done anyway. And Churchill's association with the 'camarilla' did him no good. When he sought to lead a rebellion inside the Cabinet against Lloyd George's recognition of Soviet Russia, Birkenhead himself warned him that he would only be supported by one out of ten Tory MPs, who were opposed to him on nine out of ten other issues.

A more immediate challenge to Lloyd George's government than Bolshevism was Ireland. The electoral victory of Sinn Fein was followed by a time of troubles, a terrorist campaign conducted by Sinn Fein's armed front, the Irish Republican Army, later dignified as a 'War of Independence', although it wasn't a war and Ireland didn't become independent. As all too often, brutality provoked brutality in response. Having once been ardently opposed to Home Rule, Churchill had then supported it; having preached harsh force against its Ulster opponents, he now favoured harsher force against the rebels of the IRA. Two new bodies, the 'Auxis' and the 'Black and Tans',* were raised to supplement the overstretched Royal Irish Constabulary, and soon became a byword for cruel reprisals.

With her usual humanity and sense, Clementine begged Churchill to 'use your influence now for some sort of moderation or at any rate justice in Ireland – Put yourself in the place of the Irish – if you were their leader you would not be cowed by severity & certainly not by reprisal which fall like the rain from Heaven upon the Just & upon the Unjust.' For once, Churchill took her advice, to the point of supporting a settlement. He even established something like an improbable friendship with Michael Collins, one of the IRA leaders, during the negotiations which led in December 1921 to a treaty establishing an Irish Free State, less six counties of Ulster. As Collins himself guessed, by signing the Treaty he signed his own death warrant: in 1922 a Civil War broke out between the new Free State government

---

* Auxiliary Brigade and Constabulary Reserve Force, the latter nicknamed from their makeshift uniform of dark tunic and khaki trousers; the Black and Tans were originally a pack of foxhounds in County Limerick.

and intransigent Republicans, more bloodily savage than the preceding Troubles, and Collins was among those killed.

None of the reprisals in Ireland which so distressed Clementine could compare with what happened in India on 13 April 1919. At Amritsar in the Punjab, a large crowd of unarmed men gathered at the Jallianwalla Bagh, a walled enclosure near the Golden Temple, the Sikhs' holiest shrine. Brigadier General Reginald Dyer led ninety Gurkha and Baluchi troops to the scene where they opened fire without warning. At least 380 people were killed, in a decisive moment for the decline and fall of the British Empire. Dyer was dismissed from his command, the incident was investigated, and a report was prepared. If Indians and enlightened Englishmen were dismayed by Amritsar, militarists and imperialists thought that Dyer had done his duty, and a good job too, and the *Morning Post*, flagship of reaction and Churchill's great foe, raised a large subscription for Dyer.

When the report was debated in Parliament in July 1920, Churchill defended the disciplining of Dyer, and repudiated his proclaimed policy of exemplary violence: 'We cannot admit this doctrine in any form,' Churchill told the Commons. 'Frightfulness is not a remedy known to the British pharmacopœia. I yield to no one in my detestation of Bolshevism, and of the revolutionary violence which precedes it ... But my hatred of Bolshevism and Bolsheviks is not founded on their silly system of economics, or their absurd doctrine of an impossible equality. It arises from the bloody and devastating terrorism which they practise in every land into which they have broken, and by which alone their criminal regime can be maintained.' More noble words, but, apart from the fact that 'frightfulness' or brutal violence had been very much part of the way the British Empire had been conquered and disciplined, they would one day rebound on Churchill.

In February 1921 he was shifted by Lloyd George to become Colonial Secretary. Churchill held that office for little more than twenty months, but they were of the highest importance in his career, and in history. The British Empire and its colonies for which he was responsible stretched across the whole globe, but Churchill's attention perforce turned to the Levant, then known as the Near East, the residue of the Ottoman Empire, where the British had found their last great field for expansion. A bad start had been made during the war. Wilson's pious and ill-informed 'Fourteen Points' implied the destruction of the Habsburg and Ottoman empires under the guise of 'autonomous development', with fateful effect. Those empires were indeed broken apart; and the Americans were still dealing with the consequences, from the Danube to the Tigris to the Jordan, in the next century.

But Wilson couldn't be blamed for the mutually exclusive promises to Arabs and Zionists made during the war by the British: rarely has Albion been more perfidious. Arab leaders were offered national autonomy by the London government, itself encouraged by a somewhat fanciful 'Arab revolt', and by the curious figure of T.E. Lawrence, a mixture of scholar, warrior and charlatan much admired by Churchill. After the war the Ottoman domains were cynically divided, under the guise of League of Nations 'mandates', with the French taking over Syria and carving out what was intended to be a Maronite Christian client state in Lebanon, while the British took over two territories, Mesopotamia, now renamed Irak or Iraq, where Indian and British troops had met disaster in 1916, and Palestine. As first mapped, this second British mandatory territory stretched from the Mediterranean eastwards far across the Jordan to where it met Iraq.

Much of this was Churchill's handiwork, confirmed in March 1921 at a conference in Cairo to decide the immediate future of these lands which had just been added, albeit somewhat ambiguously, to the British Empire. Thither the Colonial Secretary went, accompanied by Clementine and her maid. Churchill could claim responsibility for cobbling together the disparate territory of Iraq, extending from Kurdish lands in the north to Marsh Arabs in the south, a completely artificial country whose predominantly Shia Muslim populace was placed under a Sunni dynasty; a piece of statecraft much later described in a book with the succinct title *Winston's Folly*.* Churchill's hope was that this would be 'an independent Native State friendly to Great Britain', although he was sceptical at the same time about the 'ungrateful volcano', and called Iraq a land 'unduly stocked with peppery, pugnacious, proud politicians and theologians,' not a bad description then, or when the British joined another expedition to Basra eighty years later, although peppery, pugnacious and proud weren't bad words for Churchill himself.

---

* *Winston's Folly: How Winston Churchill's Creation of Modern Iraq led to Saddam Hussein* Christopher Catherwood, 2004.

Soon rebellion broke out in Iraq, and was suppressed, not by soldiers but by the new-born Royal Air Force. It had come under Churchill's authority as Minister for War and Air, and he played a central part in preserving its autonomy, but its driving force was Sir Hugh Trenchard, the first Chief of the Air Staff. In June 1918 he had propounded the doctrine that 'the moral effect [of bombing] at present is far greater than the material effect', using the word as in the French *moral*, or 'morale'. Trenchard meant that the object of bombing was to frighten and demoralise the civilian population through what might be called 'devastating terrorism': the RAF was built on the principle that frightfulness did indeed belong to the British pharmacopœia.

This was now practised, and not only by the British. In their new territory of Syria, the French bombed Damascus for several days to suppress a revolt, and the South Africans, who had acquired the former German South-West Africa, bombed the Bondelswarts tribesmen and burned their villages. On the day after the Amritsar massacre, British aircraft had flown over Gujranwala, fifty-five miles north of Amritsar and now in Pakistan, machine-gunning a crowd of protesters. Then the RAF bombed Kabul in what the British called the Third Afghan War, and after that Iraq. Defenceless villages were bombed, an exercise in what was called 'air policing' by Trenchard, who believed that 'in dealing with Arabs, it was necessary to take a firm line,' and just as enthusiastically conducted by the young RAF Squadron Leader Arthur Harris. He cheerfully described the way his Vickers Vernon bombers 'destroyed the villages and by air patrols kept the insurgents away from their homes as long as necessary'.

No less enthusiastically, Churchill saw that air power 'may ultimately lead to a form of control over semi-civilised countries which will be found very effective and infinitely cheaper', adding that, 'I am strongly in favour of using poisoned gas against uncivilised tribes.' Those words would be rediscovered and used against his memory in the following century, during another Iraq conflict. He was speaking of non-lethal kinds like mustard gas, which had already been used on the Western Front, and whose use had been defended by the British on grounds of humanity: gas incapacitated soldiers instead of killing or mutilating them. Poison gas was not in fact used in Iraq, while Churchill recoiled at one point and protested when he learned of the way that British airmen had driven terrified villagers into a lake and bombed them there. Nevertheless, to stimulate public enthusiasm for the new force, an annual RAF tournament was held at Hendon aerodrome in north London, where in 1925 visitors could watch aircraft dropping incendiary bombs on a model of an African village.

Returning from the Levant, the Churchills' lives were overshadowed by a series of personal tragedies. Clementine's brother Bill Hozier, a perennially indebted gambler, shot himself in a Paris hotel room. Then Winston's mother broke her leg in a fall, which led to gangrene, amputation, and her death at sixty-seven. Worst of all was the death of the Churchills' youngest and best-loved daughter Marigold, carried off by septicaemia not long after her third birthday. Clementine 'screamed like an animal undergoing torture', and came near to breakdown. She never afterwards mentioned the little girl. Churchill was sustained by a few true friends like Lord Hugh Cecil, who wrote to him, 'Meantime I am sorry for your sorrow for in spite of much disagreement and disapproval I shall always love you.'

If less tragic, political life was scarcely less fraught. Not only was the Coalition always an artificial political construct, Lloyd George's personal regimen was squalid. There was the minor fact that his wife Margaret resided in Wales, while in London he lived almost openly with Frances Stevenson, his secretary, mistress and, at very long last, second wife. More to the point, the sale of honours, which Lloyd George privately, ingeniously, and maybe not implausibly, defended as cleaner than the American system of political favours done in return for donations, had become flagrant and repellent. One exceptionally disreputable figure nominated for a peerage by Lloyd George in 1922, the South African mining magnate Sir J.B. Robinson, suffered the unique humiliation of being angrily blackballed by the House of Lords.

By now a change of mood not only about the government but about the war was perceptible, and was destined to grow over the coming years, a reaction against the official cult of heroic sacrifice and 'the glorious dead'. One forgotten but fascinating example from 1922 is 'Our Graves in Gallipoli' by E.M. Forster, a curious, bitter little satire about the futility of war and of that campaign in particular. It takes the form of a dialogue between two dead men, one English and one Turkish, with the Englishman speaking sourly from his grave of 'Churchill the Fortunate'. In truth his fortunes were very mixed, and the Straits separating Europe from Asia were anything but lucky for Churchill, however much that corner of the map obsessed him.

Seven years after Gallipoli came a crisis over Chanak, on the southern or Asian side of the Dardanelles, opposite the Gallipoli peninsula. The new national state of Turkey which had arisen under Kemal Ataturk, the victor of Gallipoli, had proven a more formidable foe than the old Ottoman Empire. In September 1922 Ataturk's army drove the Greeks out of Asia Minor, where they had lived since Antiquity, amid arson, rape and appalling bloodshed at Smyrna, before turning north. There the Turks confronted a British garrison, stationed at Chanak thanks to the postwar settlement imposed on Turkey by the Treaty of Sèvres, a far more humiliating 'Carthaginian peace' than Versailles. Needless to say, Churchill responded bellicosely to this confrontation, which might easily have turned into war. That was averted, but the crisis led to the fall of Lloyd George, taking Churchill with him.

Having resigned from the government and the leadership of the Conservatives on medical advice in the spring of 1921, Bonar Law sprang back to political life eighteen months later. On 7 October he wrote to The Times condemning the Coalition's policy at Chanak. 'The British Empire,' Bonar Law said, echoing Curzon, 'which includes the largest body of Mahomedans in any State, ought not to show any hostility or unfairness to the Turks.' Still more tellingly he wrote, 'We cannot alone act as the policemen of the world.' Despite that warning shot, the Cabinet agreed to continue as a coalition at the coming election. But the ground was shifting under them. Amid high drama, with many colloquies and cabals, enlivened by Birkenhead turning up drunk at the wrong place, a meeting of Tory MPs at the Carlton Club on 19 October voted to end the Coalition and fight the next election as a single party once more. Lloyd George immediately resigned, never to hold office again. Bonar Law became prime minister, formed a purely Tory – not to say reactionary – ministry, and then called a general election for 15 November, which the Tories won comfortably.

All of this could not have turned out worse for Churchill. He and the other Coalitionists were insultingly repudiated at the Carlton Club, and at the election he was then repudiated by the voters of Dundee after a hard-fought campaign, when Birkenhead was no help, arriving at Dundee to speak on Churchill's behalf once again intoxicated by more than rhetoric. At the count, Churchill was beaten by two candidates. One was the implacable Mr Scrymgeour, who now became the only declared Prohibitionist ever elected to the House of Commons, a nice touch in view of Churchill's habits. The other was the radical E.D. Morel, whose Union of Democratic Control had a real influence on British foreign policy.

'I look upon Churchill as such a personal force for evil that I would take up the fight against him with a whole heart,' Morel said. This was the very moment that Mussolini had come to power in Italy, supported by his Fascist party and its brutish *squadristi*, who terrorised town and country. Suppose there should be violent civil strife in Great Britain as well, said Scrymgeour. Then he would not be surprised 'if Mr Churchill were at the head of the fascisti party'.

OUR OWN MUSSOLINI

5

'Our own Mussolini'
Fleet Street 1926

Not long before her death, Mary Soames, Churchill's last surviving child, said about her father, 'The thing to remember is that he was a journalist.' So he was, and in his double career as politician and journalist, the writing enriched him, with earnings far larger than even the prime minister's salary, while also tempting him to play his habitual role as a lone wolf, free of party loyalty. Churchill always saw politics as personal adventure more than collective endeavour. He conspicuously lacked the quality Polish Communists later called 'partyness', and he might have adapted and reversed President Kennedy's phrase: Churchill asked not what he could do for his party, he asked what his party could do for him, whichever that party might be.

Before then English politics had seen plenty of other unlikely journeys. Disraeli began life as a Radical and joined the Tory 'gentlemen of England' not because he was one of them but because he could provide the brilliance and insolent wit they lacked. Gladstone entered Parliament as 'the rising hope of those stern and unbending Tories', in Macaulay's famous phrase, defending his father's slave-owning interests in Parliament, before ending his days as 'the people's William', adored by labourers and cottagers and execrated by Queen Victoria as a dangerous demagogue. Even so, Churchill's path was well-nigh unique in deserting one party for another and then deserting back again.

This was made easier by the unusual political turbulence of the time. In just over two years, from late October 1922 to early November 1924, there were three general elections, four governments and four prime ministers, along with a rare period of true three-party politics. Having ousted Lloyd George, Bonar Law was only at Number 10 for seven months. In most personal respects he was Churchill's antithesis – his recreation was chess, and he drank only milk – but he smoked, and this one vice caught up with him when he was diagnosed with terminal throat cancer and resigned in May 1923, dying five months later. He was replaced by Baldwin rather than Curzon, who expected the prize, after a murky episode in which Bonar Law's views may have been misrepresented to the king and his advisers.

Having recuperated physically and mentally in the warmth of Provence, Churchill returned to the fray refreshed, while he took advantage of enforced absence from Parliament to work on his war memoir. In December 1923, Baldwin blundered when he suddenly declared himself in favour of Protection and called an election. Churchill stood in Leicester West, still ostensibly as a Liberal though for the last time. He lost to the Labour candidate, while Baldwin lost his parliamentary majority, and couldn't prevent a first Labour government taking office. Ramsay MacDonald became prime minister in January 1924, and Churchill, who had shortly before said that a Labour government would be a grave national misfortune, wrote privately to congratulate him.

By now Clementine knew that Churchill was edging back towards the Conservative fold, and was unhappy about it, telling him: 'Do not however let the Tories get you too cheap.' He followed her advice to the extent of standing against an official Conservative, at a by-election in the Abbey Division of Westminster in March 1924. He was labelled an 'Independent Anti-Socialist' and supported by Beaverbrook's *Daily Express* and Rothermere's *Daily Mail*. After a noisy campaign, Churchill ran the Tory as close as forty-three votes. His latest turn provoked a very mixed response. For the Conservatives, it meant reluctant recognition of his star quality, and acceptance that he would return. But the *Weekly Westminster* published a cartoon of Churchill under the title 'Our Own Mussolini'. Beneath was an extended caption by Philip Guedalla, an Oxonian wit and litterateur, barrister and repeatedly unsuccessful Liberal candidate. 'High up on the short waiting-lists of England's Mussolinis stands the name of Winston Spencer Churchill,' Guedalla wrote, envisaging more colourfully than Morel had done Churchill 'marching black-shirted upon Buckingham Palace with a victorious army of genteel but bellicose persons'.

In May Churchill went to Liverpool conventionally attired rather than black-shirted to address a genteel but bellicose Tory meeting for the first time in twenty years, and in September he was adopted as the 'Constitutional' candidate for Epping, supported by the local Tories. Weeks later the Labour government fell after a 'red scare' in the form of a subversive letter published in the *Daily Mail*, purportedly from Grigory Zinoviev, one of the Soviet leaders in Moscow, which seemed to incriminate Labour as Communist stooges. Whether the letter was genuine or, as King George among many sensible people suspected, a forgery, Baldwin gained a large majority at the ensuing general election, while Churchill won Epping, and would hold it – or Woodford, as it later became – for forty years and through nine elections.

As he crept back into the Tory fold, Churchill offered an explanation: 'I am what I have always been – a Tory Democrat. Force of circumstance has compelled me to serve with another party, but my views have never changed.' He may have convinced himself, but others only saw that he had first been returned to Parliament as a Tory in a year when they won a crushing election victory, had defected to the Liberals less than four years later, had gained office less than two years after that while the Liberals won their own landslide, and now, with the Liberals in rapid decline, had deserted them for the Tories. Thanks to this remarkable agility he managed to retain salaried ministerial office from December 1905 to June 1929 with only two brief interludes of twenty and twenty-four months. Churchill engagingly said that while anyone can rat, it took someone special to re-rat, but that was really too breezy. He forgot Macaulay's words: 'In all ages and nations, fidelity to a good cause in adversity had been regarded as a virtue. In all ages and nations the politician whose practice was always to be on the side which was uppermost had been despised.' Once again, the belief that Churchill was an unprincipled opportunist may have been wrong, but it was scarcely surprising.

For years Churchill had been skating on very thin financial ice and never living within his means. Lucrative book contracts were the only answer. His great project in the 1920s was *The World Crisis*, a highly personal account of the Great War. The first two parts, dealing with 1911–14 and with 1915, both appeared in 1923; the next, on 1916–18, was published in two volumes in 1927. The indefatigable author then produced another volume in 1929, *The Aftermath*, and as afterthought to the aftermath came *The Eastern Front* in 1931. Since he was in office from July 1917 to October 1922 and then November 1924 to June

1929, he combined writing with ministerial and parliamentary duties. In that generous age, Churchill was able to dictate much of the text of these books to secretaries in his various government offices, and he was also able to use official documents, his own and others' letters and memoranda, in a way that would have given later Cabinet secretaries fits. Even then, when the serialisation of the first volumes began in 1923, Tory MPs asked questions in Parliament about Churchill's use of state documents, including the decrypts of German signals, and he was incensed when Bonar Law suggested that he might have breached his Privy Councillor's oath.

Once Baldwin formed a new cabinet in November 1924 he invited back the penitent Coalitionists, but in unsuitable posts which almost suggested that he was punishing them. With his faults, Birkenhead was a brilliant lawyer, but became Secretary of State for India; Austen Chamberlain the hereditary Protectionist was Foreign Secretary; and Churchill, a Free Trader whose grasp of public finance was no better than his management of his own money, was Chancellor of the Exchequer. He was exhilarated when asked if he would take the job – 'Will the bloody duck swim?' – but he didn't swim to much effect, and he came to believe that Baldwin had deliberately outmanoeuvred him. The economist Hubert Henderson* wasn't alone in saying that Churchill was one of the worst Chancellors there had ever been, and even Churchill would scarcely have disagreed.

At the beginning of his Chancellorship, he did proclaim his mission to Otto Niemeyer of the Treasury: 'I would rather see Finance less proud and Industry more content.' Far too few of his British successors, and his American admirers, have followed those fine words, and he himself had only limited success. His most momentous decision at the Treasury was to return to the Gold Standard. He had gathered four economic and financial authorities to argue it out, two for gold, two against. Keynes was one of the opponents; he called the gold standard 'a barbarous relic', although he would help create something remarkably similar to a gold standard at the end of the next war, when he was one of the architects of the new financial order which served

---

* Adviser to several governments and a professor at Oxford; father of Sir Nicholas Henderson, who will appear much later as British ambassador in Washington at the time of the Falklands War.

the western world so well through three decades of unexampled prosperity. Churchill nevertheless took the plunge.

What gave him particular delight was that he was now in his father's old office, and could don Lord Randolph's own Chancellor's robes.* On 28 April 1925, he presented his first Budget and announced that the Suspending Act of 1919 would not be renewed, and that Great Britain therefore was back on gold. This prompted Keynes's merry pasquinade, *The Economic Consequences of Mr Churchill*, which demolished another part of Churchill's reputation, all the more effectively because Keynes was in his most sparkling form ('Mr Baldwin, who has succeeded to the affections formerly occupied by Queen Victoria ...'). Churchill himself would later, if privately, say that returning to gold was the worst mistake of his life, a high standard indeed. Even at the time Keynes's objection was less absolute than technical: Churchill had returned to the now hopelessly overvalued prewar rate of $4.86 to the pound. Once again Churchill was living in the past, and living in hope. He couldn't grasp that the certainties – political or imperial or financial – of the days before 1914 were gone forever.

As Churchill might have foreseen, the effect of returning to gold was to damage the export industries and contribute to a rise in unemployment, so that Bevin, now the most formidable of union leaders, attacked Churchill as an enemy of the working class. That was nothing compared to Churchill's role in the general strike of 1926, a sorry affair. Nowhere was industrial strife more bitter than in the coal mines, still an industry employing more than a million men. Miners were shockingly ill-paid, by owners who apparently subscribed to the doctrines of Karl Marx, really believing that they could only make a profit by immiserating their workers, and the miners' unions were obdurate and angry in turn. Birkenhead spoke for others, maybe including Churchill, when he observed that 'It would be possible to say without exaggeration that the miners' leaders were the stupidest men in England if we had not frequent occasion to meet the owners.'

When the leaders of the other unions decided to call a national or general strike in sympathy with the miners' demand for a living wage, Churchill was at his most bellicose. The strike had been partly

---

* What happened to the Chancellor's robes, and when were they last worn?

precipitated by the refusal of printers at the *Daily Mail* to print a denunciation of the miners, and so Churchill took charge of the *British Gazette*, the government's official daily paper printed on the *Mail's* presses. Now for the first time he became something like a Fleet Street editor, denouncing with extreme vehemence the 'enemy', the working class. He insisted that the general strike was inherently unlawful and unconstitutional, which was simply false. Some of the union leaders were on the far Left, including some who had joined the new-born Communist Party of Great Britain, but others, and the members who followed them with remarkable loyalty and discipline, had no wish to overthrow the existing order, they only wanted to help the miners escape from penury.

As the unions' own journal said, the strike 'arose entirely out of industrial conditions and had entirely industrial aims', and any idea of misrepresenting it as a revolutionary threat to the constitution 'was Mr Churchill's. It is a melodramatic stunt on Sydney Street lines.' Within a week the strike collapsed, apart from the miners, who remained on strike. Churchill now played a more generous part. In September he came near to securing a better settlement, but was thwarted by the intransigence of the owners, who wanted to see the miners crushed and driven back to work by the lash of hunger, as they were. Even so, it was still understandable that the Labour politician Emmanuel Shinwell could say that Churchill was Labour's 'most valuable asset'.

Not long after Churchill himself explained his attitude in very revealing words: 'I have always urged fighting wars and other contentions with might and main till overwhelming victory, and then offering the hand of friendship to the vanquished. Thus I have always been against the Pacifists during the quarrel, and against the Jingoes at its close.' He thanked Birkenhead for a line from the *Aeneid*, 'Parcere subjectis et debellare superbos', which seemed to Churchill to embody his idea extremely well: 'Spare the conquered and wear down the proud.' And Churchill went on to say that this had been his principle throughout: 'I thought we ought to have conquered the Irish and then given them Home Rule; that we ought to have starved out the Germans, and then revictualled their country; and that after smashing the General Strike, we should have met the grievances of the miners. I always get into trouble because so few people take this line. I was once asked to devise an inscription for a monument in France. I wrote,

"In war, Resolution. In defeat, Defiance. In victory, Magnanimity. In peace, Goodwill."'

Whether or not that line was entirely original, it became, of course, the 'Moral of the Work' prefacing the six volumes of *The Second World War*. Churchill added that 'those who can win a war well can rarely make a good peace, and those who could make a good peace would never have won the war. It would perhaps be pressing the argument too far to suggest that I could do both.' But maybe the reason that 'so few people take' this line – offer no quarter and no conciliation to a foe until he is begging for mercy – is that it's debatable even in warfare, but extremely dangerous in domestic politics.

More volumes of *The World Crisis* continued to appear while Churchill was Chancellor. In the early volumes he tells how he had made the Fleet ready for war by 1914 – 'For thirty-four months of preparation and ten months of war I had borne the prime responsibility and had wielded the main executive power' – and he then mounts a detailed description, and vigorous if unconvincing defence, of the Gallipoli campaign. In all, forty-two chapters of the work cover the period up to the end of that campaign, with only twenty-three on the rest of the war. The later volumes are a sustained if restrained polemic against the strategy of the Allied generals, one in particular. Field Marshal Earl Haig of Bemersyde, as he had become in 1919, the peerage fortified with a grant of £100,000 from Parliament, died unexpectedly in January 1928. Until his death he remained ostensibly a hero to the nation and to the men whom he had commanded, or those who had survived his battles. One of the verses about the war by Churchill's friend Siegfried Sassoon is 'The General': '"He's a cheery old card," grunted Harry to Jack / As they slogged up to Arras with rifle and pack. / But he did for them both by his plan of attack.' That's not so far from Churchill's spirit, with its own bitter sarcasm and irony.

In America, the reception of Churchill's book was mixed at best, with Carlton J.H. Hayes saying that it displayed 'the mind of a militarist, and militarists are as dangerous now as they were from 1911 to 1914'. Some English readers also recoiled, both from what Churchill said and how he said it. This was an age of debunking, of irreverent derision in the spirit of Lytton Strachey's *Eminent Victorians*, of iconoclastic writers striving for unadorned language. And so the young literary critic Herbert Read, who had himself served as an infantry officer, singled out Churchill's book as an example of all that was wrong with grandiose prose: 'its literary eloquence is false because it is artificial ... the images are stale, the metaphors violent, the whole passage exhales a false dramatic atmosphere ... a volley of rhetorical imperatives.'

But then there was a quite different verdict from Keynes, and it was he who grasped Churchill's import. In 1927, writing for American readers in the *New Republic*, he published an exceptionally interesting review of the 1916–18 volumes of *The World Crisis*. Apart from saying that 'Mr Churchill writes better than any politician since Disraeli,' Keynes saw Churchill's central argument: 'in each country the professional soldiers, the "brass hats," were, on the great questions of military policy, generally wrong – wrong on the weight of the argument beforehand and wrong on the weight of the evidence afterward – whilst the professional politicians, the "frocks," ... were generally right.' Churchill had tried to show 'that wisdom lay on the whole with Asquith, Lloyd George' and himself as well as their French and even German counterparts, 'and that it was Haig and Robertson, Joffre and Nivelle, Falkenhayn and Ludendorff who jeopardised or lost the war.'

What each side signally lacked, Keynes wrote, was a Cunctator Maximus:* 'No Fabius arose to wait, to withdraw, to entice,' Keynes wrote, summarising Churchill's theme almost better than he could have done. The generals were always in a hurry, 'hurrying to disclose their possession of new weapons ... hurrying to the useless slaughter of their dreaded "pushes". The strategic surrender, the deliberate withdrawal, the attempt to lure the enemy into a pocket where he could be taken in flank, all such expedients of the higher imagination of warfare were scarcely attempted.' From beginning to end, the generals' thinking, if it could be called that, 'was elementary in the extreme – in attack, to find out the enemy in his strongest place and hurl yourself on him; in defence, to die heroically in the first ditch,' Keynes wrote. And yet it should have been clear from the beginning of the war that changes in military technology 'gave an extraordinary advantage, in the conditions of modern warfare, to the retreat as

---

* The third-century BC Roman politician and general Quintus Fabius Maximus was known as Cunctator or 'Delayer' from his tactics in the Second Punic War; the group of English progressives which included Churchill's acquaintances the Webbs and Shaw called themselves the Fabians to suggest that socialism could be achieved by patience and without revolutionary violence.

against the advance', to defence against attack: something Churchill had indeed grasped at the outset of the war.

Could there have been an answer? The author plainly thought so. In the single most significant sentence in the whole of *The World Crisis*, Churchill lamented that among the commanders on all sides 'There was altogether lacking that supreme combination of the King–Warrior–Statesman which is apparent in the persons of the great conquerors of history.' And who might that have been? Churchill could scarcely have intimated the answer more clearly: *The World Crisis* is both self-justification and lengthy job application.

Such eloquent contempt for pointless slaughter only strengthened the growing mood of disillusionment and regret about the war. It would find famous expression in a clutch of memoirs published ten years after the war, by Robert Graves, Edmund Blunden and Sassoon whom Churchill had befriended, sensitive young writers-to-be, all of whom had unexpectedly become soldiers, and who all told of the suffering and futility of the Western Front. At the same time, everything Churchill wrote about the Great War, however vivid and powerful, revealed the weakness of his own position, and invited an obvious riposte. Haig and the others might have been as wrong as he said, but when he was allowed to do his own thing it had led to disaster.

What Keynes failed to notice was just how tendentious, partisan, and even distorted Churchill's book was, not for the first or last time. It wasn't just the usual egocentricity, although Balfour's 'brilliant Autobiography, disguised as a history of the universe' was close to the mark. There are graver problems. An Australian scholar* who has closely examined the book has concluded that 'The reader is never sure that the version given by Churchill is complete, or if material damaging to the case Churchill is building up has been omitted, or if any deletions made have been indicated in the text,' and he gives further examples of Churchill's tendency to select evidence to his advantage or simply avoid inconvenient truths. This was just as it had been with *Lord Randolph Churchill* and just as it would be with *Marlborough* and *The Second World War*; Churchill was telling a tale, and he would rather bend the facts than concede an argument.

*

---

* Robin Prior, *Churchill's 'World Crisis' as History*, 1983.

His leonine personality still imposed itself on his Cabinet colleagues, and one in particular. Neville Chamberlain had made an unhappy start in life, managing a sisal farm in the Bahamas, until telling his father, the formidable Joe, that he could 'no longer see any chance of making the investment pay'. He came home and entered municipal politics like his father, and became 'a good Lord Mayor of Birmingham in a lean year', as Lloyd George sneered, before another setback during the Great War when he was a failure as Director of National Service. But he entered parliament and became Chancellor of the Exchequer briefly in 1923.

When Baldwin returned to office in December 1924, Chamberlain could have returned to the Treasury but asked instead for the more modest post of Minister of Health. In this role he was quite outstanding, much the most successful minister of the 1924–9 government, or even of the interwar years, and a man who should be a hero to this day to those who call themselves progressives. With an energy his modest demeanour belied, he announced twenty-five new Bills when he took up his post, and within little more than four years he had carried twenty-one. Between them they transformed welfare and public housing, and completely reformed and strengthened local government, with a system greatly superior not only to the one it replaced but also to the one which replaced it under another Conservative government more than forty years later.

Since the Treasury provided the funds for Chamberlain's schemes of social improvement, he had to work closely with Churchill. They were two renegades, or at least political mavericks. Churchill had deserted one party for another and then deserted back again, while Chamberlain liked to remind his Birmingham constituents that 'I was not born a little Conservative. I was brought up as a Liberal and afterwards as a Liberal Unionist.' He ardently hoped that the party to which he now belonged could 'discard the odious title of Conservative', and after his death, Lady Cecily Debenham, a family friend, wrote to his widow, 'Neville was a Radical to the end of his days. It makes my blood boil when I see his "Tory" and "Reactionary" outlook taken as a matter of course.'

Despite their lack of temperamental affinity, Churchill and Chamberlain seemed to get on well enough, while Chamberlain's diaries, and still more the copious letters he wrote to his sisters, are among the best and most vivid records we have of politics between the wars, and of Churchill. Chamberlain noted wryly that 'It is a little difficult to keep pace with Winston who has a new idea every hour,' and no one has ever pinned down Churchill so well as Chamberlain did in an acutely perceptive letter to Lord Irwin in 1928. 'One doesn't often come across a real man of genius,' Chamberlain wrote. 'Winston is such a man and he has *les défauts de ses qualités.*' It was 'sheer delight' to hear him speaking, in public or in Cabinet,

> when presently you see his whole face suffused with pink, his speech becomes more and more rapid and tempestuous until in a few minutes he will not hear of the possibility of opposition to an idea which only occurred to him a few minutes ago. In the consideration of affairs his decisions are never founded on exact knowledge, nor even on careful and prolonged consideration of the pros and cons. He seeks instinctively for the large and preferably novel idea such as is capable of representation by the broadest brush. Whether the idea is practicable or impracticable, good or bad, provided he can see himself recommending it plausibly to an enthusiastic audience, it commends itself to him ... He is a brilliant wayward child who compels admiration but who wears out his guardians with the constant strain he puts on them.

That was true not only when it was written, it would be true fifteen years later. Not that this backhanded admiration was much reciprocated. 'I have made up my mind,' Churchill told Clementine in 1929, that 'if N. Ch. [Neville Chamberlain] is made leader of the C.P. [Conservative Party] or anyone else of that kind, I clear out of politics and see if I cannot make you & the kittens a little more comfortable before I die.' Chamberlain did become leader, and was succeeded by Churchill, in circumstances neither of them could possibly have foreseen as the 1920s came to an end.

For the three years after the General Strike, politics were more placid, and so was Churchill's Chancellorship, although his treatment of public finances was sometimes alarmingly similar to his conduct of his own affairs. While supposedly adhering to the Victorian standards of fiscal restraint and balanced budgets, he lived 'mouth to hand' and conjured problems away by juggling figures, quietly moving sources of revenue to pay for unintended items of expenditure, and gambling on better times to come. Or as Peter Clarke delightfully puts it, 'he talked like Mr Gladstone but behaved like Mr Micawber.'

There were a few diversions, such as his attempt to introduce a betting tax, at a time when gambling inhabited a legal grey area. The comical consequence of Churchill's law was that 'the Customs were prosecuting bookmakers for destroying betting slips whereas the police were prosecuting bookmakers for keeping them'. Just as comically, at the next election bookies turned out with motor cars to canvass for Labour, who had promised to repeal the law.

This was a personal subject for Churchill, and for Clementine. She was unhappy about her husband's love of a bet, on the stock market or in the casino, as she knew all too much about addictive gambling from her own family, and not only from her brother Bill who had shot himself. Much of Clementine's girlhood had been spent in Dieppe, where Lady Blanche Hozier had taken her children to prevent her husband (though probably not Clementine's father) from removing them. Visiting that pretty little fishing port again in 1924, Clementine lamented that being taken to the Dieppe casino from an early age had been Bill's undoing. And when she and her mother and sister visited the casino, 'I was astounded at the reckless way in which both Mother & Nellie gambled.'

She wrote those words to a husband who himself was close to being a problem gambler. Churchill never holidayed with his children and rarely with his wife. Instead, throughout the interwar years he regularly visited France on his own, usually as a guest of the Duke of Westminster or Beaverbrook, to eat, drink, paint and gamble. While he was on one such jaunt, he was sternly counselled by Clementine, 'BEWARE CASINO', but her advice was ignored as ever: to take but one occasion, Churchill withdrew 75,000 francs (then roughly £750 or $3700, several times as much as a factory worker's annual income) from the bank at the local casino, and returned with 3250 francs.

By now Churchill was gradually giving up what Theodore Roosevelt called the strenuous life, although not his tastes for luxury, or his ill-chosen friends. Until his fifties he still played polo, rode to hounds in Kent, and hunted wild boar at Mimizan, the Duke of Westminster's estate in south-west France. 'We had a very good hunt on the last day,' he told Clementine in February 1924, when he was waiting to see when he could get back into Parliament; 'After a long chase we finally slew a sow.' There was also sport in Scotland, from grouse-shooting at Balmoral, when official business, rather than George V's liking for Churchill, took him there, to salmon-fishing with Westminster's mistress, Coco Chanel.

When 'Bendor' Westminster* died in 1953, Churchill wrote an elegy for a 'fearless, gay, and delightful' man with whom, since they first met during the Boer War, he had enjoyed 'half a century of unbroken friendship'. Westminster was in truth an immensely rich, unworthy and malevolent wastrel, 'burly, petulant, *roi des mangés*' or king of the failures, in 'Chips' Channon's words; George V in his succinct way said that Westminster was 'almost a prince, but not quite a gentleman'. Unlike the Cavendishes, Cecils and Russells, who could at least claim to have played some part in the making of English history, the Grosvenors had sat back, made prudent marriages and acquired vast wealth. In 1899 Bendor inherited the dukedom and large country estates, but more to the point 600 acres in the part of London to which one of his titles gives the name Belgravia, providing him with an annual income of £250,000.

'His most gleaming personal exploit,' Churchill claimed, was 'a daring and far-flung excursion against the Senussi.' This campaign in Libya in 1916 to deal with a Muslim people who threatened the Egyptian frontier is one of the forgotten episodes of the Great War. Westminster raised and equipped a troop of Rolls-Royce armoured cars to fight there, far from the cold and mud of Flanders. After his troop rescued a number of British prisoners held by the Senussi, Westminster ordered his men to kill all the villagers. Many years later, one of his troopers sorrowfully recalled their victims, 'especially the kiddies'. Westminster was a bigot, but spiteful antisemitism didn't exhaust his bigotry. His greatest achievement was to destroy his brother-in-law. The seventh Earl Beauchamp was an eminent statesman, a Cabinet colleague of Churchill's when the Great War began and Liberal leader in the House of Lords after it. He had married Westminster's sister Lady Lettice Grosvenor, but was none too discreetly homosexual. Westminster relentlessly persecuted the man he called 'my bugger-in-law', delating him to the king, and forcing him into exile and almost to suicide.† Churchill was never a good judge of men, nor fastidious in his choice of cronies.

---

* The nickname came from his grandfather's famous racehorse Bend Or, itself the heraldic description of the Grosvenor arms.
† Evelyn Waugh was a friend of the Lygon family, Beauchamp's children, and this story was the germ of *Brideshead Revisited*, with Lord Marchmain, *mutatis* very much *mutandis*, the exiled nobleman.

Gambling never quite got the better of Churchill, and a betting tax didn't matter greatly in the scheme of things. Defence did. In December 1924 the Locarno settlement had seemed to end the duel between France and Germany, with Great Britain and Italy acting as seconds. It was easy to think that peace had returned to Europe for good, and Churchill as Chancellor tried his best to reduce military spending. He was parsimonious with the Services, above all the Navy, whose income he steadily reduced. Behind this lay an official doctrine which Churchill not only accepted but strengthened. In August 1919, he had supported the introduction of the Ten-Year Rule. This meant that military and naval spending should be based on the assumption that 'the British Empire will not be engaged in any great war during the next ten years and that no Expeditionary Force is required for this purpose'. In 1928 he persuaded the Committee of Imperial Defence that, rather than subject to annual review, this should be an automatic rolling rule. Thanks to Churchill this remained so until March 1932, less than a year before Hitler came to power, and less than eight years before the next war began.

By the spring of 1929 Parliament was nearing its full term, and Baldwin called an election in May, the first British general election ever held under full democracy: all women as well as men over twenty-one could now vote. Churchill had opposed enfranchising women right up until they received the vote, and then opposed this last equalising of the franchise. Despite many hopes or fears, women did not tilt the vote leftward. To the contrary, over the rest of the century the Tories owed much of their dominance to the fact that women were more likely to vote Conservative than men. Churchill would have reason to be grateful for women voters, and for the presence of women in Parliament.

Nor was he more generally reconciled to the rise of the masses. Five years later, in an elegy for his cousin, the Duke of Marlborough, and for the caste to which they belonged, Churchill wrote with undisguised admiration and regret of 'The three or four hundred families which for three or four hundred years guided the fortunes of the nation from a small, struggling community to the headship of a vast and still unconquered Empire.' And Churchill lamented the good old days when he had entered politics, and there was 'a real political democracy led by a hierarchy of statesmen, and not a fluid mass distracted by newspapers'. What he meant was that in 1900 the 'real' British democracy had an electorate of 6.7 million, or some six out of ten adult men.

Three decades later, not only were those three or four hundred families in eclipse, politically, socially and economically, the electorate was now a 'fluid mass' of 28.9 million, an increase about which Churchill was at heart most uneasy. And he was even less pleased that Labour recovered from its setback in 1924. The 1929 election showed that they were now clearly the second party, with the Liberals way back in third. Tories and Labour were neck and neck in the popular vote, and for the first time Labour won the largest number of seats. Churchill bore no small responsibility for that: just as Shinwell had said, the effects of the gold standard on employment and Churchill's bellicosity during the general strike had a perverse effect in winning support for Labour, who now formed their second minority government under MacDonald.

A later holder of that great office said that there are two kinds of Chancellor, those who fail and those who get out in time. Churchill got out in time. He left the Treasury with relief and, even if his tenure had been undistinguished, it seemed that his luck had changed after so many setbacks and disasters, while his slashing of public spending and assaults on the unions won the approval of the Tory Right. His own financial position had certainly changed for the better, at least in terms of earning power. After the appearance of *The World Crisis*, he wrote a personal memoir. Along with painting, he had found another form of therapy in bricklaying at Chartwell, and when he began *My Early Life* in September 1928, he cheerfully told Baldwin that 'I have had a delightful month – building a cottage & dictating a book: 200 bricks & 2000 words per day.' Not only was his month delightful, so is the book, to this day his most engaging work, and in many ways the most revealing. It is also the last under his name of which he could say, 'All my own work.' It was written, or dictated, without the help of research assistants or ghostwriters, and it has the authentic tang of the man on every page. He ends his memoir in 1908 when 'I married and lived happily ever afterwards.' But now, for England and Europe, there was to be no happy ending.

Nazi Movement—Local Version

6

'The English-speaking races'
New Haven 1929

'But westward, look, the land is bright!' Churchill would quote the last line of Clough's poem 'Say Not the Struggle Naught Availeth' in a radio broadcast in April 1941, and in August 1929 he looked westwards to brighten his own life. He marked his freedom from the cares of office by crossing the Atlantic to make a grand tour of north America, taking him across Canada from east to west, down the Pacific coast to Los Angeles, then back to the east, Washington and New York. The journey was both luxurious and lucrative, at least temporarily, as Churchill travelled at the expense of others and met many rich, famous and powerful men, while making and losing large sums of money. But there was a deeper significance to this visit. Winston Churchill discovered America.

This was a most important turn in his story. He had an American mother, and had visited America when young, although he hadn't returned for the best part of three decades during which he had been highly critical of American policy, barely regarding the United States as a friendly country. He had railed at the American failure to enter the Great War sooner, he had better reason than most Englishmen to know how little interested most Americans were in Europe, or how little most American politicians cared about British interests, indeed how damaging American policies had been to those interests, and for most of the 1920s he had fully reciprocated what he saw as American hostility. All that was now forgotten. To suggest that Churchill changed his position on a question of the first importance for personal or professional or financial reasons might seem far-fetched, but the fact is that he shed his antipathy after this journey, and he began to think of a book – and a political departure – on the highly dubious theme of 'the English-speaking races'.

What of this country he was visiting? For more than 140 years after the Declaration of Independence no troops of the American republic had ever set foot in Europe. In 1918 the United States Army had seen hard fighting for the last seven months of the war, but had then quickly returned home, and the Americans had turned their backs again on Europe. Wilson failed to persuade the Senate to ratify the Versailles Treaty and membership of the League of Nations, his own brainchild, a failure largely due to his own vanity and obstinacy. Churchill had taken a jaundiced view of him. After Ray Stannard Baker published his eulogistic three-volume *Woodrow Wilson and the World Settlement* in 1922, Churchill derided its portrait of Wilson as 'a stainless Sir Galahad championing the superior ideals of the American people and brought to infinite distress by contact with the awful depravity of Europe and its statesmen'.

Although the 1920s are sometimes called the Roaring Twenties or the jazz age, and this was indeed the decade when America popular culture, Hollywood movies, Broadway musicals and jazz began their long global dominance, American political and social life was another story. After Wilson was laid low by the illness which led to his death, the 1920 presidential election was easily won by Republican Warren Harding, over the Democrats, James Cox and his running mate, Franklin Roosevelt. Republicans would occupy the White House for twelve years, under Harding, Calvin Coolidge and Herbert Hoover, as the United States turned in on itself. This often took curious or ugly forms, and Churchill was naturally dismayed by the puritanism expressed in Prohibition. He was anyway sardonically amused by the idea that European immigrants to America 'took away with them all the virtues and left behind all the vices of the races from which they had sprung' and had thus become 'an order of beings definitely superior in morals, in culture, and in humanity to their prototypes in Europe'.

But many Americans found little superiority in those latest newcomers. 'America is seriously alarmed by the wave of immigration from the poverty-stricken portions of Europe,' *The Times* reported in December 1920. 'In Poland alone 311,000 persons have applied for passports to the United States, and a commissioner of the Hebrew Sheltering and Aid Society, who recently returned from that country, states that, "If there were in existence a ship that could hold three million human beings, the three million Jews in Poland would board it to escape to America.'" This was a prospect which dismayed many Americans, *The Times* added. 'The leaders of the Republican Party regard the flood of immigrants as a menace to America and the Americans, and have decided to give immediate attention in Congress' to the matter. So it did, by passing flagrantly racist immigration laws in 1921 and 1924, intended to exclude Jews and Roman Catholics and maintain the predominantly Protestant north-European character of the country. Hostility to Catholics and Jews, let alone blacks, was deep-rooted through much of American society, and Ivy League colleges played their modest part by imposing quotas to restrict the number of Jews. At Harvard, this proposal was supported by Franklin Roosevelt as a member of the Board of Overseers of his old college.

Not long before, Churchill had evinced a frightening enthusiasm for eugenics, with its dread of 'racial deterioration'. This was taken a stage further by American racial theorists. Madison Grant's *The Passing of the Great Race*, published in 1916, sounded the alarm by praising the superiority of the Germanic race, but warning of the threat to it. Grant's book was admired by Hitler, who later took American laws enforcing racial purity as a model for the laws of the Third Reich. And that book was not alone. 'Civilisation's going to pieces,' Tom Buchanan tells Nick Carraway in *The Great Gatsby*. 'Have you read *The Rise of the Colored Empires* by this man Goddard? ... if we don't look out the white race will be – will be utterly submerged.' Scott Fitzgerald was alluding to Theodore Lothrop Stoddard and his 1920 book *The Rising Tide of Color against White World Supremacy*, an American bestseller at the time. Before the end of his life in 1919, Theodore Roosevelt had been dismayed by the prospect of 'race-suicide', and one reason for Wilson's initial reluctance to enter the Great War was his concern, he told his Secretary of State, that 'white civilisation and its domination over the world rested largely on our ability to keep this country intact'. Wilson had presided over the resegregation of the Federal Civil Service, and the postwar years saw a brutal reaction, with the recrudescence of the Ku Klux Klan, savage race riots from St Louis to Chicago in which many black people were murdered, and an epidemic of lynchings.

What of American foreign policy, such as it was, at this time? If any American delay in entering the war rankled with Churchill, so did the subsequent American pursuit of war debts. In the immediate postwar glow of victory, and particularly while some American goodwill could have been expected, a golden opportunity was missed for a general forgiveness of inter-allied debts. Instead, and with that inward turn, the United States was relentless in its pursuit of repayment, to Churchill's bitter resentment. In February 1921, he was elected Chairman of the English-Speaking Union, and later joked that he was an English-Speaking Union in himself, but he told Clementine that 'It was uphill work to make an enthusiastic speech about the United States at a time when so many hard things are said about us over there and when they are wringing the last penny out of their unfortunate allies.'

He was acutely aware of how very well the Americans had done out of the war, at very little cost, and even sarcastically suggested that war debts might be arranged in proportion to the casualties sustained by each nation, with the financial burden borne least by those who had lost most men. Although a figure of 116,000 is sometimes given for American fatalities in the war, more than half of those soldiers weren't killed in action but fell victim to the terrible influenza epidemic which swept through Europe in 1918. In true war dead, American losses were about one fortieth of the combined French and British toll, a proportion which would certainly have made a difference if applied to debt. When the European allies met at Genoa in April 1922 hoping to try and settle the question of debts and German reparations, the Americans declined to attend. This was not a country in a generous mood.

And what of the idea which would now become so important to Churchill: 'the English-speaking peoples'? The phrase he and others had until then used was 'the English-speaking races', whose unmistakable overtones of Anglo-Saxon white nationalism were dangerously appealing for Churchill, with his tendency to think in terms of races and 'racialism'. We have seen that the phrase and concept had a long history, with Rhodes and Conan Doyle preaching the unity of those races. As long ago as 1898 Churchill had told his mother that 'As a representative of both countries the idea of Anglo-American rapprochement is very pleasant.' Speaking on the Fourth of July 1918, he returned to that theme, claiming that 'the people of these islands' felt a deep desire 'to be truly reconciled ... with their kindred across the Atlantic Ocean'.

But this notion of 'kindred' or blood ties was already suspect. 'Some people call it Anglo-Saxon feeling. But it is not really that as between us and you,' Sir Edward Grey told Theodore Roosevelt in 1906. 'Your continent is making a new race and a new type, drawn from many sources, just as in old times the race of these Islands was evolved from many sources. So I do not dwell upon race feeling.' President Wilson emphatically agreed. Arriving in Europe in December 1918, he spoke at a dinner at Buckingham Palace. 'You must not speak of us as cousins,' the president very rightly said, 'still less as brothers; we are neither. Neither must you think of us as Anglo-Saxons, for that term can no longer be rightly applied to the people of the United States ... there are only two things which can establish and maintain closer relations between your country and mine: they are community of ideals and of interests.'

For all his enthusiastic phrases about 'kindred', Churchill himself remained distinctly cynical about American conduct and motives. He very truly said that American obduracy over war debts was 'a recognisable factor in the economic collapse which was recently to overwhelm the world, to prevent its recovery and inflame its hatreds,' and at the same time he was alarmed by increasing American naval strength. In 1890 the United States Navy was smaller than the navy of Chile, but the Great War had established the United States as a great naval power, and incidentally made the position of Under-Secretary of the Navy, held by Franklin Roosevelt, much more important. Then the Washington Naval Treaty of 1922 accepted something which would have been unthinkable to a prewar First Lord of the Admiralty: a parity between United States Navy and Royal Navy in capital ships.

Although Churchill reluctantly accepted this, he insisted that there should be British superiority in other classes, especially cruisers, the lifeline of the Empire. As Chancellor of the Exchequer in 1927 he defied the rest of the Cabinet who were ready to accept parity in all classes of ship. 'There can really be no parity between a country whose navy is its life and a power whose navy is only for prestige,' he said. 'It always seems to be assumed that it is our duty to humour the United States and minister to their vanity. They do nothing for us in return but exact the last pound of flesh.' He and Birkenhead rebelled in Cabinet against any more conciliation of the Americans, with Churchill using even more vehement language: although British ministers endlessly intoned that war with the United States was unthinkable, 'everyone knows that this is not true'.

To the contrary, he said, British policy only made sense if such a war were seen as at least a contingency. 'We do not wish to put ourselves in the power of the United States,' Churchill insisted. 'We cannot tell what they might do if at some future date they were in position to give us orders about our policy, say, in India, or Egypt or Canada.' More than a year later he told a younger colleague that the Americans were 'arrogant, fundamentally hostile to us, and that they wish to dominate world politics'. Every effort to conciliate – or appease, as he might have said – Washington only led to fresh problems, when the British had 'to start again and placate the Americans by another batch of substantial or even vital concessions'. All this was what Clementine had in mind in November 1928, by which time Churchill had tired of the Treasury and fancied moving to the Foreign Office. She reminded him of one obvious problem of his becoming Foreign Secretary: 'your known hostility to America might stand in the way.' Her words might sound astonishing in the light of later events, although Churchill's suspicions could also seem prescient. The time would come when he was leading his country, with the United States as an ally, but found that, even if he made many concessions, the Americans were indeed inclined to give him orders, about India among other things.

In November 1928, the Republican candidate Herbert Hoover won an overwhelming victory: his Democratic opponent Al Smith was Irish-Catholic, and the vote against him partly reflected the pervasive nativist bigotry of the age. Neither Hoover's victory nor the formation of the second Labour government in London three months after his inauguration meant any large change in Anglo-American relations. What changed entirely that year was Churchill's view of America following his fruitful journey. He set off that August in an all-male party, Churchill and his brother Jack with their sons, Randolph and Johnnie. Clementine might have been with them, but she was taken ill and needed to have her tonsils removed.

Apart from simply enjoying himself and relaxing, Churchill's purpose was to make friends, contacts and money. He needed it. His financial triumphs and tribulations will be related in more detail but, despite making large sums from books and journalism throughout the 1920s, and drawing the Chancellor's salary of £5000 – several hundred thousand, in either pounds or dollars, nearly a century later – he lived well beyond his means, and had been perennially in debt: that summer he was overdrawn by more than £8000, with loans of more than £5000 owed by the end of the year.

First of all Churchill agreed with Canadian Pacific that, in return for some lectures he would give in Canada, they would offer his party first-class free passage, in the *Empress of Australia* to Quebec City and then by railway across Canada. That was only a start. He had always enjoyed the company of plutocrats, and had been beholden to some of them, such as Sir Abe Bailey and Bernard Baruch. Bailey was a South African mining magnate who became prominent in England as a racehorse owner, and a political *éminence grise*; it was at his house in Bryanston Square that the meeting was held in December 1916 which led to Asquith's replacement by Lloyd George. Bailey had helped Churchill financially and in 1932 Churchill's daughter Diana would marry John Bailey, Abe's eldest son, although not for long.

When Churchill was Minister of Munitions, the ministry had arranged contracts with Charles Schwab, an American steel magnate, and Schwab now showed his gratitude by providing a special railway carriage to take them across Canada to the west coast: 'a wonderful habitation,' Churchill wrote with boyish glee. 'Jack and I have large cabins with big double beds and private bathrooms,' and 'a large dining room which I use as the office,' including a shorthand-typist. Before moving on from Vancouver to Seattle, by way of crossing the very border which had almost led to Anglo-American war eighty years before, the party stashed plenty of bottles in their luggage against the rigours of Prohibition.

Another friendship to come out of the war was with Bernard Baruch, 'the old Jewish American financier, six foot five with white hair,' as Jock Colville later called him, who was several years older than Churchill and would outlive him. Having made a fortune on the New York stock market by the age of thirty, Baruch was appointed Chairman of the War Industries Board by Wilson when the United States entered the war. After the Armistice Churchill thanked Baruch warmly for his work, and added, 'If, in order to secure complete victory, it had been unhappily necessary to prolong the war during 1920 and 1921, I am certain that co-operation would have become so intimate as almost to amount to a fusion in many respects of our war effort.' Co-operation between Churchill and Baruch had indeed become intimate, and on this visit Baruch provided further hospitality, including the railway carriage which brought them back east, as well as a list of useful financial contacts from sea to shining sea.

Driving down the Californian coast, the party stopped at the vast palace of San Simeon high above the shore, 'the Monte Carlo casino on top of the Rock of Gibraltar,' as Churchill nicely called it, built by the newspaper magnate William Randolph Hearst. More than ten years later San Simeon would become 'Xanadu' in *Citizen Kane*, and when that movie was shown during one of the wartime evenings in the private cinema at Chequers, Churchill stormed out but by then he had enjoyed a well-paid connection with his new friend Hearst and his papers. In Los Angeles, Churchill dined as a guest of honour, seated between two rascals, Hearst and Louis B. Mayer, met Hollywood stars, and struck up a friendship with Charlie Chaplin, who would later delight the company at Chartwell. He did not befriend another English expatriate. 'This was – I think – the seventh time I have been introduced to Churchill,' P.G. Wodehouse reported after another party, 'and I could see that I came upon him as a complete surprise once more.'

Wherever he went Churchill was captivated by American market mania. 'There is a stock exchange in every big hotel,' he delightedly told Clementine, who must have been less delighted. 'You go and sit and watch the figures being marked up on slates every few minutes.' In one four-day period his own turnover reached an astonishing $200,000, mostly in quick in-and-outs. He reached New York in October just as the market began to totter on 'Black Thursday', and he was homebound aboard the *Berengaria* on 29 October, 'Black Tuesday', when it plummeted like the stockbroker he described who threw himself out of his window high above Wall Street. Churchill suffered extremely heavy losses in the crash ('an episode curiously omitted from his official biography,' as David Lough drily observes in his brilliant study of Churchill's financial life*). Churchill was now dependent on Baruch, who took over his American investments on the enviable basis that he would cover losses while Churchill enjoyed any profits.

At the same time Churchill discussed another way to help rescue his fortunes. Years ago in Bangalore he had read Gibbon's masterpiece, and he may also have known the haunting passage in which the

---

* *No More Champagne: Churchill and his Money*, 2016.

author recalled the conception of that great work. It was in Rome in 1764, as Gibbon had sat one evening 'musing amid the ruins of the Capitol, while the barefooted friars were singing vespers in the Temple of Jupiter, that the idea of writing the decline and fall of the city first started to my mind'. The idea of a two-volume book on 'the English-speaking races' started to Churchill's mind on the unlike-liest (and to English eyes most incomprehensible) of occasions: a college football game. His New York publisher was the firm of Charles Scribner's Sons, and the scion of the family, Charles Scribner III, took him to New Haven to watch Yale *v.* Army.* There they talked about this new project.

Nothing came of it for the time being, and Scribner, who was to be disappointed by the sales of *My Early Life* (published in New York under the odd title *A Roving Commission*), would warn Churchill that 'unfortunately enough, from my point of view, the American people are becoming less of an Anglo-Saxon race, and the Nordic tradition with England as the mother country of the USA is less popular in the country than one might expect'. But the seed had been planted. Twelve years after Gibbon's epiphany, the first volume of *The Decline and Fall of the Roman Empire* was published, in 1776, a notable year for histo-rians of the decline of empires. Not long afterwards Gibbon was in Paris where he turned down an invitation to dine with Benjamin Franklin, since he represented an enemy country. Franklin genially replied that he would have liked 'to furnish materials to so excellent a writer for the Decline and Fall of the British Empire'.

Although Gibbon's last volume wasn't published until 1789, he was positively speedy compared with Churchill, whose *History of the English-Speaking Peoples* didn't appear for the best part of three decades after that conversation with Scribner at the Yale game, by which time the British Empire was entering the last phase of its decline and fall. After an appropriately dignified meeting in Washington with President Hoover, Churchill tried but failed to meet the new Governor of New York. Having served as Assistant Secretary of the Navy and as Cox's running mate in 1920, Franklin Roosevelt had been stricken with polio in 1921. It didn't end his political career, but it changed and hardened his character. He returned to public life and was elected governor in 1928. The following autumn he found himself too busy to meet the

---

* Yale won 23–21.

celebrated English visitor. But then Roosevelt, unlike Churchill, remembered their first meeting in 1918.

On his return to England Churchill belatedly resumed his seat on the Opposition benches of the new House of Commons. Another question now arose, and came to dominate his life, most unhappily. Edward Wood, the scion of a Yorkshire landed family, had travelled far as a young man before he entered Parliament in 1910. After serving with the army in France, his ministerial career began in 1921, when he was made Parliamentary Under-Secretary at the Colonial Office. That was despite the reluctance of the Colonial Secretary, and at first Churchill was barely civil to the man who would one day play a crucial part in his own epic. When Baldwin formed his second ministry in 1924, Wood and Churchill became Cabinet colleagues, but not for long. The following year Wood was appointed Viceroy of India.

He would be known – or even notorious – as Lord Halifax after he inherited his father's peerage in 1934, but before that he was called Lord Irwin, the title created to go with his vice-regal position. After a few initial missteps in India, the new viceroy published a declaration in October 1929 that the ultimate object of British policy was 'Dominion status'. This enraged Tory imperialists, not least the born-again Tory Churchill. He had just finished writing *My Early Life*, a book which, along with beguiling passages about the days and nights in Bangalore, made it all too clear that his views on India and the Indians were completely unaltered over the intervening decades. The British were forever destined to rule India, Churchill wrote, with its 'primitive if agreeable races'. Even that phrase was disingenuous, since Churchill all his life thought most Indians primitive, and disagreeable.

This was not language apt for the hour. Unlike Churchill, India had changed beyond recognition since he last saw it. After his meeting with Churchill in 1906, Gandhi had returned to South Africa, and then to India in 1915, assuming the leadership of the Indian National Congress in 1921 and beginning a long campaign of non-violent civil disobedience which baffled the British and saw Gandhi in and out of prison. Irwin would later be one of the group who tried to conciliate or appease Hitler; he was certainly keen to appease Gandhi, who was released from prison in January 1931 and began a series of meetings with the viceroy. Many found (and may still find) Gandhi a mystery.

Irwin told his father that 'it was rather like talking to someone who had stepped off another planet on to this for a short visit of a fortnight,' and there were Indians as well as Englishmen who knew what he meant.

That was quite different from Churchill's envenomed contempt: 'It is alarming and also nauseating to see Mr Gandhi,' Churchill said in a carefully prepared speech on 23 February 1931, 'a seditious Middle Temple lawyer, now posing as a fakir of a type well known in the East, striding half-naked up the steps of the viceregal palace, while he is still organising and conducting a defiant campaign of civil disobedience, to parley on equal terms with the representative of the king-emperor.' After Baldwin, as Leader of the Opposition, welcomed the Labour government's new policy of conciliation in India, Churchill resigned from the Conservative Business Committee or shadow cabinet in January 1931, and when an India Bill was introduced to grant a very modest degree of self-government, Churchill began a long campaign against it, inside and outside Parliament. As Baldwin rightly saw, Churchill wanted 'the Tory party to go back to pre-war and govern with a strong hand. He has become once more the subaltern of Hussars of '96,' but it was worse than that. Married to the famous Lady Diana Cooper, Duff Cooper was a notable figure in the Tory party and London society, as well as a well-known author, biographer of both Lord Haig and Talleyrand, and he would serve under Churchill during the next war. He later said that his campaign against the India Bill was 'the most unfortunate event that occurred between the two wars', and it gravely damaged Churchill's standing at a crucial moment.

That moment also saw the one occasion English history has known when unelected plutocrats seriously attempted to depose a party leader. Beaverbrook and Rothermere mounted an attack on Baldwin through their newspapers, the *Daily Express* and the *Daily Mail*, ostensibly over Beaverbrook's fatuous creed of 'Empire Free Trade'. They made much trouble for Baldwin, and began running candidates against the Tories, until a by-election in March 1931, when he saw them off with one speech and one phrase, denouncing the press lords for seeking 'power without responsibility – the prerogative of the harlot throughout the ages' (the ringing phrase was gifted to Baldwin by Kipling, who was his first cousin). Churchill wasn't directly implicated in the plot against Baldwin, but he obviously coveted his position, and he was well known to be an associate of Beaverbrook and Rothermere. Since they were loathed by decent Tories as well as by the Left, this added to his reputation as something of a harlot himself.

Very soon, MacDonald discovered the meaning of something worse, responsibility without power. In the summer of 1931 the Labour government was blown off course by an acute financial crisis. In one of his most entertaining rhetorical riffs, Churchill had derided MacDonald by saying that, as a child, he had been taken to Barnum's Circus, with its exhibition of freaks and monstrosities, of which 'The Boneless Wonder' was what he had most wanted to see. 'My parents judged that the spectacle would be too demoralising and revolting for my youthful eye and I have waited fifty years, to see the Boneless Wonder sitting on the Treasury Bench.' Whether MacDonald showed too little backbone or too much in the face of the new crisis may be debated, but he agreed, under strong pressure from the king, not to resign, as he could and maybe should have done. Instead, he formed a 'National' government, in practice mostly Conservatives under his leadership and Baldwin's, which tried to restore confidence among what would later be called the investors and the markets by means of harsh cuts in unemployment benefit and other public spending. The Labour Party split wide apart, and was routed when an election was held in October.

No part was played in these events by Churchill, who chose to estivate in the south of France for the vital summer months of 1931. Thanks to his stance on India he had in any case excluded himself from the new government, few of whose members wanted him, and not only for political reasons: those who had sat in Cabinet with him before remembered his overbearing manner and tendency to dominate discussion. Now working harmoniously with Baldwin, not least over India, MacDonald remained prime minister until Baldwin succeeded him in June 1935. From November 1931 to May 1937 Neville Chamberlain was Chancellor of the Exchequer, in which office, at a far more difficult time, he was considerably more successful than Churchill had been.

Poor Chamberlain was one of the unlucky men of history, and nothing can rescue him, for all his remarkable achievements as Health Minister and then Chancellor. There were unattractive sides to his personality. He could be vain, resentful of criticism, and quick to punish dissent. But there was another side, solitary and melancholy, with a deep love of nature. Political rivalry apart, Chamberlain was rueful about Baldwin's pose as a simple rustic squire, when in fact he was a rich manufacturer. 'I know every flower; S.B. knows none. I know every tree; S.B. knows none. I shoot and fish; S.B. does neither. Yet he is known as the countryman, and I am known as the townsman.' Not only every flower, Chamberlain knew every bird also. In January 1933, when the Chancellor was wrestling with the aftershock of an immense economic crisis, *The Times* published what may be the most touching letter ever written by anyone engaged in such great affairs of state:

> Sir, Walking through St James's Park today, I noticed a grey wagtail running about on the now temporarily dry bed of the lake, near the dam below the bridge, and occasionally picking small insects out of the cracks in the dam.
>
> Probably the occurrence of this bird in the heart of London has been recorded before, but I have not myself previously noted one in the park.
>
> I am your obedient servant,
>
> Neville Chamberlain
>
> P.S. For the purpose of removing doubts, as we say in the House of Commons, I should perhaps add that I mean a grey wagtail and not a pied.

But love of nature did him no good when he had to deal with another supreme challenge.

In late 1931, Churchill found time to return to America for a lecture tour, which nearly ended in disaster when he was knocked down by a vehicle in the street in New York. He recovered, to repeat his new-found theme of Anglo-American amity, lecturing on 'The Pathway of the English-Speaking Peoples' to large audiences in New York, Hartford, Cleveland, Chicago, Detroit and Washington among other cities, but the applause, and the useful £7500 he collected, may have deluded him. Rhetorical profession of such amity was easy enough, but meant very little in practical terms. The *Washington Post* sarcastically observed that, not long before, closer ties with the United States 'would have been repulsive to British statesmen', which was truer of Churchill than most could have known. But now 'Mr Churchill is trying to flatter the United States into taking over some of Britain's liabilities'. If he read those words, they should have been a warning. The Americans had no wish, then or later, to share such liabilities, least of all in Europe.

In November 1932, Roosevelt won the presidency, and the Democrats won both the House and the Senate, but they were little less isolationist than the Republicans; maybe rather more. All that Americans cared about at that moment was the disaster of the Great Depression, with scores of millions out of work, the stock market at rock bottom, and much of industry and agriculture on the brink of collapse. If any foreign question did exercise Roosevelt it wasn't Europe but Japan, although even there he, like his predecessor, shrank from directly confronting aggression. Japan had invaded Manchuria in 1931, and a legend grew up that the Americans would have joined resolute international action to punish her, but legend is what it was. Nor would such action have been approved by Churchill. 'I hope we in England shall try to understand a little the position of Japan,' he said, 'an ancient State with the highest state sense of national honour', threatened by Soviet Russia and by the Communists who had taken over part of China. He was lucky that those words were forgotten ten years later.

And still Churchill was a would-be leader with no followers. Not only did those who supported Baldwin see his fight over the India Bill as a cynical grab for power: even those with whom he fought, the group of reactionary, but sincere, Tory imperialists opposed to the Bill, looked askance on their most prominent spokesman. 'He *discredits* us,' said Lord Wolmer, one of their number. '*We* are acting from conviction but everybody knows Winston has no convictions; he has only joined us for what he can get out of it.' Churchill had recently written that he had found a capacity to express the deepest sentiments of strong Conservatives, 'although they have never liked or trusted me'. They liked and trusted him no more now, and for some time to come.

His critics were still voluble, and Gallipoli wouldn't go away. In 1931 Victor Wallace Germains, a military correspondent (one of whose previous books had actually been called *The Gathering Storm*), published *The Tragedy of Winston Churchill*. The book is an assault on Churchill's strategic record, and on *The World Crisis*, which Germains showed up as a highly partisan and tendentious account, 'the work of a man specially trained in sifting and arranging the evidence'. Or as he put it in words which were, had been before, and would be again, all too true, 'Churchill the writer is the specialist successful in his own sphere; Churchill, the military leader, is the amateur who blundered.'

This personal isolation was at just the moment when Churchill was about to find a truly worthy cause. The constitutional Weimar Republic which had arisen from the ashes of the Hohenzollern Second Reich had been troubled from the start. Early in the 1920s, a tiny group with little following, the National Socialist German Workers Party, found a compelling orator, Adolf Hitler, a failed Austrian painter who had served on the Western Front. He inspired an abortive armed putsch in Munich in 1923, was imprisoned, and wrote his testament *Mein Kampf,* with its ferocious themes of national revenge and Jew-hatred. It seemed unimaginable that he and his party would ever take power, until the disastrous financial and economic collapse of 1931 gravely weakened the republic.

In 1932, Churchill visited Germany by way of research for his life of Marlborough, to look at the battlefield of Blenheim where his forebear had won his greatest victory. While Churchill and Randolph were staying in Munich, they were contacted by 'Putzi' von Hanfstaengl, Hitler's playboy fixer, who wanted Churchill to meet Hitler. A tentative arrangement was made, but Hitler failed to turn up. Churchill sent him a guardedly friendly message, though warning him against demagogic antisemitism. Randolph was another matter. In July, a general election was held in Germany and the National Socialists won 37 per cent of the popular vote: not a majority but much more than any other party and more than the combined votes for the parties of the Left, Social Democrats and Communists. Randolph sent Hitler a telegram of congratulations, an early intimation of what an embarrassment the boy would become.

In an absurd phrase which he and then many others would use, Churchill called the 1930s his 'wilderness years', blasphemously echoing John the Baptist, after Isaiah: 'I am the voice of one crying in the wilderness.' As a description of Churchill's career, this was nonsensical, but then many other fanciful phrases would be written about that 'low, dishonest decade', or alternatively 'the Red decade'. Liberal constitutionalism, market capitalism and the rule of law seemed discredited, while the European mood darkened. And yet, far from 'Red', it might rather be called a Black decade: the black of the radical Right, or fascism, which was much more successful than Communism, from Italy to Portugal and then Germany.

Nor was Churchill so remote from this tendency. His attachment to constitutional government in his own country was sincere, but it stopped at Dover, all the more so since his hatred of Bolshevism had unbalanced him. 'What a swine Mussolini is,' Churchill told Clementine in September 1923. 'I see Rothermere is supporting him,' not for the last time, as it proved. But when Clementine stayed in Rome in March 1926, she had tea with the Duce, and found him 'most impressive – quite simple & natural, very dignified, has a charming smile & the most beautiful golden brown piercing eyes.' The following year Churchill visited Italy himself, and saluted Mussolini: 'If I had been an Italian, I am sure I should have been whole-heartedly with you from the start to finish in your triumphant struggle against the bestial appetites and passions of Leninism.'

More egregiously still, as late as February 1933 Churchill called Mussolini 'the greatest law-giver among men'. These were grotesque words to use about a posturing mountebank whose brutish followers beat up his opponents, who bore direct responsibility for the murder of the socialists Giacomo Matteotti and Carlo and Nello Rosselli, and whose regime was in any case a total sham, politically, economically, morally and – as events would show – militarily rotten through and through. Il fascismo did Italy no good at all even before the Duce, or Leader, led his country to war and catastrophic defeat. The Nottingham Evening Post's headline 'Winston a fascist' may have been a little sharp, but it showed how damaging as well as disgraceful his praise for Mussolini had been.

In January 1933, Hitler became Chancellor, thanks to a cynical and stupid manoeuvre by conservative politicians. 'Don't worry, we've hired him,' said the former Chancellor, Franz von Papen, with shocking frivolity. It was André François-Poncet, the French ambassador in Berlin, who rightly saw what had happened: those politicians thought they were 'ridding themselves of the wolf by introducing him into the sheepfold'. Many Englishmen were appalled. Sir Austen Chamberlain, Neville's elder half-brother, had been briefly Tory leader, and then Foreign Secretary. 'What is this new spirit of German nationalism?' he asked. 'The worst of the old-Prussian Imperialism, with an added savagery, a racial pride.'

Churchill also saw the danger of Hitler and resurgent German might, while condemning from the outset the antisemitism of what was now called the Third Reich. Two months after Hitler took power Churchill told the Commons that a good many people were now saying to themselves what he had been saying for years, 'Thank God for the French army!' although those words infuriated many Tories. And he went on: 'When we read about Germany, when we watch with surprise and distress the tumultuous insurgence of ferocity and war spirit, the pitiless ill-treatment of minorities, the denial of normal protection of civilised society, the persecution of large numbers of individuals solely on the grounds of race – when we see all that occurring in one of the most gifted, learned, and scientific and formidable nations in the world, one cannot help feeling glad, that the fierce passions that are raging in Germany have not found, as yet, any other outlet but upon themselves.'

Those were splendid words, and it was Churchill at his best, with his clear perception of the danger Hitler represented. But what was the danger his countrymen saw in him? Given his adulation of Mussolini, it was scarcely surprising that many, from Morel in 1922 and Guedalla in 1924, had already imagined Churchill a potential English Duce, and with repellent allies in the press. In October 1932, Sir Oswald Mosley, a vainglorious demagogue who had passed through three parties – Tory, Labour and his own short-lived 'New Party' – launched the British Union of Fascists, with meetings guarded by blackshirted louts in imitation of Mussolini's squadristi. Churchill had come to share Rothermere's admiration for the 'swine' Mussolini, but Rothermere now went further still. In 1934, he published in his *Daily Mail* under his own name an article headed 'Hurrah for the Blackshirts'. When a boycott of Hitler's regime was proposed, the news provoked a front-page headline in Beaverbrook's *Daily Express*, 'Judea Declares War on Germany'. Beaverbrook himself merely told his readers, 'I am no authority on European politics. I don't speak their languages. I don't want to. I don't know their politicians. I don't like them. I don't want alliances with European states.'

Both Rothermere and Beaverbook were friends of Churchill's, and yet theirs weren't the only newspapers. The one paper which supported the Labour Party was the *Daily Herald*, for long a foe of Churchill's, and a *bête noire* to him. In 1929 it had published a photograph of him carrying a book on whose front cover the word 'WAR' was clearly visible; or, as the *Herald* cheekily captioned it, a book on 'one of his favourite subjects'. Fake news! cried a furious Churchill: the photographer had obviously 'faked or forged a copy of the photograph'. The *Herald* stood its ground and suggested that the High Tory *Morning Post* should adjudicate, which it did, finding no evidence of tampering with the photograph. It transpired that Churchill had picked up without noticing a copy of a book indeed called *War* – a translation of the German anti-war novel *Krieg* by Ludwig Renn – and he had to back down.

By 1933 London newspapers were engaged in a fierce circulation war, attracting subscribers by offering everything from encyclopedias to stockings. By the time it was called off it had been won not by the *Express* or *Mail* but by the *Daily Herald*, which reached sales of more than two million just after Hitler came to power. Two months later, this huge readership was treated to an unambiguous cartoon by Will Dyson mocking Churchill's campaign against the India Bill. He was depicted in *Sturmabteilung* uniform, with pistols on his hip and hand raised in salute, under the banner of the 'Nationalist Association of the Zouaves of India', spelling 'Nazi' and figured like a swastika. After many difficulties, the India Bill was finally passed in 1935. Churchill was left high and dry, with even fewer close colleagues, even less public support, and even smaller prospects of leadership.

All events seemed to conspire against him. In May 1935, George V celebrated his Silver Jubilee amid much simple public rejoicing; in June Baldwin took over from MacDonald as prime minister; in December a general election saw the National government easily returned to office, although Labour recovered ground in a way that should have made it clear that its collapse in 1931 was temporary. Far from ignoring the threat from aggressive dictators, Baldwin's government had now accepted that disarmament had failed, that 'collective security' would also very likely fail, and that rearmament was needed. Baldwin embarked on it, to a degree for which he was never given credit, then or since, least of all by Churchill, who was by now 'consumed with contempt, jealousy, if indeed not hatred for Baldwin,' a contemporary reported after one conversation.

In October 1935, after much bluster by Mussolini, the Italian army invaded Abyssinia, later known as Ethiopia, the only independent kingdom to have survived the partition of Africa. The League of

Nations for once applied economic sanctions, but London hesitated to take any stronger action, having no wish to fight a Mediterranean war, and in any case hoping that Mussolini could still be enlisted against Hitler. In December Sir Samuel Hoare, the Foreign Secretary, went to Paris to meet Pierre Laval,* the French prime minister, who was on a strange voyage from far-left agitator to premier of the wartime Vichy regime to execution as a traitor. Hoare proposed a compromise to satisfy or appease Mussolini, with most of the fertile plains of Abyssinia going to Italy.

When news of this leaked in the Paris papers, it ignited an explosion in England. Everyone from the Left to the Archbishops of Canterbury and York to *The Times* roared with indignation at the betrayal, and Hoare resigned, or was thrown to the wolves. Nothing more happened, and the brutal Italian conquest continued. As this winter storm of outrage blew, no word was heard from Churchill, nor sight seen of him. He later said that he should have been in England for this crisis, although by hibernating in Morocco and Spain, he avoided the need to take sides or express an opinion, and he was still convinced that Italy must be kept sweet. At length he returned home for the high dramas of 1936.

---

* This journey prompted a last royal jest from George V, shortly before his death: 'Coals to Newcastle, Hoares to Paris, eh?'.

J.L. CARSTAIRS

7

'A higher-grade race'
Palestine 1937

While not an especially beautiful or historic house, Chartwell has a lovely setting. The genius of the English landscape is great effects from small causes: a drop of a few hundred feet can create a more breathtaking panorama than thousands of feet in the Alps, and Chartwell has a glorious view southwards from the North Downs across the Weald of Kent. This corner of England had become Churchill's home by roundabout ways, and with important consequences. During his earlier period of disgrace in 1916, Clementine had written to him to say that the elder children 'are becoming so grown up and intelligent & look forward to the time when you come back to me & we will have a little country basket & in the intervals of your work we will all curl up together in it and be so happy. Only you must not become too famous or you won't have time for these pastoral joys! You must promise me that in future, however full of work & ideas you are, you will keep out of every day an hour & every week a day & every year six weeks for the small things of life.'

In hindsight, this letter is deeply poignant, because of its unfulfilled hopes. Churchill spoiled his children but neglected them. He certainly became 'too famous', but Chartwell was never that little country basket of Clementine's dreams. It became rather the centre of Churchill's working life, political but still more literary, a veritable word factory. As a journalist, biographer and historian, he was now one of the most prolific and best-paid writers of his age. He always wrote to make a point, and to make money, not necessarily in that order. And his political career can only be understood in the light of his frantic need to keep afloat financially.

His acquisition of Chartwell had begun with a chain of events out of a Victorian novel, going back to the age of *Vanity Fair*. During the

Regency years, with Waterloo and the Congress of Vienna, the Foreign Secretary was Lord Castlereagh, briefly Marquess of Londonderry, whose 'cool, collected temperament was stiffened with disdain,' as Churchill put it, and whose suicide in 1822 prompted Byron's unforgiving lines, 'So Castlereagh has cut his throat! – The worst / Of this is, – that his own was not the first.' His titles passed to his brother, and the family acquired more broad lands, including the Garron Towers estate in County Antrim, while intermarrying with other families, including the Churchills: Lord Randolph's mother Frances, Duchess of Marlborough, was the daughter of the third Marquess of Londonderry and his enormously rich wife.

One more descendant was Lord Henry Vane-Tempest, a bachelor who lived at Plas Machynlleth in Montgomeryshire in north-west Wales. On 26 January 1921 Lord Henry was travelling* between Welshpool and Newtown when his train collided with another, and he was among those killed. Thanks to a chain of inheritance which would have delighted Trollope, Churchill now came into the Garron Towers estate. Ever the optimist, he decided that he could buy a country house, to the great concern of Clementine. Even with the Garron money she thought that a large house would be a permanent drain on their impermanent resources, and she was more right than she could have feared. Churchill went ahead and bought Chartwell without telling her in September 1922, for £5500. Within two years £18,000 more had been spent on renovation, and Churchill thought it best not to tell Clementine that the estate agents Knight Frank & Rutley had just valued the property at £12,000. In the end, the purchase and rebuilding of Chartwell would cost £40,000, three times the original estimate, and far more than its market value. Had this been publicly known it could only have added to Churchill's reputation as a reckless adventurer. And there was another consequence for Churchill. Before acquiring Chartwell, making money had been desirable; with Chartwell, it became essential.

In 1965, shortly after Churchill died, his son Randolph published *Twenty-One Years*, an affable if flimsy account of his upbringing, which begins facetiously with his own birth in 1911 'to poor but honest parents'. That wasn't even funny. When Randolph was born his father

---

* On the railway line which still runs from Birmingham airport across north Wales to Harlech.

was Home Secretary, with a salary of £5000, and income tax was paid by those British citizens, a million or so, earning £160 a year or more. At no time in his life was Churchill ever poor as the poor knew it. He never lacked necessities for material comfort or even luxury. At no time did he live frugally, even when in the trenches; he boasted that there had never been a time when he couldn't buy a bottle of champagne for himself and another for his friend; he always employed a valet, he never cooked a meal in his life, he never carried money. And yet he was acutely conscious that friends like the Dukes of Westminster and Marlborough, the press lords Beaverbrook and Rothermere, the moneymen Bailey and Baruch, were very rich in a way that he wasn't.

Since his ministerial salary never began to meet Churchill's needs, he had to write, and so he did continuously throughout the interwar years. In late 1920, while he was War Minister, he had decided to write a personal history of the Great War, and decided also that he needed £20,000 for the project. With the help of Curtis Brown, an American who had set up as a literary agent in London, he did better than that. Thornton Butterworth offered £9000 for British book rights, Scribner in New York offered £5000 for American rights, on top of which came munificent bids for serial rights, £5000 from *The Times* and a remarkable £8000 for American serialisation. The *Times* offer was only accepted by Churchill once Wickham Steed, the editor, had given him not one assurance but two that his paper wouldn't criticise Gallipoli. That made some £27,000 in all.

Along with journalism, that occupied his literary energies for most of the 1920s, and Keynes wasn't alone in wondering how someone with a full-time Cabinet office was able to produce such a work. Even Maurice Ashley, one of his literary assistants, admitted that *The Eastern Front* tacked on to *The World Crisis* was written 'primarily to earn money', and since it was a subject about which Churchill knew little, he engaged military historians to help, and then more: before long he had assembled a team of researchers and ghostwriters. And so by the 1930s it is often difficult to know how much of the books and journalism he published was actually written by him.

All of this ceaseless literary production was against a background of tax demands, debt and stock market speculation which was often perilous and sometimes calamitous. All his life until 1940 Churchill was barely solvent. He lived from mouth to hand, as he put it, always looking for money in the future to pay for the past, always aware that he was on a treadmill and that, if it stopped, he was bust. During his American journey of 1929 Churchill and Clementine had managed to speak occasionally by transatlantic telephone, then unusual, and in a letter from Santa Barbara on 19 September, after writing 'It was delightful to hear your voice,' Churchill told his wife that 'extraordinary good fortune has attended me lately in finances,' in gleeful but ill-fated words at a moment when notable ill fortune was about to attend him.

His losses with the Wall Street crash meant that, rather in the spirit of Sir Walter Scott, he had to write his way frantically out of debt. 'It is a wonderful thing to have all these contracts satisfactorily settled,' he had written to Clementine as his ship approached Canada in 1929, 'and to feel that two or three years agreeable work is mapped out and, if completed, will certainly be rewarded.' This 'agreeable work' was a biography of the great Duke of Marlborough, his famous forebear, a project he had been nurturing for some years and which had been settled after a most enjoyable bidding war. Butterworth were the London publishers of *The World Crisis*, and they offered £15,000 for world rights in *Marlborough,* including American rights, while George Harrap, whose firm was better known for textbooks, offered £10,000 for British rights, with £4000 on signature. When the deal was closed in Harrap's favour, Charlie Scribner made a direct offer of $25,000 for American rights. Bevin had bitterly complained that Churchill's return to the gold standard had hurt the working class; Churchill now had his own reason to rue his earlier decision, since Scribner's offer would have been worth considerably more at a realistic lower exchange rate.

Even then, with £5000 for British serial rights, this time from the *Daily Telegraph*, it made a package of around £20,000, more than a million pounds or dollars today. Churchill's financial woes were also eased by his rich friends, Baruch in New York, and at home the industrialist Sir Harry McGowan, chairman of ICI, who had been buying and selling shares in London on Churchill's account and made £5000 for him. Besides that there was journalism: £1350 from *Nash's Magazine* for three biographical sketches, a contract 'for articles on American tour (not yet done) £2750', and various other items, the whole impressively totalling £21,825 – 'enough to make us comfortable and well-mounted in London this autumn', he told Clementine.

From then on it was ceaseless word-spinning, with the help of a team of literary underlings, and Churchill was ready to take on pretty well any kind of hackwork if the money was good. The money paid by the *News of the World* was very good indeed. That unique Sunday newspaper was owned by Lord Riddell, confidant of Lloyd George, diarist, and incidentally the first guilty party in a divorce case to be made a peer. He had bought the paper when it was selling 30,000 copies a week, and taken the circulation to seven million, with a staple diet of court reports: murder, rape, clergymen and schoolmasters who had loved young boys not wisely but too well, divorce cases related in the most lurid and sometimes anatomical detail, all soberly presented but the more salacious the better. From the proceeds, Riddell could offer lavish fees to writers.

Maybe some sense of the ridiculous held Churchill back when Riddell wanted him to write 'Great Bible Stories Retold', but he did agree to 'Great Stories of the World Retold', potted versions of anything from *Uncle Tom's Cabin* to *Anna Karenina*. Riddell was no fool, and told Churchill, 'Copy to be written by you personally,' at which Churchill, wonderously oblivious to any normal standards, immediately set a ghostwriter to work. These ghosts were very skilful in mastering the great man's voice. A reader of the distinctly personal preface to Churchill's 1932 collection *Thoughts and Adventures*, for example, would certainly have supposed it was by Churchill, and not 'rather a good pastiche!' in the justifiably proud words of its author, Adam Marshall Diston, an obscure journalist who became one of the team of ghosts. Churchill knew that this series of 'Riddells', as he called them, was undignified for a former First Lord and Chancellor, and unsatisfactory in 'artistic' terms, as he sheepishly said, but then he was getting £1000 for three articles, or £333 per piece, when the actual work was done by ghosts for £25 each.

In late 1932, the first volume of *Marlborough* had not yet been published, but with the same brazen indifference to contractual obligations Churchill proposed an entirely different book to a different London publisher. This was the one he had mooted to Scribner three years earlier at the Yale game, and he now wanted £20,000 for his proposed history of 'the English-Speaking Peoples'. He got it, from Cassell & Co., as a single payment for outright purchase of all rights in the book, 'waiving all interest in further royalties'. This seems astonishing. Authors had fought long and hard to establish the principle of copyright – that had been the purpose of Charles Dickens's first American visit, rather than curiosity about the young country – and of royalties on sales, but the explanation was simple, and fiscal. A publisher's advance is literally money advanced in anticipation of earned royalties (even if the words 'unearned advance' are familiar on many an author's royalty statement), and is thus income for tax purposes. An outright sale such as Churchill effected was a capital gain, like selling any other kind of asset or property. And as English law then stood it was free of tax.

He made a point of regarding certain contracts, like those with the *Daily Mail* or *Collier's* magazine in America, as so important that he actually wrote the pieces himself, and some of his journalism at this time was authentic and pungent. But not all. The imposing *Collected Essays of Sir Winston Churchill* was published in a four-volume deluxe edition in the centennial year of 1974 when its editors may not have known how much of its content was ghostwritten – it includes all the 'Riddells', for example – and a reader could try making a guess on internal evidence as to which are by Churchill himself. Anyone who writes for a living can only envy Churchill the amounts he earned, and no one who has rowed in the same galleys of popular journalism can merely deride him for the nonsense that sometimes appeared under his name. And yet if anything like the truth about his literary life had been known – the huge fees, the ghostwriting, the double-dealing with publishers, the energetic tax avoidance – it would only have added to the suspicion and disdain so widely felt for him.

'Let us now praise famous men', begins a famous passage in Ecclesiasticus, and Churchill relished the subsequent line, 'Rich men furnished with ability, living peaceably in their habitations', which he would echo in *The Gathering Storm*: 'Thus I never had a dull or idle moment from morning till midnight, and with my happy family around me dwelt at peace within my habitation.' This was one more case of his talent for inventing his own reality. A rich man he now was, not by the standards of those dukes or millionaires but by those of almost all his compatriots. From 1929 to 1937 Churchill's annual income assessed for tax averaged £12,738. By some calculations that was about the same as £500,000 or $2 million (at the then exchange rate) eighty-five years later, but trying to translate money values from one age to another in a way that makes sense is highly problematic.

A much more useful comparison is between what Churchill made and what others earned at the time. Most of the dozen or so servants at Chartwell were paid less than £100 a year, the housemaids no more than £50. A British industrial worker made annually between £150 and £200. Like other MPs Churchill received a stipend fixed at £400 a year when Members were first paid in 1911, though reduced to £360 along with other 10 per cent cuts in public pay in 1931. In the parlance of the day, 'a four-figure man', earning £1000 a year or more, was a well-to-do doctor or manager or the like.* The prime minister's salary was £5000, less than half Churchill's income, which put him in the top 10,000 or so of British taxpayers.

A new financial source arrived in 1934 in the form of Alexander Korda, the Hungarian-born film producer. He engaged Churchill to write two screenplays, one about the Great War, the other about the life of George V. In the former, an American fighter pilot who has pretended to be a Canadian to join the Royal Flying Corps hears the news that his country has entered the war and says, 'Oh! I'm so glad! I was brought up on George Washington, who never told a lie,' which would have delighted later American votaries of the Churchill cult. Maybe it was as well that neither of Churchill's two screenplays was filmed, but Churchill did receive £10,000 from Korda, who would continue to play a very important part in his financial life.

But 'my happy family' was sadly far from the mark. As Tolstoy might have said, the Churchill family were unhappy in their own way. The baby of the family was Mary, who did have a happy childhood at Chartwell, with nannies and ponies and skiing holidays. Among Mary's girlhood memories was being taken out on the lawn at Chartwell late at night on 30 November 1936 – her father's sixty-second birthday as it happened – to see a distant conflagration. Paxton's mighty iron-and-glass edifice built in Hyde Park for the Great Exhibition of 1851 had been transported to Sydenham Hill in south London, where it gave its name to the district, and football team, Crystal Palace, before it was engulfed by fire that night. 'I think perhaps,' Mary remembered, 'this had the same effect on me as the sinking of the Titanic had on

---

* In *Scoop*, Evelyn Waugh's classic 1938 Fleet Street comedy of errors, invitations to Lord Copper's gruesome banquet arrive 'on the desks of all the four-figure men in the office', meaning senior editors and executives.

an earlier generation: the unthinkable could happen.' She was a brides-maid when her sister Diana married John Bailey, and was dismayed when the marriage soon ended. Diana made an apparently more successful second marriage, to Duncan Sandys, a Tory MP who became one of Churchill's few supporters, but her other sister, Sarah, caused more family woe by marrying Vic Oliver, a Viennese entertainer, and 'common as dirt' in Churchill's eyes.

More revealingly, Mary said that 'the book which made the deepest impression on me' as an adolescent was *Testament of Youth* by Vera Brittain. Both memoir and pacifist tract, it did indeed profoundly influence a generation when it was published in 1933, with its unbear-ably poignant account of how the author's fiancé, brother and two closest men-friends, along with another three-quarters of a million British soldiers, had been consumed in the charnel house of the Great War. Churchill had an uphill task when he began to preach the need for rearmament and resistance to growing German might. But was it so strange that few English people wanted another war?

That left Randolph. A fascinating glimpse of how Churchill was seen at the time is found in the unpublished diaries of Sir Basil Bartlett, 'the actor-baronet', as the popular papers called him, and an astute observer. 'Winston Churchill is making inflammatory speeches again,' Bartlett wrote in May 1936: 'He is a curious character. A sort of Mary Queen of Scots of modern politics. He is bound to emerge histori-cally as a romantic and glamorous figure, but he is surrounded by corpses. No-one who has ever served him or been in any way connected to his career, has ever survived to tell the story.' And Bartlett added that 'His worst contribution so far to the life of the nation is his insufferable son Randolph.' Sir Samuel Hoare was blunter still: 'I do not know which is the more offensive or mischievous, Winston or his son.'

That insufferable son had now emerged onto the public stage, and for years to come he would provide a farcical counterpoint to his father's epic, Sancho Panza to the Quixotic hero, or, as his friend Christopher Sykes said, 'a caricature of his father at his worst'. Relations between father and son were fraught from first to last, and a lifetime later Mary still associated Randolph's visits to Chartwell 'with shouting, banging doors, and rows'. Haunted by his own emotionally bleak upbringing, Churchill pampered Randolph, who was introduced early to the temptations of gambling and drinking, while despite his ostensible education at Eton and Oxford he remained invincibly ignorant of most literary, cultural and historical matters.

He wanted to follow his father into politics, and in February 1935 he stood, aged twenty-three and without consulting Churchill, at a by-election at Liverpool Wavertree as an independent Conservative opposed to the National Government and its concessions to India. Only one commentator found words to praise the rogue candidate, the crazed Dame Lucy Houston. A woman of obscure origins and dubious repute, she had married a rich man and used his money to buy the once-esteemed *Saturday Review*, which she moved to a political position reminiscent of that Tsarist minister of the interior of whom it was said that the only thing further to the Right of him was the wall. Dame Lucy was so excited that she burst into verse:

> When the TRUTH is told to Wavertree,
> Wavertree will set INDIA free ...
> To save them from the horrors you cannot see
> YOU AND RANDOLPH can set them free.

But the party leadership was less amused when Randolph succeeded in splitting the Tory vote and letting Labour in.

Those tensions in family life may be connected with some kind of personal crisis which his biographers have overlooked, but which there is reason to think that Churchill underwent as he approached his sixties. One of its symptoms was drinking. He had always moved in bibulous masculine society, and Parliament had always flown with wine by the evening. William Pitt the Younger was reputedly the worse for drink when he sat on the Treasury Bench as prime minister,* and Asquith certainly was, as Churchill's 1911 letter to Clementine about 'what risks' the prime minister ran made clear. Churchill knew other cases. His closest friend Birkenhead ran many risks of his own before drinking himself to death in 1930 at only fifty-eight.

By that time, Churchill's own consumption was well known. He would later claim that he had taken more out of alcohol than it had

---

* Contemporary doggerel imagined Pitt returning to the Commons from a drinking bout with his crony Henry Dundas: 'Cannot shee the Shpeaker, Hal, can you?' / 'What, cannot shee the Shpeaker? I shee two.'

taken out of him, and he also claimed that he had been brought up to despise drunkenness, whether among common solders or 'the boozy scholars of the Universities', but his own booziness has been variously explained away. His friend T.E. Scott said flippantly that 'He couldn't have been an alcoholic because no alcoholic could have drunk that much,' and a recent admirer says oddly that 'he 'drank heavily, as other people did in the 1930s', when it might be better said that he drank heavily, as other people did who drank heavily. Most people didn't. Neither Chamberlain nor Attlee, Churchill's predecessor and successor as prime minister, was a hard drinker, although Chamberlain enjoyed good claret, especially his favourite Chateau Margaux which he served to favoured guests at Downing Street.

For years Churchill had been reckoned able to hold his drink. 'Winston doesn't get drunk,' Duff Cooper had noted after a convivial evening in 1921, 'but takes a great deal.' It should be no surprise if 'doesn't get drunk' began to change. Like other physical capacities, holding drink, or metabolising alcohol, becomes harder with age. Churchill had a very strong constitution, but he taxed it severely. Robert Bruce Lockhart was a secret agent-turned-journalist, who worked for a time on the 'Londoner's Diary' of the *Evening Standard*, as so many have done. In the early 1930s he often saw Churchill. 'Winston is very weak these days – like a schoolboy trying to get into the team,' he noted in September 1931. 'He is nearly always slightly the worse for drink.' Not long after that, following an erratic parliamentary performance by Churchill, Chamberlain said, 'I fancy the explanation is to be found in the incredible quantity of alcohol he is in the habit of taking ... he went to the Smoke Room three times before his speech to have a whisky & soda. That must tell on his nerves and his liver.' Two years later, Chamberlain waspishly told his sister how 'Winston makes a good many speeches considerably fortified by cocktails and old brandies.'

They didn't come cheap. Churchill's bill from his wine merchant for 1935 was £515. He was never an enophile or true connoisseur of fine wine like Chamberlain, but had acquired a taste for champagne, as well as whisky and brandy, drunk steadily through the day, and now Bruce Lockhart and Chamberlain weren't the only ones who noticed him as he had once noticed Asquith. At the New Year of 1936 Churchill was enjoying the warmth of Morocco in the company of Rothermere, who bet him £2000 to give up alcohol until his sixty-second birthday the following November – an offer Rothermere would scarcely have made if he hadn't thought this a matter of concern.

'Life would not be worth living' on that basis, said Churchill, but he did accept an offer of £600 to refrain from brandy and other spirits. Even this doesn't seem to have cramped his style. Soon afterwards he was seen drinking quantities of beer at lunch in London, followed by 'five large glasses of port'. In the summer of 1937, Sir Archibald Sinclair, Churchill's battalion second-in-command in 1916 and now leader of the Liberal Party, gave a dinner for Chaim Weizmann to meet leading British politicians. 'Baffy' Dugdale, Balfour's niece and a prominent gentile Zionist, described the dinner, where the guests included 'Winston in his most brilliant style, but very drunk'. All this only strengthened the view, across the parties, Left and Right, that he was too erratic and unreliable to be trusted or heeded.

Between Chamberlain's jibe about cocktails and that dinner came the dramas of 1936. The year saw three kings on the throne of England, the German reoccupation of the Rhineland, the Spanish Civil War and the Moscow Trials, before it ended with Churchill's fortunes falling still lower. In January George V died, just as Churchill came home from the warm south. He had befriended the new king Edward VIII, whom the world had known for many years as a glamorous if rather feckless Prince of Wales, before he succeeded his father, briefly as it turned out. A set of first editions of Marlborough presented and inscribed by Churchill was sold at auction in London in 2009, with inscriptions telling a forlorn story. The first two volumes are signed 'To The Prince of Wales', the third, in October 1936, 'To The King', the last, a year later, 'For the Duke of Windsor': that is, the same person known by three names even in the course of one year – Prince of Wales until January, king for less than eleven months, Duke of Windsor when he was given that title after he abdicated. Alas, this affection was one more case of Churchill's lamentable judgement of character.

In March Hitler reoccupied the Rhineland, demilitarised under the Versailles settlement, and Churchill sounded the alarm. 'The violation of the Rhineland is serious from the point of view of the menace to which it exposes Holland, Belgium and France,' he told Parliament. 'It will be a barrier across Germany's front door, which will leave her free to sally out eastward and southward.' But he didn't advocate any military response, only saying that 'We should endeavour now with great resolution to establish collective security.' This was a comparatively reticent response, partly because Churchill hoped that, with the India Bill out of the way, he might return to government, and partly because he privately recognised how difficult the government's position was. Self-serving German generals later said very dubiously that Hitler would have been obliged to withdraw if ordered to by the British and French, but if he hadn't, it could have meant war. Harold Nicolson knew that 'the people of this country absolutely refuse to have a war,' and Churchill knew that too.

In July General Franco's rebellion began the Spanish Civil War, and August saw the first of the astonishing and horrible Moscow Trials. Ostensibly neutral over the Spanish war, Churchill was more partial to Franco than the Republic as it rapidly fell under Communist domination. By the spring of 1937 he would say, 'I will not pretend that, if I had to choose between Communism and Nazi-ism, I would choose Communism. I hope not to be called upon to survive in a world under a Government of either of these dispensations.' ('You would not,' shouted James Maxton, the fiery leftwing socialist from Clydeside.) This may have been honest, but it was tactically clumsy at a time when Churchill needed, and for a time enjoyed, support from Left as well as Right. He changed his mind again and came round to seeing Franco as the greater threat, but not until 1939, by which time the Spanish republic had been crushed.

By the late autumn of 1936 the king's attachment to the American divorcee Wallis Simpson, and his determination to marry her, turned into a constitutional crisis which ended in abdication. And throughout the abdication crisis, as one historian has said, 'Churchill made every possible blunder.' One of the more absurd travesties of Churchill on screen is in *The King's Speech*, where Timothy Spall is not only an unlikely incarnation but is seen encouraging the Duke of York against his elder brother the king. This is the exact opposite of what happened: Churchill took up Edward's cause with reckless zeal. At the climax on 7 December he pleaded the king's case in the Commons and was angrily shouted down, with MPs jeering 'Drop it!' and 'Twister!', with the Speaker rebuking him because he 'insists on going beyond a simple question', and with some of those present murmuring that he was the worse for drink. However that might have been, the letters he fired off late at night encouraging Edward to stand firm certainly read – 'Sir, News from all fronts! No pistol to be held at the King's head! ... It's a long way to Tipperary ...' – as though they were dictated *in vino*, if not *veritas*.

Having renounced the throne, the Duke of Windsor, as Edward now was, went into exile and soon showed just how lucky his country had been to lose him by dallying with the leaders of the Third Reich. He was succeeded by the Duke of York, who was crowned in Westminster Abbey. 'The Yorks will do it very well,' the new king's mother Queen Mary said. So they did, and Churchill soon agreed. He and Clementine attended the Coronation that May, where in one of his rather rare admissions of error, he told her that he had been wrong, and that 'the other one' would never have done. At all events, by the new year of 1937 Churchill's fortunes had sunk lower than ever, and he was oppressed by failure and mortality. In February he wrote to Clementine on the perennially fraught subject of domestic finances and conceded that they might sell Chartwell, 'having regard to the fact that our children are almost all flown, and my life is probably in its closing decade'. He would live for nearly three more decades.

Whether or not the Duke of Windsor used his new leisure to read *Marlborough*, others did, and the book, handsomely produced with many maps, found an appreciative readership. There is much to enjoy in it, particularly the vivid descriptions of battles, but it displays Churchill's defects at least as much as his qualities. His scheme of self-education in Bangalore had included Macaulay's *History of England*, that magnificent work which implanted the 'Whig interpretation of history' for generations. Magnificent in learning and style and sheer vigour, Macaulay also displays the gravest of faults, which the historian Lord Acton described in words that might have applied to Churchill: 'He knew nothing respectably before the seventeenth century. He knew nothing of foreign history, or of religion, philosophy, or art.' Macaulay was brilliant, but utterly biased, so that his heroes, above all William of Orange, can do no wrong, nor his villains do right, from William Penn, the gentle Quaker, to 'John of Marlborough', who is pilloried at length for his treachery and venality, with Macaulay at his most zestful praising Marlborough for 'that decorum which he never failed to preserve in the midst of guilt and dishonour'.

In reply, Churchill had been inspired by the elderly Lord Rosebery, Lord Randolph's friend and contemporary, who showed him a forgotten publication which seemed to exonerate Marlborough from the worst charges. And he enjoyed a great advantage: before his cousin 'Sunny' Marlborough died in 1934 he had given Churchill free access to the Blenheim archives. While he tried to demolish Macaulay, Churchill learned much from that master of narrative, that combative controversialist, that confident, cocksure, and sometimes barely honest partisan. In all those respects Churchill was an enthusiastic pupil, quite as biased as his model. Keith Feiling was a history don at Christ Church who had attempted to teach Randolph during his brief sojourn in Oxford. He now helped Churchill with research and provided clever young men like Maurice Ashley to help him further. But although they could assist Churchill with books and documents, they could never teach him the virtues of true scholarship or objectivity. Not that he wanted to be taught them. It was Ashley whom he asked for the facts which he could twist 'the way I want to suit my argument'. Said to shock, this was a true word spoken in jest.

Many years later, in 1964, only months before Churchill died, his son gave a set of *Marlborough* to an on-and-off friend whom he wanted to please and impress. It was not a success. Evelyn Waugh had already described Churchill as a writer with 'no specifically literary talent but a gift of lucid self-expression', and had written slyly that his books, 'though highly creditable for a man with so much else to occupy him, do not really survive close attention. He can seldom offer the keen, unmistakable aesthetic pleasure of the genuine artist.' Now he thanked Randolph for *Marlborough* with brutal candour: 'I was everywhere outraged by his partisanship & naïve assumption of superior virtue. It is a shifty barrister's case not a work of literature.' To borrow a phrase from Churchill, that is a not unjust reflection. 'He is, I am persuaded, grossly, basely unfair,' Acton said of Macaulay, and that could sometimes be said of Churchill. 'Read him therefore,' Acton continued, 'to find out how it comes that the most unsympathetic of critics can think him very nearly the greatest of English writers.' And that by contrast cannot be said of Churchill, enjoyable as his work often is.

Before the end of 1936 Mussolini had crushed Abyssinia, although Italian troops continued their repulsive slaughter there while the emperor Haile Selassie, driven from his country, made a forlornly dignified speech at the League of Nations in Geneva, and settled in exile in Bath. Hitler made no further move, so that, with the large exception of Spain, Europe was peaceable enough in 1937. Palestine was not. An Arab Revolt against the British and the Zionists had broken out in 1936 and lasted until 1939, harshly repressed by methods reminiscent of earlier days, with more than a hundred Palestinian Arabs hanged, sometimes for trivial offences, although there were newer means also. The RAF continued what Churchill had seen as its primary task of disciplining the empire. Having once bombed Iraqi villagers, Arthur Harris was now at Middle East Command in Egypt, and recommended that the Revolt could be dealt with by 'one 250 lb or 500 lb bomb in each village that speaks out of turn'.

By now Churchill's personal engagement with Zionism had lasted more than thirty years, from his first meeting with Chaim Weizmann in Manchester in 1905. We can take up the story again from when Turkey entered the war, and soon thereafter when its dissolution seemed possible or even desirable. Now the project of restoring the Jews to the Holy Land took on a more practical aspect, the more so when a British army advanced through Ottoman Palestine. By 1915 Churchill had whimsically suggested that Palestine should be given to 'Christian, liberal, noble' Belgium, and he rejoined the government in 1917 shortly before the Balfour Declaration, favouring a homeland for the Jewish people in Palestine. The Declaration contained its own contradiction, when it added that, while a Jewish homeland should be encouraged, it was 'clearly understood that nothing shall be done which may prejudice the civil and religious rights of existing non-Jewish communities in Palestine, or the rights and political status enjoyed by Jews in other countries'.

As soon became grimly clear, the Arabs, who were still a large majority, believed that their rights were very much prejudiced by Jewish immigration, let alone a 'national home' or a Jewish state. That was what many Zionists dreamed of privately, and that was what those new converts to the Zionist cause, Balfour and Lloyd George, also envisaged, although likewise privately. Their problem wasn't far to seek. 'The weak point of our position of course,' Balfour wrote revealingly to Lloyd George in 1919, 'is that in the case of Palestine we deliberately and rightly decline to accept the principle of self-determination. If the present inhabitants were consulted they would unquestionably give an anti-Jewish verdict.' That 'weak point' never troubled Churchill. On occasion he expressed resentment at the way that 'the Jews ... take it for granted that the local population will be cleared out to suit their convenience'. But he never denied – or regretted – the fact that Zionism was a colonial enterprise, carried out like any other without regard to the wishes of the indigenous population.

Behind Churchill's renewed Zionist zeal lay his horror at the Russian revolution. He saw that a number of the Bolshevik leaders were Jewish, he worried about the appeal of Communism to other Jews, and he thought Zionism might offer an alternative and a cure. In February 1920 he voiced this concern in a weird article on 'Zionism versus Bolshevism', published in the *Illustrated Sunday Herald*. Churchill distinguished between 'what may be called the "National Jews" in many lands' and '"the schemes of the International Jews".' Listing Marx, Trotsky, Bela Kun, Rosa Luxemburg and Emma Goldman, he saw them as part of a 'world-wide conspiracy for the overthrow of civilisation and for the reconstitution of society on the basis of arrested development, of envious malevolence, and impossible equality'.

He claimed that the Jews had played a chief part in the French Revolution, and that, among those directing the Bolshevik revolution, apart from Lenin 'the majority of the leading figures are Jews'. It was true, and almost inevitable after years of persecution and pogroms, that many Jews were drawn to revolutionary socialism, and that a number of prominent Bolsheviks were Jewish, just as a disproportionate number of the victims of Stalin's terror would be. Churchill was all the more encouraged by Zionism, which 'presents to the Jew a national idea of a commanding character'. While recognising that a majority of 'national Jews' would not want to go to Palestine, Churchill nevertheless hoped to see 'in our lifetime by the banks of the Jordan a Jewish State under the protection of the British Crown, which might comprise three or four millions of Jews ... which would ... be especially in harmony with the truest interests of the British Empire.' He lived to see a Jewish state, although whether it was in harmony with British interests was another matter.

A year after writing that article he became Colonial Secretary with responsibility for Palestine, and following the 1921 Cairo conference he visited Jerusalem. By then even Zionist sympathisers in London had begun to see the sheer intractability of the burden they had light-heartedly undertaken. Churchill warned Lloyd George of the increasing cost of Palestine, recognising that 'The Zionist movement will cause continued friction with the Arabs,' and agreed with Lloyd George when he suggested that perhaps the Americans could be persuaded to take on the Palestine mandate. They certainly could not have been, although it remains a teasing 'if' of history.

This problem was made clearer still when Churchill went to see for himself. In Cairo, 'a disorderly rabble gathered outside Shepheard's [Hotel] crying "Down with Churchill", but they were dispersed speedily'. At the Cairo conference Churchill had taken another fateful decision, not to unite, as in Iraq, but to divide. 'At a stroke', as he boasted, Palestine was cut into two along the Jordan. 'Palestine' now meant the Cis-Jordanian territory between river and sea, including the West Bank, which has been controlled by Israel since 1967, while the land to the east of the river was called Trans-Jordan. The British had placed a Hashemite prince, King Feisal, on the throne of the new kingdom of Iraq, and Churchill now decreed that Abdullah, a cousin of Feisal's, would rule this adjacent kingdom of Trans-Jordan. In a case of continuity and survival very rare indeed in those parts, land and dynasty are still with us as the kingdom of Jordan and its king.

On his visit to Jerusalem, Churchill's main object was meeting Abdullah to discuss the difficulties ahead. Sir Herbert Samuel was now the High Commissioner for Palestine, and said with masterly under-statement that there was 'some probability of controversy in Palestine for some years on the question of Zionism'. That was indeed the question Abdullah wanted Churchill to answer: 'He would very much like to know what British policy really aimed at.' Did the British 'mean to establish a Jewish kingdom west of the Jordan and to turn out the non-Jewish population?' Abdullah asked. 'If so, it would be better to tell the Arabs and not keep them in suspense.' Churchill was also confronted with a memorandum from Palestinian Arabs insisting that the Balfour Declaration had been 'a gross injustice', and demanding an end to Jewish immigration.

All this fell on the deaf ears of a partisan. Churchill was much moved by the Zionist pioneers, and waxed eloquent about these 'splendid open air men, beautiful women; and they have made the desert blossom like the rose', thus creating 'a standard of living far superior to that of the indigenous Arabs'. It would be quite shocking, he thought, if the British were to 'cast it all aside and leave it to be rudely and brutally overturned by the incursion of a fanatical attack'.

Replying robustly to the Arab memorandum, he said that 'It is manifestly right that the Jews who are scattered all over the world, should have a national centre and National Home where some of them may be reunited. And where else could this be but in this land of Palestine, with which for more than 3000 years they have been intimately and profoundly associated.'

He insisted that the Zionist project was 'good for the world, good for the Jews, and good for the British Empire, and it is also good for the Arabs living in Palestine ... they shall not be supplanted nor suffer but shall share in the benefits,' a dubious prediction. Planting a tree at the new Hebrew University on Mount Scopus he declared: 'You Jews of Palestine have a very great responsibility; you are the representatives of the Jewish nation all over the world, and your conduct should prove an example for, and do honour to, Jews in all countries.' And he hoped, in what now seem ironical words, that 'peace and prosperity may return to Palestine'. A hundred years later, prosperity may have returned to many of its inhabitants, but not lasting peace.

What Churchill had done rather than said prompted a scission within the Zionist movement. Although his old friend Weizmann disliked partition and the severance of Trans-Jordan, he accepted it. Vladimir Jabotinsky did not. This formidable man now broke away to form the New Zionist Organisation, known as the Revisionists from his desire to rescind or revise that partition, and he campaigned on the starkly simple slogan, 'A Jewish state with a Jewish majority on both banks of the Jordan.' At the time, Jabotinsky was barely a name to Churchill, but their paths would cross.

After June 1929 Churchill had treated freedom from office as an opportunity to pursue an independent policy, with disdain for the new Labour government, and even his own party. American publications offered him a forum to write about any subject, however sensitive, and no question was more so than Palestine. Just as Churchill voyaged westwards that August, violence flared up there, partly provoked by the Betar, the militant wing of Jabotinsky's Revisionists, demonstrating in Jerusalem. More than a hundred Jews were killed by Arab mobs, some in peculiarly grim circumstances, while more than a hundred Arabs were killed by the British police, and 'Jabo', as both his followers and the British knew him, was exiled from Palestine. One thing the Palestine administration did not need was Churchill returning to the subject, but so he did.

His list of earnings at the time includes £300 for articles for 'Jewish papers', among them a piece for the *Zionist Record* of New York which was widely syndicated in America. British obligations towards Jews and Arabs were 'of equal weight, but they are different in character', Churchill asserted. 'The first obligation is positive and creative, the second obligation is safeguarding and conciliatory.' Whatever that may have meant, it was enough to enrage the British Ambassador in Washington. The effect of Churchill's words, Sir Ronald Lindsay wrote, 'can only be to induce Jews in America who might wish to take a moderate view, to refrain from doing so. They will expect a purely Zionist policy from the Conservatives when they come into office again and will hamper any move toward settlement till then, and then the chickens will come home to roost with Mr Winston Churchill.'

Six years later they had come home to roost with the Arab Revolt. A Royal Commission on Palestine was set up, chaired by Lord Peel, an eminent statesman who had been a Tory MP, Secretary of State for India in 1922–4, and a member of the Indian Round Table Conference in 1930–31 at the very time that Churchill's opposition to self-government had hardened into defiance. Although its practical effect at the time was small, the Peel Commission's report would later be called by Isaiah Berlin the fullest and most dispassionate examination of the question there has been, after Peel and his colleagues had heard evidence from representatives of every possible group and every strand of opinion – Arabs, Zionists of varying factions, British officials, and Churchill.

In 2007 his reputation was momentarily darkened when the typescript of an unpublished 1937 article came to light, called 'How the Jews Can Combat Persecution'. Churchill had said, 'It may be that, unwittingly, they are inviting persecution – that they have been partly responsible for the antagonism from which they suffer,' and that 'There is the feeling that the Jew is an incorrigible alien, that his first loyalty will always be toward his own race.' It then transpired that this shocking piece didn't reflect badly on Churchill's personal prejudices, only on his casual working methods in charge of the word-factory: the dubious article was in fact by his ghostwriter Diston, who may have been asked by Churchill to write about the subject. It was most fortunately never published.

When Churchill gave evidence before Peel it was in private so that he could speak freely, maybe sensing how provocative his views might seem. He strongly defended the Balfour Declaration, in accordance with which the British ought now to be 'bringing in as many [Jewish immigrants] as we can', although that was not in fact the official position of the government. Thanks to the Declaration, he claimed, 'we gained great advantages in the War. We did not adopt Zionism entirely out of altruistic love ... It was a potent factor on public opinion in America.' While he thought there might a be 'a State in which there was a great majority of Jews', he also continued to see Palestine above all in imperial terms – 'If British mastery disappears you had better be quit of the whole show ... clear out' – and he had no time for the Palestinian Arabs, who had fought for the Ottomans and lost: 'They were beaten out of the place.'

Then he reiterated his lifelong contempt for Arabs and Islam. 'When the Mohammedan upset occurred in world history', the Muslim hordes 'broke it all up, smashed it all up'. The Zionists were today cultivating lands which under Arab rule had remained a desert, and 'will never be cultivated by the Arabs'. Asked if the Muslims had not created a fine civilisation in mediaeval Spain, Churchill replied briskly, 'I am glad they were thrown out.' And in all too revealing words, he said bluntly that the British faced an inescapable choice: either 'facilitate the establishment of the Jewish National Home, or we are to hand over the government of the country to the people who happen to live there at the moment.' As he added, 'You cannot do both,' which was true enough.

When asked by Peel whether there shouldn't be some compunction about 'downing the Arabs' merely because they wanted to remain in their own country, Churchill was more than blunt. The Palestinian Arabs could not be allowed to dictate the future of the country simply because they had lived there so long. 'I do not admit that right. I do not admit, for instance, that a great wrong has been done to the Red Indians of America, or the black people of Australia. I do not admit that a wrong has been done to these people by the fact that a stronger race, a higher-grade race, or, at any rate, a more worldly-wise race, to put it that way, has come in and taken their place.' That was what was happening in Palestine, Churchill thought: the Jews were taking over, and a good thing too, since they were 'a higher-grade race' than the Arabs.

This was of a piece with his long-held view of Zionism. Beatrice Webb had likened the Zionist settlers in Palestine to the white settlers in Kenya, but then Edwin Montagu, a fierce Jewish opponent of Zionism, listened to one outburst from Churchill in Cabinet in 1920 about 'the very lowest class of coolies' who were migrating to Kenya, and told him that he sounded like 'a European settler of the most fanatical type'. Churchill wouldn't have been distressed by either comparison. Colonial settlement had built the empire, as well America, he thought, and now the Zionists were following in the footsteps of those earlier pioneers who had made Canada, Australia and South Africa by way of supplanting the indigenous savage inhabitants.

'To arrive at a just estimate of a renowned man's character one must judge it by the standards of his time, not ours,' Mark Twain very rightly said, and nothing is more dangerous for any historian than prochronism or 'presentism': judging the past through today's eyes. That is true not least where colonialism and racism are concerned. But we can indeed judge Churchill's views on race and empire by the standards 'of his time'.* Churchill's views were already retrograde in his own age, not ours, and whereas over the course of his long life other people's racial attitudes softened, his if anything hardened. His colleague Desmond Morton recorded how Churchill liked to talk of Africans as 'niggers', Chinese as 'pigtails' and Indians as 'baboos'. By the 1930s many people were already ceasing to think in crude terms of higher and lower races. One other man did so, of course. Hitler believed that the Jews were a lower-grade race, who deserved to be persecuted and in the end exterminated. Churchill thought the Jews a higher-grade race who deserved to take over the Holy Land from the Palestinian Arabs. Were we forced to choose, Churchill is preferable to Hitler, but many did not wish to make that choice even when he spoke, let alone today.

Before Churchill, the Peel commission had heard evidence from another extraordinary figure, to this day perhaps the one man of genius the Zionist movement has produced. Now exiled from Palestine,

---

* In his 2018 biography of Churchill, Andrew Roberts says that 'modern sensibilities' might be offended by Churchill's attitude to lower- and 'higher-grade races', but that 'it was perfectly orthodox thinking at the time'. He contradicts himself. His collection of essays, *Eminent Churchillians*, published in 1994, includes an important essay on Churchill and race, in which Roberts said correctly that what we now think unacceptable views about races were much more widely held in Churchill's day, but added, also correctly, that 'Churchill was more profoundly racist than most.'

Jabotinsky was still leading the Revisionist Zionists, whose uniformed group Betar was picking bloody fights there with Arabs, as well as street fights with Hitler's supporters in Vienna. Jabo gave a bravura performance before Peel, insisting on the need for a Jewish state and unlimited immigration: 'Our demand for a Jewish majority is not our maximum – it is our minimum: it is just an inevitable stage, if we are allowed to go on salvaging our people.' And in a haunting phrase, Jabo said that, if the Arab claim to Palestine were compared with 'the Jewish demand to be saved, it is like the claims of appetite versus the claims of starvation'.

When the report was published in July 1937, it recommended partition between the two communities, in proportions roughly two-thirds Arab to one-third Jewish. This was rejected out of hand by the Arabs, and tentatively though tearfully accepted by Weizmann *faute de mieux*. But it was passionately opposed by Jabotinsky, whose path Churchill now crossed. In July Jabo approached Churchill through the good offices of Lady Violet Bonham Carter, Asquith's daughter, Churchill's friend for more than thirty years, and by now one more patrician Zionist lady. Jabo wrote to Churchill, with a covering note from Lady Violet begging him to read the letter and detailed memorandum. 'People are so ignorant of the geographical proportions and strategic position of the tiny corner now allotted the Jews,' she wrote. A parliamentary debate on the Peel report was imminent and Jabo implored Churchill to intervene, while offering to meet him: 'I would come to Chartwell if necessary.'

Five days later they did meet at Westminster, for a long conversation shortly before the debate, 'and the results were excellent', Jabotinsky's devout biographer records. Churchill duly spoke in the Commons and, having now made up his mind, he opposed partition. More than that, he wrote for the *Evening Standard* a column which, like his speech, was unmistakably influenced by Jabotinsky. Partition was a counsel of despair, Churchill wrote. 'One wonders whether, in reality, the difficulties of carrying out the Zionist scheme are so great as they are portrayed.'

After this, Parliament shelved the report, and in 1939 the government published yet another hand-wringing White Paper, which proposed strict limits on Jewish immigration, to Zionist rage. By then Hitler had given an unambiguous warning. In his speech to the Reichstag on 30 January, he said, 'Today I will once more be a prophet.

If the international Jewish financiers, inside and outside Europe, succeed in plunging the nations once more into a world war, then the result will not be the Bolshevisation of the earth, and thus the victory of Jewry, but the annihilation of the Jewish race in Europe!' Other countries, notably the United States, showed no enthusiasm for accepting more than a handful of refugees, and so the desperate Jews of Europe awaited a fate horrible beyond imagining.

CALLING MR. CHURCHILL

8

'A bitter cup'

Munich 1938

'I have been so hampered in my work by politics that I am behindhand with Marlborough.' Churchill's letter to Keith Feiling in the autumn of 1935 seems almost comical, as though mere politics was a distraction from the first priority of writing, which indeed it was in financial terms. The combination of frantic literary output with a political career inevitably placed a strain on Churchill, and in any case his 'work in politics' for the past four or more years had been his lamentable and futile fight against the India Bill, on which he had wasted so much energy to no effect except the damage to his reputation.

But then he had taken up another great question: warning about the revival of Germany as an aggressive military power, preaching the need for rearmament against that threat, and denouncing what became known as the policy of appeasement. This is the story he told so vividly in *The Gathering Storm*, which has coloured all accounts of the 1930s to this day, withstanding any number of critiques, however well informed or well reasoned. 'A prophet is not without honour, but in his own country,' Jesus said, and, as if the comparison with John the Baptist crying in the wilderness weren't impious enough, Churchill would represent himself as such an unhonoured prophet. 'I saw it all coming and cried aloud to my own fellow-countrymen and to the world, but no one paid any attention,' he claimed in his famous Fulton speech in 1946, and then he said it again and again. He might as well have prefaced *The Gathering Storm* with Byron's lines: 'Of all the horrid, hideous notes of woe, / Sadder than owl-songs or the midnight blast; / Is that portentous phrase, 'I told you so.''

A solemn 'theme' prefaces *The Gathering Storm*: 'How the English-speaking peoples through their unwisdom, carelessness and good nature allowed the wicked to rearm.' In case readers had missed his point, several pages later Churchill repeats, 'how easily the tragedy of the Second World War could have been prevented: how the malice of the wicked was reinforced by the weakness of the virtuous.' And again: 'There never was a war in all history easier to prevent by timely action than the one which has just desolated such great areas of the globe. It could have been prevented in my belief without the firing of a single shot.' This became the great argument of Churchill's life; and never have so many questions been begged in so few words. His claim was reinforced by a kind of moral bullying: since the war was so terrible, and since everyone afterwards wished that it hadn't happened, those who had failed to prevent it 'by timely action' must have been knaves and fools. But what form could that timely action have taken, and what had Churchill's own record really been?

For one thing, the picture of a prophet crying unhonoured in the wilderness is most misleading. Even if Churchill had damaged himself so much, that didn't mean that he was totally excluded from the centre of power, or that he was a consistent opponent of the government, or that he had to rely on clandestine sources for information about German rearmament, for all that he later contrived to give that impression, which was then endlessly played out on screens large and small. Over and again, Desmond Morton is seen bravely supplying Churchill with information about German rearmament which the government ignored or even tried to conceal. Morton was a notable figure, if not quite as notable as he liked to think: a former Gunner major with a wartime Military Cross who was now head of the industrial intelligence centre for the Committee of Imperial Defence. He lived close to Chartwell and regularly visited Churchill, and his reward came in 1940, when he became a senior intelligence aide at Downing Street and Sir Desmond.

But to represent him as a brave clandestine whistle-blower is quite wrong. In 1932 Morton had been granted permission by MacDonald to communicate with Churchill, permission confirmed by MacDonald's successors as prime minister, Baldwin and Chamberlain. Churchill joined a secret government defence committee in 1936, at Baldwin's invitation, and senior naval officers were authorised to talk to him by Hoare, who had returned to the Cabinet as First Lord of the Admiralty after a brief period of penance. When Baldwin retired at last after the Coronation in May 1937, he was succeeded by Chamberlain as his recognised heir. Eight years earlier Churchill had told Clementine that he would leave politics if Chamberlain became Conservative leader;

now he seconded the formal motion by Tory MPs approving Chamberlain.

In reality, Churchill was anything but an outsider. Along with Lloyd George, Sir Austen Chamberlain, Sir Herbert Samuel and Sir John Simon, Churchill enjoyed a special place in Parliament as one of the veterans who had been Cabinet ministers before 1914. After the passage of the India Bill ended Churchill's self-inflicted estrangement from the government, he continued to sit below the gangway, the front bench in the Commons to the right of the Treasury Bench where eminences who were out of office sat. But his position was as a friendly critic rather than an opponent of the government, almost like a minister arguing in Cabinet against his colleagues, something he had done often enough in the past.

On that great matter of the German threat and the need to counter it, Churchill's views over the years were complicated, and far from coherent. Sometimes he stated the obvious, as when he warned of a resurgent Germany, and sometimes he was plain wrong. Everyone could see the problem facing the former allied powers, meaning the French and British, since the Americans and the Russians had both gone missing, and Italy was a problem of its own. 'It was perfectly obvious,' as A.J.P. Taylor put it, 'that Germany would seek to become a Great Power again; obvious after 1933 that her domination would be of a peculiarly barbaric sort.' As early as 1925 Churchill had seen what others saw, that 'from one end of Germany to the other an intense hatred of France unites the whole population ... the soul of Germany smoulders with dreams of a war of Liberation or Revenge. These ideas are restrained at the present moment only by physical impotence ... Germany is a far stronger entity than France, and cannot be kept in permanent subjugation.'

Nor did he want to do so. Even after the war, Churchill could look back to 1932, when the two might have met, and say, 'I had no national prejudices against Hitler at this time. I knew little of his doctrines or record and nothing of his character,' an odd admission since there was ample evidence of all of those. 'I always admire men who stand up for their country in defeat ... He had a perfect right to be a patriotic German ... I had always wanted England, France and Germany to be friends.' In 1935, Churchill wrote that 'the world lives in hopes that the worst is over, and that we yet live to see Hitler a gentler figure in a happier age.' And as late as 1938 he added, 'I have always said that if Great Britain were defeated in war I hoped we should find a Hitler to lead us back to our rightful position among the nations. I am sorry, however, that he has not been mellowed by the great success that has attended him. The whole world would rejoice to see the Hitler of peace and tolerance.'

These words shouldn't be quoted simply to deride Churchill, although a list of his speeches and writings at the time might confirm Beaverbrook's claim that over the years he had held every possible position on every known subject. What they do mean is that he was as perplexed as other politicians by the German problem, and by no means had any more idea how to deal with it. When in November 1932 Churchill told the Commons that Germany was looking for revenge, he was again saying what everyone knew. Gerhard Starcke was a student in Berlin in the late 1920s. Looking back thirty years after the war he recalled one pervasive belief which ran right across all German classes and parties, 'that the injustice of Versailles was to blame for EVERYTHING'. And so even Germans with misgivings about Hitler's dictatorship were pleased when in October 1933, nine months after coming to power, he withdrew from the international Disarmament Conference, and demanded that Germany should be allowed a conscript army.

At this crucial point Churchill was still wasting his political substance in a bitter phase of his Indian campaign, more resented by former colleagues than ever, more reviled by liberal opinion, and more out of step with the public mood. Much was made, far too much in fact, of the debate in the Oxford Union in February 1933 when a majority voted that they would 'not fight for King and Country'. Randolph dashed back to the university he had briefly attended to try and reverse the vote, but only succeeded in increasing it, while Churchill called the resolution 'an abject, squalid, shameless avowal', as though an undergraduate debating society really mattered. Months later Baldwin was more seriously shaken when a government candidate at a by-election in East Fulham lost to Labour. Baldwin interpreted, or more likely misinterpreted, this as a vote against rearmament.

But random expressions of discontent from a few self-important young men or disgruntled Londoners were almost beside the point: no one in England or France, let alone America, wanted war – and many were inclined to dismiss it as an impossibility. They included Churchill. During these so-called wilderness years, with no responsibilities of office to restrain his fertile imagination and loquacious tongue, he made many very specific predictions about war and peace, matters military and naval, which were wild and foolish in the extreme and would come back to haunt him in wartime. More broadly, in 1930 Churchill wrote that 'War, which used to be cruel and magnificent, has now become cruel and squalid ... we now have entire populations, including even women and children, pitted against one another in brutish mutual extermination,' in which case it surely made sense to avoid it at all costs.

Then again, 'I don't believe we shall see another great war in our lifetime,' Churchill said in March 1932, in a radio interview in New York after he had recovered from his street accident. 'War is now nothing but toil, blood, death squalor and lying propaganda,' he went on. 'Besides, as long as the French keep a strong army, and Great Britain and the United States have good navies, no great war is likely to occur.' In July 1935 he told English newspaper readers that 'Another great war would cost us our wealth, our freedom, and our culture, and cast what we have so slowly garnered to different packs of ravening wolves. It would,' he added, 'be like the last war – only worse.' That was in many ways all too true as a prediction. The next great war proved to be much worse than the last in terms of death and devastation, and for the British it did 'cost us our wealth'. To say that could only mean that such a war should be avoided. But how? British politicians were now in the same bind as their predecessors had been before the Great War. Either a clear commitment to military intervention or a policy of absolute non-intervention might have kept England out of war, or even, very hypothetically, have prevented war at all. The path somewhere in between, although understandable, might have made war more likely. But then Churchill himself kept falling between stools, and there was no clear course in his thought.

In 1930 he wrote an article for the *Saturday Evening Post* called 'A United States of Europe'. Many mistakes and misapprehensions sprang from this single phrase, which Churchill would repeat during the war and afterwards. Phrase and concept had a long history. The story of Washington telling Lafayette that, now that a United States of America had been created, it should be followed by a United States of Europe, may be apocryphal. But by the 1840s that phrase was being used by Carlo Cattaneo and by the *Moniteur*, an Italian radical writer and a Parisian radical paper, and the political flavour wasn't an accident. Nor was the phrase itself hard to understand, as Europeans watched with awe, envy and sometimes alarm as the vigorous young republic burgeoned across the Atlantic.

Or as Churchill put it, Europe saw 'the economic and financial portent of the United States', with its vast resources and educated inhabitants who were progressing and prospering 'at a degree never before witnessed'. And he wondered, 'What are the causes which are favouring the New World, and hindering the old?' That was a good question, with many answers, but the wrong conclusion was to suppose that Europe could copy the American example by forming a political union. As Samuel Johnson truly said, 'Almost all absurdity of conduct arises from the imitation of those whom we cannot resemble.' Europe did not, does not, and cannot resemble America, and any attempt by a European Union to imitate the American Union was, and has remained, doomed to failure. Churchill should have seen that before lightly using the phrase.

Eight years later he employed the same title for another article, in the *News of the World*, and addressed the question of what the British role would be in such a United States of Europe. 'We are with Europe, but not of it,' he said in oracular words he would later reprise. 'We are linked but not compromised. We are interested and associated, but not absorbed. And should European statesmen address us in the words which were used of old, "Wouldst thou be spoken for to the king, or to the captain of the host?" we should reply with the Shunamite woman, "I dwell among my own people".' (from the Second Book of Kings, and one more memory from Harrow chapel). Such words were still being echoed by 'Eurosceptics' eighty years later, although Churchill's 'interested and associated, but not absorbed' might mean anything or nothing, as indeed could 'a United States of Europe'. But a Concert of Europe did mean something. Such a concert had kept the peace between the European Powers for a generation after the Congress of Vienna in 1815, and for another after the Congress of Berlin in 1878. It was the tragically unfulfilled hope of at least some of those who met in Paris in 1919, and of those who brought the League of Nations and its Covenant into being, that they might do the same.

To this day the League has been much maligned. More than eighty years after it was founded, President Bush the Younger was still sneering at the League as a way of deriding the United Nations. One of his aides or speechwriters might have reminded him that the League's greatest weakness throughout its existence was that the United States had never joined. At the 1920 presidential election, when he was Cox's running mate, Franklin Roosevelt had supported Wilson's campaign for American membership of the League, but by the time he became president himself in 1933, when it was still possible for the United States to join, he had changed his mind.

In 1938 a collection of Churchill's speeches was published, entitled *Arms and the Covenant*. By then the Covenant of the Leagues was a lost cause as a way of restraining German aggression. So what of the arms, or what sort of arms should they be? Churchill sounded the alarm about German revanchism and rearmament early on, and from 1934 until war came he spoke repeatedly about the threat of German air power. He was quite wrong, twice over. In March 1933 he hoped 'that we shall be permitted to live in our island without being again drawn into the perils of the continent of Europe'. But 'we have to be strong enough to defend our neutrality ... I am strongly of the opinion that we require to strengthen our armaments in the air.' This was to be his persistent theme, but it is essential to understand what he meant by 'armaments in the air'.

Like all his compatriots, Churchill was obsessed by memories of 1916: not only of the slaughter of the Somme, but also of the bombing of London by German airships and aircraft. By later standards death and destruction had been almost insignificant but the psychological effect had been shattering. Politicians and airmen, not to mention H.G. Wells and other future-shock writers, had warned that from now on war would mean the obliteration of cities from the air. It's hard now to recall how much bombing was dreaded, or to understand how far that dread affected all British politicians. And it was not for Americans then, or now, to sneer at such anxieties. How many bombs fell on American cities in the twentieth century?

For ever after, Baldwin would be damned for telling British citizens in 1932 they should know that 'The bomber will always get through'. That sounded like a counsel of despair, and yet it was what everyone then thought, not least Churchill. In February 1934 he painted a lurid picture of 'the crash of bombs exploding in London and cataracts of masonry and fire and smoke will apprise us of any inadequacy which has been permitted in our aerial defences.' That November he spoke of 'the great new fact' that 'Germany is rearming', and said that 'one could hardly expect that less than 30,000 to 40,000 people would be killed or maimed' in the first ten days of war 'under the pressure of continuous air attack', and that three or four million would have to flee the capital. In the event, some 60,000 people were killed by bombing in all British cities over nearly five years.

Not only did Churchill claim that German armament factories were 'working practically under war conditions', he challenged Baldwin's figures on German front-line aircraft with figures of his own suggesting that Germany enjoyed a clear superiority. His figures were partly inspired by his *éminence grise* (though much darker than grey) F.A. Lindemann. This sinister personage, who will play a much larger part in our story, German-born but violently Germanophobic, had become a professor at Oxford largely thanks to his personal fortune, and a friend of the Churchill family partly because he partnered Clementine at tennis. Churchill knew nothing of science and greatly overrated Lindemann's professional competence, beginning with his fallacious statistics about German air strength. To explain this fully would require a lengthy excursus, but it is enough to say that Baldwin was basically right about the strength of the Luftwaffe, and Churchill wrong. He may have been wrong unwittingly, led astray by Lindemann's incompetence, although Churchill did later slyly admit that 'In these endeavours no doubt I painted the picture darker than it was.'

He was wrong also in the policy he was commending. Churchill's belief that whole cities would be obliterated when war began meant that, in 1934 or 1936 or even later, he didn't foresee the revolution in air war which would be brought about by the end of the decade through the advent of the fast monoplane fighter and of radar. He was even wrong to suppose that the Luftwaffe was intended for long-distance bombing, rather than for supporting the army. The Germans had to improvise a bombing campaign in 1940, and even then required something Churchill certainly didn't foresee before the war, the defeat of the French army which provided the Luftwaffe with airfields just across the Channel, rather than in Germany. And beyond that, Churchill was wrong to believe in the doctrine of 'air power', as preached first by Smuts and Trenchard and then by the RAF and the Air Ministry. Since there could be no defence against bombers, this doctrine held, the only answer was to build more bombers in return: defence through a balance of terror.

He was even more broadly wrong about German rearmament. Detailed research after the war showed that there had in fact been little such rearmament before 1936, or little more than the gradual evasion of the Versailles Treaty and strengthening of the army which governments of the German republic had begun before it was succeeded by the Third Reich. And here, above all, Churchill failed to see that the real threat was not in the air but on the ground. After his rhetorical demand for the right to a conscript army, Hitler acted unilaterally in March 1935 in defiance of Versailles by introducing conscription. Within less than four years a quite small standing army had become the mighty Wehrmacht, the most ferociously effective and murderous, army Europe would ever know, which conquered the continent from North Cape to Pyrenees to Caucasus.

But what should the response be? While Churchill fulminated about air power, he insisted that all would be well if the French army and the Royal Navy remained strong enough, and if Bomber Command, as it had been designated in 1936, were strengthened. At no time did he advocate the two courses that might actually have deterred Hitler: a commitment to a continental strategy through an alliance with France, and conscription to match the French army. Right up until the spring of 1939 Churchill maintained that 'I do not think we need a great conscript army on the continental model.' This was all of a piece with what he had said for years, and it was at the heart of Churchill's problem: his failure to understand modern war. Through two great wars and between them he refused to recognise the importance of mass, or sheer numbers. Before he called his Great War book *The World Crisis* he had thought of 'The Great Amphibian' as a possible title, intending England's unique position as a maritime power which could strike here and there by seaborne campaigns rather than full-scale land war, and he persisted in this belief.

He persisted also in overestimating the strength of England's continental friend. 'As long as the French keep a strong army ...', he claimed in 1932, and in the same year, 'Thank God for the French army.' The Third Republic was a constitutional democracy, up to a point, though backward in some ways: until 1939 the Parisian public could still watch condemned men guillotined in public, and while British and American women had been enfranchised after 1918, French women couldn't vote until 1945. And this harsh masculine republic was also notoriously unstable and corrupt, politicians and press alike. More than that, France was fundamentally weakened by its internal divisions, between Catholic and anticlerical, royalist and republican, and now fascist and communist. In February 1934, less than two years after Churchill's 'Thank God', far-right riots in Paris saw fifteen people killed and a prime minister forced to resign. Even in November 1937 Churchill could tell Lord Linlithgow, the Viceroy of India, 'The peace of Europe dwells under the shield of the French army.' He said that at the very moment when that army was riven by the Cagoulard conspiracy, which revealed the degree of extreme right-wing sympathies among French officers. Churchill's lifelong Francophilia was attractive, but it misled him when he insisted, 'I hope and trust that the French will look after their own safety.' Hope and trust weren't enough.

Having succeeded MacDonald in June 1935, seen off Edward VIII the following year, and witnessed the coronation of George VI, Baldwin made way for Chamberlain in May 1937. Churchill never felt for Chamberlain the venomous hostility he had for Baldwin. 'No closer parallel exists in history than that presented by the Tory conduct in the years 1696–9 with their squalid conduct in the years 1932–7,' the latter dates being of course when Baldwin led the Tories. That line came from *The History of the English-Speaking Peoples*, which Churchill was working on at the time, and continues well-nigh spitefully: 'In each case, short-sighted opinions, agreeable to the party spirit, pernicious to national interests, banished all purpose from the State and prepared a deadly resumption of the main struggle of a Continental war. These recurring fits of squalor in the Tory record.' Churchill had been consistently out-played by Baldwin and settled the score by never giving him any credit for having begun to rearm – work which Chamberlain continued. And he didn't know what Baldwin had said about him to a colleague in 1935: 'if there is going to be a war – and no one can say there is not – then we must keep him fresh to be our war Prime Minister.'

Now Chamberlain pursued more vigorously a policy whose very name would become a curse, what he called 'world appeasement'. So toxic would that word become that its origins are forgotten, to the point where one ignorant reviewer of Tim Bouverie's 2019 book *Appeasing Hitler* could say that he had never before realised that 'appeasement' was originally 'a term embraced by its proponents'. The word had been used in English from the sixteenth century, always in a neutral or even positive sense: to appease or satisfy a natural appetite or proper demand. That was the sense which Churchill had intended when he slipped back into French in 1911 to tell Asquith, 'I hope we may be able to pursue *une politique d'apaisement,*' intending mollification of their Tory opponents. Ten years later in 1921 Churchill had hoped to see an 'appeasement of the fearful hatreds and antagonisms which exist in Europe'. Such appeasement had been the consistent aim of British governments since then. One initiative, one conference after another tried to find a way of settling differences between hostile countries with conflicting ambitions.

In that sense, appeasement was the purpose of the League of Nations, which had settled the Manchurian question in 1931 by appeasing or satisfying Japan, very much as Churchill wished. Italy would have been appeased by the Hoare–Laval agreement, and was in effect appeased when Mussolini was allowed to conquer Abyssinia anyway. Churchill remained an unwavering appeaser towards Italy, partly out of his misplaced admiration for Mussolini and partly from the understandable view that one potential European enemy at a time was quite enough, and that a hostile Italy would threaten the Mediterranean Fleet and the British lifeline to Suez and India.

In the case of Germany, the policy of appeasement was coloured by the belief, first propagated by Keynes and more and more widely held since, that Germany had been harshly treated by Versailles, and that the Wilsonian doctrine of self-determination had been illogically or hypocritically applied, to German detriment. Indeed it had been: 'national justice' was granted to the Slovenes of the ancient Habsburg duchies of Styria and Carinthia in the south, which were sliced through to make the new state of Yugoslavia, but not to the Germans of the ancient kingdom of Bohemia, which retained its traditional boundaries and its German population.

There was and is a strong case against that very doctrine. In a confidential memorandum in December 1918, Wilson's Secretary of State, Robert Lansing, had said that self-determination was a phrase 'simply loaded with dynamite', and in 1944, Walter Lippmann, who had once been a confidant of Wilson and had helped draft the Fourteen Points but had at last seen where they had led, wrote that 'Self-determination, which has nothing to do with self-government but has become confused with it, is barbarous and reactionary: by sanctioning secession, it invites majorities and minorities to be intransigent and irreconcilable. It is stipulated in the principle of self-determination that they need not be compatriots because they will soon be aliens. There is no end to this atomisation of human society. Within the minorities who have seceded there will tend to appear other minorities who in their turn will wish to secede.'

Much of the experience of the twentieth century is summed up in those words. And yet the democracies all paid lip service to the principle of self-determination, even Churchill himself on occasion, although his deepest instincts weren't for 'national justice' but for British greatness and the balance of power. He was ill-equipped to grasp the problem. In his anachronistic way he never ceased to think of 'Prussia' as the foe. He failed to grasp that National Socialism, although it would gain widespread support in northern Germany, had its roots not in Berlin but in Vienna, where Hitler had learned his politics early in the century: the antisemitism and appeal to the 'little man' of Dr Karl Lueger combined with the pan-German nationalism of Georg von Schönerer. That meant that Hitler intended to undo not only Versailles but the work of Bismarck half a century earlier. In 1866 Bismarck had engineered the Austro-Prussian War, the second of the three ruthless diplomatic wars by way of which he created a predominantly Protestant Reich under Prussian leadership, and Prussia had defeated Austria at Königgrätz, a defeat much lamented by Churchill.* Bismarck excluded Austria, including Bohemia, from his version of Germany, although they had been immemorially as much 'German' as Brandenburg or Württemberg.

When the whole map of central and eastern Europe was redrawn after the Great War, supposedly in accordance with 'self-determination', there were in reality winners and losers, the losers not surprisingly being those who had already lost in the war. The Habsburg monarchy had been damned as a 'prison house of nations', and when it fell apart those nations were ostensibly granted freedom, with the signal exception of the people of the German-speaking Habsburg rump (the present-day Austrian republic), who were flagrantly denied self-determination, or merely their simplest wishes. In March 1919, the democratically

---

* In 1978, when I published in the *Spectator* a column of sentimental lament for the Habsburg monarchy, the late Alastair Forbes, a great friend of the Churchills, wrote to me, 'Winston would have approved. He liked young Englishmen who regretted the result of Königgrätz.'

elected Austrian National Assembly unanimously approved union with Germany and, as the *Daily Telegraph* reported, the Assembly moreover 'desires that the act of union should also include German Bohemia'. This was hoped for as well by Ebert, leader of the German Social Democrats, if not by all Germans.

Instead, 'Austria' was made a separate state, whose future would have to be decided by the League of Nations, although Keynes pointed out that really meant the French: Clemenceau thought that there were quite enough Germans without the Austrians. A hitherto unknown country called 'Czechoslovakia' was created from the old kingdom of Bohemia and the margravate of Moravia, with 'Slovakia' tacked on, although for a thousand years this had been simply the northern counties of the kingdom of Hungary, and despite speaking similar languages its inhabitants had no historical connection whatever with the Czech lands, nor any keen desire to be part of this new country.

And so in practice the supposedly national states of the postwar settlement, either revived like Poland, or enlarged like Rumania, or created brand-new like Yugoslavia and Czechoslovakia, were as much prison houses of the nations as the old multi-national empires, with their intransigent and irreconcilable majorities and minorities of Lippmann's phrase. 'German Bohemia' meant the three and a half million Deutschböhmen or Sudeten Germans from the hills in the north-east, part of the ring of hills encircling Bohemia and Moravia, with towns like Pilsen and Budweis made famous by the beer they brewed, and the spas of Carlsbad and Marienbad once so much frequented by the rich and the royal. Not only German nationalists but English liberals and socialists saw a grave injustice. In 1920, H.N. Brailsford, the leading radical English commentator on foreign affairs, echoed the party policy document of the year before called 'The Labour Party, Labour and the Peace Treaty' when he wrote that, of all the wrongs of the postwar settlement, 'the worst offence was the subjection of over three million Germans to Czech rule'.

As Chamberlain began to address those questions in his methodical way, the first person who defied him was the clever, young and handsome Anthony Eden. He was no hero to Churchill: 'I think you will see what a lightweight Eden is,' Churchill had written to Clementine when Eden was appointed Foreign Secretary in January 1936, about a man who would serve as his own Foreign Secretary not once but twice, before succeeding him as prime minister. Two years after that letter, in February 1938, Eden resigned over a somewhat technical difference with Chamberlain which could be represented as opposition to the appeasement of Mussolini. A small circle of dissident MPs gravitated towards him, derisively known as 'the glamour boys', but Churchill still kept his political options open: after Eden's resignation, Churchill's name appeared among a list of 150 Tory MPs pledging Chamberlain their resolute support.

Then on 13 March 1938, in the wake of much dark intrigue, independent Austria disappeared and the country was absorbed by Germany in an 'Anschluss' or union, while Hitler arrived in Vienna to an ecstatic welcome. 'We were now confronted,' Churchill told Parliament the following day, 'with a programme of aggression nicely calculated and timed, unfolding stage by stage.' More than twenty years later, in 1961, this view was challenged by A.J.P. Taylor in his controversial book *The Origins of the Second World War*. Hitler had 'no precise plans of aggression', Taylor wrote, 'only an intention, which he held in common with most Germans, to make Germany the most powerful state in Europe and a readiness to take advantage of events.' However that might be, could this Anschluss really be an act of 'aggression', as Churchill called it? A plebiscite confirming the union passed almost unanimously. It was held under conditions of terror, the Gestapo and SS already about their business in the streets of Vienna, with many willing new hands there to help them. But a genuinely free vote would without doubt have been little different. For that matter, had the German regime been of a different character, the majority of Austrians supporting Anschluss could have included Social Democrats, liberals and Jews.

This was Hitler's fourth successful such vote,* which was why both Clement Attlee and Margaret Thatcher later reprehended what she called 'the referendum ... a device of dictators and demagogues'. Those votes weren't held in a free country, but the Saarland plebiscite had been. This small territory on the French border, with its rich coalfields and vineyards, had been detached from the new German republic after the war to placate the French, but with a promise that it would one day have the opportunity to rejoin Germany, when its people could vote. They did so in January 1935. By then, two years after Hitler had come to power, the nature of his Reich was clear for

---

* After referendums on abolishing the presidency, withdrawing from the League of Nations, and reoccupying the Rhineland.

all to see. Refugees came to this little corner of free German soil to warn the Saarlanders of the meaning of National Socialism: their Roman Catholic Church would be circumscribed, their trade unions and Social Democratic party would be destroyed, free speech would be silenced, the Gestapo would exert a reign of terror, persecution would rule. And in what all observers recognised as a free vote, with a startling turnout of 98 per cent, 91 per cent of the people in Saarland voted to join the Reich. Sir Nevile Henderson was British ambassador in Berlin and acquired an exaggerated reputation as an appeaser too sympathetic to Germany: in fact, after Munich, he told Halifax 'I never want to work with Germans again.' But he had said in August 1938, 'The British Empire cannot set its face against the principle of self-determination.' Any consistent opposition to appeasement had to begin by ignoring that principle, and national rights.

Many British people were repelled by Hitler's hysterical rhetoric and cruel persecution. A few grasped the way that National Socialism combined demonic rage with modernity. The travel writer Robert Byron visited Germany in 1938 and watched the Nuremberg rally, where he was struck by just this: 'The whole ceremonial is of a remarkable kind ... and it is new in that it incorporates, indeed is based on, the last resources of the age.' Byron ruefully added that it was unsettling to live at a time 'when only Winston Churchill talks sense'. Indeed he talked much more sense on far stronger ground in condemning the character of the Third Reich. In May 1938, he gave a grand speech at the Free Trade Hall in Manchester, which has been called the one great public building named not for a man or a place but for an idea, and an idea which Churchill had always cherished.

'Undoubtedly our government could make an agreement with Germany,' he said with bitter irony. We would only need 'to muzzle the British press and platform by a law of censorship, and to give Herr Hitler a free hand to spread the Nazi system and dominance far and wide through Central Europe.... We should be the helpless, silent, gagged, apparently consenting spectators of the horrors.' But this could never happen, he said, on the note of high optimism he would sound more famously two years later, since no British government which capitulated to Hitler would survive: 'The mere instance of self-preservation would make it impossible for us to purchase a fleeting and precarious immunity at the cost of the ruin and enslavement of Europe.'

Those noble words echoed what he had said at the time Hitler took power about 'the tumultuous insurgence of ferocity and war spirit, the pitiless ill-treatment of minorities,' but Churchill's heroic spirit was expressed in ways that went far beyond the bounds of realism, when he claimed that the British people would have favoured resistance had they not been misled and betrayed by Baldwin and Chamberlain. In a notorious index entry in *The Gathering Storm*, Churchill listed under 'Baldwin', 'Admits putting party before country,' by which he meant Baldwin's telling Parliament that he could have proceeded with rearmament only as fast as the public wished. But that, in a democracy, was no more than the truth. As Baldwin rightly said, the dictator was always two years ahead of democratic politicians. That applied to both British and American leaders: to this day Roosevelt has been habitually defended for doing just what Baldwin said he was doing, refraining from military confrontation with the aggressors until he had his people behind him; and a long American wait it proved to be.

To whom was Churchill appealing? Around this time, Nick Jenkins, Anthony Powell's narrator in his great novel sequence *A Dance to the Music of Time*, lunches with the absurd but ubiquitous Widmerpool. 'People talk of rearming,' Widmerpool says, 'I am glad to say the Labour Party is against it to a man – and the more enlightened Tories, too.' Apart from 'to a man', that was true. Under the leadership of George Lansbury, the Labour Party had veered towards outright pacifism: not only did it regularly vote against the military estimates in Parliament, at one point its annual conference nearly passed a resolution calling for the abolition of the Royal Air Force. In the autumn of 1935 the party was pulled back by Ernest Bevin, the great leader of the Transport and General Union, with his savage attack on Lansbury for 'hawking your conscience'. This philippic ended Lansbury's career, although his successor, the Oxonian sometime infantry officer C.R. Attlee, continued to speak of war as a capitalist conspiracy. When Hitler reoccupied the Rhineland, Hugh Dalton, a former Gunner officer and one of the few Labour politicians who shared Churchill's view, said that Labour would certainly not have supported any military response.

Nor would they in 1938. After the disappearance of Austria, Konrad Henlein visited London several times in the spring and summer. The leader of the Sudeten Germans persuaded many people with his call for 'Home Rule' or political autonomy for the Germans within Czechoslovakia, which he claimed was all he wanted. Churchill was among those so persuaded. There was no doubt, he wrote in June, that Henlein was working honourably with Beneš, the Czech president, 'and that a good settlement is possible between them on the basis of Home Rule for the Sudeten Germans within the Czechoslovakian State. Why, then, should this not be achieved? The Czechoslovakian Government owe it to France and Great Britain that nothing which reason and justice can claim should be withheld.' Still more tellingly, Churchill admitted that 'without the championship of armed Germany, Sudeten wrongs might never have been redressed'. He may not have been what one of Chamberlain's most loyal parliamentary supporters called him that summer, 'old Winston Churchill, now the most dangerous man in Europe,' but his position was far from coherent.

Hoping to redress them, Chamberlain was also desperate to avoid war, an anxiety which played into the hands of Hitler, master of bluff and bullying. The crisis escalated through the summer and into September, when war seemed to be close at hand and thirty-eight million gas masks were distributed around the country. Speaking on the radio on 27 September Chamberlain told the British people how fantastic it was that these preparations for war should be made 'because of a quarrel in a far away country between people of whom we know nothing'. Those words would ever after be quoted in derision, although for the British, and still more the Americans, a far away country and people of whom we know little would be an excellent description of many another place, from Vietnam to Iraq. Chamberlain flew three times to see Hitler, first presenting him with a statement 'symbolic of the desire of our two peoples never to go to war with one another again' and finally, on 30 September, concluding the agreement which ceded the German-speaking territory of Czechoslovakia to the Reich. Chamberlain returned to cheering crowds, and defended his deal with the fatal words 'peace for our time ... peace with honour'.

This was the Munich agreement, whose very name would become another curse, thanks to Churchill. When it was debated in Parliament he made a speech which staked his claim, and a brilliant speech it was. He began by stating 'what everybody would like to ignore or forget but which must nevertheless be stated, namely, that we have sustained a total and unmitigated defeat, and that France has suffered even more than we have.'* Some of what Churchill said was all too true: 'The German dictator, instead of snatching his victuals from the table, has been content to have them served to him course by course ... £1 was demanded at the pistol's point. When it was given, £2 were demanded at the pistol's point. Finally, the dictator consented to take £1 17s. 6d. and the rest in promises of good will for the future.'

That was a good description of the way Chamberlain handled the crisis, so anxious to placate Hitler that he offered concessions before they had been asked for. Then Churchill ended with a grand perora- tion: 'And do not suppose that this is the end. This is only the beginning of the reckoning. This is only the first sip, the first foretaste of a bitter cup which will be proffered to us year by year unless by a supreme recovery of moral health and martial vigour, we arise again and take our stand for freedom as in the olden time.' In those exalted words Churchill anticipated his great speeches in the finest hour to come. But he could not have known what a cup he himself had filled, how bitter the fruits of 'Munich' – or of his speech – would indeed be.

Even at the time, Churchill's argument was confused. For one thing, he privately felt more sympathy for Chamberlain in his frightful dilemma: 'We stand to lose everything by failing to take strong action. Yet if we take strong action London will be a shambles in half an hour.' But in any case he gave himself away in that speech when he referred to 'the rape of Austria' six months before Munich. The word 'rape' should never be used lightly in any context, literal or figurative, but rarely has it been less apt, since consent was so obvious. And so it was with the Sudetens also, as Churchill well knew. In the Commons debate, Sir John Simon, now Chancellor of the Exchequer, neatly quoted Churchill against himself. 'Bohemia and Moravia contained at least three million German-speaking population,' he had written, 'often concentrated, usually in the ascendant, a strong competent stock, holding firmly together like the Ulstermen in Ireland.' Indeed

---

* *Hansard* records here a shout of 'Nonsense!' from his old sparring partner Lady Astor. St Mary Aldermanbury is the Wren church transplanted to Fulton in Missouri, and now the grandest of Churchillian shrines. In its crypt the walls are dotted about with sundry pieces of Churchillian wit and wisdom, including the exchange: 'If I was your wife, Winston, I'd put poison in your coffee;' 'And if I was your husband, Nancy, I'd drink it.' That may be apocryphal, but Sir Isaiah Berlin recalled that, in the very first words he ever heard him utter when they met, Churchill had said, 'The world would be a better place if all members of the Astor family were shot.'

Churchill had expressed it even more lucidly: 'To exclude the German-speaking population from the new State of Czechoslovakia was deeply and perhaps fatally to weaken the new State; to include them was to affront the principle of self-determination.'

With the Munich deed done, Churchill renewed his attack from another flank, weaving a larger tapestry of imagination. He now claimed that a frustrated German resistance existed, which had only needed a little encouragement from outside to throw off Hitler's yoke. On this utterly misleading theme others would play endless variations, and it became one of the foundation myths of the postwar German Republic. Churchill began early. Shortly after Munich, in a broadcast to the United States on 17 October, he again condemned the agreement, and went on: 'If the risks of war which were run by France and Britain at the last moment had been boldly faced in good time and plain declarations had been made and meant, how different would our prospects have been today ... [Had Hitler faced] a formidable array of peace-defending powers ... this would have been an opportunity for all peace-loving and moderate forces in Germany, together with the chiefs of the German army, to make a great effort to re-establish something like sane and civilised conditions in their country.'

This would be central to Churchill's authorised version, endlessly reiterated, before and after the war, and widely accepted to this day. Speaking in Brussels in November 1945, he said, 'If the allies had resisted Hitler strongly in his early stages ... the chance would have been given to the sane elements in German life, which were very powerful – especially in the High Command – to save Germany from the maniacal grip into which she was falling.' On this text he would preach in *The Gathering Storm* his far larger sermon, about the easiest of all wars to avoid.

What was the truth? Since Hitler took power, there had been little sign of dissidence in the German army. Its officers had sworn a personal oath of loyalty to the Führer, and done so moreover immediately after the butchery of the 'night of the long knives' in 1934, when dozens of Hitler's erstwhile comrades had been murdered. Some generals disliked and distrusted him, among them General Werner von Fritsch, the commander-in-chief of the German army, although he shared Hitler's belief that 'international Jewry' was the enemy. But in April 1938 von Fritsch was falsely charged with homosexual offences and dismissed. Any chances of an effective plot to remove Hitler dwindled after his departure and the promotion of Wilhelm Keitel and Alfred Jodl, who were both subsequently made field marshals, and subsequent to that both hanged as war criminals.

In any case a plot to overthrow Hitler would have enraged many if not most Germans. Hitler had destroyed constitutional government, but he had first used it. As one cynical supporter said, he was 'chosen by parliament and confirmed by democracy'. His party may never have won a majority of the vote, but then no party ever did or does in multi-party European democracies, and the National Socialists did win a large plurality in a free election. After that his popularity only increased. Many Germans hated Hitler, but they were either silent or they fled. Jews were increasingly desperate to escape, and many did, to the impoverishment of Germany and the great intellectual and cultural enrichment of the countries where they found refuge. Sigmund Freud was received with honour when he reached London, the conductor Fritz Busch, who wasn't Jewish but detested the National Socialists, came to England and helped create the Glyndebourne opera festival, the Upper West Side of New York became facetiously known as the Fourth Reich for the number of German scholars and writers living there in exile, although the same could have been said of Los Angeles with its own constellation of illustrious emigrés, Thomas Mann among them. But far more Germans chose *innere Emigration*, that characteristic phrase: 'internal emigration' had indeed had been the path taken by so many of the brightest and the best Germans ever since the failure of liberal revolution in 1848, who withdrew into private life and tried to ignore the public horror.

There were no free elections under the Third Reich, but if there had been one in Germany in 1938, the vote for the National Socialists and their leader would without any question have been much higher than the 37 per cent the party had won in 1932. By now, Hitler was far and away the most popular leader Germany had ever had. What Churchill, and all those who have accepted his version ever since, failed to see when decrying 'Munich' is that denunciations of the appeasers turn too easily into extenuations of the Germans. Hitler was not Neville Chamberlain's fault. He was the leader many if not most Germans wanted, and the man whom, as events would show, they were prepared to serve and obey, whatever he ordered them to do.

This was dreadfully illustrated less than seven weeks after Munich by 'Kristallnacht'. In the most savage pogrom to date, a trail of broken glass – *Kristall* – was left as Jewish shops were ransacked, synagogues were burned, and Jews were beaten and killed, while not a single church in Germany opened its doors to the victims. No German could possibly now plead ignorance of Hitler's character or his intentions, not that November, nor eleven weeks later when he promised 'the annihilation of the Jewish race'. Even the former Kaiser, still full of sour Jew-hatred in his Dutch exile, was dismayed by the savagery of Kristallnacht. Chamberlain was appalled. This outrage was a humiliation for him, and he pleaded in Cabinet for a more generous admission of Jewish refugees. The previous prime minister, now Earl Baldwin of Bewdley, came out of retirement to speak on the radio on behalf of a charity for settling Jewish refugees. A humanitarian scheme was devised for rescuing 10,000 Jewish children and bringing them to the West. That might have included the United States, until a poll found that two out of three Americans were opposed to giving those Jewish children refuge in America. In the event, some 9000 came to England, while all of 269 went to America. The 9000 were the famous Kindertransport, whose grateful beneficiaries adorned English life into the next century.

And who were Churchill's 'peace-defending powers'? Within less than two years of Munich he would learn how gravely he had exaggerated the capacity of the French army. In the end Hitler would be crushed by a combination of Russian blood and American money, but in 1938 Soviet Russia and the United States were two sleeping giants asking only to be left alone. What could be expected from them? After the first Moscow trials exterminated the Old Bolsheviks, Stalin's oldest and closest comrades, a much greater and wider terror saw hundreds of thousands shot and millions imprisoned at Vorkuta and Kolyma and a myriad other camps in the vast 'Gulag archipelago'. Then Stalin turned upon the Red Army in a ferocious purge which saw almost every officer over the rank of lieutenant-colonel shot, making it no easier to take Russia seriously as a military power in any immediate future.

As often, Churchill's response was unpredictable. He who had once denounced 'the foul baboonery of Bolshevism' and proposed to crush the new-born Soviet state, now opened private contact with Ivan Maisky, the Russian ambassador in London throughout the 1930s, a posting which probably saved his life. One of the weirdest passages in *The Gathering Storm* mentions the 'military and Old Guard Communist conspiracy to overthrow Stalin ... Thereafter there followed the merciless, *but perhaps not needless*, military and political purge in Russia ...

the Old-Guard Communists ... were certainly filled with jealousy of Stalin who had ousted them ... (italics added).' This was a grotesque travesty of the truth: Stalin was a cruel and paranoid tyrant, morally equivalent to Hitler if in some ways different from him. But then, in the more than ten years between the terror and his book, Churchill had embraced Stalin and even come to like him.

As to the other sleeping giant, having expressed such deep private resentment of the United States before his rediscovery of America in 1929, Churchill was now engaged in writing his history of 'the English-speaking peoples'. But he still knew little about the realities of American life, or politics, or popular sentiment, above all the intensity of isolationist feeling. Churchill didn't know that Chamberlain went to meet Hitler fortified by a signal from Roosevelt, 'Good man,' and that the president then told his ambassador in Rome that there was nothing in the agreement he could object to. And yet there was much else that Churchill could have seen for himself.

In one of his most eccentric appointments, Roosevelt had sent as American ambassador to the Court of St James's Joseph Kennedy, a rich, corrupt, bigoted, antisemitic appeaser. Kennedy now preached reconciliation between the democracies and dictatorships: 'After all, we have to live together.' His son John had come to England but was now back in America, whence he congratulated his father on a speech that, 'while it seemed to be unpopular with the Jews etc. was considered to be very good by everyone who wasn't bitterly anti-Fascist'. Jack Kennedy and his sister Kathleen or 'Kick' enjoyed great popularity in upper-class English society, but Kick grumbled that autumn of 1938 that 'all you can hear or talk about at this point is the future war which is bound to come. Am so darn sick of it.' When war did come, Jack wrote to a friend in London that the American people were united in their determination 'to fight to the last Englishman', another true word in jest.

Any idea that the Americans – either the political leaders or 'we the people' – were eager to fight was a fantasy. Since his inauguration only weeks after Hitler took power, Roosevelt had been overwhelmingly preoccupied with domestic problems, and disinclined to look abroad. In common with many Americans, he disliked Hitler; in common with most Americans, he had no wish to play any part in European conflicts if it could be avoided – or in Pacific conflicts for that matter. Even when Japan invaded China in July 1937 Roosevelt continued to watch with perplexity, aware of the mood of the

American people, and when in October he did speak publicly of the
need to 'quarantine the aggressors', Lippmann recorded that the
speech had 'an exceedingly unfavourable popular reaction'.

From the Armistice in November 1918 to Pearl Harbor in December
1941 the American people remained acutely averse to war. Every
survey showed most of them emphatic in their determination not to
fight in another European conflict. Informed guesses about opinion
became more solid after Gallup began organised polling in 1935. Apart
from the overwhelming majority against another war, a 1937 Gallup
poll found that 70 per cent of Americans thought it had been a mistake
to fight in the Great War, and 71 per cent opposed any American
action against foreign tyrants. More alarmingly, another poll in the
summer of 1938 found that more than half of Americans thought the
Jews had too much power in their country.

All of American society was isolationist and pacifistic, much of it
was nativist and racist, and antisemitism flourished in places low – as
that poll showed – and high. Eleanor Roosevelt, the president's wife,
who became a sainted liberal heroine, described Felix Frankfurter, the
famous judge, as 'an interesting little man, if very Jew', and complained
after being entertained by Churchill's friend Bernard Baruch that 'The
Jew party was appalling,' with its vulgar conversation about furs and
jewellery. Having supported a Jewish *numerus clausus* at Harvard, her
husband later told a Roman Catholic colleague that America was a
Protestant country and that Catholics and Jews must know they were
there on sufferance. This did not mean that the Roosevelts were
crypto-Nazis. It meant that they were characteristic Americans of their
age and class. It was Chamberlain who was right when he said, 'It is
always best to count on nothing from the Americans except words,'
and Churchill who was wrong about potential American support,
deluded by his airy notion of 'the English-speaking peoples'.

What could never be doubted was Churchill's courage and indomitable
will. They were needed. Over the winter following Munich his unpopularity was deeper than ever, so much so that he only narrowly survived
a serious and concerted attempt by the Conservatives in Epping to
disown him as their MP. Had that happened he would have had the
Conservative whip removed and would almost certainly have felt
obliged to resign and stand in a by-election which, given the mood
of the moment, he would very likely have lost and been out of
Parliament when war came.

Not that he had any support to speak of in Parliament. One of the best-informed historians of the Conservative Party in this period has written that throughout the 1930s scarcely any important public figure believed that Churchill would become prime minister, and very few Tories had any close relationship with him. 'No serious pre-war politician was a Churchillian,' Stuart Ball correctly says. 'Churchill's praetorian guard was therefore a rag-tag and bobtail of outsiders and amateurs.' Or to be precise, as 1939 began, in a House of Commons of 615 Members, more than 450 of them from the Conservative Party to which Churchill belonged, his personal parliamentary fellowing consisted of little more than three men, Brendan Bracken, Robert Boothby, and Duncan Sandys: two charlatans and his son-in-law.

Defiant but also morose and restless, the lonely heresiarch sat at Chartwell surrounded by his shady court, while receiving unlikely visitors who came to consult him. Unlikeliest of all was Guy Burgess, whose career had taken him from Eton and Cambridge to the BBC, the British secret service, and the Soviet intelligence agencies, to whom he betrayed his country. His later claim that Churchill had said, 'Here am I, an old man, and without party. What help shall I give?' may be ignored, but two journalists a great deal more eminent than Burgess also visited Chartwell in early 1939, Henry Wickham Steed and Kingsley Martin. Three years older than Churchill, Wickham Steed had been a young correspondent in Berlin* at the time Churchill was in Bangalore with the 4th Hussars. Twenty-five years later he was editor of *The Times*, at the awkward moment when its owner, Lord Northcliffe, was going mad. He then became a widely-read commentator on international affairs. Interviewing Churchill for the popular magazine *Picture Post*, Steed wrote presciently that 'Should some great emergency arise his qualities and experience might then be national assets; and the true greatness, which he has often seemed to miss by a hair's breadth, might by common consent be his.'

As editor of the radical *New Statesman*, Martin personified the Left's anguished confusion, standing 'against fascism and war'. He now asked Churchill, 'In view of the strength and character of the totalitarian states,

---

* When he alone identified the aged Bismarck as the anonymous author of highly controversial newspaper articles; Steed then reported for *The Times* from Vienna for ten years, and in 1913 published *The Hapsburg Monarchy*, still one of the best of foreign correspondents' books.

is it possible to combine the reality of democratic freedom with efficient military organisation?' Churchill replied that democracies should be able to defend themselves without sacrificing the fundamental principles of a free society under a rule of law: 'I am convinced that with adequate leadership, democracy can be a more efficient form of government than Fascism.' More ominously, this was the occasion when he said, 'I do not think we need a great conscript army on the continental model.'

And yet for all of Churchill's isolation, there was another side to the story; for all the cheers that had greeted Chamberlain on his return from Germany, many Englishmen and women in their hearts felt what Léon Blum, the great French socialist leader, said was his private response to Munich: a mixture of shame and relief. Gradually shame came to predominate, especially after Kristallnacht, and with it came also the lurking sense that Churchill might have been right after all: a supposed victory for reason and justice was really a cowardly capitulation to brute force, just as he had said. Vindication came sooner than he might have guessed.

On 15 March Czecho-Slovakia – significantly hyphenated since Munich – fell apart, and with it also fell apart Chamberlain's entire case for an honourable settlement. Slovakia became a German puppet state, 'Czechia' was declared a German protectorate, and Hitler arrived triumphantly in Prague, where the Gestapo was soon busy. Now at last Chamberlain declared that any further aggression would be resisted, in effect a guarantee to Poland. By May, a poll found 56 per cent wanting Churchill back in the Cabinet, and a clamour for his return began in papers as different as the *Daily Telegraph* and *Daily Mirror*, but Chamberlain ignored them.

Despite his new promises, he still hoped to avert war; even when Hitler made fresh demands on Danzig; even after the die was cast with the Molotov–Ribbentrop Pact on 23 August, a non-aggression treaty in which Soviet Socialist Russia and National Socialist Germany became practical allies as well as the spiritual kin they already were. This moment was brilliantly caught by Low's cartoon in the *Evening Standard* of the two leaders beaming and bowing towards one another in courtly fashion over the corpse of freedom, while Hitler says, 'The scum of the earth, I believe?' and Stalin replies with a smile, 'The bloody assassin of the workers, I presume?' This cleared Hitler's path to the east, and on 1 September Germany invaded Poland.

9

'United and with clean hearts'
Downing Street 1940

'I felt as if I were walking with destiny,' Churchill wrote in a famous and exalted passage about the day he took office as prime minister, 10 May 1940, 'and that all my past life had been but a preparation for this hour and for this trial.' Whether or not this really made sense, Churchill surely passed at that moment into the realm of legend, where truth and myth are hard to distinguish, lying almost beyond the reach of history. This was done with words, the power of language, those beguiling words 'walking with destiny' among them. The American broadcaster Edward Murrow said that Churchill had 'mobilised the English language and sent it into battle', words later borrowed by President Kennedy, but that could be put another way, and put better, as Churchill so often did. On 15 June, with France on the verge of collapse, Churchill sent off a flurry of telegrams about the gravity of the situation to Roosevelt, adding drily to a colleague, 'If words counted, we should win this war.' Words did count, and there is nothing mythical about the effect of Churchill's rhetoric. Words didn't win the war, but they were all he had at that moment. Words sustained the British people, and inspired them, as well as many others. Words also misled the British, and others, and have continued to mislead to this day.

His new epic had begun on Saturday 2 September 1939. The House of Commons heard Chamberlain condemn the German assault on Poland, but he didn't say what action he would take, and he sat down amid embarrassed silence. Arthur Greenwood was deputising as Opposition leader for the indisposed Attlee. Sitting behind Chamberlain on the Tory benches was the old Tory imperialist Leo Amery, whom Churchill had known since schooldays at Harrow a lifetime before, when the bumptious Winston had pushed the older boy into the swimming pool. As Greenwood rose to speak, Amery shouted across the chamber, 'Speak for England, Arthur.' Later that day Chamberlain was told by his closest colleagues that he could prevaricate no more. An ultimatum was delivered demanding the withdrawal of German troops, and was ignored by Hitler.

On Sunday, an unhappy prime minister addressed the nation on the radio to say that the country was now at war with Germany. Although Chamberlain was self-pitying – 'You can imagine what a bitter blow it is to me that all my long struggle to win peace has failed' – his last words were said with a feeling and eloquence that might have been Churchill's: 'It is the evil things that we shall be fighting against – brute force, bad faith, injustice, oppression and persecution – and against them I am certain that the right will prevail.' Before the end of the day Chamberlain had bowed to the inevitable in another way and asked Churchill to return to the Cabinet as First Lord of the Admiralty, the office from which he had been ignominiously driven more than a quarter-century before. A signal was sent to the fleet: 'Winston is back' – or so the story has it. No record of the signal has been found, but that scarcely matters since it became part of the great pageant that was now about to unfold, a line endlessly echoed, from the eminent American historian Arthur Marder's book on Churchill at the Admiralty entitled *Winston is Back* to the last scene of the television drama *The Gathering Storm,* where Albert Finney as Churchill arrives at the Admiralty to be told about that signal by a Marine clerk, and replies, 'Yes he bloody well is.'

When the Commons met for a short session that Sunday, Churchill spoke briefly but beautifully:

In this solemn hour it is a consolation to recall and to dwell upon our repeated efforts for peace. All have been ill-starred, but all have been faithful and sincere. This is of the highest moral value – and not only moral value, but practical value – at the present time, because the wholehearted concurrence of scores of millions of men and women, whose co-operation is indispensable and whose comradeship and brotherhood are indispensable, is the only foundation upon which the trial and tribulation of modern war can be endured and surmounted. This moral conviction alone affords that ever-fresh resilience which renews the strength and energy of people in long, doubtful and dark days. Outside, the storms of war may blow and the lands may be lashed with the fury of its gales, but in our own hearts this Sunday morning there is peace. Our hands may be active, but our consciences are at rest.

The significance of this almost forgotten speech would be very great, well into the following century. Now that he was Chamberlain's colleague Churchill couldn't very well dissociate himself from 'our repeated efforts for peace', but he meant what he said. Churchill had never in any way advocated a 'pre-emptive' war. By refraining as long as possible from taking up arms, and only fighting – to use a later distinction – a war of necessity rather than a war of choice, the British had, as he rightly said, gained an incalculable moral advantage: an advantage they would not have enjoyed if war had come a year earlier over Czechoslovakia.

With the German army completing its brutal conquest of Poland, Russia entered that unhappy country from the east in the spirit of the Molotov–Ribbentrop Pact to complete, as Polish leaders had foreseen, 'the fourth partition of Poland'. Meantime, the French and British armies stood still on the French border while the Wehrmacht stood still on the other side. The curious nature of that 'phoney war' is illustrated by the fact that, in the four months from declaration of war to the new year, only three British soldiers died on active service, while more than four thousand people were killed on British roads.* It was much more dangerous to be a pedestrian in the London blackout than a soldier at the front. In France they called this phoney war the *drôle de guerre*, and there was almost a drollery about Churchill's war at this time, with his insatiable capacity for intervening in all matters great and very small.

His own hands were certainly active, as he directed the Navy in all parts of the globe, with its fifty-six cruisers and 180 destroyers, so many of which would be sunk in heroic fighting retreats over the next few years from Norway to Crete to the East Indies, its twelve battle-ships, which was too many, and its six aircraft carriers, which was too few. As Churchill worked sometimes from 7:30 a.m. to 1:30 a.m., besides speaking in Parliament and on the BBC, his immense energy

---

* In all 8272 people were killed in British road accidents in 1939, when there were just over three million motor cars; in 2018 there were more than 35 million cars, and 1784 deaths.

was unleashed in every direction. At one moment he would be giving
operational orders, and then at another telling a caste-ridden Navy
that a man with a Cockney accent shouldn't be prevented from
becoming an officer; at yet another recommending backgammon in
the ward-room ('A better game than cards for the circumstances of
wartime afloat'), then trying to secure an honour for the painter
Walter Sickert who had once painted his portrait. Better still was a
masterly reply to the Duke of Windsor, who had petulantly complained
about some footling breach of protocol. Only Churchill could have
written under guise of sympathy while putting this foolish man so
firmly in his place: 'At a time like this, when everybody is being ordered
about, and millions of men are taken from their homes to fight, it
may be for long years, and many others ruined, it is especially necessary to be defended in one's spirit against external misfortunes.'

In November the Churchills entertained the Chamberlains to dinner
in their flat at the Admiralty. Churchill pumped Chamberlain for
reminiscences of his early days as a not very successful sisal planter
in the Bahamas, and he later wrote, not very convincingly, that Hitler
had reckoned without this doughty pioneer of the far-flung Empire.
Relations between them seemed cordial, although Chamberlain was
shrewd enough to see what Churchill was up to. As soon as he returned
to the Admiralty Churchill began bombarding his colleagues with long
letters and memoranda, which were quite unnecessary since they all
continually met in the little village of Westminster and Whitehall. But
'of course,' Chamberlain told his sister, 'I realise that these letters are
for the purposes of quotation in the Book he will write hereafter.'
That was quite so: from the beginning, Churchill was writing the war
as well as fighting it. He was searching for a strategy but also telling
his own story, in Parliament or on the radio, as others besides
Chamberlain saw. Evelyn Waugh had laid aside his latest novel to join
the Royal Marines and a new elite unit known by what was then the
exotic name of 'Commandos', borrowed from the Boers forty years
back. Or, as Waugh put it in a letter to Lady Diana Cooper at that
first Christmas of the war, he was serving 'in a very fine force which
Winston is raising in order to provide himself with material for his
broadcasts'.

That book 'hereafter' wasn't the immediate problem; the *English-
Speaking Peoples* was. Although Churchill's income tax status was again
hurriedly changed so that he was no longer an 'author by profession',

as he had been for ten years, he was still frantically trying to finish his book, with a team of literary assistants toiling away in a room the First Lord had commandeered at the Admiralty. Years before, when its delivery date had been agreed as 31 December 1939, no one could have guessed what that date would mean. The chairman of Cassell & Co. was Newman Flower, nearly as old as Churchill and no respecter of persons. Churchill was told that he must deliver by the end of the year or face ruinous cancellation of the contract and return of the huge advance. By Christmas Churchill did hand in a manuscript of sorts, but on 27 December, Desmond Flower, Newman's son, bluntly informed him that this draft was unformed, unfinished and unpublishable. Facing financial disaster, Churchill used Brendan Bracken, his loyal supporter and factotum, to bargain with and threaten the publisher by telephone, pleading the emergency and Churchill's importance to the nation. Cassell's were silenced, for their own good as it turned out: they had to wait a long time, but Churchill would prove the best investment they ever made.

After seven months the war suddenly ceased to be phoney or droll. On 4 April, Chamberlain foolishly said that 'Hitler has missed the bus'; four days later the Germans overran Denmark and invaded Norway, at which Churchill, no less foolishly, boasted that 'Every German ship using the Kattegat will be sunk': words falsified as quickly as Chamberlain's. An expeditionary force was sent to Norway, but it was doomed almost as soon as it landed, one more unhappy 'amphibious' operation to Churchill's name, ending with an ignominious evacuation of the last British forces from Narvik on 28 May, by which time Norway was forgotten as well as lost.

On 7 May, Chamberlain opened a two-day debate in the Commons on the failure in Norway. Churchill did his best to defend the government, and he knew very well that he bore as much responsibility as anyone for the affair, if not more. But the mood had changed. Sir Roger Keyes, a naval hero of the last war, donned his uniform as Admiral of the Fleet to denounce Chamberlain, and Amery echoed Cromwell as he told the prime minister, 'In the name of God, go!' Just at this moment Hitler struck in the west, invading Holland, Belgium and France, and Chamberlain thought that the new crisis was no time for him to resign. Many MPs were in uniform, like Ronald Cartland, an idealistic young Tory who came home to Westminster to vote against Chamberlain, before he returned to his regiment in France, and was killed on the retreat to Dunkirk. The twenty-five-year-old John Profumo, also in Territorial Army uniform, had only just become a Tory MP at a by-election. He, too, voted against the government. The next day he was hauled before the Chief Whip, Captain Margesson, who gave him a magnificent dressing down: 'You utterly contemptible little shit ... for the rest of your life you will be ashamed of what you did last night.' But time had run out for Margesson.

And for Chamberlain also. Labour said they wouldn't serve in a coalition under him, and Chamberlain recognised that he had to give way. An attempt to make Halifax prime minister in his place came to nothing, to the regret of many Tories, and also of the king, who told Chamberlain that he had been treated badly, and said of Halifax, 'I was sorry not to have him as PM.' At six in the afternoon on 10 May Churchill was summoned to the Palace. Another cinematic travesty, in *Darkest Hour*, has the king stuttering oddly, 'It is my duty to invite you to take up the position of prime minister of this United Kingdom.' In Churchill's own plausible and amusing version, the king asked whimsically if Churchill knew why he had been sent for. 'Adopting his mood, I replied, "Sir, I simply couldn't imagine why." He laughed, and then said "I want to ask you to form a Government." I said I would certainly do so.'

That evening Churchill began forming a new ministry – and he began creating a new narrative, beginning with the highly dubious words, 'Eleven years in the political wilderness had freed me from ordinary Party antagonisms.' That was true only in the sense that during those years he had wilfully excluded himself from office, and had been distrusted by Tories as much as by Labour. Attlee now became Lord Privy Seal and deputy prime minister in effect, though not formally until a reshuffle in February 1942. Bevin, who had not long before said that Labour would never forgive Churchill for his crimes against the working class, became Minister of Labour. Sinclair, Churchill's old second-in-command at 'Plugstreet', became Secretary of State for Air, where he would be responsible for the most distinctive, and contentious, British campaign of the war.

For years Churchill had been conscious that no one was listening to him. Now everyone was listening to him, albeit reluctantly in the case of some of his old foes and critics. He gave his first great speech as prime minister to the Commons on 13 May: 'I have nothing to offer but blood, toil, tears and sweat ...You ask, what is our aim? I can answer in one word, it is victory, victory at all costs, victory in spite of victory however long and hard the road may be; for without victory, there is no survival. Let that be realised; no survival for the British Empire.' These were grand words, but their ultimate import was far from clear at the time. What 'all costs' would mean was a war waged with many morally repulsive compromises, ending with Churchill's country an enfeebled and impoverished dependency of the United States, with half of Europe under Soviet domination, and indeed with 'no survival for the British Empire'.

What immediately faced Churchill was military disaster. In a brilliant coup, the German army broke through in the Ardennes forest into France and drove deep between the allied armies, forcing the British Expeditionary Force back to the Channel. Two years before, Churchill had written that the tank, which he had once sponsored, was no longer a weapon of importance: 'I, personally, doubt whether it will ever see again the palmy days of 1918 ... the anti-tank rifle and the anti-tank gun have made such great strides that the poor tank cannot carry enough thick skin to stay up to them.' He had also said that 'so far as the fighting troops are concerned, aircraft are an additional complication rather than a decisive weapon'. As the German tanks smashed through the Allied armies, they had palmier days than ever, as did the air weapon, notably the Stuka dive-bomber whose mere sight and sound, a high-pitched scream as it dived, played a decisive part in further demoralising Allied troops.

In 1938 Churchill had written 'How Wars of the Future Will Be Waged', confidently predicting that armies would have 'great prepared lines of fortifications which it will be very difficult for the other army to break through ... the idea that enormous masses of armoured vehicles and tanks will be able to overrun these fortifications will probably turn out to be a disappointment'. He later sheepishly admitted that he hadn't grasped the revolution effected 'by the incursion of a mass of fast-moving armour. I knew about it, but it had not altered my convictions as it should have done.' Nor had it, but this was a man who had staked his whole claim on his gifts of prophecy.

Before the rescue from Dunkirk was accomplished, Churchill warned of 'heavy tidings' that could yet come. They might have been heavier still, and the old Churchill hadn't changed his colours. Even when the main British Expeditionary Force was doomed to evacuation at best, Churchill stubbornly insisted on landing another large British force in France, to the west of the Seine. Most of these managed to escape home, without firing a shot and leaving behind almost all their equipment, but not all were saved. The 51st Highland Division had been detached from the larger BEF and placed under the French Third Army before they were cut off by the German offensive. After a fighting retreat, the 51st reached the port of Saint-Valéry-en-Caux whence they could have retired west if Churchill had given the order, but he didn't, and more than 10,000 men were trapped there, to be taken into captivity on 12 June,* nearly a third of the more than 30,000 British soldiers who became prisoners in the short campaign.

On 27 May the evacuation from Dunkirk began but it seemed unlikely that many would escape. When Churchill met a larger group of ministers from outside the War Cabinet on 28 May he said, in electrifying words, 'Of course, whatever happens at Dunkirk we shall fight on.' But the miracle came about. By 3 June, the last of 388,226 men were brought back, most in destroyers but some in the 'little ships': river ferries, fishing smacks and pleasure launches. In the course of several brave flights Churchill made to France to rally its despondent leaders, it became clear that the battle was lost, although more than 100,000 French soldiers would be killed before the end.

Quite why it was lost so quickly and calamitously is still debated, and far from obvious. 'The proximate reason the Third Republic fell,' the historian Alan Allport has asserted, 'was that its army failed to mount an effective counter-attack against the German bridgeheads over the Meuse between 14 and 16 May,' and for what it may be worth, computer simulations of the battle tend to give victory to the French and British. The great French historian Marc Bloch had served in the army in the last war and was an officer again in 1940; he later joined the Resistance, was captured by the Germans, tortured and shot, after writing the powerful short book *L'Étrange Défaite* (*Strange Defeat*) about 1940. 'Our leaders, or those who acted in their names, were incapable of thinking in terms of a new war,' Bloch wrote. 'The German victory was, essentially, an intellectual victory.' That was so, and not only was Churchill's 'The peace of Europe dwells under the shield of the French

---

* The late Brian McIrvine, an actor by trade and my wife's uncle, had been commissioned in the Seaforth Highlanders just in time to go to France with the 51st Division, and to spend five years in prison camp.

army' now an embarrassing memory, he also had been incapable of thinking in terms of a new war.

A bitterly divided Third Republic came to its ignominious end on 22 June when the aged Marshall Pétain signed an armistice on humiliating terms in the same railway carriage in which the Germans had signed the previous armistice in 1918. One Frenchman refused to accept this verdict. On one of his visits to France, Churchill met Brigadier-General Charles de Gaulle, and later claimed to have thought, in a Shakespearean phrase, 'Here is the Constable of France.' De Gaulle escaped to London, declared over the BBC on 18 June that 'France had lost a battle but not a war,' set about creating 'Free France' as a challenge to the new collaborationist government at Vichy, and began building a myth as beguiling and misleading as anything of Churchill's.

On 4 June, Churchill spoke again, using a sentence President Bush the Younger would borrow more than sixty years later: 'We shall not flag or fail. We shall go on to the end. We shall fight in France, we shall fight on the seas and oceans, we shall fight with growing confidence and growing strength in the air, we shall defend our island, whatever the cost may be. We shall fight on the beaches, we shall fight on the landing grounds, we shall fight in the fields and in the streets, we shall fight in the hills; we shall never surrender.' Some of his speeches were broadcast after he had delivered them in Parliament, and George Orwell noticed that ordinary Londoners were affected by them, even when puzzled by the more high-flown passages. Not that everyone did hear every speech. Just as many Frenchmen later claimed to have heard de Gaulle broadcasting from London that summer, when it's certain that only a tiny handful did, many British people thought they could remember hearing him say 'we shall fight on the beaches' on the radio, when in fact it wasn't broadcast at the time, and Churchill only recorded the speech after the war.

All the same, the effect was real, and had an explanation. 'He is a brilliant but wayward child,' Chamberlain had said in his perceptive letter of 1928. 'One doesn't often come across a real man of genius. Winston is such a man and he has les défauts de ses qualités.' Not only was that exactly right, for most of his career the defects were displayed again and again: the bare-knuckled pugnacity which so often looked irresponsible, the restless originality which seemed unbalanced. Now, for one extraordinary moment, all his defects became qualities. All his past follies, errors and transgressions ceased to matter. Churchill was like the stopped clock which is bound to be right every twelve hours, and this was that moment: for once he told the right time. His own words about Haig now applied to Churchill himself: 'He had often been wrong in the past. He was right in the end.'

With all his foolish earlier words of admiration about the Führer, he now intuitively understood that Hitler's National Socialist regime was 'a monstrous tyranny, never surpassed in the dark lamentable catalogue of human crime', whose triumph would mean 'a new dark age made more sinister, and perhaps more protracted, by the lights of a perverted science'. There may even have been some uncanny affinity between Churchill and Hitler, although light against dark, rather as Wotan in Wagner's *Ring* calls himself 'Licht-Alberich' against his evil antagonist 'Schwarz-Alberich'. Both Englishman and German were fervent nationalists with a passionate belief in their countries' greatness, both believed in 'race' and the superiority of some races over others. Indeed, Hitler horribly magnified some of the worst and most repellent sides of Churchill, his belief in 'higher-grade races' and in the need to purify the racial stock through eugenic breeding. Both men were inspired by a demonic sense of providence and personal destiny, both had more than a touch of megalomania. And it may even be that such affinity enabled Churchill to understand Hitler better than more normal people could.

For so long, Churchill's piratical indifference to convention, his defiance of the rules, his disreputable record as a political renegade, had counted against him. Now they, too, were advantages. As Orwell said, he might be the grandson of a duke, but Winston Churchill was not a gentleman. That was also in his favour. For years England had been governed by decent if inadequate men, who were quite incapable of dealing with someone like Hitler, or even recognising his full terrifying nature. An honourable Conservative or respectable democratic socialist could not have shown the necessary ruthlessness that the rascally Churchill did. Even his voice helped. As we can hear from recordings, most of the ruling elite then spoke with a strangulated accent sometimes called 'educated' or 'received', which had become the official voice of the BBC, and which now sounds slightly weird; an accent which Orwell rightly said was disliked by those English people who didn't speak with it, and not much liked by those who did. But Churchill, 'too old to have acquired the modern "educated" accent,' as Orwell observed, 'speaks with the Edwardian upper-class twang who to the average man's ear sounds like cockney.'

And his detachment from reality was itself also now an advantage. Churchill had never heard of Antonio Gramsci, the Communist organiser and brilliant political writer imprisoned by Mussolini, but he perfectly exemplified Gramsci's maxim, 'Pessimism of the intellect, optimism of the will.' Or in Churchill's own private phrase, 'KBO': keep buggering on. That was his greatest contribution to ultimate victory. 'I have always believed what I wanted to believe,' he had said. With superb optimism of the will, he now wanted to believe that England could survive against Hitler's omnipotent Reich, when pessimism of the intellect, or practical evidence, suggested otherwise. His capacity for willing the ends but not the means, and taking the word for the deed, had led to disaster before and would do so again, but now they were essential: he willed the end of victory at a time when there were no means at all to achieve it. The angry defiance which had so often been grossly inappropriate – directed against every party in turn, against Ulster Unionists and then Irish rebels, against British working men and against Indian nationalists – for once found a wholly fitting object.

Then again, Churchill's inspirational quality that year also meant that he was constructing his own reality. Even his exalted phrase about 'walking with destiny', and his claim that his whole life had been a preparation for that hour and that trial, were highly dubious. To quote Michael Howard once more, the puzzle is not that Churchill's advice was ignored for so long, 'but how it was that a man with so unpromising a background and so disastrous a track record could emerge in 1940 as the saviour of his country'. There had been no conspiracy to silence a great statesman or ignore a wise seer: 'his arrogance, his egocentricity, his flamboyance, his emotionalism, his unpredictability', not to mention his horrible associates and his self-indulgent way of life, had all made him in some ways an outsider, until the country, or at any rate a small group of politicians, 'turned to him in despair because there was no one else to whom they could turn'.

Now that disastrous, disliked and distrusted outsider was transmuted by some strange alchemy into a national hero. And he could rewrite his own story. Looking back later at his first months of the war as First Lord, when he delighted to speak in Parliament and on the radio about the Royal Navy's triumphs, he wrote that 'I had a good tale to tell.' Those words offer the key to Churchill. His whole life had been spent telling tales, spinning yarns, speaking and writing stories, often questionably and unconvincingly. It was not just that so many people regarded him as a failure and that his life had seemed a fascinating but sorry waste. More than that, he had lost the argument, again and again.

He had failed to persuade others that his desertion of the Tories for the Liberals had been a matter of principle rather than of ambition. He had failed to persuade others that Gallipoli had been a brilliant but unlucky enterprise. He had failed to persuade others that the advent of a Labour government would be a national catastrophe, he had failed to persuade others that the return to the gold standard was wise, he had failed to persuade others not to grant any measure of self-government to India, and he had signally failed to persuade others that Edward VIII should be allowed to keep his throne as well as Mrs Simpson. Given this record, it wasn't so surprising that he also failed to persuade others of the need for resistance to Germany.

Now in that amazing summer he had new tales to tell, and new arguments to win. Many of them were what Giovanni Giolitti had called the 'beautiful national legends' that sustain a country; they were *fables convenues*, necessary myths, and they really were needed at the time. Churchill was weaving his own beautiful legends. At the time they were essential; it was only later that their consequences would become so dangerous and damaging.

First was the tale of national unity. Churchill's very first words in the House of Commons as prime minister, at the beginning of his 'blood, toil ...' speech, were moving the resolution 'That this House welcomes the formation of a Government representing the united and inflexible resolve of the nation to prosecute the war with Germany to a victorious conclusion.' He later declared, 'Had I at this juncture faltered at all in the leading of the nation, I should have been hurled out of office. I was sure that every Minister was ready to be killed quite soon, and have all his family and possessions destroyed, rather than give in.' That was given pictorial expression in Low's cartoon of the new government, Churchill right marker in the front rank, Attlee, Bevin and Morrison for Labour as well as Eden and Chamberlain, rolling up their shirtsleeves as they march, with the caption, 'All behind you, Winston.'

This was fine stuff, but far from the whole truth. Several senior ministers still wavered after Churchill became prime minister. For the time being he very shrewdly didn't purge the old appeasers, apart from Hoare, who was sent with a *hasta la vista* to be ambassador in Madrid, as well as the lamentable Duke of Windsor, who was despatched further still as Governor of the Bahamas. By the end of the year Halifax had also most reluctantly been exiled, as ambassador in Washington, while Simon was kicked upstairs as Lord Chancellor. Most importantly, Chamberlain remained in the government. And yet some of them were incorrigible in their pessimism, still keener to discuss peace than fighting on in what seemed a hopeless cause. Indeed, before the deliverance from Dunkirk was certain, even Churchill talked for a time of concessions that might have to be made to Germany.

His appointment disgusted Tories like R.A. Butler, Halifax's Under-Secretary at the Foreign Office, and a committed appeaser. 'Rab' lamented that 'the good clean tradition of English politics ... had been sold to the greatest adventurer of modern political history,' the 'half-breed American', while he and 'Chips' Channon, the rich socialite MP, and Lord Dunglass, who had been Chamberlain's Parliamentary Private Secretary, drank a toast in champagne to Chamberlain, 'the king over the water'. These were not marginal figures. Butler would introduce a famous Education Act in 1944, before serving as Chancellor in Churchill's postwar government, and would twice nearly become prime minister, pipped on the second occasion in 1963 by Dunglass, or Lord Home as he by then was.

Again, 'It fell to me in these coming days and months, to express the British people's sentiments on suitable occasions,' Churchill later said. 'This I was able to do because they were mine also. There was a white glow, overpowering, sublime, which ran through our island from end to end.' That was also untrue, in so far as it can be said about something as elusive as popular sentiment. The point can be made by literary comparison, between the opening years of two wars. In 1914–15 Rupert Brooke had seen his generation 'as swimmers into cleanness leaping, / Glad from a world grown old and cold and weary,' while Julian Grenfell wrote 'Into Battle', much anthologised at the time but now even harder to stomach: 'And he is dead who will not fight; / And who dies fighting has increase.' No poet wrote anything like that in 1939–40, not least because Brooke and Grenfell were both dead within a year of writing, and the zeal for battle they expressed had been washed away by the blood and mud of the Somme. We know from newspapers, polls, diaries and Mass Observation reports that the mood of the British people in the summer of 1940 was defiant, sullen or dogged, but not 'sublime' or exalted.

Linked with that was another myth, which others now joined Churchill in propagating. The runaway British bestseller in the summer of 1940 was a polemic called *Guilty Men* by 'Cato', a ferocious indictment of appeasement and the 'men of Munich'. It was published in July and before the end of August had gone through seventeen printings and sold more than 200,000 copies. *Guilty Men* is a despicable little book, written in the worst sort of sabre-rattling style – 'this land of Britain is rich in heroes' – which immediately suggests the work of a non-combatant, as was the case. One of the few heroes of the book is Beaverbrook, which might also suggest that its author were in his employ, as was again the case. 'Cato' was in fact three people, Michael Foot, Peter Howard and Frank Owen, all civilians, and all journalists working for Churchill's odious crony. Foot would shortly be made editor of Beaverbrook's *Evening Standard*.

Amid the sycophantic praise heaped on Beaverbrook, they don't mention that he had been an arch-appeaser, and that the slogan 'Britain will not be involved in a European war this year or next' ran every day across the masthead of the *Daily Express* through late 1938 and much of 1939. Venomous and utterly one-sided, the spirit of *Guilty Men* is set by the epigraph, about 'the people' who disrupted the National Convention in France in 1793 and did not want 'a lot of phrases. They demand a dozen guilty men,' or scapegoats to be sacrificed to the blood-lust of the mob. As an historical account of the prewar years *Guilty Men* is worthless, but it was very important in blackening the names of the appeasers, and it was most convenient for Churchill that this assault on men who were now his colleagues should come from a distant source.

Then there was the tale of victory. 'You ask, what is our aim?' Churchill said in that first great speech as prime minister. 'I can answer in one word: It is victory, victory at all costs, victory in spite of all terror, victory, however long and hard the road may be.' This was surely sublime optimism of the will. After the fall of France Churchill knew better than anyone that, although he might hope against hope for his country's survival, any idea that it could defeat Germany was fantastic. One apocryphal fable circulating in pubs and factories held that, at the words 'we shall fight on the landing grounds, we shall fight in the fields and in the streets', there had been a hubbub of approval from MPs, under which Churchill had turned and said to Attlee *sotto voce*, 'We'll fight them with bloody bottles, which is all we've got.'

Had he said it, he wouldn't have been so far wrong. Words were mobilised because they were all he had. On the quite different subject of communal canteens for people who had been bombed out, Churchill suggested that they should be called 'British restaurants', since 'Everybody associates the word "restaurant" with a good meal, and they may as well have the name if they cannot get anything else.' That was very much his general principle. You might as well think that victory was attainable, even if on any objective consideration it wasn't. No doubt the British people wanted their country to win, and admired Churchill, but not a few people also saw that 'he thinks that a speech is a substitute for victory,' as one listener put it.

When Clementine said years later that Churchill had become a legend, she added, 'I think it was those speeches in 1940,' and so it was. If the speeches achieved immortality it wasn't by accident. After reading a Foreign Office draft later in the year, Churchill regretted that 'The ideas set forth appeared to me to err in trying to be too clever, to enter into refinements of policy unsuited to the tragic simplicity and grandeur of the times and the issues at stake.' No one could miss the tragic simplicity and grandeur of his own speeches. While he was happy to use ghostwriters for much of his journalism and books, he would never have imagined using a speechwriter.* The speeches were all his own work, and he treated them as literary compositions, dictated first, typed and revised and retyped, often in short lines so that they looked like blank verse, or 'like the printing of the Psalms', as they struck Lord Halifax.

He drew on his wide reading, with his very retentive memory, and he was a veritable Rossini of rhetoric, forever reusing his own material, as well as other people's. In January he said, when defying Hitler, 'Let us go forward together and put these grave matters to the test,' words

---

* Jock Colville, later Sir John, served as Churchill's assistant private secretary for much of the war, when he learned to draft less important missives in the Churchillian style, and ten years later as his principal private secretary, when he sometimes did draft speeches, although never those Churchill gave in Parliament.

he had first spoken in 1914 when defying the Ulster Unionists, and the Tories, his once and future party. In his first speech as prime minister, short as it is, there are two borrowings, from 'old Clemenceau', as Churchill called him, and from Garibaldi. Clemenceau had told the French Assembly on 20 November 1917, 'Finally you ask what are my war aims? Gentlemen, they are very simple: Victory!'; Churchill said, 'You ask, What is our aim? I can answer in one word: It is victory.' Garibaldi had told his recruits in 1849, 'I offer no pay, no quarters, no provisions. I offer hunger, thirst, battles and death';* Churchill said, 'I have nothing to offer but blood, toil, tears and sweat.' His famous tribute on 20 August to the fighter pilots waging the Battle of Britain – 'Never in the field of human conflict was so much owed by so many to so few' – used a rhetorical device – 'Never ... so many ... so few' – he had employed at least six times in speeches since 1899.

Even when speaking extempore in private, addressing his ministers on 28 May, he used rousing words which must have been a conscious or unconscious echo of an ancient source. 'If this long island story of ours is to end at last,' Churchill told his colleagues, 'let it end only when each of us lies choking in his own blood upon the ground.' In his Third Philippic of 20 December 44 BC, Cicero had said, 'And if now ... that worst of fates shall befall the republic, then, as brave gladiators take care to perish with honour, let us too ... fall with dignity rather than live as slaves in ignominy.' Churchill's Classical studies had not prospered at Harrow, but during his self-education in Bangalore he had read Cicero in translation, and that passage must have lurked at the back of his mind. Altogether he was waging a very literary war, not merely mobilising language for battle but deliberately constructing a great epic, with himself as the hero and the British people as the chorus.

'We are fighting by ourselves alone,' Churchill said on 14 April, pointedly adding, 'but not for ourselves alone.' This was given visual form in another famous Low cartoon, of a Tommy on the English clifftops above the breaking sea, punching his fist defiantly upwards with the words, 'Very well, alone.' But of course Great Britain was anything but alone. There were the Dominions, Australia, Canada, New Zealand and South Africa, who had all entered the war freely

---

* 'Non offro nè paga, nè quartiere, nè provvigioni. Offro fame, sete, marce forzate, battaglie e morte.'

after parliamentary votes, who possessed vast material resources, and whose combined citizenry of well over twenty million,* when added to the British, made them roughly equal to Germany in population. Their soldiers served in most of the British campaigns of the war, with Australians fighting in the Western Desert and New Zealanders in Crete, while many Canadians flew – and many died – in Bomber Command.

Then there was India, which didn't enjoy democratic government but whose army serving the king-emperor was entirely manned by volunteers, and swelled from 200,000 at the beginning of the war to 2.5 million at its end. Many Indians were fighting bravely for a Raj which was about to expire, though maybe also fighting indirectly for a new nation (or nations) to come. And there were the conquered nations of Europe, whose governments and fighting forces found exile in England, along with their monarchs. The formidable Queen Wilhelmina of the Netherlands had already reigned for fifty years since she had inherited the throne as a girl; surveying the exiled leaders in London, Churchill called her the only man among them, and she was the first woman since the Middle Ages admitted to the Order of the Garter.

In Norway, King Haakon VII wouldn't collaborate with the German invaders and refused to appoint their chosen figurehead Vidkun Quisling as prime minister. They appointed him anyway and gave the world a synonym for treason. Haakon left aboard HMS *Devonshire*, and wouldn't see his country again for five years. Meantime the Norwegian resistance gave heroic and invaluable service to the Allies, whose resources were augmented by the large Norwegian merchant marine. Czech pilots helped win the Battle of Britain, and a Polish division would raise their red and white flag on the ruins of Monte Cassino in 1944. The role of the Free French was more ambiguous, for all de Gaulle's own heroic national legend, but one day French and North African troops would also be fighting the Wehrmacht.

Along with this ran the contradictory tale of 'the English-speaking peoples', whose history Churchill had just been writing. After Dunkirk, Churchill believed, apart from the illusory hopes he pinned on bombing, that Germany could be defeated only with the United States

---

* In the case of South Africa, both parliamentary vote and population bore the qualification 'whites only'.

as an ally. His 'we shall fight on the beaches' speech ended with a peroration: 'and even if, which I do not for a moment believe, this Island or a large part of it were subjugated and starving, then our Empire beyond the seas, armed and guarded by the British Fleet, would carry on the struggle, until, in God's good time, the New World, with all its power and might, steps forth to the rescue and the liberation of the old.' Later, in his 'never in the field of human conflict' speech, he ended with another peroration in which he mentioned the possibility of granting the Americans naval and air facilities in Newfoundland and the West Indies, which came to pass as the 'Lease' of Lend-Lease.

Then he claimed that 'these two great organisations of the English-speaking democracies, the British Empire and the United States, will have to be somewhat mixed up together in some of their affairs for mutual and general advantage. For my own part, looking out upon the future, I do not view the process with any misgivings. I could not stop it if I wished; no one can stop it. Like the Mississippi, it just keeps rolling along. Let it roll. Let it roll on full flood, inexorable, irresist-ible, benignant, to broader lands and better days.' All in all, Churchill spoke throughout 1940 and 1941 as if the United States were already to all intents an ally, and that Roosevelt was anxiously waiting to join the fight, which was simply untrue.

When Churchill told the Commons on 4 June that 'We shall fight on the beaches, we shall fight on the landing grounds, we shall fight in the fields and in the streets, we shall fight in the hills,' he could only have meant fighting against a German invasion of England. It never came, and must remain one of the many hypothetical ques-tions of the war, but it may never have been very likely. Hitler gave orders to prepare for a potential cross-Channel operation, but the difficulties were enormous. Had a large German army landed in England it might well have conquered the country, but first it had to land. In June 1944, the Allies crossed to Normandy after years of planning, by which point the Germans were in full retreat on the eastern front, and the Allies enjoyed total control of sea and air, as well as huge superiority in armaments. None of that was true of the Germans in 1940.

At the moment he used the phrase, Churchill clearly believed that 'the Battle of Britain' would be fought on British soil, but now it meant a war in the air. It began as an attack by the Luftwaffe on RAF airfields, which provided an epic of its own for generations to come, an image retained on the national retina ever after and captured by the painter Paul Nash of the skies of Kent and Sussex criss-crossed by Spitfires and Hurricanes chasing German Junker bombers and Messerschmidt 109 fighters. In September, Goering, head of the Luftwaffe, made a foolish mistake when, in frustration, he turned from bombing RAF aerodromes, which had come close to success, to night bombing of London and then other cities. But then, supposing that the RAF had been apparently defeated, the Germans well knew the overwhelming strength of the Royal Navy. Even so, the invasion which might come (but never did) became part of the national epic. Church bells hung silent, only to be rung when the invader came, while Churchill cheerfully proposed the sanguinary slogan 'You can always take one with you.'

There were other fateful steps taken by Churchill that summer which would set the course of events for years to come, sometimes summed up by three-word phrases. A pile of red stickers was printed for the prime minister to place on his missives, shouting 'Action this day', and he ordered many an action on many a day, well-considered or otherwise. Shortly after the fall of France he took 'a hateful decision, the most unnatural and painful in which I have ever been concerned', to neutralise the French fleet in the Mediterranean by any means necessary, persuasion or violence. At the Algerian port of Mers-el-Kébir French ships were bombarded and two battleships destroyed with great loss of life. This action was detested by Admiral Sir James Somerville, who was ordered to carry it out, and was almost certainly unnecessary. The French commander wasn't given the clear choice of sailing to a neutral port, and when the Germans occupied Vichy France in November 1942, the officers of the French fleet at Toulon scuttled their ships before they could fall into German hands. But still, when Churchill announced this perfidious coup de Jarnac in the Commons, he received ringing Tory applause for the first time: 'All joined in solemn stentorian accord.' One other man who admired Churchill's decision was de Gaulle, which might seem surprising, but he always respected ruthless 'sacred egoism'.

'Collar the lot' was Churchill's brutal instruction to intern 'enemy aliens' in the form of German or Austrian citizens, who were almost all Jews or other refugees from a regime they hated. Having ordered their internment, Churchill then pretended he hadn't, brazenly telling Parliament in August that 'the Fifth Column danger' no longer existed if it ever had: 'I always thought it exaggerated.'

Another three words were still more ominous. Hugh Dalton was a formidable if improbable and unlovable figure. 'Canon Dalton's horrid little boy', as Queen Victoria had called him, was the son of a clergyman who had been a tutor to the royal children at Windsor, educated at Eton and Cambridge, an economist by profession and a socialist by conviction. Dalton had served as a Gunner officer in the Great War and had been one of the few Labour politicians who had opposed appeasement and his own party's pacifism. In June, the Special Operations Executive was created to foment resistance and insurrection in the occupied continent, and Churchill chose Dalton to head it, with the order to 'Set Europe ablaze!'

Never in the field of human conflict have so few words caused so much suffering to so little effect. One of Churchill's most persistent delusions was that people longed to be free of despotic rule and were willing to pay any price to achieve their freedom. Over the next four or more years large resources were lavished on the SOE and the Political Warfare Executive. With the highly ambiguous exception of Yugoslavia, resistance movements played an insignificant part in the defeat of Germany, and the extreme savagery of German retribution right up until the end of the war was an awful price to pay for so little achieved. The one undoubted consequence of encouraging those resistance movements was indirect, and certainly unintended by Churchill: it greatly strengthened the Communists in Italy and France as well as the Balkans.

But the most ominous words of all were those here italicised, in a letter Churchill wrote to Beaverbrook on 8 July: 'There is one thing that will bring Hitler down, and that is an *absolutely devastating, exterminating attack* by very heavy bombers on the Nazi homeland, without which I do not see a way through.' Chilling as these words were, they were of a piece with Mers-el-Kébir, 'collar the lot', and 'set Europe ablaze': all part of Churchill's determination to show that he really meant it, and would stop at nothing in pursuit of 'victory at all costs'. And yet he remained a mass of contradictions. In September he decried 'These cruel, wanton, indiscriminate bombings of London', forgetting for the moment his own wish for 'devastating, exterminating attacks' against Germany. It was only later that the costs came to be counted: strategic, political and moral.

If the British were a united people, and if the summer of 1940 really was a finest hour, one reason is easily forgotten. For five months, from 10 May until 9 October, Churchill was a true national chief above party, as the head of a government which included the leaders of the great political parties. There was the Labour leader Attlee, who served Churchill as his deputy for five years with a loyalty and decency not always repaid. There was Sinclair of the Liberals as Air Secretary. And there was Chamberlain, who displayed even greater loyalty by remaining in office under his successor, with the nominal role of Lord President of the Council. Had he sulked like Asquith in 1916 and refused to serve he might have split the Conservatives as the Liberals had been split, and made life very difficult for Churchill.

But Chamberlain was still Conservative party leader, and even expected to continue in the post, seeing Churchill as a 'hostilities only' premier, like a National Service conscript, who was there for the necessary but temporary work of winning the war, and Churchill initially agreed, telling Chamberlain in May that 'as Prime Minister of a National government formed on the widest basis, and comprising the three parties, I feel that it would be better for me not to undertake the Leadership of any one political Party'. Yet by the late summer, Chamberlain was diagnosed with bowel cancer and underwent an operation, but too late. Only on 9 September, six days before Fighter Command enjoyed its most successful day against the Luftwaffe, now marked as Battle of Britain Day on 15 September, did Chamberlain recognise the truth: 'I know that [a political return] is out of the question.' His prognosis was soon terminal; he resigned from the government on 30 September and as Conservative leader on 4 October.

Now Churchill was determined to seize the prize which had so long eluded him. Clementine was much less enthusiastic. He might have abandoned the Liberal sympathies which he had proclaimed when they met and married, but she hadn't. She voted Liberal at least until 1945,* and the dislike so many Tories felt for her husband was

---

* Since the Churchills never lived in the parliamentary constituencies he represented, she never voted for a Liberal standing against her husband in person.

still warmly reciprocated by her. She told Churchill wisely that, if he became Tory leader, he would alienate the working class and lose the unique position he had enjoyed since May as 'the voice of the whole nation'. As usual his will prevailed. He had become prime minister in unique, unprecedented and unrepeatable circumstances, and he became leader of the Conservative Party on 9 October also in the only circumstances in which he could ever have achieved this. He would have been surprised – and Clementine would have been appalled – to know that he would lead the party for nearly fifteen years.

A sad story ended when Chamberlain died on 9 November. In the Commons three days later Churchill delivered an elegy. He couldn't very well say that Chamberlain had been right at the time of Munich, and it would have been offensive (as well as politically inadvisable) for Churchill to say merely that he had been right and Chamberlain wrong. He dealt with this in one of the greatest and most moving speeches he ever gave:

> In paying a tribute of respect and of regard to an eminent man who has been taken from us, no one is obliged to alter the opinions which he has formed or expressed upon issues which have become a part of history ... It is not given to human beings, happily for them, for otherwise life would be intolerable, to foresee or to predict to any large extent the unfolding course of events. In one phase men seem to have been right, in another they seem to have been wrong.... History with its flickering lamp stumbles along the trail of the past, trying to reconstruct its scenes, to revive its echoes, and kindle with pale gleams the passion of former days ...
>
> It fell to Neville Chamberlain in one of the supreme crises of the world to be contradicted by events, to be disappointed in his hopes, and to be deceived and cheated by a wicked man. But what were these hopes in which he was disappointed? What were these wishes in which he was frustrated? What was that faith that was abused? They were surely among the most noble and benevolent instincts of the human heart – the love of peace, the toil for peace, the strife for peace, the pursuit of peace.

He then reiterated what he had said on the first day of the war. The British knew, and so should all others, that 'However dark may be the clouds which overhang our path,' it was thanks to that 'toil for peace' that 'we were guiltless of the bloodshed, terror and misery which have engulfed so many lands and peoples, and yet seek new victims still.... Long and hard, hazardous years lie before us, but at least we entered upon them united and with clean hearts.' Although Churchill said privately and puckishly, 'I could have done it the other way round,' that didn't mean that his words were insincere. For all his opposition to appeasement, that farewell to Chamberlain, and the speech he had given on 3 September 1939, were together a complete repudiation of pre-emptive war.

Now he was leading a country united and with clean hearts in a war the British had not wanted but knew they must win. Churchill faced a greater challenge than ever. In so many ways the summer of 1940 set the course of British history for the next five years – or maybe eighty.

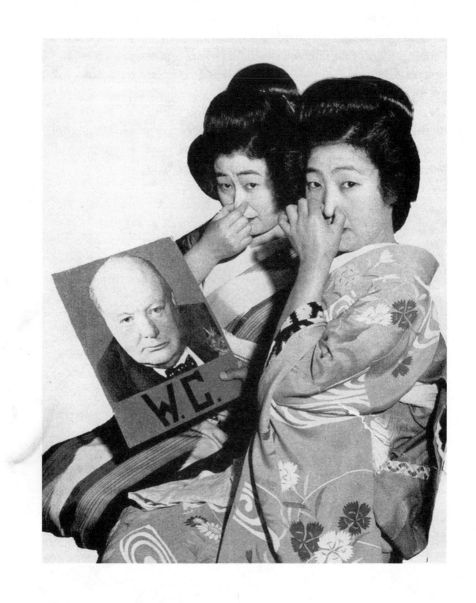

10

'Unpleasant surprises'
Placentia Bay 1941

After London was bombed every night from 7 September to 2 November, the Luftwaffe moved on to attack provincial towns and western ports, before returning to the capital, and on the night of 29 December the historic City of London was badly hit by incendiary bombs. Just to the north of St Paul's Cathedral was the ancient centre of London printing and publishing, and publishers' stock was kept in a huge wholesale warehouse in Paternoster Row. That night it was set ablaze and millions of books were consumed, while flames raged around St Paul's, threatening to destroy it also. Churchill ordered the firemen to do everything possible to save the cathedral, and they did. Herbert Mason saved it in another way. A staff photographer with the *Daily Mail*, he was fire-watching on the roof of his newspaper office south of Fleet Street, with a direct view of St Paul's, and he had his camera with him.

Some images acquire a talismanic significance, not least photographs of that war. Later came the silhouetted riflemen going into action at Alamein, Robert Capa's GIs landing on Omaha Beach, almost more vivid because the film was blurred by faulty processing, and Joe Rosenthal's 'frozen flash of history', the Marines raising the Stars and Stripes on Iwo Jima. In the 'War's greatest picture', as the *Daily Mail* immediately called the photograph Mason took that December night, there is no human being, just Wren's magnificent building, its great dome rising through flame and smoke. The photograph found its way to Germany, where the *Berliner Illustrierte Zeitung* published it to boast of the destruction wrought by Goering's bombers, but to the British, and Americans also, it demonstrated something quite different. That night St Paul's became a symbol of sheer defiance.

And Winston Churchill was another. His image – truly an icon – was seen everywhere that year, in newspapers, on newsreels, on posters, on pieces of crockery (Toby jugs with Churchill's face were on sale, as well as chamber pots with Hitler's face on the bottom), even if the words on one poster, 'Let us go forward together' may have suggested a national spirit more resolute than it really was. And yet at the same time the old Churchill began to reassert itself. This went beyond his impulsive strategical conduct. Churchill was by no means an easy, loveable man. The dislike he had long inspired was partly personal, a response to his haughty and arrogant manner. When George Lansbury briefly and unsuccessfully led the Labour Party he complained about the way Churchill behaved 'like God Almighty' turning up at the Commons to give an oration and then stalking out. On the other side, Margaret Fuller, who worked as secretary at Conservative Central Office throughout the 1930s and knew many of the political leaders, recalled years later that Churchill was thought rather boorish: 'He would walk boldly into a room and casually let his coat fall from his shoulders, confident that someone else would pick it up.'

As prime minister he treated people in a 'manner brusque, off-handed, even as I thought then piggish', in the words or Walter Thompson, his personal detective for many years. 'He could be violently offensive to those who worked for him,' said Colville, and he was 'curiously inconsiderate'. Clementine knew this. She wrote to her husband in June 1940 about the 'danger of your being disliked by your rough sarcastic & overbearing manner ... I must confess that I have noticed a deterioration in your manners; & you are not so kind as you used to be ... Besides you will not get the same results by irascibility and rudeness.'

Even so, Thompson and Colville both added that those who worked for him would in the end be devoted to him. His harsh manners were the other side of an irrepressible bonhomie. In words very similar to Colville's, General Ismay, Churchill's chief of staff, insisted that Churchill was completely unlike anyone else they, or anyone, would ever meet. He was also unlike any of the other wartime leaders. Here was a man who, at one moment of acute crisis, lay on a sofa talking to his staff before telling 'one or two dirty stories', then, 'saying "goodnight, my children," he went to bed at 1.30 am'; who was wont to burst into music-hall song, 'Run rabbit, run rabbit, run, run, run,' or 'Roll Out the Barrel' (in the corridor at Buckingham Palace); or who at another time of crisis took two younger colleagues from Downing Street on the spur of the moment to Buck's, his favourite London club, where they lunched on oysters and champagne, steak and kidney pudding and Guinness.

His immense personality, brutal and genial, mercurial and melancholy, angry and generous, distinguished him from friend as well foe: it's quite impossible to imagine Roosevelt carousing or lunching like that, let alone Stalin (who employed a personal poisoner, so eating with him could be hazardous), or Hitler. And yet this was also a problem. Churchill was 'as un-understanding as he is of personalities' as ever. He remained the poor judge of character he had always been, too often underrating able and honourable men while promoting self-confident charlatans, and his intimates were a gruesome bunch. Churchill was at his worst in Downing Street, caballing with his frightful personal court or kitchen cabinet, Beaverbrook, Bracken and Lindemann. The influence of Lindemann would have very grave consequences, while Beaverbrook first betrayed Churchill, which Churchill either didn't notice or didn't mind, then inflamed animosity within the War Cabinet, and finally led Churchill badly astray. And un-understanding of personalities would also mislead Churchill when he dealt with his allies.

But he was at his very best in the House of Commons, where he treated other 'parliament men' of all parties in candid and comradely spirit, and in the Cabinet War Rooms, where he dealt with Attlee, Eden and Bevin as colleagues. Even eighty years on, the aura of the Churchill War Rooms, as they now are, can be sensed by a visitor, although an effort is needed to conjure up the physical atmosphere, with Churchill endlessly relighting his Havanas, Attlee puffing on a pungent pipe, and Bevin chain-smoking the full-strength cigarettes which would shorten his life. What those barely ventilated rooms were like for non-smokers is not a happy thought. But even if Churchill treated the War Cabinet, and the Chiefs of Staff, with respect, his guiding principle was expressed in his cheeky words, 'All I wanted was compliance with my wishes after a reasonable period of discussion.' Compliance with his wishes too often had woeful results.

Over the winter and into the spring of 1941, survival rather than victory was still at stake. In his 'so many to so few' speech the previous August, Churchill had declared that 'The Front line runs through the factories', and that this was a war between 'the whole of the warring nations, not just soldiers, but the entire population, men, women and children'. His language of heroic determination was far from the whole truth, and morale among Londoners was more shaken by the Blitz than the government chose to acknowledge. 'London can take it' became another heroic slogan, though one Cockney put it differently. 'Everyone's sticking it?' he told an American correspondent. 'And just what the bloody hell do you think anyone can do? You'd think we had some bloody choice in the matter!'

All the same, Churchill's rhetoric did have its effect, in fashioning a glorious narrative. If *Guilty Men* had been the surprise bestseller of 1940, there was another in 1941. In May the Air Ministry published a short pamphlet called *The Battle of Britain*, hoping that they might at least sell the first printing of 30,000. Well before the year ended it had sold a million copies. Like 'so many ... so few', the very name of that battle had been coined by Churchill. The 1942 biopic *The First of the Few* tells the story of R.J. Mitchell, played by Leslie Howard, the aeronautical designer who was the father of the Supermarine Spitfire, and who died of cancer just as the first prototypes were airborne. As he lies dying in the last reel, ethereal images of Spitfire squadrons appear overhead. This was one of the four films released in 1942 which had music by William Walton, who turned his score into the popular 'Spitfire Prelude and Fugue'. It was among the many ways in which the Churchillian epic was now being amplified, from high art – T.S. Eliot pronouncing sonorously that 'History is now and England' – to mass culture: Vera Lynn singing 'We'll meet again'.

And yet this ideal of living in a heroic age jarred against the hard fact of failure, too often self-inflicted. Churchill had encouraged de Gaulle to continue his quixotic fight, but their first joint venture was disastrous. In September as the Battle of Britain still raged, a British and Free French expedition to Dakar, the capital of the French colony of Senegal on the west African coast, was meant to rally the garrison there for the Gaullist cause. It was a fiasco. Dakar remained loyal to Vichy, the Royal Navy sustained futile losses, and 'Dakar' became yet another unhappy name on Churchill's charge sheet, with plenty more to come.

Even Dakar was trivial beside the larger strategical problem. Much of what was dignified as British 'grand strategy' in this war could have been summed up by another line Churchill liked to chant, one of the wonderful songs the Tommies had sung in the trenches in the previous war: 'We're 'ere because we're 'ere because we're 'ere.' Only that can explain what would seem otherwise inexplicable, that for the best part of three years the main battlefield between the armies of the British Empire and those of the Axis should have been in north-east Africa. The British had been ''ere' in the Mediterranean since acquiring Gibraltar in 1713, they had based a fleet at Malta since Napoleon's time, and since Gladstone's shameful bombardment of Alexandria in 1882 Egypt had largely been administered by British officials. A British garrison was stationed there, although Egypt never became a formal part of the Empire. Indeed it was a curiosity that Egypt was a member of the League of Nations and throughout the war remained in theory not only independent but neutral. On the one occasion when the sybaritic young King Farouk vaguely tried to assert his neutrality his palace was surrounded by British tanks and he soon saw the error of his ways.

To the west, Egypt bordered Libya, which Italy had seized in 1912 in her first vulgar spasm of acquisitive imperialism, and where Mussolini's grotesque vision of a 'new Roman Empire' had meant brutally subduing the Libyans while he tried to settle the land with reluctant Italian peasants. On 10 July 1940, eighteen days after France signed the armistice, the new Caesar declared war on France and Great Britain. This was one of the greatest mistakes of the twentieth century. Mussolini's fellow Latin dictators, Antonio Salazar of Portugal and Francisco Franco of Spain, both sat out the war as neutrals. Had Mussolini done the same, he might have died in his bed like them (at the age of eighty-one in Salazar's case, eighty-three in Franco's, after each had ruled or misruled his country for thirty-six years). Instead, puffed up with vanity and playing the jackal, as Churchill rightly said, Mussolini thought he could pick at the carcasses of two defeated powers. And so 'the greatest lawgiver among men', as Churchill had once called him, condemned his army to endless defeat, his country to years of suffering, and himself to a squalid death.

For years past Churchill had been consistently indulgent towards Mussolini and Italy. 'There is a school of British strategists,' he sarcastically said in April 1939, 'who hold that in a world struggle with Nazidom it would be a positive advantage to have Italy as an enemy.' But those 'strategists' weren't so wrong. When Mussolini declared war, Churchill told Jock Colville that 'People who go to Italy to look at ruins won't have to go as far as Naples and Pompeii,' adding that, if Germany now had the Italians as allies, that was only fair: 'We had them last time.' It was true enough. Even under Mussolini the Italians remained one of the most civilised peoples in Europe, whose lack of enthusiasm for fighting for him was no disgrace. But Italy became a heavy burden for Germany, and Mussolini did Churchill a favour, by presenting him with the one force even the British Army could beat. No one foresaw that this was the beginning of a strange campaign in the desert which would capture the imagination of the British people.* We don't think of 'the Anglo-Italian war', but for the best part of three years the British army, including forces from the Commonwealth and Empire, did much of their fighting against the Italians, and one cynic later said that the story of the war was that the Russians defeated the Germans, the Americans defeated the Japanese, and the British defeated the Italians.

Before he declared war, Mussolini's fantasies of military glory had already been inflamed by the brutal conquest of Abyssinia. Then again, in the spring of 1939, with the eyes of most of Europe fixed on Prague, the Italians invaded Albania, one more country small and weak enough for them to defeat, and King Zog joined Haile Selassie in English exile. Mussolini promised to respect Greek independence and the British promised to defend it. Then on 27 October 1940 Churchill admonished ministers, 'I do not agree with your suggestion that at the present time we should make any further promises to Greece and Turkey.' The next day Mussolini invaded Greece, and Churchill immediately changed his mind, insisting that British troops should be sent there. In September Marshal Graziani, the Italian commander in Libya, advanced into Egypt with a force of 300,000 and the British, with little

---

* And the Americans also: when Humphrey Bogart wins the desert campaign in *Sahara*, his last words in the movie are 'We stopped them at Alamein,' an interesting use of 'we'.

more than a tenth of that number, prudently withdrew. On 8 December Lieutenant-General Richard O'Connor, under General Sir Archibald Wavell, the Commander in Chief in the Middle East, launched what was meant to be no more than a 'raid in force' against Graziani's army, with 25,000 men, largely Australian. The Italians collapsed. Within two months O'Connor's small army advanced 350 miles and took 130,000 prisoners, losing 500 men. Had O'Connor possessed the logistical as well as military resources, the Italians might have been driven out of North Africa completely, but part of the British army was now diverted to Abyssinia, and another part to Greece.

'I am beginning to feel very hopeful about this war if we can get round the next three or four months,' Churchill had written to Roosevelt on 31 July 1940; or as he told Parliament, if they could get through the next three months, they could get through the next three years. His optimism was not shared across the Atlantic. In April Roosevelt had been told by Kennedy, his ambassador in London, that 'Mr Churchill's sun has been called to set very rapidly by the situation in Norway,' and even when his sun rose the following month, Roosevelt's scepticism about Churchill from their first distant meeting was strengthened by private reports he had received from Americans who visited London: now the president was prepared to think that the new prime minister was probably the best man for the job, 'even if he is drunk half of his time'. When in late June 1940 a poll found that only one American in three expected the British to win the war, Roosevelt himself wasn't much more confident. By December, Churchill's optimism seemed rather more justified. But if he knew that he could defy Hitler, he also knew that he couldn't defeat him, or not without allies.

In the spring of 1940, as Roosevelt's books and papers had been moved from the White House to his home at Hyde Park on the Hudson, there were signs that he wanted to retire, after what would have been eight gruelling years. No president had ever served more than two terms before, although the Constitution didn't then forbid this; Woodrow Wilson, who was often on Roosevelt's mind, had thought of running for a third term in 1920 until political and medical events conspired against him. After Dunkirk and the Fall of France Roosevelt decided he must run again, but not on a promise of war, rather the opposite. In 1916 Wilson had campaigned for re-election on the slogan 'He kept us out of the war,' and Roosevelt was blunter still that autumn of 1940. On 30 October, ten weeks after Churchill's 'Let it roll' speech, and six days before Election Day, he spoke at Fenway Park, home of the Red Sox in Boston, the most Anglophobic city in America, the most Irish and, as the *Boston Globe* columnist Jeff Jacoby has rightly written, the most antisemitic. 'I have said this before, but I shall say it again and again and again,' Roosevelt told this audience. 'Your boys are not going to be sent into any foreign wars.'

Much energy has been expended by American historians on arguing that, on the one hand, Roosevelt couldn't enter the war until his country was ready – exactly the point which, when made by Baldwin, had earned Churchill's contempt – and, on the other, that he was all along trying to prepare the Americans for war. Roosevelt did 'something that Churchill couldn't do', Jon Meacham has claimed. 'He shrewdly managed American public opinion to a moment when the world's greatest democracy was willing to project force to defend its values in a distant land.' But these admirers can't have it both ways. If Roosevelt really did think of entering the war when he spoke at Fenway Park, then he was even more devious and deceitful than his worst enemies alleged. 'Your boys are not going to be sent into any foreign wars' is a strange way of managing opinion in favour of such a war, and the fact is that, after Roosevelt's re-election, another year would pass before the United States entered the conflict, and then involuntarily.

As it was, with the British facing a profoundly unwarlike American people, and an intensely suspicious Congress, a Lend-Lease agreement was awkwardly reached, and acclaimed by Churchill as 'the most unsordid act' in history. Few of his phrases were quite so wrong-headed. The British received some modest supplies, in the first place a number of obsolescent destroyers. In return the United States was granted valuable naval bases from Newfoundland down to the Bahamas by way of Bermuda and all the way through the West Indies to British Guiana, the colony over whose border the United States had nearly gone to war with England at the time of Churchill's first American visit in 1895. Eden described this cession as 'a grievous blow at our authority and ultimately ... at our sovereignty', which it plainly was.

More painfully still, the British had to divest themselves of overseas investments, dollar assets and gold, and relinquish their export markets under duress. The story that horrible old Joe Kennedy called Lend-Lease 'the best goddam fire sale in history' may be apocryphal, but that was what it was. In one notorious case which stood for many, the Courtauld company's American subsidiary, Viscose Corporation, possibly the single most profitable British holding in north America, was bought by an American banking consortium for $54 million, less than half its real worth. As his years at the Treasury, let alone his private affairs, had shown, Churchill never properly understood finance, but Keynes did, and it was he who said that Washington was treating England as if it were the most feckless Balkan nation. He also said later that the Americans had taken the opportunity of the war to 'pick out the eyes of the British Empire' economically.

There was no mystery here. The eminent American historian Walter Russell Mead has described Roosevelt as the most Anglophobic president of the twentieth century, something Churchill never began to grasp. If Roosevelt didn't want Hitler to win, he also disliked the British Empire and British financial supremacy. Charles Lindbergh, who in 1927 had become the first aviator to fly alone across the Atlantic, now led an isolationist group called 'America First' which attracted many adherents, among them Gerald Ford and Potter Stewart, a future president and a future justice of the Supreme Court.

And yet 'America first' was Roosevelt's principle too. 'The world must be made safe for democracy,' Wilson had told Congress as the United States entered the Great War in 1917, words tragically belied by events. Roosevelt's aim was less exalted: to make the world safe for America. If indirectly or later directly combatting Germany could also mean impoverishing Great Britain and weakening her empire, then so much the better. Roosevelt even proposed sending an American cruiser to the Simonstown naval base at Cape Town, the nearest British equivalent to Fort Knox, to collect gold bullion as down payment, which an American writer has compared to a looter stealing the watch and wallet from a dying trooper.

On 9 February 1941 Churchill broadcast to the United States. He ended with another of his rhetorical flourishes, 'Give us the tools and we will finish the job.' This implied that, were the Americans to provide enough aircraft, tanks, ships and ammunition, the British on their own could defeat Hitler's Reich, although no one knew better than Churchill how absurd that was. 'Our affairs have prospered in several directions during these last four or five months,' he boasted. 'Mussolini attacked and invaded Greece, only to be hurled back ignominiously by the heroic Greek Army,' while in Libya there was another 'considerable event upon which we may dwell with some satisfaction'.

One listener had found his earlier speeches 'painfully boastful and usually followed by some disaster, as if in Kipling's "Recessional"'. This oration was quite boastful enough and, as before, hubris was followed by nemesis, bragging by disaster. Two days after the broadcast, Hitler summoned General Erwin Rommel to give him command of a new force of two armoured divisions to fight in Libya, and Rommel flew there immediately. With his eye already fixed on Russia, Hitler had no wish for his resources to be depleted, but he couldn't let Mussolini be humiliated, in Africa or Greece. Rommel's new force attacked on 30 March, and this time it was the British who collapsed, rapidly retreating far into Egypt with many soldiers taken prisoner. Then the Germans seized Yugoslavia on the way to Greece, where the British force was soon sent packing: 50,000 of 62,000 men got away, again leaving behind almost all their equipment. Twenty years before, Low's cartoon 'Winston's Bag' showed him with dead cats labelled 'Antwerp Blunder', 'Gallipoli Mistake', 'Russian Bungle'. The bag was even fuller now. As Churchill himself morosely said to Eden, 'Remember that on my breast are the medals of the Dardanelles, Antwerp, Dakar and Greece.'

One debacle in Greece was followed by another in Crete, which the British had garrisoned but with far too few fighter aircraft. On 20 May German parachute forces quickly secured the airfield at Maleme, after which troops poured in and the battle was lost. The British withdrew on 27 May leaving more than 10,000 soldiers behind to be taken prisoner.* And one more episode in Churchill's life returned to haunt him when in Iraq, his very own creation, a government friendly to the Axis took power and unleashed a murderous pogrom against

---

* Among the British prisoners that spring were my uncles, my mother's brothers. Geoffrey Reed, who worked in the oil business, had been commissioned in the Royal Engineers; his unit was surrounded in Rommel's first rapid advance. Robert Reed, who later led a blameless life as a commercial solicitor in the City, had joined the Commandos and was one of the soldiers left behind on Crete.

the Jewish community, while German aircraft were seen in Syria, controlled by the Vichy French.

As ever taking his word for the deed, Churchill ordered Wavell to deal with both those problems, and then attack in the desert. Iraq and Syria were settled quite easily, but the counter-offensive against Rommel in June was a failure and Churchill relieved Wavell, replacing him with General Sir Claude Auchinleck. He likewise achieved one victory, only to be frustrated both by an Axis counter-attack, and by Churchill's endless prodding. Such consolations as there were came at sea. The Fleet Air Arm won a famous victory on 11 November 1940 when twenty-one Swordfish biplanes, an aircraft already obsolescent when the war began, found the Italian battle fleet lying at anchor at Taranto and torpedoed three battleships.

Then on the night of 28–9 March 1941, at Cape Matapan south of Greece, the squadron of four new heavy cruisers which were Mussolini's pride and joy was caught napping by the Mediterranean Fleet, which sank three of them, with 2300 Italian sailors killed and three British.* In May the *Bismarck*, the magnificent new German battleship, broke out into the Atlantic. After she was engaged south of Greenland by two British warships, the *Prince of Wales* and the *Hood*, and blew up the *Hood* with her fifth salvo, the *Bismarck* escaped into the depths of the ocean and might have escaped to a French port. But she was spotted by an aircraft flying from Lough Erne in Northern Ireland and then crippled by torpedoes from aircraft of the Fleet Air Arm, before ships closed in to finish her off. On 27 May Churchill was in the Commons to speak about Crete when he was passed a note by Bracken, and asked indulgence to interrupt another speaker: 'I have just received news that the Bismarck has been sunk.' Amid the jubilant cheering he forgot that Taranto and *Bismarck* showed the new importance of air power at sea. He would soon be reminded the hard way.

In that unlucky February broadcast Churchill had insisted, 'But this is not a war of vast armies, firing immense masses of shells at one another. We do not need the gallant armies which are forming

---

* The searchlight officer in HMS *Valiant* was the nineteen-year-old Sub-Lieutenant Philip Mountbatten, later Prince Philip, Duke of Edinburgh.

throughout the American Union,' meaning the partial conscription Congress had introduced with the Selective Training and Service Act the previous September. 'We do not need them this year, nor next year; nor any year that I can foresee.' Even allowing that they were said to placate Americans who had no wish to join the war, these were unusually foolish words, and would soon be totally falsified. By 1945 the conscripted British Army – which six years earlier Churchill had deemed unnecessary – numbered three million, while the United States Army – which four years earlier Churchill had said would never be wanted – had grown to more than eight million men, nearly two million of them serving in Europe. And vast armies, firing immense masses of shells at one another, described in truth the only way such a war could be won.

Nor were Churchill's troubles merely military. On becoming prime minister, he would write, 'At last I had the authority to give directions over the whole scene.' He had assumed an exceptional degree of control over the conduct of the war by appointing himself Minister of Defence, albeit with no ministry, as a way of avoiding the losing battles that civilians had waged with the generals in the previous war. But his authority over the political scene was less than complete. The Churchillian legend has obscured just how disliked and distrusted he had been, and in a good many eyes remained. In *Men at Arms*, the first part of Evelyn Waugh's war trilogy, 'Guy Crouchback', the hero, has joined the imaginary 'Halbardiers' as his creator joined the Royal Marines. He is in the officers' mess when they hear the news of Churchill's appointment: 'Guy knew of Mr Churchill only as a professional politician, a master of sham-Augustan prose, a Zionist, an advocate of the Popular Front in Europe, an associate of the press-lords and of Lloyd George.'

This fictional character spoke for plenty of instinctive Conservatives, some in uniform, some even in government. They have been derided as the 'Respectable Tendency', but many of them were the best elements in English public life, and might better be called the Honest Tendency. At the time Churchill became prime minister, and for some time after, any disdain Butler felt for the 'half-breed American' was far from rare. Halifax made way for Churchill, but thought that 'The gangsters will shortly be in complete control.' Lord (formerly J.C.C.) Davidson, Baldwin's old *éminence grise*, and an important figure in the Conservative Party, said the same: 'The crooks are on top as they were in the last war,' while Sir Alexander Cadogan, the Permanent Under-Secretary of the Foreign Office, was 'afraid that Winston will build up a "Garden City" at No. 10, with the most awful people'.* An even blunter verdict came from the Conservative journalist Collin Brooks. 'Poor old Neville' was 'a good fellow', Brooks lamented, who 'simply doesn't know that there are shits in the world.... Now, Winston knows that shits exist – *and he likes 'em.'*

Another quintessential Tory was Thomas Dugdale, a Yorkshire squire who had fought in the Great War with the Royal Scots Grey, a long-serving MP and at one time Baldwin's PPS. By 1941 he was Deputy Chief Whip, and Chairman of the Conservative Party the next year, before later serving as a minister in Churchill's peacetime government and ending as Lord Crathorne. Abroad on active service, Dugdale corresponded with his wife Nancy, a clever and strong-willed woman from the celebrated Tennant family. Her letters offer a startling contrast to Churchill's claim that the nation – and his party – was united behind him. 'I could hardly control myself,' Nancy told her husband when Churchill became prime minister, and she made little effort to do so. Tory MPs regarded the new prime minister 'with complete mistrust as you know, and they hate his boasting broadcasts. W.C. is really the counterpart of Goering in England, full of the desire for blood, "Blitzkrieg" and bloated with ego and over-feeding, the same treachery running through his veins, punctuated by heroics and hot air.' Worst of all, she thought, 'Now all these reptile satellites – Duff Cooper – Bob Boothby – Brendan Bracken, etc – will ooze into jobs they are utterly unfitted for.'

Just as these malcontents suspected, the 'crooks' or 'shits' were now promoted. They were a disparate bunch. As a very young MP, Robert Boothby had been Churchill's Parliamentary Private Secretary when he was Chancellor. Handsome and superficially charming, he was a mountebank and adventurer, sexual as well as political, best known (among the very small minority who knew everything) as the lover for many years of Lady Dorothy Macmillan, the wife of his Conservative colleague Harold Macmillan, and possibly the father of

---

* The 'garden suburb' or city was the nickname given to the collection of temporary buildings erected behind Downing Street in the previous war, in which Lloyd George had installed his new ministries and his new men.

one of her children. He was also bisexual and predatory, skating on very thin and scandalous ice later in life. In 1940, Churchill rewarded him with a junior ministerial job, but not for long as Boothby was implicated in shady financial dealings and forced to resign.

At least Boothby's background wasn't mysterious, whereas Brendan Bracken did everything possible to make his origins even unlikelier than they actually were. He came in fact from Tipperary, but was shipped off to Australia at the age of fifteen. On his return he managed to spend a term at Sedburgh, the Yorkshire boarding school, pretending to be still fifteen though by now nineteen. Having invented an Australian background and a public-school education, he thrust himself into London life, journalistic and financial, even though he was 'a loud-mouthed know-all, impervious to rebuffs, who gatecrashed parties and insulted everyone with reckless abandon'. Succinctly described by Chips Channon as 'red-haired, garrulous, lying', Bracken was always ready with 'the latest gossip, sexual and political'. He nevertheless made a great deal of money quickly, acquiring the *Financial News* and a half-share in *The Economist* before he bluffed his way into a parliamentary seat in 1929 and became a devoted follower of Churchill.

Their friendship barely survived a rumour, which Bracken may have started, and didn't discourage, that he was Churchill's natural son. This caused a rupture with Clementine, who with her usual good sense never trusted Bracken, but Churchill nevertheless appointed him his PPS when he returned to office in 1939. Colville wasn't alone in finding Bracken 'a cad ... rather too talkative and apt to make the most ridiculous pronouncements'. The following year Bracken was made a Privy Councillor, at the new prime minister's insistence and despite the king's understandable objection. A year later he replaced Duff Cooper as Minister for Information, while remaining Churchill's most trusted servant in public and private matters. Bracken had used, and would use again, bare-knuckle tactics with publishers and film companies hugely to increase Churchill's wartime income.

Neither of those was as dangerous as 'the Beaver' and 'the Prof'. ('The Beaver' was the nickname conferred on Beaverbrook by those who didn't know him; his friends called him Max. F.A. Lindemann, Lord Cherwell from 1941, was widely known as 'the Prof'; apart from Churchill, he didn't have any friends.) We have seen how Beaverbrook emerged from Canadian obscurity, leaving behind him the blackest of financial reputations, to forge a precocious career in British newspapers and politics, which he polluted for more than half a century. The fact that he and his *Express* papers had supported appeasement until war came didn't stop Churchill making him Minister of Aircraft Production, an appointment opposed by the king 'in view of the effect likely to be produced in Canada'. Having acquired a reputation as an organiser, he would later prove a relentlessly treacherous friend to Churchill, just as Clementine guessed.

And what were the origins of Frederick Alexander Lindemann, Churchill's other consigliere? 'He is so violently anti-Semitic and anti-German that I suspect them to be German-Jewish,' said the Oxford historian Hugh Trevor-Roper, who knew him very well as a colleague at Christ Church, in a long and brilliant letter written in 1952 but not published for more than sixty years. Lindemann claimed to have been born in Baden to a German (or Alsatian) father naturalised as a British subject. He was mostly educated in Germany; at Berlin University he met Henry Tizard, who later helped him and whom he betrayed in return. In 1919 he became Professor of Experimental Philosophy, as Oxford quaintly called physics, still in his mid-thirties and at Tizard's recommendation, although Lindemann's personal fortune helped, and would be used to fund his laboratory.

A man who neither smoked nor drank and subsisted on a curious diet of egg white was an unlikely friend for Churchill. And in words which no one could possibly have used about his patron, Lindemann did not have 'a rich personality', Trevor-Roper said. Instead,

> He has made himself appear interesting by elaborate concealment of his real character ... he lacks all those human interests and weaknesses which make people interesting to other people ... He is impersonal, inured against the revelation of weakness by a systematic asceticism, an undeviating pursuit of power, a carefully fabricated aura of mystery ... I like the old wretch myself, because I like wicked men (others pretend to like him because they like to know powerful men), but I can see why those who don't share my perhaps curious taste regard him as a real menace, especially if they dislike his politics – which indeed are the blackest reaction. Fundamentally the Prof believes in an absolutely mechanical society, managed with scientific efficiency, and therefore without any concessions to liberalism, in the interest of the old ruling classes: a sort of 1984 run by the House of Lords.

Lindemann was an ardent eugenicist who hated the working classes as well as the Jews, and such a racist that when, later in life, a doctor advised him to recuperate from an operation by wintering in the West Indies, the Prof said he couldn't do so because he loathed black people too much.

That characteristic 'I like the old wretch myself' made Trevor-Roper well-nigh unique among Lindemann's colleagues and confreres, almost all of whom hated him as intensely as he hated most of humanity. A.J.P. Taylor had 'never met anyone more dislikable'; he was 'a genuinely horrible figure'; Isaiah Berlin said, 'the only person, I think, whom I have ardently wished to murder'. In the highly misleading 1983 television series *The Wilderness Years*, Churchill is dining at Blenheim in the 1930s when he explains who the Prof is: 'He is a great man, my dear, a physicist extraordinary, a mathematician of genius.' But Lindemann was nothing of the kind. For all his Oxford professorship, the truly great physicist Ernest Rutherford called him a 'scientist *manqué*'.

This reactionary racist became nevertheless one of the most important figures in Churchill's entourage, with consequences as serious as they were lamentable. He had already intrigued against one enemy. Sir Henry Tizard was one of the great Englishmen of his age, who had interrupted his career as an academic scientist at Oxford specialising in chemical thermodynamics to join the Royal Flying Corps and serve as a test pilot. He was later, besides many other distinctions, the President of Magdalen College, but more than that he was one of the few people who may be said to have saved their country. Tizard was a go-between straddling the worlds of scientific research and Whitehall, and without his crucial work in seeing that radar was installed round the coastline by 1940, the Battle of Britain would have been lost. By contrast, Lindemann wasted a good deal of other people's time with his crackpot notion of 'aerial torpedoes'. But he was much more successful in relentlessly urging another policy: 'bombing must be directed to working class houses' and their inhabitants, Lindemann demanded.

Short of annihilating German workers, none of these cronies had any clearer idea than Churchill himself of how Germany should be defeated, or by whom. That question was answered dramatically on

22 June 1941 by 'Barbarossa'. As soon as he heard the news of the German invasion of Russia, Churchill didn't hesitate. Broadcasting that evening, he proclaimed an unconditional Anglo-Russian alliance. After slyly saying, 'I gave clear and precise warnings to Stalin of what was coming,' and denouncing Hitler once more as 'a monster of wickedness, insatiable in his lust for blood and plunder', he cheerfully acknowledged his own record: 'No one has been a more consistent opponent of Communism than I have for the last twenty-five years. I will unsay no words that I've spoken about it. But all this fades away before the spectacle which is now unfolding. The past, with its crimes, its follies and its tragedies, flashes away.'

Now he could only see Russian soldiers 'standing on the threshold of their native land, guarding the fields which their fathers have tilled from time immemorial ... I see the 10,000 villages of Russia, where there are still primordial human joys, where maidens laugh and children play. I see advancing upon all this, in hideous onslaught, the Nazi war machine, with its clanking, heel-clicking, dandified Prussian officers.' And Churchill said emphatically, 'Any man or State who fights against Nazism will have our aid. Any man or State who marches with Hitler is our foe.' This view was by no means universally echoed across the Atlantic. Senator Harry Truman of Missouri spoke for many Americans when he said that the United States should have nothing to do with the great war in eastern Europe, but stand aside and let Germany and Russia cut each another's throats. Churchill saw it differently, and added in an unimproveable private aside, 'If Hitler had invaded Hell I should have made at least a favourable mention of the Devil in the House of Commons.' But as Faust learned, a pact with the Devil had a price.

Having gained one ally, Churchill now sought another. Six weeks after the German attack on Russia, he sailed westwards in the handsome new battleship the *Prince of Wales*, recently in action against the *Bismarck*, to meet President Roosevelt at Placentia Bay on the coast of Newfoundland. After getting over the initial embarrassment that Churchill had quite forgotten their first meeting in 1918, the two men discussed what became known as the Atlantic Charter. In contrast to Wilson's pedantic and pernicious Fourteen Points, this vague and lofty statement of war aims – in a war that Roosevelt still hadn't entered, and showed no very lively enthusiasm for entering – was nevertheless open to contention. The British quibbled over 'access on equal terms to the trade and raw materials of the world'.

But what really provoked Churchill's ire were the words 'the rights of all peoples to choose the form of government under which they will live'. While this was nodded through, Churchill assured Parliament on his return that it referred only to Europe. As he noted grimly, the possible application of this sentence to Asia and Africa 'requires much thought': he had no intention of allowing the Charter to be cited by enemies of British imperial rule. Still more revealingly, he observed that, if this principle of democratic self-government were taken literally in the Levant, 'the Arabs might claim by majority they could expel the Jews from Palestine, or at any rate forbid all further immigration. I am wedded to the Zionist policy, of which I was one of the authors.' Once more he recognised a fundamental contradiction between that 'Zionist policy' and the principles of democracy.

For all the appearance of camaraderie at Placentia Bay, the warmth was, and would remain, on one side: Churchill was consoling himself with an imaginary idea of Roosevelt, and of an American people eager for war. When men like Lindbergh and Senator General Nye of North Dakota blamed the English and the Jews for trying to drag the United States into the war, they didn't necessarily speak for many Americans, but maybe Una Mae Carlisle sang for more. Some of that delightful jazz singer's recordings are more memorable because she was accompanied by the great Lester Young, but one of them is 'Blitzkrieg Baby', which is memorable anyway for its lyrics: 'Blitzkrieg baby, you can't bomb me / Cos I'm pleading neutrality ... I don't want no infantry / Blitzkrieg baby, you can't bomb me.' That was an American hit song in May 1941. While Londoners were picking through the rubble of the Blitz, and British infantry were trying to stave off Rommel in Egypt, America was still pleading neutrality. And Churchill now knew that. For a year he 'had been assuring his colleagues in London that Roosevelt was itching to fight', as one historian has said, but after the meeting at Placentia he 'had to come to terms with the possibility that the president really meant it when he said he wanted to keep America out of the war.'

On his return, Churchill described his meeting with Roosevelt in a broadcast on 24 August. He then touched on the conflict on the eastern front, which had now become a war of national subjugation and racial extermination, as Churchill well knew. 'Scores of thousands, literally scores of thousands of executions in cold blood are being perpetrated by the German police troops upon the Russian patriots who defend their native soil,' he declared. 'We are in the presence of a crime without a name.' One day it would acquire a name, or more than one: the Final Solution, the Holocaust, the Shoah. This project of exterminating the Jews of Europe, which Hitler had publicly promised would be a consequence of war, had begun not with death camps and gas chambers but with the butchering of Jews in broad daylight wherever the Wehrmacht advanced. Every German soldier on the eastern front knew that, Feldmarschall or Feldwebel. '150 Jews from this place were shot, men, women and children. The Jews are being completely exterminated,' one soldier wrote to his wife in Bremen on 7 August, less than seven weeks after the invasion of Russia began. 'Please don't think about it. That's how it has to be.'

If the full import of Churchill's words failed to register with everyone who heard them, there were two dismayed private responses. He had merely spoken of 'Russian patriots' being killed, and Chaim Weizmann telegraphed to say, 'Impossible convey you shock reaction here to Prime Minister's failure to mention Jews.' Weizmann had his own sources of information, and he knew all too much about the fate of his people at German hands. This first phase of the great murder reached a climax at the end of September when more than 30,000 Jews in Kiev were rounded up, taken to Babi Yar outside the city, and shot. In all, a million Jews would be killed within six months.

But the other shocked private reaction was from the intelligence services. Churchill had committed the cardinal sin of compromising sources. As the Germans immediately realised, he could only have been aware of those horrors thanks to intercepted and decrypted signals in which the Germans matter-of-factly described their murder. Churchill knew this thanks to 'Ultra' and Bletchley Park. This unprepossessing country house, fifty-five miles north of London and equidistant between Oxford and Cambridge on a cross-country railway line, witnessed the greatest British contribution to defeating the Third Reich, not to say one of the greatest British achievements of the twentieth century.

During the Great War, the celebrated Room 40 at the Admiralty had broken the German naval cyphers, but a generation later these were far more complex thanks to the technically very advanced Enigma coding machine, which the Germans understandably believed was unbreakable. By now the riveting story of how an Enigma machine worked and how its codes were cracked at Bletchley has often been told, although it remained a closely-guarded secret not only at the time but for many decades after the war. Churchill was privately thrilled by his 'golden eggs', the decrypts which the British called Ultra, but in his postwar book he could only coyly refer to 'our spies in Germany' as his source of intelligence. Those Ultra decrypts gave the British Army an important advantage in North Africa and in later campaigns, if not a decisive one. Where they were crucial was in the Battle of the Atlantic.

'The undoubted obsolescence of the submarine as a decisive war weapon,' Churchill had said in 1938, 'should give a feeling of confidence and security so far as the seas and oceans are concerned, to the western democracies.' Just how wrong he was had become horribly clear as the Royal Navy waged a gruelling campaign against a few score U-boats, which at times came near to starving Great Britain and throttling the island economically: the only battle of the war that really frightened Churchill, he said, and with reason. Over more than three years it swung this way and that in seemingly inexplicable fashion. At times sinkings of merchantmen by U-boats mounted to an almost unsustainable level, until the tide quite abruptly turned, and instead it was one U-boat after another sent with its crew to a watery grave. What this meant was that Allied losses increased when the Germans changed their Enigma settings and for the time being baffled the Bletchley team, before another triumphant moment when 'a way in' was spotted, and a mixture of human genius and technological sophistication broke the code. The technology was the huge 'bombes' which look like something from an old science-fiction B-movie. And yet, as they whirred and purred at Bletchley, running through innumerable permutations, the modern computer was conceived: from those Bletchley bombes, everyone's lap-top descends.

Nor were the U-boats the only problem for the prime minister as 1941 wore on, or the only thing he had been utterly wrong about. 'But why should there be war with Japan?' Churchill had written to Baldwin in 1924. 'I do not believe there is the slightest chance of it in our lifetime.' He was Chancellor at the time, and in that spirit he had parsimoniously reduced spending on the naval base at Singapore. Painfully short-sighted as those words would seem, they were explicable. What Churchill meant wasn't so much that war with Japan was unthinkable, as that it didn't bear thinking about, which was true enough. Great Britain was stretched to the limit fighting Germany and Italy, and now aiding Russia; fighting against Japan as well was an unbearable prospect – but an increasingly real one. As Japan continued its brutal war in China, Roosevelt attempted to help the Chinese government, such as it was, by tightening the economic screws on Japan, to the point where the military junta in Tokyo felt they had to choose between humiliating withdrawal or war: an American policy deeply harmful to British interests.

Now Churchill was haunted by two nightmares, neither so remote from reality: that the United States might go to war with Japan but not with Germany, or that Japan, desperate for natural resources, would strike south towards the European colonial empires without making war on the United States at all. That would indeed have been the rational course for the Japanese. They already controlled French Indo-China. British Malaya with its rubber and tin, and the Dutch East Indies with its oil, now beckoned temptingly, and no serious obstacle stood in the way except Singapore. On 10 November Churchill announced that 'should the United States become involved in a war with Japan a British declaration of war would follow within the hour.' He then awaited a reciprocal undertaking from Washington, and waited in vain, for nearly four weeks.

On Sunday 7 December, Japanese aircraft bombed the American fleet at Pearl Harbor. This exploit was as militarily brilliant as it was politically foolish: to send a fleet undetected nearly 3500 miles across the Pacific and then launch a devastating airborne strike was one of the great feats in the history of warfare. But the Japanese, as a few of their more intelligent leaders such as Admiral Isoroku Yamamoto knew, had picked a fight they could never win in the long run. The Japanese also attacked in the south, and a whole further series of disasters began to unfold for the British. Even so, at the end of that fateful Sunday, Churchill recalled, in one more hallowed passage, that he had gone to bed late, exhausted but triumphant: 'Now at this very moment I knew that the United States was in the war, up to the neck and in to the death. So we had won after all!'

If he did think as much on that Sunday night, then he was right, but for the wrong reason. At that moment, the Americans weren't 'in the war' at all, at least not in the war against the Third Reich, which had occupied most of Churchill's waking thoughts for years past. And for four days it wasn't certain that they would be. Congress immediately declared war on Japan, but not until 11 December did Hitler himself resolve the matter by declaring war on the United States and 'the circle of Jews around Roosevelt'. Once more Hitler had come to Churchill's rescue. Why he did so is one of the unknowable mysteries of his dark and terrible mind, and one of the strangest 'ifs' of the war is what would have happened if Hitler had not declared war but instead said that he would remain neutral in the war between Japan and its enemies: at the least, it would have been very difficult for Roosevelt to join the European war.

What Churchill barely grasped was that a great turning point really had taken place, coinciding with Pearl Harbor but more than 7000 miles from Hawaii and in the European rather than Pacific war. Whereas Yamamoto didn't believe that Japan could defeat the United States, Hitler and his generals thought that Germany would beat Russia and, for all Churchill's defiant rhetoric, many Englishmen and Americans thought the same. That was understandable enough so soon after Stalin had shot most of the senior officers of the Red Army, which had then been heroically held at bay by little Finland during the four months of the 1939–40 Winter War. And for months after the invasion of Russia, pessimism seemed justified, as the Red Army was thrown back on all fronts. One general after another who had dissatisfied Stalin was recalled to Moscow and shot, a resource not available to Churchill, although he sometimes made robust jokes about it. At last the Germans came so close to Moscow that they reached the outer terminus of the tramway, and could see the winter sun glittering on the domes of the Kremlin.

And then, in the first days of December, after endless defeat and retreat, the Russians stood their ground and successfully counterattacked. This Battle of Moscow was truly one of 'the decisive battles of the world', as Victorian writers called them, utterly dwarfing any battles the British were fighting: the recent sortie for the relief of Tobruk in Libya had seen 237,000 soldiers engaged and 68,000 casualties; in the fighting for Moscow that December, more than three million men fought, with 400,000 casualties, a contrast which would persist throughout the war. That check before Moscow didn't mean that the Germans had lost. And yet, without a quick victory, they faced a long, grim war against a vast horde-army with seemingly endless resources, for whom casualties on any scale had no meaning; against the endless steppes; and against those famous Russian military heroes, General January and General February, with what would prove four grim winters to come. The western Allies would fight long campaigns of their own, on a smaller scale, and would provide Russia with quantities of material aid. But in the end, and whatever Churchill said, the Third Reich drowned in Russian blood.

As soon as the United States was at war, Churchill invited himself to Washington and, despite a distinctly tepid response from Roosevelt, arrived to spend Christmas at the White House. He received a standing ovation from Congress, for a speech which marked a crucial point in Churchill's assimilation as an American hero, though not in his relationship with the president, and Roosevelt warmed to Churchill little more whenever he was cheered to the echo by Americans. His boisterous manner was no help. Eleanor Roosevelt was shocked by his drinking, and Churchill got his relationship with her husband completely wrong, in larger ways and smaller. He insisted on pushing the president into the dining room in his wheelchair, when a more sensitive man night have guessed that Roosevelt hated being patronised or reminded of his affliction.

This was one more case of un-understanding of personalities – and a relationship which has been un-understood to this day. Endless books with titles like *Franklin and Winston* are given visible form by a kitschy sculpture at the bottom of Bond Street in Mayfair. Paid for by local tradesmen 'to commemorate fifty years of peace' and made by Lawrence Holofcener, it was unveiled in May 1995 by Princess Margaret, but detested by Mary Soames since the likeness of her father is so poor. Churchill sits at one end of a bench with Roosevelt at the other, smiling at one another with a space between them where a tourist can sit and be photographed, suggesting an intimacy between the two men which in fact never existed.

With all his outward conviviality, Churchill was a very private man, who had some cronies but few real friends, maybe no very close friend since Birkenhead died, with the ambiguous and unfortunate exception of Beaverbrook. But Roosevelt was much more remote.

Of all the leaders of the war, the American president remains to this day the most inscrutable: Stalin is an open book compared to FDR. Churchill's cronies might have been deplorable, but at least he had some, and Roosevelt did not. He was close to two women, neither of whom was his wife. In contrast to the Churchills' sometimes heated but very strong marriage, the Roosevelts had been privately estranged since 1918, when Eleanor discovered that Lucy Mercer Rutherfurd, her private secretary, was also her husband's mistress. For politics' sake there was no divorce, but the marriage was thereafter a formality, and Rutherfurd remained Roosevelt's intimate friend. The other woman in his close confidence was his secretary, Marguerite 'Missy' LeHand. And it was she who said of him that 'he was really incapable of a personal friendship with anyone'. Churchill could be an impossible man to deal with, but he wasn't mysterious or withdrawn, whereas Roosevelt's nearest colleagues never really knew what he was thinking.

When Churchill addressed Congress, after the inevitable ingratiating mention of his ancestry – 'I cannot help reflecting that if my father had been American and my mother British, instead of the other way round, I might have got here on my own' – he was candid about the immediate prospect: 'Many disappointments and unpleasant surprises await us ... I speak of a long and hard war. But our peoples would rather know the truth.' And there were also words which were the very best of Churchill: 'I owe my advance entirely to the House of Commons, whose servant I am. In my country, as in yours, public men are proud to be the servants of the State and would be ashamed to be its masters.' Not all his successors at 10 Downing Street would remember that.

As Churchill soon learned, 'disappointments and unpleasant surprises' was an understatement. One unpleasant surprise was medical. While at the White House he suffered a small heart attack, or so his doctor thought. He was accompanied to Washington by Sir Charles Wilson, who would be made Lord Moran in 1943, and who had been his personal physician since he became prime minister, on the recommendation of two former patients, Beaverbrook and Bracken. Other doctors who saw Churchill on his return to London weren't certain it had been a heart attack; either way Wilson made sure that the public knew nothing at all about it, or other medical difficulties. They hadn't stopped Churchill making a detour to Ottawa to give another bravura performance before the Canadian parliament. Altogether, one more north American tour had been exhilarating for Churchill. Then he came home to face the music.

11

'The Liquidation of the British Empire'
Mansion House 1942

Without victory there would be 'no survival for the British Empire', Churchill had said in May 1940, and in his 'finest hour' speech five weeks later he spoke of 'the long continuity of our institutions and our Empire'. These high-flown words were followed by two years of miserable defeat, and the first part of 1942 was in some ways the worst period of the whole war for Churchill, a combination of military disaster and political weakness which Clementine called 'the valley of humiliation'. It was a striking aspect of that humiliation, and a reflection on the curious nature of this war, that in its first three years, not only were more British soldiers taken prisoner than killed, but more British civilians than servicemen were killed. At last the tide of war was turned and by 10 November 1942, when Churchill spoke at the Mansion House in the City of London he was able to say, 'Now this is not the end. It is not even the beginning of the end. But it is, perhaps, the end of the beginning,' and he went on to say: 'I have not become the King's First Minister in order to preside over the liquidation of the British Empire.'

But he had. Many years later an unusually astute observer saw this. 'Although he didn't like to do so, Mr Churchill ended the stage of the British Empire,' Chou En-Lai told Henry Kissinger in 1969. He might not have wanted to or meant to, the Chinese prime minister added, 'But objectively he ended the British Empire.' In a life rich with irony, this was the bitterest irony of all for Churchill to accept, so much so that he could barely acknowledge it. As the Russians first held at bay and then destroyed the Third Reich, and as the Americans first held at bay and then destroyed the Japanese empire, the truth stared Churchill in the face: he might believe that he was fighting for the continuity of British institutions and Empire, but did he imagine that Stalin and Roosevelt were? Hard as it was for Churchill to accept, 'liquidation' followed inexorably from his own record as war leader.

That record was part of *The British Way in Warfare*, the title of a book published by Captain B.H. Liddell Hart, the self-appointed, and sometimes self-important, military oracle, in which he returned to his pet theme: England's greatness had formerly rested on indirect attack and limited aims, a policy tragically forgotten in 1914, he thought. Writing about the book in November 1942, Orwell summarised this 'traditional strategy' favoured by Hart, and by Churchill: 'You attack your enemy chiefly by means of blockade, privateering and seaborne "commando" raids. You avoid raising a mass army and leave the land fighting as far as possible to continental allies.' What few people seemed to have noticed, Orwell said, was that for the past three years we had 'waged the kind of war that Captain Liddell Hart advocated', and yet neither he 'nor anyone else would argue that this war has gone well for us.'

Throughout 1942, Churchill remained wedded to that 'kind of war' by indirect strategy in the hope of avoiding a frontal conflict with the German army in Europe. Bombing was one form of indirection, the 'Mediterranean strategy' another, and commando raids one more. They were personified by three men Churchill promoted: Arthur Harris, Bernard Montgomery and Louis Mountbatten. As it happened, Orwell wrote at the moment when the war did in fact begin 'to go well for us', but that was because in one other crucial respect Churchill had indeed stuck to traditional strategy, by 'leaving the land fighting as far as possible to continental allies', or to one, the Russians, with consequences he should have foreseen.

Before 1941 ended, another disaster had already occurred, for which Churchill bore the blame in more ways than one. He had ordered the *Prince of Wales*, in which he had so recently sailed to Placentia Bay, to sail to Singapore accompanied by the battlecruiser *Repulse*, and 'exercise a vague menace', in his own words, which were quite vague enough. In July 1938, he had written that all evidence 'would seem to show that warships, even if isolated, are practically immune from aircraft attack', words which already rang hollow after Taranto, the *Bismarck* and Pearl Harbor. On 10 December, after much confusion, steaming one way and then another, the *Prince of Wales* and *Repulse* were caught by Japanese aircraft off the coast of Malaya and sunk with the loss of 840 men, including Admiral Sir Tom Phillips, who was flying his flag in

Prince of Wales and chose to go down with her. To be sure, 'the air menace' was now very much of a decisive character.

But as poor mad Edgar knew, 'The worst is not / So long as we can say "This is the worst".' Japanese forces landed in Malaya, and by 31 January 1942 they reached the far south to gaze across the straits at Singapore, having comprehensively outfought a larger British force. At Singapore, Lieutenant-General Arthur Perceval commanded a garrison of more than 100,000 men, among them 33,000 British and 17,000 Australians. As the situation became more desperate, Churchill signalled to Wavell, who was now Commander-in-Chief in south-east Asia: 'There must at this stage be no thought of saving the troops or sparing the population. The battle must be fought to the bitter end at all costs.... . Commanders and senior officers should die with their troops. The honour of the British Empire and of the British Army is at stake. I rely on you to show no mercy to weakness in any form. With the Russians fighting as they are and the Americans so stubborn at Luzon [in the Philippines], the whole reputation of our country and our race is involved.'

His words meant nothing. On 15 February Perceval surrendered, after sustaining only modest casualties. This was 'the worst disaster and largest capitulation in British history', as Churchill said, and for him an indelible shame. But he chose to overlook his own record. In one more famous passage, he would write about the inadequate landward defences of Singapore, 'I ought to have known. My advisers ought to have known, and I ought to have been told, and I ought to have asked.' This was nonsense. No one was in a better position to know than he, and few bore more responsibility, from his saying that there would never be war with Japan to his starving Singapore of resources when he was Chancellor to his characteristic derision of the fighting quality of the Japanese: 'The Japs are the Wops of Asia'.

And yet when Churchill added that 'Defeat is one thing, disgrace is another,' he was right. The capitulation was disgraceful, not only in itself but in the way that Australian and British soldiers frantically scrambled for departing ships, pushing civilians out of the way. Shortly before the victorious Japanese marked their triumph with a massacre of Singapore Chinese, an explosion had rent the air as the British garrison blew up the causeway linking Singapore to Malaya. One Chinese schoolboy did escape, to be famous in time. When the

principal of Raffles College asked what the noise was, young Lee
Kwan Yew replied, 'That is the end of the British Empire.'

For Churchill this was a highly unpalatable truth, but truth it was, and
his son told him another unwelcome truth. In war as in peace,
Randolph provided a comic sub-plot to his father's heroic drama,
including a marital farce sharply contrasting with the bond between
Churchill and Clementine. Shortly after the war began in 1939,
Randolph met Pamela Digby, the pert and pretty nineteen-year-old
daughter of an obscure peer. He proposed to her on their first evening,
and they married shortly afterwards. In November 1940 their marriage
produced a son, christened Winston, but it was not otherwise a success.
And marriage did not improve Randolph, who was 'one of the most
objectionable people I had ever met', Colville thought at Chequers in
June 1940: 'noisy, self-assertive, whining and frankly unpleasant', even
before an evening's drinking, when he was 'in a horrible state, gross,
coarse and aggressive. I felt ashamed of him for Winston's sake.'

By the time his son was born, Randolph was nevertheless an officer
in the 4th Hussars, and a Conservative MP, although both of these
were misleading dignities. The prime minister's old regiment could
scarcely refuse him, and he only became the Member for Preston at
a by-election thanks to the electoral truce between the parties. In late
1940, he joined No 8 Commando, as Evelyn Waugh had done, and
he provides a running commentary on Randolph's career. After
training in Scotland, the Commando sailed to Egypt in February 1941,
with Randolph now quite out of control. He was playing wildly at
the card table: one night in the troopship he lost £400, more than
twice a working man's annual wage. Beaverbrook subsequently bailed
out his gambling debts, and established one more hold over the
Churchills.

And of course Randolph was also drinking copiously, while holding
forth bombastically. After the usual delays and foul-ups of military
life, a soldier graffitied wittily that never in the field of human conflict
'have so few been buggered about by so many', which was, Waugh
drily added, 'funnier if you are as familiar as Randolph makes us with
Winston's speeches'. When they arrived in Cairo, Randolph dined
with Sir Miles Lampson, the British ambassador, who sent a sycophantic signal to Downing Street: 'Your son is at my house. He has
the light of battle in his eye.' Unfortunately, when the message was

encrypted for transmission, the cypher clerk made a slip, so that 'light of *battle*' arrived as 'light of *bottle*'. As Waugh added, 'All too true.'

With Randolph away, Pamela looked elsewhere for amusement, with a penchant for Americans. Among the wartime visitors to England who became her lovers were Jock Whitney, who later returned as ambassador, Bill Paley, the president of CBS, and the broadcaster Edward Murrow. But much the most significant was Averell Harriman, nearly twenty years older than Randolph, and nearly thirty years older than Pamela. A millionaire thanks to the Union Pacific Railway family fortune, Harriman became an amateur diplomatist, and a very important one. In 1941, he came to London as Roosevelt's personal representative, dealing among other things with the Lend-Lease programme, and stayed there until sent to Moscow in 1943. That ended his connection with Pamela for the time being, though not forever, as they eventually married.

Not only was this liaison encouraged by Beaverbrook; some suspected that Churchill condoned his own son's cuckolding with this politically important visitor, and Randolph himself came to believe that. Either way, Pamela had embarked on a career in its way much more remarkable than Randolph's, if also more reminiscent of the days of Charles II or Louis Quinze than of the twentieth century. An English girl with 'kitten eyes full of innocent fun' but no formal education would become the last great courtesan, who progressed through the bedrooms of many rich and powerful men to emerge as Pamela Harriman, grandest of Washington hostesses, prominent supporter of the Democrat Party and, in a barely imaginable last act, American ambassador to Paris.

In March 1941, another ambassador arrived at the Court of St James's, when Kennedy was replaced after far too long, though not after another year of insisting that England was finished. His successor was Gilbert ('Gil') Winant, a former Republican governor of New Hampshire and a man of considerable charm, who said on arrival, 'I'm very glad to be here. There is no place I'd rather be at this time than in England.' In his five years in London he did a great deal for Anglo-American relations, politically and personally. Before long he began a discreet liaison with Sarah Churchill, whose marriage to Vic Oliver was petering out. These may seem frivolous matters, but sometimes the personal really is political, and it was not without significance that at the height of this great conflict the prime minister's daughter-in-law was sleeping with the president's personal representative, and the prime minister's daughter was sleeping with the American ambassador. Special relationships indeed. Later meetings between Randolph and his father were not happy. Churchill implied as much in a letter to Clementine, with an oblique mention of Randolph's marriage: 'No reference was made by either of us to family matters. He is a lonely figure.'

And yet, lonely or not, Randolph had seen just enough of the war to say, on one return to Downing Street, 'Father, the trouble is your soldiers won't fight.' That sounds harsh, and it went very much against the Churchillian grain, with its legend of British valour, but the fact was the British were regularly bested by the Germans, and the Japanese too. In the desert Auchinleck drove the Axis forces back to where they were in December 1940, but in early 1942 Rommel drove the British back again almost to Alexandria. Trying to explain away repeated failure, Churchill told the Commons, 'We have a very daring and skilful opponent against us, and, may I say across the havoc of war, a great general.' This might have seemed chivalrous but, as Goebbels sarcastically observed, Churchill lauded Rommel's individual genius because he didn't want to admit that the British were simply being outfought by the Afrika Korps.

An even harsher verdict at that time came from the American military attaché in Cairo: 'With numerically superior forces, with tanks, planes, artillery, means of transport and reserves of every kind, the British army has twice failed to defeat the Axis forces in Libya.' Its morale was low, 'its tactical conceptions were always wrong, it neglected completely co-operation between the various arms; its reactions to the lightning changes of the battlefield were always slow.' That was at a time of defeat, in early 1942, and yet even at a time of victory a year later, when the Eighth Army was finally pushing Rommel's men back through Libya and into Tunisia, Churchill could see the truth for himself 'Not happy about fighting,' he minuted in March 1943. 'We uniformly had the worst of it. Looks as if Germany is beating us unit for unit.'

He found it very difficult to come to terms with the fact that British soldiers, though of the same 'race' as their fathers and grandfathers, were men of a different type, no longer mute subjects of the king ready to accept death or glory but citizens of a democracy to which they felt at best a conditional allegiance. Churchill's gradual, reluctant recognition of this lay behind his determination that the British should not, or not for as long as possible, fight 'a war of vast armies, firing immense masses of shells at one another'. His addiction to 'the British way of war' and indirect methods brought him into conflict with the Americans as well as the Russians, both of whom he deceived. Although the Americans were lured unwillingly into a Mediterranean campaign, they thought it another Gallipoli on a larger scale, a 'side-show' or attempt to win through a backdoor approach, and fought moreover, they thought, for sinister British imperial purposes.

Apart from what would be called the Mediterranean strategy, 1942 saw the full implications of two of Churchill's phrases from the summer of 1940, 'devastating, exterminating' bombing and 'Set Europe ablaze'. A much larger bombing offensive began, while at the same time Churchill became ever more infatuated with the idea of popular insurrection, to the point where he absurdly persuaded himself that this might obviate the need for a formal military campaign to defeat Germany. In December 1941 he said that there was no need to suppose 'that great numbers of men' – British soldiers – 'are required' for the liberation of Europe. 'The uprising of the local population, for whom weapons must be brought, will supply the corpus of the liberating offensive.' The following year he was captivated by John Steinbeck's novel *The Moon is Down*, set in an unnamed country where the patriotic inhabitants ask for British arms to be dropped in to be used against the Germans. 'It stresses, I think quite rightly,' Churchill excitedly wrote, 'the importance of providing the conquered nations with simple weapons, such as sticks of dynamite, which could easily be concealed and are easy in operation.'

In vain did Lord Selborne, now head of Special Operations Executive, tell Churchill that such a policy would only expose civilians to German reprisals, which were indeed utterly brutal: when a single German soldier was killed, as many as a hundred people from a neighbouring village would be shot, or in France dozens of prisoners who were held hostage for the purpose. In June, two Czechs trained by SOE were dropped into their country and assassinated Reinhard Heydrich, the 'Deputy Protector of Bohemia and Moravia', and also one of the principal authors of the 'Final Solution'. The immediate response from the SS was to destroy the village of Lidice and execute 173 people. Hearing this news, Churchill proposed sending bombers to obliterate a German village in revenge, to which Attlee asked whether 'it is useful to enter into competition in frightfulness with the Germans', as if Bomber Command weren't doing that already. Even so, many more brave men, British or foreign, were sent into the darkness of Hitler's Europe, often to their deaths, to very little purpose. It seems doubtful whether these heroic exploits shortened the war at all and, whatever Churchill thought in 1942, it says something that, in the whole of the six volumes of *The Second World War*, SOE is mentioned just once, in an appendix.

An even greater drain on British resources were the 'special forces' and operations so beloved by Churchill. Beginning with the Commandos, a whole series of such forces was raised to carry out acts of derring-do: the Special Air Service, the Special Boat Service, the Long Range Desert Group and more besides. These were viewed askance by the army, with good reason. One fictional officer voiced the perfectly sensible view of the general staff: such a force could 'either become a corps d'élite, in which case it must seriously weaken other branches of the service, or a Foreign Legion of drop-outs, in which case it's hard to see them making a serious contribution to the war effort.' But 'Winston adored funny operations,' said Desmond Morton, Churchill's prewar informant who was now working at Downing Street, adding that he saw them like 'a miniature railway in his garden. Unfortunately he seems unable to connect up funny operations with the great strategic plans.'

Three such funny operations in 1942 tell the story. On 28 March Operation Chariot saw the *Campbeltown*, an elderly destroyer packed with explosives, steam up the Loire to St Nazaire and ram into the dry dock, the only one west of Calais which could hold German capital ships, while a party of Commandos went ashore and shot up the defenders. As Churchill gleefully described it, there was a 'faulty fuze', and it wasn't until the next day 'when a large party of German officers and technicians' was inspecting the wreck of the ship jammed in the gates that the ship blew up with devastating force, killing hundreds of Germans 'and shattering the great lock for the rest of the war'.

That may have done some good, although at no small cost: out of 511 British servicemen who took part in Operation Chariot, a third were killed and two-fifths were taken prisoner. Much costlier in proportional casualties was Operation Frankton in December, remembered only because of one of the worst British war movies of the 1950s. As

The Cockleshell Heroes tells it, a ten-man party of Royal Marines was landed from a submarine to paddle up the Gironde estuary in canoes and plant underwater limpet bombs on the hulls of ships moored there. 'We were just wiped out without doing any good,' says Trevor Howard, playing Captain Hugh Thompson. He's speaking about the Great War, but with unconscious irony. In the cinematic operation, almost all his men are captured. Two are put on their own in cells with pencils and paper by the Germans, who say that they can describe their operation, and no one will know, or be shot at dawn. One writes 'Rule Britannia', the other 'Drop dead'. At dawn they are lined up in front of a firing squad, and Howard tells them, 'Keep the line straight, men,' before they hear the limpet bombs exploding in the harbour; then the camera pans round to the German rifles opening fire. In reality, five ships were damaged but quickly repaired; of the ten men, two died of hypothermia, two escaped and six were executed, 'wiped out without doing any good'. 'Funny' is one word for this Churchillian operation.

But the greatest of all self-inflicted disasters was Operation Jubilee, for which Churchill bore indirect but clear responsibility. Although Canada had loyally entered the war in 1939, after the fall of France the only fighting the British army engaged in for three years was in North Africa and the eastern Mediterranean, which the Ottawa government thought too remote for Canadian troops to take part in. And so they kicked their heels in England, until 19 August 1942. That day a 'raid in force' was launched across the Channel against Dieppe, the pleasant little fishing port and resort on the coast of Normandy long popular with English visitors: as prime minister, Lord Salisbury escaped when he could to the Chalet Cecil, the villa he had built outside Dieppe, Oscar Wilde went there for a different kind of exile, and Clementine Churchill had spent part of her girlhood there.

From beginning to end the raid was a catastrophe, as might have been foreseen by anyone who had ever crossed to Dieppe on the Newhaven packet, and seen from the deck the small beach dominated by cliffs on either side. Tanks struggled to get ashore, the Germans responded rapidly and fiercely, and of the 6,086, mostly Canadian, men who landed, 907 were killed, 586 wounded and 1946 captured, a casualty rate not seen since the worst days of the Great War. Among those who witnessed the fiasco from a destroyer offshore was Ian Fleming, a journalist serving as a naval intelligence officer. This experience lay in the background of his James Bond novels in the 1950s, with their undertones of British decline.

One man bore the greatest blame for this dismal episode. Lord Louis Mountbatten was a courtier, a charlatan, and one of those curious people whose careers see one failure after another, leading every time to higher promotion. His mother was Princess Victoria of Hesse, making him one of Queen Victoria's many great-grandsons, his father, Prince Louis Battenberg, Princess Victoria's first cousin, had been First Sea Lord before the Great War when Churchill was First Lord of the Admiralty.* As the war approached in 1914, Battenberg took the decision to mobilise the fleet. Churchill approved and claimed the credit for this, but couldn't then prevent Battenberg from being hounded from office by hysterical Teutonophobia. His indulgent attitude towards the son may have been tinged with guilt, although Churchill was anyway taken in by Mountbatten's spuriously dashing personality.

Later in that first war, 'Battenberg' was anglicised to 'Mountbatten', Prince Louis was made a marquess, and his son became Lord Louis, and began an ascent eased by charm, connections and money. He served and befriended the Prince of Wales and married Edwina Ashley, granddaughter of Edward VII's financial adviser Sir Ernest Cassel, from whom she inherited a fortune. After years spent as much as a playboy as a naval officer, Mountbatten took command of the destroyer *Kelly* and Fifth Destroyer flotilla in 1939. Within a matter of months at sea he nearly capsized his ship, collided with another destroyer, was mined once, torpedoed twice, and then sunk by enemy aircraft. Even a sympathetic biographer admits that in the eyes of most other naval officers Mountbatten 'lacked "sea sense", the quality that ensures a ship is doing the right thing in the right place at the right time'. When *Kelly* was sunk off Crete in May 1941, Mountbatten was saved, and was about to be given command of an aircraft carrier when Churchill pushed him higher still, as Head of Combined Operations, against considerable opposition from other service chiefs. Churchill hoped that this glamorous if dubious figure could justify his faith in England as what he had called 'the great amphibian', striking at will across the seas.

---

* From when the old office of Lord High Admiral had been 'placed in commission' under Queen Anne, the Lordships of the Admiralty were headed by the First Lord, a civilian and cabinet minister; the First Sea Lord was the senior naval officer.

In that capacity Mountbatten bore full responsibility for the disaster at Dieppe. As the enormity became clear he began an elaborate cover-up, signalling that the morale of the retiring troops was 'excellent. All I have seen are in great form.' His obfuscation continued after the war, in a way which confirmed what Gerald Templer, a general in the North African and Italian campaigns who would become Chief of Imperial General Staff, later said to him: 'Dickie, you're so crooked that if you swallowed a nail you'd shit a corkscrew.' Churchill knew that the raid had been a disaster, and suspected that there was something fishy about Mountbatten's account, but nevertheless wrote that, while Dieppe had been 'disappointing' and that the very heavy casualties were 'out of proportion to the results', the raid was 'costly but not unfruitful', when in fact it had been costly and entirely fruitless. But Mountbatten rivalled or even surpassed Churchill as a master of self-publicity, which reached new heights with *In Which We Serve*. This was patently a Mountbatten biopic, in whose making he eagerly assisted; an enjoyable flag-waver written and directed by Noel Coward, and starring him as Captain Kinross of HMS *Orrin*, otherwise Mountbatten of the *Kelly*.

Such self-publicity was after all very Churchillian. From his first speeches onwards, Churchill had seen the war as a contest in rhetoric, not to say advertising or publicity. He created a noble legend of the Finest Hour, Dunkirk, the Battle of Britain and the Blitz. By 1942 the three men he had promoted, Harris, Montgomery and Mountbatten, all had grave shortcomings as commanders but were themselves masters of publicity. Each created a legend of himself: 'Bomber Harris' planning 'your target for tonight'; 'Monty' with his quaint uniform and his caustic speech; the elegantly debonair Lord Louis incarnated as 'Captain Kinross'. And Churchill would then find that each in his way was a Frankenstein's monster beyond his control.

Not even Mountbatten said anything as grotesque as the words, 'The Germans cannot afford any more Dieppes either on land or in the air. Two or three simultaneous raids on a large scale would be too much for the three solitary Panzer divisions in France.' That was the editorial opinion of the *Evening Standard* on 21 August, now edited by Michael Foot but speaking as ever with Beaverbrook's voice. Nothing was stranger in Churchill's war, or his life, than his relationship with Beaverbrook, and nothing better illustrated his un-understanding of personalities. Throughout the war Beaverbrook entertained and amused Churchill, while making trouble for him, or simply betraying him. As ever it was Clementine who saw this, urging Churchill to keep Beaverbrook out of the government: 'Is not hostility without better than intrigue and treachery and rattledom [as in rattlesnake] within?'

That was in early 1942. In February Beaverbrook had left the government after many threats to do so, but to the relief of his colleagues. Visiting Moscow, this capitalist robber baron found a new enthusiasm, for Soviet Communism, lauding Stalin and the Red Army in a BBC broadcast. He also became an advocate of Russian acquisition of the Baltic states, which was indeed grimly accomplished after the war. When Beaverbrook left the government he behaved in the most petulant and self-dramatising way but, whatever Clementine thought, this rattlesnake was even more dangerous outside. 'I have a deep respect for the Prime Minister,' he told Eden shortly afterwards; 'I will not do or say anything to weaken his authority,' before going on to do and say all he could to weaken it. Two weeks after writing that, Beaverbrook lunched at the Savoy Hotel with Leslie Hore-Belisha, who was dropped as War Secretary in January 1940 and who would speak against Churchill in a July 1942 debate. Beaverbrook 'had decided to oppose the Gov't', Hore-Belisha recorded. Beaverbrook asked another MP whether he would 'join him in forming an anti-Churchill party', and told a leading businessman that he would never return to government 'unless I join as Prime Minister'.

In March Beaverbrook visited America, where he said that 'The hopes of humanity … are all centred on the fight that Joseph Stalin and the Red Armies are making against the invaders of Russia,' and that the Anglo-Americans must now take 'offensive action' by invading France. When he saw Halifax, the ambassador in Washington, he told him, 'I might be the best man to run the war. It wants a ruthless, unscrupulous harsh man, and I believe I could do it.' Then in a speech in New York, an astonishing mixture of spite and insolence, he said that he had heard that Churchill 'will fall before the summer is out. You must help me to kill that bad rumour.' Far worse, Beaverbrook declared that 'Communism under Stalin has provided us with examples of patriotism equal to the finest annals of history,' and went on, 'Persecution of Christianity? Not so. There is no religious persecution … Racial persecution? Not at all. Jews live like other men. Political purges? Of course. But it is now clear that the men who were shot down would have betrayed Russia to her German enemy.'

Back in England, Beaverbrook addressed the Birmingham Committee for Anglo-Soviet Unity in June, demanding 'No unnecessary delay in sending forth our second expeditionary force to fight on the Second Front. ... Tanks for the Second Front. Airplanes for the Second Front. Ships for the Second Front.... . What we have got Russia is entitled to share. What we can give should be sent to them willingly, gladly, rejoicing as we go.' He then repeated his eulogy of Stalin and his regime to a bemused House of Lords. And yet no combination of public disloyalty and private treachery could temper Churchill's strange dependence on this evil man. 'Needy' is not a word that usually comes to mind with Churchill, but somehow or other he needed Beaverbrook.

As Beaverbrook well knew, he was undermining Churchill at his weakest moment. After the fall of Singapore the Japanese were within touching distance of Australia, bombing Port Darwin on the northern coast. The Australians were supposedly among Churchill's 'English-speaking races', although after Singapore he thought privately that 'inferior stock' explained the conduct of Australian troops. For their part, the Australians were increasingly sceptical about the 'mother country', and ever more inclined to look towards America for protection. In the summer came a new disaster. Churchill had promised Stalin as much aid as could be supplied, and most of this was sent by the perilous route round the north cape of Norway to Archangel and Murmansk, where convoys were highly vulnerable to attack by U-boats and aircraft. In June, convoy PQ17 was ordered to disperse in the false belief that large German warships were nearby, and twenty-four out of thirty-four ships were sunk.

Undaunted by failure, Churchill continued the great travels which were such a feature of his wartime leadership, and distinguished him from friend and foe: Roosevelt had never been in an aircraft before 1932 when he melodramatically flew to the Democratic convention in Chicago to accept the presidential nomination (as Hitler flew to the Nuremberg rally in 1935, shown in Leni Riefenstahl's brilliant but loathsome film *Triumph of the Will*), and he would only once fly abroad, to and from his meeting with Churchill at Casablanca in January 1943. Stalin remained in Russia, Hitler remained in Germany, although that included his headquarters in East Prussia. But Churchill had not only flown before the Great War, he made enormously long and sometimes perilous flights during this war, for which alone General Douglas MacArthur, no Anglophile, said he deserved the Victoria Cross.

In the summer of 1941, Churchill had rhetorically embraced Stalin as an ally and crossed the Atlantic to meet Roosevelt. In the summer of 1942 he met them both again, in unhappy circumstances. June really was a low point for Churchill. It was the worst month of the whole war for shipping losses: 173 ships or 834,196 tons sunk, largely in the Caribbean and the Gulf of Mexico, where the U-boats made hay and the United States Navy showed that it had much to learn about anti-submarine warfare. Rommel's latest offensive had left Tobruk as an isolated outpost by 14 June, when Churchill told Auchinleck that 'there is no serious question in any case of giving up Tobruk'. He then flew to Washington, where Roosevelt was elated by a great victory for his navy. At Midway in the centre of the Pacific ocean, from 4 to 7 June, for the first time in the history of naval warfare two fleets fought far out of each other's sight, by way of aircraft flown from carriers. Admiral Chester Nimitz's American force lost one carrier, but sank four Japanese carriers and a cruiser, stemming the Japanese flood tide six months after it had risen, with curious synchronicity matching the way the Red Army had stemmed the German tide at Moscow almost six months after Barbarossa. Readers of Churchill's war history would later be most inadequately informed about the importance of the battles of Moscow or of Midway, and much else concerning the Russian and Pacific wars.

In the White House on 21 June Churchill was talking to Roosevelt when the president passed him a signal saying that Tobruk had surrendered, with 33,000 men, all their arms, and large supplies of petrol. For Churchill this was 'one of the heaviest blows I can recall during the war. Not only were its military effects grievous, but it had affected the reputation of the British army.' On his return to London, he faced and won a vote of confidence in the Commons, helped by a Tory critic, Sir John Wardlaw-Milne, who proposed that the Duke of Gloucester* should be appointed Commander in Chief, at which the House was swept with laughter. Even so victory remained elusive.

On the day of the Dieppe fiasco Churchill was in Cairo, after a dramatic detour to Moscow. There he had his first meeting with Stalin,

---

* Younger brother of Kings Edward VIII and George VI and uncle of Queen Elizabeth II, the duke was a simple soldier with the plain humour of his Hanoverian forebears. His favourite evening entertainment was to have the company, regardless of age and sex, sing the song 'My grandfather's clock', omitting the letter 'l', and, once asked whether he had read *Wuthering Heights*, the duke replied, ' Yes, indeed, jolly funny.'

a most curious confrontation between an Englishman who had once denounced the incomparable foulness of Bolshevism and the tyrant whose mass murder had made it much fouler. Stalin alternately harangued and besought Churchill, insulted him, derided British failures, and demanded immediate assistance, repeating his preposterous requests for fighter squadrons and even infantry divisions to be sent to Russia, but above all insisting on 'Second Front Now'. That was the slogan plastered by Communists across walls in London and echoed by Beaverbrook, meaning an immediate allied invasion of northern Europe. It had also been advocated by the Americans, led by General George Marshall, the Chief of Staff, from the moment they entered the war. Marshall proposed a landing in Normandy: even if it was no more than a forlorn hope, with most men killed or captured, it would relieve pressure on Russia and show that the western allies meant to fight. This was bitterly resented by the British: the Americans had sat out the war for more than two years and were now proposing a bloody sacrifice, most of whose victims would be British.

Any idea of a French landing in 1942 soon withered, and in Moscow Churchill broke the news to Stalin. 'I have a somewhat raw job,' he understandably said to Harriman, who accompanied him to Moscow, as he endured Stalin's taunts, which were near the knuckle: 'You can't win wars if you aren't willing to take risks,' and 'You must not be so afraid of the Germans.' Churchill had persuaded the reluctant Americans that their army would land in North Africa, and now told Stalin about this, something which, as well as the fact that there would be no landing in France, Stalin already knew perfectly well thanks to his traitorous informants highly placed in both London and Washington.

It was then, according to Harriman, that 'the Prime Minister drew a picture of a crocodile and pointed out that it was as well to strike the belly as the snout'. On this occasion Churchill didn't utter the phrase with which he would be notoriously associated, the 'soft underbelly' of the Axis, but he did use it later, among his staff, and evidently to Montgomery and Eisenhower, who both mention it in their memoirs. This concept of striking from below at a softer target unquestionably animated his Mediterranean strategy. And it was wholly fallacious: one result of both great wars was to demonstrate that Europe has no soft underbelly in any sense. More than that, the implication of the drawing and phrase, as Stalin reasonably surmised, was that someone else would have the bloodier task of attacking the 'crocodile' head-on.

Back in Egypt, Churchill saw the sorry condition of the desert army after their latest failure at Gazala in May and June when the Eighth Army, on favourable terms, was again defeated by the Afrika Korps. The blame fell on Auchinleck, and Churchill yet again did what Lloyd George would have liked to do by sacking a general and looking for another. The replacements were not always an obvious improvement, although to be fair to Churchill anyone looking for the highest qualities of leadership and strategical brilliance among the British general officers of the 1940s was not spoiled for choice. Churchill's pick this time as commander of the Eighth Army was Lieutenant-General William Gott,* but on 7 August the aircraft in which Gott was travelling back to Cairo was shot down and he was killed. In his place, Churchill now chose Montgomery.

Although few military historians today would account Montgomery as a great commander, he answered Napoleon's question about any general – 'But is he lucky?' – with a loud affirmative. His luck was in from the moment that he was appointed, and his timing was faultless. Montgomery had been involved in planning the Dieppe raid, but Gott's death meant that before it took place he was on his way to Egypt, and far from obloquy. In North Africa as well, the new commander's luck was in. When the oppressively boisterous Colonel Cantwell orders 'a montgomery' in Ernest Hemingway's 1950 novel *Across the River and Into the Trees*, he intends a martini made fifteen parts gin to one of vermouth, since the general allegedly required such a superiority of forces before he attacked. That was literary licence, but Montgomery was certainly the most cautious of generals, who refused to make a precipitate attack and insisted on an overwhelming weight of men and arms before his offensive began on 23 October. It was the news of the breakthrough at Alamein which had Churchill, at Buckingham Palace during a banquet for Eleanor Roosevelt, swaying down the palace corridor singing 'Roll out the Barrel'. His glee was premature, and for the next few days the battle stalled, but by 12 November the Eighth Army had reached Tobruk, and Benghazi by the 19th, although they wouldn't reach Tripoli in

---

* Known as 'Strafer' from the German imprecation in the previous war, '*Gott strafe England*' ('May God punish England'). English army officers of his generation as matter of course acquired nicknames, so that anyone following the military history of this war needs to know who Strafer, Tiny, Jumbo, Pug, Maori and Boy were.

the west of Libya for another two months, even though the Germans were now fighting to their west as well.

Despite American suspicions of being dragged into a Mediterranean campaign to bolster British imperial interests, Roosevelt had agreed to a landing of American as well as British troops in north-west Africa, the French colonies of Morocco and Algeria, partly for domestic political reasons: he hoped that the sight of GIs actually fighting the Germans for the first time after nearly a year of war would boost the Democrats ahead of the midterm elections on 3 November. Alas for such cunning, the exigencies of war meant that the landings didn't take place until 8 November, after the Democrats had lost eight Senate seats to Republicans, and forty-two seats in the House. American officers had derided the British military record, but when the United States Army first encountered the Wehrmacht in the Kasserine Pass in southern Tunisia, the Americans got a very bloody nose of their own.

Part of the Churchillian myth held that, despite early defeats, British and then American soldiers had shown their mettle by beating Germany in the end. It was many years before a new generation of English military historians could admit that 'They were better.' Those are the blunt words of Max Hastings, one of those historians, writing about Antony Beevor, another of them: 'Man for man, German soldiers fought more effectively in World War II than their Allied counterparts did.' That had already been ruefully and still more eloquently admitted by the doyen of military historians, and Sir Michael Howard wrote with intimate knowledge. After his first taste of action at Salerno in 1943, he was sent on an intelligence course to learn 'everything that was to be learned about the German army: its organisation, uniforms, doctrine, personnel, tactics, weapons – everything except why it was so *bloody good*, which still, after half a century, remains something of a mystery to me.'

In 1940 the Wehrmacht had conquered Norway, the Low Countries and, still with numerically inferior forces, France in the space of less than eleven weeks. Despite greatly superior Allied forces, from the first artillery bombardment at Alamein until General Alexander's grandiloquent signal to Churchill the following 13 May, 'Sir, it is my duty to report that the Tunisian campaign is over. All enemy resistance has ceased. We are masters of the African shore,' was more like seven months. It would then take the best part of two years for the Allies to drive the Germans out of Sicily and Italy, and the next campaign took nearly a year from Normandy to the Elbe, when most of the German army was still fighting in the east.

Maybe it wasn't such a mystery as Howard found it, and maybe too much has now been made of German military brilliance. The Wehrmacht was the best army in history, and it was fighting for the worst cause. No myth of British or American bravery was as pernicious as another nourishing legend, 'the purity of arms of the Wehrmacht', which Churchill did nothing to discourage. That myth held that, apart from a handful of criminals, the German army had fought an honourable war. In reality the whole Wehrmacht on the eastern front was aware of mass murder, and complicit in it. More than that, the Germans were inspired by zealous tribal passion, by the spurious glamour of National Socialism, and by ferocious discipline.

In the Great War, far more British soldiers were killed than taken prisoner; in Churchill's war, 218,000 British soldiers were killed against 260,000 taken prisoner. Again, in the Great War, more than 300 British soldiers had been executed for desertion or cowardice, which was more than the German soldiers likewise shot. From 1939 to 1945, no British soldier was executed for the same offences, and only one American,* while more than 20,000 German servicemen were shot, hanged or guillotined for dereliction of duty – and that paled into insignificance beside the numbers of Russians executed. As the desert campaign wore on, Churchill continually grumbled about the teeth-to-tail ratio, the disparity between fighting units and ration strength in the Eighth Army. But armies – or western armies – had entirely changed. The army Churchill had known on the Western Front in 1916 meant essentially rifle battalions, 130 of them attacking on the first day on the Somme, with lesser numbers of supporting units.

There were days at Alamein, or later at Anzio and in Normandy, when individual rifle companies suffered casualties reminiscent of the Somme, but such front-line units were now a much smaller part of the whole army, whose 'tail' did swell hugely, and inexorably. Churchill took a long time to see that, unlike the men he had commanded in 1897 or 1916, the British Army of 1943 was manned by citizen-soldiers, reluctant conscripts who couldn't be disciplined as their fathers had been (and as German and Russian soldiers still were). Although many

---

* An episode of which Carl Foreman made heavy weather in his lugubrious 1963 'anti-war' movie *The Victors*.

of those soldiers taken prisoner had no choice, and were ordered to surrender, there is no doubt that the fighting spirit of the British army was not what it had been a quarter-century earlier. Some regiments in North Africa and Italy were notoriously 'sticky', and while some fought bravely, few showed the complete, almost suicidal obedience of the men who died on the Somme. For the most part, British soldiers wanted to do their duty but no more, and to come home again.

That was at least as true of the Americans. The United States Army and the Red Army were fighting in the same year of 1943, but they might have come from different centuries. The GIs were supported by a vaster tail, not only of supply trains, mechanical engineers and medical and dental units, but of entertainers, newspapers, movies, PX supplies, ice-cream-making machines such as landed in Morocco, Coca Cola bottling plants, and altogether everything that could be laid on to sustain morale. Not only were any such amenities unknown to Russian soldiers, the Red Army, as it developed into an immensely powerful offensive force, was utterly unlike the western armies. Elite units, sometimes now called Guards, spearheaded attacks, and when they had broken through the German line they were followed by a torrential horde of savage, barely trained men, killing, pillaging and raping, until order was restored by the all-important police units, who shot the worst offenders and restored discipline.

Human life had always been cheap in Russia, but never cheaper than 'under socialism'. Even now it's impossible to say how many of the Russian war dead should be reckoned Hitler's victims or Stalin's, and the comparison between Anglo-American and Russian fatalities is simply not comparing like with like. For years, the British and American publics were told endlessly about the courage of the Red Army, which in one sense was true, but that takes on a different aspect since we have learned that more than 300,000 Russians soldiers died not in battle 'fighting fascism' but were shot by their own army for cowardice or desertion; more than 13,500 Russian soldiers were executed at Stalingrad alone *pour encourager les autres*. As Marshall Zhukov said with a touch of dry Bolshevik humour, it took a very brave man to be a coward in the Red Army – and Zhukov, a brilliant general, had the advantage over his western counterparts that he could command his armies with a total indifference to casualties.

Was this army fighting a 'good war'? It was certainly fighting a more important one. While the Anglo-American armies slowly advanced in

Africa, a far vaster battle was being fought at Stalingrad, where the
German Sixth Army reached the banks of the Volga in November,
and was then surrounded, before General Friedrich Paulus surrendered
with what was left of his army. Of the 90,000 Germans taken prisoner,
barely 6000 ever returned home; in all, the Germans took 5.7 million
Russians prisoner, 3 million of whom died in captivity, some butchered,
many more starved to death. In all, more than a million men had
fought on either side at Stalingrad, which emphasises the absurdity of
Churchill's words: 'No one could doubt the magnitude of the victory
of Tunis,' he later wrote. *'It held its own with Stalingrad.'*

By a wholly unforeseen coincidence, one of the most famous of all
movies was released in January 1943, and while audiences relished
Casablanca, Churchill and Roosevelt met at the city of that name in
Morocco. The movie was an enjoyable farrago, but then there was a
certain fictional quality about the Casablanca Conference, which was
far from the start of a beautiful friendship, in Rick's last line. Roosevelt
was his usual genial, inscrutable self, allowing Churchill once more
to foster his delusion that a warm personal relationship existed between
them. Although a cross-Channel invasion that year wasn't yet ruled
out, the Americans agreed reluctantly to follow the North African
campaign with an invasion of Sicily, and implicitly of mainland Italy.
This turned out to be an ineluctable process: since the victory in Africa
was so tardy, Sicily wasn't invaded until July and southern Italy not
until September, by which time an invasion of France was no longer
possible that year, if it had ever been.

At Casablanca, Roosevelt and Churchill did agree on one seemingly
weighty policy, of 'unconditional surrender', for which they would be
much reprobated by critics. In one light it was just a turn of phrase:
Italy and Japan surrendered on elaborate conditions, and unconditional
surrender almost certainly did nothing to prolong the war with
Germany. But it was a surety to Stalin that the western allies wouldn't
conclude a separate peace with Germany, which was just what some
Germans hoped for, including those who would try to kill Hitler in
July 1944. Above all, 'unconditional surrender' was a belated rebuke
to Woodrow Wilson's disastrous 'peace without victory'. This time
the Germans would be left in no doubt that they had lost, and would
have no room for another *Dolchstosslegende.*

In one other way Casablanca was truly a turning point. More than seventy years later, William Waldegrave, a sometime Conservative Cabinet minister who hadn't been born when this war ended, looked back on an Anglo-American alliance 'which, at least after the Casablanca Conference of 1943, had stopped having even the facade of equality'. At Casablanca, Churchill got his way for the last time, but from then on, for all appearances of allied amity, Great Britain was unmistakably a junior partner, something Churchill found very painful to accept, until he found a way around the awkward truth, by pretending that the two nations were one.

From Casablanca Churchill flew to Cairo, where he arrived in the early morning and was offered tea but asked instead for a glass of wine, telling Lady Lampson, the ambassador's wife, 'I have already had two whiskies and sodas and two cigars.' He was accompanied by his even thirstier son, to general displeasure. Randolph was 'a dreadful young man. He has been an incubus on our party ever since Casablanca,' thought Sir Alexander Cadogan, the head of the Foreign Office, 'Very silly of Winston to take him about.' Then from Cairo, Churchill made a stranger journey, which his cabinet had tried to prevent, to meet İsmet İnönü, the Turkish president, in a railway carriage in southern Anatolia.

This *idée fixe*, Churchill's dream of inducing Turkey to enter the war on the Allied side, persisted from beginning to end. Brought up as a good Turkophile Tory, he had once incited a disastrous campaign against the Turks, whose fighting qualities he underestimated to his cost, while urging the destruction of the Ottoman Empire. It duly collapsed after the Great War, and Churchill became Turkophile all over again, ruefully impressed by the army Ataturk led at Gallipoli, and the national state he had created and İnönü now led. In the railway carriage Churchill pleaded again, in his version of French, to no effect. Here was a broader question where better strategical judgement was shown by Hitler than Churchill: Hitler could see that a country, Sweden or Switzerland in his case, can be more advantageous as a neutral than as an ally, certainly an ally like Italy. İnönü politely rebuffed Churchill, but why wouldn't he? He had nothing to gain from joining the war, potentially much to lose, and good reason to sit it out. But Churchill's addiction to the eastern Mediterranean was to have more woeful consequences before the year was over.

"Himmel! It's That Man Again"

12

'Are we beasts?'
Hamburg 1943

With his clarion call in May 1940 to fight 'against a monstrous tyranny, never surpassed in the dark, lamentable catalogue of human crime', Churchill had invested the war with a unique moral quality. And he had been right. With all its faults, Churchill's country in its finest hour stood for the forces of virtue, while the Third Reich was the embodiment of evil. Within two years it had become more evil still. Churchill had mentioned mass killings in the east as early as his August 1941 broadcast, and that was before the Germans plotted a more methodical means of murdering the Jews with something unknown in history, camps built for the purpose of mass extermination by means of gas chambers and crematoria. Killing the three million Polish Jews in death camps began in the spring of 1942, and most of them were dead within a year.

In October 1942, Churchill wrote a public letter to the Archbishop of Canterbury in which he said, 'The systematic cruelties to which the Jewish people – men, women and children – have been exposed under the Nazi regime are amongst the most terrible events of history. Free men and women denounce these vile crimes, and when this world struggle ends with the enthronement of human rights, racial persecution will be ended.' On 14 December, the War Cabinet discussed the question. Churchill asked about reports that the killing was being done 'by mass electrical methods' and Eden said that something of the kind seemed to be true. It was poison gas pellets rather than electricity, but this was a clear intimation that the British leaders knew that murder of a quite new kind and on a previously unimaginable scale was under way.

Three days later Eden published the Allied Declaration. The Germans, it stated, were 'now carrying into effect Hitler's oft repeated intention to exterminate the Jewish people in Europe. From all the occupied countries Jews are being transported, in conditions of appalling horror and brutality, to Eastern Europe,' and Poland 'has been made the principal Nazi slaughterhouse'. The Declaration promised retribution against the murderers. At the end of dignified speeches, the Commons rose spontaneously and stood in silence out of respect for the victims. This did little to help them, but Churchill's, and his country's, response was at any rate better than Roosevelt's refusal even to contemplate the horror. Whatever the sufferings of the European Jews, he did not propose to offer them refuge in America: his administration, and in particular antisemitic officials in the State Department, went to some lengths, helped by mendacious statistics, to keep out Jews. At the same time, Churchill's clear knowledge of the Final Solution should be borne in mind: he would later try to deny having known what he had known.

And yet, if the Third Reich was an epitome of evil, the purity of Churchill's own cause had been gravely compromised. The twelve months of 1943 were punctuated with place names, beginning and ending with meetings at Casablanca and Tehran. Between them, Katyn, Hamburg and Bengal had sombre resonances, illustrating the way that the war had been sullied by awful moral compromises. On 18 April, between one Allied victory at Stalingrad and another in Tunisia, the Germans announced that the bodies of 14,000 Polish officers had been found in the forest of Katyn, and that the Soviets had shot them. The Russians immediately denied this, and claimed that the Germans themselves had done it, but the Polish government in exile in London produced conclusive evidence of Russian guilt. In all, 22,000 Polish officers and other members of the educated elite had been seized when Stalin grabbed his slice of Poland in the autumn of 1939, and in the spring taken to the forests and shot one by one.

Although this was a small figure beside the hundreds of thousands Stalin had butchered in his recent purges, or the millions in all who perished by execution, deliberate famine or slow death in labour camps during his terrible quarter-century reign, Katyn still occupies a special place of perfidy and cruelty. When Churchill learned the truth, by way of Eden and Sir Owen O'Malley, the British liaison official with the London Poles, he said nothing. Or rather, he told Harold Nicolson and another MP, 'The less said about that the better,' and he told General Władysław Sikorski, the exiled Polish leader, 'Alas, the German revelations are probably true,' adding somewhat superfluously, 'The

Bolsheviks can be very cruel.' Not only did the British government publicly accept the Russian version, maintained by the Russians themselves until the fall of the Soviet regime, but the Foreign Office peddled this until long after the war.

Although Poland was the very cause for which England had gone to war in September 1939, it was becoming ever clearer that Stalin would expect to keep eastern Poland as well as the Baltic states. On 4 July Sikorski was killed when his aircraft crashed taking off in Gibraltar, which would one day lead to a grotesque conspiracy theory that Churchill had arranged this, so as to get the awkward man out of the way. That was monstrously false, but it was true that the Poles became an embarrassment to Churchill, and over the next two years he would spend many bitter hours with other Polish leaders telling them that they would have to accept new frontiers, even before Stalin imposed a quisling regime on whatever Polish state remained.

And were the means by which the British themselves were fighting as noble as Churchill had once proclaimed? No other British war movie, not the utterly inferior *Cockleshell Heroes* nor the greatly superior *The Cruel Sea*, with its unsparing account of men fighting the epic Battle of the Atlantic, ever achieved the fame of *The Dam Busters*, which delighted Churchill when it was released in 1955; and few films were so misleading. We have seen that the Royal Air Force had been created with the deliberate purpose of attacking enemy cities and their inhabitants, when Churchill had advocated dropping 'not five tons but five hundred tons of bombs each night on the cities and manufacturing establishments', and that between the wars the RAF had been used to cower unarmed civilians in Afghanistan, India, Iraq and Palestine.

Some efforts had been made to restrain this new horror. In the 1922 Washington Treaty, one article on the Rules of Warfare specifically prohibited 'Aerial bombardment for the purpose of terrorising the civilian population, of destroying or damaging civilian property not of a military character, or of injuring non-combatants.' Signatories included the United States, Japan, France – and Great Britain, hypocritically so, since those words described the very purpose of the RAF. Again in September 1938, the League of Nations resolved unanimously that 'The intentional bombing of civilian populations is illegal,' although the RAF was bombing civilians at that time in Palestine. Some English people were disturbed by this. In May 1939, one wrote to the Archbishop of Canterbury with his concern. The archbishop had been assured, this correspondent was told, 'that the Government and the RAF itself would recoil from any policy which would aim at reducing the civil population to panic and demoralisation by deliberate attacks on non-fortified and thickly populated areas'.

As the war began in September 1939, Roosevelt condemned 'the ruthless bombing from the air of civilians' and addressed an 'urgent appeal' to any warring powers that their 'armed forces shall in no event, and under no circumstances, undertake the bombardment from the air of civilian populations'. In response, Chamberlain told Parliament that 'whatever lengths to which others may go, His Majesty's Government will never resort to the deliberate attack on women and children, and other civilians, for the purpose of mere terrorism,' and his chiefs of staff proclaimed their intention of 'refraining from attacks on civil population as such for the purpose of demoralisation'. In 1940 Bomber Command did in fact try for a time to attack specific targets in Germany by daylight with squadrons of obsolete bombers, which were cut to shreds by German fighters.

And so the RAF began to bomb by night. Unbeknownst to the public, who were still told that military targets were being attacked, the War Cabinet had decided as early as 30 October 1940 that, in the unlovely euphemism that was to characterise this story, 'the civilian population around the target areas must be made to feel the weight of the war'. The following May, Trenchard wrote a weirdly wrong-headed memorandum, infused by prejudice: 'the German nation is peculiarly susceptible to air bombing, being unable to crack jokes while sheltering'. In August, David Bensusan-Butt,* a young Air Ministry official, conducted an impartial bombing survey which demonstrated in detail that one out of three bombers failed to attack the target area, and only one in four got within five miles of it. Almost no damage had been inflicted on German industry, and the 1941 bombing offensive killed more British aircrew than Germans, a futility epitomised by one raid in September which killed thirty-six Berliners while fifteen aircraft and eighty-seven aircrew were lost.

*

---

* An economist by profession, a favourite pupil at Cambridge of Keynes, for whose *General Theory* he compiled the index.

For all his past record, from 'five hundred tons' to his claim in July 1940 that only 'devastating, exterminating' bombers would defeat Germany, Churchill blew hot and cold about bombing. 'It is very disputable whether bombing by itself will be a decisive factor in the present war,' he wrote in September 1941, directly challenging the RAF's doctrine. 'On the contrary, all that we have learnt since the war began shows that its effects both physical and moral, are greatly exaggerated.' In October he amplified that: 'Even if all the towns of Germany were rendered largely uninhabitable, it does not follow that the military control would be weakened ... The Air Staff would make a mistake to put their claims too high.' This was one of his more prescient utterances: towards the end of the war, the towns of Germany were in rubble, but the Germans were still fighting in that rubble, and all the boastful claims of the airmen would have been shown to be hollow.

More than one choice was now available to Churchill. He could have suspended or diminished the bombing offensive, at least until the means had been found of bombing military targets accurately by day, as the Americans did later find. Or any pretence of attacking military targets could be dropped, in favour of saturation bombing, or area bombing, or terror bombing. That was the decision now taken, urged by Lindemann. Animated by his intense hatred of Germans, he provided false statistics to exaggerate the effect of bombing. The decision was personified in February 1942 by the appointment of Air Chief Marshal Sir Arthur Harris, as he now was, as Commander-in-Chief of Bomber Command. Formidable, coarse and brutal, Harris knew that his bombers were incapable of hitting precise targets, but having once terrified Iraqi and Palestinian villagers he was now determined to terrify the Germans by killing them on a scale quite unknown before.

He cleverly saw his new campaign in terms of publicity, announcing his arrival on 28 March with the bombing of Lübeck, a beautiful mediaeval Hanseatic city, home of Thomas Mann (and the Buddenbrooks), strategically insignificant but, as Harris put it, 'more like a fire-lighter than a human habitation', and it burned very well. In May came an even bigger coup, the 'thousand-bomber raid' on the great cathedral city of Cologne. This was only the start of a campaign Harris described candidly, but privately, as aimed at 'the destruction of the German cities, the killing of German workers, and the disruption of civilised life throughout Germany ... the creation of a refugee problem on an unprecedented scale, and the breakdown of morale

... by fear of extended and intensified bombing.' To avoid any doubt, he added that 'these are not by-products of attempts to hit factories', and he always resented any attempt to divert his force from its task of mass destruction to hitting military targets. Even so, the bombing campaign of 1942 inflicted so little damage on the German war economy that maybe half a percentage point of production was lost, while bomber losses rose inexorably. Bombing had failed again.

In 1943 an undaunted Harris renewed his, or his aircrews', efforts with an assault on the Ruhr, still determined to avoid what he derided as 'panaceas', or attacks on specific targets. One such panacea was nevertheless attempted. Operation Chastise was an ingenious attempt to breach three dams whose reservoirs held much of the Ruhr's water supply. On the night of 16 – 17 May, nineteen Avro Lancaster bombers of 617 Squadron took off loaded with specially designed 'bouncing bombs', which hand-picked aircrew had been trained to land precisely on the water so that they would drop down the side of the dams and blow through them. This all required the greatest skill and courage from airmen flying barely above ground level. Two dams, the Möhne and Edersee, were breached, but the Sorpe was not, which to some extent nullified the purpose of the operation. Severe flooding killed more than 1600 civilians, at least 800 of them female forced labourers from Russia and Poland, but the dams were soon repaired. Only eleven out of nineteen aircraft returned; the others were shot down or crashed; of 133 aircrew who took off, fifty-three were killed, thirteen of them Canadian.

Before the raid, Harris called the 'Dam Busters' plan 'tripe of the wildest description. There is not the smallest chance of it working.' After it, he immediately claimed the credit. Churchill was in Washington for an Anglo-American conference, and due to address Congress again. These speeches delighted senators and congressmen, who lamented that they had to wait for a visit from the prime minister to hear the kind of grand, inspiring survey their own president never gave them. In the Capitol on 19 May, Churchill was able to boast of the 'unparalleled devastation' wrought by British bombing, and the 'gallant operation' to destroy the dams of which they had just heard, which would, he said with gross exaggeration, 'play a very far-reaching part in reducing the Germans munitions output'. That was not so, but the raid boosted Churchill, whose purpose in Washington was to argue yet again against an invasion of France, in 1943 or maybe even in 1944.

Chastise was nothing beside Operation Gomorrah, one more all too revealing name: Sodom and Gomorrah were the Cities of the Plain which an implacable Jehovah had destroyed with fire and brimstone. Harris turned away from the Ruhr to Hamburg, and in late July the great Hanseatic port, with a long tradition of Anglophilia through trading links with England, was bombed on successive nights. On the 27th, as 787 bombers attacked the city with high explosives and incendiaries, and, thanks to a coincidence of clear skies, a new device called 'window' (small strips of foil dropped from aircraft which baffled the defenders' radar), and hot dry weather, something quite new happened. Just before midnight Hamburg was set alight. A vast firestorm engulfed several square miles and burned for hours at hundreds of degrees. No living creature could survive within the inferno, and at least 40,000 people died, incinerated or asphyxiated as the firestorm burned off the oxygen. Most were women and girls. More than 10,000 were children.

While the Churchill government had privately said that the German working class must be made 'to feel the weight of the war', it had insisted publicly that bombing was directed at military targets. Whether the public really believed this is another matter. For much of the war, the bombing campaign was closest to home for the English in more senses than one. The Eighth Army was far away in the Mediterranean, the Fourteenth Army further still in the Far East, and ships of the Royal Navy were sailing across distant seas. But the bombers were stationed on English soil and lived on bases among the rest of the populace who heard, night after night, the roar of hundreds of Rolls Royce Merlin engines overhead as they drove Wellington and Lancaster bombers to the Ruhr and Berlin, and the bombers' deeds were boastfully reported day by day.

Along with 'the wireless', the great wartime entertainment was 'the pictures', with millions going each week to see the latest Hollywood or sometimes home-grown movie, and newsreels as well, the television news of that age. Shortly after Gomorrah, the newsreel included footage filmed from a British aircraft. It showed the city engulfed in a huge sea of flame, while the commentary intoned, 'Hamburg is being liquidated. The second city of the Reich is being liquidated.' That didn't leave much to the imagination, and was all too literally true, since many bodies were in fact turned to liquid by the heat.

And what of Churchill? He was a man of extreme contrasts, great brutality mixed with true chivalry, and on no other question was he more confused and conflicted than bombing. We have seen that in 1901 he had said all too truly that 'the wars of peoples will be more terrible than the wars of kings'; in 1914 he had denounced 'the baby killers of Scarborough' when the German navy had killed a handful of children; in 1920 he had said that 'Frightfulness is not a remedy known to the British pharmacopœia'; in 1930 he had lamented 'cruel and squalid' modern war with 'chauffeurs pulling at the levers of aeroplanes' and 'entire populations, including even women and children, pitted against one another in brutish mutual extermination'; in September 1940 he had decried the 'wanton' killing of Londoners by the Luftwaffe. That summer of the Hamburg firestorm, Churchill was sitting in his little cinema at Chequers, watching a newsreel which showed another blazing German city. Turning to his neighbour, he asked, 'Are we beasts? Have we taken this too far?' He might well have asked, and wondered how posterity would judge the baby killers of Hamburg, and him.

From the Ruhr and Hamburg, Bomber Command turned to Berlin in late 1943, and bombed the capital relentlessly. An ever more frenzied Harris told Churchill in November, 'We can wreck Berlin from end to end if the USAAF* will come in on it. It will cost us 400–500 aircraft. It will cost Germany the war.' Or again, he claimed that he could kill 900,000 German civilians and end the war. A myth took root, and still hasn't been eradicated, that bombing, whatever its ethical implications, was a means of winning wars and did help to win this war. Churchill bore much of the blame. In 1934 he had said that London would be devastated by German bombing in a matter of days, and in 1940 he had said, in words now carved on the Bomber Command memorial at Hyde Park Corner, 'the bomber alone provides the means of victory'.

Just after the 'dam busters' raid, Sinclair, the Air Secretary, said that there was only one hope of getting to Berlin without the terrible slaughter which 'the land battles of the last war entailed, and that is the paralysis of German war power by Bomber Command'. But German war power wasn't paralysed by bombing. German industrial war production increased steadily until the autumn of 1944, by which time Germany was defeated anyway; bombing achieved a solitary success, with the systematic American attacks on the factories which

---

* United States Army Air Forces. There was no separate US Air Force until 1948.

1. One symbol
of defiance:
Herbert Mason's
photograph of
St Paul's Cathedral
amid the fires
and smoke of
German bombs,
29 December 1940.

2. And another: Churchill
in characteristic pose, 1940.

3. With 'the Winston of Germany', Kaiser Wilhelm II, on German army manoeuvres. Breslau, 1906.

4. With Marshal Stalin. Churchill said, 'I can't help it, I like that man.' Moscow, 1943.

5. With two of the few richer writers than himself, Somerset Maugham and H.G. Wells. Cap Ferrat, 1937.

6. The bench unveiled by Princess Margaret on Bond Street, 1995, but disliked by Mary Soames. 'Missy' LeHand, Roosevelt's secretary, said that 'he was really incapable of a personal friendship with anyone,' while Sir Alan Lascelles, the king's private secretary, remarked in June 1944 that Winston was not sure 'that he really likes FDR.'

7. Chartwell in Kent, Churchill's home and word-factory.

8. St Mary Aldermanbury, the Wren church transported to Westminster College in Fulton, Missouri. Beside it, recalling the 'iron curtain' of which he spoke at Fulton, is a fragment of the Berlin Wall.

9. The 'victory watch,' given to Churchill by the burghers of Geneva in 1945, sold by his grandson in 1998 for £485,000.

10. 'The Tower of the Koutoubia Mosque,' painted by Churchill in Marrakesh in 1943, sold in 2021 for £7 million.

11. President Reagan in the Situation Room at the White House during the 1987 Iran–Contra crisis, with the poster behind him, in which Churchill urges: 'Let us go forward together.'

12. President Bush the Younger in the Oval Office with the bust which kept watch over him.

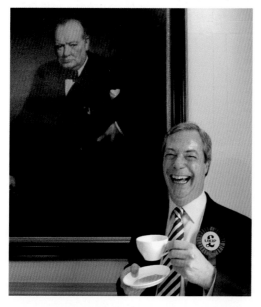

13. Nigel Farage of the United Kingdom Independence Party with the inspiration for Brexit.

14. Richard Burton in *The Gathering Storm*, 1974.

15. Albert Finney in *The Gathering Storm*, 2002.

16. Robert Hardy in the ITV mini-series *Winston Churchill: The Wilderness Years*, 1981.

17. Gary Oldman in *Darkest Hour*, 2017.

18. As adorned with turf by a
May Day demonstrator, 2000.

19. The statue in Parliament Square
unveiled by Clementine, Lady
Spencer-Churchill, 1973.

20. 'Turf War' by Banksy:
signed copies of the
screen print cost £15,000.

21. Bronze casts of Ivor Roberts-Jones's original maquette for the statue on sale for £275,000 each.

22. The icon invoked, February 2017.

23. The statue daubed, 2020.

24. Eighty years on, Mason's photograph of St Paul's echoed by Peter Brookes of *The Times* as the different scourge of Covid sweeps England, March 2020.

25. The author of *The Churchill Factor* as seen by Ingram Pinn of the *Financial Times*.

supplied the Luftwaffe with artificial oil. Even then, an astonishing 80 per cent of German industrial plant capacity remained intact, as Ben Steill has shown: 'Germany exited the war with a *greater* functioning machine tool stock than it had on entering it.' It was quite a feat to kill nearly half a million civilians while barely affecting the German war economy. No doubt German morale was affected by the destruction of every city, but in the last year of the war the Germans were still fighting fiercely in Normandy and the Ardennes, as well as on the Eastern Front.

Since it subsequently became undeniable that Bomber Command had failed in its proclaimed purpose, another argument was advanced by its defenders, clutching at straws: bombing at least diverted Germany's weaponry and manpower from the great conflict in the east, thereby helping the Russians, and it's true that maybe a third of the Germans' 88mm guns, the best artillery piece of the war, also lethally effective anti-tank weapons, were used defending Germany from bombers. But this cuts two ways. British military-industrial resources were decidedly finite (one consequence of the war was the discovery that American military-industrial resources were almost infinite). Although the figure is still disputed, bombing seems to have absorbed something between a quarter and a third of British industrial war production. And every squadron of Lancasters built meant so many tanks, landing craft, escort vessels and fighters not built, all weaponry of which the British were painfully short throughout the war.

Both Sinclair and Harris claimed that bombing avoided the terrible carnage of the Somme, a claim repeated much later by Richard Overy, a prominent English historian of the subject, although he has, over forty years, turned an almost complete circle, from bombing sceptic to ardent defender of Bomber Command to sceptic again. He had previously, and correctly, said, 'the resources devoted to strategic bombing might more usefully have been used in other ways', and latterly, also correctly, that 'Bombing in Europe was never a war-winning weapon and the other services knew it.' But during his phase as an enthusiast, he wrote that 'Bomber Command made a larger contribution to victory in Europe than any other element in Britain's armed services,' and he echoed Sinclair by writing that 'Harris's enduring belief during the war that bombing would in the end save the allied nations a very high bloodletting was vindicated'.

This managed to be utterly wrong twice over. By the end of the war, 55,000 of Harris's men had been killed, almost half of all active Bomber Command aircrew, a fatality rate far exceeding those of any other branch of the Allied services in this war. Or even of larger units in the Great War: some rifle companies sustained very high casualties in 1916, but the whole Fourth Army on the Somme – which would be a more valid comparison with Bomber Command – didn't lose half its men. For some squadrons the toll was still heavier. Of the 133 aircrew who took off for the Dam Busters raid, only thirty-two were still alive when the war ended: within two years of that famous night, three out of four of the brave men of 617 Squadron had been killed. Far from avoiding another carnage, 'strategic bombing' was the Passchendaele of this war, and Harris its Haig.

In any case, Sinclair was wholly mistaken about avoiding 'land battles', just as Churchill had been two years earlier, with his 'this is not a war of vast armies, firing immense masses of shells at one another', let alone Overy's Allies spared 'a very high bloodletting'. To the contrary, vast armies fought horribly bloody land battles firing immense masses of shells but, rather than Loos or Verdun, they were called Stalingrad and Kursk. The British, and Americans, did recognise that, if half-consciously. Even as Churchill tried to delay an invasion of France, there was an *arrière-pensée*, occasionally voiced, that the more Russian soldiers killed the fewer British and American soldiers would have to be. That was ignoble enough, but Churchill wilfully put out of his mind what would follow if the Russians did most of the fighting.

Another kind of horror was more distant, and the story of India in this war is a dismal one. When Churchill was at his lowest political ebb in 1942, the one other person besides Beaverbrook who seemed to challenge him was the unlikely figure of Sir Stafford Cripps. Apart from the fact that they were both in their ways eccentrics, no two men ever had fewer elective affinities than Cripps and Churchill. Cripps was a well-to-do scientist, barrister and Labour MP, much concerned in Christian affairs and the unity of the churches, a puritan who had given up smoking and foresworn drink 'as a protest against the alcoholism' among Labour MPs, according to Beatrice Webb, who was his aunt. Or as Churchill said, 'He has all of the virtues I dislike, and none of the vices I admire.' In the 1930s Cripps moved to the far Left as leader of the Socialist League, denouncing the League of Nations as an 'International Burglars Union' while extenuating the Moscow Trials and colluding with the Communist Party, until he was expelled from the Labour Party.

He was nevertheless sent as ambassador to Moscow in June 1940, and when he returned to London in early 1942 and was hailed, quite wrongly, as the man who had brought Russia into the war, Churchill reluctantly brought him into the War Cabinet. With the Japanese army advancing through Burma towards Bengal, Cripps left for India in March to search for a political settlement with the Indian nationalists. He embarked on frenetic negotiations with Indian politicians, principally Gandhi and Jawaharlal Nehru, the leader of the nationalist – ostensibly secular but in practice Hindu – Congress Party, and Mohamed Ali Jinnah of the Muslim League. A resulting 'Cripps offer' promised self-government for India with a constituent assembly after the war.

Despite later mythology, Jinnah was favourable, while Gandhi derided the offer as 'a post-dated cheque', and it was characteristic of his lack of realism to think that any government in the middle of a desperate war could offer India immediate independence. If Cripps received little help from an unenthusiastic Viceroy, Lord Linlithgow, Churchill was even less enthusiastic. He couldn't express himself publicly on the unfitness of the Indians for self-government as he had done ten years before, but in private, he told the Russian ambassador Maisky that 'the Moslems will become masters' of India eventually, 'because they are warriors while the Hindus are windbags', undone by 'their internal flabbiness'. Maisky shrewdly noted that 'Churchill is a considerable man and a major statesman ... but something of the small boy lives on in him ... India is a toy he dislikes.'

The failure of the Cripps mission suited Churchill very well, as it seemed to put Gandhi in the wrong, not least in the eyes of the Americans, who had been prodding the British, although in the end nothing Churchill could do would stop the coming of Indian independence, which arrived little more than five years later. It may be that a united independent India was always an impossibility, but Churchill's claim that there would be civil war after the British left was close to self-fulfilling prophecy, and one made almost with relish. While the English hadn't invented the sectarian conflict in India, they had sometimes exploited it, but Churchill was almost unique in

wanting to encourage it. 'Winston rejoiced,' Colville recorded in April
1940, 'in the quarrel which has broken out afresh between Hindus
and Muslims. Said he hoped it would remain bitter and bloody.' He
would have his wish granted before long.

In the summer of 1943 Bengal was swept by terrible famine, in
which as many as three million people died. It has been heatedly
debated ever since, and Churchill stands indicted by some Indian historians, notably Madhusree Mukerjee in *Churchill's Secret War*. The headline on Joseph Lelyveld's review of that book in the *New York Review
of Books* asked, 'Did Churchill Let Them Starve?', which doesn't have
a simple answer, and the story of the famine is complex and fraught
and the celebrated Indian economist Amartya Sen has taken issue with
Mukerjee's polemical account, pointing out that the Japanese conquest
of Burma had cut off the main supply of rice for Bengal, that Indian
merchants hoarded rice supplies in the hope that prices would rise,
and that prices did shoot up in rural Bengal despite, as Sen observes,
'very little overall decline in food output or aggregate supply'.

All that may be true, but Churchill's partisans have a hopeless task
when they try to defend his conduct during the famine. He was influenced by the appalling Lord Cherwell, as Lindemann had become in
1941, whose racism was more intense than Churchill's own and who
urged hanging hoarders as a simple remedy. 'No matter how famine
is *caused*,' Sen has written, 'methods of *breaking* it call for a large
supply of food in the public distribution system,' and there was none
such since Churchill had no wish for it. But above all he is damned
not so much by what he did or didn't do as what he said and thought,
and what his colleagues said and thought of him. Before the famine,
when Gandhi had gone on hunger strike, Churchill had said that it
should be made clear to him that nothing would be done to stop him
dying and, when news of the famine first came, Churchill wondered
why, if the Indians were starving, Gandhi was still alive. In any case,
he said, 'The starvation of anyway underfed Bengalis matters less than
that of sturdy Greeks.'

Not much later he told Colville that 'the Hindus were a foul race
protected by their mere pullulation from the doom that is their due,'
and sardonically suggested that Harris should send his bomber squadrons to India to finish them off. This might have dismayed but would
not have astonished Wavell. He had been moved to India as
Commander-in-Chief, and he became Viceroy, as Field Marshal Lord

Wavell, in 1943, when the famine was his first great crisis. He successfully forced the provincial government to adopt a more active policy,
but unsuccessfully pleaded with London for more grain to be sent,
angrily saying, 'I feel that the vital problems of India are being treated
by His Majesty's Government with neglect, even sometimes with
hostility and contempt.' More than two years later, during the Dutch
'Hungerwinter' of 1944–5 which followed the disastrous British failure
at Arnhem, the RAF mounted a huge operation to drop food into the
Netherlands. There seemed to be 'a very different attitude,' Wavell
noted bitterly, 'towards feeding a starving population when the starvation is in Europe.' Churchill would not have denied that his attitude
was different. His conduct only reinforced Leo Amery's view of him.
Churchill had made his contemporary and fellow imperialist Secretary
of State for India in 1940 and he held the office until 1945. 'I am by
no means quite sure whether on this subject of India he is really quite
sane,' Amery wrote in his diary. He even told Churchill to his face
that he 'didn't see much difference between his outlook and Hitler's'.

Differences over strategy apart, India was a persistent cause of mutual
resentment between Churchill and Roosevelt, increased by Roosevelt's
baiting. The president would chide Churchill about the Raj, to which
Churchill replied by comparing the Indians of India, who had multiplied greatly in numbers under British rule, with the fate of the Indians
of North America, expropriated and well-nigh exterminated. This
wasn't a new argument, nor Churchill the first Englishman to make
it to a Roosevelt. During Kipling's American sojourn, he had befriended
Theodore Roosevelt, with whom he used (in a more relaxed age) to
walk through Washington, and the Smithsonian Institute. As Kipling
later wrote, 'I never got over the wonder of a people who, having
extirpated the aboriginal of their continent more completely than any
modern race had ever done, honestly believed they were a godly New
England community, setting examples to brute mankind. This wonder
I used to explain to Theodore Roosevelt, who made the glass cases
of Indian relics shake with his rebuttals.' Even so, the Bengal famine
was scarcely the best time to repeat this theme.

Then Roosevelt said that he had visited Gambia, one of the most
poverty-stricken British colonies in Africa, on his way to Casablanca,
and suggested that there should be an international commission after
the war to investigate such places, to which Churchill sourly replied

that the commission should include the American South in its investigations. That was a much better argument. Like his 'progressive' predecessor Woodrow Wilson, Roosevelt had relied for his electoral victories, and for Congressional support, on the Solid South, the eleven states of the former Confederacy which were at once a racial oligarchy ruled by violence and a huge 'rotten borough', providing the Democrats for generations with twenty-two senators and scores of congressmen, often returned unopposed. The Democrats were the party of the New Deal, and they were the party of the lynch mob. And Southern ways had been imposed on the military: the United States waged this war against the worst racial tyranny in history with rigorously segregated armed forces.

This became a new source of Anglo-American tension with the arrival of American servicemen in England. The GIs aroused mixed feelings in any case. Better paid, better fed, with better-quality uniforms, not to mention better teeth than British soldiers, they inevitably attracted English girls. 'It is difficult to go anywhere in London without having the feeling that Britain is now Occupied Territory,' Orwell wrote as the huge American invasion swelled. And he added that 'The general consensus of opinion seems to be that the only American soldiers with decent manners are the Negroes.' American insistence that black people, their own soldiers or others, should be excluded from pubs and restaurants where white Americans went, was much resented: one pub landlord put up a sign saying 'This place for the exclusive use of Englishmen and American Negro Soldiers.'

More seriously, rape was a capital offence under military law, and the fact that a disproportionate number of American servicemen executed were black dismayed the English. When Leroy Henry, a black GI, was falsely accused of rape by a woman in Combe Down* near Bath and sentenced to be hanged, he was saved by vociferous local protests. This revulsion wasn't shared by Churchill. A man from Sierra Leone who worked in the Colonial Office in London used to take his lunch in a nearby restaurant, until the Americans demanded that he should be kept out: after all, no black man could eat in a restaurant in Washington. Lord Cranborne, the Colonial Secretary, raised the matter in Cabinet, to which Churchill replied that he couldn't see a problem: 'If he takes his banjo with him, they'll think he's one of the

---

* Where this book was written.

band.' But his colleagues didn't think it was funny, and resolved that nothing should be done by the British authorities 'to assist [the Americans] in enforcing a policy of segregation', and that in all public places there should be 'no restriction of the facilities hitherto extended to coloured persons as a result of the arrival of United States troops in this country,' although the weight of American money made this principle hard to stick to.

At the Guildhall in the City of London on 30 June 1943 Churchill spoke about the Anglo-American alliance, and he would expand on this in a speech five weeks later at Harvard, without mentioning the black GIs, or the banjo. In between those speeches, the Allies had followed Churchill's impulse and landed in Sicily on 9 July. The island was taken after a campaign which reflected much more credit on the 50,000 German defenders, who for five weeks conducted a fighting retreat against almost half a million Allied soldiers, and were then mostly allowed to escape. One folly was followed by another. Marshal Pietro Badoglio was one of the less successful Italian generals of that age, not a high standard anyway, and one of the less admirable Italians, who had brutally repressed the peoples of Libya and Abyssinia before he was sidelined by Mussolini, but if nothing else he knew the way the wind was blowing. In March, Milan and Turin were shaken by great strikes, and on 23 July, two weeks after the Allies landed in Sicily, Mussolini was dismissed by the fatuous king Victor Emmanuel III, and arrested. At that point a golden chance might have existed to remove Italy from the war. With its indefatigable zeal for destruction, the RAF, and the Americans as well, were already bombing Italian cities heavily. In *Il Gattopardo* (*The Leopard*), Giuseppe Tomasi di Lampedusa's great novel set in late-nineteenth-century Sicily, a melancholy line describes the hero Prince Fabrizio's love for his beautiful palace in Palermo, in fact the author's own palace, where 'from the ceiling the gods, reclining on gilded couches ... thought themselves eternal; but a bomb manufactured in Pittsburgh, Penn., was to prove the contrary in 1943'. At the other end of Italy the Palazzo Archinto in Milan was decorated with glorious frescoes by Tiepolo. On 12 August, palace and paintings were destroyed, many Milanese were killed, and placards appeared on ruined homes, 'This house was destroyed by our liberators.'

★

If Churchill's relationship with Roosevelt was often strained, this was not for want of frequent meetings. Churchill visited America seven times during the course of the war, and met the president nine times, spending in all about 120 days with him. In May 1943, when he addressed Congress, Churchill also hosted a lunch at the British Embassy in Washington attended by a number of senior American officials. He now began to expiate on his idea of a 'fraternal association' been the two countries: 'There might even be some form of common passport' or 'some form of common citizenship', so that Americans and citizens of the British Commonwealth could reside in each others' countries, vote there and perhaps 'be eligible for public office'.

In August, Churchill made his longest transatlantic visit of the war. At an acrimonious Allied conference in Quebec, he pressed the merits of the Italian campaign, while the Americans believed that he really wanted to postpone a cross-Channel invasion until the Greek calends. Then he made a detour to Harvard to receive an honorary degree, and to expand on his theme. In June, he had said that if the Americans and the British 'walk, or if need be march, together in harmony and in accordance with the moral and political conceptions to which the English-speaking peoples have given birth, and which are frequently referred to in the Atlantic Charter, all will be well.' And he added: 'Upon the fraternal association and intimate alignment of policy of the USA and the British Commonwealth depends, more than on any other factor, the immediate future of the world.' Now, speaking to the young men of Harvard, many of them in uniform, he waxed more eloquent still.

'Twice in my lifetime,' Churchill told them, 'the long arm of destiny has reached across the oceans' to bring the Americans into a great war. Unconsciously echoing Kipling's call for the Americans to take up the white man's burden, Churchill said that 'The price of greatness is responsibility.' And he went on: 'You will find in the British Commonwealth and Empire good comrades to whom you are united by other ties besides those of State policy and public need. To a large extent, they are the ties of blood and history ... it may well some day become the foundation of a common citizenship. I like to think of British and Americans moving about freely over each other's wide estates with hardly a sense of being foreigners to one another.'

This has been called 'one of the central addresses of his life', in which Churchill conveyed his 'vision for the future of the

English-speaking peoples'. Another way of looking at it is that it was an enormous misconception, and self-deception, although one which may be easily explained. It was not by accident that, after years of suspicion and hostility towards the United States, Churchill had decided to write about 'the English-speaking races' in 1929 while on a lucrative American tour. And it was not by accident that he should have spoken of 'the foundation of a common citizenship' in 1943, 'the year when', it has been correctly observed, 'world leadership moved from Great Britain to the United States'. Difficult as it was for Churchill to accept this, presaging as it did the eclipse of the British Empire and of British might and greatness, maybe there was a way of disguising that loss of leadership – by pretending that England and its successor as world leader were really one and the same!

That summer two other Englishmen were talking in Algiers, where Eisenhower's Allied Forces Headquarters (AFHQ) were based. Harold Macmillan was a former infantry officer and a future prime minister, who had, like Churchill, an American mother. Badly wounded serving with the Grenadier Guards in 1916, he had become a Tory MP, an opponent of appeasement who had voted against Chamberlain in the Norway debate, and had been rewarded with office, serving for a time under Beaverbrook (although there were 'aspects of his character which I found distasteful'), before being sent by Churchill as minister resident in Algiers. Another 'Greats man' or Oxford Classicist like Macmillan, Richard Crossman, the author of *Plato Today*, was a former don and a future Labour Cabinet minister, who was then working for the Ministry of Economic Warfare in the murky field of propaganda.

'We, my dear Crossman,' said Macmillan, 'are Greeks in this American empire. You will find the Americans much as the Greeks found the Romans – great big, vulgar, bustling people, more vigorous than we are but also more idle, with more unspoiled virtues but also more corrupt. We must run the AFHQ as the Greek slaves ran the operations of the Emperor Claudius.' This idea, that the sophisticated worldly-wise English would guide and restrain the powerful but uncouth Americans, was a refinement of, or variation on, Churchill's 'ties of blood and history', and it would have potent appeal for English politicians for generations to come after it was elaborated as a 'special relationship'.

And yet, like Churchill, Macmillan was trying to evade the most obvious truth. The United States is a sovereign country. That's the point of the Fourth of July. Both of them had forgotten Palmerston's principle: 'We have no eternal allies and we have no perpetual enemies. Our interests are eternal and perpetual.' And for all his phrases of amity, Churchill was learning for himself the hard way what Palmerston had also meant when he said that there are no alliances between equals. Macmillan half-consciously hinted at that when he recalled that those wise Greek mentors in imperial Roman households were in fact slaves. At no time then or later did the Americans ever reciprocate any idea of a common citizenship, or kinship, or special relationship, and why would they? At no time then or later did they need or want the guidance of worldly-wise 'Greeks' in London to mentor or restrain them.

On 3 September, four years to the day after the war had begun and three days before Churchill's Harvard speech, the new Italian government agreed to an armistice and British troops crossed to the mainland, to be followed a week later by a larger American landing at Salerno. But the timing had gone awry. By now the Germans had rushed reinforcements to the south where they were waiting for the invaders, and nearly pushed them into the sea. Harvard and Salerno coincided with a grotesque episode which was all Churchill's own work, and one which maybe more than any other in his life disposed of his claim to have been 'that supreme combination of the King–Warrior–Statesman', or merely a serious strategist.

Still inexplicably obsessed by Turkey and its neighbouring seas, Churchill insisted on an outlandish operation in which a British force was despatched to seize Rhodes and other islands of the Dodecanese group in the eastern Aegean, midway between Crete and the Turkish coast. Eisenhower washed his hands of the whole business and insisted that no American forces took part, thus avoiding any share in a humiliating and totally pointless disaster. The British were quickly and abjectly evicted from the islands by the Germans, losing the best part of five infantry battalions, several warships and 113 aircraft. The famous Long Range Desert Group, one of Churchill's beloved special forces, lost more men in six weeks than in the previous three years, all thanks to a deplorable and unforgivable folly. It has been claimed by his defenders that, although Churchill made mistakes, including

Gallipoli, he learned from them. To the contrary, A.J.P. Taylor was right when he said that, throughout this second war, 'Gallipoli was never far from his mind – as example, not warning.' The Aegean folly was almost a parody of Gallipoli twenty-eight years before, and with even less purpose: as with Gallipoli, the Dodecanese campaign 'could only have succeeded if it had been fought somewhere else'.

No sooner had Italy been invaded than the huge difficulties of this strange campaign became clear, as the Allies made their way north-wards to the Volturno river, were held there for months to come, then reached the next barrier on the Garigliano, where they were still fighting in May. Even without hindsight, the Italian campaign was baffling, and one wonders again if Churchill had ever travelled the length of the peninsula or studied enough maps. 'No battlefield could have been worse chosen,' Michael Howard wrote from bitter experi-ence. 'For nearly two years the Allied armies had to fight for mountain after mountain, hill after hill, in a theatre that might have been specifi-cally designed for defensive war.' Almost that point had been made many years before: 'The peculiar difficulty which attends mountain warfare,' the young Churchill had written in 1899, 'is that there are no general actions on a large scale, no brilliant successes, no important surrenders, no chance for a *coup de théâtre.*' He had forgotten those words by 1943.

He would later say that Aneurin Bevan, the left-wing Labour MP, had been 'a squalid nuisance' during the war, and there was some-thing, if not squalid, then unattractive, about an agitator who had been of military age in 1916 but had avoided serving, but who now became an armchair or backbench strategist. All the same, Bevan was near the knuckle that December when he asked, on behalf of 'the whole country': 'What strategical question behind the war put the British and American armies to fight their way right up the whole peninsula in the autumn and winter. Is that "the soft underbelly of the Axis"? We are climbing up the backbone.' A sharper verdict still came from the other side. General Fridolin von Senger und Etterlin was a patrician German officer and sometime Rhodes Scholar, who had risen to command a Panzer Corps in Italy, and later became a leading figure in the Federal Republic, the new-born German democ-racy, and the Bundeswehr, its likewise democratic army. At a confer-ence years after the war, he met Howard, who had now embarked on his own academic career. 'May I give you a word of advice?' the German asked the Englishman. 'Next time you invade Italy, do not start at the bottom.'

Despite those setbacks, Churchill always felt in his element at conferences with other Allied leaders, and he now wanted to hold another, the first meeting of the 'Big Three'. He hoped this might be in London, but Stalin wouldn't come to the west, and Roosevelt didn't want to come to England, for the unavowed reason that this would be politically disadvantageous ahead of the following year's election, when he was already thinking of running for a fourth term. After the Russians entered the war in 1941, they and the British had divided Persia into two spheres without asking the inhabitants, and it became a very important route for American supplies to Russia. Now the Persian capital Tehran was proposed for a conference, and thither Churchill went in November by way of Cairo for a preliminary meeting with Roosevelt. Even now Churchill was trying to twist the Americans' arms. Major-General John Kennedy, recently promoted to assistant head of the British Army, recorded that Churchill wanted the Americans 'to accept a postponement of Overlord', as the cross-Channel landing had been codenamed.

When Roosevelt arrived in Cairo, Churchill showed him the Pyramids, before they went on to meet another Sphinx in Tehran, where his un-understanding of personalities persisted. Churchill thought he liked Stalin, and wanted Stalin to befriend him in return. It didn't occur to him that, with a man who had ordained the torture and execution of most of his oldest and closest comrades, friendship and 'liking' might have rather limited meaning. But then again, when Churchill regularly spoke in private and public of Roosevelt as another friend, it was just as much a misreading of the man Dwight Macdonald called 'the shrewdest and most amoral political strategist of our day'. That shrewdness was limited to domestic politics. Roosevelt hoped to create a United Nations with a prominent American role, succeeding where Wilson had failed, although he hoped its strength would rest on the Great Powers, particularly the Americans and the Russians. He had already told Churchill in early 1942 that he would establish a better rapport with Stalin than Churchill or his Foreign Office could, and he then said fatuously of Stalin, 'I think that if I give him everything I possibly can and ask nothing from him in return, noblesse oblige, he will not try to annex anything and will work with me for a world of democracy and peace.'

From 28 November to 1 December the three leaders discussed the path to victory and the peace to come. And it was at Tehran that Churchill recognised the truth. 'There I sat with the great Russian bear on one side of me, with paws outstretched, and on the other side the great American buffalo, and between the two sat the poor little English donkey who was the only one ...who knew the right way home.' Those last words were vanity – Churchill had by now been given ample opportunity to show the right way, and had too often shown the wrong way – but what he said about the increasing insignificance of poor little England was all too true.

A year which began with one meeting at Casablanca and ended with another at Tehran was indeed *The Hinge of Fate*, as Churchill portentously called the fourth volume of *The Second World War*, but that title of the whole work is itself a problem, in more ways than one. The war of 1914–18 was known at the time as the European War, and then, not surprisingly, as the Great War. In 1920, the military writer Charles Repington published *The First World War*, its title intended as a warning lest there be more such wars, and that name became more widely used during the war of 1939–45, which itself became officially known as the Second World War even while it was being waged (World Wars I and II in American parlance). But these were really misnomers. As Churchill himself said, if there was a 'first world war' it was the Seven Years' War of 1756–63, which was waged from Europe to India, North America to West Africa. The Great War saw naval battles off the coast of Chile and off the Falkland Islands as well as three different campaigns in Africa and two in western Asia, while in Europe fighting ranged from the Baltic to Gallipoli, the southern Balkans to the Dolomites. But then, and even although Russia suffered grave losses in the long course of its defeat, the essential focus of the war was the narrow blood-soaked ribbon of land called the Western Front.

With the second great conflict there is a different problem of looking at and understanding it. We speak of the Second World War, or just 'the war', but we should really speak of 'the wars'. Between 1941 and 1945 two great, historically decisive wars were fought, between Germany and Russia for mastery of eastern Europe, and between

Japan and the United States for mastery of the western Pacific. One was incomparably the greatest land war in history and the other incomparably the greatest sea war: by 1945 the Red Army deployed more than 400 rifle divisions, and the United States Navy had more than 100 aircraft carriers afloat. Nothing else had ever matched that, or has since. Other countries played secondary roles, inglorious in the case of Italy, defiant in the case of Great Britain. And yet, by the end, the best succinct description of how the Third Reich was defeated came from Stalin: England provided the time, America provided the money and Russia provided the blood.

If anything, Churchill's own strategical interventions were consciously or unconsciously shaped by his recognition of British decline, and his memories of the Great War. An American army officer who was frustrated by listening once to Churchill's endless objections to a French landing was told by a British colleague, 'You are arguing with the Somme.' In that war, each side had signally lacked a Cunctator or Delayer – or so Keynes said when writing about Churchill's account of that war – who could wait, withdraw and entice. By 1943, British forces under Churchill had withdrawn quite often enough, if involuntarily, and he certainly played a waiting game, the Delayer whose last major, if negative, impact on Allied strategy was thwarting the Americans in their desire for an invasion of northern Europe, in 1942, or 1943.

An invasion of Normandy in June 1944 succeeded, whereas it's quite certain that an invasion of northern France in 1942 could only have been a bloody disaster in which almost all the casualties would have been British. Some historians have commended Churchill for preventing an invasion of France in 1943, though not all. John Grigg served as a subaltern in the Grenadier Guards in the last years of the war before he became a journalist and author, whose lasting memorial is his biography of Lloyd George, sadly uncompleted when Grigg died. In 1980 he published *1943: The Victory That Never Was*, making a careful and well-argued case that an invasion of northern France could have been accomplished that summer. We can't judge events which did not take place, and that has to be conjecture. 'The terrible "ifs" multiply,' as Churchill might say, and too many 'ifs' would have had to be answered: if the Axis had been cleared from North Africa more quickly and the Allies had stopped there rather than invading Sicily and Italy; if the tide of the Battle of the Atlantic had turned sooner, which would have meant diverting the resources lavished on Bomber Command to long-range aircraft against U-boats; and if much else besides. What we do know is that the invasion was delayed until June 1944, with very great consequences.

Meantime the Italian campaign was inspired by Churchill's belief that in war it's better to do something than nothing, although that dubious principle had been the argument for the Somme and 'the ghastly crime of Passchendaele'. Then again, he told the Commons that the British had to fight the Germans somewhere, or else 'sit back and let the Russians do all the fighting'. But that was what he was really doing in any case. Seen in perspective, the 'Mediterranean strategy', the Italian campaign and 'strategic bombing', not to mention 'set Europe ablaze', all look like 'virtual war', or displacement activities whose purpose was to delay as long as possible the only serious contribution the western Allies could make to the defeat of Germany: the invasion of France.

In turn this meant that for the three years from Barbarossa to D-Day almost all the real fighting against Germany was done by the Russians. The figures are awe-inspiring. In the course of 1943, some 70,000 western servicemen died fighting Germany and its allies: British, American, Canadian and many others, soldiers, sailors, airmen, including bomber aircrew. In that same year, almost two and a quarter million Russian soldiers were killed. While Rommel was being slowly driven out of Africa, a far vaster battle was being waged at Stalingrad; while the western Allies took their time forcing 50,000 Germans from Sicily, nearly a million German soldiers were defeated by the Red Army in the immense battle of Kursk, where the Wehrmacht lost more than a thousand tanks and over a hundred thousand men.

Although Churchill would admit that the Red Army 'tore the guts out' of the Third Reich, it's difficult or even painful even now for Americans and the British to recognise how modest a part their countries played in the defeat of Germany. By the end of the war, nearly nine out of ten German soldiers who died had been killed in the east, which is where the Third Reich met its end. Churchill's 1931 book on *The Eastern Front* was dedicated 'To our faithful allies and comrades in the Russian imperial armies.' He might well have dedicated a volume of *The Second World War* 'to our allies and comrades of the Red Army'. They had won the war.

13

'Our Allies will win it'
Champs-Élysées 1944

The emperors Caligula and Nero were both born in Antium, on the Italian coast a little more than thirty miles south of Rome, and they often visited it to escape city heat for sea air. It wasn't there that Caligula made his horse a consul, but Nero razed the existing villa at Antium to build another much bigger and more vainglorious. Some nineteen hundred years later a scheme was hatched, if not quite of Caligulan or Neronian madness, then tinged with fatal optimism and folly, to land an army at Antium, now called Anzio. This was Operation Shingle, one last outing for Churchill the great amphibian and, as Samuel Johnson might have said, one more triumph of hope over experience. Before 1944 ended Churchill was hankering after another such, but was mercifully foiled. The first was bad enough.

On 22 January 1944, American troops, and some British, landed at Anzio behind German lines, but in inadequate numbers: boys sent to do a man's job, as the American official naval historian has it. There they were caught by a fierce German counter-attack, and penned under fire for weeks and then months. Churchill complained when the expedition went awry but he had strongly favoured it, and General John Lucas, the American commander, said that Anzio was Gallipoli all over again, 'and with the same coach on the bench'. So far from a brilliant coup shortening the campaign, it would be almost six months before the Allies took Rome.

For all his reluctance, Churchill could no longer delay the invasion of northern France, but his relations with his allies became increasingly fraught. His attempts to communicate more closely with Roosevelt were frustrated by something very few were aware of at the time. Churchill certainly didn't understand the real state of Roosevelt's health, and it may be that Roosevelt himself had not learned the full truth: by the spring of 1944 he was already a dying man. Churchill was in his seventieth year, and no doctor would say that he had taken good care of himself, after consuming over the years great quantities of champagne, brandy and cigars. He had suffered what appeared to be a minor heart attack in December 1941, and then two bouts of pneumonia. The second, in December 1943 while in North Africa on his way back from Tehran, was serious enough that his life seemed in danger, and might have been lost but for 'M & B' drugs, the first generation of the antibiotics which would transform hundreds of millions of lives.

By contrast, Roosevelt was nearly ten years younger. The polio which crippled him twenty years before was a random affliction, and he had never lived intemperately, apart from smoking the cigarettes which almost certainly shortened his life, as they did the lives of many people of that age, including George VI. His personal doctor, equivalent to Moran with Churchill, was Ross McIntire. Officially serving in the United States Navy, he was promoted, to some adverse comment, from lieutenant-commander to admiral without a day of active service or sea time, except when accompanying the president on foreign journeys, and he saw his duty as issuing excessively optimistic bulletins about his health. In March, while Roosevelt was still pondering whether to run for re-election in November, adding a fourth term to his already unprecedented third, he was examined by Howard Bruenn, an eminent cardiologist, and a better physician than McIntire, who recognised that Roosevelt had congestive heart disease. He told McIntire that Roosevelt was most unlikely to survive another term. Indeed he doubted whether the president would live more than a year, and if Roosevelt had any inkling of that then his decision to run again was grossly irresponsible. As it was, he was ill enough to spend some weeks convalescing at the White House.

Then in April the president vanished. He boarded his magnificent personal train, the 'Ferdinand Magellan', at a platform unknown to the public, beneath the Bureau of Engraving and Printing, which stood five blocks from the White House, and disappeared into the night. For the next four weeks, he rested at Hobcaw Barony, a vast estate in South Carolina owned by Baruch, whose hospitality and financial support Churchill had long enjoyed. And so for nearly two vital months while the great invasion drew near, the president was *hors de combat*. Unlike Churchill, Roosevelt rarely interfered in strategy or gave orders to his generals, and during his time at

Hobcaw he had only one telephone conversation with General Mark Clark, the American commander in Italy. Churchill continually wrote to the president, still concerned about the Normandy landing, but these overwrought missives, and importunate suggestions of another meeting, were brushed off with vague, reticent replies written by Marshall. All of this only increased Churchill's frustration, and his resentment.

Less than a fortnight before D-Day, he treated the Commons to one of his *tours d'horizon*. This 24 May speech is little remembered, but caused much comment and even anger at the time. To read it is to be struck by just what an extraordinary creature Churchill was, that he could deliver such an oration with full vigour in his seventieth year and after four exhausting years of war; and to be struck also by his capacity for self-delusion. What enraged American liberals and the English Left was his saying, 'I am here today speaking kindly words about Spain,' praising Franco for not having helped Germany, and saying that 'Internal political problems in Spain are a matter for the Spaniards themselves. It is not for us – that is, the Government – to meddle in such affairs.' But then the whole tenor of this speech was that 'As this war has progressed, it has become less ideological in its character.' That was what shocked the editors of the *New York Times*, and the *New Republic*, which moaned, 'No, Mr Churchill, it will not do.' They were dismayed when he derided liberal 'newspaper editors, broadcasters, calumnists, or columnists' who thought that the war was fought for ideals like democracy, and said playfully that 'the word "Empire" is permitted to be used, which may be a great shock to certain strains of intellectual opinion'.

And yet what today seems most shocking is not what Churchill said about Spain but his words about Yugoslavia and Russia. From when Yugoslavia had been overrun by Germany in 1941, the British had supported the Chetniks, the Serb royalist resistance movement led by Dragoljub Mihailović, which originally co-operated with the Communist Partisans under Josip Broz, known as Tito. This soon turned into a complex of civil wars among Chetniks, Partisans and Ustashe, the militia of the fascist Croat statelet led by Ante Pavelić. These wars within wars were fought with extreme savagery on all sides, with many atrocities, and with little obvious right or wrong. Mihailović sometimes

made temporary accommodations with the Germans, but so did Tito
on at least one occasion, in order to turn his forces on the Chetniks.

In any case, the Germans were only in Yugoslavia in the first place
by accident, when forced to occupy the Balkans in order to save
Mussolini from another humiliation. The country served mainly as
a route to Greece and as a covering flank. But the achievements of
the Partisans were much exaggerated, in good faith by Bill Deakin,
Churchill's once and future research assistant, who was dropped into
the country, and in bad faith by James Klugmann, who held, quite
incredibly, a senior post in SOE in Cairo, although he was known to
be an active Communist, and was in fact a Russian spy. Churchill was
persuaded to abandon Mihailović, who 'has not been fighting the
enemy', he told the Commons. Months earlier, in Cairo in December,
Churchill had seen Fitzroy Maclean, a diplomatist and recently elected
MP who had already been in Yugoslavia with the Partisans. Maclean
warned him that Tito was a dedicated Communist. 'Do you intend
to make your home in Yugoslavia after the war?' Churchill asked,
and Maclean said not.* 'Neither do I,' said Churchill. 'Don't you think
we should leave it to the Yugoslavs to work out their own form of
government?' That was exactly what Bevin had said about Russia
twenty-five years before – 'we have no right to determine their
government' – when Churchill very much wanted to determine it
by violence.

Even so and despite what Maclean had told him, Churchill assured
Parliament that Tito 'has largely sunk his Communist aspect in his
character as a Yugoslav patriot leader. He repeatedly proclaims he has
no intention of reversing the property and social systems which prevail
in Serbia, but these facts are not accepted yet by the other side.' Nor
should they have been, as these 'facts' were quite absurd. Then
Churchill said, 'The terms offered by Russia to Rumania made no
suggestion of altering the standards of society in that country and
were in many respects, if not in all, remarkably generous'; all this
about a country where a Stalinist terror-state was already being
imposed.

---

* In fact, after the war Maclean acquired a house on a pretty island on the Yugoslav
coast.

He went on to claim that 'Profound changes have taken place in Soviet Russia; the Trotskyite form of Communism has been completely wiped out.* The victories of the Russian Armies have been attended by a great rise in the strength of the Russian State, and a remarkable broadening of its views. The religious side of Russian life has had a wonderful rebirth. The discipline and military etiquette of the Russian Armies are unsurpassed.' Two weeks after he spoke, Operation Overlord began at last, two weeks after that the Red Army began its great offensive Operation Bagration, and within a year, millions of Hungarian, Austrian and German women had their own taste of that 'military etiquette'.

With victory now assured, if far from imminent, what did peace hold for Churchill's country, and for him personally, in political, or financial terms? In December 1940 he had told Colville, 'He would retire to Chartwell and write a book on the war, which he already had mapped out in his mind chapter by chapter,' an exorbitant feat since at the time the war had barely begun and no one, including Churchill, then had any idea what course it would take. More than a year later he had told Cripps that 'I have my niche in history, nothing can displace me,' which was true but suggested that he might be surveying the scene from that Olympian niche. But he didn't really want to think about the political future, and when he reiterated, 'Everything for the war however controversial, nothing controversial if not for the war,' it was really a way of postponing any thought of the morrow.

In September 1940, and again in November 1941, Churchill promised Eden that he would be his successor, and before he left for Washington in June 1942 Churchill recommended to the king that, in the event of his death, he should appoint Eden, 'who is in my mind the outstanding Minister in the largest political party in the House of Commons and in the National Government'. Eden didn't imagine that he would wait nearly fifteen years for the promise to be honoured. He and other

---

* This prompted a shout, 'There never was such a thing,' from William Gallacher, the Communist Member for West Fife, with whom Churchill developed something like a friendship. Gallacher's two sons died in infancy and he adopted his brother's two sons. The death of both on active service in 1944 prompted a touching exchange of letters between Churchill and Gallacher.

Tories like Duff Cooper were anxious to look ahead for postwar Europe, while Labour men were equally keen to discuss domestic reform. Apart from vague musings about a united Europe, with possible groupings such as a Danubian federation where the Habsburg monarchy had been, and his expressed hope that there would be no continuing American presence in Europe, Churchill had little to offer. It was Eden who supported de Gaulle, believing that a strong France would be needed to contain Germany, and also to help balance Europe against American dominance. And when Duff Cooper tried to impress on Churchill that England would have the leadership of Europe for the taking when peace came, his urgings fell on deaf ears.

And so with domestic politics. If the runaway bestsellers of 1940 and 1941 had been *Guilty Men* and *The Battle of Britain*, their even more surprising successor in 1942 was an official document unenticingly called 'Social Insurance and Allied Services', although known to history as the Beveridge Report. Sir William Beveridge was an economist, and a child of the Raj like many notable figures who remade British life at the time. The prime minister had known, and not much liked, Beveridge since he had worked for the Board of Trade thirty-five years before. His Report portrayed in the language of Bunyan 'the five giants' to be overcome: idleness, ignorance, disease, squalor and want. Churchill and Lloyd George had once helped lay the foundations of social security or the welfare state (a phrase Beveridge hated), and interwar ministers, above all Chamberlain, had added much to the structure. But Beveridge now proposed a far more comprehensive programme of a national health service, family allowances, social insurance, full employment, for every citizen from cradle to grave. Churchill had lost his youthful radical zeal, but he couldn't ignore the fact that this Report sold 70,000 copies within days, and that a rare parliamentary rebellion forced the government to take formal note of it.

His indifference to Beveridge was of a piece with the way Churchill gave little thought to postwar politics, or the future of a Conservative party he had come by accident to lead. The Tories had won effortlessly in 1935, and then that Parliament had prolonged its life for the duration of the war, with somewhat mediocre personnel, as Churchill observed. An election had to come when the war ended, and there were warning signs for the Tories if Churchill had read them. The aberrant crisis of 1931 had set Labour far back, but they had gradually recovered their position through the 1930s, and the war years had given further evidence of Tory weakness. The party truce accompanying the formation of the government in May 1940 meant that two of the three main parties would stand aside in a by-election in a constituency held by one of the others, but there was nothing to stop independent candidates standing, and independents won a string of by-elections.

One dramatic by-election was held in February 1944, in West Derbyshire, a safe Conservative seat long represented by a member of the Cavendish family headed by the Duke of Devonshire, the great local magnate. The new candidate was the Marquess of Hartington, elder son of the duke and a twenty-six-year-old officer in the Coldstream Guards. He was in love with Kick Kennedy, daughter of the former American ambassador and sister of a future president, but marriage had been delayed by the religious difference, with the old duke a 'black Protestant' and Kick's Irish Catholic mother Rose equally horrified at her daughter marrying a Protestant.

At the by-election Hartington was cruelly derided in the popular press as the nepotistic representative of a dying order, to the point that Churchill personally intervened with a letter of support: 'My dear Hartington, I see that they are attacking you because your family has been identified with the Parliamentary representation of West Derbyshire. It ought, on the contrary, to be a matter of pride to the constituency to have such long traditions of constancy and fidelity through so many changing scenes and circumstances.' And he continued with a ripe flourish of Whig history, how the great families had long been 'on the side of the people's rights and progress', the Glorious Revolution and the Constitutional Monarchy, the Reform Bill, the Repeal of the Corn Laws and all: 'Most English people are proud of the past of their country.' But not proud enough on this occasion, and Billy Hartington was defeated by a local independent. Had he won, he wouldn't have been an MP for long. Those objections overcome, Hartington and Kick were married at long last and had a brief honeymoon before he rejoined his regiment. In September he was killed at the head of his men in Belgium.

Had Churchill paid more attention he would have seen the significance of that sad story: what the by-election had said about the eclipse of the old order to which he was so attached, and how far his dream of England was from the present reality. The whole tenor of the age tended towards collectivism, a tendency hugely encouraged by the 'war socialism' Churchill had preached in 1917 and had practised to an extreme degree in this war. Indeed, the war years have been called the nearest England ever came to totalitarianism, with state direction of labour and industry, police control of personal finance, censorship of the press, compulsory labour in the mines* and imprisonment without trial. Since his government had done so much to accustom the British to 'war socialism' and being told what to do by the state it was foolish of Churchill to suppose, as he would, that he could terrify them with the spectre of bureaucratic regimentation.

Although Churchill never repented Gallipoli, he was apprehensive about Normandy, telling Clementine on the night before D-Day that he might be responsible for 10,000 deaths by the next evening. In the event, around 3000 Allied soldiers were killed on 6 June, fewer than on some days later in the Normandy campaign, and of course far fewer than on some days in the Great War, not to say on many days that summer on the eastern front. The beachhead was secured but the breakout was slow and, just as the battle for Normandy developed, London faced another ordeal.

By now four years had wrought a great change in Churchill. The immense energy and bravura of 1940 were dissipated, he was tetchy and petulant, with drink taking an unmistakable toll. 'A frightful meeting with Winston,' Brooke recorded, 'quite the worst we have had with him. He was very tired as a result of his speech in the House concerning the flying bombs.' These were the VI 'doodlebugs', jet-propelled pilotless aircraft packed with explosive, which added a new misery to life in London, killing more than 6000 people from the first a week after D-Day until the autumn, and giving Churchill yet another problem. On this occasion 'he had tried to recuperate with drink,' Brooke recorded; 'he was in a maudlin, bad-tempered, drunken mood.' Attlee wrote Churchill a private letter of reproach about his conduct of business and treatment of colleagues, and the unity of the War Cabinet had anyway been impaired since July 1943 when Churchill insisted on bringing back Beaverbrook, despite the opposition of Lord Salisbury, who called him 'a very wicked man', and of Attlee, who

* The 'Bevin boys', named after the Minister of Labour, called up for National Service and sent to work as miners rather than serve in the army.

rightly said that Beaverbrook was 'the man in public life who is most widely distrusted by decent men of all parties'.

But for all that frustration, exhaustion and sense of impotence alongside his two more powerful allies, Churchill was still a master of narrative. And it was story-telling, literary and cinematic, which now saw a complete change in his personal fortunes. The war years made Churchill a very rich man for the first time, after a succession of attritional battles with publishers, tax authorities and movie moguls: a personal equivalent to the military victories which had long eluded him but had come at last. To return to the first year of the war: having left the *English-Speaking Peoples* unfinished in December 1939, Churchill was still in acute financial straits when he became prime minister. Rescue came in the form of Sir Henry Strakosch, a very rich Austrian-born financier who had made a fortune in South African mines. In the spring of 1940 he gave Churchill a precious tax-free gift of £5000, tactfully routed through Bracken, and when Strakosch died in 1943 he bequeathed Churchill another £20,000, which cleared him of debt for the first time in his life. He was still obsessed with minimising his liability for tax, which was now being charged at far higher rates than ever before to meet the cost of the war. That was true for the rich, paying marginal rates up to 97.5 per cent on their highest income, and for the working class. Churchill's saying that the front line ran through the factories was true not least fiscally: during this war factory workers were introduced to the delights of income tax for the first time by way of 'PAYE', pay as you earn, or deduction from pay packets.

With immediate financial pressure relieved, Churchill's literary income rose steadily, much improved by the publication in February 1941 of *Into Battle*, his first collection of wartime speeches, which sold briskly in America as well as England. It was followed by a series of such lucrative volumes. Newspapers were eager to publish anything by him, however incongruous: the *News of the World* dug up and ran an old piece called 'Are There Men in the Moon', and other papers printed extracts from his earlier books. This led to an unseemly tussle with the Inland Revenue about the rate at which these payments, and the sale of earlier copyrights, should be taxed, a wrangle which continued until shortly before Alamein. Both sides were naturally keen that the dispute should remain confidential, and so lawyers for Churchill and for the Revenue presented their cases to a private tribunal. It ruled in Churchill's favour and, since the alternative was now a public appeal to the courts, Sir Cornelius Gregg, the chairman of the Inland Revenue, conceded defeat with one rueful word, 'Acquiesce'. It was very much to the credit of English life that the Revenue should have pursued the prime minister as far as it did in the middle of a war. How creditable Churchill's conduct was, in doing everything he could to avoid the onerous taxes his compatriots were paying towards the war, may be variously estimated.

Although Cassell had agreed to postpone the unfinished *English-Speaking Peoples*, Churchill was in an awkward contractual tangle wholly of his own making. Well before finishing that book for Cassell he had signed another contract with another publisher, or publishers, for another book, with Harcourt Brace in New York, and in London with G. Harrap & Co., who had published *Marlborough*. The new book was to be called *After Armageddon*, but not a word of it had been written, and in 1940 Churchill tried to cancel the contract and return the advance. But he was now the hottest possible literary property and, while Harrap were ready to forget about the non-existent book, that contract had included an option on any next book Churchill might write, which they expected him to honour. By 1942 Harrap told Churchill that they would be happy to pay him more money for a revised contract 'if you feel you are able to write a different book', envisaging a war memoir.

But it wasn't only Cassell and Harrap. Nearly forty years before, Churchill's life of Lord Randolph had been published by Macmillan & Co., the firm founded in 1843 by two brothers who sprang from a Scottish crofting family, to become one of the leading houses in London. They had passed on *The World Crisis*, which was published by Butterworth. The contract for that book had been negotiated by Curtis Brown, who had kept in touch with Churchill since then and sometimes done deals for him, or tried to: at the time of the Munich crisis Curtis Brown had told him that an American newspaper would pay $1000 per piece for a 'war diary'.

By 1941, Churchill had recovered the copyrights for his earlier books, now out of print. Bracken proposed an enticing deal with Macmillan, similar to the unusual, and highly lucrative, arrangements both Kipling and Shaw had made with that firm, on commission while retaining copyright. Bracken thought he could extract terms from Macmillan so that 'you will take the major part of the profits which they earn ... I think this is an admirable arrangement,' whether or not it was an admirable business for a minister of the Crown to be handling on behalf of the prime minister in the middle of a great war. When a contract was drawn up it appeared to offer Macmillan first refusal on Churchill's future books, including the war memoir.

There were thus at least three London publishers potentially concerned with 'the Book he will write hereafter', although far more would have liked it. While many publishers assumed that Curtis Brown was still acting for Churchill, he had made the mistake of having no written agreement with him. Now Curtis Brown kept what he called a 'dossier' of offers for the war memoirs, but when he wrote to say that he had received a much higher offer of £250,000 – 'It is a letter of such importance that perhaps the Prime Minister would like to see it' – he had in return an ice-cold letter from Churchill's secretary. Curtis Brown should not 'be under any misapprehension: the "dossier" to which you repeatedly refer has no existence ... Would you please be good enough to let this correspondence end with the assurance that if Mr Churchill has need of your services at any time, he will not hesitate to ask you for them.' Churchill wanted a completely free hand to make deals for himself.

Before then there had been another gratifying battle between film producers keenly interested in Churchill, in particular Korda, for whom he had worked before the war. He proposed buying the film rights of the unpublished and unfinished *English-Speaking Peoples,* but Churchill's attentive secretary Kathleen Hill looked again at the original contract with Cassell and found that the outright, tax-free sale had given the publishers 'the complete and entire copyright', including film rights. Rather than put out money to buy them back, Churchill offered Cassell first refusal on any war memoir in return for ceding the film rights. Tense negotiations were conducted through lawyers but also by way of Bracken and Churchill's friend Lord Camrose of the *Daily Telegraph.* His intervention was far from disinterested: by helping Cassell establish a claim on 'any history of the War written by our friend', Camrose established a similar claim to newspaper serial rights.

In early 1944 Harrap renewed their own claim, suggesting legal arbitration, but now the web Churchill had woven became more tangled still when Daniel Macmillan again asserted his firm's right to any postwar book by Churchill. Between the wars, Daniel's brother Harold had taken an active part in the family business while continuing his political career, but Harold Macmillan was now far away in the Mediterranean as Churchill's plenipotentiary, his hands full with everything from French admirals to Italian politicians, as well as dreams of playing Greeks to the new Romans. And so, as David Lough writes in his enthralling book on Churchill and his money,* 'With D-Day less than two months away, Churchill now faced two competing legal claims to his postwar memoirs from Macmillan and Harrap, each potentially blocking the exchange he wanted to make with a third publisher, Cassell, so that he could sell Sir Alexander Korda the film rights.'

Just as the chiefs of staff tried to restrain Churchill's wildest military impulses, so Churchill's legal advisors tried to keep him within the proprieties of the law once they found out what he had been up to. They recognised that both Harrap and Macmillan had contractual rights which couldn't simply be brushed aside with Churchillian bluster. One lawyer, Charles Nicholl, saw how weak Churchill's position was with regard to Harrap, who could claim that the 'After Armageddon' contract 'might be held to include the whole or part of the period of the present War', and told Churchill to desist from all further correspondence with Cassell and Korda. Macmillan finally tired of the struggle and Churchill paid them off with a cheque for £7000, and a barefaced letter saying 'Please do not think that I am giving the notice because of other commitments as that is not the case,' which it was.

Now Harrap offered to cancel the existing contract in return for a new one on his next book, which was just what Churchill didn't want. His advisers urged him to accept this, but his heart had hardened against Harrap, who 'have been using this contract all this time as a blackmailing lever. The conduct of this firm, and particularly of Mr George Harrap, has been in my opinion so at variance with the usual conditions prevailing between author and publisher, that I do not wish to have any further dealings of any kind with them,' to which Harrap might have retorted something about his own conduct. Inconclusive talks were held by Bracken, until Harrap at last gave up, not because they didn't have legal and contractual right on their side, as they plainly did, but because 'it is distasteful to us, whether we are right or wrong, that we should be compelled to litigate the matter with a man to whom every one of us is indebted'. Churchill had

---

* *No More Champagne*, 2015.

always made his own rules. Now, as victory approached in Europe, he enjoyed a different kind of outright victory and, in a way that 'affronted the concept of a contract as a binding two-sided agreement, Churchill was able to walk away from commitments that he had previously given while pocketing all the proceeds himself, tax-free'.

While barrage and counter-barrage were fired in that campaign with publishers, there was a separate battle-front over movie rights. In July 1943 Korda wanted to buy *Marlborough* with the backing of MGM, and offered £20,000, but there was another player in the game. Filippo Del Giudice was a Jewish lawyer from Trani who had left Italy for England to escape Mussolini's dictatorship even before 'the greatest lawgiver's' antisemitic laws were introduced. He went into film production, was interned in 1940 and released. Having been a protegé of Korda's he was now a rival, and he bid for *Marlborough*. This news leaked, in garbled form, and Hannen Swaffer* revealed in the *Daily Herald* the 'astounding' news that *Marlborough* had been sold for £55,000. He added that since 'any scenario writer of skill' could write a screenplay of Marlborough's life from standard biographies and histories, Churchill was being paid for little more than his name. If this was mildly malicious, it wasn't so far from the truth. 'Mr Del' hadn't in fact offered as much, but now did raise his bid to £50,000, with £30,000 paid on signature. Korda had some consolation, when he was allowed to buy rights in *English-Speaking Peoples*, also for £50,000. His deal allowed him to make up to four movies from the book but not to cover Marlborough's life. Churchill paid no income tax on either deal, and more than seventy-five years later no movie of either book has been made. Altogether, far away from gunfire, Churchill won another two splendid victories of his own.

Military victory was more elusive. In the ambitious plans for D-Day – another echo of Gallipoli and Achi Baba – the British were to advance from Juno and Gold beaches that day and take Caen ten miles inland. Caen was taken, or what was left of it, on 21 July after a slow slog by Montgomery's army. General George Patton's US Third Army was

---

* Now quite forgotten, the bibulous and bombastic Swaffer was a famous Fleet Street figure in his day. The *Daily Herald* was the paper which once supported Labour and had portrayed Churchill as a Brownshirt in 1933; after many vicissitudes, it descended to what is today Rupert Murdoch's *Sun*.

a different story. Patton was a brilliant commander, and barely sane, with foibles which ranged from slapping shell-shocked soldiers in hospital to delivering a final speech to his army before D-Day so profane that it couldn't be broadcast or reported ('We don't want yellow cowards in this army. They should be killed off like flies. If not, they will go back home and breed more cowards. We've got to save the fucking for the fighting men.')

Not long before that Patton had opened an Anglo-American service club in London with the words, 'The idea of these clubs could not be better because undoubtedly it is the destiny of the English and American peoples to rule the world, and the more we see of each other the better.' Although that was quite close to Churchill's sentiment at Harvard, Patton's bluntness caused a scandal. That was forgotten as his Third Army broke through and delivered a right hook which encircled the Germans at Falaise. As usual, Montgomery was much slower in pursuit, just as he had been the previous summer in Sicily. And as usual, Montgomery tried to rewrite history by claiming falsely that a battle of attrition had been his purpose.

By now Hitler had lost the war. But was Churchill winning it? He was acutely aware of how far British power was diminished, and how far he had to compromise, however unwillingly, with the Russians and Americans. Publicly he praised the Russians; privately he said that, if his shirt were taken off, his belly could be seen scarred by his crawling to Stalin. Publicly he expressed devoted friendship for Roosevelt; privately, 'Winston is very bitter' about his disputes with Roosevelt, the king's secretary Tommy Lascelles recorded, 'and not so sure as he was that he really likes FDR.' Churchill would have winced at the line Orwell heard in a London pub, 'Chamberlain appeased Germany, Churchill appeases America,' but he would have understood it, and he sourly said that he was tired of being made to 'sit up and beg like Fala', Roosevelt's Scottish terrier.

As to his third ally, Churchill's relations with de Gaulle had been intermittently tempestuous for four years. At one moment Churchill acclaimed de Gaulle as the saviour of France, at another he told a secret session of the Commons that de Gaulle was deeply hostile to England, which his language and conduct did sometimes suggest. Clementine liked de Gaulle, something of an acquired taste, and could talk to him in her excellent French, but she asked him why he had to be so harsh towards his friends. Arrogant and graceless, de Gaulle seemed to have taken as his watchword Prince Schwarzenberg's saying in 1849, 'They will be astonished by our ingratitude.' He owed everything to Churchill, and Eden also, but his national and personal pride made it impossible for him to acknowledge that. He created the most extravagant of national legends, that he himself had personified the French people, and that they would liberate themselves. Fantastical as all this was, Churchill could not but feel some admiration and kinship, since he had after all created a comparable national and personal legend of his own.

Meetings between the two men became ever more heated until what Lascelles called one of their 'stormier interviews', when the prime minister, who insisted on speaking his own version of the language of Chateaubriand, shouted at de Gaulle, 'Et marquez mes mots, mon ami – si vous me double-crosserez, je vous liquiderai.' In slightly calmer vein, he said to de Gaulle, 'Look here! I am the leader of a strong, unbeaten nation. Yet every morning when I wake my first thought is how I can please President Roosevelt, and my second thought is how I can conciliate Marshal Stalin. Your situation is very different. Why then should your first waking thought be how you can snap your fingers at the British and Americans?'

Two days before D-Day, he told de Gaulle, 'There's something you need to know. Each time we must choose between Europe and the open sea [le grand large], we shall always choose the open sea. Each time I must choose between you and Roosevelt, I shall always choose Roosevelt.' De Gaulle never forgot those words. To his rage, he wasn't allowed to land in Normandy immediately after D-Day, but his speech the following day couldn't be faulted for grandeur. 'The supreme battle has begun ... For the sons of France, wherever they may be, whoever they may be, the simple and sacred duty is to fight the enemy by all the means available ... Behind the heavy clouds of our blood and our tears, the sunshine of our grandeur is re-emerging.' As Churchill drily observed to Roosevelt, the speech was 'remarkable, as he has not a single soldier in the great battle' (not literally true: a small number of Free French commandos had in fact landed with the British on D-Day).

And yet by 25 August Churchill was at de Gaulle's side as they made an unforgettable walk down the Champs-Élysées to Notre Dame cathedral in the heart of a liberated city, with Churchill in floods of tears, and an unsmiling de Gaulle towering above him. In de Gaulle's wonderfully vainglorious words, now inscribed on his statue in the

Place de la Concorde, the city was *'Paris outragé, Paris brisé, Paris matyrisé, mais Paris liberé, et par lui-même,'* the last phrase in particular is flagrantly untrue: Paris, and France, had not been liberated 'by herself'. Antoine de Saint-Exupéry, the airman and writer who will always be remembered for his children's book *The Little Prince*, was serving with the Free French. Five days after that walk in Paris, he took off from Corsica and was never seen again, but he had already put a brutal finger on de Gaulle's pretences: 'Tell the truth, General, we lost the war. Our allies will win it.' True enough; and something of the same might have been said to Churchill, if anyone had dared.

By a nice irony, in a lifetime during which the great amphibian Churchill had been associated so often with so many distant landings, the only one he ever witnessed in person was one he had bitterly opposed. He had wanted to watch the D-Day landings from a ship offshore, but the king forbade him. Instead, on 15 August he watched from a ship as Operation Dragoon landed allied troops on the 'Azure Coast' of Provence, where he had spent so many happy days and nights. He admired through gritted teeth the great Allied fleet 'spread along twenty miles of coast with poor St Tropez in the centre'. By a further irony, this was one of the most successful campaigns of the war. Of course the German army was already fighting on three fronts, in Italy, Normandy and above all in the east, and the invasion of southern France was barely opposed. All the same, these invaders advanced so fast up the Rhone valley that within less than four weeks they had made contact with Eisenhower's army to the north, before turning east, where by 24 November, within a hundred days of landing, Lieutenant-General Jacob Devers's Sixth Army Group had reached the Rhine at Strasbourg. One of the unanswered questions of the war is what would have happened if Devers's army had crossed into Germany as he wanted.

But by then Eisenhower's habitual caution had been strengthened by disaster in the north. For once in his life Montgomery had shown daring, with an over-optimistic plan to seize two bridges in the Netherlands by airborne landings, but he bungled the ill-planned and ill-directed campaign. The British Airborne Division was broken at Arnhem, suffering 7000 casualties before its remnants were withdrawn. '"Not in vain" may be the pride of those who have survived and the epitaph of those who fell,' Churchill most inadequately told the Commons after Arnhem, adding that 'We must not forget that we owe a great debt to the blunders – the extraordinary blunders – of the Germans,' although the Germans had owed a debt to some of Churchill's own blunders, and those of his chosen commanders. It remained for Arnhem to become another name on the list of heroic failures, a story told or garbled in the epic 1977 movie *A Bridge Too Far*, which with all its highly paid stars in cameo roles quite missed the point that Operation Market Garden was a self-inflicted disaster, for which 'Monty' should have been sacked.

Still yearning for one more amphibious operation, Churchill proposed a landing at Istria, with the object of taking Trieste and driving towards a supposed 'Ljubljana gap' and then the Danube valley. This newly-hatched dream of reaching Vienna, Berlin and Prague before the Russians, which aroused much retrospective debate after the war, was militarily far-fetched in the extreme. Istria is a pretty, hilly peninsula, which had once, with the whole eastern Adriatic coast, belonged to the Venetian Republic, and then to the Habsburg empire, whose fleet was based at Pola on the tip of the peninsula with its splendid Roman amphitheatre. After the Great War, the Italians had tried to claim it, and the posturing proto-fascist poet Gabriele d'Annunzio briefly seized 'Fiume' on the easterly base of the peninsula before it was ceded to the new Yugoslavia under the name Rijeka.*

There is no 'Ljubljana gap'. Beyond Istria, mountains stretch north and east, and as the Südbahn railway – one of the glories of Habsburg days – wends its way from Trieste to Vienna, it passes through tunnels cut into land which is anything but suited for infantry and armour. Yet again Churchill doesn't seem to have had the right maps. This adventure was mercifully thwarted, by Brooke and still more by Eisenhower, with the brisk words: 'In my opinion to contemplate wandering off overland via Trieste to Ljubljana repeat Ljubljana is to indulge in conjecture to an unwarrantable degree ... I am unable to repeat unable to see how over-riding necessity for exploiting the early success of Overlord is thereby assisted.' A final Gallipoli was averted.

In October, oppressed by the course of events, Churchill flew to Moscow to see Stalin, the man whose army had won the war. Churchill's

---

* The three new Italian cruisers sunk by the British at Cape Matapan in March 1941 bore aggressively irredentist names: in the Italian forms, the *Fiume*, *Pola* and *Zara*. The three towns are now in Croatia, called Rijeka, Pula and Zadar.

statement that 'no suggestion of altering the standards of society' in Rumania had been foolish enough in May, and five months later they rang hideously hollow: the Red Army had 'liberated' or conquered Rumania and Bulgaria, and was advancing into Hungary, accompanied by the secret police, who quickly imposed a reign of terror as a basis for quisling dictatorships. In Moscow Churchill proposed a deal, based on the bluntest realpolitik or spheres of influence. Russia would have a 90 per cent interest in Rumania, 75 per cent in Bulgaria and 50 per cent in Hungary and Yugoslavia, with 'the others', presumably the British, taking 10, 25 and 50 per cent respectively. Only in Greece would 'the others' have 90 per cent, the Russians 10. Churchill wrote out this 'naughty document', as he later called it, and showed it to Stalin, who ticked it. 'We have settled a lot of things about the Balkans,' Churchill told Clementine. 'I have had v[er]y nice talks with the Old Bear. I like him the more I see him. *Now* they respect us here & I am sure they wish to work with us.'

There were two problems, Churchill added the Americans and the Poles. 'I have to keep the President in constant touch & this is the delicate side,' which indeed it was, since Roosevelt still believed that he himself could deal with Stalin to create a new world order, and still maintained that he hated spheres of influence. To European eyes, that was further American hypocrisy since, from the Monroe Declaration to Roosevelt's day, Washington had jealously guarded its own sphere of influence in Latin America. As Walter Lippmann wrote at this very point, 'We have never thought of acknowledging the "right" of Cuba or Haiti or the Republic of Panama – all of them independent sovereign states – to contract alliances which were inconsistent with the concert of the whole North American region.'

But the fate of Poland was bitterest of all. One of Wilson's Fourteen Points in 1917 had been 'An independent Polish state', and in September 1939 Great Britain and France had gone to war with Germany in defence of Polish independence. A Polish government in exile had been established in London, Polish help had been crucial in unlocking the Enigma code, and hundreds of thousands of Poles had fought gallantly in the Allied forces. Once Russia entered the war, the story took a different and grim turn. Stalin had his eyes on that eastern territory which had once been ruled by Russia, and would be again if he won the war. By 1943 the news about Katyn had only reinforced the Poles' natural hatred of Stalin and Russia. And yet, as the Germans were driven from eastern

Europe by the Red Army, it gradually became clear that Poland would lose not only its prewar territory but its independence.

In August 1944, an heroic but inopportune patriotic rising in Warsaw was brutally crushed by the Germans and most of the city destroyed, while the Red Army sat watching from the far bank of the Vistula. Stalin was delighted to see these patriots disposed of, since he had already created a 'Lublin committee' of Polish Communists in opposition to the London exiles, ready to take over the country and install a quisling regime. Churchill told the king, 'Our lot from London are, as your Majesty knows, a decent but feeble lot of fools, but the delegates from Lublin seem to be the greatest villains imaginable.' He returned having really settled nothing except to quieten for the moment his uneasy conscience, with little justification. Chamberlain was damned by Churchill and has been by posterity for betraying the Czechs in 1938 but, as betrayal of 'a faraway country' or countries, Munich paled beside Churchill's 'percentages' deal.

After the debacle at Arnhem, the Allied advance resumed, until December when a last throw of the dice by Hitler, like Ludendorff's March attack in 1918, caught the Americans unawares in the Ardennes. This Battle of the Bulge saw the heaviest fighting of the campaign since Normandy, with more than 20,000 Americans killed. Montgomery distinguished himself by his insolence and bombast, causing deep American resentment. Nor was Montgomery the only commander who should have been dismissed had he not been inflated by Churchillian publicity. By the late summer the British 'strategic bombing offensive' had conclusively failed, as more and more German cities were destroyed, and German industrial war production steadily increased. The Americans had suffered their own chastening casualties until they began to deploy long-range Mustang fighters which could accompany bombers and allow them to bomb accurately, with devastating effect on German oil production: exactly the 'panacea' Harris had so long derided.

By now he was thoroughly insubordinate, but Churchill found that he had made 'Bomber Harris' a popular hero, and to dismiss him would be to call into question the whole terror-bombing campaign. In fact it had already been questioned, by the heroic Dr George Bell, Bishop of Chichester, speaking in the House of Lords; by Richard Stokes, a contrarian backbench Labour MP, a Great War veteran and holder of the Military Cross, in the House of Commons; and by military theorists like Liddell Hart and J.F.C. Fuller, although when

Fuller wrote a column for the *Evening Standard* criticising area bombing, it was rejected by the editor, none other than Michael Foot. Even some aircrew hated what they were doing. 'Whatever statesmen and braided air marshals may say or write it was barbarous in the extreme,' one said later. '"Whoever harms a hair of one of these little ones ..." I expect no mercy in the life to come. The Teacher told us clearly. We disobeyed.' And of course Churchill himself had asked 'Are we beasts?' If that troubled him in the summer of 1943, then what should he have felt by early 1945? In the eleven months from D-Day to VE Day, more bombs were dropped on Germany, and more civilians killed, than in the previous four years, as one city after another was 'browned', in Bomber Command's unlovely, presumably cloacal, turn of phrase.

This culminated on 13 to 14 February with the destruction of Dresden, a baroque gem, 'the Florence on the Elbe' once much admired by English and American visitors, laid waste with at least 25,000 people killed, although a much higher figure would be given later, not necessarily with respectable motives. Apart from the evocative name, what made this seem exceptional was a despatch by Howard Cowan, an Associated Press correspondent at Allied Headquarters, who wrote that 'The Allied air commanders have made the long-awaited decision to adopt deliberate terror bombing of German population centres.' That was not so: there had been no change of policy at all, and Dresden was no different from Hamburg and Berlin, Hanover and Darmstadt. But Churchill's complicated or conflicted attitude to bombing now came back to haunt him, along with the ugly fact that, as Martin Middlebrook, one of the best historians of the subject, has said, the bombing campaign had been 'a three-year period of deceit practised on the British public and on world opinion'. Churchill had been complicit in this deceit, and was now impaled by it.

Before the destruction of Dresden, there had been a second and final meeting between Churchill, Stalin and Roosevelt. At Stalin's insistence, and to the intense inconvenience of the British and, even more, the Americans, it was held from 4 to 11 February at Yalta on the Crimean peninsula, where the British army had fought an unlikely campaign ninety years before. This was a wretched experience, a gruelling journey, squalid conditions in quarters that were bugged twice over: verminous, and wired by Soviet spies. Stalin enjoyed another advantage, in the physical condition of Roosevelt, which was no better for victory in November in an election in which he should never have run. When Churchill met the president at Malta before travelling on to Yalta, he bafflingly or untruthfully told Clementine that 'My friend has arrived in the best of health and the best of spirits.' Even by his standards of believing what he wanted to believe, those were extraordinary words. Others in the party, particularly those British officials who hadn't seen Roosevelt since Tehran more than a year before, were shocked by his deterioration. His appearance 'was, frankly, terrible', said Gladwyn Jebb.

Some matters were settled at Yalta, for better or very much for worse. Once Germany was defeated, she would be partitioned into sectors controlled by the victors, including France at Churchill's demand, for which he received no thanks from de Gaulle. Poland would lose her eastern territories but would be compensated to the west. The political character of this restored and relocated Poland was another matter. At the end of the conference a joint communiqué merely asserted that the Polish government would be 'reorganised on a broader democratic basis with the inclusion of democratic leaders from Poland itself and from Poles abroad'. That meant anything and nothing. There was in truth an insoluble problem: Stalin wanted a Polish government friendly to Russia, which no truly representative government could be. Now Poland was occupied by the Russians, who were soon busy arresting and then disposing of any real or imagined political opponents.

One other question which set Roosevelt at odds with Churchill was Palestine. During the war Churchill had kept in touch with Weizmann, whose loyalty to the Allied cause had found poignant personal expression when his son Michael was killed as an RAF pilot. Palestine was a harder problem than ever for the British government, with desperate Jews trying to escape Europe, but the Arabs resolutely opposed to Jewish immigration, and the British again trapped by their own contradictory promises. Despite his personal sympathy for Zionism, not shared by several of his colleagues in the government, Churchill had kept his distance from Zionist leaders, even Weizmann whom he had known so long. They did meet at last in November 1944, when Weizmann was consumed by the horror that had befallen his people in Europe. Churchill could do no more than hope for better times when the war ended.

On the day after they met, Lord Moyne was assassinated in Cairo. Walter Guinness was an eminent public man, decorated soldier, traveller, MP, minister, ennobled in 1932, and 'a most agreeable, intelligent and unusual friend', in Churchill's words, not to say a generous host in whose yacht Clementine had visited the East Indies in 1935. In January 1944 Churchill had appointed Moyne minister resident in the Middle East. He was shot by two men of the Lehi, known to the British as the Stern Gang, a more extreme faction of Jabotinsky's followers known as the Irgun. The assassination was directed by Yitzhak Shamir, who had taken the codename 'Michael' in homage to Michael Collins, and to the IRA's earlier campaign of violence. In 1983, 'Michael' would become prime minister of Israel.

This almost ended Churchill's support for a movement he had favoured for forty years. 'If our dreams for Zionism are to end in the smoke of assassins' pistols,' he told the Commons, 'and our labours for its future to produce only a new set of gangsters worthy of Nazi Germany, many like myself will have to reconsider the position we have maintained so consistently and so long in the past.' He knew the suspicions of MI5, the intelligence agency, that he himself was a possible target for assassination, and he would later stand accused of doing nothing to help the Hungarian Jews.

Since the Great War and the Trianon Treaty which was imposed on Hungary and removed two-thirds of her territory, Admiral Miklós Horthy had governed this diminished country, ostensibly as Regent for a monarchy, 'an admiral without a fleet ruling a kingdom without a king'. His regime had been autocratic, reactionary and antisemitic, but not actually murderous, and although he had competed for Hitler's favour to regain territory from Rumania, and had sent Hungarian troops to fight on the eastern front, he had kept the Germans out of Hungary, until they took over in March 1944. The Third Reich were determined that, even if they faced defeat and destruction, they would kill as many Jews as possible before they went. In the summer of 1944, half a million Hungarian Jews were rounded up and deported to Auschwitz and death. 'The Romanians survived, the Bulgarians survived, the Hungarians did not. That's on Churchill's conscience,' in the lurid words of Edward Luttwak, implying that he could and should have done something to prevent the murder, without saying what that something was. 'In 1944, Churchill, lifelong friend of the Jews, became Hitler's remaining Holocaust ally.'

Those are outrageous words, and there is a grave moral danger in suggesting that the Allies, through however many sins of omission, shared the guilt of the murderers. Claims of ignorance of the great killing are another matter. 'There is no doubt,' Churchill wrote to Eden on 11 July, as the Hungarian horror unfolded, 'that this is probably the greatest and most horrible crime ever committed in the whole history of the world,' adding that 'all concerned in this crime who may fall into our hands, including the people who only obeyed orders by carrying out the butcheries, should be put to death after their association with the murders has been proved.' If that had been taken literally after the war it would have meant a bloodbath, since so many had some 'association' with the great murder.

After Yalta, Roosevelt went on to meet Ibn Saud, the king of Saudi Arabia, in the forlorn hope of persuading him to accept a Jewish homeland in Palestine. When Stalin asked what he could offer the king as inducement, Roosevelt answered 'with a smile' that he could offer him six million American Jews. But the meeting aboard an American warship in the Red Sea was not a success. Nothing Roosevelt could do would bend Ibn Saud's implacable opposition to the Zionists and, when Roosevelt spoke of the horrors suffered by the European Jews, the king made the telling reply, 'Give the Jews the choicest lands of the Germans who oppressed them. Amends should be made by the criminal, not by the innocent bystander.' After the meeting Admiral William Leahy, the chief of staff, said to Roosevelt, 'the king sure told you, didn't he? ... If you put any more kikes in Palestine, he's going to kill them,' at which Roosevelt laughed. He returned across the Atlantic, with only months to live, and never saw Churchill again.

On his own return home from Yalta, Churchill had other problems to face. He was busy covering his tracks, and preparing a new narrative, even if it meant contradicting himself. Writing urgently to Roosevelt, Churchill said: 'you and I by putting our names to the Crimean settlement have underwritten a fraudulent prospectus.' And yet, on 23 January, before Yalta, he had said to Colville, 'Make no mistake, all the Balkans, except Greece, are going to be bolshevised; and there is nothing I can do to prevent it. There is nothing I can do for poor Poland either.' On 27 February he nevertheless told the Commons that the 'most solemn declarations have been made by Marshal Stalin' about Polish elections, although adding, 'The Poles will have their future in their own hands, with the single limitation that they must honestly follow ... a policy friendly to Russia. That is surely reasonable.' He said moreover that 'I know of no government which stands to its obligations, even in its own despite, more solidly than the Russian Soviet Government,' and angrily repudiated 'any suggestion that we are making a questionable compromise or yielding to force or fear', as he plainly was. Over a drink in the Smoking Room that evening, he said to Harold Nicolson and Lord de la Warr that he didn't see what choice he'd had at Yalta other than to accept Stalin's word.

At last in late March the western armies reached the Rhine, and Churchill flew to join the headquarters of the British Second Army. Unlike any previous prime minister, he had worn uniform while in office, indeed a variety of them, and on this occasion he was dressed as Colonel of the Fourth Hussars, fifty years after he had joined the regiment. He insisted on visiting the bank of the Rhine and unbuttoned and emptied his bladder into the great river. On a more elevated note, he attended a church parade, 'the first time I have known the PM to go to church,' noted Colville, who had been with him for five years. Churchill delighted in the sound of gunfire again, regardless of personal danger. Many years later, when enfeebled and dejected, he said, 'I wish I had died in 1945,' and even at the time the old hussar might not have minded a soldier's glorious death.

Now victory was near, but whose victory was it? For three-quarters of a century since, the Americans and the British have been nourished on the glorious myths of liberation, with endless books on the Normandy campaign, and on Arnhem and the Battle of the Bulge, movies about D-Day from *The Longest Day* to *Saving Private Ryan*, as well as television programmes like *Band of Brothers*; myths nourished by Churchill with his emphasis on the battles fought by the western allies, with his preposterous claim that Normandy had been 'the greatest and most decisive single battle of the whole war'. This has been a grave distortion. One eminent military historian, who has studied the war for many years, has said (in private rather than in print, so disturbing might this be to his readers) that he now doubts whether the campaign which began on D-Day shortened the war by more than a few weeks, or even a week. Much the greatest part of the German army was still fighting in the east. In the eleven months from D-Day to VE Day, some 110,000 American soldiers were killed in north-western Europe, and about half as many British (including Canadians and others), formidable figures by twenty-first century standards. In the same period, more than half a million soldiers of the Red Army were killed.

If Churchill deluded himself about the balance of the war, he did so as well about his allies. Churchill had told Clementine that Stalin respected him, when in fact Stalin held Churchill in genial contempt, and enjoyed toying with him. If Churchill said he hated being made to sit up and beg like Roosevelt's Scottish terrier, the Russians only changed the breed of dog. Sergo Beria, son of the murderous NKVD chief Lavrentia Beria, quipped that the Russians 'compared Churchill to a poodle wagging its tail to please Stalin'. And Churchill had deluded himself just as much about his other ally. After his re-election, Roosevelt replaced Cordell Hull, his Secretary of State, with Edward Stettinius, who infuriated Churchill by publicly criticising him for trying to restore monarchies in Greece and Italy: 'We expect the Italians to work out their own problems of government along democratic lines without influence from outside,' Stettinius, adding to Roosevelt that the problem lay in the 'emotional difficulty which anyone, particularly an Englishman, has in adjusting to a secondary role after always accepting a leading role as a national right', which was true. And Roosevelt agreed, contemptuously comparing the British with the Argentines, whom he despised. 'No lover ever wooed his mistress as ardently as I wooed Roosevelt,' Churchill claimed. The seduction remained unrequited. 'It is very apparent,' Stettinius noted after talking to Roosevelt, 'that he distrusts the British and dislikes them immensely.'

Many years before, in May 1901, Churchill had startled the Commons with his prophecy that 'a European war could only end in the ruin of the vanquished and the scarcely less fatal commercial dislocation and exhaustion of the conquerors,' and he had since had ample opportunity to ponder that truth. Forty years later in October 1940 he had said to Colville, 'A lot of people talked a lot of nonsense when they said wars never settled anything; nothing in history was ever settled except by wars.' This is a bleak doctrine, that no human betterment can be achieved but by killing and dying, although it's true enough that wars do wreak great changes. And yet, as Churchill had better reason than most to know, and was being reminded again as what he called this 'new, disgusting year' of 1945 began, the changes wrought by war are very often unforeseen, unwanted, unintended, and highly unwelcome, to victors as well as vanquished.

TWO CHURCHILLS

14

'Some sort of Gestapo'
Whitehall 1945

'This is your victory,' Churchill told a vast cheering crowd in Whitehall, to which they shouted back, 'No, it is yours.' He beamed at what seemed the universal approbation of the people, and they cheered louder still when he appeared with the king and queen at Buckingham Palace. Earlier that day, 8 May, as the German surrender was formally announced, the Commons adjourned and Members walked across to a service of thanksgiving at St Margaret's, Westminster, Parliament's own parish church. Another service was held at St Paul's on the following Sunday, where the Archbishop of Canterbury pronounced, 'This is such a national thanksgiving as never was before.' It was true. Over the centuries, the bells of St Paul's had rung out for other victories, Marlborough's among them, and then the Armistice in 1918, but none like this. A huge congregation in the cathedral was headed by the king and queen and the two princesses, Elizabeth and Margaret, along with the prime minister and Mrs Churchill, and their daughter Mary. She had commanded an anti-aircraft battery of the ATS, in whose ranks Princess Elizabeth had served as a mechanic, emblematic of national unity and the way that members of the two most famous families in the country had played their part. Even then the mood of elation was qualified. As the *Manchester Guardian* reported, 'There was much singing and shouting, but less of the hysteria and none of the blind, unthinking optimism of November 1918.'

While Churchill basked in glory, he thought of the future. One reason for the subdued mood was that the war wasn't yet finished. Churchill scarcely needed to remind anyone that 'Japan, with all her treachery and greed, remains unsubdued. The injury she has inflicted on Great Britain, the United States, and other countries, and her detestable cruelties, call for justice and retribution.' Those were grim words to the ears of soldiers who had just fought the European war to its gruelling conclusion. In his deranged address to the men of the US Third Army before D-Day, General Patton had concluded by saying that Germany must be crushed, 'And then we'll have to take a little jaunt against the purple pissing Japs and clean them out before the Marines get all the credit.'

By the following spring, such a 'cleaning out' was no cheerful prospect for the GIs of the Third Army, or for British soldiers either. Seven weeks before VE Day, Iwo Jima was taken by the Americans, after thirty-five days of brutal fighting in which almost the entire Japanese garrison of 22,000 was wiped out, and 6821 Marines were killed, all to take an island a quarter the size of Manhattan. Few men in uniform looked forward to another 'little jaunt' like that. Nor did Churchill, for whom the Pacific war was very remote, and not only geographically, although it had just acquired a poignant personal resonance. Days before the landing on Iwo Jima, another landing in the Marshall Islands had seen heavy casualties. Among the dead was Stephen Hopkins.

In 1941, Roosevelt had sent Harry Hopkins as a personal emissary to London, where he and the prime minister had established more of a real friendship than Churchill ever enjoyed with Roosevelt, and Hopkins had believed in Anglo-American amity in a way that his president never did. He had brought tears to Churchill's eyes by quoting 'Whither thou goest, I will go,' Ruth's beautiful lines: 'thy people shall be my people,' something Roosevelt certainly didn't feel. Stephen was his son. Now Churchill sent his friend no mere letter of condolence but a parchment bearing the words from *Macbeth*, 'Thy son, my lord, has paid a soldier's debt.' Twenty-first century readers, familiar with politicians who delight in waging wars in which they and their sons would never dream of serving, may be struck by this: not the sorrow of bereavement, or consoling eloquence, but the fact that, once upon a time, one of the most important and influential men in America could lose a son killed serving as a private in the Marines.

For Churchill there was an even closer reminder to come, when Eden learned that his elder son Simon, an RAF pilot, was missing in Burma. Eden heard this while he and Churchill were at the first sessions of the Potsdam conference, the last great summit of the war for the Big Three. He asked for the news to be suppressed for the moment as he did not want to seem to appeal for sympathy.

Eden was acquainted with grief. He had lost his eldest brother, John, killed with the 12th Lancers in October 1914, and then his beloved younger brother Nicholas, killed at Jutland as a sixteen-year-old midshipman in HMS *Indefatigable*. That was just after Anthony arrived in France to serve with the 60th Rifles at Ploegsteert Wood, the 'Plugstreet' where Churchill had served shortly before. The following year Eden won the Military Cross for saving his wounded sergeant under fire. He was still in Potsdam when Simon's death was confirmed.

He was one of the casualties of a strange campaign, fought by the British Fourteenth Army, the most international and multi-racial army of the war, under General Sir William Slim, the most gifted and like-able British general of the war, even if that might not be saying much. In 1942 the British had been routed and driven back to the border of India. Slim took command at the worst moment, and then justified Clausewitz's saying that no one can be considered a great commander who has not conducted the most difficult of all military tasks, a fighting retreat. The Fourteenth Army had at last stood its ground at Kohima and then, in 1944, went on an offensive which, by the time the war ended in Europe, had driven the Japanese out of most of Burma and taken Rangoon, inflicting what by some measures was the worst defeat the Japanese army ever suffered.

This was accomplished by an army which was 'British' as of the Empire, but only about one-sixth of Slim's force was from the British Isles: the rest were Indians, Gurkhas, and among others also Africans who had volunteered for a war in a distant country which few of them had heard of. One foot-soldier serving in Burma with the Border Regiment was George MacDonald Fraser, who would one day achieve fame as the author of the splendid 'Flashman' novels. Many years later he looked back on that harsh struggle in Burma, against monsoons, leeches and disease, as well as against an enemy for whom he and his comrades felt 'a deep abiding hatred', although 'as well as hating they respected and even admired him'. He and his fellow soldiers were of course 'racist', MacDonald Fraser observed sardonically, 'but they were racists who had a loyalty and devotion to their Indian and African and Chinese and Burmese and Afghan and Gurkha comrades which no modern liberal could even begin to understand.'

Nor did Churchill. Even though family as well as imperial pride might have made him want to recover a land which his father had acquired for Queen Victoria, he brusquely told his chiefs of staff in September 1944 'that the minimum of effort should be employed in this disease-ridden country'. He didn't share any devotion to black and brown soldiers. And he never appreciated the gifts of Slim, inflicting on him as 'Supreme Allied Commander in South-East Asia' the preening Mountbatten, who vaingloriously chose 'Mountbatten of Burma' as his peerage, as though he had been responsible for the victory. Nor did Slim's plain speaking endear him to Churchill. 'Well, Prime Minister, I know one thing. My Army won't be voting for you,' Slim cheerfully said on a brief return to London.

Other soldiers could have told him the same. When Churchill gave his victory broadcast in May, a troop of Welsh Guards serving in tanks commanded by Kenneth Rose, later a journalist and biographer, had stopped and dismounted to listen. A lifetime later Rose recalled how the Guardsmen heard the peroration – 'Advance, Britannia! Long live the cause of freedom! God save the King!' – and fell silent, until the troop sergeant said, 'Sounds as if the old bugger's pissed.' And when Michael Howard helped organise an election debate in his battalion of the Coldstream Guards, now in northern Italy, speeches were made on behalf of the three parties, before a Guardsman said to Howard afterwards that it didn't make much difference: 'But the likes of us – we're all Labour, aren't we? So we'll vote Labour.'

That might have warned Churchill about the general election now approaching. The existing Parliament had been elected as long ago as November 1935 and had artificially prolonged its life for the duration of the war. Six months before the victory in Europe, on 31 October 1944, Churchill had told the Commons that it would be wrong to prolong it any more once Germany was defeated. Then he changed his mind, and on 18 May he suggested that the coalition should continue until Japan was defeated. At that time almost no one knew about distant events in New Mexico, or foresaw how soon, or with what terrifying abruptness, that eastern war would end; the war against Japan was expected to last at least another eighteen months. Then Churchill floated the quaint notion of a referendum on the continuance of Parliament and Coalition. Attlee dismissed the suggestion with admirable words which should have been remembered many years later: 'I could not consent to the introduction into our national life of a device so alien to all our traditions as the referendum, which has only too often been the instrument of Nazism and fascism.'

In late May the Labour Party conference met in Blackpool. Five years earlier their conference at the more genteel seaside resort of Bournemouth had helped bring Churchill to power; now the conference ended the Coalition by rejecting his proposal. Churchill thought that, if an election were coming, then it should be sooner rather than later. He resigned as prime minister on 23 May, entertaining the chief ministers of the departing Coalition with the words, 'the light of history will shine on all your helmets,' while he returned to office at the head of a 'caretaker' Tory government. Parliament was dissolved and the election called for 5 July. In the exceptional circumstances, in contrast to 1918, and in a very fine display of democracy in action, the result wasn't to be declared until 26 July, so that the forces could vote and have their ballots retrieved from wherever they were, up to 5000 miles away.

In this new battle, Churchill would lead the Conservatives rather than the nation, much against his wife's wishes. Clementine had been unenthusiastic about Churchill's return to the Tory fold in 1924 and so she was again about his assumption of the party leadership in October 1940. In August 1944, she implored him to resign the Conservative leadership when the war ended: 'You shouldn't use your great prestige to get them in again. They don't deserve it.' She had shown much courage and fortitude of her own, flying to Russia on behalf of the Red Cross, but the war had been a huge strain on her nerves. Churchill had turned seventy in November 1944, and she would be sixty the following April. She was longing for her husband to retire from politics at last and come home to the 'basket' she had fondly imagined during the previous war. As usual, Churchill ignored her.

His about-turn on the election was one sign that Churchill was losing his grip, or even complete contact with reality. There were more signs, as he now began to pick fights which made him look foolish. One was with Eamon de Valera and his Irish statelet. Churchill had a point. Many Irishmen from north and south, Catholic and Protestant, had served bravely with the Irish Guards, the 8th Royal Irish Hussars, the Royal Ulster Rifles, the Royal Navy and the Royal Air Force. But the record of the Dublin government had been contemptible. In 1921, Churchill had played his part in negotiating the Anglo-Irish Treaty which established the Free State. Its provisions included continued British possession of the 'treaty ports' on the coast of the new Free State, Lough Swilly in the north west, Berehaven in the south west, and Queenstown, the port of Cork City. These had played a crucial part in the campaign against U-boats in the Great War and, after the Americans finally entered the war in 1917, a number of their young naval officers who would later be senior commanders in the Pacific war first cut their teeth sailing from the Queenstown station. In that war, the Germans had no U-boat bases further west than Zeebrugge on the coast of occupied Belgium.

By 1940 the balance had been drastically tilted the other way. In another gesture of appeasement by Chamberlain in 1938, hoping to placate de Valera, though to Churchill's rage, the treaty ports were relinquished. Two years later this meant that, whereas Hitler had U-boat bases as far west as Brest in Brittany, the Royal Navy no longer had its Irish ports, apart from Belfast Lough. In September 1939, de Valera proclaimed a strict neutrality, while the militant Irish Republican Army wasn't neutral at all. Having declared that the war had begun because the London government was in the hands of Jewish finance, the IRA now did what they could to help Hitler. In the summer of 1940, Sean Russell, the grandiosely named 'Chief of Staff' of the IRA, went on a clandestine mission to Berlin, where he met von Ribbentrop, then foreign minister and subsequently hanged at Nuremberg. They concluded cordial discussions by announcing, 'Our ideas have much in common,' which was true enough.

Neutrality was adhered to throughout the war although, as Orwell pointed out at the time, vaunted Irish sovereignty and neutrality were really meaningless, since they depended entirely on British naval and military strength. The Swiss would later be criticised for their neutrality, but it was unavoidable, it was genuine, with the country well-armed for defence, and it didn't seriously damage or impede the Allied cause. Irish neutrality differed in all these respects, especially the last. The loss of the ports, with convoys obliged to take a much longer route around the north of the island, certainly prolonged the defeat of Germany, with all that implies. And German representatives remained in Dublin throughout the war until the very end.

All news of German atrocities had been censored in the Irish media. Even when Cardinal Hinsley, the head of the Roman Catholic church in England, preached a sermon denouncing those atrocities, Irish papers were forbidden to mention the sermon, and when newsreels now showed liberated Belsen, de Valera complained that this was 'anti-national propaganda'. He then visited the German legation, which had remained open in Dublin throughout the war despite British and then American protests, to pay the condolences of the Irish government and people upon the death of the German leader, Adolf Hitler, making Dublin the only capital on earth where the Führer was publicly mourned, a grotesque action which caused outrage on both sides of the Atlantic. As the *New York Times* put it, de Valera might have thought he was following neutral protocol, in which case, 'Considering the character and record of the man for whose death he was expressing grief, there is obviously something wrong with the protocol, the neutrality, or Mr de Valera.'

In view of all that, it was quite a feat to make de Valera look good, but Churchill managed it. A brutal aside in his Victory Broadcast denounced the Dublin government and prime minister: 'If it had not been for the loyalty and friendship of Northern Ireland we should have been forced to come to close quarters with Mr de Valera or perish for ever from the earth. However, with a restraint and a poise to which, I say, history will find few parallels, His Majesty's Government never laid a violent hand upon them ... and we left the de Valera government to frolic with the Germans and later with the Japanese representatives to their heart's content.' De Valera waited some weeks before replying in a broadcast of his own, in which he asked Churchill, with an appearance of dignity, if he could not find it in his heart to acknowledge 'that there is a small nation that stood alone, not only for a year or two, but for several hundred years against aggression'. As Churchill ruefully admitted, de Valera won the exchange.

Far more serious was 'Operation Unthinkable', as it was secretly called. Churchill was now consumed with apprehension at the Russian advance into Europe, which was so much a consequence of his own actions. Roosevelt had died on 12 April, less than four weeks before victory. He was succeeded by his vice president, Harry Truman, whom Churchill now warned that an 'iron curtain' was falling across Europe, a phrase he would make much more famous the following year in Truman's home state. After he had failed to get his way with his hare-brained scheme for a landing at the head of the Adriatic, Churchill had urged Eisenhower to press straight for Berlin so as to reach it ahead of the Russians. Eisenhower knew as well as Churchill that the partitioning of Germany into occupied zones had effectively been agreed, and he quite rightly declined to risk the lives of any soldiers under his command for a political gesture, and almost certainly a pointless one at that.

In his frustration, Churchill now began to think of another war. On 24 May he ordered his chiefs of staff to prepare plans to 'impose upon Russia the will of the United States and the British Empire' by 1 July. 'If we are to embark on war with Russia, we must be prepared to be committed to a total war, which will be long and costly.' Brooke was even more angrily derisive than usual: 'The idea is of course fantastic and the chances of success quite impossible.' Not only fantastic, 'Operation Unthinkable' was barely sane. British and American soldiers had fought long and hard, and wanted to go home, having been told moreover for years that the Red Army were their heroic allies. Any order to make war on the Russians would have provoked mutiny.

When the election campaign opened, Churchill made an almost graver mistake. On 4 June he gave a Conservative 'PPB', one of the carefully allotted party political radio broadcasts each party was allowed to present on the BBC. His theme was the encroaching power of the state, which had of course hugely increased under his own wartime government. But a Labour government would be a much more serious threat, he warned: 'No Socialist Government conducting the entire life and industry of the country could afford to allow free, sharp or violently worded expressions of public discontent. They would have to fall back on some sort of Gestapo, no doubt very humanely directed in the first instance.'

Even now it's hard to believe that he uttered words so disgraceful, and so stupid. He was implying that Attlee and Bevin, two patriotic democratic socialists who had loyally served in his war cabinet for five years, were crypto-Nazis. The word 'Gestapo' was made worse not better by the Churchillian sarcasm 'no doubt very humanely directed', and was simply intolerable only weeks after the British had been given a harrowing radio report by Richard Dimbleby of the horrors of Belsen, that hell on earth filled by the Gestapo. When

Clementine saw the script beforehand, she was dismayed by the inflammatory word 'Gestapo', and begged Churchill not to use it, good advice again ignored. Sarah was shocked when she listened, and told her father so.

His words now rebounded in a way that might have been foreseen. Most people recognised the disastrous error, and the shocking vulgarity, exacerbated by the front page of Beaverbrook's *Daily Express* the next morning, shouting 'GESTAPO IN BRITAIN IF SOCIALISTS WIN'. Ordinary citizens recorded their disgust, and many thought that this was a pot calling the kettle black. The *New Statesman* published little topical verses, and one such witty ditty entitled 'Plagiarism' caught the mood: 'One Empire; One Leader; One Folk; / Is the Tory campaign master-stroke. / As a National jest, / It is one of the best, / But it's not an original joke.' This neat echo of the Hitlerite slogan 'Ein Reich, Ein Volk, Ein Führer' suggested that if anyone was a potential dictator it wasn't the reticent, quietly formidable Attlee, but the man who had traduced him.

It was generally believed that Churchill had been egged on by Beaverbrook, who was regarded with contempt by all decent people, and that Churchill was also under the influence of Friedrich von Hayek, a distinguished emigré economist teaching at the London School of Economics who, with compatriots like Ludwig von Mises, formed an 'Austrian school' which kept alive the tradition of classical free-market liberalism. The year before, von Hayek had published *The Road to Serfdom*, arguing that all collectivist political and economic systems, Communist or National Socialist, resembled each other, and that any centrally planned society must be destructive of freedom. The book is more intellectually sophisticated than its lurid title suggests, but like many such sophisticated arguments it could easily be simplified and distorted.

Whether Churchill had actually read *The Road to Serfdom* or, as seems more likely, someone had given him the gist of it, the consequences proved to be a huge self-inflicted wound. In his masterly reply on the radio the following evening, Attlee was at his cool, dry best. The Tories had hoped, he said, to persuade voters that 'Winston Churchill, the great leader in war of a united nation' was the same man who should now be followed as the leader of the Conservative Party: 'I thank him for having disillusioned them so thoroughly.' Attlee wouldn't waste his time on 'a second-hand version of the academic views of an Austrian professor,' he said, adding lethally, 'The voice we heard last night was that of Mr Churchill, but the mind was that of Lord Beaverbrook.' This exchange was a complete victory for Attlee, and lost Churchill many more votes than it won.

Despite that, and as a proper courtesy, Churchill invited Attlee to accompany him on 17 July to the last great conference of the war at Potsdam, which for the Hohenzollerns had been to Berlin what Windsor was to London for the English monarchs, a grand residence conveniently near the capital, although a more potent symbol of Prussian rule. Churchill was photographed in a trio for the last time, sitting in an easy chair to the right of Truman, who had Stalin to his left. Less happily for the prime minister, when the two party leaders passed British troops in Berlin, some present noticed how Attlee was loudly cheered by the Tommies, Churchill scarcely at all. Had he paid more attention to that, and to Slim's words, he might not have been as shocked as he shortly was.

Since Stalin was always well informed about Churchill's plans by Soviet agents in London, he was more than usually detached and sardonic when they met. For his part, and for all of 'Operation Unthinkable', Churchill was pleased to see his old acquaintance. 'He is again under Stalin's spell,' Eden wrote. 'He kept repeating "I like that man."' Stalin undertook to join in the war against Japan, and in one of their last decisions as allies he and the others agreed on a partition of Vietnam, a distant and seemingly trivial question which had risen from the debris of war in the East and which would one day spell disaster for Truman's successors in the White House. Having returned to London, Churchill never saw Stalin again, and when the conference resumed, his place was taken, to Stalin's great surprise, by Attlee.

On 26 July Churchill heard the election results at Number 10 in the mephitic company of Beaverbrook and Bracken, and with mounting dismay. In one of the great landslides in British political history, Labour gained 393 out of 640 seats. Ten years before, the Tories had won 432 seats; they now collapsed to 213. As usual the system distorted the result in favour of the winner, although Labour's 47.8 per cent of the vote to the Tories 39.8 per cent was impressive enough. The poor Liberals, Churchill's party for twenty years, suffered most of all, still taking 9 per cent of the vote but rewarded with no more than twelve seats.

Once he had absorbed the result, Churchill summoned 'my carriage' and was conveyed in his Rolls Royce to Buckingham Palace where he resigned, recommended his successor, and took leave of the king. Shortly afterwards, Attlee followed him to be appointed prime minister, driven to the Palace by his wife in a small family motor car. There could not have been a more apt contrast between departing grandeur and the new age of austerity and equality. As for Violet Attlee's predecessor as chatelaine of Number 10, although Clementine couldn't express the deep relief she really felt, she remarked that the defeat might be a blessing in disguise, to which Churchill replied, 'At the moment it seems quite effectively disguised.' She urged him again to retire, and plenty of his colleagues, led by Eden, who was longing to take over, were anxious for him to go.

But that wasn't at all how Churchill saw it. Once again it would be 'In Defeat: Defiance'. Churchill was not just defiant but resentful. He always wanted the last word and to be able to claim victory, and he saw the election as a political Dunkirk, which must be avenged by a political D-Day, with him still in command. Exhausted though he might be in his eighth decade, he had unfinished business: with the Tory party who must now accept him as their leader for as long as he wanted; with the British electorate who must also repent by making him prime minister again; and with posterity.

He knew how fraught his position was. For all the glorious victory, so much had gone wrong. Churchill had never used a phrase as trite as 'the good war', but his speeches in 1940 had unmistakably imbued the war with a noble moral character: he would wage war against a monstrous tyranny, never surpassed in the dark, lamentable catalogue of human crime; it was the British people's finest hour. And that was true, at the beginning of Churchill's war. It was not true at the end. The two wars that mattered, between Germany and Russia in eastern Europe and the United States and Japan in the Pacific, not only dwarfed anything the British knew, neither could possibly assume any noble or 'finest' quality.

Most people in the west had no idea of the real character of the war on the eastern front, or even fully grasped the disparity of scale between their war and the Russians'. The British were certainly awed by what they knew about the Red Army's sacrifice, and a 'Sword of Stalingrad' was made by English craftsmen and presented to Stalin, but little was known about how his armies were treated by him. If the Germans fought a war of extermination, in which millions of innocents were murdered, the Russians fought brutally in their own way, not least by executing their soldiers on a vast scale: by the end, the equivalent of twenty infantry divisions of its own men had been shot.

Whether or not this made the Russians fight harder, it surely brutalised them, and their victorious advance towards Vienna and Berlin saw another terrifying regression into barbarism, a carnival of murder, pillage and, above all, gang rape. A year after Churchill had said that 'The discipline and military etiquette of the Russian Armies are unsurpassed,' as many as two million German women were savagely raped by Russians, often repeatedly, sometimes fatally, sometimes with the victims begging for death. This was done with Stalin's approval. When Milovan Djilas, the Yugoslav Communist, very bravely remonstrated with him about this great orgy of rape, Stalin said that his boys had fought a long hard war and deserved some fun.

Still more retribution was wrought on the Germans. As agreed at Tehran and then Yalta, Poland was moved bodily to the west, like a line of soldiers on parade marking to the left, as Churchill breezily put it, losing the lands in the east which were mostly inhabited by White Russians and Lithuanians, although by many Poles also, while acquiring the ancient German lands of East Prussia, Further Pomerania and Silesia. Such drastic redrawing of borders was far from unprecedented in European history – Poland had been brutally partitioned in the late-eighteenth century and reconstituted after 1918 – but there had been little movement of peoples. Now, with the consent of Churchill and Truman at Potsdam, well over twelve million Germans were expelled, or ethnically cleansed, as a later phrase would have it, from lands where their forebears had lived since the Middle Ages. Three million more Germans were driven out of Czechoslovakia on the orders of Edvard Beneš, once again Czech president, a grim revenge for the Munich agreement.

Nor were those the only *Victims of Yalta*. That was the title of a polemical book published in 1977 by Nikolai Tolstoy, which brought a subterranean horror to light: the forcible handing over by the British Army of Cossacks and 'White Russians' (in the political rather than geographical sense, refugees from the Soviet state) to Stalin, and of Croats to Tito by the British Army in May 1945. The story wasn't simple, politically or morally. Some of the Cossacks who had wandered west and ended in Austria had fought for Hitler, and some had taken part in his atrocities. Many of the Croats were from the Ustashe, the blood-stained militia of Ante Pavelić's fascist regime, which had committed frightful crimes of its own. Then again, some of the Russians had left at the time of the Revolution and were in no possible legal sense Soviet citizens, and many were women and children, lost in the fog of war.

Although Churchill had agreed to the general principle of 'repatriation' at Yalta, with the implication that this might be involuntary, it was two colleagues, both future Tory prime ministers, who were much more complicit. Eden as Foreign Secretary was insistent that all should be sent back without delay, and Macmillan, as Churchill's plenipotentiary, was on the spot in Klagenfurt. He knew what he was doing. He wrote in his diary that 'Among the surrendered Germans are about 40,000 Cossacks and "White" Russians, with their wives and children. To hand them over to the Russians is condemning them to slavery, torture and probably death. To refuse, is deeply to offend the Russians, and incidentally break the Yalta agreement. We have decided to hand them over.'

What made the episode so repulsive, and sickened the British soldiers ordered to carry it out, was the deceit and treachery. Lieutenant-Colonel Robin Rose Price of the Welsh Guards wrote in his diary, 'Order of most sinister duplicity received i.e. to send Croats to their foes, i.e. Tits to Yugoslavia under the impression they were to go to Italy.' The Croats were put on trains, where they suddenly found themselves in the hands of 'Tits', or Tito's Partisans, and they immediately knew their fate. Once back over the border, many thousands of them had their hands bound with barbed wire before they were driven into the country and killed. On one occasion, British soldiers who forced prisoners across a bridge into Yugoslav territory could hear them being shot on the other side.

'We have proclaimed ourselves the strong supporters of Marshal Tito because of his heroic and massive struggle against the German armies,' Churchill had said a year earlier. 'Tito has largely sunk his Communist aspect in his character as a Yugoslav patriot leader. He repeatedly proclaims he has no intention of reversing the property and social systems which prevail in Serbia, but these facts are not accepted yet by the other side.' Even by Churchill's standards, his words in May 1944 had been a fantasy, as Tito now demonstrated, by ruthlessly 'reversing the property and social system', persecuting the

churches, and settling the score with Mihailović, the Serb leader whom
Churchill had supported and then abandoned.

There were other problems with Churchill's rhetoric of a noble war
fought for freedom and justice. If there were really two great wars,
between Germany and Russia, and between Japan and the United
States, neither could be invested with any profound moral quality.
The war in eastern Europe was utterly barbarous, with the mass
murder of the Jews as a supreme wickedness, while it left eastern
Europe under a hateful Russian despotism. And what possible moral
quality was there to the Pacific war? It was at best an old-fashioned
imperial contest for hegemony, at worst a primitive racial duel. The
Japanese army was shockingly cruel to prisoners of war, but that was
dwarfed by the far greater horrors Japan inflicted on Asian peoples
they conquered, as many as twenty million of whom may have
perished. On the other hand there was no war for freedom when
British, French and Dutch colonies were reconquered, except to the
wholly unforeseen extent that they became independent after the war,
although not without a further series of bitter little wars.

More than that, racial hatred was far from only on the Japanese
side. In 1944, Admiral William 'Bull' Halsey, commander of the Third
Fleet in the Pacific and a popular figure with the public, proclaimed
on a newsreel, 'We are drowning and burning the bestial apes all over
the Pacific and it gives just as much pleasure to burn them as to drown
them.' And in a supposedly off-the-record dinner with Washington
journalists he expanded on his theme: 'I hate Japs. I'm telling you men
that if I met a pregnant Japanese woman I'd kick her in the belly.'
Blunter still was Paul McNutt, the War Manpower Commissioner,
when he proposed a simple solution, once the war was won:
'Extermination of the Japanese – *in toto.*'

And with all that, 'Not the least ironical aspect of this most ironical
of wars,' Dwight Macdonald correctly noted in early 1945, was that
'the war in the Pacific has always been more popular with all classes
of Americans than the war in Europe.' For most Americans for most
of the time from December 1941 to August 1945 'the war' had meant
the Pacific war, which is where American blood was shed first and
last in ceaseless, brutal conflict. It's significant that no subsequent
American president had fought in the European war (apart of course
from Eisenhower as supreme commander) but that four future

presidents – Kennedy, Nixon, Ford, Bush the Elder – saw action as naval officers fighting Japan. So here were two epic struggles, in eastern Europe and the Pacific, which couldn't possibly be seen as noble contests between good and evil. Churchill's task would be to create a narrative of 'the Second World War' which evaded all such complexities and ambiguities, and ignored or explained away as far as possible the larger outcome in terms of the liquidation of the Empire, the decline of British power, the disastrous economic outcome for England, and the inexorable Soviet dominance over eastern Europe, all by placing his little country, and himself, at the centre.

One last question haunted Churchill. When Allied soldiers reached Germany they found a scene of desolation. Every town and city lay in rubble. Even now, the exact number of Germans killed by bombing is unsure, but it was almost certainly more than 400,000, maybe 500,000, which was not only several times more than the number of British civilians killed by the Luftwaffe, it was considerably more than the number of British combatant servicemen who died in the war. Indeed, in consequence of the zeal for destruction, British victims of bombing were outnumbered by French civilians killed by British and American bombs, as part of the 'liberation'.

Just as the war was reaching its conclusion, Churchill had second thoughts about 'strategic bombing', or maybe third or fourth thoughts. On 28 March, six weeks after the destruction of Dresden, he wrote to Ismay, his representative on the Chiefs of Staff committee: 'It seems to me that the moment has come when the question of bombing of German cities simply for the sake of increasing the terror, though under other pretexts, should be reviewed. Otherwise we shall come into control of an utterly ruined land ... The destruction of Dresden remains a serious query against the conduct of Allied bombing ... I feel the need for more precise concentration upon military objectives such as oil and communications behind the immediate battle-zone, rather than on mere acts of terror and wanton destruction, however impressive.'

That Dresden memorandum might be thought the most discreditable action of Churchill's career. Harris and Sinclair were understandably enraged, and Churchill was persuaded to withdraw it and tone down his words, which were outrageously hypocritical. It was Churchill who had favoured bombing from the Great War onwards, and had preserved the RAF for that purpose, he who had wanted a 'devastating, exterminating' attack by heavy bombers in July 1940, he who had appointed Harris in February 1942 with a clear brief to destroy whole cities, he who, despite intermittent qualms – 'Are we beasts?' – had supported him thereafter, even when Harris insubordinately disobeyed orders, defiantly and correctly thinking that Sinclair, and Churchill, wouldn't dare sack him. But if he couldn't stop Harris, Churchill now tried to ignore him, and his men, who had not only inflicted great suffering but had endured it: the surviving airmen never forgot that they were only half of active Bomber Command still alive at the end of the war. But Churchill made no mention of the bombers in his victory broadcast, no campaign medal was struck for Bomber Command, Harris wasn't allowed to issue a final dispatch, and he didn't receive the peerage that all equivalent British commanders were granted.

Nothing in this story should suggest any 'moral equivalence' between the Allies and the Axis, as some German writers later attempted to do. The suffering endured by Germans will always be contrasted with the incomparably greater suffering inflicted by Germans on others. More than twelve million Germans were brutally expelled from their homes and more than 400,000 Germans were killed by bombing; nearly six million Jews had been expelled from life itself, a deed committed, as Günter Grass would later insist, not 'in the name of Germany', but by Germans. British and American troops were horrified by the destruction and carnage they found in Germany, but when they saw camps like Belsen and Dachau they were inclined to think the Germans had received their just desserts. Like other camps in Germany which the Anglo-American forces liberated, Belsen was intended for internment and punishment rather than mass murder. It was some time before everyone in the west fully realised the enormity of what had happened in the dark night of the east, the industrial extermination of millions at Auschwitz, Treblinka and Maidanek.

For the Germans themselves this was *Stunde Null*, zero hour, a moral as well as physical abyss without precedent, and the complete bankruptcy of National Socialism was marked by an epidemic of suicides. Almost all the senior leaders of the Third Reich killed themselves. Having seen the contemptible fate of Mussolini, butchered by partisans and strung upside-down in the marketplace in Milan, Hitler had no wish to follow him. His fifty-sixth, and last, birthday was celebrated on 20 April in a weird quasi-diplomatic gathering attended by the representatives of a handful of clerical or fascist regimes, including an Irish official. On the 30th, after marrying Eva Braun and watching her swallow cyanide, Hitler shot himself. Magda Goebbels poisoned her six children before her husband shot her and then himself. Himmler escaped from Berlin, was arrested by British soldiers near the Danish border, and broke the cyanide capsule behind his teeth. Goering would also take poison, but not for another eighteen months, on the night before he was due to be hanged at Nuremberg. Fifty-three out of 554 German generals killed themselves, and many lesser folk as well.

And yet for the western Allies, the difficulty was that, fighting a just and necessary war in a good cause against a wicked enemy, they had been brutalised and coarsened themselves. No one could have better described this than Churchill. In 1930 he had written that 'War, which used to be cruel and magnificent, has now become cruel and squalid.' Those words exactly applied to this war, the greatest and most terrible of all, from the magnificent first year of 'Churchill's war' in 1940–41 to the squalid last year in 1944–5. Sooner than anyone guessed, the Pacific war ended, also in a cloud of moral perplexity, which was moreover humiliating for Churchill. The discovery that the atom could be split had been made before the war by scientists in Cambridge, under the tutelage of Ernest Rutherford (who would tell visitors at the time that, while it had been a technically fascinating experiment, it had of course no practical application at all). Until the early years of the war, the British were still well ahead in nuclear research, in part because among the scientists specialising in the field were Jewish refugees who were technically 'enemy aliens' and thus forbidden to work in fields of military importance, then considered to include radar, but not nuclear physics.

By September 1941, Churchill and a few colleagues had decided in utmost secrecy to proceed with what scientists had told them would be now feasible, making a bomb from uranium that was equivalent 'to 1,800 tons of TNT' and whose radioactive after-effect 'would make places near to where the bomb exploded dangerous to human life'. But if British scientific knowledge led to nuclear fission, only the United States possessed the immense financial and industrial resources needed to take it further, and it was in America that the vast project was put in train.

At the Quebec conference in August 1943 it had been agreed that this was a joint Anglo-American venture and that British consent would be needed to use any weapon that might result, but this was an informal oral agreement between Roosevelt and Churchill, who fatally failed to have it sealed in writing. By the time the first bomb was detonated in New Mexico on 16 July 1945, just before the leaders met at Potsdam, Truman had forgotten about this condition. British consent was sought as an afterthought, and the bombing of Hiroshima on 6 August and Nagasaki three days later represented a further clear abdication and diminution of British power. A year later, in August 1946, Congress passed the McMahon Act which abruptly and arbitrarily stopped any nuclear agreement with the British.

As the war ended, and in the exultation of victory, few grasped the full extent to which British interests had been damaged, by the over-turning of the balance of power in Europe, and in the East also. Nevertheless there were clear intimations that 'the liquidation of the British Empire' over which Churchill had insisted he would never preside was indeed imminent, largely in consequence of the war. From the first year, when Churchill commanded the landscape as the one leader determined to fight Hitler, and when England seemed, even if in illusory fashion, to be a truly great power, the last year or more had seen Churchill squeezed between Roosevelt and Stalin, and the British position much reduced, the country now in practice a power of the second rank, however painful that was for Churchill to accept.

This had been the first great radio war, and it would be the last. Many leaders broadcast to their people, even if not every voice was equally familiar. Before the war Churchill had broadcast quite often, and then to far larger numbers in 1940. For years Roosevelt had given his 'fireside chats' to scores of millions of Americans, huge numbers of Germans listened to the controlled hysteria of Hitler's tirades over the radio. By contrast de Gaulle's first broadcasts from London were heard by very few people in France and, more than a year later, when Stalin made his first ever broadcast, to 'Comrades, citizens, brothers and sisters, men of our Army and Navy!' on 3 July 1941, only a tiny minority of Russians can have heard him, while those who did were puzzled by his Georgian accent.

Likewise, only a few Japanese heard Emperor Hirohito speak by radio for the first time on 15 August 1945, and they were likewise perplexed by his sing-song court accent and classical Japanese. His words were in fact a recording, made days earlier, which had survived an attempt to capture and destroy it by fanatical army officers, determined to fight to the last man, woman and child. Japan was prostrate, with more than two million of its armed forces dead, with most of the Imperial Navy and almost all of its merchant fleet on the ocean floor where American submarines had sent them, with the country devastated and starving, with Tokyo in ashes, including the ashes of 100,000 people, and with Hiroshima, Nagasaki and 150,000 more people obliterated from the face of the earth. Faced with these facts, Hirohito still couldn't use the word 'surrender', even though that was in reality what he was announcing. Instead he resorted to exquisite evasion and masterly meiosis: 'Despite the best that has been done by everyone – the gallant fighting of the military and naval forces, the diligence and assiduity of Our servants of the State, and the devoted service of Our one hundred million people – the war situation has developed not necessarily to Japan's advantage, while the general trends of the world have all turned against her interest.'

Any thought of using such words would have appalled Churchill. And yet they applied to him also. The truth was that, by the summer of 1945, the war situation had developed not necessarily to England's advantage, while the general trends of the world had turned against her interest – and Churchill's. However wonderful his rhetoric had been five summers before, however heroic his own role in ensuring the defence of freedom and civilisation, Great Britain had not emerged from the war happily placed. One further indirect effect of the atomic bomb was that the end of the Japanese war also ended Lend-Lease, with nary a care on Truman's part. The American economy had been completely transformed by the war. Four years of explosive growth had not only pulled the country at last out of the Depression, but brought the Americans full employment and undreamt-of prosperity, with average wages around 50 per cent higher in real terms in 1944 than in 1941. The Russian people had won the war, but with immense suffering, and still lived in a nightmare of mad despotism where returning prisoners of war were sent to labour camps, and any word of criticism of the regime meant death.

Although the British had fought for a good cause, ending in victory, and although their country, unlike Russia, was still free, they felt like the captain answering St Paul, 'With a great sum obtained I this freedom.' They had made huge sacrifices for the common good – as Keynes put it: 'We threw good housekeeping to the winds. But we saved ourselves and helped save the world' – and as their reward they now faced what he called 'a financial Dunkirk', after a war in which the country had lost around a third of its national wealth.

Altogether the outlook was bleak – unless Churchill could present it otherwise. For all his setbacks, he had one great resource, and one huge advantage. The resource was his command of language. In 1940 he had used exalted rhetoric to express his optimism of will at a time when England's position was objectively hopeless and winning the war was something that could only be dreamt of in words. Now he had another battle ahead of him. At that moment in 1945, Churchill had won two great victories, the first in a war against Germany, the second in the battle over his reputation which had raged since the beginning of the century. But that second victory seemed to him less secure after his rejection by the electorate, and with his acute sense of diminished national power. Now he would use language again as his weapon.

His advantage was that he was the survivor. Low's cartoon 'Two Churchills' contrasted the disconsolate 'Party Leader' with 'The Leader of Humanity', and if he was indeed the leader of humanity, it was by default, or elimination. He was in a truly extraordinary position. In the one month of April not only had Hitler and Mussolini met violent ends, Roosevelt had died also. Stalin was alive but remained an enigma, and whatever else he might be capable of, and despite the later ingenious imaginations of novelists like Robert Harris, he did not keep a journal, let alone write his memoirs.

That left Churchill with the field to himself. In this crucial phase of his life he could seize the opportunity to propagate an unchallenged version of how the World War had come about, of how it had been waged, and of how another war should be avoided. He had won the war, but he might appear to have lost the peace. He had lost the election; he now had to win the argument. After the great task of the war, there was now his next great task of imposing his version of events on the world and on posterity. In 1940 he had invented one truth. With the war over he had to invent another. 'I had a good tale to tell,' he would say about his speeches early in the war. Now he had to tell the best tale of all.

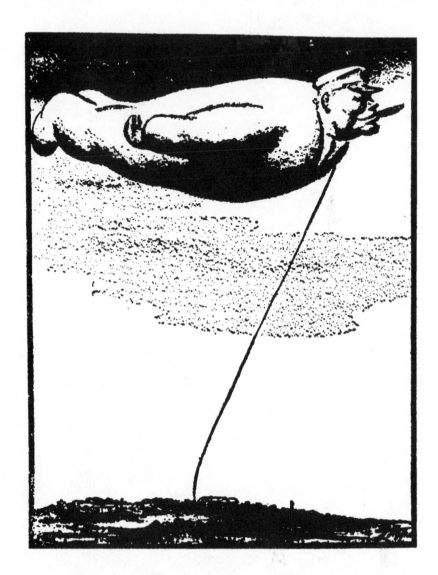

"Fulton's Finest Hour."

15

'A special relationship'
Fulton 1946

Until 1946 no Englishman, and not many Americans, had heard of Fulton in Missouri in the very middle of Middle America, or of Westminster College which resides there. On 5 March Fulton became world-famous. The president of Westminster, Dr Frank McCluer, had an audacious idea: he invited the most illustrious man alive to give the John Findley Green Lecture. Churchill wouldn't have given the invitation a second glance had it not ended with a hand-written note: 'This is a wonderful school in my home state. Hope you can do it. I'll introduce you. Best regards – Harry S. Truman.' This changed Churchill's mind, and he travelled west to give what would be one of the most famous of all his speeches.

An American visit came as healing balm, at a moment when Churchill was still embittered by the election, and unable to see his future clearly. But of course, Clementine had been right: the electoral defeat of 1945 wasn't just a blessing in disguise, it was one of the greatest strokes of luck in Churchill's life. 'Churchill the fortunate,' E.M. Forster's British soldier had sourly said from his grave in Gallipoli, but Churchill had suffered from more than his share of misfortune, albeit often misfortunes he had invited. Now his luck had changed for good. The king offered him the most ancient of chivalric titles, but Churchill said that he didn't think he should accept the Order of the Garter when the electorate had just awarded him the order of the boot. He could also have had a peerage, indeed a dukedom, but he had no intention of leaving the Commons, and he thought that a heritable peerage would impede Randolph's political career, fancifully supposing that Randolph had such a career to impede: having entered Parliament only thanks to the wartime party truce, he had been swept away by the Labour landslide, and would never be an MP again.

At the same time, by vacating Downing Street for Attlee, Churchill avoided responsibility for some of the most intractable tasks any British government had ever faced. The Attlee ministry of 1945–51 may fairly be called one of the only two British governments since the war which have changed the country, and changed the political landscape. The other was the Thatcher government of 1979–90, and they were both very much of their time, with great deeds to their names and great failures. If there was a real weakness with the Attlee government it was that it was too Churchillian. They tried to build their New Jerusalem by way of cradle-to-grave social security but at the same time maintained, or even increased, military and imperial commitments. Bevin now became Attlee's Foreign Secretary, partly because King George disliked Hugh Dalton so much and thought he would see less of him if he were Chancellor rather than Foreign Secretary.

A biography of Bevin many years later was predictably subtitled 'Labour's Churchill', and Churchill himself somewhat condescendingly called Bevin 'a working-class John Bull'. He was quite bullish enough. Bevin loudly insisted that Great Britain was still a great power when facts and figures belied this. The 'financial Dunkirk' cast a most ironic light on Churchill's talk of Anglo-American unity, as well as his claim that American aid had been 'unsordid'. Within a year of the ending of Lend-Lease by Truman, the Attlee government faced a financial crisis so acute that an American loan was sought. Like Lend-Lease before it, it came on highly onerous terms. Import controls had to be ended, and sterling had to become fully convertible within a year. In consequence, the attempt to deal with each financial crisis only led to another and worse crisis, as import costs soared, the balance of payments spun out of control, and convertibility had to be suspended only weeks after it was introduced.

And so Churchill should have blessed his luck in not having to deal with problems which would have been no easier for him than they were for Attlee. To begin with he wisely said that the country should be left to get at ease with the new government. In any case Churchill was poorly placed to criticise much of Labour's work in expanding welfare, above all the creation of a National Health Service by Aneurin Bevan, now Minister of Health. Churchill derided him as the 'Minister of Disease', but Bevan was only continuing the work which Churchill had once helped begin, and had always defended.

At the new year of 1945, Lloyd George at last left the Commons, where he had represented Caernarvon Boroughs for fifty-five years, for that House of Lords he had once mocked so merrily, but the first Earl Lloyd-George of Dwyfor survived for less than three months. On 28 March, two days after his death, Churchill saluted his memory. It was Lloyd George, he told the Commons, 'who launched the Liberal and Radical forces of this country effectively into *the broad stream of social betterment and social security along which all modern parties now steer,* [italics added] ... His warm heart was stirred by the many perils ... the health of the bread winner, the fate of his widow, the nourishment and upbringing of his children, the meagre and haphazard provision of medical treatment and sanatoria, and the lack of any organised accessible medical service of a kind worthy of the age from which the mass of the wage earners and the poor suffered.'

Despite his later rightward turn, Churchill never abandoned that commitment he and Lloyd George had once shared. In a radio broadcast from Chequers in March 1943 he had said that, after victory, 'We must establish on broad and solid foundations a National Health Service,' and the Conservative manifesto at the 1945 election promised 'a comprehensive health service covering the whole range of medical treatment from the general practitioner to the specialist ... available to all citizens'. Churchill could boast that he had helped lay the foundations of an edifice of social security, which Chamberlain had built upon between the wars, and which Labour was now topping out.

In any case, Churchill took his duties as Leader of the Opposition very lightly. How much pleasanter to travel abroad and be garlanded as the greatest man of his age, than to engage in tedious scrutiny of Bills and White Papers! On the personal front, or specifically the financial front, his outlook had never been brighter. Years later his grandson 'little Winston' would claim that Churchill ended the war almost bankrupt, which was absurd. The war years had transformed him financially, and the best was yet to come. Having accepted the invitation from Presidents McCluer and Truman, Churchill, Clementine and Sarah sailed westwards in the *Queen Elizabeth* along with many Canadian troops, some of them returning home for the first time in five years. 'What a glory shines on the brave and the true!' he told them in a hastily composed speech extolling the Commonwealth and

Canada's contribution to victory, which had indeed been disproportionate, and not always recognised.

When he reached New York he was immediately asked by the press
about his memoirs, and he repeated his official line for the moment,
that he didn't know whether he would write a book about the war
or whether it would be published in his lifetime. That was thoroughly
disingenuous, since 'this atomic bomb of an Englishman', as one
American journalist called him, was now a red-hot property in the
literary marketplace, and Churchill was already sounding out the
market. After sunning himself in Florida and visiting Cuba just over
fifty years after he had marked his twenty-first birthday there, he
returned to Washington. Such luxuriating at length in sunny climes
while his country shivered in the bleak midwinter caused vexation at
home, not least in the party he was meant to be leading. 'I think it is
quite wrong of Winston to have gone abroad at such a time as this
and for so long,' Lord Derby wrote to Beaverbrook. The octogenarian
'king of Lancashire', a man whose biography Randolph would one
day write, thought that 'to be left as we are now without any controlling power in our Party is to my mind bad statesmanship.' When Lord
Salisbury, another Tory elder statesmen, said, 'Winston's day is over,'
he was expressing the silent view of many in the party. Little did they
guess that, for Churchill, his day had barely begun, in his new roles
as historian of the war, and international oracle.

At Fulton, clad in the gown of his newly-conferred honorary
doctorate, Churchill spoke a few pleasantries about the way the name
'Westminster' seemed somehow familiar, before embarking on what
would become one of his most famous speeches, and one sentence
in particular: 'From Stettin in the Baltic to Trieste in the Adriatic, an
iron curtain has descended across the Continent.' The phrase was far
from new. From everyday German theatrical usage, the *eiserner Vorhang*
or iron curtain is simply the safety curtain in a theatre which can be
dropped to prevent fire spreading. An Englishwoman visiting the new-
born Soviet Union shortly after the Revolution had called the impen-
etrable barrier separating Russia from the West an 'iron curtain', and
Churchill himself had warned Truman the previous May about an
iron curtain dividing Europe. Churchill's words were unconsciously
and eerily similar to what Karl Marx had written almost a century
before, 'it would appear that the natural frontier of Russia was from
Danzig or perhaps Stettin to Trieste', when Marx added his hope that

the English would hold back this Russian advance. Still less happily for Churchill, Goebbels had written in January 1945 that, thanks to the Yalta agreement, 'An iron curtain would fall over this enormous territory controlled by the Soviet Union, behind which nations would be slaughtered.'

One later school of 'revisionist' historians argued that the Cold War was all the fault of Truman and Churchill, the United States and the West, and Churchill's Fulton speech was held up as a declaration of that conflict – as it also has been by some of Churchill's admirers. As late as 2013, a writer in the *Spectator* could fatuously claim that Churchill said 'the previously unsayable. Up until this point, everyone has been politely pretending that the Soviets are pretty decent fellows on the whole ... Churchill isn't having this nonsense ... he comes with his declaration of a new war, this time against the Red peril.' This is claptrap. If anyone had pretended that Stalin was a 'decent fellow' it was Churchill.

But then the revisionists are also quite wrong to claim that Stalin's acquisition of eastern Europe was no more than a response to western provocation, in particular the expulsion of Communists from the coalition governments in France and Italy which they had joined after the liberation. This commits the greatest of historians' sins, falsification of chronology. What Churchill called the bolshevisation of Rumania, Bulgaria, Hungary, and above all Poland, had begun as soon as the Red Army and secret police arrived, well before the departure of the French and Italian Communists from office in the 'May crisis' of 1947. And Churchill's speech of 6 March had been anticipated four weeks earlier by Stalin's little remembered but no less significant speech of 9 February. This bluntly declared an end to the wartime alliance, or as bluntly as Stalin's language allowed.* Where Churchill would blame the war on western faintheartedness, Stalin blamed it on 'monopoly capitalism'. More plausibly, he said that 'it was the

---

* As Dwight Macdonald observed at the time, Stalin 'always says everything three times ("Moreover, after this war no one dared any more to deny that vitality of the Soviet state system. Now it is no longer a question of the vitality of the Soviet state system, since there can be no doubt of its vitality any more.") On the evidence of Stalin's barbarous oratory alone, one could deduce the bureaucratic inhumanity and the primitiveness of modern Soviet society.'

Soviet armed forces that won. Our Red Army has won'; less plausibly, he attributed this to the strength of the 'Soviet social system'.

If Churchill's speech was misinterpreted, that was partly his fault, through a slip an experienced newspaperman shouldn't have made. He called his speech 'The Sinews of Peace', but only at the last moment, after reporters had already seen the text; without that name to guide them, they took the speech as a call to arms, beginning with the local paper: 'CHURCHILL WARNS OF RED BID FOR POWER' trumpeted the *Fulton Daily Sun-Gazette*. And the speech seemed all too bellicose to the Americans. Churchill still refused to see the contradiction between the survival of a British Empire which meant so much to him and close friendship with a United States which was so strongly – if hypocritically – hostile to British imperialism. Hence the ferocious critical reaction. While the *Chicago Sun* called Churchill's speech 'poisonous', it was criticised also by the *Wall Street Journal* (in those days, its twenty-first-century readers may be surprised to know, a paper of liberal Republican and mildly pacificist tendency), and Walter Lippmann in the *Washington Post* dismissed the idea that there could be any special relationship between the imperialist British and 'a people as deeply imbued as the Americans with the tradition and the conviction that empires are at best a necessary evil, to be liquidated as soon as possible'. With his usual mixture of acuity and obtusity, Lippmann failed to see that the British Empire would indeed soon come to an end, and be succeeded by an American imperium. That was Churchill's doing as much as anyone's.

A more telling criticism of the Fulton speech than Lippmann's might have been made. Soon thereafter, Soviet aggression began to frighten Americans, and a 'myth of Yalta' was born on the American Right, in its way as pernicious as the myth of Munich. Roosevelt had betrayed the Poles and other east Europeans, it was said, by handing them over to Stalin at Yalta. No one knew better what nonsense this was than Churchill. He would have resented a German journalist saying as late as 2014 that 'Yalta was Churchill's Munich'.* And he knew all too well that no one had 'given' Stalin eastern Europe: he had taken it, or won it with the blood of the Red Army.

---

* Thomas Kielinger, the long-serving London correspondent of the *Welt*, in his 2014 book *Winston Churchill: Der späte Held*.

Although Churchill would escape the anathemata of the American Right, and later become a hero to many of them, he knew in his heart that, if an iron curtain had fallen across Europe, and as far west as a line from Stettin to Trieste, then few people alive were more responsible for this than himself. Soviet domination of eastern Europe was almost implicit in the words 'victory at all costs' in his first great speech as prime minister in May 1940, still more so in his embrace of Stalin as an ally in June 1941, and above all in his endless procrastination over a landing in north-western Europe, which meant that the Red Army did most of the fighting, and Stalin claimed his reward. If Churchill had managed to delay the invasion of France any longer, the iron curtain could have fallen even further west, maybe from Hamburg to Genoa rather than Stettin to Trieste. Later Churchill would muse that 'we could have done it', that the British and Americans could have defeated Germany without the Russians. If that meant that the Anglo-American armies, instead of the Red Army, would have accepted millions of soldiers killed it was pure fantasy.

From June 1941 on, Churchill's purpose, unspoken and almost unconscious, was to let the Wehrmacht be destroyed in a vast war of attrition in the east while the British fought leisurely peripheral campaigns with far fewer casualties. Churchill had told the Commons about the 'remarkably generous' terms offered by Russia to Romania, he had made his outrageous 'percentages' deal with Stalin in October 1944, and the following February he had told Parliament that 'I know of no Government which stands to its obligation, even to its own despite, more solidly than the Russian Soviet Government' while he privately acknowledged that eastern Europe was 'going to be bolshevised'.

Strange as the words 'stands to its obligation' may sound – and how they should shock Churchill's later American devotees! – they were true enough in one case. Stalin had kept his bargain where Greece was concerned. There was a much stronger indigenous Communist movement in Greece than in almost any other Balkan or east European country, and it had provided a large part of the wartime resistance. But at the end of 1944 Stalin had stood aside and allowed the Communists to be crushed, with Churchill's help, and gave them little support in the ensuing bloody civil war. Nor did he give any encouragement to the Italian and French Communists to try to seize power: indeed, he restrained them.

Where Churchill was entirely wrong was when he told Parliament that no 'spheres of influence' were being created. To the contrary, that was precisely what was happening, and he had played his part, as he knew very well: he had told Stalin that they shouldn't use the phrase 'dividing into spheres', since 'the Americans might be shocked'. Although Churchill was unaware of the conversations between Stalin and Djilas in the last year of the war, he should have understood what Stalin had said to Djilas: 'This war is not as in the past; whoever occupies a territory imposes on it his social system as far as his army can reach. It cannot be otherwise.' Actually, this was very much 'as in the past': *cuius regio eius religio* writ new, the principle on which the bloody religious wars of the sixteenth and seventeenth centuries had been ended, that the people would follow the faith of their prince. The lands of western Europe which the Anglo-American Allies recovered became liberal democracies with free-market economies mitigated by social security, and the lands east of the Elbe became Leninist one-party dictatorships, dignified by the odious pleonasm 'people's democracies', or the still more absurd 'workers' states'.

In view of that, Churchill's Fulton speech might be considered misleading enough, but he had other themes, still more dubious. He asserted yet again that 'There never was a war in all history easier to prevent by timely action than the one which has just desolated such great areas of the globe.' Churchill made this another text in his Authorised Version, although it begged far too many questions. Whose 'timely action' should it have been? The British and French peoples, who were so anxious to avoid war? The Americans, who had no intention at all of entering a European war until they were left with no choice?

Then he came 'to the crux of what I have travelled here to say. Neither the sure prevention of war, nor the continuous rise of world organisation will be gained without what I have called the fraternal association of the English-speaking peoples. This means a special relationship between the British Commonwealth and Empire and the United States,' and his gaudy peroration:

> Let no man underrate the abiding power of the British Empire and Commonwealth ... Do not suppose that we shall not come through these dark years of privation as we have come through the glorious years of agony, or that half a century from now, you will not see 70

or 80 millions of Britons spread about the world and united in defence of our traditions, our way of life, and of the world causes which you and we espouse.

This was empty eloquence. It took a very long time for the British to recognise how little this 'special relationship', or the Commonwealth, really meant. And yet if they had looked harder, just how dubious Churchill's claims were would be made clear shortly after he spoke, and in a context which had intermittently absorbed him for forty years.

Two of the many problems he no longer had to deal with, as opposed to comment on unhelpfully, were Palestine and India. In 1946 violence flared up again in Palestine. Jabotinsky had died in 1940 but his heirs in the Irgun began a self-proclaimed campaign of terror against the British and the Arabs. In July 1946, they blew up the King David Hotel in Jerusalem with heavy loss of life: British, Arab and Jewish; and the following year they would capture and hang two British sergeants, Clifford Martin and Mervyn Paice, National Service conscripts, or draftees. The Irgun was led by Menahim Begin, a future prime minister of Israel, like Shamir who had ordered the assassination of Moyne, and these savage events imprinted themselves on the mind of Margaret Roberts, an Oxford undergraduate, who would never forget them. Churchill thought for a moment of asking the United States to take over responsibility for 'the painful and thankless task' of governing Palestine, just as he had after the Great War, but that was the last thing the Americans wanted.

On his return from Fulton, Parliament debated the Palestine question. 'Had I had the opportunity of guiding the course of events after the war was won a year ago,' he said, 'I should have faithfully pursued the Zionist cause as I have defined it; and I have not abandoned it today, although this is not a very popular moment to espouse it.' It certainly was not, notably in his own party, as he conceded when he mentioned the 'honourable friends' – other Tories – who didn't share his enthusiasm. One was Christopher Soames, who was soon to become Churchill's latest son-in-law when he married Mary on what she recalled as 'a freezing February day' in 1947. Soames was then an officer in the Coldstream Guards but he would leave the army and enter Parliament in 1950; when Churchill returned to Downing Street the following year, Soames became his parliamentary private secretary, and closest confidant. Before that, Soames had warned Churchill that his support for Zionism was not widely shared in the party or the country.

In that same speech, Churchill touched on the event which, in a way few then realised, would one day condition our whole view of the war. 'I must say, that I had no idea, when the war came to an end, of the horrible massacres which had occurred,' Churchill declared; 'the millions and millions that have been slaughtered. That dawned on us gradually after the struggle was over.' That was a lie. It was true that only the murderers and the murdered knew exactly what was happening at the time in the death camps, but the plea that 'we didn't know' was as unconvincing from western leaders as from the German people. If they hadn't known, it was because they hadn't wanted to know. And in fact they did know a great deal. Churchill had been more aware than anyone else in the West about 'the horrible massacres', from August 1941 onwards, when he had spoken of 'a crime without name' in the form of mass killings in the east. From late 1942 he was aware of industrial extermination, and the Commons had stood in silence to honour the victims, to May 1943 when Victor Cazalet told the Commons of 'the horrors of the massacres at a camp called Treblinka', to July 1944 when Churchill had told Eden that this was 'the greatest and most horrible crime ever committed in the whole history of the world'.

To make his denial worse, Churchill derided Bevin as he tried to steer an even course through the Palestine maelstrom and find a way for the British to extricate themselves with dignity, or the least indignity. It's hard to see what else Churchill would have done himself. As Keynes told Weizmann, England was simply too poor and tired to bear any more a burden which brought nothing but obloquy from all sides. Later Churchill said morosely that he could have saved the British Empire from anything except the British people. That was not so: the age of European empire was over, and united national determination would have made no difference. But it was true enough that no such determination existed. The real British spirit in these years was succinctly expressed by a graffito exchange on a wall in Jerusalem. A Zionist militant had painted 'Tommy go home!', underneath which one such Tommy replied, 'I wish I fucking well could.' So spoke millions of young men who were reluctantly 'called up' while National

Service or conscription remained in force until the end of the 1950s, and that soldier may have spoken for most of the British people, during the decline and fall of the British Empire.

Throughout this bleak story, the Americans were no help at all. The Zionists demanded the immediate admission of 100,000 Jews to Palestine, which would have provoked another Arab revolt, and then, only months after escorting Churchill to Fulton, Truman gave his 'Yom Kippur speech' of October 1946, timed for the midterm congressional elections, in which he joined demands for the admission of the 100,000. Attlee lost patience, and bitterly rebuked Truman for not having consulted the prime minister 'of the country which has the actual responsibility for the government of Palestine in order that he might acquaint you with the actual situation and probable results of your action'.

Like Roosevelt before him, Truman harried and harassed the British, while refusing to offer any practical assistance – as he breezily said, 'I have no desire to send 500,000 American soldiers there to make peace in Palestine' – and at the same time going to some trouble, before, during and after the great murder in Europe, to restrict Jewish immigration to America. Speaking with his usual sarcastic bluntness, Bevin said that the American campaign for admission of Jews to Palestine was pursued 'from the purest of motives. They did not want too many Jews in New York.' This caused much anger in America, and it was certainly a shocking and offensive thing to say. It was also quite true. However coarsely phrased, Bevin's words might have referred to the nativist or racist immigration laws passed after the Great War and the overwhelming American sentiment against Jewish immigration thereafter. The lengths to which the Roosevelt and Truman administrations had gone to restrict the numbers of Jews seeking American refuge to a bare minimum was not made any more attractive by official mendacity, suggesting that many more Jews had been admitted than was the case.

In 1947, amid escalating violence, one more committee, under the auspices of the newborn United Nations, visited the Holy Land, and again recommended partition. Rather than Peel's proposed 65 per cent Arab to 35 per cent Jewish ten years before, the committee now allotted 57 per cent of British Palestine to a Jewish state and 43 per cent to an Arab state. The Zionists were ready to accept a bird in the hand, but the Arabs, who were still two-thirds of the whole population, and, ominously enough, almost half the population in the Jewish sector, were adamantly opposed. So were Attlee, and Bevin, who rashly assured Parliament that the United Nations wouldn't approve the partition plan when it was debated and voted on in the General Assembly, a claim which excited further derision from Churchill.

But partition was crucially supported by Truman, and his administration twisted every arm to vote in favour, west European states as well as the Latin American republics which then mostly did the State Department's bidding: with no more than sixty-five member-states in the General Assembly, less than a third of the number sixty years later, 'the Americas' were the largest single bloc. Far from least, there were the Commonwealth countries, which were also leaned on by Washington. When the debate was held in November at the United Nations' temporary headquarters in the suburbs of New York, London cautiously told its representative to abstain, but still hoped that the vote in favour of partition would fail to reach the required two-thirds of votes cast. The debate was attended by Harold Beeley of the Foreign Office, in the course of a distinguished diplomatic career which would later see him as British representative at the United Nations: 'The galleries were packed with an almost exclusively Zionist audience,' Beeley said. 'They applauded declarations of support for Zionism. They hissed Arab speakers. They created the atmosphere of a football match, with the Arabs as the away team.' The home terraces got the result they wanted, by thirty-three votes to thirteen, and there was rejoicing from New York to Tel Aviv.

More significant than the numbers was the way the vote divided. For the moment, Stalin supported the Zionists, so that made three votes: Soviet Russia along with the 'sovereign' Ukrainian and Byelorussian Soviet republics (more aptly known by the traditional names of Little Russia and White Russia) to which Churchill and Roosevelt had allowed membership to the United Nations as a sop to Stalin before he acquired a tame block of satellites. Whatever Stalin's motive, it wasn't philosemitism, as he would shortly show when he launched a savage campaign against 'rootless cosmopolitans' in Russia, his polysyllabic expression for Jews when he wanted to shoot a few more of them. The majority also included eleven countries which would later belong to Nato. Of the minority of thirteen, nine were Muslim countries.

But most telling of all was the division within the British Commonwealth, until then a cohesive diplomatic bloc. For the first time, the old – or 'white' – Commonwealth followed Washington rather than London, with Australia, Canada, New Zealand and South Africa all voting for partition. And yet the Commonwealth had just changed character. After years of Churchill's nagging resistance to Indian independence, and his endless lamentations about the 'scuttle' from empire, he had finally admitted defeat, and the Tories accepted the Attlee government's legislation granting India her freedom in August 1947, although it was two states rather than one which became independent.

Writing in 1945 for an American, and leftist, audience in the famous 'little magazine' *Partisan Review*, Orwell had observed that what was called progressive sentiment in the west, among American liberals, European social democrats and, not least, the British Labour Party, was then 'strongly committed to support the Jews against the Arabs' in Palestine. Such sentiment was exemplified in 1946 by a little pamphlet with the resonant title *A Palestine Munich*, written by two newly elected Labour MPs, on the Left of the party, R.H.S. Crossman and Michael Foot. The former was the man to whom Macmillan had proposed his 'Greeks to their Romans' conceit three years earlier, the latter was the co-author of the wretched *Guilty Men*. With 'Munich' now established as a synonym for betrayal, those being betrayed, the authors claimed, were the Jews.

They had no difficulty in showing that the Labour Party had for many years made warm offers of sympathy and support for the Zionists, to the extent that the party's manifesto for the 1945 election had recommended not only the founding of a Jewish state but its creation by means of ethnic cleansing, or at any rate 'transfer of population': 'Let the Arabs be encouraged to move out as the Jews move in,' which was one way of describing what did happen three years later. Crossman and Foot showed little more sympathy than Churchill for the Palestinian Arabs. What they forgot was what Orwell had added: 'the Palestine issue is partly a colour issue,' in which 'an Indian nationalist, for example, would probably side with the Arabs.' That one flash of insight illuminated many bitter years to come. 'An Indian nationalist, for example', did indeed side with the Arabs: antagonistic as they were, the new Indian and Pakistani republics voted on the same side, in one of their earliest appearances at the United Nations, which is to say they voted against the Zionists, the United States and the white Commonwealth.

Not that it mattered for the moment. As the man Churchill had called 'the great Bismarck' so truly said, 'The great issues of our time are not decided by speeches and majority votes, but by iron and blood,' and once again he was proved right. In May 1948 the state of Israel declared its independence and fought fiercely against Arab neighbours which ineffectually made war on the new state, while hundreds of thousands of Palestinian Arabs were driven out. By the time the fighting stopped, the new-born Jewish state controlled not Peel's 35 per cent, or the 57 per cent recommended by the United Nations, but 78 per cent of what had been Mandatory Palestine.

Shortly afterwards, an Israeli ambassador was appointed to London, and went to see Churchill at Hyde Park Gate, the Churchills' recently acquired London home. The ambassador was startled to find the Leader of the Opposition in bed late in the morning cradling a bottle of wine, but there were warm exchanges of esteem. Churchill made another intervention in January 1949 when he told the Commons that the Palestinian Arabs had voluntarily fled the country: 'All this Arab population fled in terror to behind the advancing forces of their own religion.' This fiction was maintained by the Israeli government for many years before Benny Morris and other 'new historians' revealed the true story of 1948; if anything, more to the point, Yitzhak Rabin, a future Labour prime minister, and martyr, described how he, serving in the Palmach militia, had given the orders at the behest of David Ben Gurion, leader of the new state: 'The inhabitants of Lydda must be expelled quickly without attention to age . . . Implement immediately.'

While Churchill would acquire heroic status in Israel as an honorary founding father, all unnoticed was the final, and supreme, irony of his career. He was a lifelong imperialist, he strongly favoured European colonial settlement, and he believed in racial superiority. Those beliefs always underlay his support for Zionism. In 1937 he had said that the British shouldn't 'hand over' Palestine 'to the people who happen to live there at the moment', and in 1941 he had reiterated that he didn't want to see the Arabs claim Palestine 'by majority'. More forthrightly still, he had said that he favoured the Jews as 'a higher-grade race' than the Arabs. Since those words Churchill had led his country to victory against the most hateful racial tyranny in history, which had committed against the Jews an act of murder without parallel, inspired by a belief that the Jews were a lower-grade race. Now a Jewish state had risen from the ashes. And yet, thanks to Hitler, his Third Reich and his 'Final Solution', the very language Churchill had used nine years earlier in praise of Zionism had become intolerable.

As to his high-sounding words at Fulton, less than two years since that speech the United States had betrayed its supposed British friend on a question of the highest importance for London. How 'special' could their relationship really be? Churchill had also said that no one should underestimate 'the abiding power of the British Empire and Commonwealth'. What 'abiding power' was there in a group which had split three ways on what was to prove the most bitterly contentious question dividing the world into the next century? In itself that one vote at the United Nations in November 1947 exposed the emptiness of Churchill's words.

A foolish and ignorant thesis would be propounded that departing imperial powers divided or partitioned the territories they were leaving out of malice aforethought.* This has no foundation. Churchill himself had been an early convert to the idea of 'Pakistan' but, just as all contemporary evidence shows that the Asquith government in which Churchill had served had not wanted to partition Ireland, all contemporary evidence shows that the Attlee government he now opposed did not want to partition India, or Palestine either. But as time was running out, Churchill's shadow fell even more heavily over India than Palestine. If he made an indirect contribution to the ensuing horror, it was in the person of Mountbatten, whom he had praised and raised above his modest abilities. Had it not been for Churchill's foolish earlier patronage, Mountbatten would never have been able to take the next step in a life of over-promotion when he was appointed the last Viceroy of India in December 1946. He already had the Garter to add to his beloved collection of honorific and initials, and would now become the last GCSI and GCIE, Knight Grand Commander of the Order of the Star of India and of the Most Eminent Order of the Indian Empire, an empire which was about to expire.

By the time Mountbatten reached India, unity had been effectively if tacitly abandoned by every important political leader there. Having

* For example by Christopher Hitchens in 'The Perils of Partition', in *Arguably*, 2012.

first named June 1948 as the date the British would leave, Mountbatten found that events were slipping out of his control, and he despairingly advanced the date to August 1947. In New Delhi, the viceroy and his wife formed a warm relationship with Jawaharlal Nehru, which became even closer: Indian historians to this day believe that Nehru and Edwina Mountbatten were lovers, another case of 'the personal is political'. And Mountbatten flagrantly favoured the Congress party, notionally non-sectarian but in practice representing the Hindu majority, while he was deeply antipathetic toward Mohamed Ali Jinnah, leader of the Muslim League. Here Mountbatten clearly did not share Churchill's prejudices: with all his contempt for Islam, Churchill admired the Muslim 'martial races' of the Raj as much he despised the 'foul race' of Hindus.

We have seen that Churchill actively welcomed the rivalry between Hindu and Muslim and hoped that it 'would remain bitter and bloody'. And if Mountbatten didn't instigate the terrible bloodshed which followed partition, he bears much blame, for his precipitancy over the timetable and his incompetence over the actual lines of partition. The map-making was the work of Sir Cyril Radcliffe, who knew nothing whatever about India until he arrived and was given just five weeks to draw the border. The line of partition had inevitably left the Punjab with huge minorities on the wrong side, Muslims in India and Hindus in Pakistan. Mountbatten characteristically authorised this arbitrary map-drawing behind the scenes, and thereafter denied that he had done so. Independence Day was greeted in both the new states with joy which was soon hideously extinguished. Seven years earlier Churchill had hoped that the conflict between Muslim and Hindu 'would remain bitter and bloody,' and his wish was more than granted. Awful communal violence saw expulsions and massacres in which more than ten million fled and nearly two million were killed.

In November Mountbatten left India for what was for him in every way a much happier event, the wedding of the young Princess Elizabeth to his nephew Lieutenant Philip Mountbatten: Lord Mountbatten would later make a great nuisance of himself after Elizabeth had acceded to the throne by demanding that the name of the royal family should be changed from Windsor to Mountbatten-Windsor. Apart from him, no one was more delighted by the royal wedding than Churchill. 'The news has certainly given the keenest pleasure to all classes,' he told the King, 'and the marriage will be an occasion for national rejoicing, standing out all the more against the background of our lives.'

By this time there was a new dissonance between Churchill, the extraordinary 'leader of humanity', and the distinctly ordinary party leader, just as Low's cartoon and Attlee's broadcast reply had suggested at the time of the election. Even as the leader of humanity, he could seem confused and conflicted. Six months after Fulton, he made another and greater speech in Zurich, where he spoke as a voice of reconciliation, at a time of retribution. During the war, the Allies had debated at length what was to be done with Germany, and its leaders. The British had favoured summary executions, and at one moment Churchill had spoken cheerfully of importing American electric chairs to dispose of the German leaders – 'electric chairs for gangsters' – but when at Tehran Stalin suggested shooting 50,000 German officers and Roosevelt for a moment seemed to agree, Churchill indignantly said that it was unthinkable.

Now it was the Americans who favoured formal trials, which were duly held in Nuremberg over nearly a year, ending in October 1946 with the conviction and execution of twelve defendants. The tribunal unwisely indicted defendants not only for the unparalleled atrocities of the Reich but for 'crimes against peace', or 'conspiracy to wage aggressive war', a most dubious charge. In 1919 when the victorious allies had discussed putting the Kaiser and other German leaders on trial for having begun the war, Churchill had been sceptical: there was 'a great deal to be said about Russia, if you unfolded the question', he said, and about Austria-Hungary, and Serbia, among others, he could have added.

In 1946 there was even more to be said about Russia if you unfolded the question, or about Stalin's murderous tyranny, from the Ukrainian famine and the bloodbath of the show trials and the great terror to the Molotov–Ribbentrop Pact in 1939 to the butchery of Katyn to the gang rape at the end of the war. And the Russian invasion of Finland in 1939 was 'a crime against peace' if ever there was one. Now two judges appointed by Stalin sat on the bench in Nuremberg. Churchill at his wisest saw how dubious the very idea was of the victors prosecuting the vanquished for having waged war at all. As he sardonically said to Ismay, if you lead a country in a war, 'it is supremely important to win it. You and I would be in a pretty pickle if we had lost,' which remains the most succinct criticism of any such proceeding.

However the leaders of the Reich were dealt with, what should Germany, and Europe, look like? By the Moscow Declaration of 1943, the Anschluss of 1938 was nullified, and 'the Governments of the United Kingdom, the Soviet Union and the United States of America are agreed that Austria, the first free country to fall a victim to Hitlerite aggression, shall be liberated from German domination'. Then Prussia was formally abolished by the Allies in a pointlessly vindictive gesture. These perverse decisions overlooked the fact that it was in Vienna that Hitler had learned his politics long before he was welcomed back there in 1938 by the most rapturous crowds he ever saw, that a disproportionate number of the leading figures, and worst criminals, of the Reich had been Austrian, and that Prussia had a distinctly better record of resistance to Hitler than Austria. But it reflected Churchill's prejudices, his old sympathy for Austria and his contempt for 'clanking, heel-clicking, dandified Prussian officers'.

In November 1942, Eden's private secretary had recorded Churchill saying that 'the only way to run Europe after the war was for Great Britain and Russia to keep out and for Europe to be run by a Grand Council of "the Great Powers including Prussia, Italy, Spain and the Scandinavian Confederacy". He did not want America in Europe.' Now speaking in Zurich on 19 September 1946, he proposed a remedy 'which, if it were generally and spontaneously adopted by the great majority of people in many lands, would as by a miracle transform the whole scene and would in a few years make all Europe, or the greater part of it, as free and happy as Switzerland is today. What is this sovereign remedy? It is to recreate the European fabric, or as much of it as we can, and to provide it with a structure under which it can dwell in peace, safety and freedom. We must build a kind of United States of Europe.'

That phrase 'United States of Europe' had been current since the first half of the nineteenth century, and Churchill himself had written a somewhat cloudy article entitled 'A United States of Europe' for American readers in 1930. In Zurich he now said, 'The guilty must be punished. Germany must be deprived of the power to rearm and make another aggressive war. But when all this has been done ... There must be what Mr Gladstone many years ago called a "blessed act of oblivion".'

And he went on, 'I am now going to say something that will astonish you. The first step in the re-creation of the European family must be a partnership between France and Germany. In this way only can France recover the moral and cultural leadership of Europe. There can be no revival of Europe without a spiritually great France and a spiritually great Germany.' After recommending a Council of Europe as the first practical steps which were needed, he ended with the ringing words: 'Therefore I say to you "Let Europe arise!"' These were truly noble sentiments, but there remained an underlying ambiguity which Churchill never resolved: if there were a partnership between France and Germany as the basis for a kind of United States of Europe, what would be the British role be?

And what would Churchill's role be? In Missouri or Zurich, he bestrode the world stage, but back home he seemed a diminished figure. From middle age there had been something of the big baby about his appearance, all the more so when he wore his wartime 'siren suit' which looked like rompers, and he was now sometimes babyish in manner as well, petulant and wilful, a point made in a most astute and candid portrait of Churchill in 1947 by the American journalist Raymond Daniell. After his 'painful and unhappy transition' from supreme power to opposition, he now seemed 'an embittered, troubled man who for perhaps the first time in his career cannot see how his country or the world is going'. In Parliament Churchill cut a surly figure, childishly baiting Herbert Morrison, his own Home Secretary not long before and now Leader of the House, on occasion even sticking his tongue out. In 1940 and 1941, at times when the news was very bad, Churchill would go to the Smoking Room, to talk affably to other MPs or to sit intently reading the *Evening News* as he sipped his drink with wonderful insouciance. Now he came to the Smoking Room to sulk, glowering if his whisky wasn't brought by his favourite waiter. 'Newspaper men who were once on speaking terms with him find it advisable to let him alone,' Daniell wrote, and he might have added that any younger journalist rash enough to approach Churchill would be met with a withering, 'Do I know you?'

Even Harold Nicolson, who hero-worshipped Churchill, knew that younger Tories thought Churchill too old or even 'embarrassing', and after Churchill's old friend Jan Smuts had spoken to a number of eminent people, he sadly wrote, 'They all feel that Winston must go.' An American newspaperman who polled sixty leading political and military figures in his country found only two who saw a political future for Churchill. Sometimes rumours reached the London press. While Churchill had been in America, a story appeared in the *Evening News*, 'Churchill will "Hand Over" Soon',' which read as if planted by one or more of his colleagues. But when James Stuart, the Tory Whip, saw Churchill and tried gently to raise the question of a succession, he was sent away with a flea in his ear.

One thing Daniell misunderstood was Churchill's literary career. He said correctly that Churchill was at work again on the *English-Speaking Peoples*, which had been left unfinished and unpublishable at the end of 1939. Now more research assistants had been hired, including the Cambridge don D.W. Brogan, as the text was expanded and revised. But Daniell suggested that this work was unwelcome for Churchill, since 'he was in the same embarrassing situation as many another author who has taken an advance from a publisher and then spent it before completing the work'. That had often been true of Churchill in the past, but since he had routed his publishers in 1944 he had no financial concern about the uncompleted *English-Speaking Peoples*, which others would get into shape for future publication while he approached his new great task: what Chamberlain as long ago as 1939 had called 'the Book he will write hereafter'.

Not the least reason that Churchill was a fainéant Leader of the Opposition was that his real life was led not at Westminster but at Chartwell. It had been closed for the duration of the war, but the Churchills returned there when peace came. In 1938 Churchill had reluctantly told Clementine that they might have to sell the house. It remained a drain on financial resources even when closed, and Churchill was horrified when his cousin the Duke of Marlborough intimated that he might sell Blenheim. But now that problem was solved. Lord Camrose assembled a somewhat random group of rich men who clubbed together to help Churchill. Some of them could be called friends or colleagues of his, such as Lord Portal, as the wartime head of the RAF now was, Jimmy de Rothschild, and Camrose himself; others, like the cinema magnate J. Arthur Rank and the motor manufacturer Lord Nuffield, were merely happy to be associated with such an illustrious cause.* They bought the house from Churchill for £50,000 and presented it to the National Trust along with another capital sum of £35,000 to pay for its maintenance, with the condition that Winston and Clementine Churchill could live there undisturbed for the rest of their lives, in effect national treasures themselves.

By contrast with these exaltations, Churchill's relationship with Parliament, and his own party, remained delicate. In June 1948, a Conservative lunch was given for him at the Savoy, where he optimistically promised to win the next election with a three-figure majority. And yet 'gone is the rapture of yesteryear', noted 'Chips' Channon, who was present. 'His reception was tepid ... the Party resents both his unimpaired criticism of Munich, recently published, and his alleged pro-Zionist leanings.' The 'recently published' book was *The Gathering Storm*, the first volume of *The Second World War* with its attack on Baldwin and Chamberlain and the years of appeasement from 1936 to 1939 – and on the Conservatives he was now leading: most of such Tory MPs as had survived the great cull in 1945 had formerly supported appeasement.

A new generation of liberal-minded Tories, Edward Heath, Iain Macleod, Reginald Maudling and Enoch Powell, had served in the war, and were not yet in Parliament. Some of them were working for the Conservative Party, and trying to reconcile it with the new age, not least with a new conciliatory approach to the trade unions, a repudiation of Churchill's own former bellicosity. Churchill was suspicious of the progressive and collectivist tendencies of these youngsters, whom he genially called 'my pink pansies', while grumbling that he was being asked to make speeches on industrial policy which he didn't believe in.

By 1950, the parliament elected five years before was approaching its end and an election was held in February. With a very high turnout of 84 per cent, never surpassed before or since, Labour retained a

---

* The full list is recorded on a plaque at Chartwell: Edward Peacock, Viscount Camrose, Viscount Bearsted, Sir Hugo Cunliffe-Owen, Lord Glendyne, Lord Leathers, Mr James De Rothschild, Sir Frederick Stewart, Mr J. Arthur Rank, Viscount Portal of Laverstoke, Sir Edward Mountain, Sir James Lithgow, Lord Kenilworth, Lord Bicester, Sir James Caird, Lord Catto and Viscount Nuffield.

parliamentary majority, but much reduced, and the Tories recovered to within striking distance, while a famous vintage saw Heath, Maudling, Macleod, Powell and other younger Tories elected for the first time. By June the Korean War was added to the government's troubles, and in October 1951, under improper pressure from King George to clarify the position of his small majority, Attlee wrote a private letter to 'My dear Churchill', to say that he had agreed to a dissolution of Parliament and an election would be held on 25 October, only a year and nine months after the last one.

An old saw of British politics holds that Oppositions don't win elections, governments lose them. Never was that truer than of the Attlee government. It had fulfilled its historic mission, but was worn out, with Attlee himself and several of his colleagues mentally and physically exhausted after eleven extraordinary and gruelling years in office. Churchill had derided Baldwin as little more than an effective 'party manager'. He was certainly the more successful electioneer of the two. Baldwin led the Tories in five general elections and, even when Labour twice formed the subsequent government, the Tories won the largest vote in all five. Churchill led the party in three elections, and never secured a plurality, not in 1945 or 1950, and not now in 1951, when the Tories gained a majority of seats through the vagaries of the electoral system but actually won a smaller popular vote than Labour.

One of the most misleading rewritings of Churchill's life, in a small way, comes at this point in *The Crown*, when the king, welcoming Churchill back, says he never got on with his dull predecessor, to which Churchill growls, 'An empty taxi stopped at the House of Commons and Mr Attlee got out,' at which they both chuckle. That 'joke' was certainly current at the time: it's quoted by a character in *The Wrong Set* in 1949, Angus Wilson's first book. But Churchill disapproved of others mocking Attlee, whom he would defend as a brave officer and patriot, telling one young Tory MP who had sneered at 'silly old Attlee' that he would be asked to leave if he said that again.

And so a new regime began, if new it was. Two great men had seen the difficulty. Keynes had died in 1946, worn out by his exertions to the extent that he may be said to have died for his country. Not long before he died, Keynes said what could have been a rebuke to Churchill: 'England is sticky with self-pity and not prepared to accept peacefully and wisely the fact that her position and her resources are not what they once were.' And in 1949, Sir Henry Tizard wrote a brief minute. The man whose work installing radar before 1940, despite Lindemann's incompetent meddling, helped save the country, now saw with great penetration. 'We persist in regarding ourselves as a Great Power,' Tizard wrote, 'capable of everything and only temporarily handicapped by economic difficulties. We are not a Great Power and never will be again. We are a great nation, but if we continue to behave like a Great Power we shall soon cease to be a great nation.' His words would seem ever more prophetic with the coming years.

Man goeth forth unto his work and to his labour until the evening.

16

'It is not history, it is my case'
Windsor 1953

Inside the ancient chancel of St George's Chapel in Windsor Castle, from where royal weddings are now watched on television by hundreds of millions, scores of millions of Americans among them, hang the banners of the Knights of the Garter, while the walls bear small brass plaques commemorating knights of yore. They include Sir Winston Churchill. Having twice declined the Order of the Garter he finally accepted, and was splendidly installed on St George's Day 1953. A portrait depicted him in his Garter robes, including the first Marlborough's insignia, with the new knight's son and grandson dressed as his pages, Randolph auditioning for the role of 'Jack Falstaff ... page to Thomas Mowbray, Duke of Norfolk'. It was Churchill's *annus mirabilis*, a second finest hour for him. In 1953, he was prime minister once again, he published the sixth and last volume of *The Second World War*, he received the Garter, and he was awarded the Nobel Prize in Literature.

Less than six weeks after that ceremony at Windsor there was still more splendid ceremony in Westminster Abbey when a young queen was crowned. It might seem paradoxical that citizens of an American republic which had begun life by rebellion against the king of England should be absorbed by such gaudy pageants – nothing could surely be more 'un-American' – but the coronation received vast coverage in the American media,* betokening an American fascination with all things English and grand, which would only grow over the years until the age of *Downton Abbey* and *The Crown*. And more than anything there was an increasing American obsession with Churchill.

---

* One of the reporters covering it was twenty-two-year-old Jacqueline Bouvier, who later that year would marry Senator John Kennedy.

We have seen how Churchill rediscovered America from 1929, but it took longer for America to discover Winston Churchill. Between the wars his name was well known, as author and journalist, though by no means a bestseller, and his various American publishers regularly found themselves looking at large unearned advances. He was also known as a statesman to that very small number of Americans who took a serious interest in British politics, or any foreign affairs at all, although known didn't always mean loved. He did have American admirers as well as detractors. The *Washington Post*, not as important a paper as it later became but nevertheless the parish journal for the administration and Capitol Hill, carried a torch for Churchill over many years.

In 1917, the *Post* believed that 'Half a dozen Winston Churchills in the British cabinet prior to the European war would have saved England from the folly for which she is now paying a frightful toll.' When Churchill returned to America in late 1931 for his highly lucrative lecture tour on 'The Pathway of the English-Speaking Peoples', that great subject he had now lighted on, the *Post* took a more sceptical line. Churchill was in the United States 'for the general purpose of trying to hitch the American wagon to the British star,' the *Post* said. 'Not many years ago political and economic unity with the Yankees would have been repulsive to British statesmen ... now the tables are turned and Mr Churchill is trying to flatter the United States into taking over some of Britain's liabilities,' as indeed he was and would be. But by July 1939, the *Washington Post* had returned to its admiring mode. Chamberlain hesitated to bring Churchill into his government, the *Post* said, since this 'would mean his own eclipse. Churchill is a man of such brilliance as inevitably to throw the present collection of mediocrities in the British Cabinet into complete obscurity, but no step could be more salutary for Great Britain and for Europe's peace than that.'

Admiration for Churchill grew much stronger in the war years: first of all in the finest hour of 1940 and 1941, when Americans watched an embattled England from afar with a mixture of admiration and guilt. Churchill was *Time*'s Man of the Year in 1940, and Congress, which had been so surly and insular not only between the wars but through the first years of the war, welcomed him as a new-found hero when he spoke on Capitol Hill. By the end of the war, the mood had turned once more towards withdrawal: America wanted to go home again. All that was to change very quickly, so quickly that it took on the misleading appearance of inevitability – and Churchill was reborn in his role as prophet.

Even as early as 1945, an American journalist could observe that Churchill was 'much more criticised and less believed as a superman in England than in the United States', words given heavier emphasis only months after they were written when the British people ejected Churchill from Downing Street. By 1952, Alistair Cooke could write that in England 'Mr Churchill suffers (though with aplomb) from a popular reaction against the American idolatry of him'. His aplomb had good reason by then: the conception, gestation and publication of Churchill's huge book *The Second World War* was if anything more an American than a British story, and another victory for Churchill.

During and after the war he had been attacked by some American writers, among them Harry Butcher, Ralph Ingersoll and Elliott Roosevelt, the president's obnoxious blabbermouth son. His 1946 book, *As He Saw It*, which dismayed his own family, had FDR saying that Churchill couldn't abide General Marshall, 'And needless to say, it's because Marshall's right.' Those writers charged that Churchill had tricked the Americans into his Mediterranean campaign before trying to trick them into a Balkan campaign, and that he had been as much concerned with preserving the British Empire as with winning the war. Churchill found such critiques 'very offensive and disparaging to this country and to my personal conduct of the war', and one of his aims was to vindicate that conduct in American eyes. His many and lengthy letters to Roosevelt had likewise been written with an eye for the future. Since these could tenuously claim to have formed a private correspondence they were free from the Official Secrets Act, or so Churchill maintained.

Throughout the war that correspondence and many other papers were printed, collected and bound monthly, and when Churchill lost office in July 1945 this huge trove of sixty-eight volumes was removed bodily from Downing Street to Chartwell in a convoy of army lorries. Although official regulations had just been changed in a more generous sense, to allow ministers to keep and quote their own papers, it was far from clear in any interpretation of the law that the immense archive Churchill had removed belonged to him rather than to the Crown, or to the British people. More than twenty years before, Tory MPs had queried his use of official documents for *The World Crisis*; now

Adam McKinley, a Labour MP, told the Commons that it was 'grossly offensive' for official documents to be 'sold to the highest bidder' by former ministers. He proposed that the state should receive half of all proceeds from 'books or newspaper articles based on official documents collected during their term of office'. He was brushed aside, although the whole question of the legal status of these papers would resurface many years later. Attlee showed an indulgent lack of concern, but then it suited him for Churchill to be an absentee leader of the opposition while attending to his mighty work.

This great enterprise was launched in 1946 with a series of calculated manoeuvres, to secure the best possible terms for publication, but also to deal with the crucial question of tax. Not a few successful English writers were dismayed by high taxation at this time. J.B. Priestley, the erstwhile radical, was one, and Evelyn Waugh another. 'In a civilised age this unexpected moment of popularity would have endowed me with a competency for life,' Waugh sardonically wrote after hitting his own jackpot with *Brideshead Revisited*. 'But perhaps in a civilised age I should not be so popular. As it is the politicians confiscate my earnings.' No writer felt that more bitterly than Churchill, although he had been one of those confiscating politicians. During the war in which he had led his country, the British people had paid taxes on a scale never before imagined, from the rich, with their top marginal rate of 97.5 per cent on highest incomes, to the working class: the four million who paid Income Tax when the war began had tripled to twelve million by the time it ended.

After he lost the election, Churchill met Walter Graebner of Time-Life who offered $75,000 for three articles in *Life* magazine. This was much more than Churchill had ever received before for his journalism but he replied that if he returned to writing now, 'I would have to pay taxes of nineteen and six in the pound, so what's the use?'* He suggested instead that the magazine might like to publish his paintings, for which Graebner offered $20,000. On his American visit, Henry Luce himself, the publisher of *Time* and *Life*, offered Churchill an eye-watering $25,000 for a single radio broadcast.

---

* In the happy days of £.s.d. before the British currency was decimalised there were twelve pence in a shilling and twenty shillings in a pound, so 'nineteen and six' was 97.5 per cent.

But he was now guided by Charles Graham-Dixon, an Inner Temple barrister and tax specialist, who warned him, 'Speak for love but not for money.' How then to avoid that fatal nineteen and six? Graham-Dixon saw a solution which combined baroque ingenuity with classical simplicity. First a Literary Trust was created in which ownership of the papers was vested, on the highly dubious assumption that ownership was actually Churchill's to vest. Publishers would then pay only modest advances to Churchill as author in the usual way, but would have to pay the Trust far larger sums for rights to the papers. And those purchases, unlike the advances, wouldn't be liable to Income Tax. So brilliantly successful did this wheeze prove that, by the 1949–50 tax year, Churchill's gross income was nearly £80,000, but he paid tax on only £5000. No wonder that in April and May 1949, 454 bottles of champagne were consumed at Chartwell, along with fifty-eight of brandy, fifty-six of Black Label whisky and sixty-nine of port.

Another useful friend was Camrose, the rescuer of Chartwell. After Cassell bought British book rights to the war memoir for £40,000, Camrose paid £500,000 for British serial rights, the bulk of it borne by his *Daily Telegraph*. He also offered to auction the book in America. Camrose set off for New York on 16 October 1946 in the newly refurbished *Queen Mary*, where he was displeased to find someone else on board. Imre Révész was a Hungarian Jew who had created a syndication agency in the 1930s, and had enlarged Churchill's income when he took him on as a client. In return, partly with Churchill's help, Révész became a British subject and 'Emery Reves', Churchill's literary factotum. He had been summoned from Paris by Churchill to accompany and encourage Camrose, although Churchill also quaintly told Reves, 'you must realise that you do not actually represent me.' After one bid of $1.1 million for all American rights, Henry Luce was approached. But Reves wanted his own piece of the action, and so he rushed to Boston to lunch with Henry Laughlin, the president of Houghton Mifflin, who offered $250,000 for book rights. Camrose then closed with Luce at $1,150,000 for serial, or 'total 1400', as Camrose cheerfully cabled back. The average annual wage in the United States at the time was $2600, and would be $88,000 in 2020, so that $1.4 million might be reckoned at nearly $34 million by the following century. It only remained for Keith Murdoch to pay £75,000 for Australian newspaper rights, a remarkable sum considering how

little Churchill wrote about the Australians, and how little he thought
of them.

Now a team had to be recruited, who would assemble the material
and write the basic text. Many years before, Churchill had said that
'a Syndicate can compile an encyclopedia. Only a man can write a
book,' but he had quite forgotten those words when he called this
team of researchers and ghostwriters 'the Syndicate'. After working
for Churchill before the war, Bill Deakin had joined the Royal
Oxfordshire Hussars, Churchill's old yeomanry regiment, and then
SOE. As a liaison officer to Tito, Deakin had shown that 'great spirit
and courage' which Feiling had mentioned in originally commending
him to Churchill, while Deakin was partly responsible for his decision
to abandon Mihailović and switch to Tito. Whatever the supposedly
pragmatic arguments for this, Deakin must have known better than
anyone how absurd Churchill's claim had been in May 1944 that
'Marshal Tito has largely sunk his Communist aspect'. And in 1946
neither Churchill nor Deakin can have taken much pride in the show
trial in Belgrade of Mihailović and a number of his former comrades.
'I wanted much,' Mihailović's last statement read. 'I began much; but
the gale of the world carried away me and my work.' He was shot
on 15 July, when it was reported that he had not required the traditional blindfold, since his socialist captors had gouged out his eyes
before shooting him.

Now Deakin returned to Chartwell to head the Syndicate. There
were also 'Pug', General Sir Hastings Ismay, who had been Churchill's
military secretary to the chiefs of staff and would be the first Secretary-
General of NATO, and General Sir Henry Pownall, Vice Chief of
Imperial General Staff from 1941, and just as significantly now a
member of the advisory committee for the great series of official
histories of the war in all its aspects and campaigns which the government was commissioning. Most curious of all was the personal role
of Sir Edward Bridges, the Cabinet Secretary and head of the British
Civil Service. He had hampered the publication of memoirs by other
former ministers, but Churchill was not merely an exception to that
rule: Bridges gave any help or made any information needed available
to him.

This was all much odder and more questionable than was recognised
at the time, because of the glaring ambiguities. Was Churchill an

active political leader engaged in everyday party strife, or was he a uniquely venerable world statesman standing above such conflicts? Was he an author writing a personal account for private gain, or was he in some sense an official historian of the war? In the event he was treated as all of these things. And what was his work, if 'his' was the word? The basic method of its composition was for the Syndicate to take the raw material, the mighty trove of documents, and knock them into some kind of shape, cutting and pasting and writing the connecting narrative as a first draft, to which Churchill would then add his own touches.

As it rolled forwards like a mighty offensive, indeed more formidable in its way than some British offensives had been during the war, it became the publishing phenomenon of the age. Its six volumes ultimately appeared in eighteen languages in fifty countries, and it was serialised, often at enormous length, in eighty newspapers and magazines. But American publication was the most important and influential. With each of the six volumes American publication preceded British, sometimes by nearly a year.* This was partly for copyright reasons, but it was appropriate enough, since American readers were central to the enterprise, and the American reception was crucial.

By far the most important volume of the six was the first. *The Gathering Storm* was a lengthy and elaborate set of variations on the themes 'There never was a war in all history easier to prevent by timely action' and 'I saw it all coming and cried aloud to my own fellow-countrymen and to the world, but no one paid any attention.' What few readers or reviewers grasped was one of the chief problems with the book. 'Germany existed before the Gestapo,' Churchill at his most admirable had said during the war, then as he saw the hungry Germans scrabbling for food amid the rubble of Potsdam, 'I cannot hate them now,' then again at Zurich the next year, 'There can be no revival of Europe without a spiritually great France and a spiritually great Germany,' and, as a typical aside, he wanted to see Germany 'fat but impotent'.

---

* I *The Gathering Storm*, 21 Jun. American and 4 Oct. 1948 British publication; II *Their Finest Hour*, 29 Mar. and 27 Jun. 1949; III *The Grand Alliance*, 24 Apr. and 20 Jul. 1950; IV *The Hinge of Fate* 27 Nov. 1950 and 3 Aug. 1951; V *Closing the Ring* 23 Nov. 1951 and 3 Sept. 1952; VI *Triumph and Tragedy* 30 Nov. 1953 and 26 Apr.1954.

And yet he who had done so much to burnish the British national legend 'We are fighting by ourselves alone' also indirectly contributed to a new German national legend. In later years, it has often been supposed that Germany faced up to the horrors of the Third Reich with seemly guilt and remorse, through *Vergangenheitsbewältigung*, or coming to terms with the past, but that was far from the whole truth. In the postwar years there was instead a comforting view that Hitler, National Socialism and the Third Reich had been an unfortunate misadventure which befell the German people while they weren't concentrating, 'an accident in the factory', in one cynical phrase. After the Nuremberg trials, as well as some lesser trials, and a process of 'denazification' for many others, Germany returned as best it could to life as normal.

This was accomplished with a degree of wilful blindness, indirectly encouraged by Churchill. In 1938 he had claimed quite wrongly that the German generals longed to overthrow Hitler if only they were given some encouragement, and had grossly exaggerated the strength of opposition to Hitler. Now that story had been gleefully embroidered by those generals themselves, in Allied captivity, and then when on trial, for obvious reasons. As Churchill's book was drafted, his advisors warned him that he was being too credulous. Sir Orme Sargent had been deputy under-secretary at the Foreign Office at the time of the Munich agreement, which he opposed, and he alerted Churchill to the danger 'of overrating the possibility of an army revolt in September 1938'. Some of the generals may have thought from time to time about overthrowing Hitler, Sargent said, but they always shrank from action, at any rate until July 1944, when the war was lost and Germany faced total destruction.

One of the captured generals was Franz Halder, at one time Hitler's chief of staff, who had been arrested after the July Plot. He was not one of the conspirators though he was lucky to survive, and even luckier that no action was taken against him after the war, when he was removed to America. Churchill was also warned about taking him too seriously by Deakin, and by General Pownall: 'Halder, as you know, is apt to "shoot a line".' Churchill was persuaded to temper his enthusiasm and admit that the supposed resisters always drew back, while grudgingly conceding that 'It was to the interest of the parties concerned after they were prisoners of the Allies to dwell on their efforts for peace.'

Even so, Churchill helped in his way to foster a dangerous myth. While some generals were put on trial after the war, and Wilhelm Keitel, head of the Army Supreme High Command, and Alfred Jodl, Chief of Operations Staff, were hanged at Nuremberg, many went unpunished. Some even published self-justifying and self-glorifying memoirs, like Erich von Manstein's *Lost Victories*, Heinz Guderian's *Panzer Leader*, and Albert Kesselring's *A Soldier to the Last Day*. From all we now know, each of these had loyally served Hitler's genocidal regime, to the last day indeed, each was in the full sense a war criminal, and each deserved to be hanged quite as much as Jodl and Keitel. That was true of very many others.

From when the tide of war turned in late 1942 and the British advanced, a number of senior German officers were captured. The most important generals were incarcerated at Trent Park, north of London, a country house piquantly owned by the Jewish millionaire Sir Philip Sassoon, who had entertained Churchill there. The officers' comfortable quarters were bugged, as was the garden where they walked, and their candid recorded conversations were translated by refugees now serving in the British Army. One of these was Eric Mark, who had escaped Germany as a child but whose parents were murdered in Treblinka. Listening to the captured Germans 'was one of the most difficult times I ever had,' Mark later recalled. 'Most of them liked to boast about how many Jews they had killed, saying things like "I knocked off about 1500".' These were 'the chiefs of the German army' who, Churchill had claimed, had wanted to restore 'sane and civilised conditions in their country'.

That contrasts bleakly with the healing legend expressed by Konrad Adenauer. He had been mayor of Cologne until Hitler took power in 1933 and he was dismissed, although before then he had advocated co-operation between his Centre party and the National Socialists, and under the Third Reich he opted for *innere Emigration* rather than active resistance. Not much more than a year younger than Churchill, Adenauer was already seventy-three when he became the first Chancellor of the new Federal Republic, and would hold office until 1963, when he was eighty-seven. Soon after it was born, the Federal Republic established diplomatic relations with Israel, and Adenauer declared that 'The vast majority of the German people rejected the crimes which were committed against the Jews and did not participate in them.'

Like Churchill's plea of ignorance of the genocide, this was close to falsehood. Most Germans might not have participated in the crimes against the Jews, but the vast majority were well aware of them: everyone in every German city, small town and village knew that the Jews were vanishing, and none of the millions of Germans who served on the eastern front could plead ignorance to the mass murder of the Jews. More than that, many of the men running the republic in the postwar decades had been loyal servants of the Third Reich, something ignored until truth-seeking led to *Achtundsechsiger* rage, the ferocious reaction of the 1968 generation.

None of this was properly understood at the time in England, where the reception of *The Gathering Storm* was mostly respectful, although privately, as Channon noted, older Tories resented the book. Only one really spiteful review appeared, in the socialist weekly *Tribune* under the headline 'Churchill's *Mein Kampf*', by none other than Michael Foot, co-author of *Guilty Men* and *A Palestine Munich*? But American reviewers were not so much respectful as reverential, the tone set in the *Christian Science Monitor*: reading Churchill was 'like entering a cathedral. The hush of greatness is all around.' One reviewer after another bowed down before Churchill's stature not only as a leader but as a writer. And they all believed that this 'great literary achieve-ment' bore the stamp of the man's own hand in every line. In what became an almost ritual comment, the *Newark News* claimed that 'A ghostwriter for Churchill would be the height of the incredible.' Even in the supposedly sophisticated pages of the *New Yorker*, Hamilton Basso wrote that the most engaging thing was that 'he wrote it himself'. *The Gathering Storm* comprised 261,000 words of text as well as appendices, published less than three years after the war ended, and the text of all six volumes, published over little more than five years, came to 1.63 million words. It occurred to none of these star-struck admirers to wonder whether a man who was still a party leader in a great democracy, while travelling to speak from Missouri to Zurich to The Hague, could really have written such a book unaided.

None of these eulogies matched the grandiloquent heights of an essay published in the *Atlantic Monthly* in September 1949 entitled simply 'Mr Churchill', ostensibly a review of *Their Finest Hour*, the second volume. Isaiah Berlin was born in Riga into a prosperous Jewish family. Taken to St Petersburg (by then Petrograd), the little boy witnessed the October Revolution and was horrified by its violence. The family were lucky enough to escape to England, where Berlin went to Oxford and became the first Jew elected to All Souls College. With plenty of excursions, he spent the rest of his life in Oxford enjoying brilliant social as well as professional success, and repaid it with ardent Anglophilia.

He was known to Churchill. During the war, Berlin was attached to the British embassy in Washington, and the sharp, stylish commentaries on the American political scene signed 'I. Berlin' had caught the prime minister's eye. When a Downing Street aide noticed that 'Mr I. Berlin' was staying in London he was bidden to lunch. Mutual incomprehension grew, as the prime minister put more and more searching questions about the mood of Congress to his baffled visitor, until at last Churchill asked Berlin what was his favourite among his own works, and was told 'White Christmas'. This story of the confusion of Isaiah with Irving is authentic, even if it might well seem 'too good to be true', which was Churchill's private verdict on the *Atlantic* essay. Later still, very much in private, Berlin admitted that he had never really liked Churchill: 'too brutal'.

No one reading his essay would have guessed that, and nor were readers made aware that Berlin had been paid a handsome fee by the author to read the book before publication. Berlin didn't stint the superlatives, or his own purple prose, not least the rhetorical characteristic he shared with Stalin, of saying everything three times: 'His heroic, highly coloured, sometimes oversimple and even naive, but always absolutely genuine, vision of life.' Berlin warmly defended Churchill as a writer against modern critics like Herbert Read, who had earlier held up a passage from *The World Crisis* as a model of how not to write: 'Such eloquence is false because it is artificial,' Read had written in 1928; 'the images are stale, the metaphors violent, the whole passage exhales a false dramatic atmosphere ... a volley of rhetorical imperatives.'

For Berlin, Churchill was a contrarian figure in his own age precisely because of his 'inspired, if unconscious, attempt at revival, a deliberate return to a formal mode of English utterance which extends from Gibbon and Dr Johnson to Peacock and Macaulay, a weapon created by Mr Churchill in order to convey his particular vision. In the bleak and deflationary twenties it was too bright, too big, too vivid, too unsubtle for the sensitive and sophisticated epigoni of the age of imperialism, who, living an inner life of absorbing complexity and delicacy, became unable and certainly unwilling to admire the light of a day which had destroyed so much of what they had trusted and loved.'

These raptures were amusing enough in view of the way that the Syndicate had actually compiled the book, the manner in which Churchill had dealt with it, and also the response from publishers. Henry Luce could be obtuse or narrow-minded, but the creator of *Time* and *Life* did have a newspaperman's instinct for simple narrative. When he saw the first drafts he had paid so much for, he rebuked Churchill, and received an ingratiating reply in which Churchill promised to polish the text further. Another publisher was 'terribly disappointed' with what Churchill provided, while John Shaw Billings, an executive at Luce's company, found one manuscript so dull that he thought 'The old boy is chiselling on us.' There were similar *obiter dicta* in Churchill's own country. Anthony Quinton had returned from the RAF to Oxford, where he would become a philosophy don at New College and then President of Trinity, as well as a Tory peer. Many years later he recalled attending a lecture by the economic historian J.P. Cooper, who remarked in passing that Churchill's book 'reflects the gravest discredit on the historical jam-making factory responsible for its production'.

'Who now reads Bolingbroke?' Edmund Burke asked scathingly about the eighteenth-century politician Henry St John, Viscount Bolingbroke, a man with an even more erratic career than Churchill's, and a voluminous political and philosophical writer. 'Who ever read him through?' Seventy years later devotees still read Churchill, but it may be wondered how many people have actually read through those six volumes. A detached reader must be puzzled by the book, and disappointed. Nor is this hindsight: if only Churchill had listened to his womenfolk. Had he taken Clementine's advice and retired from political leadership at the war's end, it could only have enhanced his reputation, to which nothing was added by his postwar ten years of political leadership.

And he should have taken more advice from his daughter Sarah. In December 1947, Churchill and his entourage went to Marrakech at Luce's expense to knock the first volume into final shape, and Sarah joined them. She looked at the early drafts, with their endless rehashed documents, and was downcast. What her father should do, Sarah told him plaintively, was to put the mountain of paperwork aside and to 'write this book from the heart of yourself'. Had he done that, and written a book in the authentic manner of *My Early Life*, if on a far larger scale and with a much mightier theme, a frankly personal account of his wartime leadership which made no pretence to being a history of the war, it might not have made him as much money as the groaning six volumes did, but it could have been a masterpiece relished to this day, instead of a very dubious source, to be drawn on carefully, and less and less read as the years go by.

In a draft of a reply to Stalin in January 1944, Churchill had said, 'I agree that we had better leave the past to history, but remember if I live long enough I may be one of the historians.' He enjoyed the joke enough to repeat it in a parliamentary debate in January 1948: 'For my part, I consider that it will be found much better by all Parties to leave the past to history, especially as I propose to write that history myself.' This was more than just a jest. As David Reynolds says in *In Command of History*, his splendid book on the writing of *The Second World War*, Churchill's great aim with that book '(apart from making money) was the search for vindication', and Churchill admitted as much himself, saying that it wasn't history, but 'a contribution to history', or again, 'It is not history, it is my case.'

Finding the right sonorous titles for the volumes was tricky. Potential titles for the first volume included 'The Downward Path' and 'Toward Catastrophe', which his publishers thought dispiriting. It was the faithful Reves who came up with *The Gathering Storm* only weeks before serialisation began. Other titles were less problematic, at least until translated: the second volume entitled *Their Finest Hour* appeared in French as *L'Heure tragique*. But the real difficulty stems from the title of the whole. Compare *The Second World War* with books by great contemporaries. Lloyd George's account of the Great War wasn't published until fifteen years after the Armistice, well after *The World Crisis*, to which it is partly a reply. De Gaulle would also wait, so that the first of his three volumes on the World War appeared in 1954. But Lloyd George's book was called *War Memoirs*, de Gaulle's *Mémoires de Guerre*. Churchill didn't call his work 'Memoirs', nor did he say publicly 'this is my case'. His book again merits Balfour's jibe about *The World Crisis*: it was another autobiography posing as history, a pose that begins with the title *The Second World War*.

'This monumental work may not be Literature,' Churchill had said about Lloyd George's *War Memoirs*, 'but it is certainly History.' *The Second World War* may be Literature, but it is certainly not History.

Even as an account by a leading player in the drama, Churchill's book compares unfavourably with Lloyd George's and de Gaulle's books, or for that matter with *The World Crisis*. And 'my case' is almost an understatement. While Churchill sometimes admitted error on his part and failure on the part of British forces, the book is as notable for what it does not say as for what it does. Favoured colleagues were allowed to see, and censor, passages which concerned them. An egregious case was the Dieppe raid. Mountbatten was able to doctor and twist the draft so as to absolve himself of richly deserved blame, while Churchill wrote what he knew very well was a euphemistic account of that disaster. With other awkward questions, such as terror-bombing, or the likewise costly but mostly fruitless activities in occupied Europe, Churchill's technique was simply to avoid them. Apart from mention of 'Bomber' Harris's 'vigorous leadership', he said little about the bombing campaign.

But there was a still greater difficulty. The book is not only inevitably egocentric but Anglocentric, to an absurd degree. The two really great conflicts of 1941–5, in eastern Europe and in the Pacific, are treated in the most cursory way, dashed off by the Syndicate with a carelessness which led to great embarrassment. Samuel Eliot Morison was an eminent American historian, for many years a professor at Harvard – his statue now gazes seaward from outside the St Botolph Club in Boston – whose largest work was the fifteen-volume *History of United States Naval Operations in World War II*. When Morison came to look at Churchill's book he was startled to find that he was reading himself, since chapters on the Pacific war had been lifted almost wholesale from his work by the Syndicate, with little time to conceal the plagiarism. Morison had no wish to sue the saviour of civilisation, and the matter was settled discreetly, with later impressions carrying a fulsome acknowledgement of Morison.

Such difficulties were forgotten as events conspired to give Churchill's book completely fresh significance. Although Stalin had kept his side of the bargain with Churchill in Greece, he had subjugated all of eastern Europe. It may be debated to this day whether Stalin really believed that socialist revolution would triumph throughout the world, or even in western Europe. He often did little enough to bring this about, ordering Communists to take no advantage of any potential revolutionary situation, while he consolidated his rampart. Even so, by March 1947, Truman was so alarmed by the appearance of Soviet aggression that he asked Congress for $400 million in loans to Greece and Turkey, to save them from Communism, or to prop up their reactionary regimes, according to taste. He had remembered the Iron Curtain warning Churchill had given at Fulton, and picked up the torch lit by Churchill when he flew to Athens at Christmas 1944 to forestall a Communist coup.

Then came 1948, one of the most dramatic and formative years of modern times. It saw the creation of Israel, the triumph of the Afrikaner Nationalists in South Africa, and a memorable American presidential election in which Truman snatched last-minute victory; all this beside turmoil in Europe. In Poland, Rumania, Bulgaria and Hungary, Stalin's agents had already used the same methods they had practised in Spain a decade earlier, the infiltration of key ministries by the Russian secret police and their local allies, using local Communists and purging them, stealing elections by intimidation and violence. But even then it took one event to transform western sentiment. On 10 March 1948 the Czech foreign minister Jan Masaryk, son of Tomáš Masaryk, founding father of Czechoslovakia, was found dead on the ground beneath his upper rooms of the ministry, purportedly a suicide though it looked very much like murder. This was a prelude to a complete Communist takeover. In March 1939, Hitler's entry into Prague had seemingly proved Churchill right in his condemnation of Munich five months before. Now Masaryk's death and the coup in that same city seemingly proved Churchill right in his Fulton speech two years before. Once more, just as he had said in 1938, 'mournful, abandoned, broken, Czechoslovakia recedes into the darkness'.

As the war ended the British, Americans, Russians and French had partitioned Germany for the purposes of occupation. The eastern border of Germany was now on the river Oder and its tributary the Neisse, so that Danzig, over which the war had begun, was now Polish 'Gdansk', and 'Stettin in the Baltic' of which Churchill had spoken at Fulton was now 'Szczecin'. Between Oder and Elbe was the Soviet zone, with Berlin an island in the middle, itself divided into four sectors. After many other provocations, the Soviets stopped road and rail traffic from the west into the city on 18 June – three days before *The Gathering Storm* appeared in American bookstores! – and the western allies responded with an airlift. British and American aircraft which not long before had been dropping incendiaries on the city now became 'raisin bombers', flying in food and fuel. No book's timing could have seemed more apt. The political message of Churchill's book appeared more valid than ever as echoes from the 1930s grew louder.

And so this Cold War reached an early crescendo with a Churchillian descant over the main theme. *Their Finest Hour* was published in America in March 1949, a week before the North Atlantic Treaty Organisation came into being; on 29 August Russia exploded its first atomic bomb; on 1 October Mao proclaimed the People's Republic of China, having driven out Chiang Kai-chek's Nationalists. As if to complement the most famous history of the age, written by a man called Winston Churchill, the most famous novel of the age was also published in 1949, with a hero called Winston Smith. *Nineteen Eighty-Four* offered a horrifying vision of totalitarianism, which would be read later by Poles, Hungarians and Russians as something close to social realism.

In April 1950, Churchill's third volume was published in America, and in June the Cold War turned hot. The coincidence was ironical: the title of *The Grand Alliance* was an echo linking the Anglo-Soviet-American alliance to the original Grand Alliance which Marlborough had led to victory, and the book appeared just at the moment when that later alliance had broken, to the point that American and British soldiers found themselves fighting, if not Stalin's Red Army, then his surrogates, in the form of the North Korean troops. By a quirk of history, the Russians were temporarily boycotting the United Nations and were unable to veto a Security Council resolution authorising the use of force against the aggressor. The alliance, albeit dominated by the Americans, was the only one which was ever fought under the formal banner of the United Nations, with American and British troops joined by Canadian, French, Indian, Turkish and Fijian contingents.

Although Churchill was heartily grateful that the prime minister who had taken the country into the Korean War was Attlee and not himself, thanking the Almighty: 'The old man is very good to me. I could not have managed this situation had I been in Attlee's place. I would have been called a warmonger,' his imprint on the war was huge. He hadn't mentioned 'Munich' at Fulton, but he did say, 'Our difficulties and dangers will not be removed by closing our eyes to them. They will not be removed by merely waiting to see what happens; nor will they be removed by a policy of appeasement.' Sure enough, Truman invoked Munich when he called for resistance to Communist aggression – and he then saw for himself what this could lead to. After initial disasters, the imperious General Douglas MacArthur landed behind enemy lines at Inchon and drove the invading forces back deep into North Korea. As he approached the border with China on the Yalu river, he was warned that any further advance might provoke Chinese intervention, but MacArthur haughtily replied that to stop would be to appease the Chinese as the British had appeased Hitler. He duly advanced to the Yalu, whereupon the Chinese army fell ferociously on his forces and drove them far back again.

This was the first really notable demonstration of how dangerous the spectre of Munich – and Churchill's shadow – could be. Even Churchill began to notice, and to step back. 'The word "appeasement" is not popular, but appeasement has its place in all policy,' he said, even if he had a nerve to say it. 'Make sure you put it in the right place. Appease the weak, defy the strong ... appeasement from strength is magnanimous and noble and might be the surest and perhaps the only path to world peace.' Little as it was understood by his American admirers, Churchill the great warrior was now oppressed by thoughts of war.

In August 1951, Churchill's fourth volume appeared in London, and by the end of October he was back at Number 10, for his eerie second prime ministership of three-and-a-quarter years. A heavy pall of reminiscence hung over this sad episode, like a fading star's farewell performance, which really ought not to have been given. For all Churchill's remarkable constitution, life had taken a toll on him. After his serious wartime illnesses, with pneumonia and heart attacks, he suffered a stroke in 1949, again unknown to the public. By the last year of the war he had been fractious, inebriated and exhausted, and although he had remarkable powers of recovery, his years as Leader of the Opposition had done him little credit.

Now in his late seventies, with his physical and mental powers faltering, Churchill was deaf and inattentive during Cabinet meetings. A box of the famous red 'Action This Day' stickers was placed on his desk, but this time they were never used. He could still manage a performance in the Commons, but when he spoke at the Conservative Party Conference, his intimates worried less about what he said than whether he would get through the speech at all. And the Cabinet which Churchill formed was like an Old Boys reunion, full of his wartime comrades: 'Pug' Ismay, the frightful Cherwell, and 'Alex', now Field Marshall Earl Alexander of Tunis, who was made Minister of Defence, a post he didn't want, but 'I simply can't refuse Winston.'

At the same time, much of Churchill's rhetoric about 'setting the people free' from the oppression of the Labour government was hollow. 'The modified Socialism that's being carried out today is the only possible course,' says Alan Craddock in Angus Wilson's novel *Hemlock and After,* written and set just before Churchill's return. 'As a matter of fact, I doubt if a Tory government could act any differently as things stand, whatever they might wish.' That proved largely true. The National Health Service and the welfare reforms of the Attlee government were left untouched, while the nationalised coal and railway industries weren't returned to private ownership. And Churchill's earlier life was in some ways reversed, with unhappy consequences.

He had been the most bellicose minister in crushing the General Strike, when the miners, with the strongest possible case, asking only for a living wage, were starved out. Together with unemployment in the 1930s, that had left the Tories, even Churchill, with a bad conscience. Now Sir Walter Monckton was made Minister of Labour with a brief to maintain full employment and placate the unions at almost any cost: much too high a cost, as it later turned out. When asked by a minister on whose terms a dispute provoked by one union should be settled, Churchill said, 'On theirs, old cock,' and it was now that the combination of backward industries, incompetent management and aggressive unions began the long years of British comparative economic decline.

Little more than three months after Churchill's return, in February 1952, King George VI died, aged only fifty-six but worn out by ceaseless worry and cigarettes. Churchill was entranced by the pretty young queen, not quite as young as the eighteen-year-old Victoria when she acceded, but at twenty-five captivating to her elderly prime minister. Addressing the nation by radio, Churchill spoke affectionately of the king, with whom he had established much warmer relations than seemed possible at the time of the Abdication. Now death had come to him 'as a friend', after 'a happy day of sunshine and sport'. And so 'I, whose youth was passed in the august, unchallenged and tranquil glories of the Victorian Era, may well feel a thrill in invoking, once more, the prayer and the Anthem "God Save the Queen!"'

He still had his eye on America. On a visit in 1949 Churchill had found time to go to Boston to be entertained by his publishers Houghton Mifflin, genially remarking that a Boston lunch party was more agreeable than a Boston tea party. But if his American popularity seemed to be increasing all the time there were still a few ornery dissenters, and not every American had yet become a Churchillian. When he was about to return to America in December 1952, Senator William Langer, a Republican from North Dakota, suggested that the Old North Church in Boston, which in 1775 had lit lanterns to pass on Paul Revere's warning that the Redcoats were coming, 'should put the country on guard against the arrival soon of Prime Minister Winston Churchill'.

After Dwight Eisenhower was nominated as the Republican candidate for the presidency and then went on to win an easy victory over Adlai Stevenson, Churchill was alarmed. The last volume of *The Second World War* hadn't yet appeared when Eisenhower was elected: *Triumph and Tragedy* came out a year later, in November 1953, and Churchill ingratiatingly told Eisenhower that he had scanned the text carefully to remove anything that might hint that there had been serious dissension between the British and the Americans in the last year of the war, as of course there had been.

At the same time, Churchill was oppressed by thoughts of war, memories of wars past, fears of wars to come, and revulsion from the means of waging them. In 1952 he was dismayed by what he heard about the effects of napalm. 'We should make a great mistake to commit ourselves to approval of a very cruel form of warfare affecting the civilian population,' he told Lord Alexander, his defence minister. This might seem the height of hypocrisy from the man not long before ultimately responsible for the killing of hundreds of thousands of civilians with incendiaries. Or it might seem the stirrings of a troubled conscience.

These concerns lay behind his urgent desire to avert a new – and possibly final – war. 'If only I could dine with Stalin once a week, there would be no trouble at all,' he had said in early 1944. 'We get on like a house on fire.' In March 1950 he had hoped for 'another talk with Soviet Russia upon the highest level. The idea appeals to me of a supreme effort to bridge the gulf between the two worlds so that each can live its life if not in friendship, at least without the hatreds and manoeuvres of the cold war,' and back in office he continued to hope for a 'parley at the summit', an expression Churchill put into currency. He never did see the Russian leader again: Stalin died in March 1953, seven weeks after Eisenhower's inauguration, taking his horrible mystery to the grave, and no such summit with his successors took place before Churchill retired two years later.

As to Eisenhower, not only were Churchill's fears that he would be a bellicose leader completely groundless, there was a grave reciprocal misunderstanding. In truth, both those old warriors now longed for peace. At the 1951 election the *Daily Mirror* ran the alarmist headline 'Whose finger on the trigger?' implying that Churchill was still the warmonger he had always been, but he replied, 'If I remain in public life at this juncture it is because I believe I may be able to make an important contribution to the prevention of a third world war,' and he meant it. And yet his old American comrade in arms felt the same. The only American president to have seen action in the Great War was the young Missouri haberdasher Harry Truman, who had served as an artillery officer and wrote bloodthirsty letters home about his zeal to kill Germans. Unlike him, Eisenhower was a career army officer, but to his subsequent chagrin he spent 1917–18 on American soil engaged in recruiting and training. Then from D-Day to VE Day he had commanded one of the mightiest armies that ever fought, in a campaign in which 110,000 GIs had been killed.

Now Eisenhower never wanted to see more young Americans die. After the election but before he was inaugurated, he paid a secret visit to Korea to see how the war could be wound up, and as soon as he took office he began to disengage. General Mark Clark, who had been the inadequate commander of the US Fifth Army in Italy, was appointed to take over command of the forces in Korea shortly before the war ended with an armistice which in effect recognised a drawn match. Although Clark complained that he had 'the unenviable distinction of being the first US Army commander to sign an armistice without victory', it would not be the last war the Americans failed to win.

Then in April 1953, only weeks after his inauguration and just after Stalin's death, Eisenhower made an extraordinary speech, on 'that issue that comes first of all in the hearts and minds of all of us – that issue which most urgently challenges and summons the wisdom and the courage of our whole people. This issue is peace.' While insisting on 'every nation's right to a form of government and an economic system of its own' and that 'Any nation's attempt to dictate to other nations their form of government is indefensible,' Eisenhower reminded his audience that 'The cost of one modern heavy bomber is this: a modern brick school in more than thirty cities ... It is two fine, fully equipped hospitals.' And he would govern in that spirit. After the Korean armistice, no American soldier was killed fighting a war for the remaining seven years of Eisenhower's presidency, an astonishing record which confuted all of Churchill's apprehensions.

Such words bitterly disappointed American conservatives. But if they turned to Churchill as a standard-bearer in the war on Communism, they misunderstood him as much as he had misunderstood Eisenhower. He would reiterate his fears about war in his last great parliamentary speech, but even before that, in May 1953, two months after Stalin's death, he told the Commons that it was 'a mistake to assume that nothing can be settled with the Soviet Union unless or until everything is settled'. More than that he recognised that Russia was entitled to expect friendly neighbouring states: 'I do not believe that the immense problem of reconciling the security of Russia with the freedom and safety of Western Europe is insoluble. Russia has a right to feel assured that as far as human arrangements can run the terrible events of the Hitler invasion will never be repeated, and that Poland will remain a friendly Power and a buffer, though not, I trust, a puppet State.' These words had the truly comical consequence that Winston Churchill himself was now denounced as an appeaser, by Senator William Knowland.

Before he died, Stalin had proposed a reunited but neutral Germany. Some in the West saw this as a ruse, but Churchill grasped at it, although he fancifully supposed that Great Britain could be the guarantor of European peace, a fine illustration of what Tizard had meant by the continuing illusion that we were still a great power. Indian independence had taken the heart out of Churchill's imperialism, and ended his appetite for clinging on to the vestiges of empire. He favoured withdrawing western troops from Korea – 'I'd never heard of the bloody place till I was seventy-four' – and added that 'Indo-China, too, does not really matter. We gave up India. Why shouldn't France give up Indo-China?'

'What curious attitudes he goes into!' says Alice about the messenger in *Through the Looking Glass*, to which the White King replies, 'Not at all. He's an Anglo-Saxon Messenger – and those are Anglo-Saxon attitudes. He only does them when he's happy.' Churchill was an Anglo-Saxon messenger, and he had Anglo-Saxon attitudes. It has been argued that those attitudes may even have stood him in good stead in 1940, when his belief in British superiority sustained him in an almost hopeless position, although they were very dangerous as well. He had called the Japanese 'the wops of Asia', and then, when warned of the threat from Mao's Chinese army in Korea, he had said, 'Four million pigtails don't make an army.'

Nor had his Anglo-Saxon attitudes much changed. Churchill had to be restrained from praising the Afrikaner Nationalist regime which had ousted his old friend Smuts in 1948 and instituted a system of strict segregation which they called 'apartness' or apartheid, and which differed from Smut's (and Churchill's) white supremacism mainly in its starker dogmatic foundation. Churchill's private secretary was now David Hunt, later Sir David, who recalled how 'anti-black' Churchill had been, and how he wanted to send Dr D.F. Malan, the Nationalist prime minister, a telegram of encouragement, telling him *'Alles sal reg kom'* (everything will be all right), and 'Keep on skelping the kaffirs!' (whacking the blacks). He also greatly disliked one of the unforeseen consequences of the last days of empire: the arrival in Great Britain of 'coloured' immigrants from what would be called 'the New Commonwealth', the West Indies, and the Indian sub-continent, and what he foresaw with distaste as a 'magpie society'. In one of the last Cabinet meetings over which he presided, Churchill suggested that the Tories should campaign at the coming election on the slogan, 'Keep England White'.

He had mellowed all the same. Churchill even welcomed to Downing Street bitter old enemies – de Valera whom he had once so abused, and Nehru, his fellow Old Harrovian, whom he had once imprisoned as a rebel and whom he now acclaimed as 'the light of Asia'. And he had lost any zeal for 'jolly little wars against barbarous people'. The colonial powers fought a series of far from jolly campaigns as their empires declined and fell, with the British handling their withdrawal well only by comparison with the French, who fought horribly bloody, and unsuccessful, wars in Indo-China and Algeria. The British defeated Communist insurgents in Malaya, and the Mau Mau, Kikuyu rebels in Kenya, but with a brutality which distressed Churchill.

When Michael Blundell, supposedly one of the more liberal voices among the white settlers in Kenya, went to see Churchill he got whisky and soda at three in the afternoon. But for all the stories in the press about atrocities committed by the Mau Mau (more than a thousand of whom would be hanged by the British), Churchill recalled the Kikuyu from more than forty years before as 'happy, naked, charming people' and told Blundell that it was essential to negotiate with the Kikuyu: they were 'persons of considerable fibre and ability and steel, who could be brought to our side by just and wise treatment'. It was as if Churchill wanted to put behind him a lifetime of blood, toil and tears.

'What is called, somewhat oddly, the Middle East,' as he had phrased it years before, was an altogether different matter. There were no longer any formal British possessions there, but nascent Arab nationalism threatened British oil supplies, as well as the Suez Canal, the old lifeline of the Empire and still believed to be an economically essential route. Nationalists were contending for power in Egypt, which Churchill had known in peace and war. Shortly after he returned to Number 10, there was a long and bibulous evening there, with animated conversation between Churchill and Eden, himself back yet again for his third term as Foreign Secretary. Now Churchill instructed Eden on how to deal with the troublesome Egyptians. Sir Evelyn Shuckburgh of the Foreign Office was present, and recalled how, 'Rising from his chair, the old man advanced on Anthony with clenched fists, saying with the inimitable Churchill growl, "Tell them that if we have any more of their cheek we will set the Jews on them and drive them into the gutter, from which they should never have emerged."' Events would suggest that Eden took these words to heart.

One other country east of Suez which much concerned Churchill was Persia, now called Iran by nationalists, as indeed it had concerned him at intervals for more than forty-five years. In 1907 he had been a member of the government which concluded the Anglo-Russian entente dividing Persia into spheres of influence. He had himself acquired Anglo-Persian Oil before the Great War to fuel the Royal Navy, and in 1941 he had agreed to another Anglo-Russian partition of Persia, and the restoration of the Shah. There was plenty of reason for Persian resentment of England. Now a democratically elected government under Mohammad Mosaddegh was threatening to nationalise his country's oil, and perhaps allow Russia a path to the Gulf. No one was more infuriated than Churchill by 'Messy Duck', as he called him. In 1941, he had said about the occupation of Persia that 'We had been doing something for which we had justification but no right,' an interesting distinction which he might also have made about the events of 1953.

On 23 June Churchill gave a dinner for Alcide De Gasperi, the Italian prime minister. After the guests had left, Churchill sat down and then slumped, with one side of his mouth sagging ominously. 'I think something has happened,' Soames told Colville, and so it had, a stroke severe enough to incapacitate Churchill and cause anxiety that he might not survive. For several weeks the country was in effect run by a handful of senior ministers and Soames, while a conspiracy among the press lords, principally Beaverbrook and Camrose, kept the public in complete ignorance of Churchill's condition. To make matters worse, not only the prime minister but the Foreign Secretary was incapacitated; Eden was in Boston for an operation to repair a previous botched operation for gallstones and couldn't have taken the reins even if Churchill had wanted to hand them over.

On 19 August, while Churchill was still *hors de combat*, a coup backed by the CIA and MI6 overthrew Messy Duck and replaced him with the restored Shah. Churchill knew about this beforehand even if some of his ministers didn't, but when he returned to chair the Cabinet on 25 August, he spoke with a straight face about the coup as a bolt from the blue. Chief among the conspirators was 'Kim' Roosevelt, yet another member of the clan, grandson of Theodore, and now head of the CIA's Middle East division (where he was a strong critic of American partisanship towards Israel). *Guys and Dolls* was still running on Broadway, and on the night of the coup Roosevelt sat in his Tehran apartment playing 'Luck Be a Lady Tonight' over and over again on his gramophone. She was a lady for the Shah, if not his country. For a quarter-century the oil would flow while the Shah's rule became ever more despotic and megalomaniacal. In 1979 he was deposed and replaced by religious zealots and fierce nationalists, implacably hostile to the United States, to Israel, and not least – or not without reason – to Great Britain, leaving an utterly intractable problem for the West.

If Churchill's mind was made up about the Levant, he was in two minds about Europe, or maybe many more than two. He had written 'A United States of Europe' in 1930, then, over the dark winter of 1940–41 he had ruminated that 'there must be a United States of Europe' and he believed it should be built by the English; if the Russians built it, there would be communism and squalor; if the Germans built it there would be tyranny and brute force. In Zurich in 1946 he had advocated reconciliation between France and Germany, and 'some kind of United States of Europe', and in 1947 he favoured the United Europe movement in which Tories like his son-in-law Duncan Sandys and his former intimate Robert Boothby played prominent parts.

This was now more than a pipe-dream. In 1950 Robert Schuman, the French foreign minister, proposed joint Franco-German control of coal and steel – the sinews of war, which such control should prevent forever. In April 1951 'the Six' – France, West Germany, Italy, the Low Countries of Belgium, the Netherlands and Luxembourg, now known by the less pleasing portmanteau 'Benelux' – signed the treaty creating the European Coal and Steel Community. By 1956 these Six would be meeting at Messina to draw up what they would sign in 1957 as the Treaty of Rome. It brought into being the European Economic Community, informally known as the Common Market, which in the fullness of time would become the European Community and then the European Union.

Throughout the early years of this adventure the British stood aloof, watching at first without even much interest. Labour evinced its own bluff patriotism personified by Bevin, and the Attlee government treated these European advances with disdain. So did Churchill's government after 1951, and he seemed to have forgotten his dream of ten years before of a Europe built by the English, undone by his illusions or even fantasies about Anglo-American unity and the strength of the Commonwealth. In May 1953 he told the Commons:

Where do we stand? We are not members of the European Defence Community, nor do we intend to be merged in a Federal European system. We feel we have a special relation to both. This can be expressed

by prepositions, by the preposition 'with' but not 'of' – we are with
them, but not of them. We have our own Commonwealth and Empire.
One of the anxieties of France is lest Germany, even partitioned as she
is now, will be so strong that France will be outweighed in United
Europe or in the European Defence Community ... But, anyhow, I
have always believed, as an active friend of France for nearly 50 years,
that our fortunes lie together.

Those words would be quoted sixty or more years later by English
'Eurosceptics' or Brexiteers, and Churchill was right about what would
prove continual French nervosity of German dominance. Whether he
was right about '"with" but not "of"', whatever that meant, or 'a
special relation', he was plainly wrong about his other proclaimed
'special relationship', as would soon be seen.

In all too many ways, Churchill's last political phase was a long
look back, an exercise in reminiscence, and not only on his part. Even
as he conjured up the 'tranquil glories' of the Victorian era and its
empire, 'The media wrote excitedly about a new Elizabethan age,'
Michael Howard recalled, but did so 'more accurately than they knew,
for once again we were, as we had been then, a power of the second
rank, teetering on the verge of bankruptcy and punching far beyond
our weight in international affairs.' No one had done more to
encourage these reveries than Churchill. In 1940 he had been an
anachronism, but a magnificent anachronism. Fifteen years later he
was a voice from the past.

17

'Great sovereign state'
British Embassy 1963

Only one prime minister older than Churchill had ever held office, and before he retired in 1894 aged eighty-four, Gladstone had been sarcastically called 'an old man in a hurry' by Lord Randolph Churchill. By the time Churchill marked his eightieth birthday he was an old man in no hurry at all, not even to retire as prime minister or leave Parliament. The last ten years of his life were sad, as he lost all capacity to enjoy life, and as he also became almost an inanimate object of veneration, in his own country, but even more in America.

On 30 November 1954 tens of thousands of birthday cards reached Downing Street, as well as a floral arrangement in the shape of a cigar from Israel, and a sixpenny postal order, the pocket money of a boy from Hereford. A ceremonial presentation by both Houses of Parliament took place in Westminster Hall, in front of 2500 people including the Cabinet and most MPs, as well as television cameras. When the Churchills entered, a drummer beat out the Morse 'V for victory' which had so often been heard on the BBC during the war. Tributes were led by Attlee, still Labour leader after nearly twenty years, who called Churchill 'the last of the great orators who can touch the heights'. In a graceful reply, Churchill said he never believed that he had 'inspired the nation', since 'Their will was resolute and remorseless, and as it proved unconquerable. It was the nation and the race dwelling all round the globe that had the lion's heart. I had the luck to be called upon to give the roar.'

Less happy were the gifts, or at least one of them. An illuminated book signed by almost every member of parliament was presented by David Grenfell, the Father of the House, or the member with longest continuous service, a man who had gone to work in a mine at the age of twelve and had been a Labour MP since 1922, the year Churchill had lost his seat in Dundee. A portrait painted by Graham

Sutherland, the gift of both Houses, was another matter, seeming to show Churchill not only full of years but wearing his burden heavily. 'I am now nearing the end of my journey,' Churchill said in Westminster Hall, although 'I hope I still have some service to render.' The truth was that Churchill was deeply conscious of his age and infirmity, and hated Sutherland's portrait all the more because it seemed to display that frailty, making him look 'half-witted and half dead'.

Months before, a cartoon by Leslie Illingworth had appeared in *Punch*, the weekly magazine which had been subversively satirical in early Victorian days, then for long a bastion of middle-class complacency, but was now enjoying a few livelier years under the idiosyncratic editorship of Malcolm Muggeridge. Over the caption, from Psalm 114, 'Man goeth forth unto his work and to his labour until the evening,' the caricature showed the great man bent and inert, while on the facing page Muggeridge wrote an editorial headed 'A Story Without an Ending', which purported to describe the decline of the Byzantine emperor Bellarius: 'By this time he had reached an advanced age and might have been expected to settle down to an honourable retirement ... Instead he clung to power with tenacious intensity. His splendid faculties ... began to falter. The spectacle of him thus clutching wearily at all the appurtenances and responsibilities of an authority he could no longer fully exercise was to his admirers infinitely sorrowful, and to his enemies infinitely derisory.' This was all the more cruel since editor and cartoonist – unlike most readers – certainly knew about Churchill's stroke.

After that, Churchill accepted the Sutherland painting with ill grace and some sour remarks about this specimen of 'modern art', before it vanished and was never seen again. Much later it transpired that it had been destroyed on the orders of a loyal and angry Clementine. Churchill was later 'very annoyed' by another portrait, by Ruskin Spear, exhibited at the Royal Academy summer exhibition in 1957, and he wasn't alone: Attlee called the painting 'a disgusting caricature', and Jo Grimond, the leader of the Liberal Party, said it made Churchill look like 'a white slug'. The next year a sculpture commissioned for Churchill's constituency at Woodford by David McFall, who claimed that he had 'tried to portray Sir Winston as a man intellect and a poet of fortitude,' struck local people as 'gorilla-like'.

Unlikely as an eighty-year-old prime minister was, it was an unlikely time, as though history was frozen for the moment, and in 1955 an array of men born in the nineteenth century still held power. Eisenhower was a stripling of sixty-five beside the seventy-three-year-old French president, René Coty. The prime ministers of Australia (Robert Menzies), Canada (Louis St Laurent) and Japan were all in their seventies, and at seventy-nine Adenauer, the German chancellor, almost matched Churchill. But at last he could prevaricate no more, and 5 April 1955* was announced as the date of his departure, almost half a century since he had first been appointed to government office.

In 1954, he had chaired the cabinet committee which decided to proceed with making an 'independent' British hydrogen bomb, although like the atomic bomb it depended on American technical support. And yet the prospect of nuclear catastrophe now filled the old warrior with a dismay which rang through his very moving words on 1 March 1955, in his last speech as prime minister: 'Which way shall we turn to save our lives and the future of the world? It does not matter so much to old people; they are going soon anyway; but I find it poignant to look at youth in all its activity and ardour and, most of all, to watch little children playing their merry games, and wonder what would lie before them if God wearied of mankind.' And he ended on a note which was more resigned than optimistic: 'The day may dawn when fair play, love for one's fellow-men, respect for justice and freedom, will enable tormented generations to march forth serene and triumphant from the hideous epoch in which we have to dwell. Meanwhile, never flinch, never weary, never despair.'

On the evening before his departure, he gave a splendid dinner at Downing Street for fifty people, from the Queen to officials and family friends. Looking more than ever like a Toby jug, Churchill wore formal evening dress, knee breeches and silk stockings to go with the Garter regalia. When the festivities were ended and he had bidden farewell to his Sovereign, Churchill went to his bedroom accompanied by Jock Colville. 'For several minutes he did not speak,' which Colville took to be melancholy at the prospect of departure. 'Then suddenly he stared at me and said with vehemence, "I don't believe Anthony can do it."' Nor could he. Eden's prime ministership lasted less than two

---

* The date had been chosen partly for a frivolous reason by Soames, who had re-introduced his father-in-law to the pleasures of the Turf: April the Fifth had won the Derby in 1932.

years, ruined by the Suez debacle, which seemed like a bitter joke played on the great Churchillian age by an ironical Providence.

After the sybaritic Anglophile King Farouk of Egypt was forced to abdicate in 1952, Colonel Abdul Nasser seized power in Egypt, ordered British troops to leave the Canal Zone, and then nationalised the canal itself. One name hung over the events now about to unfold so disastrously: 'Munich'. That the word had become established in the central vocabulary of politics was the most baleful of Churchill's legacies. While he was still prime minister, he had been infuriated by what he thought was Eden's conciliation of Nasser, flying into 'a rage against A.E., speaking of "appeasement" and saying that he never knew before that Munich was situated in the Nile'. Soon the same language could be heard on all sides, however inaptly or absurdly. The usually sagacious French *politicologue* Raymond Aron foolishly called Nasser 'Hitler on the Nile', and Hugh Gaitskell, the Labour Leader of the Opposition, told Parliament that Nasser's bellicosity was 'exactly the same that we encountered from Mussolini and Hitler in those years before the war'. There was even a Jewish joke to be heard: 'What happened to Hitler? He crossed the water and became Nasser.' (*Nasser* means 'more wet' in Yiddish.)

By the summer of 1956 Eden and his colleagues had privately resolved to overthrow Nasser. Since this meant, as Conor Cruise O'Brien later drily observed, the delicate task of destroying the most popular of Arab leaders without forfeiting Arab support, it meant in turn some form of deception. And so the British government colluded in the deepest secrecy with the Israelis, who saw Nasser as their greatest enemy, and the French, who believed that he had fomented the rebellion in Algeria, which in truth had needed no fomenting from outside. 'Set the Jews on them,' Churchill had told Eden, and now at Sèvres outside Paris a plot was hatched in greatest secrecy among those three countries. Sure enough, Israel would attack Egypt, whereupon the British and French would intervene, ostensibly as disinterested arbiters.

On 3 September Eisenhower presciently warned Eden that if he took military action against Egypt, not only the peoples of the Middle East but 'all of Asia and Africa, would be consolidated against the West to a degree which, I fear, could not be overcome in a generation'. As the operation unfolded, Eisenhower was appalled. He asked

Eden if he had gone out of his mind, and then used the power of the dollar to pull the rug from under the conspirators, so that the British and French were obliged to beat an ignominious retreat. The imposture had been seen through before British troops landed at Suez, but Eden was obliged to dig himself in deeper, falsely assuring the Commons on 20 December that 'there was not foreknowledge that Israel would attack Egypt'. It was no good. Eden was finished, and resigned on 10 January 1957, pleading ill health, and went to recuperate, or lick his wounds, at Ian Fleming's house in Jamaica. Insult would be added to injury when Randolph published *The Rise and Fall of Sir Anthony Eden*, a contemptuous account of his father's successor.

After the debacle, Eden was succeeded by Macmillan, who outplayed, or backstabbed, his colleague R.A. Butler, as he would do again when he himself retired, after six largely empty years as prime minister, while British industry palpably lagged behind the Germans, not to mention the Japanese, the nations who lost the war but won the peace. Two men came to power in the wake of Suez. It may be that both understood Palmerston's saying that there are no alliances between equals, but they drew contrary lessons. Macmillan decided to follow Churchill's 'Never be parted from the Americans'. Even though his own 'Greeks to their Romans' had been made to look more absurd than ever, Macmillan decided to embrace the Americans more closely than ever.

More than a year later, de Gaulle returned to power in France, as prime minister from June 1958 and then from the following January as president of a Fifth Republic which was created by and for him. He returned in consequence to the appalling conflict in Algeria, which he ended with a fine display of 'sacred egoism' and sinuous guile. He first appeared as a defender of '*Algérie française*', which the French had continued to treat not as a colony but as an integral part of the French republic that would never be relinquished. He told the *pieds noirs* or white French Algerians in oracular words, '*Je vous ai compris*', which turned out to mean that he had understood them, and was going to abandon them. It was said of the Bourbons that they had learned nothing and forgotten nothing. De Gaulle did learn, from Eisenhower's desertion of the French and British in 1956. The Americans could never be trusted, he thought, and Europe must find its own destiny, naturally under French leadership. But he truly forgot nothing, neither his contemptuous treatment by Roosevelt nor his endless rows with Churchill, memories of which would deeply affect his conduct.

After Churchill left Downing Street, his *History of the English-Speaking Peoples* was at last published, in four volumes, two each in 1956 and in 1957, almost thirty years after he had first discussed it at the Yale game. The draft left unfinished in 1939 had to be completed and revised by Churchill's assistants, and as much to the point the payments for the book were also entirely revised. Cassell & Co. had made an outright payment for world rights in the book as long ago as 1933 but Anthony Moir, Churchill's solicitor, now proposed that the payment should be regarded as an advance. The old problem remained, of how to pay as little tax as possible. The book had been begun before the fanciful Literary Trust was created, so that ruse couldn't be used, but Moir proposed a series of payments, during the course of which Churchill would 'retire' as an author once more and for good, so that remaining payments would be tax-free capital gains.

This ruse wouldn't be available for much longer – in the year of Churchill's death, James Callaghan, Chancellor of the Exchequer in a Labour government, at last introduced a tax on capital gains – but it saw Churchill out. Once again Emery Reves got in on the act, once again Henry Luce and *Life* bought serial rights, for $150,000, once again so did the *Daily Telegraph*. Churchill's loyal friend, the first Lord Camrose who had done so much for him, had died in 1954, and the paper was in the hands of his second son Michael Berry, who wasn't quite as generous as his father, offering £40,000 but asking for previous loans to Churchill of £32,000 to be offset.

If the book is competent and readable, so it should be, considering the people who had helped to assemble it. But that means that it largely reads 'like a carefully polished synthesis of the drafts prepared for him by academic historians,' as Paul Addison says, and there is not much Churchillian sparkle. It was a sad envoi to his literary career. He had shown in *My Early Life* that he could write a beguilingly and vividly personal memoir and, for all their faults and despite their inadequacies as historical records, *The World Crisis* and *The Second World War* are important primary sources. But *English-Speaking Peoples* is neither especially personal nor valuable, and a final verdict on Churchill's writing must be disappointment.

He wasn't the worst writer to win the Nobel Prize in Literature (not when the list includes Pearl S. Buck), but in truth he was never destined to be a great writer. At his best his work is intelligent, vigorous and readable, and he could have written better books than he did. This last book nevertheless predictably not only became a bestseller but was showered with reflexive praise: 'as noble and moving as anything he has ever written', wrote the *Baltimore Sun*, 'the legacy of a man of superhuman energy, great intellectual powers and the utmost simplicity of soul', eulogised the *New York Times* in the reverential tones which were now conventional for Americans describing Churchill.

In the year the last two volumes appeared, a very different book was published. Keeping a diary had been forbidden to all ranks in the wartime armed forces, and had been the most widely disobeyed of all such orders, by everyone from ordinary soldiers to the Chief of the Imperial General Staff himself. When General Sir Alan Brooke began to keep a diary, he solemnly wrote on its first page, 'On no account must the contents of this book be published,' and nor were they in full until 2001, the best part of forty years after his death. But in 1957, there appeared *The Turn of the Tide*, and two years later *Triumph in the West*. These were ostensibly by Arthur Bryant, but based on the diaries of Lord Alanbrooke, as he had become; and a murky tale this was.

Before the war Bryant had made his name as a popular patriotic historian; and if ever patriotism was a last refuge, this scoundrel justified Johnson's phrase. With all his parade of Englishry, Bryant had much admired the Third Reich, praising Hitler in 1934 as a 'mystic' helping Germany 'find her soul', and he was a thoroughgoing appeaser and critic of 'warmongers' like Churchill. As late as January 1940, in a manner as recklessly foolish as it was repellent, Bryant published *Unfinished Victory*, which explained how 'the native Germans' had been 'confronted with a problem – that of rescuing their indigenous culture from an alien hand' – the Jews, in case that wasn't clear – 'and restoring it to their own race', before a peroration saluting that German victory. Much of this had been written earlier and Bryant hadn't bothered to revise it after the war began. He quickly realised his mistake and recalled and destroyed as many copies of the book as he could.

That should have ended his career, but he returned to waving flags and boiling pots with *English Saga* and books about the Napoleonic wars. It's astonishing all the same that he should have been knighted after the war, or chosen by Alanbrooke for this task. Although Bryant heavily toned down the ceaseless frustration and even bitterness towards Churchill which Alanbrooke had expressed in his diaries, the Churchills weren't deceived by the fulsome inscription on the copy Alanbrooke sent. 'Brookie wants to have it both ways,' Clementine understandably observed, and Montgomery told Bryant that Churchill was 'very angry indeed'. In 1958, Montgomery published his own memoirs, which weren't as overtly hostile towards Churchill but whose bombastic vanity, rewriting of history to show himself in a better light than he deserved, and contemptuous criticism of the Americans, notably General – now President – Eisenhower, damaged the author's reputation, such as it was.

A larger 'battle of the books' was under way, with serious scrutiny of the war, and Churchill's record, including not least the series of official histories of the war in all its aspects and campaigns commissioned by the government. These were inevitably a mixed bunch in terms of quality or even candour. Some are thoroughly inadequate, some are admirable and valuable to this day, such as the *Grand Strategy* series, notably the volumes by Michael Howard and John Ehrman, or S.W. Roskill's three volumes on *The War at Sea*. But one work stands out in its ruthless impartiality. *The Strategic Air Offensive Against Germany* was commissioned from Sir Charles Webster, a distinguished professor of diplomatic history, and Noble Frankland, who had interrupted his budding academic career to serve as a Bomber Command navigator, and knew whereof he wrote.

For nearly ten years another campaign was waged, by the authors against the obstruction of the RAF and the Air Ministry, before their remarkable four-volume work could be published in 1960. The RAF's dismay was understandable. Although Webster and Frankland didn't enter any moral verdict against the bombing campaign, they made very clear how ineffectual bombing had been for most of the war, in terms of damaging Germany's ability to wage war, rather than killing women and children, and they conceded the essential point that German industrial war production had risen steadily until late 1944. In 1965 when A.J.P. Taylor published *English History 1914–1945*, the last volume in the old Oxford History of England series (before the names 'England' and 'English' were expunged from universities and replaced by 'Britain' and 'British', a foretaste of other expurgations) he drew heavily on Webster and Frankland. Arthur Harris was still alive – in fact he died in 1984 at the age of ninety-one – but if he had read Taylor's book, he would not have been happy with its verdict, summed up by the running heads at the top of pages: 'Bombing ineffective … Bombing fails again … Final failure of bombing'.

As early as 1950, Webster and Frankland wrote to Churchill, asking him among other things about the bombing of Dresden, to which he replied shamelessly, 'I knew nothing about it. I thought the Americans did it.' One very different writer thought he did know about it. David Irving was a self-educated energetic young Englishman who had lived in Germany and began to publish in the popular *Neue Illustrierte* a series of articles called 'Wie Deutschlands Städte starben' ('How Germany's Cities Died'). These in turn became *The Destruction of Dresden*, his first book, published in 1963. His claim that between 100,000 and 250,000 people had died in Dresden was far more than previous estimates, or than subsequent research would confirm. But Irving wouldn't go away.

As in 1955, the Tories won the 1959 general election easily enough. In 1939 Churchill had nearly been disowned by the Conservative Party in his Woodford constituency. Twenty years later, the Tories of Epping, as his seat was now named, hoped very much, albeit privately, that he would retire, and that they could have an active MP rather than a silent figurehead, but Churchill obstinately stayed put. And yet for all his lustre, and the Tory successes, there was a new mood of unrest and rebellion among young English people, given expression by the Campaign for Nuclear Disarmament and mass protests against Suez. This sceptical and derisive spirit didn't spare Churchill, as the frontiers of taste were pushed back further than Muggeridge had dared.

A 'satire boom' in the early 1960s saw the BBC's 'That Was The Week That Was', with British politicians lampooned on television for the first time, as well as the birth of the magazine *Private Eye*. The cover of its first issue in October 1961 bore the spoof headline 'Churchill cult next for party axe?' and in February 1963 it carried a still more transgressive cartoon feature, 'The Greatest Dying Englishman', which outraged Churchill's family. Then there was the stage revue, *Beyond the Fringe*, which played to packed houses in London before Broadway, to begin the careers of Alan Bennett, Peter Cook, Jonathan Miller and Dudley Moore. The prime minister of the day, Harold Macmillan, was cruelly mimicked by Cook, more cruelly than ever one evening when Macmillan was in the audience, while Cook also played a senior RAF officer in a sketch, called 'The Aftermyth of the War'. Miller is a young pilot ordered on a perilous mission over Germany, and 'Don't come back,' Cook tells him: 'We need a futile gesture at this stage. It will raise the whole tone of the war.' This wasn't such a bad description of the Churchillian instinct that had underlain sundry military woes.

What a contrast there was across the Atlantic! Through the 1950s, what Alistair Cooke had called American 'idolatry' of Churchill increased with the doting reception of *A History of the English-Speaking Peoples*. A first climax came in 1959 when the film and television rights to Churchill's *Second World War* were sold to Jack Le Vien, an American producer with big ideas: he originally hoped that the narrator for his project would be Prince Philip, until persuaded that this was unlikely. It became *The Valiant Years*, a twenty-seven part television series with Richard Burton speaking Churchill's words and a stirring score by Richard Rodgers, which enjoyed huge viewing figures in 1960–61. Significantly enough, the series ran during the presidential election campaign and past Inauguration Day. Significantly also, John Kennedy was the first president who consciously invoked the aura of Churchill. The past three had never done so, but then Roosevelt, Truman and Eisenhower were nearer to Churchill in age, all born within sixteen years of him, and they had all worked with him. They not only knew Churchill, but all had misgivings about him born of that knowledge.

More than forty years younger than Churchill, in fact younger than any of his children apart from Mary, Kennedy could become a whole-hearted Churchillian. The candidate's mother Rose Kennedy reminded voters that Jack had met Churchill before the war began in 1939, although that was a delicate matter. Kennedy's Harvard senior thesis, 'Appeasement in Munich', was turned with a good deal of help into a book which was then published in 1940 with even more help from his rich family, as *Why England Slept,* the title a deliberate echo.* Churchill heard enough to tease his 'Munichois' assistant Colville, 'You slept too,

---

* A collection of Churchill's speeches, published in 1938 and tendentiously edited by Randolph, was called *Arms and the Covenant* in its London edition, but appeared in America as *While England Slept* and sold very well.

didn't you!'. Had he actually read Kennedy's book beyond its title paying homage to himself, Churchill might have been surprised, since Kennedy shows some sympathy and understanding for the appeasers, and doubts whether earlier military action by the British would have been wise or effectual.

And of course no one had 'slept' more than old Joe Kennedy, who was still alive in 1960. His son was lucky that nothing was made of his father's record as an appeaser and defeatist. Instead, Kennedy's admirers compared him with Churchill, from when Jack was a boy ill in hospital and had devoured *The World Crisis*, to his cry during the election campaign of a 'missile gap' between Russia and the United States, which was said to echo Churchill's warnings about German rearmament in the 1930s. In fact, the one thing they had in common was that their claims were untrue. Churchill may have broadly believed what he had said about the strength of the Luftwaffe, even if he knew he was exaggerating, whereas Kennedy's claims about Russian missiles were a conscious falsehood. It worked all the same. Apart from the artful work of Senator Lyndon Johnson, Kennedy's running mate, and the Cook County Democratic machine, in ensuring that Kennedy carried Texas and Illinois, Kennedy's scaremongering, and maybe *The Valiant Years*, helped him achieve his photo-finish victory in November 1960, leading the popular vote over Richard Nixon by one-fifth of a percentage point.

For Macmillan, the Anglo-American relationship now seemed more special, more personal, and more poignant than ever: his wife Lady Dorothy Macmillan was the sister of the ninth Duke of Devonshire, whose grandson, Lady Dorothy's great-nephew, was the Lord Hartington who had married the new president's sister Kick Kennedy in 1944. That August, Kick Kennedy's eldest brother, Joe Jr, in whom old Joe's fondest hopes had been invested, was killed flying on a perilous mission, confirming his father's view that the war should never have been fought. Weeks later Billy Hartington was killed in Belgium leading his Coldstreamers, and four years after that Kick was killed in an air crash. This was the beginning of the Greek tragedy which would seem to engulf the Kennedys.

With his family connection, Macmillan was as mistaken as ever in thinking that the 'big bustling' backward and ignorant Americans needed guiding and mentoring by the 'Greeks', the sophisticated and worldly-wise English. In the autumn of 1962 that notion, and the

Churchillian idea of the unity of the English-speaking peoples, were once more falsified in political practice, before being witheringly derided by an American elder statesman. October saw the Cuban missile crisis, the nearest the two super-powers, the United States and Soviet Russia, ever came to nuclear war, when the Russians shipped missiles capable of reaching the United States to Cuba, where Fidel Castro had established a pro-Soviet dictatorship. In the end both Kennedy and Nikita Khrushchev, with all their public bluster, showed a restraint which suggested that they knew as well as Churchill how catastrophic such a war would be.

Many years after he had marked his twenty-first birthday in Cuba, Churchill's shadow still fell heavily over the island, although 'Churchillism' could be unpredictable. Two years before the crisis, Castro had visited New York for the United Nations General Assembly, when he said cheekily that he had been reading Churchill's *Second World War*, and had been much inspired by the story of a small island nation defying a much larger continental enemy. On the other hand there was General Curtis LeMay, who had once directed the great incendiary raids of 1944–5 – 'fire jobs,' in his defiant phrase – in which hundreds of thousands of Japanese civilians had been incinerated, cheerfully saying that he expected to be tried as a war criminal if his country lost, and whose career would end in 1968 as running mate to the segregationist George Wallace.

In between, LeMay was Chief of Staff of the US Air Force, and during the crisis he was gung-ho to bomb Cuba, angrily telling Kennedy to his face that his refusal to bomb was 'almost as bad as the appeasement at Munich'. But Macmillan's later claim that 'We were "in on" and took full part in (and almost responsibility for) every American move' during the crisis was much exaggerated. London played no guiding part at critical moments, either when American aircraft armed with hydrogen bombs were circling the Arctic coast of Russia on the level of alert just below war, or when Robert Kennedy cut a secret deal with the Russians on his brother's behalf by agreeing to withdraw missiles from Turkey as a quid pro quo for the removal of Soviet missiles from Cuba.

One man Kennedy did consult during the crisis was Dean Acheson, the imperious former Secretary of State. Product of an American patrician establishment which no longer exists, Acheson was the son of an Episcopalian clergyman, the Bishop of Connecticut, and had

passed through Groton, Yale, Harvard Law School and Covington &
Burling, the fashionable Washington law firm, before briefly serving
in the Roosevelt administration. Then when President Truman chose
him as his Secretary of State from 1949 to 1953, Acheson played a
key part in the creation of NATO, while dealing both with the threat
abroad from Communist Russia under Joseph Stalin, and the threat
at home from the anti-Communist demagoguery of Senator Joseph
McCarthy, the two Joes together making rational conduct of foreign
policy very difficult. His nativist foes accused Acheson of excessive
Anglophilia, unaware that, when he found officials at the State
Department working on a definition of the Anglo-American 'special
relationship', he ordered them to stop immediately and destroy all
their work. He forbade the very use of the phrase: any suggestion
that his officials were serving the interests of another country –
including Great Britain – was ammunition for 'the McCarthys'.

Shortly after the Cuban crisis, Acheson wrote to his friend Lady
Pamela Berry, the London hostess and wife of Michael Berry, owner
of the *Daily Telegraph*. 'Three things of my own are about to burst
on the world,' Acheson told Lady Pamela. They were 'a leader in the
December issue of *Foreign Affairs* ... a speech at West Point ... and a
piece about my childhood in the Connecticut valley.' It was characteristic of Acheson's self-regard that he should have thought the first
and last of these would 'burst' anywhere, but he was more right about
the second than he can have guessed. On 5 December 1962, Acheson
gave that speech, and it did indeed explode across the Atlantic like a
verbal intercontinental missile.

He had been invited to give a keynote address at West Point by
General William Westmoreland, the superintendent of the military
academy, but declined until pressed by his friend General Maxwell
Taylor. And so Acheson spoke to the cadets on 'Our Atlantic alliance:
the political and economic strands'. Most of the speech was a conventional *tour d'horizon* about the continuing Soviet threat and the need
to strengthen American political and economic ties with Europe, which
might not even have been reported by Fleet Street or noticed at
Westminster, but for what was almost an aside: 'Great Britain has lost
an empire and has not yet found a role. The attempt to play a separate
power role – that is, a role apart from Europe, a role based on a "special
relationship" with the United States, a role based on being head of a
"commonwealth" which has no political structure, or unity, or strength

– this role is about played out. Great Britain, attempting to be a broker between the United States and Russia, has seemed to conduct policy as weak as its military power.' Today it's hard to recapture, or understand, the almost hysterical response those words provoked in London. The *Daily Express* screamed about a 'stab in the back' from someone who was supposed to be a friend, while the *Daily Telegraph* sneered that Acheson was 'More immaculate in dress than in judgement'. The *Spectator* took a more measured view, but hoped, in pained terms, that 'in this transitional period we have a right to ask that our friends should not make matters worse. It is the nature of nations diminished in power to feel humiliated when that fact is called to their attention.'

Among those who felt especially humiliated was Macmillan. The prime minister was so stung by Acheson's denigration of 'the will and resolution of the British people', as he put it, that he not only complained bitterly in private but, despite Kennedy warning him against any exaggerated reaction, publicly and petulantly snorted that Acheson had made 'an error which had been made by quite a lot of people in the last four hundred years, including Philip of Spain, Louis XIV, Napoleon, the Kaiser and Hitler'. But then resentment cut across party lines. A few weeks after Acheson's speech, Gaitskell died and Harold Wilson was elected Labour leader, to become prime minister in 1964. Several years later, another intervention by Acheson prompted Wilson to say in the Commons that 'Mr Acheson was a distinguished figure who had lost a State Department and not found a role.'

Nowhere did Acheson mention Churchill, but he scarcely needed to. From one campus to another, the West Point speech of December 1962 was a direct rebuttal of the Fulton speech of March 1946, after an interval in which events had already contradicted Churchill. He had advocated 'a special relationship between the British Commonwealth and Empire and the United States'; Acheson called that an illusion. Churchill had said, 'Let no man underrate the abiding power of the British Empire and Commonwealth'; Acheson pointed out that the Commonwealth had no political structure, or unity, or strength. Macmillan irritably responded that 'Mr Acheson seems wholly to misunderstand the role of the Commonwealth in world affairs,' but just what was that role meant to be?

This controversy passed Churchill by, as he could now pay little attention to events. In May 1959 he had crossed the Atlantic as a personal guest of President Eisenhower, and was shown the battlefield at Gettysburg from a helicopter. The final dubious crony to befriend Churchill was the Greek shipping magnate Aristotle Onassis, to whom Randolph had introduced his father but whom Clementine deplored: 'Somehow I don't want to be beholden to this rich and powerful man.' But Churchill was happy to enjoy cruising in Onassis's yacht. On one journey through the Aegean towards the city Churchill still called Constantinople, Onassis told his captain to steam through the Dardanelles at night lest his eminent guest should be disturbed by unhappy memories by seeing Gallipoli in daylight. In 1961 Churchill made his last, somewhat anticlimactic American visit, sailing in Onassis's yacht. He saw his old friend Bernard Baruch in New York, but was too weak to accept Kennedy's invitation to visit Washington.

What might also have aroused disagreeable memories was a visit paid to Churchill at his London home in March 1960. Like Churchill, de Gaulle had returned to power, and like him had become an object of veneration to some, although there was at least no equivalent at Chartwell of the strange woman who for years was sometimes found outside the gates at Colombey-les-deux-Eglises claiming that she had been sent by the Blessed Virgin to bear the general's child. The French president had given a virtuoso speech to both Houses of Parliament and had enjoyed an amicable audience with the Queen, who may or may not by then have read her inscribed copy of his *Mémoires de Guerre*.*

Both in public and in private de Gaulle expressed his admiration for the continuity and stability of English political tradition, as well he might given the instability in France which had preceded his return and still threatened him. A final meeting of the old *frères ennemis* at Hyde Park Gate lasted all of eighteen minutes, at the end of which Churchill seemed to say, *'Vive la France!'* Talking to his confidant Alain Peyrefitte, de Gaulle took a rather different line from his speech in Westminster Hall, dismayed that the English had so lost their historic self-confidence and ambition that they had allowed their country to become an American satellite. 'Churchill was magnificent until 1942,' de Gaulle said. 'Then, as if exhausted by excess of effort, he passed

---

* Much about de Gaulle could be learned from the brief list of recipients of inscribed copies: the Pope, the President of the French Republic, the Comte de Paris whom royalists thought the rightful King of France, and the Queen of England.

the flame on to the Americans and abased himself before them.' He also recalled, over and again, Churchill's words in 1944 about choosing the 'open sea' over Europe.

By 1963 Churchill was much too frail to cross the Atlantic and attend the ceremony in which American citizenship was conferred upon him. He was represented in Washington on 9 April by his children Randolph and Mary, and his grandson little Winston. Three of President Roosevelt's sons were present, as well as Harriman, and the extraordinary Baruch, even older than Churchill. A graceful reply from the new citizen was read by Sir David Ormsby Gore, the British Ambassador in Washington. Churchill expressed his delight that the former prime minister of a great sovereign state should thus be received as an honorary citizen of another:

> I say 'great sovereign state' with design and emphasis, for I reject the view that Britain and the Commonwealth should now be relegated to a tame, and minor role in the world. Our past is the key to our future ...
>
> I am, as you know, half American by blood ... In this century of storm and tragedy, I contemplate with high satisfaction the constant factor of the interwoven and upward progress of our peoples. Our comradeship and our brotherhood in war were unexampled ...
>
> Mr President, your action illuminates the theme of unity of the English-speaking peoples, to which I have devoted a large part of my life.

This echoed the themes which he had been playing for many years past. They had less meaning than ever.

Shortly before the ceremony in Washington, there had been one worse humiliation for Macmillan, and one more baleful legacy of Churchill. Having become prime minister in the wake of Suez, and having decided to cling tightly to Washington, Macmillan had belatedly woken up to the challenge – and the potential opportunity – of the European Economic Community, whose conception in 1955 at Messina and birth in 1957 in Rome the British had disdainfully ignored. This Common Market, as it was known, was just what Churchill had called for so often, the 'appeasement of the fearful hatreds and antagonisms which exist in Europe' by way of the 'partnership between France and Germany' he had advocated in 1946.

Those were the two leading members of the original Six countries in the Common Market, all of whom had strong motives for commonality. The French were frightened of the Germans, the Germans were frightened of themselves, while the Italians reversed Groucho Marx's quip and wanted to be a member of any club that would have them or appear to take them seriously. And since the Low Countries, Belgium, the Netherlands and Luxembourg, had immemorially been 'the cockpit of Europe' whose landscape was scarred with the battlefields of many centuries up to 1945, they longed for no more battles. Churchill warmly welcomed this European union, while saying that Great Britain could remain a friendly neighbour and sponsor rather than a member. Since then, his idea of England as the centre of overlapping power circles, the Commonwealth, Europe and the Anglo-America alliance, had looked less convincing with every year. And although Macmillan had famously said that 'most of our people have never had it so good', that was only true by contrast with the domestic past rather than the foreign present: the comparison with the defeated Germans and the *Wirtschaftswunder*, their economic miracle over the previous decade, was painful for the erstwhile victors to behold.

Now Macmillan decided that Great Britain must 'join Europe' after all, although it was too late for the English to build it, as Churchill had once hoped, and without their help it had already been created in a way which was by no means favourable for Great Britain. A formal application for membership of the Common Market was nevertheless tabled in August 1961, and Macmillan reshuffled his government to provide for this enterprise a team of ministers who were pro-European – and Churchillian. One son-in-law, Christopher Soames, was agriculture minister, another was now Commonwealth Secretary, although 'ex-' was operative, as Duncan Sandys and Diana had recently divorced. And Edward Heath, who had held junior office under Churchill, was given the formal office of Lord Privy Seal (who was, as Churchill once remarked, neither a lord nor a privy nor a seal) and put in charge of the negotiations.

Of all the crosses he had to bear during the war, Churchill had once said, the heaviest was the Cross of Lorraine, the symbol of de Gaulle's Free France. Now the cross was planted firmly in the way of the British. After meeting de Gaulle in June 1962, Macmillan recorded, 'I am not at all sure how far de Gaulle and the French really feel it to be in France's interest to have us in.' All the same, he continued with blind optimism to think he could get past de Gaulle. They met at Rambouillet in December 1962, shortly after Acheson's philippic although also just after Macmillan had flown to the Bahamas and frantically begged Kennedy to provide the British with a new missile system, whose ostensible 'independence' was belied by those very circumstances. The details are now forgotten, but they confirmed de Gaulle's belief that England was an American dependency, and would be a Trojan horse for Washington inside Europe.

On 14 January 1963, he announced his veto on the British application. 'England is indeed insular, she is maritime,' he said at the fatal press conference. She was linked 'to the most distant countries. She has in all her doings very marked and very original habits and traditions.' In these words a deafening echo could be heard, of what Churchill had told de Gaulle less than twenty years before. Churchill had said that he would always choose Roosevelt over de Gaulle, and would always choose the open sea over Europe. If revenge is a dish best eaten cold, de Gaulle had feasted on a *buffet froid* of Churchill's own words.

There is a coda to this sorry story. In retirement Eden wrote his memoirs, for the large part as tedious as most other prime ministerial autobiographies. But in one fascinating passage he looked back at the war, and the part played by the French leader. Although de Gaulle's conduct had seemed 'contumacious, especially to our American allies, perhaps we should have learned from it. Some of the faults of later years might have been avoided if we had shown some of the same spirit.' Those words were one more repudiation of Churchill and the 'special relationship'.

Before that year was out there were two lamentable deaths. It may seem unkind to dwell on the woes of Churchill's children, but at the time they were difficult to avoid, so often were Randolph's antics in the newspapers, as well as Sarah's inebriated brushes with the law, in America as well as England, as her career as an actress continued intermittently. A pall of sorrow sometimes seemed to hang over the family. Sarah's wartime romance with Gil Winant had ended by the time he gave up the ambassadorship in London and returned home in 1946. Beset by financial and other worries, he fell into a decline, wrote a memoir and, on its publication day in 1947, shot himself. Two years later Sarah married Anthony Beauchamp, a photographer, without telling her parents; eight years later he too took his own life. Diana's marriage to Sandys had produced a son and two daughters, including Edwina Sandys, a sculptor whose work would celebrate her grandfather, but by the time of her second divorce Diana's life had grown ever sadder. In October 1963 she ended it with an overdose of barbiturates, awful news her father could just about take in. It was scarcely surprising that Clementine was hospitalised for depression.

That tragedy coincided with Macmillan's resignation and his replacement as prime minister, to general astonishment, by the Earl of Home, who as Lord Dunglass had sat in the Commons and served as Chamberlain's Parliamentary Private Secretary at the time of Munich. He who was now able to take advantage of a recent change in the law, disclaim his peerage, and return to the Commons as Sir Alec Douglas-Home, all so that Macmillan could once again cheat Butler of the prime ministership. A month later, Churchill's admirer President Kennedy was assassinated in Dallas. He was succeeded by Lyndon Johnson, his vice-president, who was re-elected by a huge majority in November 1964. In October 1964, the Tories under Douglas-Home had very narrowly lost the election to Labour led by Harold Wilson, ending what Labour eloquently called 'thirteen wasted years' of Conservative government.

Those years had begun with Churchill's return to Downing Street and continued under his influence. Few would now claim, as Churchill's official biographer loyally does, that his second prime ministership of 1951–5 was a success, and few will say that the way Macmillan rigged Douglas-Home's succession was creditable, or wise. Macmillan's biographer D.R. Thorpe writes that 'Macmillan and Home both came in time to think that it might have been better if Rab Butler had become prime minister in 1963,' to which Ferdinand Mount adds, 'I would go a lot further. It might have been better if Butler had succeeded Eden in 1957, or even Churchill in 1955.' One might put the date back further still, and imagine another history of England since the war. Suppose that Churchill had done what Clementine begged him to do and retired at the end of the war to be succeeded as party leader by Eden. He would have led the Tories to defeat in 1945 and back to power in 1951, but would have retired honourably when illness struck him down in 1953, to be succeeded by Butler.

'The country would undoubtedly have been better governed,' as Mount says. 'There would have been no Suez, no inflationary stampede, no botched attempt to join the EEC but rather a careful development of a European Free Trade Area. Social reform and economic modernisation would have been pursued in a more serious and systematic fashion. It would have been a more sober time, without the showmanship with which Macmillan delighted some and repelled others. We would not have been told we had never had it so good; but we might have been better off.'

And England would have escaped from Churchill's shadow, with all his dreams of glory, and accepted sooner a more modest place in the world. As it was there was another turning point: 1964 was the first election of the twentieth century when the name Winston Churchill hadn't appeared on a ballot paper. He had stood sixteen times at general elections, twenty times in all counting by-elections, losing six, winning fourteen. As he approached his ninetieth birthday, not only political life but life itself was draining from him at last.

18

'It was a triumph'
St Paul's 1965

'I want lots of soldiers and bands.' Sir Winston Churchill's cheerfully defiant words echoed what he had said before, that he had loved life but did not fear death, and it was true. As a young soldier, he had been fearless in battle. As a famous politician, already in his forties, he had commanded an infantry battalion in the front line of one great war. As the leader of his country in its next and greatest war, he had flown tens of thousands of miles with notable disregard for danger as well as discomfort. But the Psalmist's words were sadly apt: 'though men be so strong that they come to fourscore years: yet is their strength then but labour and sorrow.' By the age of ninety, Churchill's faculties were long faded, he could no longer love life with such relish and, far from fearing death, he may have inwardly welcomed this final rest. Those instructions showed how much he had relished the thought of his funeral. As Andrew Roberts has said, 'Few have set out with more cold-blooded deliberation to become first a hero and then a Great Man,' and he was scarcely less deliberate in his determination to create his legacy as the man of the century, above and beyond history.

Dawn on that unforgettable day of 30 January 1965 saw a chilly, misty London at a standstill, as a magnificent piece of visual and aural rhetoric was about to be played out on the streets of the capital and in St Paul's Cathedral. It would be the culmination of a lifetime's work by Churchill, spent not only constructing a political career unlike any other but also crafting his own reputation, commanding narrative, and brilliantly exploiting the power of language and symbolism, of 'beautiful national legends', and the myths which he himself had said were so needed in wartime. What even he could not know was that this January day would be a milestone in another story, the great mythos and cult of Churchill, which had already taken form and would burgeon steadily.

According to old custom the lying-in-state had begun on the fourth day after death, to be followed by the funeral on the eighth. Vast numbers filed past his body in Westminster Hall for hours on end, as Guardsmen stood at the four corners of the bier, immobile with heads bent. Then on the appointed day, it was as though every element was tailored so as to present a panorama of Churchill's life, and highlight different sides of his character and career. In some ways this biographical epic gave a decidedly coloured or distorted version of events, but then that was something he knew all about himself.

No one loved soldiers and bands more than he, nor better understood their symbolic importance. 'Even quite small parades are highly beneficial,' he had told Eden in a note dated July 1940. 'In fact wherever there are troops and leisure for it there should be an attempt at military display.' Now lots of soldiers and bands was what he wanted, and lots was what he got, along with military display as had rarely been seen. A first guard at Westminster was mounted by cadets from Harrow, his old school. Further guards of honour were found by the Queen's Royal Irish Hussars, the 17th/21st Lancers and the Royal Scots Fusiliers. The first of these was the descendant of the 4th Hussars with whom young Winston had served the Queen-Empress Victoria in Bangalore seventy years before, the second of the 21st Lancers with whom he had charged at Omdurman in 1898. Then during the Great War, he had left the Cabinet involuntarily and London voluntarily following the Gallipoli debacle, and spent three months in early 1916 commanding a battalion of the Royal Scots Fusiliers on the Western Front.

His coffin was removed by a bearer party of Grenadier Guards, with whom he had briefly trained, before the body of the 'Former Naval Person' was drawn from Westminster to St Paul's by blue-jackets, a crew of ratings from the Royal Navy paying tribute to a man who had twice been First Lord of the Admiralty, at a twenty-five year interval, and embroiled in controversy both times. Then when the hearse reached St Paul's the Irish Guards formed the guard of honour, while a solemn minute gun was fired by the King's Troop of the Royal Horse Artillery. A party of Grenadiers carried the coffin up the steps, and there was almost an awful moment. Ahead of them slowly walked Earl Attlee, as Churchill's old adversary and colleague now was, aged eighty-two, frail and stooping in his greatcoat and silk hat. He stumbled, and the front Guardsmen instinctively hesitated and broke step, so that for a split second it looked as though the coffin might be dropped. But the big men recovered their balance and bore the body to the west door, to be met by the Archbishop of Canterbury, the Royal Family and foreign dignitaries, and the immense congregation, including the government, a fair representation of the Lords Temporal and Spiritual, and hundreds of Members of Parliament.

Only two men outside the royal family – Wellington and Gladstone – had previously been granted state funerals, and Queen Victoria had attended neither of them. Now Churchill became the third, with Queen Elizabeth II leading the mourners, and George's widowed consort at the side of his daughter. Queen Elizabeth the Queen Mother had been by no means a lifelong devotee of Churchill, and there were mixed memories in her steely heart. Her husband had been placed on the throne thanks to the abdication of Edward VIII in 1936, after Churchill, at nearly the lowest point in his career, had tried to rally support for Edward; Churchill's loyalty towards her wayward brother-in-law was a lingering source of resentment for the Queen Mother. But then she also resented the way that the abdication had made her husband king, to be worn out by office, above all during the war, dying before his time and leaving her with a widowhood that would last more than fifty years.

Her son-in-law the Duke of Edinburgh and her grandson the Prince of Wales were both wearing naval uniform, as the former was more than many others entitled to do. Philip had served as a naval officer throughout the war and had been mentioned in despatches after the glorious battle of Cape Matapan in March 1941. His uniform was, as it happened, one of the few that Churchill had never worn. In that note to Eden, he had written that 'peculiarities of uniform and regimental distinctions should be encouraged,' and he knew all about them. He understood that uniforms, apart from their function of distinguishing a group of men in battle, have a histrionic purpose. They make a statement, which is one reason Churchill spent so much of his time in uniform, to a degree that embarrassed even Clementine.

Accompanying the coffin were the pallbearers. The funeral had been long and meticulously planned under the aegis of the Duke of Norfolk, in his role as Earl Marshal or master of state ceremonies, but his list of grandees was regularly revised since, as Mountbatten put it, 'the pallbearers kept dying and Churchill kept living'. The

chosen band who survived until that January day were Sir Robert
Menzies, Harold Macmillan, Field Marshal Sir Gerald Templer, Lord
Normanbrook, Lord Bridges, Lord Ismay, Field Marshal Viscount Slim,
Marshal of the Royal Air Force Viscount Portal of Hungerford, the
Earl of Avon (as Sir Anthony Eden now was), Earl Attlee, Field Marshal
Alexander of Tunis and Admiral of the Fleet Earl Mountbatten of
Burma. It was a sign of how much Churchill's life, and his country's,
had been marked by war in that century that nine of them had seen
action as officers in the Great War, and all had served under Churchill
in one capacity or another during the next war.

That line had now ended. Macmillan was the last of four successive
prime ministers to have served as an infantry officer in the Great War.
His successor, Douglas-Home, was precluded by severe illness from
military service in 1940. When Labour narrowly won the October
1964 election he was succeeded by the signally un-Churchillian figure
of Harold Wilson, a young don in 1939 when (as one biographer
derisively puts it) 'more a clerk than a captain ... it does not seem to
have occurred to him to seek enlistment in the forces', and he served
instead as a government statistician in Whitehall. The Labour and
Tory leaders were joined at St Paul's by Jo Grimond, the leader of
the Liberal Party, an amiable man who had served as a staff officer
in Churchill's war, and had not long before the funeral excited mild
derision, by telling his party conference (at a time when there were
fewer than a dozen Liberal MPs) to advance 'toward the sound of
gunfire'. And so here was British democracy embodied by the leaders
of the three famous parties, two of which Churchill had belonged to,
and all of which had served in his great wartime coalition government,
and had at different times and for different reasons abhorred him.

One man was missing. Field Marshal Viscount Montgomery of
Alamein was abroad when Churchill died, and he had disliked funerals
all his life, according to his brother. Even so, 'I have always been
somewhat at a loss to understand why he did not come home to
attend the funeral of his old friend.' But maybe they weren't such
friends after all. Churchill had always disliked Montgomery's bombast
and vanity, a dislike increased, and widely shared, after the publication
in 1958 of Montgomery's insufferably conceited and tendentious
Memoirs. As if 'Monty's' stock weren't low enough, he harangued the
House of Lords about the evils of sodomy, while uniquely applauding
both South African apartheid and Mao's murderous regime in China.

Gathered in St Paul's were the most potent, grave and reverend signiors sent by the nations of the world, many of them telling a tale by their presence, although there were equally eloquent absences. One man was as ever physically conspicuous. Only a little over a year before, President Charles de Gaulle of France had attended an event as sombre but more tragic, the Requiem Mass in Washington for the murdered President John Kennedy. There, he had been even more than usually visible when he followed French Catholic liturgical practice, sometimes standing during the service in the Washington cathedral while others were sitting or kneeling. De Gaulle conformed to local ways in St Paul's, but still towered over his neighbours.

Only twenty years earlier Soviet Russia had been an ally and the Red Army had played overwhelmingly the largest part in the defeat of the Third Reich. That army was represented by another great survivor, Marshall Ivan Koniev, a man old enough to have served the Tsar before becoming a Bolshevik and, having by luck or agility lived through the purges that almost entirely exterminated the senior officer corps, had gone on to play a part in the defence of Moscow in 1941. But the Soviet government itself was represented by no more than a deputy prime minister.

Other absences were more pointed. The presidents of Iceland and Uruguay had come, but not those of Ireland or India, or their prime ministers either. The first prime minister of independent India was Jawaharlal Nehru, who had died eight months earlier, and who might well have attended. As it was, the representation of India by no more than her foreign minister hinted at the way many Indians reciprocated Churchill's contempt for them. One man who would have matched de Gaulle in height was Eamon de Valera, now titular president of the Irish Republic after his very long years governing or misgoverning the country, becoming prime minister the year Roosevelt was elected president and resigning the year before Kennedy was. 'Dev' was eighty-two when Churchill died but age didn't explain his absence, since he was conspicuously active the following year at the fiftieth anniversary of the Easter Rising. But another young country showed its deep gratitude to Churchill. Israel was represented by the formidable septuagenarian David Ben Gurion, who had served as prime minister from 1948 to1963.

Although the service wasn't long, it was magnificently crafted, from 'The Battle Hymn of the Republic' as a reminder of Churchill's maternal descent (and maybe of the 'special relationship'), to the Hussar trumpeter sounding Cavalry Last Post and Reveille, symbolising death and resurrection, even if Churchill had never pretended seriously to believe Christian doctrine. At last the Queen bade farewell to Clementine and her family as they left the cathedral and followed the coffin to the Thames, where it was placed aboard the launch *Havengore* and carried upriver to Festival Pier, while aircraft from the RAF flew overhead to pay one tribute, and the big cranes on the wharves bent forward in homage to pay another.* Then the last stage of all was a circuitous railway journey from Waterloo station to Woodstock, and to the simple village church at Bladon, just south of Blenheim, where Churchill was laid to rest in the presence of his family.

'It wasn't a funeral,' Clementine said at the end of the day, 'it was a triumph.' So it seemed, but it was an ambiguous triumph. One person after another expressed the same sense of loss, and of a drastic historical moment. 'England without him!' Macmillan wrote in his diary. 'It seems impossible.' In another diary, Crossman wrote, 'It felt like the end of an epoch, possibly even the end of a nation.' And most brutally of all, de Gaulle said that, in burying Churchill, they were also burying the British Empire and British greatness.

And yet that was far from the whole story. 'As He died to make men holy, let us live to make men free,' they sang in St Paul's. Churchill had made no pretence to holiness, but could have claimed that he lived to make men free. When Julia Ward Howe wrote 'His truth is marching on' in her 'Battle Hymn', she was echoing 'John Brown's Body', whose tune she had taken. And if not 'his truth', then like Brown's, Churchill's spirit was marching on, with consequences quite unforeseen that day at St Paul's. At the same time, for all the near-religious veneration, Churchill's reputation was far from uncontested: 'the Churchill wars' would be still waged for many years to come. To be sure, his name and example would be endlessly invoked; but it became an almost constant pattern that such invocations were a prelude to disaster.

*

---

* Fifty years later, Churchill's grandson Nicholas Soames said that it was the bowed cranes 'that really broke me up', although at that same time one of the surviving crane drivers spoiled the effect by saying that they had all hated Churchill and had only been induced by additional money to pay this seemingly spontaneous tribute.

When the obsequies were ended, the monument-making began in earnest. First of all came the memoirs, some from people who had long been chafing at the bit for death to allow publication. Quickest off the mark was Violet Bonham Carter.* She had met Churchill at a dinner party in 1906, when she was a girl entering adulthood and he, still in his early thirties, was a bumptious ministerial colleague of her father, H.H. Asquith. This new friend fascinated and repelled and attracted Violet in turns, telling her, 'We are all worms. But I really think I am a glowworm.' The next day Violet told her father that she fancied she had been in the presence of genius. 'Well,' Asquith replied, 'Winston would certainly agree with you there, even if not everyone else would.' In 1937 it was she who had introduced Churchill to Jabotinsky, and now that vivacious young girl was an imperious old lady.

She died little more than four years after Churchill, and no one could resent the speed with which her *Winston Churchill as I Knew Him* came out. It was widely read and on the whole warmly received, although A.J.P. Taylor was sarcastic about Lady Asquith's defence not only of her father but of Churchill against Lloyd George, one of Taylor's ill-chosen heroes along with Beaverbrook: 'Churchill's eccentricities are made endearing, Lloyd George's discreditable,' and when Lloyd George agreed with someone's description of Churchill as 'frank without being straight', Taylor derided Lady Asquith's 'prim disapproval', before making a distinction only he could, between 'the two men, one of whom, Lloyd George, was certainly great and the other, Churchill, was at any rate unusual'.

But another intimate portrait of Churchill, published little more than a year after his death, caused outrage. By birth a Yorkshire Irishman, Charles McMoran Wilson had qualified as a doctor a few years before the Great War. Between the wars he rose high in his profession, as head of St Mary's Medical School in London, but it was the two wars that changed his life. In 1914, he joined the Royal Fusiliers as a medical officer, and served with courage notable even by the famously high standards of the Royal Army Medical Corps, winning

---

* Successively Miss Violet Asquith, Mrs Maurice Bonham Carter after she married her father's private secretary 'Bongie', Lady Violet Bonham Carter when her father was created an earl, Dame Violet when made a DBE at Churchill's instigation in 1953, and Lady Asquith of Yarnbury when created a life peeress in 1964.

the Military Cross on the Somme and later writing a monograph on the effects of mustard gas.

Two weeks after Churchill was made prime minister in May 1940, Sir Charles Wilson, as he by then was, before he became Lord Moran in 1943 as a mark of the prime minister's esteem, was appointed Churchill's personal physician. For the rest of his life Churchill was attended by Moran, and in his later years was his only patient, after Moran had otherwise retired from practice. Their relationship was especially close during the war, when doctor saw patient regularly and accompanied him on his arduous foreign travels. Moran was one of only a very few people who knew about Churchill's suspected minor heart attack in 1941, about the seriousness of his related bouts of pneumonia in the later years of the war, or about his strokes, less grave in 1949, incapacitating in 1953.

Because of these two wars, Moran was able to produce two remarkable books. In 1945, he published *The Anatomy of Courage*, a wise and humane book based on the notes he had kept in the trenches thirty years before while he witnessed at close quarters awful suffering, inspiring valour and human weakness. If that book caused little stir and had a modest readership, *Winston Churchill: The Struggle for Survival, 1940–1965* was a contrast indeed. Published in the spring of 1966, and also based on Moran's contemporary notes over those years, it was a uniquely detailed and intimate portrayal – or betrayal. Every subsequent biographer has drawn on Moran, the official biographer more than he cared to acknowledge, and anyone interested in Churchill has read the book. It may well be that, as John Grigg wrote when reviewing the final volume of the official life in 1988, that 'Churchill employed Moran not only as a doctor but also, knowingly, as a Boswell', and Churchill's personality shines through the pages, with endless, often fascinating, lines from his conversation. But then Boswell wasn't Johnson's doctor, and here the bitter controversy began.

A first salvo of criticism was fired by the *Lancet*, most august journal of the British medical profession, in a stern editorial published while the book was still being serialised and hadn't yet been seen in the shops. The book was no doubt interesting, said the *Lancet*, but its publication was still reprehensible: 'Lord Moran would have done well to avoid clinical details.' Public trust in the medical profession must depend on confidentiality between patient and doctor, which applied alike to rich and poor, famous or unknown – and just as much to the dead as to the living. Popular newspaper columnists weighed in, with 'Cassandra' of the *Daily Mirror* (William Connor), who had robustly criticised Churchill during the war, condemning the book as a public post-mortem.

In reply, Moran argued that normal professional obligations didn't apply 'to a great historical figure', whose health was a matter of public interest. He claimed that he had sought the advice of George Macaulay Trevelyan, the last of the Whig historians and a Harrow contemporary of Churchill's.* Trevelyan had supposedly told Moran, 'This is history, you ought to get it on paper,' and had silenced Moran's own scruples by saying, 'Let us have the truth.' Whether those words were themselves the truth no one could well say, since Trevelyan had conveniently died several years before Churchill. This was not only a self-serving but a feeble argument, and Moran was about to be blown out of the water. He also claimed that he had told Churchill about his proposed book and that Churchill had given his approval, again invoking the word of a man who could no longer contradict him, and who in any case, as Moran knew better than anyone, had been a frail shadow of himself in his later years.

'I know nothing of this, nor does my mother,' Randolph thunderously retorted. When Churchill was still alive, Clementine had told Moran on behalf of her husband that she hoped he wouldn't publish anything; she had subsequently asked to see the book in proof, Randolph said, but 'Lord Moran refused'. In answer to another correspondent who suggested that Sir Winston belonged to history and 'not to Mr Randolph Churchill', Randolph said that this was self-evident. He asked no special favours because of his father's eminence, only that Churchill, alive or dead, was entitled to that 'confidentiality between patient and doctor' the humblest citizen expected of a family doctor. And with stinging contempt, Randolph added that in recent years 'Members of the Royal Family have found it necessary to enter into covenants with their domestic staffs inhibiting them from writing

---

* Who didn't forget him: in the autumn of 1940, the prime minister offered Trevelyan the Mastership of Trinity College, Cambridge, making his life 'as happy', the historian said, 'as anyone's can be during the fall of European civilisation'.

anything they learn when in service.* It looks as if eminent people would be well advised in future to enter into similar covenants with their physicians.'

Although Randolph couldn't prevent publication, he won this sharp exchange outright, and the medical profession behaved cravenly, over-awed not by Churchill's eminence but by Moran's. Any ordinary doctor who had betrayed a patient's confidence in such a fashion would have been very severely disciplined, but that wasn't so easy with a sometime President of the Royal College of Physicians. In the end, and apart from the deplorable 'clinical detail', starting with the obnoxious title 'Struggle for Survival' for an account of a dying man, Moran needs to be read with caution, as he clearly embellished his contemporary notes. Some of what he wrote was all too true, not to say obvious: 'Winston thinks only of the colour of their skin,' when he expressed his contempt for Chiang Kai-shek and the Chinese. 'It is when he talks of India or China that you remember he is a Victorian,' although it didn't really need his doctor to tell us that, and even as a Boswell, Moran might compare unfavourably with John Colville, Churchill's assistant private secretary, whose fascinating wartime diary was published after a decent interval in 1985 as *The Fringes of Power.*

Throughout this episode Randolph displayed the innate pugnacity and eloquence which had often been dissipated during his colourful, disas-trous, thwarted life. We last saw him during the war. In its final year, he and Waugh served together again, as part of an incongruous military mission to the Yugoslav Partisans in a corner of Croatia. Waugh soon found Randolph wearisome: 'His endless coughing and farting make him a poor companion in wet weather.' They were joined by Freddie, Lord Birkenhead, son of Churchill's boon companion, and the two of them 'endlessly retell the memorable retorts their respec-tive fathers made at one time or another to various public personages,' Waugh told his wife, although 'even with that vast repertoire they repeat themselves every day or two, sometimes every hour or two.' Finally Randolph's bibulous garrulity became too much for both his companions and to shut him up they bet him large sums that he couldn't read through the whole Bible. Randolph struggled manfully

---

* This followed in particular from the publication of the sentimental reminiscences of 'Crawfie', who had been nanny to the Queen and her sister as little girls.

for a while, then gave up and paid up, though not before he had
perused a good deal of the unfamiliar text, looking up from time to
time to exclaim, 'God! Isn't God a shit!'

Having lost his parliamentary seat at the 1945 election, Randolph
bumped into Waugh in the spring of 1947 in Hollywood, where Waugh
had gone on a luxurious trip at MGM's expense to discuss a movie of
Brideshead Revisited which, in the event, wasn't made. Randolph
'behaved abominably,' Waugh wrote. 'I thought he could never shock
me any more but he did. Brutishly drunk all the time, soliciting respectable women at luncheon parties.' Even then Randolph still, astonishingly enough, cherished hopes of a political career, and made two more
attempts to get back into Parliament, at the 1950 and 1951 elections,*
Randolph gave up and turned to journalism after a fashion, though he
also spent much time denouncing the popular papers for pornographic
vulgarity, and suing them for libel. In 1956 he won large damages from
the *People*, which had called him a mercenary 'hack', prompting a public
and a private response. Waugh wrote a very funny article about the
case in the *Spectator*, entitled 'Randolph's Finest Hour' and opening
with the bravura words, 'No one who knows Mr Randolph Churchill
and wishes to express distaste for him should ever be at a loss for words
both apt and opprobrious,' before saying that the paper's description
of him as a hired 'hack' was one of the few inapt insults imaginable.
Churchill was less amused, writing to Clementine, who had been
'ashamed and mortified' by the libel suit: 'I admit I was astonished that
Randolph won ... I did not think the jury would draw so firmly the
very refined distinction between his vocabulary and the *People's*.'

None of this much enhanced Randolph's standing as an *homme
sérieux*. Nor did two high-speed books he produced, on *The Rise and
Fall of Sir Anthony Eden* and then a dishonest account of the Tory
leadership contest in October 1963, each a brutal attack on a man
who had served his father, Eden and R.A. Butler. Least of all did a
magnificently inebriated appearance on television, still gratefully
remembered by those lucky enough to have seen it. But a serious
reputation was what he had been desperate to establish, so as to secure
his credentials for what he believed was his life's supreme and

---

* When he was beaten by Michael Foot. It was 'nice for the boy to have an opponent
just as beastly as himself and just the same way,' Waugh wrote. 'Up till now he has
always stood against decent old buffers.'

redeeming task, as his father's biographer. To that end he published a full-dress biography of the seventeenth Earl of Derby, a minor politician and a dull man, which was received with respect if no great enthusiasm.

All this might seem marginal to our story, and a reader might by now have begun to tire of Randolph, as his friends so often did. But he wasn't only his father's son, he saw himself as his champion and chronicler. Randolph knew that he had wasted his life, but hoped that redemption might be possible. Churchill had agreed, with whatever inner misgivings, that Randolph should write his official 'Life', and make terms with publishers and newspapers, although dealing with this particular author was trickier than with most. When the editor of the *Sunday Telegraph* came to Churchill's house at East Bergholt to discuss the book, he found himself being chased round the dining room by Randolph brandishing a carving knife and shouting, 'Shits like you should have been shot by my father in 1940.'

Despite concerns on some sides, *Youth 1874–1900*, the first volume of the official life of Sir Winston S. Churchill, was published in October 1966, followed the next year by a second volume, *Young Statesman 1901–1914*; as it proved, the last under Randolph's name. Since *The Times* was one of Randolph's favourite whipping boys, it wasn't to be expected that the newspaper would greet his biography generously. Even so, the unsigned review which appeared, in a position which made it seem like an editorial, was almost malicious. 'Had there been open competition' for writing the biography, sneered the reviewer, 'Mr Randolph Churchill might not have come in first.' No doubt the same might once have been said of Winston Churchill when he wrote Lord Randolph's biography, but then Churchill was a young man of brilliant promise at the time, while Randolph could scarcely claim any such indulgence: cruel words to remind the reader that he was a man whose promise, such as it was, had long gone.

And the writer slyly emphasised the author's copious acknowledgement of help received, a broad hint of what was well known, that Randolph employed a team of researchers and ghostwriters like his father before him, in Randolph's case a crew of young men including Martin Gilbert and Michael Wolff. Even with their help Randolph didn't live to finish the third volume. He died in June 1968, less than four years after his father, at the age of only fifty-seven, worn out by ceaseless drinking, smoking and shouting. There were different contenders to take over the project, and a sharp tussle. Heinemann, the London publisher, first favoured Wolff, but then, to his bitter disappointment, decided on Little Winston, Randolph's son, who had recently written a quickie book with his father on the 1967 Six Day War. In a further twist, Lord Hartwell, as Michael Berry had just been created, whose *Daily Telegraph* had serial rights, proposed Lord Birkenhead, 'FE's' son and Randolph's companion in Croatia. But Houghton Mifflin, the American publisher, had the last word, and chose Gilbert.

Fifteen tons of Churchill's papers were transferred under police escort to the basement of the Bodleian Library in Oxford, where Gilbert was ensconced at Merton College, and he embarked on what would be a two-decade labour, and a somewhat erratic career of publishing the mighty work. Some volumes came out with disconcerting speed, with volumes four and five in successive years, some more slowly, seven years between the fifth and sixth; some were very long for the period covered, one volume of 988 pages for 1914–16, but some too short by comparison – 1167 pages for 1922–39. Some of the problems with the work, and its deficiencies, were explained by Gilbert many years later when he described the difficulties under which he had laboured. When Churchill signed his original contract for the *English-Speaking Peoples* he relinquished all royalties, but his huge payment was tax-free and maintained its value during the deflationary 1930s. By unhappy contrast, Gilbert's contract was for a fixed fee per volume, but in the rampantly inflationary 1970s, the value of these payments was sharply diminished; hence both the interrupted progress of the biography and the endless line of other books Gilbert turned out to keep himself afloat.

Before he died Randolph had witnessed another row almost more bitter than the dispute over Moran; a further indication of just how controversial Churchill's legacy remained. In January 1967 there was passing mention of a new play soon to be premiered in Germany and then performed in London, possibly with Richard Burton playing Churchill. There were no further details, but by the time of its summer premiere in Berlin a journalist could call it the most famous unperformed play in theatrical history. This was *Die Soldaten (The Soldiers)*, a 'drama-documentary' by the German playwright Rolf Hochhuth, set during the war, and with Churchill a central figure. It became the *cause célèbre* of the day, the more so when the National Theatre planned to put on *Soldiers*, or rather Kenneth Tynan, literary advisor at the National, wanted to.

In an alarmingly precocious career, which shot up in his twenties and fizzled out like a burnt rocket before his early death, Tynan exemplified Karl Kraus's definition: a journalist is someone with nothing to say and who knows how to say it. He combined a wonderful wit and a deadly gift for phrase with childish opinions, political and otherwise, and by this time, no longer an *enfant* but still *terrible*, he sought sensation and controversy; and they were readily provided by *Soldiers*. It proposed the grotesque conspiracy theory that Churchill had ordained the air crash at Gibraltar in July 1943, in which the Polish General Władysław Sikorski was killed, along with a number of others, including Victor Cazalet, a Tory MP and friend of Churchill's. Apart from anything else, no dark explanation was required, given the great danger of flying during the war, which Churchill had survived but many senior personages had not.

Less absurd was Hochhuth's portrayal of a heartless and brutal Churchill, egged on by 'the Prof' to bomb German cities and annihilate their inhabitants. This provoked an angry reply from several of Churchill's wartime intimates, among them Colville, Ian Jacob and Portal. They deplored the depiction of Churchill 'as a ruthless war leader' – which he surely was, and was admired for it – who deliberately 'destroyed women and children' – which was clearly true if the language of 'dehousing' and attacking civilian morale was stripped of its euphemism. 'From start to finish,' they wrote, 'Sir Winston Churchill was resolved to fight the war which was forced upon us with total determination but without more human suffering and loss of life on either side than was necessary for victory. The casualties involved in strategic and industrial bombing were for him a deplorable consequence of the strategy fully endorsed by the War Cabinet.' But the greatest possible 'loss of life' was what Harris boasted was his objective at the time and, although the protestors called the play a gross caricature, their own letter was also near caricature.

After the books came the effigies. In April 1966, another statue of Churchill was unveiled, in Washington. With somewhat blatant symbolism, the great man's figure stood legs apart, one foot on the territory of the British embassy, and one grounded in the American republic. To make the point even clearer, a little soil was added on either side, from his home at Chartwell and from the birthplace of Churchill's mother in Brooklyn.* The ceremony was performed in the presence of two of the children, Randolph and Mary, by Dean Rusk. The Secretary of State said that Churchill would always personify the Anglo-American commitment to human liberties and the rule of law, with 'the English-speaking peoples standing together', and added a tribute from President Johnson, acclaiming Churchill the 'brave ally, cherished friend and honoured citizen'.

And yet 'brave ally' wasn't at all how Johnson felt about Churchill's country at that time, or about his latest successor in Downing Street. Eisenhower had come to the funeral, but not Johnson, whose absence was never properly explained. He didn't even send his vice president, Hubert Humphrey, and the United States was represented instead by Earl Warren, the Chief Justice. Churchill had failed to attend Roosevelt's funeral twenty years before, but there was more to it this time. As Johnson escalated the war in Indochina, he had asked the British and Australian prime ministers to send troops to Vietnam, less as a serious military contribution than a gesture of solidarity. Sir Robert Menzies had been prime minister of Australia during the first two years of the World War before he was ousted by Labour in August 1941, returning to office in 1949 for a long premiership until 1966. 'Ming' (his nickname from the traditional Scottish pronunciation of his name) was devoted to the Empire, the 'mother country', the 'white Australia' policy' and to Churchill, even if Churchill never went so far as to visit Australia. His devotion was repaid by the accolade of Knight of the Thistle (the ancient Scottish equivalent of the Garter) in 1963, and the invitation to act as a pallbearer at Churchill's funeral, while he took Churchill's 'English-speaking peoples' seriously enough to comply with Johnson's request, so that an Australian battalion fought in Bien Hoa.

But Wilson did not oblige. Although he expressed sympathy with the American war, to the loud rage of much of his party, he adroitly avoided committing a single British soldier, to the silent rage of Washington. 'All we wanted was one goddam battalion of the Black Watch,' Dean Rusk, the Secretary of State, later told an English visitor.

---

* Or supposedly her birthplace: it later transpired that the house where she had grown up had been confused with the house where she was born.

Wilson was supported by at least one Conservative. Enoch Powell would later become an oracle to the Tory Right, for his various campaigns from opposition to Commonwealth immigration to hostility to the European Community, but his zealous obsession with national sovereignty was at least consistent. In 1943 he had attended the Casablanca conference as a staff officer, and come to believe 'that America's main war aim, and in the peace that followed its main foreign policy aim, was to extinguish British imperial and strategic power'. This was at least as logical an interpretation as 'Greeks to their Romans', and at the 1966 Conservative conference, when Powell was shadow defence spokesman, he told the Tories that the British should have nothing to do with the Americans and their doomed war in Vietnam.

Now the ghost of Munich haunted Johnson as it had haunted MacArthur in Korea and Eden at Suez. An American commitment to defend South Vietnam had begun under Kennedy, and Johnson as vice president had visited Saigon and implausibly hailed Ngo Dinh Diem, the South Vietnamese president, as 'the Churchill of Asia', although that didn't stop Washington giving a nod to the coup which deposed and then killed Diem at the beginning of November 1963, as it turned out only three weeks before Kennedy himself was shot. By then the number of American troops in Vietnam had increased to 14,500, but it was Johnson who turned an intervention into a full-scale war, a disaster and a tragedy. Johnson rapidly raised the number of troops until by 1968 it would be half a million.

And one impulse drove him on. 'Everything I knew about history,' he said, 'told me that if I got out of Vietnam and let Ho Chi Minh run through the streets of Saigon, then I'd be doing exactly what Chamberlain did in World War II. I'd be giving a big fat reward to aggression.' Nor would surrender in Vietnam bring peace, Johnson added, 'because we learned from Hitler at Munich that success only feeds the appetite of aggression'. An American defeat in Vietnam 'would encourage those who seek to conquer all free nations within their reach', he repeated. 'This is the dearest lesson of our time. From Munich until today we have learned that to yield to aggression brings only greater threats.' Just in case the point still wasn't clear, the administration sponsored a film called *Why Vietnam?* Running through it was a flickering image of Chamberlain at Munich.

He was seconded by the Secretary of State: 'aggression must be dealt with wherever it occurs', said Rusk, echoing what American strategists called the 'domino theory' in south-east Asia, with one country after another supposedly in danger of falling to Communism. 'The rearmament of the Rhineland was regarded as regrettable but not worth a shooting war. Yet after that came Austria, and after Austria came Czechoslovakia. Then Poland.' Henry Cabot Lodge Jr, who had been successively Republican senator from Massachusetts, American ambassador to the United Nations and Nixon's running mate in 1960, and was now ambassador to South Vietnam, insisted that there was 'a greater threat to start World War III if we don't go in. Can't we see the similarity to our own indolence at Munich?' And the administration was supported offstage by Eisenhower, who said that 'Munichs win nothing'. There was only one clear dissenting voice. 'I think that no episode, perhaps, in modern history has been more misleading than that of the Munich conference,' George Kennan told a Senate hearing on Vietnam, in the year of Churchill's death, but he went unheard.

However it might be with Munich, there was another echo from the past in Vietnam: Churchill's 'devastating, exterminating' attack by very heavy bombers was taken a step further. Although wartime bombing may have been less debated in America than England, the 1960s began and ended with two famous and very relevant American novels drawn from personal experience. Joseph Heller's *Catch-22* in 1961 was a dark comedy about an American bomber pilot who uses every strategy to avoid combat missions, and in 1968 *Slaughterhouse-Five* by Kurt Vonnegut was based on the author's memories of Dresden, where he had found himself, as a prisoner of war captured in the Ardennes offensive, during the fire-bombing of February 1945. When Vonnegut's book was published the Americans were bombing in a way that surpassed anything Harris had done: before the war ended more than twice the weight of bombs would have been dropped on Vietnam as was dropped on Germany in the last war.

While the war in Indo-China intensified, America was riven by its own great domestic drama, over civil rights. As Churchill had rightly suggested to Roosevelt more than twenty years before, the condition of the South, with segregation and the continuing violence against African Americans, put America in a weak place to preach justice and democracy elsewhere. Johnson heroically passed the 1965 Voting

Rights Act, but the Southern segregationists and their allies didn't give up without a fight. In the month that Churchill died, two celebrated Americans, James Baldwin and William Buckley, came to England to debate at the Cambridge Union, where Buckley said that if 'radical solutions' were needed to 'the Negro problem', threatening 'that civilization which we consider to be the faith of our fathers ... we will fight it as you were only recently called to do on the beaches and in the hills and on mountains and on landing grounds'. This deserves to be remembered as what may remain the most ludicrous invocation of Churchill on record.

Despite transatlantic tensions, Churchill's stature as an American idol only increased. If Dr McCluer of Westminster College had had one brainwave by inviting Churchill to Fulton for his 'iron curtain' speech, then McCluer's successor as head of Westminster had another. One day in 1961 Dr Robert Davidson read an article in *Life* about the strange and sad story of the Wren churches of the City of London. After the Great Fire of London in 1666 destroyed the City of London, including St Paul's Cathedral and nearly ninety mediaeval parish churches, the City had to be rebuilt, and by glorious coincidence the greatest architect England ever produced was then in his prime. Christopher Wren designed the new St Paul's, captured in that imperishable1940 photograph, and all of fifty-one parish churches. Less than half of these now survive, and the first culprit was the Church of England itself. Bowing to Mammon, the church pulled down four churches to make room for a larger Bank of England and Royal Exchange and other projects, before an Act of 1860 reduced the number of benefices, and the church took the opportunity to demolish ten more and sell off their sites in a shameful act of simony.

Then came the Blitz. Some churches were entirely destroyed, and some were burned out. A number were restored, from St Andrew-by-the-Wardrobe to St Lawrence Jewry. But there was one more remarkable case. Davidson conceived the idea of bringing the damaged building of St Mary Aldermanbury bodily to the middle of Missouri. 'We were younger then ... and crazy,' he said, and his crazy vision came true. More than 7000 stones were shipped from London to Fulton, where St Mary was rebuilt at a cost of over $2 million. Churchill lived to know of the project, and told Davidson that he was honoured by this 'imaginative concept. It may symbolise in the eyes of the

English-speaking peoples the ideals of Anglo-American association on which rest, now as before, so many of our hopes for peace and the future of mankind.'

And so in May 1969 the church was reconsecrated on the corner of Westminster Avenue and Seventh Street in Fulton, beautifully restored, refurbished and maintained, 'a corner of a foreign field that is forever England', and forever Churchill; a sanctuary of the English Church dedicated to the Virgin which is also consciously a shrine to one man. 'Fulton's finest hour,' one journalist called it, as a large crowd gathered to hear speeches. Mary Soames said that Missouri reminded her of 'our Cotswold region in England, with its lovely rolling hills', but she was upstaged by Mountbatten, who spoke at length about his friendship with Churchill to which he certainly owed so much.

If at Fulton and elsewhere a cult was taking shape, with sacred texts and shrines, there were still dissenters. One was Robert Rhodes James, no radical but a former clerk of the House of Commons and a future Tory MP, who had written an unsparing account of the Gallipoli campaign. In 1970 he published *Churchill: A Study in Failure, 1900–1939*, the first book appearing since the funeral to offer a well-researched, thoughtful and persuasive critique. Randolph died before he could read it, but had already disowned both book and author in advance, as Rhodes James regretfully mentioned in his preface. It remains one of the better books about Churchill, and an antidote to the hagiographies, all the more valuable because it isn't written out of political animosity, and its case, summed up in its title, is unarguable: for all his brilliance and dynamism, Churchill could only have been accounted a failure if he had died on his sixty-fifth birthday in November 1939.

And yet Rhodes James's book set a pattern, by which serious critical dissection of Churchill's life would make little impression on public consciousness compared with reverence. Far fewer people read that book than watched on television when a mighty statue of Churchill was unveiled on 1 November 1973. Years before, when David Eccles, a Tory minister, was telling Churchill about plans for Parliament Square, Churchill pointed to a spot and said, 'That's where my statue will go,' and so it did. Sculpted by Ivor Roberts-Jones and standing twelve feet high, it was inspired by a photograph of Churchill in his greatcoat picking his way through the rubble of the burned-out

Commons after it had been bombed in May 1941. Roberts-Jones's first model of the head was said to look a little too much like Mussolini and was reworked. The Queen declined the honour of unveiling it, which she thought should go to Clementine, Baroness Spencer-Churchill as she had been created in 1965, but the Queen was present among the great throng. There would be many more statues and busts of Churchill, from New Orleans to Jerusalem, but this one, towering and glowering towards the Palace of Westminster, would acquire a life and significance of its own.

Also present was Edward Heath, the prime minister, and 'A Study in Failure' could have applied to his government. After the long Tory reign ended in 1964, Labour under Wilson tried but failed to cure economic sclerosis, and Heath's Conservative government of 1970–4 had no more success, nor Labour again under Wilson and then Callaghan, until his government fell in 1979. Whichever party was in office, the country seemed increasingly ungovernable. The Conservatives would be in office for all but eleven of the first forty-two years after Churchill retired, but they were as perplexed as Labour by his legacy. Heath was also the last prime minister to have seen active service in Churchill's war, as a major commanding a battery from Normandy to the Rhine. This included one experience he had never mentioned until he published his otherwise leaden memoirs in 1998, and described the grim task he had been given of commanding a firing squad which executed a young Polish soldier convicted of rape.

He was also the last prime minister to have served Churchill in Parliament. As a whip, Heath sometimes had to ferret Churchill out from dinner parties in time for the ten o'clock division, and he was invited to Chartwell nine times between 1957 and 1961, though maybe as a lame duck, on whom Clementine had taken pity. He never married or appeared to have any interest in women. On one occasion at Chartwell Heath incongruously – and expensively – found himself playing poker with Aristotle Onassis; on another he and the rest of the party were whisked off without warning by light aircraft to Newmarket to see a horse of Churchill's run.

Visiting Washington, Heath presented President Nixon with a set of *The Second World War*, setting what would become a ritual pattern. But that book was little help during his short tenure in Downing Street, when Heath found himself beset by woes – and haunted by

Churchill's ghost. Unions were more aggressive than ever, encouraged by the appeasement towards them which Churchill's peacetime government had so enthusiastically begun. Arthur Scargill, the miners' leader, tried to settle the score at last with Churchill and the General Strike, pushing Heath into a confrontation which ended his government in early 1974.

Graver still was one other question which was supposed to have been resolved by Lloyd George and Churchill a half century before, but which now erupted again. 'Then came the Great War,' Churchill had written: 'Every institution, almost, in the world was strained. Great Empires have been overturned. The whole map of Europe has been changed ... But as the deluge subsides and the waters fall short, we see the dreary steeples of Fermanagh and Tyrone emerging once again. The integrity of their quarrel is one of the few institutions that have been unaltered in the cataclysm which has swept the world.' The integrity of their quarrel endured over the years since the partition of 1920 and the creation of a Free State comprising the twenty-six southern counties and a Northern Ireland statelet, which exploded into violence in 1969, more than half a century after Lloyd George and Churchill were supposed to have solved the problem. Over the next quarter-century a reborn 'Provisional IRA' killed British soldiers, judges, politicians and ordinary Protestants, more than 2000 in total, from Jean McConville, a widowed mother of ten, murdered in 1972 on the orders of Gerry Adams, then leader of the IRA in Belfast, to one of the most famous men of his age.

One by one the Churchillians had left the stage. Cherwell died in 1957 and Brendan – by now Lord – Bracken the following year, with the *Financial Times* as his most reputable legacy, its offices in a new building called Bracken House. Beaverbrook followed in 1964 two weeks after his eighty-fifth birthday. Of the three dubious leaders Churchill had promoted, 'Monty' would live to 1976 and the age of eighty-eight, 'Bomber' Harris until 1984 and ninety-one. None had been more prominent in later years than Mountbatten. In 1969 he had starred in his own production. 'A Man for the Century' was a biographical documentary series which from its title onwards was an exercise in self-glorification egregious even by his standards, and he had appointed himself unofficial counsellor to the young Prince of Wales in matters romantic as well as constitutional.

In the summer of 1979 he was holidaying as usual in County Sligo when his small boat was blown up by an IRA bomb; his fourteen-year-old grandson, a fifteen-year-old local boy and an elderly woman were also killed. With all his shortcomings, Mountbatten had been one of the leaders of a war which defeated fascist and National Socialist tyranny, a war in which militant Irish republicans had done all they could to help Hitler, whom Gerard Adams, Gerry's father, much admired. The bullets which killed McConville and the explosive which killed Mountbatten were paid for in part, as was all the IRA's weaponry, by money openly collected in the United States, and Mountbatten's death was cheered in many an Irish bar from Boston to San Francisco.

If that problem baffled Heath and his successors, in one crucial respect Heath repudiated Churchill, by detaching himself from Washington and turning towards Europe. In 1967, while he was Leader of the Opposition, Heath had lectured at Harvard, and his otherwise forgotten text contained one riveting phrase, about 'the so-called special relationship'. He was the first prime minister openly to challenge that dubious concept, and would be the last. By 1969, de Gaulle had resigned, and his departure opened the way for the United Kingdom to 'join Europe'. In 1973 the United Kingdom joined the EEC, and it seemed that the British had now irrevocably chosen Europe rather than Churchill's open sea.

Coming as it did less than ten years after his death, Churchill's centenary in November 1974 passed with comparatively little ado. The Cambridge historian Henry Pelling published what remains one of the better single-volume lives of Churchill, and Martin Gilbert and Elizabeth Longford both produced picture-books telling his story in photographs and paintings. There was also a deluxe four-volume edition of *The Collected Essays of Sir Winston Churchill*, a grandiose name for his journalism, handsomely printed and bound but with no critical apparatus or background information. These volumes made no attempt to distinguish between the journalism under Churchill's name actually written by him and the many pieces which were ghost-written, such as his 'Riddells' for the *News of the World*, but then serious critical attention to his writing had barely begun. Still more imposing, and definitely more scholarly, was the eight-volume, 8917-page *Complete Speeches 1897–1963*, edited by Rhodes James, who wrote a valuable fifty-page introduction, and who, with his assistants, provided short settings for each speech.

These books are valuable in more senses than one: in 2020, a set of the *Collected Essays* could be bought for £950, and one of the *Complete Speeches* for £3500. These were not books for the common reader with an intelligent interest in Churchill, but holy talismans to be acquired and cherished by rich men – and they were almost always men – who bowed down at Churchill's memory. There were a few hecklers or dissenters, but they had little effect: 1974 also saw the premiere of *The Churchill Play* by Howard Brenton, a young left-wing playwright. Churchill was seen returning from the grave in a concentration camp named after him, a bizarre enough conceit, although it caused less of a stir than Hochhuth's *Soldiers*. Productions of either play have since been few and far between.

A centenary was in any case bound to be overshadowed by the political dramas of 1974, with the fall of the Heath government and two British general elections in succession, and the only presidential resignation in American history. This last was the final outcome of a clumsy attempt to burgle the Democratic headquarters in the Watergate building during the 1972 election, when Nixon easily defeated George McGovern, and the still clumsier cover-up that followed, culminating in the desertion of Nixon by his political supporters and his resignation in August, to be succeeded by Gerald Ford, his vice president. One of the Watergate burglars or bunglers was Gordon Liddy, who was later imprisoned but said that he had been consoled by Churchill's words, 'Never give in, never, never, never, never – in things great or small, large or petty.' Looking back himself on 'the very big year' of 1972, Nixon turned for solace to the same source: 'Winston Churchill once wrote that strong leaders usually do the big things well,' he said, 'but they foul up on small things and then the small things become great. I should have read that before Watergate.' Nixon later wrote a preface for *The Wit and Wisdom of Winston Churchill*, although neither wit nor wisdom had ever been among the former president's most salient characteristics.

All this was followed with rapt attention by the British as well as the Americans. Louis Heren had joined *The Times* as a fifteen-year-old office boy, served in the war as an infantry officer, rejoined the paper to cover numerous conflicts, then became Washington correspondent, before returning as deputy editor. Three days after Nixon's resignation

Heren wrote a column advising the prime minister how to deal with the new president, by shaking off Churchillian illusions and 'British reluctance to accept the diminished status of the post-imperial era', echoing what Tizard had said a quarter-century before. And he quoted Henry Kissinger, the mephistophelean figure who had risen from academic life to become Secretary of State and Nixon's consigliere. Ten years earlier, Kissinger had observed how Great Britain 'has been claiming influence out of proportion to its power'. Washington believed that the British place was in Europe, and that it 'should be treated as simply one or other European country'. Heren stated baldly that 'Mr Wilson must realise the "special relationship" is dead'. He might as well have been writing in the void.

Not that everyone was in thrall to Churchill's aura, including his own descendants. As well as a son with Pamela, Randolph had a daughter by his second marriage to June Osborne. Arabella Churchill, given the name of Marlborough's sister, mistress to James II, was born in 1949. She can be seen as a baby girl in a painting of her grandfather Sir Winston with his family in the National Portrait Gallery, and was on the cover of *Life*, described as a potential bride for Prince Charles, the queen's eldest son. When she grew up she didn't become Princess of Wales, but worked for a time in television and for a charity. Every year, Norfolk, Virginia, home of the NATO Allied command, held an International Azalea Festival and a member state was invited to send an 'Azalea queen'. In 1971 Arabella was chosen, but refused to go, instead writing a letter to *Rolling Stone* to say that she believed in peace and love and hated the war in Vietnam. Her half-brother Little Winston was 'absolutely furious with me,' Arabella recalled. 'My mother was saying "Darling, can't I just say you've had a nervous breakdown?" The whole thing was a nightmare. I felt I had let the family down.' She later led a vagabond life, had a daughter and a son by different men, and died of pancreatic cancer at only fifty-eight, in 2007. Her mother had died by her own hand in 1980. June's death meant that, in all, suicides close to Churchill included a brother-in-law, a former stepfather, a daughter's estranged lover, a former daughter-in-law, a son-in-law and a daughter. 'Greatness' could exact a heavy price.

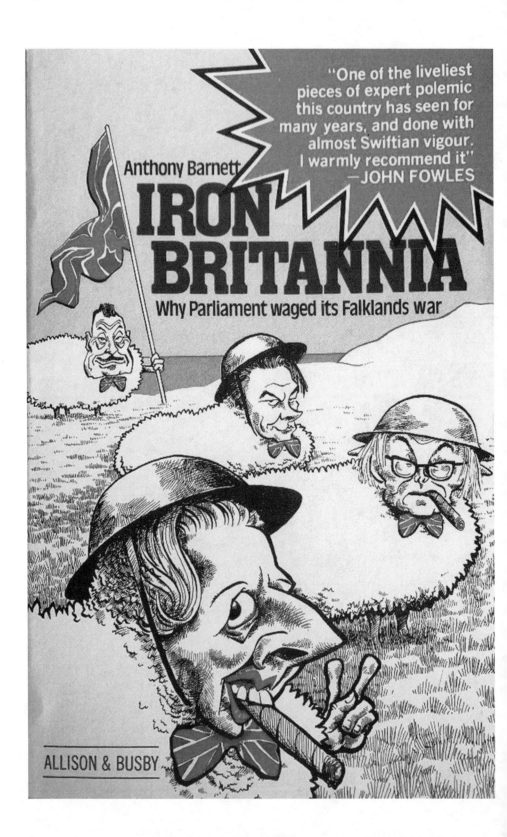

Anthony Barnett

IRON BRITANNIA

Why Parliament waged its Falklands war

"One of the liveliest pieces of expert polemic this country has seen for many years, and done with almost Swiftian vigour. I warmly recommend it"
—JOHN FOWLES

ALLISON & BUSBY

19

'Great as Churchill'
Luxembourg 1979

If the 1970s were years of frustration, decline and defeat, a dramatic change came at the end of the decade, personified by Margaret Thatcher's arrival at 10 Downing Street in May 1979 and Ronald Reagan's in the White House in January 1981: two people who would be acclaimed for having changed history before the 1980s ended with the fall of the 'iron curtain from Stettin to Trieste'. And both invoked Churchill as no leaders of their countries had done before, while Thatcher would be compared with him as no other prime minister had been before. She had briefly met him, she would be proud to sit 'where Winston sat', and she would win a military victory resonating loudly with memories of the 'Former Naval Person', amid a crescendo of what one critic decried as 'Churchillism'.

If the 1960 presidential election had been the first at which a candidate claimed Churchill's inheritance, it was very far from the last. Reagan quoted Churchill in his first inaugural, hung a poster of Churchill in the White House, and filled his administration with devotees of Churchill. By 1990 Christopher Hitchens, an English exile in America, would write an essay on 'The Churchill Cult',* and he wasn't alone in noticing how by this time Churchill was seen in America 'as a *chevalier sans peur et sans reproche*', in Michael Howard's words, 'surpassing any comparable American figure ... in his goodness and greatness.' We have seen the early days of this veneration, with 'American idolatry' of Churchill remarked on in 1952, an idolatry which had increased with every worshipful book or television programme. But it reached a new level during the Reagan years.

'There's a Me Society down at Cambridge,' the Victorian versifier J.K. Stephen wrote, mocking the vogue for Ruskin and Browning

---

* In *Blood, Class and Nostalgia: Anglo-America Ironies*, 1990.

Societies. Churchill's shade could have said 'There are Me Societies all over America'. Churchill Societies sprang up from sea to shining sea, dozens and then hundreds of them, where devotees held dinners, drank toasts and exchanged the great man's quips and rhetorical flourishes. Their members were natural customers for Chartwell Booksellers, a handsome emporium in the lobby of the Park Avenue Plaza Building between Park and Madison Avenues, which opened in 1984 as the only such shop specialising in all things Churchillian, and which is still flourishing four decades on.

Although this didn't go unnoticed, there was an unanswered or even unasked question: why *did* so many Americans make an idol of a foreign politician, rather than 'any comparable American figure'? In Washington there are memorials to Washington and Jefferson, a Lincoln Museum and Library and a Wilson Center, but no Washington or Jefferson, Lincoln or Wilson Societies meet across the country, nor FDR Societies either. Part of the answer might have been found in the 'peculiar institution' of American political history, with its complexities and ironies. When the Irish speak of 'civil war politics', they mean the way that for most of the hundred years after the inception of the Free State in 1922 the two larger parties which governed the country, the Band of Gaels and the Soldiers of Destiny (Fine Gael and Fianna Fáil in the 'first language' of the country if little spoken), descend from the Free Staters and Republicans who had fought a savage little civil war in 1922–3.

But America also has its Civil War politics. More recently Americans adopted what to Europeans seems a baffling political colour scheme, 'red states' and 'blue states' (how did the Republicans ever become 'red', the colour of radicalism and revolution?), but for a hundred years after the Civil War it should really have been 'blue against grey'. The Republicans were the party of the Union, for which all but one of its presidential candidates in the forty years after the Civil War had fought. Lincoln was the greatest of Republican presidents, and Lincoln Day the most sacred day in the party's calendar.*

And for those hundred years after Appomattox the Democrats were the party of the Confederacy, the Solid South, and segregation. At

---

* It was in a Lincoln Day speech to a Republican ladies' club in Wheeling, West Virginia, in 1950 that Senator McCarthy claimed to have in his hand a list of Communists working in the State Department, and changed American history.

the 1944 presidential election it wasn't the Democrats and Roosevelt, for all his lofty rhetoric of 'four freedoms' and the 'right of all peoples to choose the form of government under which they will live', who had a civil rights plank in their platform, it was the Republicans and Dewey. Black Americans mostly voted Republican, when they could vote at all (in the South, blacks had very little say as to 'the form of government' under which they lived), and as late as 1952, when the pious liberal Adlai Stevenson was Democratic presidential candidate, his running mate was the segregationist John Sparkman of Alabama.

Then came the great role reversal. When Johnson pushed through his civil rights legislation he said that the Democrats had lost the South for a generation. He was too optimistic: they'd lost the South forever. And Nixon seized on this with his 'southern strategy', so that the party of Lincoln became the party of the Confederate states he had defeated. It was awkward for a party which was moving to the Right and capitalising on white resentment to venerate Lincoln (or even Eisenhower, the president who had sent Federal troops to Little Rock to enforce desegregation of a high school). A further awkward-ness was that, while patriotic conservatives might have wished to revere the presidents who had led the United States in two great wars, Wilson and Roosevelt were both Democrats.

And so Churchill fitted the bill admirably. The numerous Americans who joined Churchill Societies, collected Churchill's books and Churchilliana, and lapped up adoring hagiographies like William Manchester's *The Path of the Lion,* weren't all nativist reactionaries, but it may be safely supposed that more of them tended to be conserva-tive than liberal. At their Churchill dinners they could recite his wartime speeches while overlooking his youthful radicalism, or his advocacy of universal health care in 1945 (and overlooking also the fact that, ever since he met Bourke Cockran in New York in 1895, Churchill had felt a sentimental affiliation with the Democrats!).

Moreover, he served his own cause. Churchill's cloudy notions of 'the English-speaking peoples' and a 'special relationship', however empty in practice when it came to American policy, proved very useful for his American devotees, albeit indirectly. In the finest hour of 1940–41 Americans had gazed admiringly at England from afar, even if with Blum's 'mixture of shame and relief' that they weren't them-selves at war. But when Churchill said that his country was 'fighting by ourselves alone but not for ourselves alone', and spoke as though the United States was a 'virtual ally', he salved American consciences, and made it easier for them to believe that his struggle had been their struggle also. In the fullness of time, as Americans devoured all things Churchillian and read books and watched movies about that heroic moment, they could almost persuade themselves that it was their soldiers who had beaten a fighting retreat to Dunkirk, their pilots who had won the Battle of Britain, their sailors who had sunk the *Bismarck*. And such glorious if vicarious memories were especially helpful after the humiliating final departure from Vietnam in 1975, as balm to salve the pain of that humiliation.

In England there was no need of such fantasy, but there as well history was misappropriated and misused, and inconvenient truths forgotten. Both Thatcher and Reagan had lived through Churchill's war. When it began she was a schoolgirl and he was already a Hollywood star if not quite of the first rank, although he was admired in *King's Row*, and acquired the nickname 'Gipper' from the title role in a movie about a football coach. Their experiences of war had been at a remove. In the three decades from 1960, four out of seven presidents had previously served in the United States Navy in the Pacific campaign: Nixon creditably, Kennedy, Ford and Bush the Elder heroically. By contrast, Reagan joined the Reserve before the war, but his eyesight precluded active service, and he spent the war making movies, either for Hollywood (like *Bedtime for Bonzo* and *Cattle Queen of Montana*) or for the Army Air Force and war bond drives. He never left America in wartime although, just as King George IV persuaded himself that he had fought at Waterloo, the Gipper came to believe that he had visited a liberated concentration camp.

At the 1945 election, 'the very youthful Miss M.H. Roberts, daughter of Alderman A. Roberts', as a local paper called her, had spoken in praise of Churchill, insisting that the country should not 'lose the only remaining man who had the world's confidence'. She was then a nineteen-year-old Oxford undergraduate, and a civilian. Although she would make much of her frugal upbringing as the daughter of a Methodist shopkeeper, she was understandably reticent about the Alderman Roberts's strong support for Chamberlain and his appeasement policy, and the way that she had herself evaded wartime service. When she was offered a place at Somerville, the Oxford women's college, to go up in 1943, it was without the scholarship which would have been helpful for her needy family. She could have tried again for the scholarship, but by going to Oxford a year later she might have been liable to call-up into one of the women's services, limited conscription for which had been introduced in 1941. And so, unlike Diana, Sarah and Mary Churchill or Princess Elizabeth, Margaret Roberts never wore uniform in Churchill's war.

Unable in those benighted days to join the all-male Oxford Union, Miss Roberts became President of the Oxford University Conservative Association, and an assiduous attender of party conferences. By the time she met Churchill, at a Conservative youth rally in the summer of 1950, where she proposed a vote of thanks to him, she had already stood as the Tory candidate for Dartford at the general election held the previous February, aged only twenty-four. Four years after Churchill's 'iron curtain' speech, Miss Roberts told the voters of Dartford, 'We believe in the democratic way of life. *If we serve the ideal faithfully, with tenacity of purpose, we have nothing to fear from Russian Communism.*' Those were brave and prescient words at the very moment when the mendacious demagogue Senator Joseph McCarthy had just begun to tell frightened Americans that they had everything to fear from Communism. While campaigning, the candidate had to go through the usual ordeal of pressing flesh and kissing babies, and she had enough of her Methodist upbringing to dislike visiting pubs: she never went into one on her own in all her life. But she was persuaded to visit a funfair in Orpington, where she stopped at one booth to consult a fortune-teller. In a moment uncomfortably reminiscent of the witches in *Macbeth*, this soothsayer told Miss Roberts, 'You will be great – great as Churchill.' That comparison would be made again very many years later.

By 1959, Margaret Thatcher – as she now was, having married a businessman and given birth to twin children – had entered Parliament, and she sat near the aged Churchill for five years. She ascended the ladder, as a junior minister, then a cabinet minister in Heath's unhappy government of 1970–74, and by early 1975, while many Tory MPs recognised that Heath was a failure and a liability, she was the only one with the steel to challenge him for the leadership, and win it. Weeks after her victory, Reagan visited London. He'd joined the Republicans, become a popular public figure, been elected and re-elected Governor of California, and was now thinking of running for president, but neither Harold Wilson nor James Callaghan, the

Prime Minister and Foreign Secretary, could be bothered to see him. His name may perhaps have meant more to Thatcher: as a girl she had been a constant moviegoer, and likely remembered Reagan in *Dark Victory*, the Bette Davis weepie which had once been Churchill's rather incongruous choice to show to the typists and servants at 10 Downing Street.

At any rate, she welcomed Reagan. And at their first meeting in April 1975, Winston Churchill was present. 'Little Winston', as his grandfather had called him, was now Winston S. Churchill MP, having been elected in 1970 as Member for Stretford in Manchester, not far from his grandfather's seat sixty-five years before. His role at that meeting was purely symbolic, and he was there as a kind of mascot. That didn't prove a happy augury for little Winston's career, but it did set the tone for the two leaders. 'Churchillian rhetoric,' as Richard Aldous has noted, 'would become a consistent and well-choreographed feature of Reagan and Thatcher's shared public performances,' although this led some observers to mistake the rhetoric for something more solid.

By the time Ronald Reagan was elected president in November 1980, Thatcher had been in Downing Street for eighteen months and was ready to welcome him. She had spoken of her pride in succeeding distinguished premiers, 'and of course the great Winston'. In the October after she became prime minister, she gave the Winston Churchill Memorial Lecture in Luxembourg, entitled 'Europe – the obligations of liberty': 'I have chosen liberty,' she said, 'because it is a theme closely connected with the name Churchill and crucial to my own thinking about politics. I have chosen Europe because I am in Luxembourg, a meeting place of the Council of Ministers and of the European Parliament, the seat of the European Court, and the home of Josef Bech, one of the Founding Fathers of the Community. I have chosen the problems because problems are always with us.' She spoke more truly than she knew. 'Europe' would always be an insoluble problem for Thatcher, which would bring her career to an end and would then poison her party for decades to come.

Within two years of taking office Thatcher's fortunes had fallen low, with unemployment rapidly increasing, civil disorder, and her policies denounced by whole phalanxes of academic economists. Then she was rescued by events, as Churchill had been before her. In the space of three years, she won three outright victories, in a war, in an election, and in an industrial confrontation, and she remained at Number 10 throughout the 1980s. Since Reagan was at the White House from 1981 to 1989, the decade was inevitably defined by these two Churchillians, although that didn't mean that all was mutual admiration between them, or that there was unfailing co-operation between their countries.

At the time of Reagan's death, the veteran English journalist Sir Harold Evans, long exiled in America, would claim that 'the relationship between Thatcher and President Reagan was closer even than Churchill and Roosevelt'. This was a double misunderstanding. The 1980s was the very time when historians began seriously to examine and deconstruct the wartime relationship between Churchill and Roosevelt, and to see just how fraught it had often been. And although Thatcher liked Reagan personally, and shared his free-market and anti-Communist convictions, she had no illusions about him. Not long after the inauguration, Thatcher and Lord Carrington, her Foreign Secretary, were talking over a drink one evening in Downing Street, when the conversation turned to the new president. 'Peter,' she said, tapping the side of her skull, 'there's nothing there.' Their friendship would soon be severely strained.

Albeit indirectly, and most ironically, Reagan was helped to power by another of Churchill's legacies, the 1953 coup in Tehran which had overthrown the democratic 'Messy Duck' government and restored the Shah. Since then his rule had grown ever more brutal, corrupt and insanely grandiose, until 1979 when Eisenhower's and Churchill's dark deed exploded in the faces of their successors. The Shah was overthrown by Ayatollah Khomeini, a Muslim cleric, to popular rejoicing, at first at any rate, before Khomeini created a cruel reactionary theocracy. In November youthful zealots invaded the American embassy compound in Tehran and took fifty-two Americans hostage; the following spring an attempted *coup de main* by President Jimmy Carter's administration to rescue the hostages ended in embarrassing fiasco. Reagan secured the Republican nomination, and won a landslide victory in the November presidential election, when the Iranian humiliation – and the ghosts of 1953 – helped defeat Carter.

In his inaugural speech in January 1981, Reagan inevitably, if a little quaintly, invoked the sacred name: 'To paraphrase Winston Churchill, I did not take the oath I've just taken with the intention of presiding over the dissolution of the world's strongest economy.' This was an odd choice for an American from the lucky dip of hallowed Churchillian phrases. That November 1942 speech had, as one writer put it, made it clear 'to the Americans, that Churchill did not believe the Empire's days were numbered,' even though they plainly were, in no small part thanks to him, and to American profit. But Reagan was above trivial detail. After he was shot by a would-be assassin, he neatly quoted Churchill from his hospital bed: 'There is no more exhilarating feeling than being shot without result.'

And that was only the end of the beginning. In his State of the Union address of January 1982, Reagan reminded Congress that 'from this podium, Winston Churchill asked the free world to stand together against the onslaught of aggression', and called for 'a recognition of what the Soviet empire is about ... Winston Churchill, in negotiating with the Soviets, observed that they respect only strength and resolve in their dealings with other nations.' Six months later on Memorial Day, the president continued: 'Winston Churchill said of those he knew in World War II, they seem to be the only young men who could laugh and fight at the same time.' In London only days after that, he told Parliament, 'Sir Winston Churchill refused to accept the inevitability of war or even that it was imminent,' and further quoted the sacred authority, '"I do not believe that Soviet Russia desires war. What they desire is the fruits of war and the indefinite expansion of their power and doctrines. But what we have to consider here today while time remains, is the permanent prevention of war and the establishment of conditions of freedom and democracy as rapidly as possible in all countries."'

Fine words, but what did they mean in practice? Apart from the sheer exorbitance of trying to bring freedom and democracy to the whole world, and the question of whether the United States was equipped for the task, this supposed yet again that Soviet Russia could be compared with the Third Reich. That was certainly the view of a group of men and women who would have been happy to be called Churchillians, but who became known as neoconservatives. Many of them had long before begun their political lives on the Left, often the far Left as Trotskyists or Stalinists, but had from the 1960s moved rightwards. Although neoconservatism would later be particularly associated with Israel and the Middle East, its original inspiration was the Soviet threat and the dangers of the policy called detente being pursued by Carter, which to its critics meant appeasement. In 1977, Norman Podhoretz, one of the neocon founding fathers, decried 'the latest culture of appeasement', and said that 'the parallels with England in 1937 are here'. In case that wasn't clear enough, Podhoretz's essay was accompanied by a drawing of Jimmy Carter carrying an umbrella. This would prove to be a serious misreading both of history and of the contemporary situation, but not before these anti-appeasers had made much mischief.

Few of that early generation of neocons were more prominent than Jeane Kirkpatrick, a youthful socialist who had seen the error of her ways, a professor of politics who had written contemptuously of 'the mirage of a peaceful alternative to war', which was really a defeat, and added 'The classic textbook example is Neville Chamberlain's "peace in our time" compromise at Munich.' She was also the author of the 'Kirkpatrick doctrine'. She wisely derided the idea (than which none 'holds greater sway in the mind of educated Americans') that 'it is possible to democratise governments, anytime and anywhere, under any circumstances', but from this plausible basis, she then distinguished between totalitarian countries, such as Russia and China, which must be opposed resolutely, and merely 'authoritarian' regimes, with whom Washington could do business. A prime example of the latter was the military junta which had taken power in the Argentine in 1975, which was now led by General Leopoldo Galtieri, and which in its merely 'authoritarian' way tortured and 'disappeared' tens of thousands of its opponents, sometimes by throwing them out of helicopters above the sea. 'Authoritarian' became more than an academic point after Kirkpatrick was appointed ambassador to the United Nations by Reagan, and in March 1981 Galtieri visited Washington to be warmly received by the administration. Emboldened by that warmth, Argentine forces invaded the Falkland Islands in April 1982.

By now the last rays of twilight flickered over what had been a British Empire on which the sun never set (or on which the blood never dried). At the 1945 general election, Margaret Roberts 'was very fervent in her determination to stand by the Empire', it was reported: 'The Empire must never be liquidated.' Since then she had come a long way, and the empire had gone its own way, but there was one late-imperial problem she inherited as prime minister. When Churchill wrote that the career of Cecil Rhodes had 'consequences which have yet to run their course', his words were truer than he could have known. In the 1890s, that scoundrelly adventurer had by force and fraud created a colony north of the Transvaal named 'Rhodesia'. By the 1960s, after forlorn attempts by London to create a Central African Federation, the adjacent lands of Northern Rhodesia, now called Zambia, and Nyasaland became independent states under what passed for majority rule. Southern Rhodesia remained a colony, dropping the 'Southern', with six million Africans ruled by 270,000 white settlers. In 1965 their leader, Ian Smith, a wartime fighter pilot, declared 'unilateral' independence. A savage guerrilla war ensued, waged against Smith's regime by African insurgents, while Rhodesia remained a thorn in the flesh of successive London governments until Thatcher sent a new – the last – Governor of Southern Rhodesia to pull it out, or spirit it away.

Like Churchill's other son-in-law Duncan Sandys, Christopher Soames was 'a good European'. Having lost his seat in Parliament, where he had been his father-in-law's right hand man, he served as British ambassador in Paris, and then in Brussels as the first British vice-president of the European Commission. When Thatcher took office she brought Lord Soames, as he now was, into the Cabinet, and sent him to Rhodesia to extricate the British from this last colonial tangle. In practice that meant following the advice Senator George Aiken had earlier given his own country embroiled in the Vietnam War: Declare victory and get out. With some diplomatic prestidigitation by Soames, this last colony became the independent state of Zimbabwe under 'majority rule', although the subsequent electoral victory of Robert Mugabe was very much not what Thatcher and Soames wanted, and the appallingly bloody, incompetent and corrupt decades in which Mugabe would misgovern his country and reduce it to starving penury almost made colonialism look good.

Still, it was more than a nice irony that this final stage in that 'liquidation of the British Empire' over which Churchill had sworn not to preside – and the young Thatcher had abhorred! – should be accomplished by Sir Winston's son-in-law. Not that it did Soames much good. When told that a man was a patriot, the Emperor Francis I of Austria replied, 'But is he a patriot for me?' Margaret Thatcher may have proclaimed her devotion to 'the great Winston', but she was no Churchillian for the Churchills. Not long after his return to London, Soames was summarily dropped from the government. He complained bitterly that he wouldn't have dismissed a gamekeeper in the way she dismissed him, while she said later that Soames had reacted as if he had been sacked by a housemaid.

Before that, little Winston had been dropped from the Tory team for voting against Rhodesian sanctions, and although he remained an MP from 1970 to 1997 he never held office. He did, however, display a new version of his grandfather's prejudices, supporting the apartheid regime in South Africa and railing against 'the relentless flow' of Asian immigrants, all the while entertaining the tabloids with his eventful private life. Churchill's other political grandson fared no better: Nicholas Soames, son of Mary, was elected as Member for Crawley in 1983, but he, too, was never offered ministerial office by Thatcher, serving instead as a PPS or unpaid assistant to successive ministers until he was finally made a junior minister two years after Thatcher departed.

If Rhodesia was all too glaring a problem when Thatcher became prime minister, then the invasion of the Falklands by Argentine forces on 2 April 1982 was quite unforeseen, if not necessarily unforeseeable. Either way, this was to be Thatcher's finest hour in the eyes of her admirers – and it was almost superfluous to mention Churchill. He had been First Lord of the Admiralty in December 1914 when Graf Spee's fleet was destroyed off the Falklands, and again in December 1939 when the cruiser *Admiral Graf Spee* had been caught near the islands and driven to meet her end in the River Plate. And now, Thatcher's biographer John Campbell would write, every senior politician concerned was sure 'that no male prime minister, except perhaps Churchill', would have ordered a task force to sail and then fight to reconquer the islands. This was duly, and astonishingly, accomplished. British troops entered Port Stanley on 14 June to accept the Argentine surrender, although not before the Royal Navy had lost three ships: at one point Argentine bombs better aimed or with better fuses might even have led to defeat, instead of the glorious victory of which Thatcher could boast.

In all this the prime minister had by no means received unstinting American support. Sir Nicholas Henderson had recently retired after a distinguished diplomatic career, but Thatcher shrewdly brought him back as ambassador to Washington, where he was invaluable during a conflict which cast yet more strange light on supposed Anglo-American amity. From the first, Henderson was astonished by how lukewarm the Americans were about Galtieri's aggression. Astonishment turned into outrage when he heard that Kirkpatrick had dined at the Argentine Embassy on the night of the invasion. As Henderson said, it was as if he had joined the Iranians for tea on the day that the Americans were taken hostage in Tehran. General Alexander Haig, Reagan's first Secretary of State and another man who liked to spout Churchillian phrases, visited Buenos Aires to seek a compromise, and pleaded with London to make peace.

Even when fighting began, the Americans shilly-shallied. The low point came when the United States joined Great Britain in vetoing a Security Council resolution demanding an immediate cease-fire, only for Kirkpatrick immediately to announce that this was a mistake and that she should have abstained: 'Not only had the United States sought to double-cross Britain; it had done so incompetently.' Henderson recalled that, after the Argentines were routed, Reagan impressed on the prime minister the need for magnanimity, a word he 'kept trying to put in Mrs Thatcher's vocabulary, quite unsuccessfully'. Indeed, of the lines from Churchill's 'Moral of the work', she was by nature always more disposed to 'In Defeat: Defiance' than 'In Victory: Magnanimity'. And the episode rankled. Years later, after both leaders had retired, Henderson said privately, 'If I reported to you what Mrs Thatcher really thought about President Reagan, it would damage Anglo-American relations.'

As to the larger consequences of that strange war, they were happier for the Argentines than for the British. Galtieri was deposed following the defeat and his hateful junta was ejected soon after, but the British were elated by their triumph. The echoes from 1940 were deafening: 'an island people, the cruel seas, a British defeat, Anglo-Saxon democracy challenged by a dictator and finally the quintessentially Churchillian posture – we were down but we were not out,' as Anthony Barnett put it in his radical philippic *Iron Britannia* published shortly after the war. Its cover was a cartoon of Thatcher in a Tommy's steel helmet, smoking a cigar and making a V-sign. But then her admirers said the same with no hint of irony: the radical-turned-rightwing journalist Paul Johnson compared her with Churchill's 'gigantic and leonine' personality. Behind Thatcher in that cartoon was the Labour Leader of the Opposition, also helmeted. And who should that be, but none other than Michael Foot, co-author of *Guilty Men* and *A Palestine Munich*? He had become Labour leader somewhat by accident in 1980, proved predictably incompetent in the role, and was impaled by the Falklands, almost more eager than Thatcher to strike Churchillian poses and relive the glories of 1940. For Barnett, 'Churchillism' at its most dangerous invoked the wartime spirit of national unity to drown dissent, or even serious discussion.

An official report into the conflict was chaired by Lord Franks, the very epitome of what the English half-facetiously call 'the great and the good', former head of not one but two Oxford colleges, ambassador to Washington, chairman of numberless committees, who now dutifully and absurdly exonerated Thatcher of any negligence before the invasion. 'Very simply,' Franks had said many years before, in a radio lecture in 1954, 'Britain is going to continue to be what she has been, a Great Power.' 'Simply' was scarcely the word, but nearly three decades on Thatcher gave a victory speech which claimed that 'the nation that had built an Empire and ruled a quarter of the world ... has not changed ... Today has put the Great *back* into Britain'.

That was just what wiser people feared. Michael Howard was now at the pinnacle of his career, as Regius Professor of Modern History at Oxford, so many years after he had fought in Italy, and after establishing his reputation in 1961 with the masterly *The Franco-Prussian War*. Much later, Howard observed drily that this book had never been translated into French or German; but then maybe 'the France of de Gaulle's Fifth Republic did not want to be reminded by an Englishman of their humiliation, while the Germans of Konrad Adenauer's Federal Republic were as unwilling to recall its military triumphs as were the French their military disasters'. And yet the French and the Germans weren't the only ones bemused by history: the British were all too lamentably keen to relive former days. As Howard said, 'After Suez we had gradually come to terms with our much diminished importance in the world. Then along came the Falklands, to revive all the absurd old national delusions.'

A year after that victory, Thatcher won another in the May 1983 general election, when the Tories routed Labour led by Foot. Following the election she was invited to America to receive the Winston Churchill Foundation Award. 'Like Churchill,' the citation read, 'she is known for her courage, conviction, determination and willpower. Like Churchill she thrives on adversity,' a tribute seconded by George Shultz, the Secretary of State, and Paul Volcker, Chairman of the Federal Reserve Board, who praised her 'backbone'. In 1984 she followed in Churchill's footsteps when she was invited to give a Joint Address to Congress, and declared that 'No-one understood the importance of deterrence more clearly than Winston Churchill.'

While American flattery of Thatcher concealed the tension between London and Washington, Reagan was the most prominent American devotee of Churchill, and in the years of his administration, the American version of 'Churchillism' flourished as never before. Howard noticed how 'Shrines to his memory proliferate across the United States,' from the Winston Churchill High School in Maryland, whose year-book was called 'Finest Hour', to a plethora of statues. Apart from the one outside the British Embassy in Washington there was another, cigar, V-sign and all, close to the vice-president's residence on Massachusetts Avenue. Others cropped up or popped up almost at random. In 1977, a large statue, by Ivor Roberts-Jones like the one in Parliament Square, was unveiled in New Orleans, donated by International Rivercenter, and standing outside the Hilton Hotel, close to the Mississippi River. Churchill had no connection with the city, but at the unveiling ceremony optimistic words were quoted from his 'so many to so few' speech in August 1940, when he said that the British Empire and the Americans would be 'somewhat mixed up together in some of their affairs ... Like the Mississippi, it just keeps rolling along.'

So did American veneration. In the grounds of Chartwell a faintly mawkish statue of Winston and Clementine Churchill had been placed, above the inscription 'Married Love'. Kansas City is the home of the Hallmark greeting cards company, which had promoted the American tour of Churchill's watercolours years before, and is now home also to a replica of the 'Married Love' statue. This one plays 'Blood, toil, tears and sweat' at the touch of button, and is there thanks to Joseph Jacobs, a local dentist, and Miller Nichols, who was the heir to the plaza and had decided that the young people of Kansas City needed appropriate 'symbolism' to encourage 'traditional values'.

Nor was this cult mere sentimental celebration: it had real political consequences. While Reagan installed likenesses of Churchill in the White House, his administration was a veritable nest of Churchillians. Haig reminded the American Society of Newspaper Editors what his hero had said: 'In reviewing the causes of the Second World War and prospects for peace in the future, Winston Churchill concluded: "How absolute is the need of a broad path of international action pursued by many states in common across the years, irrespective of the ebb and flow of national politics."' Even that paled beside the devotion of Casper Weinberger, the Defence Secretary for most of Reagan's eight-year presidency. A Harvard man and lawyer who had served in the Pacific war, enlisting as a private and ending as a captain on MacArthur's intelligence staff, Weinberger prospered politically under two other California Republicans, first Nixon, and then Reagan who made him state Director of Finance in 1968. Nearly twenty years later, when Weinberger retired from the Pentagon, Reagan said, 'I've occasionally called Cap "my Disraeli". But as I think of him and the service he's given the nation in the cause of freedom and peace, more than anyone else it's Churchill who comes to mind.' Weinberger had indeed assembled a large personal collection of Churchillian books and memorabilia, and often spoke at Churchill dinners and other celebrations.

Amid the cultic devotion, the Reagan administration attempted 'to invest the crusade against the "Evil Empire" with the moral aura as Hitchens wrote of Dunkirk and the Blitz'.* Enthusiasts for the 'star wars' system of ballistic missile defence gave Weinberger one more item for the collection, a framed text of the same words that Gordon Liddy had clung to, 'Never give in, never, never, never, never – in things great or small, large or petty.' Churchill had said this when speaking to the boys of Harrow, in 1941, the bleakest point of the war, which makes the sentiment more understandable, especially as Churchill continued, in words his admirers forgot: never give in 'except to convictions of honour and good sense. Never yield to force; never yield to the apparently overwhelming might of the enemy.' All of this had very little to do with what was happening in the wider world at the time.

Those devotees were nourished not only by endless books but by portrayals, as 'Winston Churchill' took on a new life as a character on screen large and small, and sometimes on stage. Apart from his own abortive but lucrative dabbling in screenplays for Korda, Churchill's

---

* There was an historical irony in those sarcastic words. Not many years after writing them, Hitchens himself would be a prominent cheerleader in another crusade waged against another 'evil empire' by another Republican president who ceaselessly invoked Churchill.

life on screen had begun life during the war with two curiosities. *Ohm Krüger* was a 1941 German agitprop film about the Boer War,* with a whisky-sodden Queen Victoria and a brutal commandant of a concentration camp. He is unnamed but bears a striking resemblance to Churchill. Two years later, *Mission to Moscow*, directed by Michael Curtiz after he had made *Casablanca*, and based on the weird memoirs of Joseph Davies, the American ambassador to Moscow, portrayed the Moscow Trials as a judicially correct punishment of fifth column-ists and traitors. On his way to Moscow Davies meets Churchill, played by Dudley Field Malone, an American lawyer and politician with a sideline as a character actor, who was thought to bear a close resem-blance to the prime minister.

After Churchill's death, *Young Winston* in 1972, based on *My Early Life* and with Simon Ward in the title part, wasn't at all a bad movie, and it paved the way. What would be a long line of television series about the purported 'wilderness years' began with *The Gathering Storm* in 1974. This was notable not least because the leading part was taken by Richard Burton, who had already narrated *The Valiant Years*, but who on this occasion incautiously told a *New York Times* reporter that 'To play Churchill is to hate him,' and recalled the loathing he had inspired in the South Wales of Burton's boyhood. Burton was not asked to play Churchill again. One small part in *Young Winston* was the headmaster of Harrow, taken by Robert Hardy. He had actually met Churchill twice: first when introduced to him as a boy by a family friend, Dr William Temple, the archbishop of York, later of Canterbury, and then in 1953 when he was playing in *Hamlet* at the Old Vic with Burton in the title role. After the play, Churchill went backstage and entered Burton's dressing room with the words, 'My Lord Hamlet, may I use your facilities?' which became one small part of the great corpus of Churchillian anecdotage. In 1981, Hardy played Churchill, with Siân Phillips as Clementine, in the television docudrama *The Wilderness Years*. Its particular significance lay in the fact that it was co-written by Martin Gilbert, and gave the unadorned Churchillian version, reprising the highly partisan account in *The Gathering Storm*.

---

* For connoisseurs of cinematic trivial pursuits, it won the best foreign movie award at that year's Venice Film Festival.

For Hardy this would be the first of very many performances as the great man, ending in 2015 with *Churchill: 100 Days That Saved Britain* and including such epiphenomena as the excruciating musical *Winnie*, which mercifully closed almost as soon as it opened in 1988. Over the years Hardy almost copyrighted the part. In 1988–9 alone, not including *Winnie*, he played Churchill three more times on television (in *The Woman He Loved*, *War and Remembrance* and *Bomber Harris*), and with his endless repertoire of mannerisms, the scowl, the growl, the flourished cigar, he helped 'fictionalise' the man, turning a real historic person into a character like Falstaff or Mr Pickwick, although not one with any obvious contemporary meaning.

Behind these quaint dramatic performances, in real life practical questions continued to divide Thatcher and Reagan. In October 1983 Reagan ordered what looked like almost a parody of the Falklands campaign the year before, an *opera buffa* invasion of the little Caribbean island of Grenada to depose a far-left government. Grenada belonged to the Commonwealth and was technically under the British Crown, but Thatcher was ignored and deceived: Reagan didn't act against her advice, he didn't even ask for it. 'We were both dumbfounded,' her Cabinet colleague Geoffrey Howe later said. 'What on earth were we to make of a relationship, special or otherwise, in which a message requesting the benefit of our advice was so quickly succeeded by another which made it brutally clear that that advice was being treated as of no consequence whatsoever?' The answer was, of course, that Washington as ever pursued its own interests and objectives with disregard for friend and foe alike. Once again, Churchillian theory – 'the unity of the English-speaking peoples' – collided with practice, the immutable laws of *Machtpolitik*.

During the following year England was convulsed by the mining strike which began in March 1984 and collapsed a year later, allowing Thatcher one more triumph after routing Galtieri and Foot. This time her adversary was Arthur Scargill, the clever but vain leader of the miners' union; his vanity was displayed when he called a national mining strike in the spring of a year that coal stocks were at a record level, a strategic decision to compare with invading Russia in November. Thatcher emulated Churchill's less justified tenacity during the General Strike, without his generous desire to meet the miners' demands. After a year the strike petered out and ended in defeat.

That autumn of 1984, Thatcher attended the Conservative Party conference in Brighton and stayed at the Grand Hotel. On the night of 18 October the hotel was blown up by a bomb previously planted by the IRA. Thatcher survived but five people, including an MP, were killed, and many severely injured. Just before Thatcher became prime minister, her friend and campaign manager, Airey Neave, an MP and decorated war hero who had escaped from the famous Colditz Castle at the time when the IRA was doing all it could to help Hitler, had been blown up in his car outside Parliament. Shortly before Thatcher was deposed her friend and parliamentary private secretary Ian Gow was killed by a car bomb at his home in Sussex. Once again, the bombs used in those murders, as in the murder of Mountbatten and so many others, were paid for in part with money openly raised in America.

An almost deeper Anglo-American rift than the Falklands or Grenada came with Reagan's Strategic Defence Initiative, or 'Star Wars'. Behind this exorbitant scheme was an ultimate goal, 'to reduce and eventually eliminate nuclear weapons'. Thatcher was disdainful, saying, 'I'm a chemist', and she knew it wouldn't work. By this time, in 1987, the president was anyway caught up in the Iran-Contra imbroglio.* At the height of the affair, Reagan was photographed sitting at his desk in the White House Situation Room. Behind him on the wall hangs one of the famous posters of 1940, Mr Churchill in bulldog mode, above the slogan, 'Let us go forward together.' With the same keenness to appropriate Churchill, if little sense of irony, Congress passed a law in 1988 declaring a 'National Sir Winston Churchill Recognition Week' from 27 November to 3 December.

Although Thatcher went forward to victory in the 1987 general election, the first time since the advent of universal suffrage that a party had won three successive elections under the same leader, there were warning signs. Charles Powell was a Foreign Office man who was appointed her private secretary in 1983, an official position. But Powell became much more, her consigliere and intimate, acting in a way that often went well beyond his supposed duties, encouraging

---

* This ludicrous caper, inspired by Sir Walter Scott's lines 'Oh what a tangled web we weave / When first we practise to deceive', saw senior officials in the Reagan administration clandestinely selling arms to Iran despite the administration's official embargo, so that the right-wing Contra rebels in Nicaragua could be armed with the proceeds.

her in her feuds with colleagues, to the point that Sir Robin Butler, the Cabinet Secretary, threatened to resign unless Powell were removed. Now Powell congratulated Thatcher on her victory.

But 'all the same,' he told her, 'I hope you will not put yourself through it again.' At some point soon, her 'reputation and standing as a historic figure' would matter more than anything more she might do. 'Your place in history will be rivalled in this century only by Churchill. That's the time to contribute in some other area!' This comparison would be made more often, though oftener in the United States, along with another such suggested likeness. Reagan's tenure at the White House was book-ended by the first two volumes of Manchester's Churchill hagiography, and the two men would later be linked by Steven F. Hayward in his book ambitiously entitled *Greatness: Reagan, Churchill, and the Making of Extraordinary Leaders*.

In the end, events caught everyone out, in a way that made Grenada and Star Wars seem footnotes of history. A day after Thatcher's third election, Reagan stood at the Brandenburg Gate, gazed at the most potent visual expression of the Iron Curtain of which Churchill had spoken four decades before, and said, 'Mr. Gorbachev, tear down this wall!' Torn down it was, in November 1989 by the Berliners, although one piece of it survives, at Westminster College in faraway Missouri. By the time the Wall fell, Reagan had left the White House but Thatcher was still at Downing Street, long enough to establish a surprisingly warm relationship with Mikhail Gorbachev, the Soviet leader, warmer if anything than she had with Reagan's vice president and successor, President George Bush the Elder, after he was inaugurated in January 1989. Failing to take Powell's advice, to listen to the urgings of her husband Denis to leave in good time, or pay attention to public and party discontent, Thatcher hung on until she was deposed in a squalid coup in November 1990.

For all those invocations and comparisons, and for all the Churchill cultists within and without the Reagan administration, the 1980s may seem in retrospect surprisingly un-Churchillian. Thatcher won one small faraway war, but Reagan fought none apart from the joke campaign in Grenada. And for all the bluster of the neocons and Cold Warriors, with their warnings about Munich, the collapse of the Soviet Union and its empire was a triumph of patience – or even appeasement. Churchill had said that 'appeasement has its place in all policy', and that 'appeasement from strength is magnanimous and noble and might be the surest and perhaps the only path to world peace'; events illustrated the truth of his words.

Already far richer than Soviet Russia in 1945, the West had only increased its economic lead over the next forty years. The Russian economy was a huge Potemkin village, or what the German Chancellor Helmut Schmidt called 'Upper Volta with rockets', and the Soviet state was long predeceased by Marxism-Leninism as a doctrine in which anyone in Russia pretended to believe. A turning point had come when Thatcher said of Gorbachev, 'We can do business.' It might have been an unhappy echo of Chamberlain's 'I have met a man, with whom I can do business,' but Gorbachev wasn't Hitler, and once he implicitly renounced the use of force to preserve the regime, its fall became inevitable. It duly came about, forty years after young Miss Roberts said, 'we have nothing to fear from Russian Communism'.

Yet again, 'what is called, somewhat oddly, the Middle East' was another matter. When the Falklands crisis had erupted in 1982 Carrington was in Israel, where the Foreign Secretary was trying to mend fraught British relations with the Israeli government. At the time of Thatcher's death, Andrew Roberts wrote a panegyric in the *Wall Street Journal* in which he said, 'her support for Israel was lifelong and unwavering'. This is most misleading. She wasn't of course an 'anti-Zionist' as usually understood. Like Churchill in Manchester once, she represented a constituency, in Finchley, with a large Jewish electorate, and she shared his philosemitism and affinity with Jews, appointing several to her cabinets.

But she had also been formed by her youthful memories. Early in her prime ministership, Shlomo Argov, the Israeli ambassador to London, told Sir Michael Palliser, Permanent Under-Secretary of the Foreign Office, that Israelis saw Carrington (and maybe Palliser himself) as characteristic of the old English elite, whose disdain for the Jewish state reflected traditional prejudice. By contrast, Argov claimed that the prime minister was truly reliable, a friend who innately sympathised with Israel. Palliser replied that he couldn't be more mistaken, in each respect. Like Palliser himself, Carrington had been a young Guards officer in 1945, when they had both entered Germany to see for themselves what the Third Reich had done to the Jews, and they had never forgotten that 'terrible suffering'.

It wasn't Carrington, Palliser said, but the prime minister 'who has never missed an opportunity to mention the two sergeants'. He meant the two young British soldiers hanged in reprisal by the Irgun in 1947. Two years before Thatcher entered Downing Street, Menahim Begin became prime minister of Israel: the former leader of the Irgun, 'the vilest gangsters', in Churchill's words, and the man who had ordered the hanging of the sergeants, an event never forgotten by Thatcher. His successor as Likud leader and premier in 1986 was Yitzhak Shamir, once chief of the Sternists, Churchill's 'new set of gangsters worthy of Nazi Germany', and the man who had ordered the assassination of Lord Moyne. Thatcher's attitude to Israel was strongly affected by the fact that, apart from an interregnum in 1984–6 when the prime minister was Shimon Peres, Israel was governed during her years in office by two men whom she regarded as terrorist murderers no different from jihadists or Irish republicans.

In June 1982, shortly before victory in the Falklands, three Palestinian terrorists attempted to assassinate Argov in London, gravely wounding him. Begin took this as an opportunity to launch a fierce reprisal into Lebanon and to bomb Beirut, where the Palestinian leader Yasser Arafat had moved his base. Twenty years earlier Kennedy and Castro had both invoked Churchill and his war. Now Begin likened the Palestinian leader to Hitler, telling an Israeli general, 'I want to see Arafat in his Bunker!' And yet when Beirut was bombed by Israeli aircraft, Arafat told *Liberation*, a local left-wing paper, that he wouldn't leave the stricken city, likening himself to another leader in 1940: 'Did Winston Churchill leave London?' Not just 'all things to all men', Churchill could be truly anything to anyone.

One coda came that same year, when *Finest Hour* was published, the latest, sixth and antepenultimate volume of Martin Gilbert's official biography. It was dedicated 'to Yuly Koshorovsky and Aba Taratuta in friendship, and in hope'. Gilbert had become much concerned with the cause of the 'refuseniks', the Soviet Jews who wanted to escape increased persecution, a cause which Little Winston had also taken up. Those two dedicatees did escape, with a million others in the end, and many refuseniks became settlers, including Koshorovsky. In 2014 he died in an accident in Beit Aryeh, the West Bank settlement where he by then lived.

*

If the Levant was one insoluble legacy of Churchill, so was Iraq where
Saddam Hussein had taken power in 1979, a Sunni despot ruling a
Shiite majority in the tradition of the princes Churchill had once
helped set on the throne. Saddam waged a savage eight-year war
against Iran with American support, and in August 1990 he invaded
Kuwait. Thatcher told Bush that it was 'no time to go wobbly', but
she needn't have feared. Bush strengthened a speech he was to give
on television, he later said, after reading Gilbert's Churchill biography,
inspired by 'the similarity I saw between the Persian Gulf and the
situation in the Rhineland in the 1930s, when Hitler simply defied the
Treaty of Versailles and marched right in'.

Three months after the invasion of Kuwait, Thatcher was deposed
and succeeded by John Major. In January 1991 a ferocious air bombardment largely destroyed Saddam's forces before a ground assault on 24
February by American forces at the head of a remarkably wide coalition, including not only British and French but Canadian, Australian,
Argentine and Saudi elements. As the bombardment began, Jack Kemp,
the Secretary of Housing and Urban Development, brought a recently
published book, *Winston and Clementine* by Richard Hough, to give to
the president. Kemp was asked to deliver a prayer, but instead read
from the book that most hallowed of passages, in which Churchill
described the end of the day on which he became prime minister: 'At
last I had the authority to give directions over the whole scene. I felt
that I was walking with Destiny, and that all my past life had been
but a preparation for this hour and this trial.' Then Kemp looked up
at Bush and said, 'Mr President, this is the moment you were elected
for. Destiny made you president for this crisis.' Once upon a time
England had fought, and lost, a Hundred Years' War. In 1918 the
British Army had fought, and won, the Hundred Days' Battle. The
total rout of Saddam's force lasted a hundred hours. Churchillian
echoes apart, Bush was the last president to have seen action in
wartime, and he showed restraint, prudently refusing to go on to
Baghdad, destroy Saddam as well as his army, and occupy Iraq: just
how wise this restraint was, his son would later demonstrate by
antithesis.

Two former leaders renewed their friendship that year, when
Thatcher visited Reagan in California, to be given a personal tour of
his as yet unfinished presidential library. The sacred name was invoked
two years later when she returned to the library in Simi Vally to see

a new exhibition, 'The Art and Treasures of Winston Churchill'. What should have been a happy occasion took a sombre turn. Thatcher spoke in praise of Reagan's courage and vision, and then Reagan proposed a graceful if platitudinous toast to his visitor. Everyone applauded as he sat down, but then he rose to his feet and, to the dismay of the audience, repeated all the words he had just said. It was a sad indication of how far his dementia was advanced, and might have been a premonition of the same fate which would overtake Thatcher.

20

'Blair's finest hour'

Fifth Avenue 2001

In 1998, the first American president and the first British prime minister born after Churchill's war dined in Washington. And yet, even if the two hadn't been alive at the time, memories of those great days hung heavy over the banquet at the White House. Giving the toast, Tony Blair recalled another dinner, in England during the war, when the host was Churchill and the guest was Harry Hopkins, Roosevelt's personal emissary. That was the occasion when, speaking of Anglo-American friendship, Hopkins had quoted Ruth's words, 'Whither thou goest, I will go; and where thou lodgest, I will lodge: thy people shall be my people.' At that, as Blair reminded his audience, Hopkins had paused before adding, 'even to the end' – and 'Churchill wept.' Hearing that story, Bill Clinton also wept. Within a few years of that lachrymose occasion there would be much more to weep about, as Churchill's shadow fell over the remnants of Yugoslavia, a country for whose character after 1945 he was largely responsible, Afghanistan, a country on whose borders he had fought in 1897, and Iraq, a country he had created in 1921.

All this was quite unforeseen when the 'iron curtain from Stettin in the Baltic to Trieste' was lifted. With the fall of the Berlin Wall and then the implosion of the Soviet Union it seemed that dawn was breaking on a new age of peace and democracy. After nearly half a century had passed since the World War, it might also have seemed that its aura, and Churchill's, would have faded, but that was very far from the case. What was also unforeseen was the way that the passage of time would only increase fascination with the war, and with Churchill. For the English this would have one outcome years later when Churchillism infused the long drama which culminated in the departure of the United Kingdom from the European Union. For the Americans, their Churchill cult would culminate when his name was relentlessly invoked as one more war began in Iraq, more foolish and criminal than anything Churchill had ever done. And, yet again, all the wrong lessons would be drawn from Munich and appeasement.

A few voices carped at that tale of Churchillian grandeur, and there was a curious contrast between transatlantic adulation and English denigration, but then the character of the denigrators sometimes served Churchill's cause. To go back to the summer of 1984: on the fortieth anniversary of D-Day a truly remarkable article appeared in the staid and patriotic pages of the *Daily Telegraph*. It was then edited by William Deedes, wartime Rifleman and Military Cross, elected an MP in 1950, later briefly a minister before returning to his first trade of journalism, and the piece was ostensibly a review of *Overlord* by Max Hastings, who would be Deedes's successor as *Telegraph* editor. The reviewer described contemptuously how, during the Normandy campaign, 'whole British units collapsed under pressure', while the Germans had fought magnificently: fallen SS men showed 'physical splendour even as they lay lifeless'. The SS general Kurt Meyer was quoted, with little sign of disagreement, telling his interrogators that Hitler was 'the best thing that has ever happened to Germany', a 'thing' which this writer found 'bewitching'. No such European 'civil war' should be fought again, because the result would be 'a barbarian annexation still more degrading than the ascendancy of material corruption – chewing gum and Chesterfields – that filled the vacuum of devastated Europe in 1945'.

That would have been startling enough in those – or almost any – pages and written by anyone at all, let alone by a minister in Mrs Thatcher's government, as this effusion was. Alan Clark was a very rich, very handsome, very arrogant flaneur, who gained fame more as a diarist and sexual adventurer than as a statesman, perhaps best remembered by posterity as the man who said he could only really enjoy a Christmas carol concert if he was having an illicit affair with a woman in the choir. He had acquired some spurious reputation as an amateur war historian with *The Donkeys,* about the British soldiers and generals of the Great War, a book described by Hastings as 'almost worthless', before *Barbarossa*, written with ill-dissembled admiration for the Wehrmacht and for Hitler.

But Clark would not be the last malcontent, and the battle of the books over Churchill continued, in ways all the more striking because of that transatlantic contrast. For all Jeane Kirkpatrick's indifference

to England at the time of the Falklands war, she and her neoconservative colleagues had proclaimed themselves ardent Churchillians, and
had adduced the great name in their attack on anyone who showed
signs of appeasing Russia, however much they needed to distort the
historical record in the process. In Churchill's own country another
group, also very much on the Right but a different quarter thereof,
began publicly to attack Churchill, and the sacred myth of the Finest
Hour. Clark's almost mystical ardour about the heroism of the
Wehrmacht was an early sign, while David Irving pursued his own
weird course which had begun with *The Destruction of Dresden* in 1963.
He went on to publish *Hitler's War* and *Churchill's War*, which scarcely
concealed his greater admiration for the former leader than the latter:
Churchill in the 'wilderness years' was an embittered, spiteful,
drunken, reckless 'busted flush', who 'leers' and 'gobbles' and
'sponges', who had 'sold his soul' to a cabal of Jewish financiers.

If Irving was the least intellectually reputable of the new revisionists, and John Charmley perhaps the most, Maurice Cowling was the
oddest, a sarcastic and perverse don with a devoted following among
his pupils at Peterhouse, his Cambridge college, who included several
Tory politicians and polemicists. Cowling had edited a collection of
Conservative Essays the year before Thatcher became prime minister,
and was associated with the *Salisbury Review*, a new journal named
after the intransigently reactionary prime minister. Writing in 1989,
Cowling decried Churchill's 'war of moral indignation', and said it
was 'wrong to assume that a dominant Germany would have been
more intolerable to Britain than the Soviet Union was to become, or
that British politicians had a duty to risk British lives to prevent Hitler
from behaving intolerably against Germans and others'.

In 1993, Charmley's book *Churchill: the End of Glory* likewise chas-
tised Churchill for having sacrificed his country's greatness. Roosevelt
was presented as an implacable foe of England, while Charmley in
effect dilated on the joke Orwell had once heard in London pubs,
'Chamberlain appeased Hitler, Churchill appeases America.' The book
ended with the woeful verdict that 'Churchill stood for the British
Empire, for British independence and for an "anti-socialist" vision of
Britain. By July 1945 the first of these was on the skids, the second
was dependent solely upon America and the third had just vanished
in a Labour victory.' An enthusiastic review appeared in *The Times*,
headed 'A reputation ripe for revision', with a cartoon of Churchill

painting at his easel for readers who hadn't guessed whose reputation this might be. Once more it was Clark, still an MP but no longer a minister, contemptuous of 'Churchill's single-minded determination to keep the war going', to the distress, he believed, of the Tories whose aim was 'to conserve – the existing social order at home, and the integrity of the empire overseas'.

There were 'several occasions when a rational leader could have got, first reasonable, then excellent terms from Germany', Clark claimed, notably in April 1941. If England had made peace then, 'the fleet and the Spitfires could have been moved to Singapore'. These revisionists had an obvious problem. If they were honest, they meant that Hitler should have been offered a free hand to do anything he liked in Europe, including mass murder, in return for leaving England and the British Empire alone. Besides, Cowling, Charmley and Clark, by suggesting that a deal could have been made with Hitler, assumed that he was a man who would have kept his word, when Stalin was only one of many who had learned the hard way that this was not so.

And yet some of what Charmley said was hard to deny. It was quite true that the war had had many unhappy outcomes for England, and not least for Churchill. His words said he would not preside over the liquidation of the British Empire, his deeds brought about just that, as Chou En-lai had observed. Nor was Charmley merely provocative when he derided Churchill's idea of the 'English-speaking peoples', and said that the Americans 'were, in fact, foreigners who disliked the British Empire even more than did Hitler,' and that Roosevelt had no love at all for the British. When Churchill succeeded Chamberlain, he had told the Tory MPs that the two supreme causes he had faithfully served were 'the maintenance and enduring greatness of Britain and her Empire and the historic certainty of our Island life'. Churchill had rhetorically evaded reality, or tried to create a reality of his own.

One man might have taken on these hecklers, but although Martin Gilbert replied to Charmley in mild terms, he evidently felt he had completed his task when the last volume of the monumental official biography appeared in 1988. He had signed off on a high note, claiming unconvincingly that Churchill's peacetime prime ministership had been a success, 'a period when he was very much alert to the many issues pressing in upon his fellow countrymen, from housing to the hydrogen bomb. His desire for a summit on the nuclear issue, and the care and precision with which he argued his case, are hardly the marks of a senile Victorian.' Meantime the documentary volumes continued to appear on a mighty scale: in 1993 *The Churchill War Papers Volume 1: At the Admiralty September 1939–May 1940* weighed in at 1370 pages, or 170 pages per month, a project scarcely feasible in commercial publishing terms.

In 1994, Gilbert published *In Search Of Churchill*, a quaint account of his life spent writing the biography. Apart from amusing memories of working for Randolph, who would shout 'Lovely grub!' when Gilbert found an interesting piece of Churchilliana, it was not a very exciting or reflective book. Gilbert described in more detail than most readers would want to know how he discovered, photocopied and arranged documents chronologically, pinning papers for each month of Churchill's life with 'a metal foldback clip'. It was also notably repetitious, as Gilbert related Churchill's enthusiasm for brick-laying for at least the fifth time in print, and sometimes absurdly padded.* At the same time the memoir was more revealing than Gilbert can have intended. Anyone who had felt that the *Life* had been altogether too uncritical would have been interested to learn that, while writing his earlier volumes, until Churchill's widow died in 1977, he had taken each chapter and read it out aloud to Clementine over lunch. Another and greater political biography was in the course of its lengthy appearance: *Means of Ascent*, the second volume of Robert A. Caro's as yet unfinished but incomparable – for there is truly nothing that quite compares with it! – life of Lyndon Johnson had been published in 1990. Anyone who knew that extraordinary work would have found it hard to imagine the author reading each chapter to Lady Bird Johnson.

After the assaults from Charmley, Clark and others, Gilbert could have taken the opportunity to reply. Instead he ignored them, merely repeating the fond portrait he had already drawn in which, as Robert Harris put it, 'Churchill is never wrong about anything. He is never cruel, never tyrannical, never ruthless, never really depressed, never vindictive, never reactionary, never hare-brained. He doesn't even drink

---

* The description of how 'the Muse of Painting came to my rescue', as Churchill put it, took two pages, including the bizarre footnote: 'The muses were the nine Greek goddesses of inspiration. There was no muse of painting,' before listing all nine names and concluding with the curious acknowledgement: 'I am grateful to my friend Erich Segal for these facts.'

very much.' Altogether this ended what in some ways was an unfortunate episode, or a missed opportunity. But the conclusion of the official *Life* at least meant that Churchill's papers were released from the biographer's grip, and a great flowering of serious Churchillian studies was about to begin.

Its starting point might be dated March 1991, just after Saddam Hussein's army had been routed, when a great colloquy was held at the University of Texas in Austin, presided over by an American and an Englishman. Wm. Roger Louis was a professor at Austin, co-editor of *The Oxford History of the British Empire*, and prolific historian of the decline and fall of that empire; Robert Blake was sometime Provost of the Queen's College, Oxford, and author, among much else, of the first good modern biography of Disraeli. They assembled a very distinguished cast to speak on almost every aspect of Churchill's life and work, and this occasion was one of the first signs of this renaissance. The resultant volume of essays, called simply *Churchill*, remains one of the best of all books on Churchill.

Even then, and for all that flowering, serious books about Churchill, from Charmley's revisionism to that fine Austin anthology, had only a fraction of the readership of pop hagiography, lapped up by Americans in particular. Their renewed obsession with Churchill and his war was easily explained. Memories of defeat in a bad war could be erased by rediscovering victory in *The Good War*, the title of Studs Terkel's 1984 collection of interviews with veterans of that war. As a means of recovering from the despondency and lack of national self-confidence that followed the humiliation of Vietnam, what better than reliving the days of wartime greatness? Harder to foresee was that, after such healing balm, the Americans might be ready for war again.

This change was reflected by Hollywood. The war movies of the 1970s and the 1980s had been about Vietnam – *Platoon*, *Full Metal Jacket*, *Apocalypse Now*, *Born on the Fourth of July* – and told unheroic stories with the bitterness of defeat, and defeat in a seemingly worthless war at that. But then as America attempted to forget Vietnam, Churchill's war was rediscovered. By the 1990s and 2000s, heroic movies and television programmes could be made again, *Saving Private Ryan* and *Band of Brothers* as prime examples. And books as well: Tom Brokaw's *Greatest Generation* sold more than a million in hardcover, and Stephen Ambrose was still more prolific, even if, like Churchill before him, he borrowed from others for his inspiring yarns of American derring-do: *D-Day, June 6, 1944: The Climactic Battle of World War II*, and *The Victors: Eisenhower and His Boys – the Men of World War II*.

Following Churchill himself, these books gave a distorted version of that war, by grossly exaggerating the importance of the western campaigns in defeating Germany. There were occasional antidotes, like Anthony Beevor's admirable *Stalingrad* in 1998, to remind readers where the war had really been won, but that still didn't cure western solipsism: to call Normandy 'the climactic battle' of the war besides Stalingrad and Kursk was as absurd as Churchill had been in calling it the greatest battle of the war. And yet this western 'good war' had the essential characteristic of a contest between virtue and vice, democracy against tyranny. That was seen in museums as well as books. The International Museum of World War II at Natick in Massachusetts, not far west of Boston, contains among other things personal papers of Roosevelt, Churchill, Eisenhower and Anne Frank's family, but also, from the forces of darkness, those of Hitler and Eichmann.

Even more striking, the National WWII Museum in New Orleans founded in 2000 has a most lavish collection of tanks, aircraft and other military hardware. But the 'Campaigns of Courage' and 'The Road to Berlin' pavilions, and the museum as a whole, might easily convey the impression that the war had been a contest between the United States and the Third Reich. Or more than that: in his 1999 book *The Holocaust in American Life* Peter Novick examined the way in which the Final Solution, an event which took place half a century earlier and thousands of miles away, had become integrated into American consciousness ever more with every passing year, as evidenced by the proliferation of Holocaust museums across America. Movies played their part, and when *Saving Private Ryan* was combined with *Schindler's List*, a perception was formed of a war waged by American democracy to destroy the evil Nazi oppressors of the Jews. As would transpire, all this affected politicians like Blair and George Bush the Younger, strengthening their zeal for conflicts in which each could see himself as a new Churchill once again combatting the forces of darkness.

When Clinton was inaugurated as president in 1993 and when Blair became leader of the Labour Party the following year, no one envisaged a new age of war. Neither man had any military experience and neither had shown any previous interest in foreign politics. Clinton had been the Governor of Arkansas, one of the less important states in middle America, and had little concern for other countries, apart maybe from a tinge of Anglophobia acquired as a reaction when he was a Rhodes Scholar at Oxford where, as Maureen Dowd of the *New York Times* put it, 'he didn't graduate, didn't inhale, and didn't get drafted'. 'Inhale' referred to Clinton's ludicrous claim that he had smoked marijuana but hadn't inhaled it; 'drafted' meant that he was using these years, followed by more at Yale Law School, to avoid military service.

This was one of the ignobler passages in American history, the way in which better-off and better-educated Americans evaded service in the Vietnam War. 'People who figured out how to work the system were exempted,' the defence secretary admitted in 1975. 'It is inconceivable that a system designed and operating the way the draft did could have produced a true cross-section of America in the military.' That was Donald Rumsfeld during his first brief sojourn at the Pentagon under President Ford. 'The price of greatness is responsibility,' Churchill had told the young men of Harvard in September 1943, and plenty of those he addressed had shown their responsibility in the fullest way by fighting for their country and, in the case of 657 Harvard men from 1941 to 1945, dying for it.* By contrast, Rumsfeld's words help to explain why, during more than eight years of war in Vietnam, only twelve Harvard men died. Churchill had admired the young men he addressed in 1943. A patrician and a soldier himself, who had risked his life in battle often enough, he would not have admired an elite who left the fighting to others.

There was no draft to dodge in England. 'The call-up' or National Service, as the British called their draft, had lasted almost fifteen years after the war and then been phased out, so that by 2020 an Englishman had to be in his late nineties to have served in the World War, and in his eighties to have done postwar National Service. Leo Blair had served in the war and risen from private to major, before becoming a barrister (and a Conservative), but his son Tony extricated himself

---

* 'Those who gave their lives' in 1941–5 is broadly defined on the list in the Memorial Church at Harvard; it includes Franklin Delano Roosevelt, Class of 1904. Another name is Joseph Patrick Kennedy, Jr, the brother of a future president.

from his school cadet corps before going to Oxford some years after Clinton. He also became a barrister, and was elected a Labour MP in 1983, the year of Thatcher's electoral triumph. For more than ten years he made his way, recognised as one of the brightest young Labour people, but his political concerns were entirely domestic. In 1992 two elections were held. The Tories won a fourth consecutive victory, to considerable surprise. There was a mild recession; the party was poisoned by the way Thatcher had been destroyed; her successor, John Major, was widely derided; and the Tories were tearing themselves apart over Europe, still baffled by Churchill's oracular 'with them but not of them'.

Political triumph in April was followed by financial disaster in September, and even that had Churchillian echoes. Great Britain had joined the European Exchange Rate Mechanism, precursor to the single currency, but with sterling at an over-optimistic rate, exactly the mistake Churchill had made when he returned to the Gold Standard in 1925 at the prewar rate. 'If you peg a relatively weak economy to a relatively strong currency it's the road to perdition,' the financial journalist Jeff Randall noted about 1992 in words that also applied to 1925. On 'Black Wednesday', 16 September, currency speculators short-selling sterling forced interest rates up from 10 per cent to 15 per cent within hours, and then forced Great Britain out of the ERM. Churchill had kept his job as Chancellor, Norman Lamont didn't keep his.

In November, Clinton defeated Bush the Elder. During the presidential election campaign, with unusual lack of scruple, the Bush team asked if Downing Street could try to dig up any dirt about Clinton when he was at Oxford and, with unusual lack of judgement, Major allowed the Conservative Central Office to do so. This didn't affect the outcome of the election, but when it became known to Clinton it affected his attitude to the Major government. A year after he was inaugurated, in January 1994, he took his revenge by granting an American visa to Gerry Adams, former head of the Irish Republican Army. John Banville, one of the most distinguished Irish novelists and critics of his generation, said that 'those of us who have always thought of the IRA, and indeed Sinn Fein, as neofascist, are deeply worried by the kind of respectability they have won now in Dublin, London and Washington'. The American reaction may be imagined if the British government had greeted a Muslim terrorist who had tried to murder an American president, but then for many Americans it made a crucial difference that Adams was a white man.

And so in the pattern of Truman over Palestine, Eisenhower over Egypt and Reagan over Grenada (and nearly over the Falklands), the Clinton administration now deserted the Major government over Northern Ireland. As Gerhard Schröder, a subsequent German Chancellor, was not the only one to notice, this Anglo-American relationship was special mainly in that only one side knew it existed. Still, by November 1995 the matter had been brushed over enough for Clinton to visit London, and address both Houses of Parliament where he announced the building of the guided missile destroyer USS *Winston S. Churchill*, the first American warship to be named after anyone but an American. By the time she was launched by Mary Soames in Bath, Maine, in April 1999, Blair was prime minister, having won a landslide election in 1997.

Before that, Churchill had returned to the news in unseemly fashion. Sarah had died in 1982, leaving only one survivor among his children, the formidable Mary Soames, whose husband Christopher had died in 1987. Of Churchill's two political grandsons, Nicholas Soames's career picked up at last after the departure of Thatcher, and he served as a junior minister for five years under John Major. Little Winston's did not, and he had few assets left apart from his name, and an archive. Following the convenient purchase of Chartwell by rich benefactors, Churchill had continued to live there, as Clementine was entitled to after his death, although in widowhood she spent little time there among so many memories, not all of them happy. After she died in 1977 aged ninety-two, Chartwell was taken over as intended by the National Trust, and turned into a handsome shrine to Churchill's memory.

Another shrine was Churchill College, founded at Cambridge in 1960 in Sir Winston's honour and housing the Churchill Library. The archive on which Gilbert worked for his biography had been moved to Oxford for his convenience, but where should those papers now go? All the papers from 1945 onwards had been donated by Clementine to the Churchill Library, which would receive many other collections of political papers, including Margaret Thatcher's. That left the rich wartime trove. Little Winston had tried selling this from the early 1970s on and off, provoking considerable private criticism, with senior officials again raising the question of whether the papers had legally been Churchill's property in the first place. Now he approached both Sotheby's and Christie's, the famous London auction houses, with a view to selling the archive on the open market, and 'got very stroppy', according to one source in the trade, 'wanting to get some value for these papers and constantly mentioned much higher figures', before another answer presented itself.

One of the Major government's innovations was a national lottery. Its superficial virtue was that a share of the proceeds would go to cultural, sporting and other good causes or worthy enterprises. In 1995 it was announced that little Winston had sold his grandfather's papers 'to the nation', which meant that the National Heritage Memorial Fund had used its lottery money to buy the papers for £12.5 million, almost half of the fund's original tranche of income. Little Winston was delighted that the papers would remain in this country, he said, and he was applauded by Lord Rothschild, chairman of the trustees at the Heritage Lottery Fund, who said that Churchill could have got more money if he had sold them piecemeal, as well by Andrew Roberts who remarked, 'I don't think the state has any right to just assume these things should be just given for free.'

That was of course exactly what Clementine had done with the other Churchill papers, and none of this passed without adverse comment, private and public. Max Hastings was at the time editor of the *Daily Telegraph*, previously a war correspondent in the Falklands and later a prolific military historian, whose books would include a study of Churchill as war leader. He now remonstrated with Sir Robin Butler, the Cabinet Secretary, at this imposture over the sale of the papers, but Butler thought that the public would resent an open battle with the Churchill family. There he may have been wrong. The *Daily Mirror* observed sourly that 'Never has so much been paid by so many to so few,' while a poll found that 52 per cent of British people believed that the papers should have been given rather than sold. Altogether, the story of Churchill's wartime papers remained as murky as ever. It was never at all clear that he had been entitled to remove the papers wholesale from Downing Street, still less to 'sell them' (while actually retaining them) to the publishers, the legal fiction on which his huge windfall from *The Second World War* was based. Alive or dead, Churchill continued to make his own rules.

And his sheer allure was greater than ever: Churchill remained the most bankable of famous names. Just how much so was demonstrated in 1998 when Sotheby's held 'The Political Sale'. On the cover of the catalogue was another image which had entered the Churchill iconography, his statue in Parliament Square photographed from behind as he glowered towards the Houses of Parliament. All the items in the sale associated with Churchill went for well above their estimates, some dramatically so, and one in particular. When peace came in 1945, a group of rich citizens of Geneva had wished to express their country's gratitude for the victorious conclusion, albeit to a war in which Switzerland had been neutral. Along with a clock given to the widowed Eleanor Roosevelt, they commissioned from the famous watch-making firm of Louis Cottier four extraordinary gold watches with different dials and hands for each recipient: the Statue of Liberty and an olive branch hour hand for President Truman, Joan of Arc planting the Cross of Lorraine on the coast of France for de Gaulle, and – wonderfully incongruous gift from that city of Calvin and capital! – a watch for Stalin, adorned with communist insignia and a worker standing in front of a blazing factory in Stalingrad.

But the grandest was Churchill's 'victory watch'. Engraved with his name and the dates 1939–1945, his watch depicted St George slaying a dragon, with a trident as the hour hand. It was presented to 'The Happy Warrior, he inspired England with courage and endurance when she was alone, defenceless and in great peril, and led her through five years to victory.' Churchill accepted it graciously, saying that it would always remind him of Switzerland's 'friendly feelings'. Fifty-three years later, there were even more friendly feelings for the unnamed vendor, presumably little Winston, when the watch was auctioned. Sotheby's had put a highest estimate of £100,000; it sold for £485,000.

And so, just as there were Churchill shrines, there were relics. In the Middle Ages rich and pious princes had paid vast prices for holy relics such as the real or supposed bones of saints; now any relic associated with the great man would sell, whether as magnificent as that watch or as mundane as Churchill's false teeth, which fetched £15,200 at auction in 2010. That was three times the estimate, and it became a regular feature that all forms of Churchilliana would sell for much more than experienced auctioneers expected.

*

In 1998 Blair appeared to find a final answer to Churchill's 'dreary steeples of Fermanagh and Tyrone'. The leaders of the various Northern Ireland factions gathered in Belfast: Protestant Unionists and Catholic nationalists. The latter were now a common front embracing the supposedly democratic Social Democratic and Labour Party, the Dublin government, and the terrorists of the IRA, in the guise of their front organisation 'Sinn Fein'. Blair himself arrived in Belfast with the unintentionally risible words, 'This is no time for soundbites. I feel the hand of history on my shoulder.' As yet he was not being compared with Churchill, though that would come. But what the Belfast negotiations demonstrated was that, although he might seem a plausible speaker, he was a very bad negotiator, as his dealings with two American presidents would show.

While Blair was privately perturbed by President Clinton's undisguised preference for the terrorists of the IRA over democratically elected politicians, Adams and Martin McGuinness, his predecessor as leader of the IRA, ran rings round him in the talks, as the Americans would run rings round him before long. One of the outstanding historians in the field of Anglo-American relations, and of Churchill, looked at Blair's record in this light, comparing him with another prime minister, but not the one whose mantle he claimed: 'A leader convinced of his rightness,' David Reynolds writes, 'whose powers of persuasion bordered on hubris. Who squeezed out professional advice, controlling policy and information from an inner circle, and who played his best hands too early at the conference table. A leader whose rhetoric became increasingly extravagant and deceptive ...' Altogether, so far from Churchillian, Blair's manner of negotiation 'had a good deal in common with that of Neville Chamberlain'.

That was not how Blair saw himself. He later said that he had begun reading in the library at Chequers about the 1930s, and had come to think how weak and wrong the appeasers with their arguments for conciliation had been, when Churchill was right. Once again Churchillism had shaped policy with lamentable, practical consequences, as another happy warrior began to nurture visions of glory. In 1940 Churchill had felt as if he were walking with destiny; already in 1994 Blair had 'felt a growing inner sense of belief, almost of destiny ... I could see it like ... an artist suddenly appreciates his own creative genius.' He was also transformed by seeing a movie. Blair sat spellbound through *Schindler's List*, talking 'about it long into the night' afterwards. As Jason Epstein pointed out in a dissenting opinion, 'Spielberg's film lets viewers take comfort and pride in his virtuous behaviour,' or to put it another way, that film illustrated something William Dean Howells long before had told Edith Wharton: what the American public always wants is tragedy with a happy ending. But it was exactly Blair's kind of movie: technically slick, historically misleading and morally simplistic.

Always lurking in the background was Churchill's idea of a war 'against a monstrous tyranny, never surpassed in the dark, lamentable catalogue of human crime'. Too soon Blair began to see himself – unconsciously, and then consciously – as a new Churchill, with more monstrous tyrannies to fight. And yet not even Churchill could have drawn so trite a moral as Blair did, that, in a world of good and evil there can be no 'bystanders': 'You participate, like it or not. You take sides by inaction as much as by action.' It was 'not very practical', he admitted, but 'The trouble is it's how I feel. Whether such reactions are wise in someone charged with leading a country is another matter.' Just how unwise they were would soon become clear.

If the creation of modern Iraq had been 'Winston's Folly', that country would lead to still greater follies more than eighty years later. Saddam Hussein was still in power after the Gulf War had destroyed his army but not him, as 'peppery, pugnacious, proud' as the predecessors Churchill had once so described. Some Americans wished he had been overthrown in 1991, and were soon advocating another war to do so. In 1998 Blair joined the Americans in air strikes on Iraq, while Clinton also ordered air strikes on Sudan, killing several innocent people, in order to distract attention from a sordid scandal in which he was embroiled.

But it was in one more of Churchill's legacies that Blair found his first true mission. Yugoslavia had been the creation of the Allies after the Great War, an artificial state in which the Catholic Slovenes in the north had almost nothing in common with the Orthodox Serbs and, along with the Croats, had little wish to live in a country dominated by Serbia. And the Yugoslavia which emerged after another war in which Churchill dubiously said it had 'found its soul' was as much his work as anyone's, impelled by his delusion that Tito was a nationalist who had 'largely sunk his Communist aspect in his character as a Yugoslav patriot leader'. After Tito had taken power with savage

blood-letting, including the killing of thousands of his foes treacher-
ously sent back by the British, he broke with Stalin in 1948, and then
became the Franco of the left. Like the Spanish leader, Tito was as
much nationalist as ideologue, each determined to impose a national
identity on fractious Catalans or Croats. As the 1950s and 1960s went
by, both men were still dictators, though less repressive than before,
and more open to the West. Alas, whereas Spain was able to return
to stable constitutional democracy after Franco died in 1975, Tito's
death in 1980 was followed by the gradual, and then accelerating,
collapse of the state Churchill had encouraged and Tito had held
together.

By the 1990s disintegration had become bloody civil war, or wars,
with Bosnia fought over by Serbs and Croats. A peace of sorts was
imposed in 1995 but then in 1998 fighting broke out in Kosovo to the
south of Serbia between forces from the Albanian majority and the
Serbs, who regarded Kosovo as their ancestral homeland much as de
Valera had said that Ulster was the ancestral heart of Catholic Gaelic
Ireland. Forces from Serbia, ruled by the nationalist Slobodan Milosevic,
drove out Albanians, while the Kosovo Liberation Army, categorised
by the State Department as terrorists, attacked Serbs. In 1999 Clinton
agreed to a bombing campaign against Serbia under the auspices of
NATO. When NATO had been created with Churchill's approval in
1949, its clearly stated purpose was as a treaty of mutual defence 'in
the North Atlantic region' when any member state was attacked. No
one explained how Serbia had threatened any NATO member, still
less, two years later, how the Pamirs had become part of the North
Atlantic region.

And yet many Americans now found a new Churchill. While the
bombing was underway, Blair gave a speech in Chicago, which won
him huge credit among American liberals: 'No one in the West who
has seen what is happening in Kosovo can doubt that NATO's military
action is justified,' he told his audience. 'Bismarck famously said the
Balkans were not worth the bones of one Pomeranian grenadier.
Anyone who has seen the tear-stained faces of the hundreds of thousands of refugees streaming across the border, heard their heart-
rending tales of cruelty or contemplated the unknown fates of those
left behind knows that Bismarck was wrong.' More than that, Blair
became the latest victim of the great false analogy from the 1930s.
In his words at Chicago, 'We have learned twice before in this century

that appeasement does not work. If we let an evil dictator range unchallenged, we will have to spill infinitely more blood and treasure to stop him later.' That was not in fact what Churchill had said, and at no time in the 1930s had he advocated pre-emptive or preventive war.

The speech was later described by the eminent English jurist Philippe Sands as reeking of 'the emotional and ahistorical interventionist instincts that later led directly to the Iraq debacle', yet it delighted many Americans, who warmed to the wholly predictable use of 'appeasement'. An American cult of Blair blossomed almost more quickly than Churchill-worship once had. Blair was hailed as 'the Prime Minister of the United States'; 'Blair for President' bumper stickers appeared; Dana Milbank declared in the *New Republic* that at last the United States had 'a leader who is acting presidential' on the international stage, before adding ruefully, 'Unfortunately, this leader is Tony Blair'; and for Paul Berman Blair was simply 'the leader of the free world'. It remained for Timothy Garton Ash to add breathlessly that 'Not since Churchill has a British leader had such a magnetic resonance.' Clinton reluctantly caught up with Blair, and justified the bombing of Serbia by musing, 'What if someone had listened to Winston Churchill and stood up to Adolf Hitler earlier?' And Blair would soon find other fields for his Churchillian zeal.

In 2000, George Bush the Younger, son of Bush the Elder, won the presidential election, or maybe one should say the Supreme Court light-heartedly decided to award Florida, and thus the national election, to Bush rather than Al Gore. In the campaign, Bush had emphasised the need for America to be 'humble' as it dealt with the larger world, but this proved highly misleading, since before long Bush would wage war with little sign of humility. And he would outdo all his predecessors in his addiction to Churchill. His administration was filled with devoted Churchillians, who had for long had their eyes on Iraq, had been advocating a war to destroy Saddam, and as soon as Bush was inaugurated on 20 January had discussed how this could be brought about.

Less than eight months later, on 11 September, 'I watched the twenty-first century begin,' Tony Judt wrote. That great historian, author of the brilliant *Postwar* on Europe since 1945, was an English exile at New York University, and it was from his window near

Washington Square that he had seen the destruction of the vast World Trade Center downtown. A handful of men, mostly Saudis, had overpowered the crews of four aircraft and turned them into human missiles. The spasm of horror Americans felt that day was a reminder of how very fortunate their country had been during the previous century. No bomb had ever fallen on any American city, and the experience of looking at a devastated cityscape was utterly traumatic.

As the rubble settled and a desperate search for survivors began, one ghostly figure seemed to emerge from the smoke and dust. It was Winston Churchill. Never had one name been invoked by so many. Until that day, Rudolph Giuliani, the mayor of New York, was highly controversial and widely disliked, as he would be once again years later when he became President Trump's personal lawyer and consigliere. Now he found his moment of greatness, and a new mantle to wear. 'Who Knew Rudy Was Really Churchill?' one newspaper headline asked. Giuliani said he was inspired by reading Roy Jenkins's new biography of Churchill, and more surprisingly Jenkins repaid the compliment: 'What Giuliani succeeded in doing is what Churchill succeeded in doing in the dreadful summer of 1940: he managed to create an illusion that we were bound to win.' After Steve Forbes interviewed the mayor, he reported that 'Hearing Giuliani talk about 9/11 was like hearing an echo of Winston Churchill describe his ascent to becoming Britain's Prime Minister as the country faced the greatest crisis in its history,' when his whole life 'had been but a preparation for that very moment.' And Edwina Sandys the granddaughter chipped in: Giuliani was 'Churchill in a baseball cap'.

Although a cartoon in a Texas newspaper made fun of this, with New Yorkers looking at a photograph of Churchill and one commenting, 'They say he was a Giuliani-esque leader,' the comparison didn't embarrass Giuliani. 'I also thought about him a lot when I went for mayor back in 1993,' he claimed months after the catastrophe, 'the way he had revived the spirit of the British people when it was down, and I used that for what I had to do. New York was floundering under too much crime and dirt.' He added correctly that 'I knew the press thought it was over-dramatising the situation to compare it to Britain during the war.' But however it might have been with street crime and garbage, he had no hesitation in comparing his role with Churchill's after 11 September: 'I used Churchill to teach

me how to reinvigorate a dying nation, and after the attack I'd talk
to him. During the worst days of the Battle of Britain Churchill never
stepped out of Downing Street and said, "I don't know what to do,"
or "I'm lost." He walked out with a direction, a purpose, even if he
had to fake it.'

Hard on Giuliani's heels was Blair. Faking it or otherwise, he claimed
that he had felt 'eerily calm' when he heard the news on 11 September.
'There was no other course; no other option; no alternative path. It
was war ... And it came with total clarity. Essentially, it stayed with
that clarity and stays still, in the same way, as clear now as it was
then.' He flew to New York where he warmly and very properly
expressed the sympathy of the British government and people for
New York in its ordeal. Then on 21 September, after a memorial
service for British victims at St Thomas's on Fifth Avenue, an
Episcopalian church more traditionally English than almost any found
by then in England, he spoke from the steps of the building. 'My
father's generation knew what it was like. They went through the
Blitz,' Blair said. 'There was one country and one people that stood
side by side with us then. That country was America, and the people
were the American people.'

He said that sixty years after 'Blitzkrieg Baby, You can't bomb me,
/ Cos I'm pleading neutrality.' By the time Una Mae Carlisle sang that
song in May 1941, Londoners had endured the Blitz for eight months,
and although the toll of 3000 people killed on that awful day in New
York was grim, it was no more than the deaths in London on one
bad night of many during the Blitz. Many people had 'stood side by
side with us' at that time, from the Commonwealth countries to the
conquered and occupied countries of Europe, but not the Americans.
Seemingly plausible at times, Blair was intellectually second-rate, and
woefully ignorant of history, but even he might have been expected
to know that the United States was conspicuously and profitably
neutral while Britain 'went through the Blitz'. Churchill wooed and
flattered Roosevelt, but he would never have pronounced such fawning
nonsense as Blair did.

Worse was to come. Blair's chief of staff, Jonathan Powell, had spoken
of his 'messiah complex', which may have been meant half-humorously
but seemed increasingly near the truth. On his return to England, Blair
addressed the Labour Party in what he later called a 'visionary' speech,
intended to be his 'We shall fight on the beaches ...', although what

was truly significant about that visionary speech was what Blair didn't say. On his latest American journey, he had met Bush and promised full British support for a campaign in Afghanistan, where Osama bin Laden, the leader of Al Qaeda, had organised the New York massacre. But Bush also told Blair, as witnessed by Sir Christopher Meyer, the British ambassador in Washington, 'When we've dealt with Afghanistan, we must come back to Iraq.'

Instead of revealing that to his party or to the British people, Blair spoke of 'The starving, the wretched, the dispossessed, the ignorant, those living in want and squalor from the deserts of Northern Africa to the slums of Gaza, to the mountain ranges of Afghanistan: they too are our cause ... The kaleidoscope has been shaken. The pieces are in flux. Soon they will settle again. Before they do, let us reorder this world around us.' Visionary or delusional, the next day Blair was garlanded in the press. Most exalted of all was the Tory *Daily Telegraph*, which rapturously saluted the prime minister in an editorial whose headline made the comparison as clearly as possible: 'Blair's Finest Hour'.

All this made it a good time to celebrate the great man. Lauded in the American press if sniffed at by some academics, Roy Jenkins's biography of Churchill was an inevitable bestseller, even if it was far from the 'authoritative' life the *New York Times* called it, let alone definitive. With no pretence to primary research, Jenkins made good use of Gilbert's official biography and its companion documentary volumes. But his book was a good deal more readable, and Jenkins, who had been introduced to Churchill as a boy, had one advantage easily overlooked. His own political career had once taken him into the Cabinet as Home Secretary and Chancellor, like Churchill before him. He had then become president of the European Commission, and he had been one of the group who bolted from Labour to form the Social Democratic Party. That apart, the House of Commons Jenkins had entered in 1948 was in many ways much closer to the Commons Churchill had entered in 1901 than to Parliament half a century later, after decades of atrophy and decline which would lead to the shameful events of March 2003, when a majority of servile and morally bankrupt Labour MPs voted for a criminal and needless war which it is certain that few of them really believed in or wanted.

By one piece of fortuitous timing, *Band of Brothers*, with its heroic account of a company of American paratroops training in England and then fighting from D-Day to the Rhine, began screening on US television on 9 September 2001 to stiffen the resolve of the American people. And by another, the following July one more Churchill drama-doc was premiered by the BBC. *The Gathering Storm* was one of the better biopics, with outstanding performances by Albert Finney as Churchill, and Vanessa Redgrave as Clementine; when Mary Soames saw her on screen, she exclaimed, 'It's Mama.' That year the BBC also broadcast its series, *100 Greatest Britons*. At its end, the public was asked to vote for the greatest, who was of course Churchill.

This exaltation of Churchill as war approached was no accident. The Bush administration skipped almost lightly from Afghanistan, where it might have had a plausible case for military action, to Iraq, where it had none, despite mendacious attempts to link Saddam with the 11 September attacks, and also to suggest a patently false analogy between those attacks and Pearl Harbor: Japan was a great military power, Al Qaeda was a group of zealots hiding in the mountains on the Afghan-Pakistan border. All the while, Bush quoted Churchill at every opportunity, and Blair was now convinced that, as he sat, like Thatcher, 'where Winston sat', he could take over his role. When David Owen, a former Foreign Secretary, pleaded caution over Iraq, Blair told him, 'Saddam is Hitler. You are Chamberlain. I am Churchill.' He was, in that case, a very inferior version. In the 1930s, Churchill had wilfully exaggerated the danger from the Luftwaffe, although he was not wrong about the threat that Hitler posed to peace and freedom. Now Blair wilfully, and disgracefully, distorted evidence of Saddam Hussein's weaponry, and also falsely claimed that Saddam represented a 'serious and current' threat to British interests. Even so, and even after two utterly specious 'dossiers' were published by Downing Street, a poll on 31 January 2003 found 30 per cent of British people in favour of war and 43 per cent against.

Still Blair would not let Churchill go. 'There are glib and sometimes foolish comparisons with the 1930s,' he said, before going on to make some more. While telling Parliament that he was 'not suggesting for a moment that anyone here is an appeaser or does not share our revulsion at the regime of Saddam', he quoted a newspaper editorial published after Munich: 'Be glad in your hearts. Give thanks to your God. People of Britain, your children are safe. Your husbands and

your sons will not march to war. Peace is a victory for all mankind
... And now let us go back to our own affairs. We have had enough
of those menaces, conjured up ... to confuse us.' But those hopes
had been disappointed, Blair said, from which he concluded that 'Now,
of course, should Hitler again appear in the same form, we would
know what to do.' But Hitler had not appeared again, in the same
form or any other form.

'Operation Iraqi Freedom' began on 20 March 2003. The Americans
were supported by far fewer countries than in 1991. 'Let no man
underrate the abiding power of the British Empire and Commonwealth,'
Churchill had said at Fulton. Fifty-seven years later, any abiding power,
or even 'the Commonwealth' itself, had barely any meaning. Pakistan
and Malaysia obviously opposed the invasion of a Muslim country,
but then so did Canada, once hailed by Churchill as 'the keystone of
the English-speaking peoples'. British troops took part, and also
Australians, sent there against much popular opposition by a right-
wing prime minister called John Winston Howard.

'Now that the United States is again engaged in battle,' Edward
Rothstein wrote, 'Churchill is again an inescapable presence.' His
descendants agreed. Little Winston endorsed the war in the *Wall Street
Journal*, reminding readers that 'it was my grandfather, Winston
Churchill, who invented Iraq and laid the foundation for much of the
modern Middle East,' as though those foundations had proved stable,
and that invention had been a success. 'If my grandfather were alive
today,' said Nicholas Soames, 'he would know instinctively on Iraq
that Britain's right position is at America's side.' As for the official
biographer, Martin Gilbert claimed that Bush and Blair 'may well,
with the passage of time and the opening of the archives join the
ranks of Roosevelt and Churchill.'

Amid all these invocations of the past, Blair was undone by personal
and national vanity, seduced by the notion of Bush and himself as the
new Franklin and Winston, and Macmillan's greater fantasy, 'Greeks
to their Romans'. Speaking privately to Labour MPs in March 2002,
Blair had said, 'my strategy is to get alongside the Americans to shape
what is to be done and that won't be done by grandstanding.' As
events would show, it wasn't done either by giving unwavering support.
Although the full truth about the conversations and correspondence
between Blair and Bush is still not publicly known, the official inquiries

under Lord Butler and Sir John Chilcot made it clear, however polite
and restrained their wording, that Blair had misled Parliament and
the people before the invasion, and that the British government thereafter had no 'shaping', guiding or restraining influence whatever on
Washington.

On 1 May, when he would have been better advised to echo
Churchill's 'Now this is not the end. It is not even the beginning of
the end,' Bush theatrically landed on USS *Abraham Lincoln* and unwisely
pronounced 'Mission accomplished'. Blair was no less hubristic. When
a statue of Saddam in Baghdad was toppled, cynics suspected what a
New Yorker investigation later demonstrated, that this had been a stunt
arranged by the Americans, but in London it was hailed by Blair, who
was lauded by the supposedly impartial BBC, in the form of its chief
political correspondent, Andrew Marr:

> The main mood [in Downing Street] is of unbridled relief ... [after]
> all these slightly tawdry arguments and scandals. That is now history.
> Mr Blair is well aware that all his critics out there in the party and
> beyond aren't going to thank him (because they're only human) for
> being right when they've been wrong. And he knows that there might
> be trouble ahead ... [but] He said that they would be able to take
> Baghdad without a bloodbath, and that in the end the Iraqis would be
> celebrating. And on both of those points he has been proved conclu-
> sively right ... tonight he stands as a larger man and a stronger prime
> minister as a result.

But Blair's own mission wasn't quite accomplished, and in one
respect he did resemble Churchill. An advertisement for a brand of
beer used to say that it 'reaches the parts other beers cannot reach'
and, just as many Americans had once thrilled to the grandeur of
Churchillian rhetoric more than to Roosevelt's less exalted speeches,
Blair could reach the parts Bush couldn't reach by selling the case for
war to American liberals and centrists chary of their own president.
As the *Wall Street Journal* put it, more tellingly than it realised, the
British prime minister was 'Bush's Ambassador to the World'. In July
Blair went to Washington and to Capitol Hill, where he had been
awarded the Congressional Gold Medal, and he addressed Congress
as Churchill had more than sixty years before. Where Churchill had
been humorous in the same forum – with an American father and

English mother rather than the other way round 'I like to think that I might have got here on my own' – Blair was merely ingratiating: 'On our way down here, Senator Frist was kind enough to show me the fireplace where, in 1814, the British had burnt the Congress Library. I know this is, kind of, late, but sorry.'

In one respect the problem was personal. If twenty-three sitting MPs had been killed in action in the Great War, and if all four prime ministers in Downing Street from 1940 to 1963 had once served as infantry officers, and Heath was the only prime minister since then to have seen a battlefield in Churchill's war, then Blair led a government of more than a hundred ministers of all ranks, not one of whom had ever seen any kind of military service at all. Not only had none heard the proverbial shot fired in action, none of them had ever worn uniform or so much as stripped a Bren gun or blancoed a belt.

Likewise, if four out of six American presidents in the three decades from 1960 had served gallantly in the United States Navy in the Pacific campaign, then by odd coincidence three of the four presidents in the next three decades had been born within ten weeks of each other in the summer of 1946. That meant that Clinton, Bush the Younger and Trump were of exactly the age to have served in the Vietnam War, and yet none of them did so. Clinton used academic deferments to avoid the draft, Bush the Younger joined the National Guard when that was notoriously a way of avoiding Vietnam and the sound of gunfire, while Donald Trump was kept out of uniform by the affliction of a heel spur (so severe that he subsequently couldn't remember which foot it was).

It was easy to be sentimental about Brokaw's 'Greatest Generation', but in the end the generation which fought in Churchill's war had been truly admirable. Whereas 'My generation has been catastrophic,' Judt said shortly before his lamentably early death in 2010. 'I am more or less the same age as George W. Bush, Bill Clinton, Hillary Clinton, Gerhard Schröder, Tony Blair and Gordon Brown – a pretty crappy generation, when you come to think of it.' Born after the war, they had grown up 'in a world of no hard choices, neither economic nor political. There were no wars they had to fight. They did not have to fight in the Vietnam War. They grew up believing that no matter what choice they made, there would be no disastrous consequences. The result is that whatever the differences of appearance, style and personality, these are people for whom making an unpopular choice is very hard.' But now there were disastrous consequences, and the Clintons, Bush and Blair left others to endure them.

All unlike Churchill's war, which began with heroic defiance in the face of endless defeat before victory dawned after a long ordeal, the Iraqi adventure war by that crappy generation began with effortless victory, and the scale of the real disaster emerged only gradually. By the new year of 2004 Blair's stock was still high enough in America for a book to be published with a title half-consciously invoking Churchill, *Tony Blair: the Making of a World Leader*, but before long he seemed less a leader than what a Beirut newspaper called 'Washington's international gofer'. As the war went horribly wrong, Bush had fewer and fewer supporters, until Maureen Dowd portrayed him alone in the White House, with no friends left except 'Barney, his Scottish terrier, and Tony, his English poodle'. In 1944, humiliated by his unmistakably decreasing influence and the demands America made on him, Churchill said that he hated being made to sit up and 'beg like Fala', FDR's Scottish terrier, but Blair never minded being made to sit up and beg like Barney. How much more humiliating would Churchill have found his country's fate? Forty years after his death, his 'ties of history and blood' found their apotheosis in the deserts of Iraq, and met their nemesis.

21

'Churchill was the first neocon'
Bagram 2007

In February 2007, Vice President Dick Cheney visited Afghanistan. His mission was fraught. At Bagram air base he woke to the sound of a bomb outside the gate, which killed twenty-three people, a reminder that the five-year American campaign to pacify Afghanistan had enjoyed somewhat limited success. But then the vice president had something inspirational to read. He was photographed on the steps of the USAF 'Spirit of Strom Thurmond'* with a book tucked under his arm, whose title could be clearly read: *A History of The English-Speaking Peoples Since 1900* by Andrew Roberts. Now the story had come full circle. In 1897 Winston Churchill had served in a military expedition to punish the unruly Pathan or Pashtun tribesmen on the Afghan border, and had written his first book about the expedition. In 1929 he conceived a work on 'the English-speaking races', and had frantically tried to complete it in 1939, although in the event *A History of the English-Speaking Peoples* wasn't published for nearly thirty years after its conception. More than a hundred years after Churchill had ridden 'my grey pony all along the skirmish lines where everyone else was lying down in cover', British troops were once more fighting in Afghanistan, this time as allies of the Americans, with Churchill again at the skirmish line, like the dead Cid tethered to his horse leading his men into battle.

*

---

* Named for the Governor of South Carolina who bolted from the Democrats to run against Truman as a 'States Rights', or segregationist, candidate in 1948, insisting that 'all the laws of Washington and all the bayonets of the Army cannot force the Negro into our homes, into our schools, our churches,' and then as a senator relentlessly opposed Civil Rights legislation. This aircraft landed in a country to which the United States claimed to be bringing justice and equality.

When Bush took office, there were two formidable groups within his administration. The rightwing nationalists Dick Cheney and Donald Rumsfeld were determined to restore American power and prestige after the humiliations of Vietnam and Iran, and formed a working alliance with the ideological neoconservatives. One thing which united the two groups was their shared reverence for Churchill. The first generation of neoconservatives from the 1960s to the 1980s had been principally concerned with the Soviet threat, invoking Chamberlain and Munich yet again to damn the policy of detente. The end of the Cold War and the fall of Soviet Russia might have perplexed them, but they had found a new obsession in the Levant, and the cause of Israel. The *New York Times* columnist David Brooks said sardonically that, as the word 'neocon' was widely understood, it had apparently become an abbreviation, in which '"con" is short for "conservative" and "neo" is short for "Jewish"'. But this really was an episode in Jewish American intellectual and political history, even if most Jewish Americans were never neoconservatives. Some of the more prominent neocons were active in Israeli as well as American politics. Two of them, Richard Perle and Douglas Feith, prepared a policy document in 1996 called 'A Clean Break: A New Strategy for Securing the Realm' on behalf of Benjamin Netanyahu, leader of the Likud party, who became prime minister of Israel that year, an office he would hold longer than any predecessor.

He had an indirect personal connection with Churchill. Likud was the ultimate heir of the Revisionists, the right-wing military branch of Zionism which Vladimir Jabotinsky had founded in the 1920s, and which had descended by way of Betar, Irgun and then Herut, the rightist opposition excluded from power in Israel for nearly thirty long years, before Begin became prime minister in 1977. In 1937 Jabotinsky had met Churchill and persuaded him to support the Revisionist line. Shortly before his death in 1940, Jabotinsky had appointed as his secretary a young mediaeval historian and activist named Benzion Netanyahu, who remained a zealous supporter of the Revisionist cause, enjoying a personal success when he persuaded the Republicans to include advocacy of a Jewish state in its platform at the 1944 election. Many years later, in a 1998 profile for the *New Yorker*, David Remnick was startled by the vehemence of the old man's views – Benzion was then in his eighties, and would live to the age of 102 by the time of his death in 2012 – and his undisguised hatred for the Arabs, 'an enemy by essence' who only responded to force and with whom there could be no compromise. Remnick added, 'To understand Bibi [Benjamin's nickname], you have to understand the father.'

From the beginning, 'Bibi' outdid any others in his endless invocations of Churchill and Munich. In 1992 he claimed that Iran was 'three to five years' away from obtaining nuclear weapons, adding, 'It's 1938, and Iran is Germany,' a comparison he repeated on the Op-Ed page of the *New York Times*. Speaking in the Knesset, he told Yitzhak Rabin, the Labour prime minister, whose secret Oslo negotiations with the Palestinians had become public knowledge, 'You are worse than Chamberlain. He put another nation in danger, but you are doing it to your own nation.' Then in his 1995 book *A Place Among the Nations*, Netanyahu dilated at length on the Israeli predicament, in terms of Hitler, Chamberlain and Munich, suggesting that Israel was Czechoslovakia and 'Judea and Samaria', or the West Bank, was the Sudetenland, a parallel he may not have fully thought through (were the settlers the Czechs or the Sudeten Germans?). As Ari Shavit, an Israeli journalist who covered Netanyahu for years, put it, 'His worldview is very clear. Iran is Nazi Germany. Israel is England. He is Churchill and America is America.' At a huge rally in October 1995, Netanyahu spoke while the crowd chanted, 'Rabin is a traitor,' and 'In blood and fire we will get rid of Rabin,' while holding up posters of Rabin in SS uniform. The following month Rabin was assassinated by a right-wing fanatic. His widow Leah never forgave Netanyahu for what he had said.

Meantime in Washington, the *Weekly Standard* had been founded in 1995 as the voice of neoconservatism, backed by Rupert Murdoch and edited by William Kristol. In 1997, Kristol, and Robert Kagan launched the Project for a New American Century, 'to promote American global leadership', which was 'good both for America and for the world'. The twenty-five people who signed its original statement included Cheney and Rumsfeld, who shared the neocons' belief that a reshaping of the Middle East must begin by overthrowing Saddam Hussein. They also shared their veneration of Churchill and, if this predated the new millennium, it was inflamed by 11 September. Gertrude Himmelfarb now wrote that what 'we are rediscovering in the past is the idea of greatness – great individuals, great causes, great civilisations. It is no accident that Churchill has re-emerged now, at a time when the West is again under assault.'

When Bush was in the Oval Office, he joked that Churchill was watching his every move, in the form of a bust. This bust would become a source of great contention, and a mystery. There were in fact two busts. One was by Sir Jacob Epstein and was given in 1965 to President Johnson by Churchill's American 'wartime friends', as Lady Bird Johnson described them, during 'an evening of nostalgia'. These friends were principally Averell Harriman, the old commanders Carl Spaatz and Ira Eaker, as well as David Bruce, a former American ambassador in London. The Franklin D. Roosevelt Jrs, Anna Roosevelt and Ed Murrow's widow were present, and Kay Halle, who had been instrumental in the granting of honorary citizenship to Churchill. 'A special guest,' Lady Bird added, 'was youthful, pink-cheeked Winston Churchill, the grandson of Sir Winston, who is touring the United States.' When Blair visited Washington in 2001, he gave Bush another bust, also by Epstein. Bush had already installed the first bust in the Oval Office, but it needed to be repaired and so he replaced it with the second one. There was further confusion when Thatcher said that she had presented Reagan with a bust of Churchill.

At any rate, however many busts there were in the White House they weren't the only ones in Washington: Feith had a Churchill bust in his Pentagon office. That was only a small sign of neocon veneration. The *Weekly Standard* acclaimed Churchill as the 'Man of the Century', and Charles Krauthammer, the peculiarly vehement neocon columnist of the *Washington Post*, provided the standard fare: 'After having single-handedly saved Western civilization from Nazi barbarism – Churchill was, of course, not sufficient in bringing victory, but he was uniquely necessary – he then immediately rose to warn prophetically against its sister barbarism, Soviet communism.' Krauthammer gave the annual Churchill Dinner speech at Hillsdale College, whose president, Larry Arn, was an adviser to the International Churchill Society and had written an essay called 'How Winston Churchill Can Save Us – Again', which was one of 122 articles mentioning Churchill published by the *Weekly Standard* in the five years to 2004. Finally William Luti, another Pentagon ideologue, spelled it out in plain terms when he declared that 'Churchill was the first neocon.'

Abstruse arguments were advanced to explain why this might be so, or at least why there was a neoconservative cult of Churchill. One man praised or blamed was Leo Strauss, the Jewish German-born philosopher, who found a home, and founded a school, at the

University of Chicago, where he reared many pupils such as Allan Bloom. When the *Weekly Standard* pronounced Churchill 'Man of the Century', they quoted Strauss at the time of Churchill's death contrasting him with Hitler: 'The contrast between the indomitable and magnanimous statesman and the insane tyrant – this spectacle in its clear simplicity was one of the greatest lessons which men can learn, at any time.' But no elaborate explanation was needed for why a Jewish refugee from National Socialism admired Churchill, while 'neoconservatism' had very specific origins in the experience and outlook of a group of Americans disillusioned with liberalism.

None of this might have mattered if the neocons had been no more than 'calumnists or columnists', in Churchill's phrase, and even the more extreme manifestations of the Churchill cult need not have had consequences. The Reagan administration had been a hive of Churchillians, but they hadn't marched to war under his banner. This was different. One more of the group was David Frum, a Canadian like Krauthammer, who had damned Roosevelt: 'FDR has to be found wanting. Of the three great killers of this century, one (Mao) was aided by Communist sympathisers within the Roosevelt administration … Another (Stalin) benefited from Roosevelt's almost wilful naiveté about the Soviet Union.' Even with Hitler, Roosevelt's record was 'spotty', Frum said, as he 'hesitated to jeopardise his hopes for an unprecedented third term by riling isolationist opinion'. These were still no more than the views of one journalist, until Frum was hired by Bush as a speechwriter, and was responsible for the fateful – or fatal – phrase 'axis of evil' which Bush used in his January 2002 State of the Union address, intending Iraq, Iran and North Korea. Only the last of those possessed nuclear weapons, and 'axis' was a curious word to use about Iraq and Iran, which had not long ago fought a lengthy, bloody war and were still deeply hostile to each other. But the phrase served its purpose to beat the drums of war.

By now, a debate had opened up on the American Right, partly in response to traditional nativist isolationists like Patrick Buchanan, who argued that America should be 'a republic, not an empire' and plausibly condemned foreign adventures, while provocatively suggesting that American boys were being sent to war on behalf of Israel. But while some neocons insisted that the United States was not and never could be an empire, others began to admit that America was indeed an imperial power, and a good thing, too. The British historian Niall Ferguson derided the United States as an 'empire in denial' and argued it should recognise the need for what he called liberal imperialism, or 'democratic realism', in the phrase preferred by Krauthammer. Max Boot spelled out 'The Case for American Empire' in the *Weekly Standard*: 'Afghanistan and other troubled lands today cry out for the sort of enlightened foreign administration once provided by self-confident Englishmen in jodhpurs and pith helmets.'

With or without pith helmets, the intervention in Afghanistan was incompetently conducted, not least because the administration already had its eyes fixed on Iraq – and its minds on Churchill. After 11 September, when Giuliani was 'Churchill in a baseball cap' and Blair gave would-be Churchillian speeches about the Blitz, Bush had done all he could to don the mantle. 'We will not tire, we will not falter, and we will not fail,' he told a joint session of Congress on 20 September, consciously echoing Churchill's words of 9 February 1941. After stating that 'I loved Churchill's stand on principle', Bush now declared a 'war on terror'. He would still be speaking of it in February 2004 when he opened an exhibition, 'Churchill and the Great Republic', at the Library of Congress. 'Our current struggles or challenges are similar to those Churchill knew,' Bush said. 'One by one, we are finding and dealing with the terrorists, drawing tight what Winston Churchill called a "closing net of doom."'

Alongside the two hijacked aircraft which had destroyed the World Trade Center in New York, another crashed in a field in Pennsylvania after passengers fought back, and a fourth hit the Pentagon, where 125 people were killed. Donald Rumsfeld, Bush's Defence Secretary, described in affecting words how he had watched the wounded and dying being brought out on stretchers. Rumsfeld had been no friend of Bush the Elder. Having been the youngest ever Defence Secretary in the brief Ford administration, Rumsfeld had hoped that he would be Reagan's choice as running mate in 1980 rather than Bush, and ever after thought wistfully that he could have been vice president, and then president. He visited Baghdad on behalf of Reagan in 1983, and met Saddam Hussein, whom the Americans were supporting in their war against Iran. Bush the Younger had then appointed Rumsfeld Defence Secretary once more, now the oldest man ever to hold the office.

And maybe the most Churchillian. Even before the attacks, while explaining the need for a missile defence programme to a Senate committee, Rumsfeld had said, 'Winston Churchill once said, "I hope I shall never see the day when the forces of right are deprived of the right of force."' Then on the day after 11 September, Rumsfeld addressed the Pentagon staff: 'At the height of peril to his own nation, Winston Churchill spoke of their finest hour. Yesterday, America and the cause of human freedom came under attack.' On 25 September, asked whether he would allow deliberate deception of the press in the course of military operations, he replied, 'This conjures up Winston Churchill's famous phrase when he said ... sometimes the truth is so precious it must be accompanied by a bodyguard of lies.'

That particular Churchillian line had become all too familiar, and had been wilfully abused. Churchill had of course been speaking of wartime deception and disinformation, the *ruse de guerre* at which the British had excelled. From the body left by a submarine to be washed up on the coast of Spain in 1943, in the uniform of a British officer and carrying highly secret information which was in fact disinformation about landings in Sardinia and Greece rather than Sicily, to the immensely elaborate scheme which tricked the Germans into believing that the landing in 1944 would be in the Pas de Calais rather than Normandy, this was the story which had been told in entertaining as well as scholarly fashion by Michael Howard in *Strategic Deception in the Second World War*. Publication of this book was held up for nearly ten years by Margaret Thatcher, despite her admiration for Howard, with her exaggerated concern for security.

But Churchill meant deception of the enemy, a bodyguard of lies once the war was being waged. What Rumsfeld, and Bush, and Cheney, and not least Blair, had engaged in gave *ruse de guerre* fresh meaning: deception of their own people to persuade them *to go to war*. In April 2002 Blair visited Bush on his ranch at Crawford in Texas, and received his marching orders in an almost literal sense. A decision was taken to invade Iraq, and Blair promised that, come what may, British troops would take part in the invasion. This was followed by a campaign of unprecedented bellicosity and mendacity waged by both the Bush administration and Blair's Downing Street, on behalf of a preventive war, the very thing Churchill had repudiated so long before.

With all the ceaseless waving of Churchill's shroud, and the crossfire of the 'Churchill wars', the debate over his reputation still continued, and few people played a more prominent part on the Churchillian side than Andrew Roberts. Having made his name in 1990 with an outstanding life of Lord Halifax, Chamberlain's Foreign Secretary who might have succeeded him in 1940, Roberts then published a collection of well-researched and fascinating essays with the catchy if somewhat misleading title *Eminent Churchillians*. Among other things, it demolished what was left of Mountbatten's reputation, showed how deeply Churchill was still resented by many Tories even after he became prime minister, and revealed the depth of his racism. At the same time Roberts began to engage in political debate, describing himself somewhat superfluously as 'extremely right-wing', and never hesitating to play the provocateur: during the bitter Balkans conflicts of the mid-1990s he was unique in advocating the use of tactical nuclear weapons against the Serbs.

He also relentlessly denounced the European Union, in the press and in his quaint 1995 dystopian thriller *The Aachen Memorandum*. It imagined England in 2015 absorbed into the United States of Europe – the phrase Churchill used often enough – after a referendum rigged by a pro-European elite, while Iain Duncan-Smith, Niall Ferguson and Michael Gove are freedom-fighters in an underground Anti-Federalist Movement, and John Redwood leads a 'Free British' group from Oslo. In a more sober vein, Roberts published in 1999 a prize-winning biography of Salisbury, dedicated to Margaret Thatcher, 'thrice-elected *illiberal* Tory', echoing Salisbury's description of himself. Every year the Crosby Kemper Lecture is given at Westminster College in Fulton, on British and frequently Churchillian themes. The inaugural lecture in 1981 was inevitably by Martin Gilbert, and he was followed by many more Churchillians: Sir William Deakin, who helped write *The Second World War* after serving in Yugoslavia during that conflict, and later became the first Warden of St Anthony's College, Oxford, Sir John Colville, Lady Soames the daughter, and Edwina Sandys the granddaughter, as well as Robert Rhodes James, the author of *A Study in Failure*, and Sir Michael Howard. In 2000 Roberts lectured at Westminster College on 'Churchill and His Critics', and by now the author of *Eminent Churchillians* had himself become a pre-eminent Churchillian.

His lecture was a defiant riposte to those critics, who were 'knocking, aggressively carping, sometimes frankly contemptuous of Churchill and his achievements'. Apart from the detractors on the

English right, Roberts correctly identified a new attack coming from American right-wing isolationists, notably Patrick Buchanan, who had laid into Churchill in his book *A Republic, Not an Empire*, and who would return to the theme. In reply, Roberts listed the standard charge sheet against Churchill – Gallipoli, the General Strike, the gold standard, Indian nationalism, Bomber Command's campaign, and the 'soft underbelly of Europe' – before concluding, 'I personally believe he made the right choice in almost every single one of those cases.' A remarkable verdict indeed, going further than Churchill himself had gone. He was impenitent about Gallipoli, but admitted that returning to the gold standard was the worst mistake he had made. Oddest on Roberts's list was 'British official recognition of Soviet guilt over the Katyn massacres': Churchill acknowledged the truth that the Russians were responsible for Katyn, but only in private. A grotesque fiction was maintained that it was the work of the Germans, and the Foreign Office, out of cowardice or sheer habit, didn't acknowledge the truth about Katyn for many years. And Roberts's claim that 'It took Britain's dogged resistance during the Blitz and the Battle of Britain to convince America of Britain's worthiness as an ally' was curious, unless of course the lecturer was finding his own destiny as an advocate of American might.

In the spring of 2002, just at the time Blair went to Texas to pledge his fealty, a very different appraisal of Churchill was offered: a long essay which challenged the heroic version beloved of Bush, the neocons and Roberts. Christopher Hitchens's 'The Medals of His Defeats' was of more than usual interest, at a time when one war was being waged in Afghanistan and another was approaching in Iraq, and the more so because the author of the essay was about to make a Churchillian about-turn of his own. A clever, pugnacious, fluent English journalist, Hitchens had made a great success in America, partly because he was so readable, partly because he seemed to Americans so erudite, and partly because his insolent or sometimes outrageous flourishes seemed refreshing amid what Michael Kinsley called an American press 'para-lysed by gentility'.

He was no respecter of persons, as Henry Kissinger, Mother Teresa, and Bill Clinton had learned, before he turned to Churchill. It was amusing that Hitchens's assault on the Man of the Century should have appeared in the *Atlantic Monthly*, the magazine where Isaiah Berlin's eulogy had been published more than half a century before.

Some of what Hitchens said was true, or even commonplace. England was not 'alone' in 1940, and the threat of invasion was never very serious. Some of it was a familiar catalogue of Churchill's follies, squaring Hitchens off against Roberts: 'Gallipoli, the calamitous return to the gold standard, his ruling-class thuggery against the labour movement, his diehard imperialism over India, and his pre-war sympathy for fascism'.

And some of it was merely silly. Hitchens claimed that the broadcasts of three famous speeches in 1940 had not been Churchill himself speaking but an actor called Norman Shelley ('Perhaps Churchill was too much incapacitated by drink to deliver the speeches himself'), which was a complete myth. It was sillier still to say, 'I would not consider as qualified in the argument about Churchill anybody who had not read Irving's work,' since a London court case had recently, and not before time, demolished David Irving's claims to be a serious historian. When Hitchens wrote of 'an increasing scholarly understanding that only when Hitler made the mistake of fighting the Soviet Union and the United States simultaneously did he condemn himself to certain defeat', he was stating the obvious, and it had not taken 'the unsealing of more and more international archives' to show that the British contribution to victory was less than Churchill's telling of the tale had suggested.

'Yet the legend of 1940 has persisted,' Hitchens wrote. But was it just a legend? At the end he had to admit grudgingly that Churchill's defiance in 1940 really had been crucial. And when he wrote about his father, a naval officer who had taken part in the sinking of the *Scharnhorst* in December 1943, and called that 'a more solid day's work than any I have ever done', there was an echo of Churchillian bellicosity, and a hint of the turn Hitchens was soon to make. Before long he would be an active cheerleader for Bush, Blair and their war in Iraq, and would be pleased to find in London that 'Old leftist friends of mine from the 1960s are now on Labour's front bench and staunchly defend the overthrow of Saddam Hussein as a part of the noble antifascist tradition.' So anyone who had wondered what the American forces had been doing in Fallujah or Abu Ghraib now knew: they were fighting fascism. Behind this was a yearning which afflicted Hitchens by no means uniquely among his contemporaries. As his American wife later said, he was one of 'those men who were never really in battle and wished they had been'.

He didn't moderate his enthusiasm for the war even when it began to go badly wrong, and nor were the Washington warriors swayed in their admiration for Blair, or for their greatest hero of all. The admiration was reciprocated. In 2002, Charles Moore, the editor of the Tory *Daily Telegraph*, met Rumsfeld in Washington, and found that 'he looks like a fit, recently retired professor at an Ivy League university,' who 'talks with a don's intellectual interest, but an executive's concern for clarity and action.' By September 2005 that concern had borne few fruits in Iraq, but when Air Force 2 carrying Rumsfeld stopped briefly at Heathrow he was met for breakfast by a group who had come to pay homage, among them Moore, Roberts and William Shawcross.*

Two years later Roberts published the book which nourished Cheney on his visit to Afghanistan. *A History of The English-Speaking Peoples Since 1900* borrowed Churchill's title, and presented itself as a sequel taking up where his four volumes left off. Roberts told 'the story of the English-speaking peoples, who successively and successfully fought the Kaiser's Germany, Axis aggression and Soviet Communism, and who are now struggling against Islamic fundamentalist terrorism,' which might have seemed something of a stretch. 'The Kaiser's Germany' was defeated by the blood-sacrifice of the French army above all, and 'Axis aggression' was defeated by the blood-sacrifice of the Red Army, with the British in the second case, and the Americans in both cases, sustaining modest casualties by comparison. Soviet Communism was defeated by its own weakness and internal contradictions, as well as by patience, and even appeasement, while the 'war' against 'Islamic fundamentalist terrorism' was not going well as the book was published.

Just after Cheney returned from Afghanistan in 2007, the book's American publication was marked by a truly unusual author tour, described by Roberts himself in a truly unusual column. In New York dinners were given for him by the intellectual conservative *New Criterion* magazine; by Jayne Wrightsman, 'one of America's foremost philanthropists'; by Harold Evans and Tina Brown, where he faced 'polite but tough questioning' from Jon Meacham, Fareed Zakaria and

---

* More curiously the party contained Mark Birley, owner of the famous nightclub Annabel's. Someone in London suggested that he might have been looking for a new customer to replace Osama bin Laden, who once frequented the *boîte*.

Adam Gopnik; and finally by Henry and Nancy Kissinger, where the guests included Michael Bloomberg, George F. Will, Peggy Noonan and the 'charming, witty, good-natured and even slightly retiring' Rupert Murdoch'. Thence to Washington where Roberts bumped into John Bolton, who as American ambassador to the United Nations had suggested ripping several floors off the top of the UN building, and would later serve as Donald Trump's National Security Advisor, but was at that time enjoying the book, he said. 'Irwin Stelzer gave a big party at the Metropolitan Club for me,' Roberts wrote, 'and his friends Irving and Bea Kristol, Charles Krauthammer, Richard Perle and Charles Murray stayed for dinner afterwards. Then there were more speeches at the Heritage Foundation, Hudson Institute and Anglosphere Institute.' This was the full roster of the neoconservative elite and its corresponding think-tanks. The 'Anglosphere' was the latest variation on Churchill's 'English-speaking races' and 'special relationship', although at times it sounded more like Kipling's 'White Man's Burden'.

On the following morning Roberts went to the White House to lecture staffers and CIA officials. Before lunch, with Karl Rove, Steve Hadley, Cheney back from his Afghan visit, 'and a small group of distinguished journalists and proprietors', Roberts was asked whether he would like to go to the Oval Office to meet 'the reviewer-in-chief'. In their forty-minute conversation, Roberts discussed the 'war on terror' with 'the Leader of the Free World', and found that President Bush 'was full of resilience and fortitude – as I'd taken for granted he would be – but he was also thoughtful, charming and widely read.' At last he returned across the Atlantic 'to Paris for an intimate dinner with Nicolas and Cecilia Sarkozy at the home of Robert and Mathilde Agostinelli'.

All this was an astonishing achievement by a single writer, but Roberts's story is of greater significance. He personified the assimilation of Churchillism with American policy. At the same time, not every reviewer or reader of his book saw that the author's description of himself as extremely right-wing wasn't merely playful. Once again, Roberts out-Churchilled Churchill. In 1901 Churchill had hated 'this miserable war' in South Africa, 'cruel and hideous in its conclusion', meaning the concentration camps in which so many Boer civilians died. But Roberts now claimed that the Boer women and children were responsible for their own death because of their insanitary habits. In 1920, Churchill had condemned the Amritsar massacre and General Dyer's policy of exemplary violence – 'frightfulness is not a remedy known to the British pharmacopœia' – but Roberts defended the massacre for having restored order in the Punjab. These were dangerous waters for an eminent Churchillian in the twenty-first century.

Weeks after Roberts met the 'reviewer-in-chief', Blair left office. By then the Iraq War had gone horribly, and predictably, wrong but Blair was impenitent. Just before the invasion, he had met Jacques Chirac, the French president, who opposed the war, and was much derided and abused in America at the time as 'Jacques Chiraq', with congressmen fatuously ordering 'freedom fries' instead of French fries in the Capitol restaurant. Chirac told Blair that he and Bush had no personal experience of war, but that he did: a lifetime before, the young Chirac had served as a conscript in the French army fighting its horrible war in Algeria, which Iraq came to resemble all too closely, and he said that no one who had ever experienced such a war would want another. He said that the Americans and British expected to be welcomed with open arms, but shouldn't count on it, adding shrewdly that, in an artificial country with a divided society like Iraq, one shouldn't mistake the mere fact of a Shiite majority for what we would call democracy. And he asked whether Blair realised that by invading Iraq, he might yet precipitate a civil war. As the British team left, Sir Stephen Wall of the Foreign Office recalled, Blair said to them, 'Poor old Jacques, he just doesn't get it!' Alas, events proved that he got it rather better than Blair did.

Nine years after the invasion and five after he had left office, Blair was interviewed by the *Financial Times* and its then editor, Lionel Barber. Asked about the appallingly bloody implosion of Iraq which had followed the botched campaign, Blair said, 'What is very clear now is that the problem is, when you take the lid off these deeply oppressive and dictatorial regimes, out comes the pouring of a whole lot of religious, tribal, cultural, ethnic poison, which is then multiplied by the actors in the region who are engaged on either side of this battle between modernisation and atavism.' To which Barber could not forbear to say, 'Yet that was exactly what a small army of experts was telling him privately and publicly before the invasion of Iraq.'

Over his long life, Churchill made very many mistakes. He could be gravely wrong, and his name is clouded by his dark prejudices, not least his contempt for Arabs and for Islam. He might perhaps have supported a brutal assault on Saddam and his regime to 'drive them into the gutter, from which they should never have emerged', as he had urged with the Egyptians more than half a century before. But at least he wouldn't have been so foolish as to think that Iraq was ripe for turning into a constitutional democracy, or that it would then become friendly to the United States, Israel and the West.

In 1914 Churchill had favoured dispatching British and imperial troops to Basra, and he was fortunate to be out of office by the time of their defeat at Kut two years later. Blair also left office before another humiliation. When British troops had arrived in Basra in 2003 it seemed that they were welcomed by the local populace. Within four years, as the non-governmental International Crisis Group reported, 'relentless attacks against British forces' had driven them off the streets 'and into increasingly secluded compounds ... Basra's residents and militiamen view this not as an orderly withdrawal but rather as an ignominious defeat. Today, the city is controlled by militias, seemingly more powerful and unconstrained than before.' An American general agreed: 'I don't know that you could see the British withdrawal from Basra in any light other than a defeat.'

Partly because this disaster, where Churchill's spirit had been invoked to invade a country he had created, had gone awry in such grim fashion, critics returned again to question the Churchillian mystique. In 2008 the sacred icon was assaulted by two American iconoclasts, one from the left and one from the right. The eccentrically brilliant novelist Nicholson Baker published *Human Smoke: The Beginnings of World War II, the End of Civilization*, and Buchanan published *Churchill, Hitler, and 'The Unnecessary War': How Britain Lost Its Empire and the West Lost the World*. Baker's book was a collage of cuttings and quotations intended with a very unusual purpose. Churchill had been criticised often enough, but rarely indeed had the value and object of the war been questioned. 'Was it a "good war"?' Baker asked. 'Did waging it help anyone who needed help?' Less debatably, Baker showed how brutal Churchill could be, when he supported bombing for didactic purposes: 'Let them have a good dose where it will hurt them most ... It is time that the Germans should be made to suffer in their own homelands and cities.' As to Buchanan's claim that the Versailles settlement had been vindictive and had caused the next war, it was a very familiar argument, even if he expressed it in a vulgar way: 'France and

Britain got the peace they had wanted. Twenty years later, they would get the war they had invited.' This was a droll line coming from such a writer: the harshness of Versailles had long been a touchstone of specifically liberal opinion, and Buchanan wasn't specifically liberal.

After the Bush presidency petered out ingloriously, the 2008 presidential election was dominated – and in effect decided – by the legacy of Iraq. John McCain was the Republican candidate, a brave man who had, unlike most of the hawks at this time, served his country in action, and endured years in Vietnamese captivity, but he was doomed to lose by way of delayed reaction to Bush and his war. The year before the election McCain had visited England and been feted at the Conservative conference and in the pages of the *Spectator*, 'The special relationship between our two countries will endure throughout the twenty-first century,' McCain told that magazine. 'I say that with total confidence because it's lasted for 200 years.' This suggested a shaky grasp of history: those '200 years' would go back to the early years of the nineteenth century, or more specifically to 1812, when the two countries were at war.

As the year wore on, it became clear that McCain would be beaten by either possible Democratic candidate, Hillary Clinton or Barack Obama. Apart from her many other drawbacks, beginning with the fact that her political career had, as Camilla Puglia bluntly observed, been based on blatant nepotism, she had supported the Iraq War, and Obama had not. As she later said, privately, bitterly and correctly, that had been the decisive factor. Not only had Obama (who wasn't yet a senator in 2003 and hadn't been faced with the choice) not supported what was by now a deeply unpopular war, he barely paid lip service to the pieties of the 'special relationship', or Churchill. Obama had already made a name with his memoir, *Dreams From My Father*, and now published a campaign book, *The Audacity of Hope*, both a cut above the average of books by politicians. *The Audacity of Hope* has several pages on Indonesia, where Obama grew up, and mentions Galesburg, Illinois six times. England, Great Britain and the United Kingdom do not appear in the text, and Churchill isn't mentioned once. Maybe this was what Boris Johnson, an ambitious English politician who was then mayor of London, meant when he decried Obama as a foe of England.

★

During the presidential campaign a new crisis erupted in the Caucasus, between Russia and Georgia, an independent republic since the break-up of the Soviet Union, over the territory of South Ossetia, which few even well-informed people in the west could until then have easily found on a map. There was brief fighting, and the Georgian forces retired. To the limited extent that rights and wrongs could be established, it seemed that the Russians had tried bullying their neighbours, but also that Mikheil Saakashvili, the recently installed Georgian leader, had provoked a show-down in the hope that the Americans would back him. But if that hope was soon dashed, there was an almost clockwork predictability about the comparison invoked. When President Nicolas Sarkozy of France went on a grandstanding visit to Moscow to act as intermediary and gain a ceasefire, one sabre-rattling columnist in *The Times* described him on his return 'waving a piece of paper and acclaiming peace in our time.' In the *Washington Post*, the neoconservative Robert Kagan compared the Russian attack on Georgia to the 1938 'Sudeten Crisis that led to Nazi Germany's invasion of Czechoslovakia'. It remained only for a more than usually well-selected gaggle of interventionist 'public intellectuals'* to ask in the *Monde*, '*Le test géorgien, un nouveau Munich?*'

But the affair was not 'a new Munich' at all, except that, if any comparison were to be made between the two crises seventy years apart, it was that the people of South Ossetia had no more wanted to be ruled by the Georgians in 2008 than the Sudeten Germans had wanted to be ruled by the Czechs. And yet nothing daunted the new 'Munichers' – not in the earlier sense of that word to intend those who had supported the agreement, but those who endlessly now used the name as a curse, and decried any talk of compromise as appeasement. President Bush had dismissed the idea of talking to terrorists: 'We have heard this foolish delusion before. As Nazi tanks crossed into Poland in 1939, an American senator declared: "Lord, if I could only have talked to Hitler, all this might have been avoided."' Donald Rumsfeld had compared opponents of the Iraq War to 1930s appeasers. A 'bitter cup', Churchill had said in his speech attacking the Munich

---

* The signatories were Vaclav Havel, Valdas Adamkus, Mart Laar, Vytautas Landsbergis, Otto de Habsbourg, Daniel Cohn-Bendit, Timothy Garton Ash, André Glucksmann, Mark Leonard, Bernard-Henri Lévy, Adam Michnik and Josep Ramoneda.

agreement. Seventy years later, after the ghost of Munich had haunted Suez, Vietnam and Iraq, the dregs of the cup were still bitter.

When Blair left Downing Street, the House of Commons and, it seemed, England itself all at once, to be signed up by J.P. Morgan and a Swiss finance company and embark on a new life as a well-rewarded advisor to sundry rulers such as the president for life of Kazakhstan, he was succeeded by Gordon Brown, Chancellor of the Exchequer for the previous ten years. The Tories had already acquired their fifth leader in those ten years, the fresh-faced David Cameron. By early 2009 Obama had been inaugurated, and British politicians were eager to meet him. Brown made his first visit to pay homage to the new president at the White House bearing gifts, both symbolic, one imaginative. A desk sits in the Oval Office made of oak taken from HMS *Resolute*, one of the ships with which the Royal Navy conducted its campaign against slavery, and Brown gave Obama a penholder carved from the timbers of HMS *Gannet*, *Resolute*'s sister ship.

But he also gave him Martin Gilbert's seven-volume biography of Churchill, even though there was very likely to have been a copy already in the White House. In return, the president gave the prime minister a set of movies on DVD, from *Citizen Kane* to *Raging Bull*. Completing the contrast between the guest's eagerness to please and his host's indifference, Brown gave young Sasha and Malia Obama outfits from Topshop; Fraser and John Brown got models of Marine One, the presidential helicopter, worth several dollars each. Then when Obama visited London, Cameron gave him CDs of British rock bands The Smiths, Radiohead and Gorillaz, and a copy of Churchill's *History of the English-Speaking Peoples*. At least he didn't give him *My African Journey*, with its disdainful descriptions of Obama's Kenyan forebears. Not long after this, Cameron said that the British were of course junior partners of the United States, 'just as we were junior partners in 1940', whereupon the tabloids summoned indignant old Desert Rats and fighter pilots to remind him that the Americans hadn't been partners at all at the time.

Not even in the United States was Churchill's name more resonant than in Israel, and one Israeli more than any liked to bask in his aura. In 2011, Netanyahu was the subject of a long and reverential interview in the *Daily Telegraph* by Charles Moore, that paper's former editor.

Just as Rumsfeld had reminded Moore of an Ivy League professor, he now found Netanyahu 'ruminative, almost professorial ... His talk is full of historical parallels and dates'. When asked about the West Bank settlements, 'He comes straight back with a historical parallel – the Sudetenland in the late 1930s: "People, especially the leading British media", considered that Czechoslovakia's possession of these German-speaking areas was "the barrier to peace with Hitler", but "It didn't work out quite like that."'

On one other point Netanyahu was equally emphatic. 'He wants to remind Europeans that Israelis are staying put: "We are not neo-Crusaders. We are not neo-colonials."' He was worried in particular about the British, once so sympathetic to Israel but no more. There were 'two streams' in British attitudes to Israel and the Jews, Netanyahu claimed. 'One, exemplified by Lloyd George's "understanding of history" in the Versailles era', was admirable, but there were also 'bad attitudes', for which he could see an explanation: 'Britain was a colonial power, and colonialism has been spurned,' Netanyahu correctly said. 'The British therefore looked at the Israeli question through their own "colonial prism",' which made them 'see us as neo-colonialists'. But that was entirely wrong: 'We are not Belgians in the Congo! We are not Brits in India!'

By now it had become a touchstone for defenders of Israel that Zionism was a movement of 'national liberation', or 'the self-determination of the Jewish people', and above all that it was in no way whatever a colonial enterprise. Apart from the awkward fact that, in 1896 when Theodor Herzl published his little book *Der Judenstaat*, adumbrating such a Jewish state, Jews were barely a twentieth of the population of the Holy Land, this denial was truly anachronistic. Political Zionism had been born in the heyday of European nationalism and colonialism, and it would have been surprising had it not partaken of both. In any case, not only was the etymology of 'colonial' benign – a *colonus* in Latin is a farmer, a *casa colonica* in Italian is a farmhouse – the word was in no way opprobrious in Churchill's early lifetime: Canada and New Zealand were happy to be known as 'the Colonies', whose leaders met in London for the Colonial Conference, and indeed for the earliest Zionists it was a matter of pride that they were *coloni* or farmers. But then Netanyahu was certainly right in saying that 'colonialism has been spurned': word and concept had gone right out of fashion by the end of the twentieth century.

And yet there was one English statesman Netanyahu revered, he said, and he moved across his office so that he could be photographed in front of the portrait of Sir Winston Churchill which hung there. It didn't occur to the interviewer to ask Netanyahu whether he was under the impression that Churchill was opposed to colonialism, or was ashamed of the British Raj in India. Was 'Bibi' unaware that Churchill had expressed his support for Zionism from the beginning in enthusiastically imperialist and colonial terms? Did he know of – or would he have agreed with? – Churchill's saying that the Jews deserved to replace the Palestinian Arabs, as the American Indians and aborigines had been replaced, because the Jews were 'a higher-grade race'?

A year after this interview, a party was given by the Israeli embassy in London for members of the Churchill family, to thank their forebear for all he had done for Zionism and the Jewish state, and a statue of Churchill was unveiled in Jerusalem by young Randolph Churchill, Sir Winston's great-grandson. As a slight interruption to this pattern of reciprocal adoration, in October 2014 the House of Commons passed a declaratory resolution recognising a notional state of Palestine, with one of those voting in favour Churchill's grandson, Sir Nicholas Soames. But then, the following year, Netanyahu gave a rapturously received address to Congress, which was a barely disguised attack on the President of the United States. Just beforehand, Steve Forbes, a magazine publisher who had worked for the Reagan administration and twice been a candidate for the Republican nomination, wrote of the importance of this address to Congress: 'Netanyahu, The Churchill Of Our Time'.

Epilogue: 'Another scale of values'
Bladon 2021

In 2020, the world was ravaged by a pandemic more virulent than any known since the influenza which had followed the Great War a hundred years earlier, and killed more people than that war itself. This time, within a year of the arrival of coronavirus in the United States, the Americans who had died of it outnumbered the fatalities of all American armed forces in every foreign war since 1776. It may be that the fears and tensions heightened by this pestilence helped fuel another rage, against the injustices of the age, and of other ages also. One form this took was a passion for erasing the ugly past. 'Every statue and street and building has been renamed,' Orwell imagined in *Nineteen Eighty-Four*, and now many statues were torn down and buildings renamed.

'His noble presence and gentle, kindly manner were sustained by religious faith and an exalted character,' Churchill wrote of the Confederate general Robert E. Lee, but the House of Representatives decided that exalted character was outweighed by his history as a slave-owner when they voted to remove Lee's statue from the Capitol. Churchill was derisive about Woodrow Wilson's pose as 'a stainless Sir Galahad championing the superior ideals of the American people', but he was unconcerned by Wilson's racial prejudices and policies, and never imagined that Princeton, where Wilson had once been the college president, would remove his name from the institute which had long borne it. While praising the mining magnate and imperial adventurer Cecil Rhodes as a man with 'the energy that often makes dreams come true', Churchill had predicted that the consequences of his career 'have yet to run their course', little guessing that one belated consequence would come when Oxford University and Oriel College, for generations the beneficiaries of Rhodes's largesse, yielded to angry demonstrators, and removed his bust which had long stared down on the High Street.

And then they came for Churchill. There are very many statues, portraits and busts of him, some celebrated, some contentious, but the most famous of all is the statue sculpted by Ivor Roberts-Jones, which stands in Parliament Square. Since it was unveiled by Churchill's widow in 1973 the statue had become a vivid embodiment of Churchill's afterlife. A photograph taken from behind, with Churchill casting a long shadow as he gazes balefully at the Palace of Westminster, has been used over and again, on sales catalogues or by the *Daily Mail* as it campaigned against British membership of the European Union. Prosperous devotees of Churchill could buy one of 500 bronze casts of the sculptor's original maquette, which were sold by the sophisticated St James's art gallery MacConnell-Mason for £275,000 each. Another art work was created by the graffitist Banksy, with a piece of turf facetiously placed along Churchill's pate like a 'Mohican' haircut.

In June 2020, demonstrators clambered on to the plinth bearing the statue, where the single name 'Churchill' is carved, and one of them daubed it so as to read 'Churchill was a racist'. The slogan was quickly erased and the statue boarded up to protect it from further assault. Outraged about this sacrilege, the *Daily Mail* began an online petition urging Boris Johnson, whom the whims of fate had now made prime minister, 'to publicly promise that Churchill's statue will *never* be torn down'. And then, following the American election in November, the interminable story of the White House bust was reprised, with the news that Joe Biden intended to replace Churchill, this time with Cesar Chavez.

Much of the story told in this book has been about images, either in the art historian's sense, or the advertising agent's, or even the hagiologist's. Churchill's image as well as his name and aura remain powerfully charged, and potentially fraught. If anything, it was surprising that those whom the Right derided as zealots of political correctness or 'woke warriors' had taken so long to catch up with Churchill, his unique stature seemingly having made him invulnerable. As it was, 2020 proved to be a year full of Churchillian resonances. On its last day, the United Kingdom left the European Union after forty-seven years, under a prime minister who had written a book on Churchill and was compared to him by admirers. And the departure of an American president who had also been compared to Churchill was accompanied by unimagined scenes of violence. Did these events mark a moment of triumph for Churchillism and the Churchill cult, or a final crisis?

Over the previous decade Churchill's memory had shone, often more brightly than ever, and echoes of the Finest Hour had never rung more loudly. In 1897, the year of Queen Victoria's Diamond Jubilee, Churchill rode his grey pony into Afghanistan. British soldiers were fighting there again in 2012, when Queen Elizabeth II celebrated her own Diamond Jubilee by becoming only the second British monarch to reach sixty years on the throne. It turned into another Churchillian triumph. Even the miserable English summer weather couldn't stop the Jubilee from being a cheerful occasion. If not quite 'From Clee to heaven the beacon burns,' there were many bonfires and street parties across the country. A grand service was held at St Paul's Cathedral, after a royal party had sat sheltering not very comfortably from the rain in a boat which made its way down the Thames, as part of a flotilla which included some of the 'little boats' which had brought the men back from Dunkirk, while a Spitfire and a Lancaster flew overhead. That summer London also staged the Olympic Games. A ridiculous opening ceremony was a mixture of kitsch and political propaganda, but the closing ceremony was still more bizarre. A giant effigy of Churchill loomed up, with Timothy Spall, an excellent actor who had been wildly miscast as Churchill in *The King's Speech*, reciting Shakespeare.

In America as well the obsession with Churchill showed no signs of abating. A very well arranged exhibition, 'Churchill: The Power of Words' at the Morgan Library in New York, was such a huge success as to take the library by surprise, with far more visitors than had been envisaged. Less surprising was the success of the final volume of *The Last Lion*, the three-part biography begun by William Manchester in 1983. His appointed successor to finish the work was Paul Reid, a newspaperman who hadn't written a book before but tried to master Manchester's style as Churchill's ghostwriters had once mastered his, albeit with unhappy effect: 'The honourable fight for British survival made the war great for Churchill ...' he wrote, 'Britons, pummelled since 1940, stood by their Winnie.'

That devotion to one famous Englishman fitted in with a continuing American infatuation with all things English, ranging from a love of English clothing (the Burberry syndrome) to Masterpiece Theater on television and a succession of English programmes giving a glossily sentimentalised version of country-house life, from *Brideshead Revisited* to *Downton Abbey* and, of course, Chartwell as it appeared in so many Churchill dramadocs or biopics. But then there was nothing exclusively American about what the French call *la mode rétro* and the English 'the heritage industry', a consuming interest in the past. To judge from the bestseller lists in the second decade of this new century, in England this meant an absorption with the things its people no longer knew personally: rural life and fighting wars. Two delightful books about communing with nature – *H is for Hawk* by Helen Macdonald in 2014, and *The Shepherd's Life* by James Rebanks the following year – were runaway successes, although falconry and shepherding in the Lake District were utterly remote from most people's lives.

So was war, an appetite for which, or rather for memories of which, seemed insatiable and if anything increased with the passing of time. A genre sardonically dubbed 'warnography' saw books pour forth, some good, many bad, on Normandy and Arnhem, on the Battle of the Atlantic and Stalingrad. In 2016, more than seventy years after VE Day, the five best-selling British history books included Beevor's *Ardennes 1944*, Hastings's *The Secret War: Spies, Codes and Guerrillas 1939–1945*, and Damien Lewis's *Churchill's Secret Warriors*. And these were the serious writers. Further down-market, in a branch of the newsagents W.H. Smith that year, one could find a large batch of magazines which included *Military History*, billing a piece on 'Hitler's Secret Weapon', *World War II* with 'The Making of a Legendary Sniper', *History of War* with 'Churchill's Cutthroats', and *Britain at War* with an article on the Avro Lancaster. As if to show that *nostalgie de la guerre* could spread to more peaceful activities – and to one which Churchill had enjoyed – that year Lancaster Bomber was the name of a promising two-year-old racehorse, owned by a syndicate who also owned horses called Churchill and Clemmie.

If naming a horse after a bomber might seem frivolous, the year of the Queen's Jubilee also saw a grimmer and more ambiguous legacy of Churchill and his war with the unveiling of a memorial to Bomber Command. Sixty-seven years after the last of its 55,573 aircrew had been killed, it might seem a belated atonement for Churchill's neglect, the oblivion to which he had consigned the bombing campaign, but that wasn't the whole story. There had been much agitation for such a memorial, and it was a gesture of defiance against liberal sentiment, and Europe, mostly paid for by an odd collection of right-wing businessmen, including a pornographer into whose hands Beaverbrook's *Daily Express* had fallen during its long decline. The aircrew deserved better than that, or than tabloid columnists still shouting that the Germans had got what they asked for – or maybe than the memorial itself. A large and ungainly structure, created by Philip Jackson, the Royal Sculptor, it stands on the edge of Green Park where Piccadilly meets Hyde Park Corner. Beneath a pillared arch is a plinth on which stand bronze statues of aircrew in flying gear as if about to board a Lancaster. Inscribed on the arch are Churchill's words, '... the bombers alone provide the means of victory,' whilst on the plinth are Pericles' words: 'Freedom is the sure possession of those alone who have the courage to defend it.'

Across the road, on the large island surrounded by incessant traffic, are several Great War memorials, among them Charles Jagger's huge bas-relief for the Royal Artillery and a much smaller sculpture commemorating the Machine Gun Corps, for whom it was thought fitting to inscribe the biblical line, 'Saul hath slain his thousands, and David his ten thousands.' That would have been apter still for Bomber Command, whose own dead were outnumbered so many times over by their victims. Although there might have been criticism and controversy surrounding the wartime campaign, it had a very real legacy – from the American bombing which had devastated Vietnam in the 1960s and 70s, to the drones which could be guided towards Afghanistan by someone in New Mexico nearly 8000 miles away to hit a group of Taliban fighters, or a wedding party as the case might be.

When Obama arrived at the White House he removed, or at any rate moved, the bust of Churchill on which his predecessor had so doted and replaced it with one of Abraham Lincoln. Moving the bust was 'a snub to Britain', Johnson had claimed, which illustrated 'the part-Kenyan president's ancestral dislike of the British empire – of which Churchill had been such a fervent defender'. When challenged about Churchill, Obama felt obliged to say, not very convincingly, 'I love the guy', but by 2012 when he ran for re-election, the *New York Times* reported that 'the question of whether Barack Obama or Mitt Romney [his Republican opponent] will occupy the White House has been overshadowed at times by the question of whether Winston

Churchill will do so.' Romney challenged Obama for having moved the bust, and promised to restore it if elected. Despite the incantation of Churchill's name by his opponent, Obama was re-elected and inaugurated again in 2013. Almost as a rebuke, yet another Churchill bust was unveiled, this time in the Capitol. In words more trite than strictly true, John Boehner, the Speaker of the House of Representatives, declared that 'Winston Spencer Churchill was the best friend the United States ever had.'

In all this Churchillolatry there was a contradiction. As in 1945, Churchill continued to be portrayed as 'the leader of humanity', which is how visitors to the Morgan Library or those watching the Olympics ceremony could doubtless imagine him. And yet he was also invoked, and his renown was claimed, in highly partisan fashion: by the neoconservatives who said he was one of theirs, by English Europhobes, by Romney and pretty well all Republicans, and by nationalists in other countries also.

No country had been solely responsible for the great crash of 2007–8, the worst economic disaster the capitalist West had known since the crash and Depression of 1929–31, until the arrival of coronavirus in 2020. No government handled it well, and no one remembered Churchill's admirable principle, 'I want to see Industry more happy, and Finance less proud,' or dared tame the pride of finance, the bankers and hedge fund managers whose recklessness had brought about the disaster. Gordon Brown had with poetic justice taken over from Tony Blair when the bubble burst and banks collapsed. Obama inherited the crisis in 2009 but was too cautious about upsetting the natural order to take failing (and dishonest) banks into public ownership, let alone see that crooked bankers were condignly punished. Maybe it was hard to foresee what the longer consequences of these events would be over the next ten or more years, harder to foresee how politically turbulent those years would be, and hardest to predict how Churchill would loom over them all until the baroque finale.

At the 2010 British election 'New Labour' were finally routed but no party won an outright parliamentary majority. After the Great War there had been a Coalition government of Tories and the Liberal faction under Lloyd George, which was warmly supported by Churchill; now, ninety years later, another coalition was formed, of Tories under David Cameron and Liberal Democrats under Nick

Clegg, which embarked on a policy of severe austerity, with spending on public services drastically reduced. Lloyd George's Coalition hadn't done the Liberals much good, and this new coalition didn't do the 'Lib Dems' much good either. Churchill jumped ship back to the Tories in 1924, and Clegg eventually left politics when he lost his parliamentary seat and landed a highly paid job as a lobbyist for Facebook. Some Churchillians found words to praise the new prime minister. Niall Ferguson was one of a new breed of television dons or 'hackademics', and in his own words 'a fully paid-up member of the neo-imperialist gang.'* In 2012 he published an admiring interview-profile of David Cameron. The young prime minister's 'dream is not a return to the England of Downton Abbey,' Ferguson averred. 'It's an authentically British dream – of a multi-ethnic United Kingdom ... Churchill would surely have approved.' Would the Churchill who complained about 'the magpie society' and at his last Cabinet meeting in 1955 commended the slogan 'Keep England White' really have approved a multi-ethnic country? The fatuous, or perhaps cynical, separation of an ideal 'Churchill' from the real man could scarcely proceed further.

In May 2013 Mary Soames died aged ninety-one. She was Churchill's last surviving child, and the only one whose life had been happy and successful. Although by no means a soft personality, she inspired much respect and affection. Widowed for a quarter-century, she had flowered in later life, emerging from the shadows of a famous husband and a far more famous father. Her biography of her mother was published in 1979 to deserved applause and won the Wolfson Prize. It wasn't just 'a delightful book', as A.J.P. Taylor called it; its candour was a reproach to some of the more hagiographical lives of Churchill. Lady Soames described a marriage between two formidable personalities which withstood the strains imposed on it by Churchill's egomania and Clementine's highly-strung and sometimes chilly temperament, although at heavy cost to their other three children.

More than twenty years later, Lady Soames published *Speaking for Themselves*, a collection of her parents' letters, and then in 2011 as a

---

* He was widely believed to be the inspiration for Irwin, the paradox-mongering historian-on-the-make in Alan Bennett's play *The History Boys*, who says, 'The Japanese were caught napping at Pearl Harbor.'

swansong her equally delightful memoir *A Daughter's Tale*, which gave the true tang of her childhood and of the war years. During Blitz and blackout, her gang of friends had met at the Players' Theatre in Covent Garden, where the young Peter Ustinov performed an 'intimate and cliquey' cabaret, making their way home as best they could at 2 a.m., until the bombing intensified and patrons were encouraged to bring pillows and blankets and stay the night. Four years later, Mary was commanding her own anti-aircraft battery, and it was hard not to think back to those days at her memorial service when 1300 people filled Westminster Abbey, led by the Prince of Wales and several members of the Order of the Garter: Lady Soames had been only the second woman admitted to the elect order which her father had also joined.

An almost more striking testimony to Churchill's aura came with the sale of her possessions. It had already become a pattern that Churchilliana, his paintings or anything else associated with him, would not only always sell, but sell for much more than experienced auctioneers expected. Sotheby's called its sale 'Daughter of History: Mary Soames and the Legacy of Churchill' and turned it into a great occasion, with a series of readings by the actors Emilia and Edward Fox, and talks by the art historian David Coombs and the author James Holland as well as by Nicholas Soames. Among the items on sale were several portraits of Churchill by Sir Oswald Birley, but the main attractions were Churchill's own paintings, above all 'The Goldfish Pool at Chartwell', which he painted in 1932 and chose to illustrate his 1948 book *Painting as a Pastime*. With a highest estimate of £80,000, it sold for £357,000. Not all of Lady Soames's collection was offered for sale. She left a gross sum of £24 million in trust for her four children, a large part of which would normally have gone to the government, but a further thirty-eight paintings by Churchill were offered to the nation in lieu of inheritance tax. Churchillian adroitness in dealing with the burden of taxation hadn't deserted the family.

A dizzying succession of events now turned British politics upside down, with American politics following close behind. The days when an English carpetbagger like Churchill could represent a Scottish seat were long gone, and a sometimes resentful vein of nationalism had not, as Blair had hoped, been stemmed but strengthened by devolved government in Edinburgh. In a referendum in 2014 the people of

Scotland did vote to remain in the Union, but then turned against the parties which supported it. In 1997, the Tories had been obliterated in Scotland, to much Labour gloating. Now, at the 2015 general election Cameron and the Tories upset polls and pundits by winning an outright parliamentary majority, and it was Labour's turn to be almost wiped out in Scotland.

There was another portent at that election: the return to Parliament of Boris Johnson, although he was still Mayor of London and held the two positions pluralistically for another year. Six months before the election he had published *The Churchill Factor*, a trite and breezy study of 'how one man made history', which clearly hinted that another man might do the same: this was a campaign autobiography posing as a tribute. Apart from one interesting chapter on Churchill's rhetoric, which drew on Johnson's Classical education, the book was written in the manner his readers had come to expect. Churchill sometimes sounds 'like a chap who has had a few too many at a golf club bar' while some of his grosser racist utterances are no more than 'the unpasteurised Churchill'. One enemy of his is an 'ocean-going creep', Bracken is a 'carrot-topped Irish fantasist', Lord Halifax is 'the beanpole-shaped appeaser,' one thing or another is 'wonky ... bonkers ... tootling'. This was the Finest Hour related by Bertie Wooster.

'Too clever' was what Churchill had said in 1940 about a draft speech which was 'unsuited to the tragic simplicity and grandeur of the times and the issues at stake'. What might he have said about Johnson's writing? But then maybe Johnson really was the man for his age, an age as incapable as himself of tragic simplicity and grandeur. Orwell's Newspeak was a language so constructed that it was strictly impossible to express any subversive sentiment. In 'Borispeak' it was equally impossible to say anything serious; if Johnson was a new Churchill, then never had tragedy been more blatantly played as farce. And yet an academic critic who dismissed the book as 'a self-aggrandising pot-boiler' spoke too soon – or perhaps too truly. It was a runaway bestseller boiling many a pot, and if it was meant to aggrandise the author then it succeeded in a way nothing Churchill wrote had ever done. Churchill didn't become prime minister because of his life of Marlborough, but *The Churchill Factor* played an unmistakable part in Johnson's ascent towards Downing Street.

★

On 30 January 2015, the fiftieth anniversary of Churchill's death, an official year of commemoration began with a wreath-laying ceremony under the auspices of the Houses of Parliament. Several television programmes looked back half a century, with Jeremy Paxman discussing Churchill's continuing significance, while the Science Museum in London displayed 'Churchill's Scientists', an exhibition showing Churchill's fascination with science and its military application from radar to the atomic bomb, and travel companies offered tours from 'In Churchill's Footsteps' to 'Commemorating Churchill: Power Houses of the Home Counties'. In May the thirty-second annual International Churchill Conference was held at Blenheim. Many of these events, and others in America, Europe and Australia, were coordinated as 'Churchill 2015', organised by 'an alliance of Churchill-related institutions from around the world ... focused on commemorating his achievements' and their 'vibrant existing legacy'. Behind all of this in turn was the International Churchill Society, the formidable body promoting 'the development of educational resources and programmes relating to the life and legacy of Sir Winston Churchill'. Alongside the success of *The Churchill Factor* the anniversary celebrations played a part in the sequence of events now unfolding.

One other portent, and surprise, at the 2015 election was the remarkable performance of the Europhobic United Kingdom Independence Party, although that was really a misnomer and UKIP was essentially an English nationalist party. Its leader was Nigel Farage, a self-confident and fluent demagogue, who liked to be photographed with a cigarette in one hand and a pint of beer in the other in front of a picture of Churchill. Now UKIP capitalised not only on hostility to European immigrants but on reciprocal English resentment of Scottish sway over national politics, and gained votes from Labour as much as from the Tories. Thanks to the rigidities of the electoral system they only won one seat, but they took a startling 12.7 per cent of the popular vote. More than ever, the relationship with Europe, and membership of the European Union, would now dominate British politics.

Until 1975 there had never been a referendum in Great Britain, and both Attlee and Thatcher had deplored what Thatcher called 'the device of dictators and demagogues'. Now, in 2015, Cameron was spooked both by UKIP and by the noisy Europhobes in his own party. Without the wit to quote Attlee and Thatcher, he promised a referendum on British membership of the European Union, as a tactical manœuvre to keep his party together, and swallowed his own poison pill. The referendum was to be held little more than a year after the election, on 23 June 2016. If the American election four years before had sometimes seemed less a contest as to whether Obama or Romney would occupy the White House than whether Churchill would, then this referendum campaign turned into a contest for Churchill's mantle. He himself bore some responsibility, as he had been so contradictory and ambiguous, from writing about 'a United States of Europe', in 1930 to telling de Gaulle in 1944 that 'we will always choose the open seas' over Europe to his 'with' but not 'of' in 1952. But Churchill had had a personal involvement in the European movement through his sons-in-law Duncan Sandys and Christopher Soames, and in 1961 he had told the chairman of the Conservative Association in his constituency: 'I am sometimes given credit for stimulating the ideals of European unity which led to the formation of the economic and the other two communities ... I think the Government are right to apply to join the European Economic Community.'

Ignoring that, the rightwing tabloids the *Sun* and the *Daily Mail* vied with images of the great man urging a Leave vote, Farage was as free and familiar as ever with his name, while one Tory right-winger after another waved the Union Jack and chanted Winston's name. And yet from the other side came a magisterial intervention, in the imposing personages of the Duke of Wellington and Sir Nicholas Soames. 'As descendants of Marlborough, Wellington and Churchill,' they wrote, 'we feel strongly that the country cannot escape the lessons of history, that Europe succumbs to division when Britain turns its back on our continent. The EU has fostered democracy in place of communist tyranny in the East and fascist dictatorship in the South. Britain's destiny and self-interest has always been to secure Europe's peace and freedom. It would be short-sighted and irresponsible to quit the EU and leave our continent to its fate.' A similar if sharper point was made by the author of *Winston's War.* Max Hastings recalled Raymond Seitz, 'the shrewdest US ambassador here in modern times', who had told him twenty years earlier, 'Always remember that the United States is interested in Britain only in so far as it is a player in Europe.' Hastings correctly added that 'the notion of a "special relationship" was invented for reasons of political expediency by Winston Churchill, who then became the first of many prime ministers to discover it to be a myth.'

Having promised the referendum in the hope that he wouldn't have to keep his promise, and then called it in the expectation of winning for Remain, Cameron began to sense the campaign slipping away. Shortly before the vote he was asked whether he was a 'twenty-first-century Neville Chamberlain'. That was 'exactly the red rag needed to bring out my bullishness', he recalled, and so he replied: 'In my office I sit two yards away from the Cabinet Room where Winston Churchill decided in May 1940 to fight on against Hitler ... He didn't quit on Europe ... he didn't quit on European freedom. We want to fight for these things today.' He called this 'My finest hour of the campaign'.

Like Wilson forty-one years before, Cameron allowed his party, and his cabinet, to differ, and take opposite sides. What he didn't expect was the desertion of two men he thought of as allies, Johnson and Michael Gove. Johnson had to decide which side to back, and even wrote two *Daily Telegraph* columns, one for Remain and one for Leave, and then chose the one which would suit his interests better. As Dominic Lawson, a former editor of the Tory *Sunday Telegraph*, and himself a committed Leaver, pointed out, 'Johnson was never in favour of Brexit, until he found it necessary to further his ambition to become Conservative leader.' He was exactly 'the transatlantic type of demagogue ("Them's my sentiments and if they don't give satisfaction they can be changed")' that Churchill had once been called well over a hundred years before, and committed Europhobes might even have felt as Lord Wolmer had felt when he joined the campaign against the India Bill: 'He *discredits* us. *We* are acting from conviction but everybody knows Winston has no convictions; he has only joined us for what he can get out of it.'

Even so, in 1940 Churchill had been passionately convinced that he was in the right and that, despite everything, he would win. In 2016 Cameron called the referendum not believing he would lose, and Johnson and Gove had backed Leave not believing they would win. Nor did most people, and the outcome – 51.89 per cent Leave, 48.11 per cent Remain – caused a real shock, to many people in England, and still more in Scotland and Northern Ireland which had both voted Remain. Cameron immediately resigned and was quickly replaced not by the egregious Johnson but by Theresa May, a stolid, unexciting vicar's daughter, to whom it was left to implement 'the will of the people'.

Maybe Churchill's ghost also spooked participants and onlookers alike in the political dramas on the other side of the Atlantic in 2016;

certainly many people found it hard to believe what was happening. When Donald Trump, a shady property dealer and star of a television reality show, entered the contest for the Republican nomination he didn't expect to win that, let alone the presidential election the following year, and neither did anyone else: bookies' odds were 4–1 against Trump up to Election Day on 8 November. Once again, clever people took a view which was a conceptual confusion: when 'respectable America' – the liberal media, college faculties, the intellectual and cultural establishment – declared that the very idea of Donald Trump as president was unthinkable, what they meant was that it didn't bear thinking about.

After he did win, he spoke to nine other national leaders before taking a telephone call from Mrs May, when he showed his own understanding of their relationship by saying, 'If you travel to the US, you should let me know.' That was only blunter than his predecessor had been, for the 'special relationship' had been regarded as 'something of a joke' inside the Obama administration, those who worked in it said. But there was one very important difference. Unlike any previous president Trump openly declared his disdain for the European Union, and his enthusiasm for what was now called 'Brexit'. He treated the formidable German chancellor Angela Merkel with open contempt (which was reciprocated in full), while befriending Farage and singing Boris Johnson's praises. His weirdly demagogic and disruptive four years at the White House would completely upend international as well as domestic politics.

For three years a Westminster Parliament with a majority of Members who had supported Remain was polarised and paralysed. May called a snap election in June 2017 hoping to increase her parliamentary majority, but instead lost it. Her government staggered on, not much helped by a visit Trump paid to England the month after the election. To his chagrin it wasn't a state visit – his unpopularity in London made a journey through the streets with the queen in a golden coach inadvisable – and he was taken by helicopter from the American ambassador's residence, itself an isolated and heavily guarded compound, to Blenheim. There Mrs May waited on a red carpet to greet the president, and the bands of the Scots, Irish and Welsh Guards inappropriately played 'Amazing Grace' as Trump paid homage in the room where Churchill was born. May had ill-advisedly made Johnson Foreign Secretary when she became prime minister,

but just before Trump's visit he deserted her as he had deserted
Cameron before, and within little more than a year the pressure of
events and the discontent of her own party and cabinet forced her to
resign, to be succeeded by the author of *The Churchill Factor*.

Political upheaval was accompanied by a new wave of Churchillism.
A new £5 note issued by the Bank of England, and designed to be
washable if not actually indestructible, showed the Queen on one side
and Churchill's growling face on the other, above the words 'I have
nothing to offer but blood, toil, tears and sweat.' In that referendum
year, yet more actors came forward to play Churchill, for all that the
role was, as A.A. Gill of the *Sunday Times* called it, 'an iceberg for
titanic thespian aspirations'. Michael Gambon played the title part in
Churchill's Secret (the secret was his stroke in 1953 and the cover-up)
and in *The Crown* John Lithgow gave what Gill called 'a marvellously
monstrous rendition of the old sot', leaving aside an historically
misleading screenplay. By further coincidence – if anything Churchillian
really was coincidental – 2017 saw the release of two Churchill biopics
and a flagwaver: *Churchill*, *Darkest Hour* and *Dunkirk*. Brian Cox took
the title part in *Churchill* with Miranda Richardson as Clementine,
which seemed to be as easy a part to play well as Churchill's was hard:
she followed not only Vanessa Redgrave but Harriet Walter in *The
Crown* and Kristin Scott Thomas in *Darkest Hour*.

Both *Churchill* and *Darkest Hour* were heroic fantasies, whose connection with reality was tenuous. In the second film there is a preposterous
moment when Churchill leaps out of his motor-car and into the
Underground. In the train, he finds a group of stout-hearted Londoners
full of the Dunkirk spirit. When he quotes Macaulay's 'Horatius at
the Bridge', his line is finished by a black passenger. Heartened by
this, Churchill arrives at the Commons to be cheered on all sides.
While this was of course cinematic drama rather than factual account,
it was one more sign that Churchill was as much fictional character
as historical figure.

All the same, Charles Moore in the *Spectator* was able to claim that,
'regardless of the film's historical accuracy,' its great current merit was
that it was 'superb Brexit propaganda. The message is that it is sometimes both possible and necessary, if continental Europe is going one
way, for Britain to go the other,' although such a message was unquestionably not the intention of those who made the movie, or those who

made *Dunkirk* either. Churchill doesn't appear in that noisy film but at the end a soldier brought back from France picks up a newspaper and reads, 'We shall fight on the beaches ...' . While *Darkest Hour* won Gary Oldman an Oscar for his portrayal of Churchill, and did well at the box office, that was dwarfed by the astonishing success of *Dunkirk,* which became the highest-grossing war movie ever, taking the best part of half a billion dollars in America, and demonstrating yet again the way that Americans had appropriated and assimilated the finest hour.

If the biography of Churchill which Andrew Roberts published in 2018 had been called superb Brexit propaganda, its author would scarcely have minded. Over less than three decades Roberts had been an astonishingly prolific author, with eighteen books to his name, and had engaged in a bewildering variety of other activities, as chairman or member of various bodies on the Europhobic or neoconservative Right, including the Bruges Group, the Freedom Association, Centre for Policy Studies, the ANZUK Union Institutes and the Friends of Israel Initiative. More detailed than Roy Jenkins's *Churchill,* and its single volume weightier in tone than the Manchester-Reid three, Roberts's *Churchill: Walking With Destiny* followed those books on to the bestsellers lists while dividing critical opinion, from Richard Toye in the *TLS* finding it 'a thousand pages of literary purgatory' to Richard Aldous in the *New York Times* calling it 'the best single-volume biography of Churchill yet written'.

What few reviewers recognised was the book's significance. Although no mere Brexit tract or apology for white nationalism, Roberts's biography was an act of undisguised hero-worship, which lengthily extenuated the darker side of Churchill, dubiously claiming that his racism was shared by most of his contemporaries, or that calling Hindus 'a foul race' worthy of extirpation was no more than 'provocative humour'. Above all, Roberts took seriously – and took as his title – Churchill's claim that he had been 'walking with destiny' in 1940, and that his whole life had been a 'preparation for this time and this trial'* – to the point that the biography is divided into two

---

* The unlikeliest invocation of those hallowed words, and one of the most extreme cases of the use and abuse of Churchill, had been in 2007 when Lord Black of Crossharbour, the former newspaper owner Conrad Black, stood trial for fraud in Chicago and from the dock produced a piece of paper with the words 'I felt that I was walking with destiny, and all my life had been but preparation for that hour.'

parts, 'The Preparation' and 'The Trial'. In early 2019 Roberts made a ten-week speaking tour to twenty-seven American cities, after which he was able to report, no doubt truly, that 'the enthusiasm for all things Churchillian in the USA is stronger now than at any time since his death,' and that 'Americans love Churchill for his foresight, humour, eloquence and physical and moral courage.'

As 2020 began, Trump was campaigning for re-election, while Johnson had achieved at any rate a temporary and tactical triumph. In August 2019 he had demanded 'to be released from the subjection of a parliament that has outlived its usefulness', a choice of words that was called 'appallingly fascistic' by the political columnist turned novelist Robert Harris; he got what he wanted, although the prorogation of Parliament was subsequently ruled to be unlawful by the Supreme Court. He purged the Conservative Party of principled pro-Europeans, including two former Cabinet ministers, a former attorney general, and Churchill's grandson Nicholas Soames; he appointed a cabinet of talentless nonentities whose only necessary qualification was unconditional support for Brexit and loyalty to Johnson himself; and, having managed to force a dissolution of Parliament, in December his purified Europhobic party won a clear parliamentary majority. All this was rapturously greeted by the right-wing press. 'It's time critics saw Boris for the Churchillian figure he is,' Tim Stanley screeched in the *Daily Telegraph*. 'Dear Boris, Hallelujah!' Andrew Roberts cheered, while he and two rich Brexiteers gave a party to celebrate the election victory at a luxurious Mayfair club, where Roberts 'gave a speech that would have befitted Henry V after Agincourt', according to 'Taki' in the *Spectator*.

A different view was taken by the last survivors of Churchill's war although by now, more than seventy years after VE Day, there weren't many of them left. Newspaper obituaries brought regular news of their departure, a Fleet Air Arm pilot who had sunk a U-boat, a man who had taken part in a commando raid in Italy, a Lancaster flight engineer, one of the 'Spitfire girls' who had flown new aircraft from factory to airfield, a fighter pilot who had shot down one of the German jets. Shortly before the 2019 election, three remarkable men died who had been decorated for courage in that conflict. Noble Frankland had won a Distinguished Flying Cross with Bomber Command before he became its historian, while Field Marshall Lord

Bramall, former Chief of Staff of the British Army, and the historian Sir Michael Howard had both won the Military Cross commanding infantry platoons, Bramall with the 60th Rifles in Belgium, Howard with the Coldstream Guards at Salerno. Both were committed Europeans and Remainers, by contrast with the sabre-rattlers of the Europhobic right, whose bellicose sub-Churchillian rhetoric was generally in inverse ratio to their experience of gunfire. Howard died in November 2019 on the day after his ninety-seventh birthday. His friend Max Hastings recorded that just before his death he had spoken about the 'extraordinary bathos' with which his long life was ending. He could remember the story of his time, from the rise of Hitler before he had fought against him. And now that story was ending 'under *the prime ministership of Boris Johnson*', words spoken with awed contempt.

Another historian must undertake the bleak task of relating the years of the Trump presidency, quite unprecedented and unlike anything many Americans had ever imagined, or could easily comprehend, right up to its lurid climax. The greatest drama of 2020 was the coronavirus pandemic which was of course unforeseen, but what might have been foreseen was the total unfitness of both Trump and Johnson to deal with it. If no country handled this disaster very well, the American and British governments handled it exceptionally badly, as attested by the bleak statistics. By early 2021, more than 400,000 Americans had died and that country's distinction of having the world's third-highest rate of deaths per million population was surpassed by the United Kingdom, with the highest rate, and more than 130,000 dead.

And yet there was undoubtedly a spirit of national unity, and the pandemic carried overtones of the finest hour. A cartoon by Peter Brookes in *The Times* mirrored the famous photograph of St Paul's in December 1940, with the sinister emblem of coronavirus instead of the smoke of Luftwaffe bombs. Tom Moore had joined the army in 1939 and served as a tank commander in Burma. In April 2020, frail in his hundredth year, he set out to walk round his garden ten times a day until he had done a hundred laps, to raise money for health care, with such a public response that 1.5 million people donated nearly £33 million, and on his hundredth birthday a Spitfire and a Hurricane flew overhead to salute him. Queen Elizabeth dubbed him Sir Tom, while she also gave an address to the nation about the pestilence, which impressed even people disdainful of the monarchy. The most striking moment was when she reminded us of her first broadcast on BBC radio, as a little girl in 1940. In that year and for the rest of the war, Vera Lynn was one of the most popular singers in England, 'the nation's sweetheart'. She enjoyed a new season of fame in great old age, before dying at 103. At the end of her broadcast, the Queen echoed one of Dame Vera's most famous wartime songs, 'We'll meet again.' A year later the Queen and the nation bade farewell to her consort Prince Philip, who died aged ninety-nine, seventy-three years after their marriage had so delighted Churchill, and eighty after Sub-Lieutenant Philip Mountbatten had been commended for his conduct in the Battle of Cape Matapan.

Despite Trump's bungling the crisis, the most remarkable thing about the presidential election of November 2020 was not that he lost but that, after all he had done and said for four years, more Americans voted for him than had for any previous presidential candidate in their country's history. Although Joe Biden gained seven million more votes than Trump in an unquestionably fair election, many Americans accepted Trump's claim that the election had been stolen, leading to the grotesque events in Washington in the new year, replete with Churchillian resonances beyond satire. After watching *Darkest Hour*, Mike Huckabee, the former governor of Arkansas, tweeted, 'in @ realDonaldTrump we have a Churchill'. On 6 January 2021, the day Congress met to certify Biden's election, That same day Trump urged a mob to come to Washington and advance on the Capitol because 'you'll never take back our country with weakness. You have to show strength.' In 2001, Rudolph Giuliani had been called 'Churchill in a baseball cap' by little Winston; now Giuliani told the mob there should be 'trial by combat'. In 2014 the Claremont Institute had presented Senator Ted Cruz of Texas with the Statesmanship Award in Honour of Winston Churchill. Now he too incited the rioters against his fellow legislators. In his long life Churchill had done and said many foolish, sometimes disastrous and even ignoble things, but he had a profound respect for constitutional government and elected legislatures, not least Congress where he had been so loudly cheered. Nothing he had ever done deserved Trump, Giuliani and Cruz.

In Churchill's own country explanations for the outrage in Washington were quickly offered by people insistent that the American Right couldn't possibly be blamed. Charles Moore claimed that responsibility for a riot in which four people had died lay with the Black

Lives Matter movement, and Churchill's biographer thought it just as obvious that those really to blame for the violence were Hollywood liberals, by way of 'the unremitting message of hundreds of Hollywood entertainment shows which constantly show office-holders as crooks and evil-doers,' and which, Roberts insisted, 'was bound to have an effect on the psyche of activist civilians'.

As to Moore's and Roberts's hero Johnson, the ignominious departure of his admirer Trump was very uncomfortable. Following the referendum, his ascent to the prime ministership, and his election victory, the logic of his position was to want the re-election of Trump, but he knew that the president was intensely disliked in England (and still more in Scotland), and Trump's lavish praise of 'Boris' had done him no good. Moreover, with Biden, the successful Democratic candidate, privately calling Johnson a 'physical and emotional clone' of Trump, publicly saying that Brexit was a disaster, and dismissing a British television reporter with the words, 'BBC? I'm Irish,' Johnson's relations with Washington were trickier than ever.

All the while, the campaign against statues or any other memorials to slave-traders and imperialists continued, with the name of John Cass, the eighteenth-century philanthropist whose money came partly from slavery, erased or cancelled from schools and streets in London which had borne it, and the famous Codrington Library at All Souls' College in Oxford losing its name. All this might seem likely to affect attitudes to Churchill, who had been passionately attached to a British Empire created in part by slavery and brutal conquest, and who had evinced racist views intransigent even in his own time. One possible response to the new iconoclasts, eager to destroy every vestige of an ugly past, was given in another context by Charles de Gaulle. In 1944, he visited the Free French Second Armoured Division in Normandy. One crew, in an excess of hatred of the foe, had painted on the side of their tank the slogan 'Mort aux cons': very roughly, 'Death to all idiots.' Seeing this, de Gaulle said with a flicker of a smile, 'Vaste programme!', or, that's a big job you've got there. The new image-breakers had a truly vast job on their hands if they were going to extirpate every remnant of the past displeasing to their sensibilities.

One of the numerous other statuary relics of Churchill's war which adorn London had been assaulted before his. This stands outside the west end of St Clement Danes in the Strand, which has become the

RAF church. To the left is Dowding, victor of the Battle of Britain, and to the right 'Bomber' Harris, whose statue has been daubed regularly with slogans calling him a war criminal. Montgomery still swaggers in Whitehall, and so does the statue of Mountbatten by Horse Guards Parade. It was criticised by naval pedants, as he's wearing formal *aiguillettes* or braided cords from the shoulder of his uniform while holding binoculars as if at sea, a combination impossible in real life, though maybe somehow apt for that vainglorious man.

For all the assaults on his statue, Churchill's sheer continuing allure was startlingly demonstrated in March 2021. After the Casablanca conference in 1943 he had relaxed in Marrakesh and painted the Koutoubia Mosque, apparently the only picture he painted during the war. He gave it as a birthday present to Roosevelt, one of whose sons sold it some years after the war, before it was eventually bought by the movie actress Angelina Jolie in 2011. When she sold it ten years later the auctioneers Christie's put a highest estimate of £2.5 million on it; it went for £8.2 million, far the highest price ever paid for one of his paintings, a price quite unrelated to its artistic value and and an extreme display of the sheer veneration of Churchillian relics.

Three days after the sale there was a different kind of celebration of the Churchill cult. On 5 March, the seventy-fifth anniversary of his "iron curtain" speech, an online virtual commemoration from the room at Westminster College in Fulton where he had given the speech saw contributions from from veteran Churchillians like Edwina Sandys and Andrew Roberts, though more surprisingly by Bob Geldof, "musician and humanitarian" and a new name in the field, as we all as a lecture on "Churchillian Realism" by the conservative columnist George F. Will, who was also installed as a Churchill Fellow, shortly before his eightieth birthday. And yet just how wide of the mark Roberts had been when he said that there was 'a settled view of Churchill's glory which no amount of historical debate will now alter' had just been demonstrated by what the tabloids called a 'Churchill race row', and moreover at his eponymous college. When it was announced a debate about Churchill's views on empire and race would be held at Churchill College, Cambridge, and that the proposed speakers included Professor Priya Gopal, a fellow of Churchill College and a 'staunch critic of the British Empire', and Kehinde Andrews, a professor of Black Studies there was a predictable reaction. 'It seems to me extremely unlikely young ladies and gentlemen will get a balanced view of Churchill's life,' Sir Nicholas Soames commented; he hoped that 'a sense of proportion' might be brought 'to this idiotic debate that's got out of control in all our universities', premature indignation preceding what might be a sober discussion of a serious subject, held in what is perhaps the most admirable of shrines to Churchill's memory.

In 1959 Churchill himself had planted the first tree on the site of the new college, and six decades later its spare modern buildings gaze across the Cam and the Backs towards the historic grandeur of Trinity and King's. Visiting Boston, he had been struck by the Massachusetts Institute for Technology, and his college was intended to encourage engineering and applied science. The college's description of itself as 'open, friendly, progressive and outward-looking' might be thought less than Churchillian, and the fact that it admitted women under-graduates from the beginning was maybe belated recompense for the Churchill who had opposed votes for women until the day they were finally enfranchised. The college houses the Churchill Archive, 'a major centre of historical research into what might be termed the Churchill Era, where scholars will be able to find a great mass of inter-related material gathered together under a single roof'. The core of what is now a huge archive, including the papers of 570 people, Margaret Thatcher among them, are Churchill's own papers: ten million words in 3000 boxes carefully arranged and tended by its excellent staff, and now digitised.

Furthest-flung but in some ways most remarkable of all the shrines is the campus of Westminster College in Fulton, Missouri, where Churchill gave his 'iron curtain' speech in March 1946. It now houses the National Churchill Museum, dominated by St Mary's Aldermanbury, the Wren church transported there from the City of London in Churchill's honour and meticulously maintained. In the crypt is a collection celebrating Churchill's life, with exhibits and memorabilia from his earliest years onwards, and dotted round the walls are his quips and *boutades*, like his reply to the lady who told him he was drunk: 'And you, madam, are very ugly, but tomorrow I shall be sober.' Next to the church stands a large statue of Churchill, and what at first glance seems a curious sight: a stretch of graffiti-covered concrete blocks, which proves to be a sculpture called 'Breakthrough' by Churchill's granddaughter Edwina Sandys, consisting of a section of the Berlin Wall donated by the East German government shortly before its demise, as the iron curtain fell.

In London, the Cabinet War Rooms survive thanks to Frankland, who saved them from demolition at the hands of heedless bureaucrats. In 1960, the year his and Webster's remarkable official history of the bombing offensive was published, he applied on the spur of the moment for the position of Director of the Imperial War Museum, which he transformed, making it one of the most successful museums in London, and beyond. The airfield at RAF Duxford in Cambridgeshire became an air museum, and HMS *Belfast*, a cruiser launched in the city of that name in 1938 and which had taken part in the sinking of the *Scharnhorst* at the Battle of North Cape and then in the Normandy landings, was brought to London and permanently moored near Tower Bridge as a naval museum, whose great popular success testifies further to *nostalgie de la guerre*, or yearning for past glories. So do the Churchill War Rooms, as the Cabinet War Rooms are now called, where innumerable visitors, notably Americans, have seen the table where Churchill sat with Attlee and Bevin, and the red scrambler telephone on which he spoke to Roosevelt.

Most personal of all shrines is Chartwell, lovingly tended by the National Trust. The public can visit the rooms where Churchill dined with Clementine and quarrelled with Randolph, the study where he dictated his books and worked on endless proofs; they can admire the numerous portraits and other memorabilia, substantially augmented since 2016. That year the Trust implausibly claimed there was a 'real risk' of future generations forgetting Churchill's legacy. It appealed to the public for £7 million in order to acquire hundreds more of Churchill's personal effects, including his Nobel Prize in Literature and the box in which he kept the notes for his speeches. The purchase of these relics from his great-grandson Randolph rounded off the story seventy years on from when Churchill filled Chartwell with official papers taken from Downing Street, which then had to be bought back by the public.

Even without any Churchillian connection, Blenheim would rank with Chatsworth, Woburn and Longleat as part of the great country-house heritage business. When the eleventh Duke of Marlborough inherited the dukedom in 1972, he embarked on what he called 'the ongoing battle of Blenheim'. He showed considerable gifts of showmanship, pulling in the crowds with boat trips and butterfly houses, letting out the house for corporate entertaining and the grounds for pop concerts and weddings. Churchill's image is used to advertise events such as 'the Great British Garden Party' in 2018, celebrating '"All things British", dance, music, lawn games and vintage cricket with live commentary from Henry Blofeld.' No longer just an icon or a totem, Churchill had become part of the entertainment industry and the heritage business.

Far less visited but most affecting of all is Churchill's grave, in the churchyard of St Martin's, the parish church of Bladon, a small village on the edge of the Blenheim estate. Near the graves of his mother and his father and his daughter Sarah, a large flat stone raised on a dais is imposing but not overbearing, and bears no more than the plain names 'Winston Leonard Spencer Churchill 1874–1965 Clementine Ogilvy Spencer Churchill 1885-1977'. There are flowers by the grave, but often no one else is in the churchyard.

This has been a long journey, and Bladon is a good place to end it, just as Churchill's own journey ended here, having begun only a mile away. For so long a bitterly controversial figure, intensely disliked and distrusted, he was transformed at one extraordinary moment into a superhuman hero, and then gradually acquired an almost mythical status which made it hard to distinguish fact from fiction. Adulation has distorted our understanding of him, as he has been travestied on screen, appropriated and misappropriated, used and abused, and invoked on behalf of any number of causes and enterprises which he might or might not have favoured. Having been so derided once, then venerated above all others, he is now the object of angry contention once again. Angry, but futile; and for those who still wonder how a reactionary racist and imperialist could have been the saviour of his country and of freedom, the best answer may be I.F. Stone's. Asked once how he, as an American radical, could possibly admire the notorious slave-owner Thomas Jefferson, Stone replied, 'Because history is a tragedy and not a melodrama.'

Those words would have been understood by Winston Churchill, for all that his life was often played, and later reenacted, as melodrama. For its first forty years his career was erratic and largely unsuccessful. His judgement as a wartime strategist was sometimes woeful, his postwar years were unsatisfactory and increasingly sad, his legacy is flawed, and his posthumous influence has been little short of disastrous. So far from being a universal oracle of wisdom and virtue, few great men have been wrong so often, have made so many mistakes, or have held so many opinions and prejudices which were repugnant even at the time. So much that Churchill believed in or advocated has withered away or simply failed. British greatness and might are great or mighty no more, the names of the regiments in which he served aren't to be found on the shrunken Army List, the Royal Navy has a fraction of of the number of ships afloat it had when he was First Lord and the great shipyards of Tyneside and Clydeside and Merseyside which once built the ships are gone as well, 'the abiding power of the British Empire and Commonwealth' abides no more, the Anglo-American 'special relationship' has repeatedly proved meaningless, and even the 'United States of Europe' Churchill dreamed of long ago has been a damaging illusion. Invocations of his name have again and again led to calamity, while in his own country, 'Churchillism' and the paralysing memory of the Finest Hour have deluded the British and prevented them from coming to terms with their true place in the world, and in America the Churchill cult has had measurably sorry consequences.

But he should have the last word. He had said of Lloyd George that he was a 'the leader, distrusted always, who was trusted most when things were worst,' and so was Churchill, at the he one irredeemably sublime moment in his life, when he saved his country and saved freedom. Wrong about much else, was not wrong about 'the tragic simplicity and grandeur of the times' in 1940, and he was not wrong either.

In his noble speech paying tribute to Chamberlain on 12 November 1940, he had declared that 'Long and hard, hazardous years lie before us, but at least we entered upon them united and with clean hearts' – something too few of those who have claimed Churchill's mantle since would be able to say. And he continued that, one day,

> we may all pass our own conduct and our own judgements under a searching review. It is not given to human beings, happily for them, for otherwise life would be intolerable, to foresee or to predict to any large extent the unfolding course of events. In one phase men seem to have been right, in another they seem to have been wrong. Then again, a few years later, when the perspective of time has lengthened, all stands in a different setting. There is a new proportion. There is

another scale of values. History with its flickering lamp stumbles along the trail of the past, trying to reconstruct its scenes, to revive its echoes, and kindle with pale gleams the passion of former days.

Those words are more fitting still for the man who spoke them. Disdaining Hitler's rabid rhetoric, Churchill asked, 'What do these ravings and outpourings count before the silence of Neville Chamberlain's tomb?' And we may ask today, what do all the years of conflict since, the endless outpourings of friend and foe, count before the silence of Winston Churchill's tomb?

Thanks

Writing this book has been a long journey, longer than it should have been, and I've accumulated many debts of gratitude on the way. I've mentioned the great colloquy on Churchill held at the University of Texas in Austin in 1991, which produced an outstanding anthology edited by Robert (Lord) Blake and Wm. Roger Louis. Robert was an old friend, whose help I acknowledged in my first book many years ago while he was still Provost of the Queen's College, Oxford, and Roger would become a new friend. From that colloquy emerged the British Studies Seminar at Austin over which he presided, as Kerr Professor of English History and Culture. For nearly twenty years I've spoken there frequently, several times on Churchillian subjects, with the talks published in successive volumes of the *Adventures With Britannia* series, and made too many kind friends in Austin to list, while becoming a long-distance Longhorns fan. But I must thank Roger especially, and Dagmar also, as well as their and my friend Tom Staley. Roger is more than merely a great historian of the decline and fall of the British Empire. One of my Austin lectures was on the 'special relationship' as the grand illusion of postwar British policy but, if the phrase can be used without irony, it was by another revered friend, Sir Michael Howard, when he once said to me, 'Roger *is* the special relationship.'

Over the years that I've visited Austin I've also written extensively about Churchill for the *New York Times*, the *Boston Globe*, the *TLS* and *Harper's Magazine*, but in particular for the *New York Review of Books*, which has published a number of Churchillian essays by me. It's effortless to say that the late Robert Silvers was the greatest editor of his age, and indeed pointless to say so: what possible rival did he have? Even so, I'd like to record that writing for Bob Silvers was not only a privilege but a pleasure, albeit a bracing one. Whenever I sent Bob a piece I felt once again like the scapegrace undergraduate I had been very long before, presenting an essay to a tutor who was stern but kindly. Any criticism from him left me downcast, warm words of praise and I was elated for days.

My father, Stephen Wheatcroft, gave me very practical help before he died aged ninety-four, just before he could live to see Brexit which would have appalled him and more than seventy years after he'd been crash-landing his aircraft on the deck of a carrier. He had already given me practical help very many years ago, when I'd made a hash of university entrance and he encouraged me to try again, finding a friend of a friend who taught at the London School of Economics (my parents' old college) to coach me for the New College scholarship which, with his help, I managed to win. My crammer was the late Donald Cameron Watt, before he became known as one of the outstanding historians in his field, culminating in his classic books *Succeeding John Bull: America in Britain's place 1900–1975* and *How War Came.* We bumped into one another at one of Roger Louis's parties at the Reform Club not long before Donald died, where I should have thanked him again more profusely.

Since I began thinking and writing about Churchill, too many others have also departed, and I would like my dear friends Rodney Milnes Blumer, Alexander Chancellor, Eric Christiansen, Michael Howard, Elisabeth Sifton and Richard West to have seen this book. My former editor Sir Peregrine Worsthorne has also departed, more than eighty years after a surprise meeting with Churchill which he entertainingly described to me. Part or all of it was read in various stages by my friends and colleagues Ian Buruma, Isaac Chotiner, Franklin Foer, Charles McGrath, Stuart Proffitt and Gina Thomas. My friends and neighbours Crispin Simon and Georgina Brown lent me many essential books while also allowing me to recuperate in their pool. Others who have helped me in ways they may have forgotten include Sir Max Hastings, Lady Selina Hastings (no kin) and Blair Worden. While we watched a happier contest between our countries at Lord's my friend Pankaj Mishra enlivened me by reminding me that 'It is not easy for an Indian to love Winston Churchill.' Over many years I have had cordial relations with some of Churchill's descendants. While I enjoyed Lady Soames's hospitality, I learned that she could be fierce with anyone who criticised her father. She might not have accepted, but I hope that her children, my old acquaintance Sir Nicholas Soames and my very old friend Emma Soames, may, my plea that I have tried to avoid either the denigration or the adulation from which their grandfather has suffered.

By now it has become repetitious to thank my great friend Robert Harris. I've done so already in the prefaces to two other books, at least one of which I'm fairly sure he hasn't read. But the fact is that there is no one else with whom I've discussed Churchill, Chamberlain, the 1930s, the war, and much else besides, over countless lunches in Wiltshire pubs, more than I have with Robert, whose knowledge of the period of course informs his splendid thrillers-with-attitude, from *Fatherland* to *Munich* and *V2*. He shares some credit (rather than blame, I trust) for what this book has become.

Visits to the Bodleian Library in Oxford, so long after the years when I should have spent more time there than in the King's Arms opposite, were more agreeable when I stayed as a guest of the Warden of New College. I was once taught history there; the last surviving of my tutors was Eric Christiansen, who became a lifelong friend, and it was at his memorial service that I met Miles Young, then recently appointed Warden, who has become a hospitable friend in turn. Much the most important to me of the libraries I used was the wonderful London Library, a home from home for fifty years. It lent me almost every book I needed, and generously acquired more at my request. And I'm sure that I speak for other members when I say that there is no sufficient praise for the splendid service the Library provided during the lockdown. It would take too long to name all the physicians, nurses, dentists, consultants and surgeons who have cut up and patched up my increasingly ramshackle frame over the past few years, but to Dr Andrew Smith, my doctor, and to all of them, and to all the health workers who have helped us through the pandemic despite an utterly incompetent government, I offer my heartfelt thanks.

The final stage of preparing the book for publication became both a team effort and a family business. I'm most grateful to my publishers, Stuart Williams at the Bodley Head, with his colleagues Lauren Howard and Jörg Hensgen who read successive drafts and offered valuable help. So did John Glusman, my publisher at W.W. Norton & Co. in New York. My thanks to his colleague Helen Thomaides, as well as to my agent Toby Mundy, who introduced me to my publishers, and also to Steve Wasserman. After he had acted as my agent when this book was first thought of long ago, we later went our own ways, he back to his native California, but I'm grateful to him for his earlier help. Fiona Brown copy-edited the text impeccably, my wife's assistant Caron Egly performed the Sisyphean task of bringing some semblance of order to the books and papers in my work room, while her husband Mike Ballard unglitched my Mac.

And finally my family, who became my colleagues as an indirect consequence of the pandemic. My niece Isobel Muir gave me valuable assistance. Then my daughter Abigail, locked down in London, helped arrange the illustrations, and my son Gabriel forced to flee Madrid where he'd been living and come home to his parents, checked quotations and compiled the references. They were both hugely helpful: my love and thanks to them both.

That leaves their mother. Authors often thank their spouses or other halves for literary advice or emotional sustenance. My debt to Sally Muir, my wife, is of a much more literal character. Without her material support my book could not have been finished. While my work languished, her career flourished, or rather her careers: as fashion designer, co-creator of the celebrated Black Sheep sweater once worn by Lady Diana Spencer and enjoying a lucrative new lease of life thanks to *The Crown*; as co-author with Joanna Osborne, her other other half, of the seminal series of books beginning with *Knit Your Own Dog*; and as a highly successful painter of animal portraits, some of which have been collected in her lovely books *A Dog a Day* and *Old Dogs* (I'm the one who can't be taught new tricks). More details can be found on https://www.sallymuir.co.uk/ When Sally once stood beside me and said 'for better for worse, for richer for poorer' she cannot have known just what that would mean, and nor did I, but there are no words appropriate here to express my gratitude and love.

Some Churchill Books

If Churchill thought a hundred years ago that 'too much has been and is being written about me,' what would his shade say today, when thousands upon thousands of books about him have been published? Any reader daunted by the sheer, immense quantity of Churchilliana might try four books to begin with. Paul Addison was an eminent historian of the twentieth century who wrote a number of longer scholarly works, but his own favourite among his books was his short biography *Churchill: The Unexpected Hero* (2005), expanded from his essay in the *Oxford Dictionary of National Biography*, itself a priceless resource, nowadays online, at little more than 250 pages a lucid and balanced *tour de force*.

Then there is the great anthology *Churchill* (1993), edited by Robert Blake and Wm. Roger Louis, which began life as a symposium at the University of Texas, and whose twenty-nine essays on subjects from 'Churchill and Social Reform' to 'Churchill and Zionism' to 'Churchill and Appeasement' to 'Churchill and the Navy' to 'Churchill and Stalin' to 'Churchill and India' form a study of the man and his career as good as most biographies. Of Churchill's own books, *My Early Life* (1930) remains the most engaging and enjoyable, and the one which gives his fullest flavour. That, and *Speaking for Themselves: the Personal Letters of Winston and Clementine Churchill*, edited by their daughter Mary Soames (1998), the unmediated and uninhibited voices of two remarkable people, and an unsurpassable portrait of a marriage.

But then all the books Churchill wrote are to some extent about himself. Burke asked if anyone had ever read all of Bolingbroke, and, if Henry Adams claimed to have done just that five times, it's possible that there are Americans today who've read Churchill through, every last page, but it's a daunting task, as can be seen from the full list of his books provided by the International Churchill

Society https://winstonchurchill.org/resources/writings-articles-and-books/the-books-of-sir-winston-churchill/. As Lady Soames said, the thing to remember about her father is that he was a journalist. His first books were what's now called reportage, vivid and often all too candid accounts of the wars on which he had reported or in which he had fought (or sometimes both). Churchill's zest for battle infuses *The Story of the Malakand Field Force* (1898), *The River War* (1899) and two books on the Boer War, *London to Ladysmith via Pretoria* and *Ian Hamilton's March* (both 1900). He also published *Savola* (1899), the novel which his more ardent devotees claim is underrated but which he himself more wisely begged his friends not to read.

His two-volume biography of his father, *Lord Randolph Churchill* (1905), forcibly displayed Churchill's qualities and faults, in particular the partisanship and waywardness with sources. *My African Journey* (1908) is readable and telling. Before the Great War he also published four collections of speeches full of radical vigour and vituperation, which are now very rare books, *Mr Brodrick's Army* (1903), *For Free Trade* (1906), *Liberalism and the Social Problem* (1909) and *The People's Rights* (1910). After *Lord Randolph*, more than fifteen years, and the cataclysm of war, passed before Churchill began his highly personal, and misleading, account of that war, the five volumes of *The World Crisis*, much of which he wrote while he held ministerial office (volumes 1 *1911–1914* and 2 *1915* were both published in 1923, volume 3 *1916–1918*, in two parts I and II, in 1927). It was rounded off by *The Aftermath* (1929) and *The Eastern Front* (1931).

He was out office from 1929 to 1939, his productive and lucrative 'wilderness years'. From about 1930 and *My Early Life* onwards, any assessment of Churchill as a writer has to begin by establishing as far as possible how much of the journalism and books that appeared under the name 'Winston S. Churchill' was actually written by him rather than by a growing team of researchers and ghostwriters. All his books thenceforth were the work of more than one hand, more and more hands as time passed. Many passages in his later books were drafted by others before Churchill applied a personal polish, and much of his journalism was ghostwritten, such as the seemingly personal Introduction to his collection *Thoughts and Adventures* (1932). Nor are all of the pen portraits in *Great Contemporaries* (1937) Churchill's own unaided work. During that decade Churchill published the four volumes of *Marlborough: His Life and Times* (1933–8), composed with the help of research assistants but with Churchill himself providing the pride and prejudice, and he supervised with even more help the writing of *A History of the English-Speaking Peoples*, although its four volumes weren't published until 1956–8.

Before then he had produced the six volumes of *The Second World War* (1948–53), the publishing phenomenon of its age which overshadowed, and distorted, the historiography of that conflict for generations. While the two biographies, and then the two multi-volume war books, can scarcely be recommended as serious and detached accounts, whether of Lord Randolph, or Marlborough, or of the two great wars, they are of considerable interest for what they say about Churchill. So is his journalism. In the centenary year of 1974 *The Collected Essays of Winston Churchill*, edited by Michael Wolff, was published in a deluxe edition handsomely printed and bound, but with no critical apparatus or commentary at all apart from place and date of original publication. A reader who picks and chooses can find some of Churchill's most vigorous, and sometimes wrong-headed, polemical writing, but the editors gave no indication that many of the newspaper pieces it includes, like 'Great Stories of the World Retold', were entirely ghostwritten.

For his true voice, the speeches are better, since he always composed them unaided, at least until his last years. More than ten years after the Great War he published an individual (and eccentric) speech on economic policy, and a collection of his unhappy speeches on India. He then published a collection of speeches every year from 1938 to 1946, sometimes more than one book a year. *Winston S. Churchill: His Complete Speeches 1897–1963* edited by Robert Rhodes James (1974) comprises eight volumes, and nearly 9000 pages, with valuable editorial commentary. Rhodes James also edited the more manageable, though still more than 900-page, single volume of selected speeches *Churchill Speaks* (1981). Since few people are going to read his entire output, a really useful book would be 'A Churchill Reader' or 'Portable Churchill', giving the choicest and most authentic extracts from books, speeches and journalism.

By one count, twenty-six biographies of Churchill were published in his lifetime and another thirty-six in the thirty-four years between his death and 2000, and that's in English alone. The first was by Alexander MacCallum Scott, who briefly worked as Churchill's private secretary and later served as a Liberal MP, and who wrote two admiring books, *Winston Spencer Churchill* in 1905, when its subject had just turned thirty, and an updated *Winston Churchill in Peace and War* in 1916, when his fortunes had sunk low. More was written about Churchill between the wars, one of the more interesting books being *The Tragedy of Winston Churchill* by Victor Wallace Germains (1931), with its well-reasoned critique of the Gallipoli campaign.

The story has been told in earlier pages of the official biography, begun by Randolph, completed by Sir Martin Gilbert, published in seven volumes from 1966 to 1988, and complemented by the monumental series of Companion Volumes, *The Churchill Documents*, now totalling twenty-three such volumes. Gilbert's endeavour was so great that it seems churlish to criticise it but, after reading the seven volumes straight through from end to end, the Tory journalist Simon Heffer, himself an accomplished historian and biographer, minced no words in calling them 'boring on a level it is almost impossible to describe'. This relentless chronicle, with no light or shade, is a pious monument rather than a critical biography, indeed it's in every sense uncritical throughout. But it remains, especially the Companion Volumes, an incomparable trove for all others. Gilbert might have written an absorbing book about the way he completed his enormous task, but *In Search of Churchill* (1994) adds little of interest.

In 1974, Henry Pelling published a biography notable because he wrote from the perspective of an historian of the Labour movement and the Left. Other short lives have been written by Piers Brendon (1984), John Keegan (2002) and Paul Johnson (2009). Enough has been said earlier about *The Last Lion* (1988–2012), the three volumes, which represent a kind of pinnacle of American Churchillolatry. In the new century there were two widely-read single-volume biographies, which were discussed earlier, by Roy Jenkins (2001) and by Andrew Roberts (2018). Since Roberts wouldn't deny that Churchill is his hero, it's fair to call his formidable book a work of hero-worship, which quotes more than 40,000 of Churchill's own words. Although 'hagiography' has become a term of abuse, it means literally 'writing about saints', and the concluding sentence 'Shortly after 8 a.m. on Sunday, 24 January 1965, the noble heart of Sir Winston Spencer-Churchill beat its last,' could come from the Lives of the Saints. Much earlier Roberts published the excellent and fascinating collection of essays *Eminent Churchillians* (1994). *Churchill: Four Faces and the Man* (1969) is a remarkable collection of essays on Churchill by five writers: A.J.P. Taylor,

Rhodes James, J.H. Plumb, Basil Liddell Hart severally looked at him as a whole, as politician, historian and strategist, and Anthony Storr provided a psychological study.

Memoirs or diaries by those who knew or worked with Churchill began immediately after his death with Violet Bonham Carter's *Churchill as I Knew Him* (1965). By contrast with the highly controversial publication of Lord Moran's *Winston Churchill: The Struggle for Survival 1940–1965* (1966), John Colville's *The Fringes of Power: Downing Street Diaries 1939–1945* (1985) was welcomed by the Churchill family, although not by everyone. My old friend Desmond Browne QC tells me that his late mother, Lady Moyra Browne, and his uncle, the Earl of Bessborough, were more than annoyed by the way that they – at the time Moyra Ponsonby and Eric Duncannon – were mentioned, she because of the implied intimacy with Colville ('Anyone would think we were walking out'), he because of the story of his ephemeral engagement to Mary Churchill. On close reading, Colville possibly, and Moran certainly, betray substantial revision of their accounts long after they were first written. *Churchill as Historian* (1968) by Maurice Ashley, who had been one of his researchers, also counts as a memoir. One other invaluable source is *The Neville Chamberlain Diary Letters* edited by Robert Self (four volumes 2000–05), from the pen of a man who, whatever his shortcomings, was a highly perceptive observer, not least of Churchill. Outside libraries, these volumes are now regrettably difficult to find, and then at exorbitant prices. A different kind of sideways glance is found in *Henry 'Chips' Channon Diaries*, volume 1 1918–1938 edited by Simon Heffer (2021).

Then there are the hostile accounts, which began with Germains's *Tragedy*. Robert Rhodes James's *Churchill: A Study in Failure 1900–1939* (1970) remains one of the best books on Churchill, although it also showed how hard it is for serious sceptical studies to penetrate public consciousness. A nicely contrasting place should be found side by side on the bookshelf for *Churchill: A Study in Greatness*, and *Churchill: A Study in Failure* the former, by Geoffrey Best (2001), being more detached and thoughtful than its title suggests. Of the critiques, those by Alan Clark and David Irving can be passed over in silence, but John Charmley's *Churchill: the End of Glory* (1993) is a serious assessment of how far Churchill failed in his own terms as war leader. Two Americans have attacked Churchill, Nicholson Baker from the left in his idiosyncratic anthology *Human Smoke: The Beginnings of World War*

II, the End of Civilization and Patrick J. Buchanan from the right in *Churchill, Hitler, and 'The Unnecessary War': How Britain Lost the Empire and the West Lost the World* (both 2008).

Beginning with Charles Eades's *Churchill: By His Contemporaries* (1953), there have been a number of studies in what the Germans call reception-history, the story of how the story was told. Rhodes James's tale was taken up by Brian Gardner in *Churchill in His Time: A Study in Reputation 1939–1945* (1968), and that was followed by *Man of the Century: Winston Churchill and His Legend Since 1945* by John Ramsden (2002) and the anthology *Winston Churchill in the Twentieth Century* edited by David Cannadine and Roland Quinault (2004). Cannadine also published a collection of essays, *In Churchill's Shadow: Confronting the Past in Modern Britain* (2002). Anthony Barnett's *Iron Britannia* (1982) looked at the way Churchill and 'Churchillism' had overshadowed the Falklands War. Christopher Hitchens's *Blood, Class and Nostalgia* (1990) included one of the finest essays on 'The Churchill Cult'. More recently, *The Churchill Myths* by Steven Fielding, Bill Schwarz and Richard Toye (2020) dissects the latest reverential manifestations of Churchillism on cinema screen or in books.

In the flowering of Churchill studies in the past thirty years, many if not most of the best books have been on discrete subjects. An incomplete list would include Addison's *Churchill on the Home Front* (1992), Paul Bew's *Churchill and Ireland* (2016), Lawrence James's *Churchill and Empire* (2013) and *Churchill's Empire* (2010) by Richard Toye, who has been a very productive Churchillian, with books including *The Roar of the Lion: the Untold Story of Churchill's World War II Speeches* (2013) and *Winston Churchill: A Life in the News* (2020), which is essentially a stroll through the press cuttings at the Churchill Archive, with many unlikely and fascinating titbits therein. *Churchill and Secret Service* by David Stafford (2013) examines his lifelong fascination with secret intelligence. For the war years, Max Hastings's *Finest Years* (2010, published as *Winston's War* in America) admires Churchill's leadership and fortitude but is unsparing about his blunders, especially the Dodecanese campaign. *Churchill's Secret War* (2010) by Madhusree Mukerjee is a well-reasoned indictment of Churchill's response to the Bengal famine. Jonathan Schneer's *Ministers at War* (2015) relates in particular Beaverbrook's appalling conduct in 1942. One book now forgotten deserves to be read: *Soft Underbelly* by Trumbull Higgins (1968) is a well-informed account and analysis of Churchill's Italian campaign and the bitter Anglo-American conflict it provoked. Of several books on Churchill and the Jews or Zionism, the best is *Churchill's Promised Land* by Michael Makosky (2012).

Three particularly good books deal with a vital aspect of Churchill's life, much neglected until recently: his writing and his money-making (the latter usually though not always by way of the former). David Reynolds has written several excellent books, *Rich Relations: the American Occupation of Britain 1942–1945* (1995) and the outstanding *The Long Shadow: the Great War and the Twentieth Century* (2013), but none better than *In Command of History: Churchill Fighting and Writing the Second World War* (2005), which describes in ruthless detail how that immensely influential, and dubious, book was compiled by Churchill and his 'Syndicate', and how he made as much money as he did from it. In effect a prequel to that, Peter Clarke's *Mr Churchill's Profession* (2012) tells the story of his career as a writer until 1945, and David Lough's *No More Champagne* (2015) for the first time relates in detail his truly hair-raising financial life. To those might be added Jonathan Rose's *The Literary Churchill: Author, Reader, Actor* (2014).

Books on Churchill and individual relationships include Toye's *Lloyd George and Churchill: Rivals for Greatness* (2007), Leo McKinstry's *Attlee and Churchill: Allies in War, Adversaries in Peace* (2021), and Jon Meacham's *Franklin and Winston: An Intimate Portrait of an Epic Friendship* (2004), which gives a rosy view of their often tense dealings. Josh Ireland's *Churchill & Son* (2021) about his relationship with Randolph, is a recent addition. Ian Buruma's *The Churchill Complex* (2020) describes the so-called 'special relationship'. Thomas E. Ricks's *Churchill and Orwell: The Fight for Freedom* (2017) contrasts two men who never met but who haunt our consciousness of their age. Lord Alanbrooke's *The War Diaries 1939–1945* (2001) give a fascinating if sharp and sometimes sour account of working closely with Churchill, while another revealing view is *The Maisky Diaries* (2015) by the Russian ambassador to London. *His Final Battle* by Jospeh Lelyveld (2016) told for first time in full and riveting detail the story of Roosevelt's last year as he approached death.

Visual images were centrally important in Churchill's life. Gilbert's *Churchill: A Photographic Portrait* and Elizabeth Longford's *Winston Churchill: A Pictorial Life Story* (both 1974) are shoddily produced but useful, now supplemented by Max Arthur's handsome *Churchill: The Life: An Authorised Pictorial Biography* (2015). Churchill wrote about his avocation in *Painting as a Pastime* (1948), to which Mary Soames added *Winston Churchill: His Life as a Painter* (1990), and Cannadine edited the collection *Churchill: The Statesman as Artist* (2018). Churchill as subject rather than painter is treated in Jonathan Black's *Winston Churchill in British Art: 1900 to the Present Day* (2017).

And yet with all this vast shelf-space, a really satisfactory, let alone definitive, biography of Churchill is still to seek. We need a life both scholarly and readable, and with the amplitude of John Ehrman's three volumes on Pitt the Younger, John C.G. Röhl's three (and 3700 pages!) on 'the Winston of Germany', Kaiser Wilhelm, or Robert Skidelsky's three on Keynes. I can only wish the best of luck to whoever undertakes this much-needed but challenging task.

Notes

Since this book is not a work of academic scholarship, nor based on archival sources, an elaborate system of references might seem otiose. Few of my readers will want to trace any more esoteric original sources, and I've already described the books which I've found most valuable and which readers might want to pursue. But then, as I've related, Churchill himself was very wayward with sources and quotations, which he would improve or rephrase, while providing no references against which they could be checked, and so I offer these Notes as at least a token of good faith that my own methods have not been quite so Churchillian. If some references are less exact than I would have wished, I must plead in extenuation that for most of the year before my book went to press all libraries were closed by the pandemic.

Abbreviations

Gilbert is the official *Life* begun by Randolph S. Churchill and completed by Martin Gilbert and published in seven volumes (the first two by Randolph) from 1967 to 1988.

Companion is the twenty-two Companion Volumes.

Essays is *The Collected Essays of Sir Winston Churchill* 4 volumes (1974).

HoC is speeches in the House of Commons. I have given dates rather than the traditional column numbers for *Hansard* (*Parliamentary Debates*), since Hansard is now available online and the full transcript for any speech can be easily located.

ODNB is the *Oxford Dictionary of National Biography*.

WSC is Winston Spencer Churchill.

References to the six volumes of *The Second World War* are to their London editions.

Sources

Prologue, pages 1–19

1 '... shrine of the world's liberties.' Will Morrisey, *Churchill and de Gaulle: The Geopolitics of Liberty* (2014), p.10.

2 '... written about me,' Andrew Roberts, *Churchill: Walking with Destiny* (2018), p.965.

2 '... give you all the facts,' Auden, *Who's Who*.

2 '... as the subject for a book in itself,' Peter Stansky, *New York Times*, 24 Nov 1974.

2 '... the historian of Opinion', John Maynard Keynes, *Journal of Political Economy*, vol.36(1).

2 '... once lay in the future.' F.W. Maitland, 'Memoranda de Parliamento' in *Selected Essays* (1968), p.66.

3 '... United States of Europe', University of Zurich speech, 19 Sep 1946.

4 '... debate will now alter,' Andrew Roberts, Kemper Lecture, 26 Mar 2000.

5 '... nothing extenuate,' Shakespeare, *Othello*, Act 5, Scene 2.

5 '... of the human heart', HoC, 12 Nov 1940.

5 '... the other way round.' Gilbert, vol.VI (1983), p.902.

5 '... to suit my argument.' John Ramsden, *Man of the Century: Churchill and his Legend since 1945* (2002), p.201.

5 '... become a legend,' Lord Moran, *Churchill: The Struggle for Survival 1940–1965* (1966), 10 April 1957.

6 '... Now bugger off.' Nicholas Soames, interview in *Gentleman's Journal*, www.thegentlemansjournal.com/the-interview-nicholas-soames.

6 '... legendary figure from the man.' Robert Blake and Wm Roger Louis (eds), *Churchill: A Major Reassessment of his Life in Peace and War* (1993), p.v.

7 '... sneer of cold command', Percy Shelley, 'Ozymandias'.

7 '... jacket of the Royal Yacht Squadron', Paul Reid, *The Last Lion: Winston Spencer Churchill, Defender of the Realm, 1940–1965* (2012), p.193.

7n '... Je suis un Frère Aîné de la Trinité,' private information.

9 '... legend of my hats.' WSC, *Strand Magazine*, June 1931.

9 '... supposed to be funny', Evelyn Waugh, *Men at Arms* (1952), ch.8 (*The Sword of Honour* trilogy, single volume, 1994), p.164.

9 '... remember *me* always.' *Evening Standard*, 31 Jul 1945.

10 '... twentieth-century British politics', Paul Addison, essay on Churchill in *ODNB*, on which *Churchill* (2007) is based.

11 '... sham-Augustan prose', Waugh, *Men at Arms*, p.164.

11 '... firing of a single shot', Fulton Missouri speech, 5 Mar 1946.

11 '... a good tale to tell,' WSC, *The Second World War* vol.I (1948), p.342.

13 '... goodness and greatness', Michael Howard, *Foreign Affairs*, Sep–Oct 1993.

13 '... ultimate and complete triumph,' Robert Rhodes James, *Churchill: A Study in Failure* (1970), p.ix.

14 '... preparation for that hour', WSC, *The Gathering Storm* (1948), p.527.

14 '... saviour of his country.' A.J.P. Taylor, *English History 1914–1945* (2001), p.4n.

14 '... unsuccessful father.' Mark Amory (ed.), *The Letters of Evelyn Waugh* (1980), p.631.

15 '... to whom they could turn.' Michael Howard, *Foreign Affairs*, Sep–Oct 1993.

16 '... with the consequences.' *New York Times,* 16 Oct 2015.

16 '... subject of conversation', Ian Parker, *New Yorker*, 9 Oct 2006.

17 '... *L'agonie de Churchill*', *Paris Jour*, 18 Jan 1965.

18 '... St George's Day.' WSC, *Triumph and Tragedy*, p.643.

18 '... she has yet attained,' WSC, *The Aftermath*, (1929), p.17.

19 '... haply strike out his teeth,' Walter Raleigh, *History of the World*, preface.

19 '... among friends and foes,' 15 Nov 1646 in *Clarendon State Papers*, p.289.

Chapter 1, pages 21–41

21 '... killed without quarter.' Randolph S. Churchill, *Companion* vol.I (1967), p.788.

21 '... things are different.' Ibid., p.793.

22 '... God has saved the Queen.' A.E. Housman, 'A Shropshire Lad'.

22 '... blood never dries.' John Newsinger, *The Blood Never Dried: A People's History of the British Empire*, epigraph.

22 '... Your loving son Winny', Gilbert, vol.I (1966), p.89.

22 '... Everest, and home', Ibid., p.90.

23 '... great personage.' WSC, *Lord Randolph Churchill*, ch.2.

23 '... relaxing our grasp', HoC, 4 May 1885.

24 '... Ulster will fight and Ulster will be right', Lord Randolph Churchill, 7 May 1886.

24 '... in English politics', *St Stephen's Review*, 9 Oct 1886.

24 '... wishes to play another', *The Chamberlains, The Churchills and Ireland, 1874–1922* (2006), p.163.

24 '... wanted it back?' R.C.K. Ensor, *England 1870–1914* (1936), p.175.

24 '... at the head of affairs.' Alfred Austin, *The Autobiography of Alfred Austin* (1911), p.248.

25 '... by inches in public.' Gilbert, vol.I (1966), p.235.

25 '... a single mistake', WSC, *My Early Life* (1930), p.18.

26 '... balance of observance', Ibid., p.110.

26 '... public school failures.' Gilbert, vol.I (1966), p.197.

26 '... vindicate his memory.' WSC, *My Early Life*, p.62.

27 '... thank God in the Street!!!' James Pope-Hennessy, *Queen Mary 1867–1953* (1959), p.335.

27 '... strangely-lighted episode', WSC, *Great Contemporaries*, 'Lord Rosebery'.

27 '... a bloated corpulent voluptuary', Jane Ridley, *The Heir Apparent* (2010).

27 '... lest we forget!' Kipling, 'Recessional'.

27 '... in pansy-left circles', George Orwell, 'Rudyard Kipling', *Horizon*, February 1942 in Peter Davidson, Ian Angus, Sheila Davidson (eds.), *The Complete Works of George Orwell* vol.XIII (1998), p.151.

28 '... make ambition virtue', Shakespeare, *Othello* Act 3, Scene 3.

28 '... against barbarous peoples', Richard Toye, *Churchill's Empire: The World That Made Him and the World He Made* (2010), p.35.

28 '... theatre of operations.' WSC, *My Early Life*, p.77.

28 '... great humanity', William Manchester, *The Last Lion: Winston Spencer Churchill Visions of Glory 1874–1932*, p.9.

29 '... Eagerness to Go to War', *New York Times*, 18 Dec 1895.

29 '... the English-speaking races.' Arthur Conan Doyle *The White Company* (1891), dedication.

29 '... for the mass of the people', WSC, *Great Contemporaries*, 'Joseph Chamberlain'.

30 '... as a foreign nation.' Toronto speech, 30 Dec 1897.

31 '... war with England.' Amanda Foreman, *A World on Fire* (2011).

31 '... transport to Canada', WSC, *My Early Life*.

31 '... could not long be held in check,' Ibid., ch.18.

31 '... popular of all wars', R.C.K. Ensor, *England* (1935), p.230.

32 '... a bad day either', WSC, *My Early Life*, pp.104–5.

32 '... accession of Commodus.' Edward Gibbon, *History Of The Decline And Fall Of The Roman Empire*, ch.3.

32 '... glories of the Victorian Era', WSC, BBC radio eulogy for George VI, 7 Feb 1952.

33 '... Australian and the gorilla.' Charles Darwin, *The Descent of Man: Selection in Relation to Sex*, ch.VI.

34 '... Goodwood in lovely weather', WSC, *My Early Life*, p.120.

35 '... can't pull up now.' *Companion* vol.I, p.807.

35 '... or hurt, very jolly.' WSC, *My Early Life*, p.131.

35 '... these odious dervishes,' Martin Gilbert, *Churchill: A Life* (2000), p.91.

36 '... and they have not.' Hilaire Belloc *The Modern Traveller* (1898), ch.VI.

36 '... Where will you beat this?' WSC, *My Early Life*, p.182.

36 '... exists in the world.' WSC, *The River War* vol.II, pp.248–55.

36 '... iron despatch box,' WSC, *Churchill* vol.I, pp.288–9.

36 '... colossal undertaking.' WSC, *My Early Life*, p.105.

37 '... wine was not excluded.' Ibid., p.207.

37 '... of entering Parliament.' Ibid., pp.196–7.

37 '... British regular troops', Ibid., p.200.

37 '... they nearly always do.' Ibid., p.222.

38 '... to be deprecated', Andrew Roberts, *Salisbury: Victorian Titan*, ch.42.

38 '... no power to England.' Iain R. Smith, *The Origins of the South African War: 1899–1902* (1996), p.367.

39 '... my Mauser pistol', WSC, *My Early Life*, p.249.

39 '... the armoured train,' Gilbert, vol.I, p.481.

39 '... the military situation.' Ibid., p. 483.

40 '... abstain from reading it.' WSC, *My Early Life*, p.153.

41 '... future prime minister of England', Martin Gilbert, *Churchill and America* (2005), p.36.

41 '... in life is money,' David Lough, *No More Champagne: Churchill and His Money* (2015), p.49.

41 '... finish up stone broke.' Ibid.

41 '... in less than two years.' Gilbert, vol.I, p.545.

Chapter 2, pages 43–63

45 '... the English have done.' Oscar Wilde, *A Woman of No Importance*, Act 3.

46 '... nineteenth centuries', David Cannadine, 'Churchill and the Pitfalls of Family Piety', in Blake and Louis (eds), *Churchill*, p.10.

47 '... fighting in the field', HoC, 18 Feb 1901.

47 '... methods of barbarism', Speech at National Reform Union dinner, 14 Jun 1901.

47 '... absurd and wrong', George Arthur, *Life of Lord Kitchener*, ch.XLIV.

47 '... than palaces in Park Lane!' Paul Addison, *Churchill on the Home Front: 1900–1955* (1992), pp.17–18.

47 '... military armaments,' Ibid., p.18.

49 '... dirty little Hebrew', Martin Gilbert, *Churchill and the Jews: A Lifelong Friendship*, ch.2.

49 '... into Gentile society.' Gilbert, vol.I, p.286.

50 '... disposition of the world among its peoples' Roger Hyam, 'Churchill and the British Empire' in Blake and Louis (eds), *Churchill*, p.161.

50 '... path of patronage', WSC, *Lord Randolph Churchill*, preface.

51 '... twenty years later', Peter Clarke, *Mr. Churchill's Profession*, p.61.

51 '... directly contrary sense', R.F. Foster, *Lord Randolph Churchill: A Political Life* (1981), p.395.

51 '... in his own image', Ibid., p.399.

51 '... cheap and vulgar egoist.' Ibid., p.400.

52 '... whom civilisation has no charms', HoC, 28 Feb 1906.

52 '... Asiatic cancer', Smuts, election speech, Oct 1906.

52 '... spoke nicely', Toye, *Churchill's Empire*, p.110.

52 '... private expedition', Gilbert, *Companion* vol.II (1969), pt.2, p.797.

53 '... an enormous scale,' Addison, *Churchill on the Home Front*, p.54.

53 '... butchery of the natives', Gilbert, *Churchill: A Life*, p.183.

53 '... would have been to us.' WSC, *My African Journey* (1908), p.125.

53 '... in German South-West Africa', Churchill, *Thoughts and Adventures* (1949), p.54.

54 '... to play polo', WSC, *Great Contemporaries*, 'Alfonso XIII'.

55 '... departure from precedent', J.A. Spender and Cyril Asquith, *Life of Herbert Henry Asquith* (1932), p.197.

55 '... My dear Winston', Gilbert, vol.I, pp.244–5.

56 '... country can rival.' WSC, *My Early Life*, p.73.

56 '... out, Out, OUT.' Sonia Purnell, *Clementine: The Life of Mrs. Winston Churchill*, pp.33–4.

56 '... speculation in English politics', A.G. Gardiner, *Prophets, Priests and Kings* (1914), pp.233–4.

56 '... has just discovered', Lucy Masterman, *History Today*, Nov–Dec 1964.

56 '... with Mrs Beatrice Webb', Addison, *Churchill on the Home Front*, p.62.

56n '... the flood of filth coming across the Channel', William Joynson-Hicks, *ODNB*.

57 '... Russia ever written', Taylor, *English History*, p.348.

57 '... than the English aristocrat.' Paul Addison, 'Churchill's Three Careers', in David Cannadine and Raymond Quinault (eds), *Winston Churchill in the Twenty-First Century* (2004), p.12.

57 '... is supposed to count.' *National Review*, Jan 1906.

58 '... feeling for literature', George Orwell, *New Leader*, 14 May 1949, in *The Complete Works of George Orwell* vol.XX, p.111.

58 '... her imperial greatness', A.J.P. Taylor, *The Struggle for Mastery in Europe, 1848–1818* (1954), p.478.

59 '... an act of sexual vice', Lord Hugh Cecil letter to *The Times*, 22 Aug 1907.

59 '... in our time, O Lord', Gilbert, vol.II, pp. 89–90.

59 '... enrichment is derived.' HoC, 4 May 1909.

60 '... cheap labour for the millionaire', Addison, *Churchill on the Home Front*, p.39.

60 '... selfish individuals.' Roberts, *Walking with Destiny*, p.121.

60 '... of all civilisations.' Addison, *Churchill on the Home Front*, p.92.

60 '... most advanced politicians.' Lucy Masterman, *History Today*, Nov 1964, p.747.

60 '... than he was in opposition', David Cannadine, *In Churchill's Shadow* (2004), p.55.

60 '... make anyone laugh.' Gilbert, vol.II (1967), p.517.

61 '... prisons is incredible,' *Daily Chronicle*, 27 May 1897.

61 '... honourable gentleman doing?' HoC, 6 Feb 1911.

62 '... story to an end.' Churchill, *Thoughts and Adventures*, p.48.

62 '... danger to the race', Addison, *Churchill on the Home Front*, p.125.

62 '... perverted science', HoC, 18 Jun 1940.

62 '... the Winston of Germany', T.G. Otte, *The Foreign Office Mind: The Making of British Foreign Policy, 1865–1914* (2011), p.351.

62 '... amazing ability and industry,' Richard Toye, *Lloyd George and Churchill: Rivals for Greatness*, ch.3.

63 '... but not impossible.' Violet Bonham-Carter, *Winston Churchill as I Knew Him* (1965), pp.220–22.

Chapter 3, pages 65–87

65 '... *une politique d'apaisement*', Gilbert, vol.II, p.349.

66 '... what risks to run.' Ibid., p.344.

66 '... of our naval affairs,' WSC, *The World Crisis* vol.I, ch.V.

67 '... tumult in the cloud.' W.B. Yeats, 'An Irish Airman Foresees His Death'.

67 '... and its traditions', Mary Soames (ed.), *Speaking for Themselves* (1999), p.64.

67 '... could go to hell,' Ibid., p.65.

68 '... asperity of party politics.' Gilbert, *Companion* vol.V (1983), p.63.

68n '... much better informed ... whatever you have on you.' Private information.

69 '... coming war with Germany', Roberts, *Churchill*, p.143.

69 '... he is going to do,' Brian Lavery, *Churchill Warrior* (2017), p.74.

69 '... Holidays at Govt. expense', Margaret MacMillan, *The War that Ended Peace* (2014), p.168.

69 '... state in the world', Misha Glenny, *The Balkans: Nationalism, War, and the Great Powers* (2012), p.219.

70 '... than those of kings.' Reichstag speech, 14 May 1890.

70 '... a soldier in mufti,' Chris Wrigley, 'Churchill and the Trade Unions', *Transactions of the Royal Historical Society* (2001), p.282.

70 '... not write in blood.' Ibid.

70 '... folly and barbarism it is.' Gilbert, vol.II, p.225.

71 '... bright red blossom.' Ibid.

72 '... to loyal Ireland,' Paul Bew, *Churchill and Ireland* (2016), p.48.

72 '... of ancient wrongs,' 8 Feb 1912, Winston S. Churchill (ed.), *Never Give In! Winston Churchill's Speeches* (2004), p.39.

72 '... of the British people.' R.C.K. Ensor, *England: 1870–1914*, p.455.

73 '... foolish in speech or action.' Bew, *Churchill and Ireland*, p.37.

73 '... *dreissig Jahr zu wenig*', Franz Grillparzer, *König Ottokars Glück und Ende*, Act I.

73 '... pulling us to pieces.' Kenneth Rose, *King George V* (1983), p.242.

73 '... Parliament as a Liberal.' Gilbert, vol.I, p. 318.

73 '... I shall go out.' Lord Riddell, 6 Jan 1914, *More Pages from My Diary, 1908–1914* (1934), p.194.

74 '... on an extended scale,' Robert Rhodes James, *Churchill: Study on Failure 1900–1939* (1970), p.62.

74 '... infamy and their own', WSC, *The World Crisis* vol.V, ch.IV.

74 '... nobody has a good word', Catriona Pennell, *A Kingdom United: Popular Responses to the Outbreak of the First World War in Britain and Ireland* (2012), p.26.

74 '... would have any effect on the world', Michael S. Neiburg, *Dance of the Furies: Europe and the Outbreak of World War I* (2011), p.23.

75 '... the map of Europe.' WSC, *The World Crisis* vol.I, p.193.

75 '... fearful moods of levity.' Soames (ed.), *Speaking for Themselves*, p.96.

75 '... to frogmarch events.' Douglas Newton, *The Darkest Days* (2014), p.52.

75 '... for a sea-fight,' H.H. Asquith, *Memories and Reflections 1952–1927* vol.2, pp.1–2.

75 '... a fearful war as this.' Michael and Eleanor Brock (eds), *Margot Asquith's Great War Diary 1914–1916: The View from Downing Street* (2014), p.106.

75 '... something like this?' Philip Guedalla, *Mr. Churchill: A Portrait*, ch.IV.

75 '. . untrained for land war', Max Hastings, *Catastrophe: Europe goes to War 1914* (2013), p.448.

76 '... detached force in the field', Gilbert, *Companion* vol.III, (1971), p.111.

76 '... Homeric laughter', Michael and Eleanor Brock (eds), *Letters to Venetia Stanley* (1982), p.263.

76 '... quite off his head', Ibid.

76 '... given a handle to my enemies.' WSC, *The World Crisis* vol.I, ch.XVI.

76 '... at the Dardanelles.' Max Hastings, *Catastrophe*, p.264.

76 '... while sailors sail the sea.' Brock (eds), *Margot Asquith's Great War Diary 1914–1916*, p.61.

77 '... the world can give me,' Lawrence James, *Churchill and Empire: Portrait of an Imperialist* (2013), p.101.

77 '... chew barbed wire in Flanders?' Gilbert, vol.III (1971), p.226.

77 '... I didn't want this.' Private information.

77 '... on that point.' Gilbert, vol.III, p.226.

78 '... still in possession!' Jonathan Schneer, *The Balfour Declaration: The Origins of the Arab–Israeli Conflict* (2010), p.42.

79 '... as I for Glory', Lord Byron, 'Written After Swimming from Sestos to Abydos'.

79 '... fleet to such peril.' Hew Strachan, *The First World War* (2003), p.113.

80 '... the actions of Mr Churchill', Gilbert, vol.III, p.460.

80 '... some of his colleagues', Ibid., p.362.

80 '... cabinet by his colleagues.' Brock (ed.), *Margot Asquith*, p.84.

80 '... ascendancy over mankind.' Manfred Weidhorn, *A Harmony of Interests: Explorations in the Mind of Sir Winston Churchill* (1992), p.22.

80 '... does not inspire trust.' Gilbert, vol.III, p.362.

80 '... quick-change political artists,' *Mr Punch's History of the Great War* (1919), p.50.

80 '... has become impossible.' Gilbert, vol.III, p.454.

81 '... amid general ignorant rejoicing', *Daily Mail*, 26 Oct 1934.

81 '... and overmastering will', HoC, 2 Nov 1915.

81 '... of the exoneration', *The Times*, 3 Nov 1915.

81 '... of the Admiralty', Gilbert, vol.III, p.564.

81 '... as he is of personalities', Brock (ed.), *Margot Asquith*, p.133.

82 '... to have gone to Antwerp,' WSC, *Thoughts and Adventures*, p.6.

82 '... British and Australasian forces.' WSC, *The World Crisis* vol.IV, ch.XVII.

82 '... from her finger-tips upwards', WSC, *The World Crisis* vol.II, ch.XXIV.

82 '... and daring strategy.' Malcolm Gladwell, *New Yorker,* July 27 2009.

82 '... fought somewhere else.' Taylor, *English History*, p.49.

83 '... won by no other means.' HoC, 15 Nov 1915.

83 '... was not cheering', *The Times*, 16 Nov 1915.

83 '... regiment is in France', Gilbert, vol.III, p.564.

84 '... in military circles,' WSC, *Thoughts and Adventures*, p.68.

84 '... we dare not be compassionate.' *The Spectator*, 11 Mar 1916.

84 '... stiff with trench-mud.' Duff Hart-Davis (ed.), *End of an Era: Letters and Journals of Sir Alan Lascelles 1887–1920* (1986), pp.196–7.

86 '... lost the war in an afternoon' WSC, *The World Crisis* vol.III ch.V.

87 '... has been a great failure.' WSC, *The World Crisis* vol.III, ch.VII.

87 '... fought for this war for years.' Gilbert, vol.III, p.454.

87 '... failure & folly.' George H. Cassar, *Asquith as War Leader* (1994), p.192.

Chapter 4, pages 89–109

89 '... outside pissing in', *The New York Times*, 31 Oct 1971.

89 '... against us every time.' Toye, *Lloyd George and Churchill*, p.172.

89 '... province or town.' David Lloyd George, *War Memoirs* vol.III, p.1067.

89 '... prevented it from always running true.' Ibid.

90 '... vanity is septic', Brock (ed.), *Margot Asquith* p.81.

90 '... industry and enterprise', Ibid., p.54.

90 '... political position is nil.' Ibid., p.279.

90 '... the shrine of the world's liberties.' Alexander MacCallum Scott, *Winston Spencer Churchill* (1905).

91 '... between the two nations', WSC, *The World Crisis* vol.III, ch.IX.

91 '... alike are condemned to live!' Ibid.

92 '... the American millions', HoC, secret session, 10 May 1917.

92 '... disasters in the War', Addison, *Winston Churchill*, p.87.

93 '... ghastly crime of Passchendaele', WSC, *Daily Mail*, 21 Sept 1934, *Essays* vol.III, p.98.

93 '... first air Member', Brett Holman, *The Next War in the Air: Britain's Fear of the Bomber, 1908–1941*, p.84.

93 '... manufacturing establishments', WSC, *The World Crisis* vol.IV, ch.II.

94 '... exile in Palestine.' David Gilmour, *Curzon: Imperial Statesman*, ch.30.

94 '... a trite *deus ex machina*', Vladimir Nabokov, *Speak, Memory*, ch.12.

96 '... against true conviction.' Toye, *Lloyd George and Churchill*, ch.8.

96 '... to a military tyranny.' WSC, *The World Crisis* vol.IV, ch.1.

97 '... by its arrogance', Anthony Trollope, *The Way We Live Now* (1875), ch.1.

98 '... rise to comment,' Michael J. Cohen, *Churchill and the Jews, 1900–1948* (2013), p.51.

98 '... mental and moral disease', Norman Rose, *Churchill, An Unruly Hero* (1994), p.146.

98 '... kiss the Hun,' Gilbert, *Churchill* (1991), p.142.

98 '... ducal blood ran cold', Addison, *Churchill on the Home Front*, p.211.

98 '... determine their government', Ferdinand Mount, *London Review of Books*, 20 Nov 2020.

99 '... rich men, bloodsuckers.' Vladimir Lenin, 11 August 1918.

99 '... proceeded to the Peace Conference.' WSC, *The World Crisis*, ch.II.

99 '... made them obviously futile', WSC, *The Gathering Storm*, p.7.

100 '... No army has overcome you.' Friedrich Ebert, 1918.

100 '... responsibility of government', Addison, *Churchill on the Home Front*, p.214.

100 '... defeat in war.' Ibid., p.229.

100 '... incompetence of the Labour Party.' *Nation*, 10 Jan 1920.

101 '... whom I ever encountered', Taylor, *English History*, p.205.

101 '... into public contempt.' Addison, *Churchill on the Home Front*, p.238.

101 '... to a lower plane.' H.L. Mencken, *On Being an American* (1922).

101n '... No, reaping.' Taylor, *English History*, p.186n.

102 '... performing an illegal operation', John Sparrow and Richard Gere (eds), *Geoffrey Madan Notebooks* (1981), p.76.

102 '... in bad taste', Soames (ed.), *Speaking for Themselves*, p.213.

103 '... & upon the Unjust.' Ibid., p.232.

104 '... can be maintained.' HoC, 8 Jul 1920.

105 '... friendly to Great Britain', Christopher Catherwood, *Churchill's Folly: How Winston Churchill Created Modern Iraq* (2004), p.168.

105 '... ungrateful volcano', Ibid., p.202.

105 '... proud politicians and theologians', HoC, 14 Jul 1921.

106 '... greater than the material effect', George K. Williams, *Biplanes and Bombsights: British Bombing in World War I* (1999), p.176.

106 '... take a firm line,' Susan Pedersen, *The Guardians: The League of Nations and the Crisis of Empire* (2015), p.265.

106 '... as long as necessary', Arthur Harris, *Bomber Offensive* (1947), p.22.

106 '... infinitely cheaper', Ronald Hyam, *Understanding the British Empire* (2010), p.236.

106 '... against uncivilised tribes.' WSC minute to War Office, 12 May 1919.

107 '... animal undergoing torture', Lough, *No More Champagne*, p.139.

107 '... I shall always love you.' Gilbert, *Companion* vol.III (1978), pt III, p.1535.

107 '... Churchill the Fortunate', E.M. Forster, *Our Graves in Gallipoli* (1922).

108 '... policemen of the world.' *The Times*, 7 Oct 1922.

109 '... with a whole heart,' Patrick Wright, *The Iron Curtain: From Stage to Cold War* (2007), p.170.

109 '... head of the fascisti party', Gilbert, vol.IV (1975), p.879.

Chapter 5, pages 111–25

111 '... was a journalist.' Private information.

111 '... stern and unbending Tories', Thomas Babington Macaulay, *Gladstone on the Church and State* (1839).

112 '... get you too cheap.' Purnell, *Clementine: The Life of Mrs Winston Churchill*, p.171.

112 '... but bellicose persons', Philip Guedalla, *Weekly Westminster*, 15 Mar 1924.

113 '... have never changed.' Addison, *Churchill On the Home Front*, p.227.

113 '... had been despised.' Thomas Babington Macaulay, *The History of England from the Accession of James II* (1848), ch.XIV.

114 '... bloody duck swim?' Gilbert, *Churchill: A Life*, p.465.

114 '... Industry more content.' Roy Jenkins, *Churchill* (2001), p.395.

114 '... barbarous relic', John Maynard Keynes, *A Tract on Monetary Reform*, ch.IV.

115 '... occupied by Queen Victoria', John Maynard Keynes, *The Economic Consequences of Mr Churchill* (1925).

115 '... meet the owners.' Frank McLynn, *The Road Not Taken: How Britain Narrowly Missed a Revolution*, ch.13.

116 '... Sydney Street lines.' *The British Worker*, 12 May 1926 in Rhodes James, *Winston Churchill: A Study in Failure*, p.174.

116 '... most valuable asset', Emanuel Shinwell in Ibid.

117 '... I could do both.' WSC, *My Early Life*, pp.327–8.

117 '... main executive power', WSC, *The World Crisis* vol.II, ch.XVIII.

117 '... plan of attack.' Siegfried Sassoon, 'The General'.

117 '... from 1911 to 1914', Jonathan Rose, *The Literary Churchill: Author, Reader, Actor* (2014), p.205.

118 '... rhetorical imperatives.' Ibid., p.197.

119 '... against the advance', John Maynard Keynes, *The New Republic*, 23 Mar 1927.

119 '... conquerors of history.' WSC, *The World Crisis* vol.III, ch.XVII.

119 '... history of the universe', Rose, *The Literary Churchill*, p.157.

119 '... indicated in the text,' Clarke, *Mr Churchill's Profession*, p.75.

120 '... Birmingham in a lean year', Lindsay Rogers, *Political Quarterly* Vol.62, No.2 (June 1947), p.289.

120 '... as a Liberal Unionist.' *The Times*, 1 Jun 1937.

120 '... odious title of Conservative', Neville Chamberlain, *ODNB*.

120 '... matter of course.' Ibid.

121 '... idea every hour,' David Dilks, *Chamberlain* vol.I (2002), p.430.

121 '... strain he puts on them.' Addison, *The Unexpected Hero*, p.123.

121 '... more comfortable before I die.' Lough, *No More Champagne*, p.187.

121 '... like Mr Micawber.' Peter Clarke, 'Churchill's Economic Ideas 1900–1930', in Blake and Louis (eds), *Churchill*, p.80.

122 '... bookmakers for keeping them', Christopher C. Hood, *The Limits of Administration* (1976), p.176.

122 '... Mother & Nellie gambled.' Soames, *Clementine Churchill* (2004), ch.14.

122 'BEWARE CASINO', Clarke, *Mr Churchill's Profession*, p.219.

122 '... slew a sow.' Soames (ed.), *Speaking for Themselves*, pp.277–8.

123 '... gay, and delightful', *The Times*, 22 Jul 1953.

123 '... unbroken friendship', David Cannadine, *Aspects of Aristocracy: Grandeur and Decline in Modern Britain* (1994), p.142.

123 '... but not quite a gentleman', private information.

123 '... against the Senussi.' *The Times*, 22 Jul 1953.

123 '... especially the kiddies', private information.

123 '... my bugger-in-law', Michael G. Brennan, *Evelyn Waugh: Fictions, Faith and Family* (2013), p.40.

124 '... for this purpose', Robin Brodhurst, *Churchill's Anchor: The Biography of Admiral Sir Dudley Pound* (2000), p. xxxviii.

124 '... still unconquered Empire.' *The Times*, 2 Jul 1934.

125 '... distracted by newspapers', WSC, *My Early Life*, p.354.

125 '... 2000 words per day.' Jenkins, *Churchill*, p.421.

125 '... happily ever afterwards.' WSC, *My Early Life*, p.367.

Chapter 6, pages 127–45

127 '... the land is bright!' WSC, broadcast 27 Apr 1941.

128 '... and its statesmen', WSC, *The World Crisis* vol.IV, ch.VII.

128 '... prototypes in Europe', Ibid.

129 '... attention in Congress', *The Times*, 8 Dec 1920.

129 '... utterly submerged.' F. Scott Fitzgerald, *The Great Gatsby* (2001), p.10.

129 '... keep this country intact', Pankaj Mishra, *From the Ruins of Empire: The Intellectuals Who Remade Asia*, p.198.

130 '... their unfortunate allies.' Soames (ed.), *Speaking for Themselves*, p.229.

130 '... rapprochement is very pleasant.' Addison, *Unexpected Hero*, p.124.

130 '... across the Atlantic Ocean', Ibid., p.125.

131 '... dwell upon race feeling.' Clarke, *Mr Churchill's Profession*, p.105.

131 '... and of interests.' Seth P. Tillman, *Anglo-American Relations at the Paris Peace Conference of 1919* (2015), p.66.

131 '... inflame its hatreds', WSC, *The Gathering Storm*, p.20.

131 '... last pound of flesh.' Addison, *Unexpected Hero*, p.126.

132 '... or Egypt or Canada.' Gilbert, *Churchill and America*, pp.104–5.

132 '... dominate world politics', Earl of Dundee paraphrasing WSC, 21 Sep 1928, in Ibid., p.109.

132 '... even vital concessions', Ibid.

132 '... might stand in the way.' Soames (ed.), *Speaking for Themselves*, p.332.

133 '... use as the office,' Lough, *No More Champagne*, p.185.

133 '... with white hair,' 6 Apr 1945, John Colville, *The Fringes of Power: Downing Street Diaries 1938–1955* (1985).

133 '... of our war effort.' Rose, *Literary Churchill*, p.202.

134 '... Rock of Gibraltar,' Gilbert, *Churchill and America*, p.115.

134 '... surprise once more.' Sophie Ratcliffe, *P.G. Wodehouse: A Life in Letters* (2011).

134 '... every few minutes.' Gilbert, *Churchill and America*, p.118.

134 '... his official biography,' Lough, *No More Champagne*, p.3.

135 '... started to my mind', Edward Gibbon, *Memoirs of My Life and Writings* (1796).

135 '... than one might expect', Rose, *Literary Churchill*, p.210.

135 '... of the British Empire', Piers Brendon, *The Decline and Fall of the British Empire* (2008), pp.10–11.

136 '... but agreeable races', WSC, *My Early Life*, p.102.

137 '... short visit of a fortnight', Earl of Birkenhead, *Halifax* (1965), pp.246–47.

137 '... of the king-emperor.' Winchester House speech, 23 Feb 1931.

137 '... subaltern of Hussars of '96,' Philip Williamson and Edward Baldwin (eds), *Baldwin Papers: Conservative Statesman, 1908–1947* (2004), p.246.

137 '... between the two wars', Duff Cooper, *Old Men Forget* (1954), p.171.

137 '... throughout the ages', St. George's speech, 17 Mar 1931.

138 '... sitting on the Treasury Bench.' HoC, 28 Jan 1931.

139 '... known as the townsman.' Robert Self, *Neville Chamberlain: A Biography* (2006), p.30.

139 '... grey wagtail and not a pied.' *The Times*, 24 Jan 1933.

140 '... some of Britain's liabilities', Robert H. Pilpel, *Churchill in America 1895–1961* (1977), p.111.

140 '... national honour', Queen's Hall, speech 17 Feb 1933.

140 '... can get out of it.' Addison, *Unexpected Hero*, p.134.

140 '... never liked or trusted me', WSC, *Thoughts and Adventures*, p.8.

141 '... amateur who blundered.' Victor Wallace Germains, *The Tragedy of Winston Churchill* (1931), p.47.

141 '... crying in the wilderness.' John 1:23.

142 '... Rothermere is supporting him.' Soames (ed.), *Speaking for Themselves*, p.275.

142 '... piercing eyes.' Soames, *Clementine Churchill*, ch.14.

142 '... passions of Leninism.' Gilbert, vol.V (1976), p.226.

142 '... among living men', Anti-Socialist and Anti-Communist Union speech, 17 Feb 1933.

142 '... into the sheepfold', Richard J. Evans, *The Coming of The Third Reich* (2004).

142 '... a racial pride.' HoC, 13 Apr 1933.

143 '... but upon themselves.' HoC, 23 Mar 1933.

143 '... for the Blackshirts', *Daily Mail*, 15 Jan 1934.

143 '... War on Germany', *Daily Express,* 24 Mar 1933.

143 '... with European states.' *Daily Express*, 11 Sep 1934.

144 '... of the photograph', Richard Toye, *Winston Churchill: A Life in the News* (2020), p.1.

145n '... more Hoares to Paris' George V in William Manchester, *The Last Lion: Winston Spencer Churchill: Alone, 1932–1940* (1988), p.166.

Chapter 7, pages 147–69

147 '... the small things of life.' Soames, *Clementine Churchill*, ch.11.

148 '... stiffened with disdain', WSC, *History of the English-Speaking Peoples* vol.IV, ch.1.

148 '... was not the first.' Lord Byron, 'Epigrams'.

148 '... poor but honest parents', Randolph S. Churchill, *Twenty-One Years* (1966), p.3.

149 '... primarily to earn money', Maurice Ashley, *Churchill as Historian* (1968), p.122.

150 '... lately in finances,' Soames (ed.), *Speaking for Themselves*, p.345.

150 '... certainly be rewarded.' 8 Aug 1929, Ibid., p.336.

150 '... in London this autumn', 19 Sept 1929, Ibid., p.345.

151 '... by you personally,' Lough, *No More Champagne*, p.230.

151 '... a good pastiche!' Ibid., p.217.

151 '... in further royalties', Clarke, *Mr Churchill's Profession*, p.150.

152 '... praise famous men', Ecclesiasticus 44:1.

152 '... in their habitations', Ibid., 44:6.

152 '... within my habitation.' WSC, *The Gathering Storm*, p.62.

153 '... who never told a lie,' Clarke, *Mr Churchill's Profession*, p.183.

153n '... four-figure men in the office', *Scoop*, Evelyn Waugh, Book 3, Ch.1.

154 '... unthinkable could happen.' Mary Soames, *A Daughter's Tale: The Memoir of Winston Churchill's Youngest Child* (2012), p.107.

154 '... common as dirt', Soames (ed.), *Speaking for Themselves*, p.412.

154 '... deepest impression on me', Soames, *A Daughter's Tale*, p.105.

154 '... insufferable son Randolph.' From the unpublished diaries of Sir Basil Bartlett. I owe this quotation to my friend Lady Selina Hastings.

154 '... his father at his worst' Christopher Sykes, 'Randolph Churchill', in Kay Halle (ed.), *Randolph Churchill: The Young Unpretender* (1971), p.240.

154 '... banging doors, and rows', Soames, *A Daughter's Tale*, p.89.

156 '... the boozy scholars of Oxford', WSC, *My Early Life*, p.125.

156 '... drunk that much,' *The Times*, 2 June 2020.

156 '... people did in the 1930s', Roberts, *Walking with Destiny*, p.969.

156 '... does not get drunk.' Duff Cooper, 5 November 1921, in John Julius Norwich (ed.), *The Duff Cooper Diaries: 1915–1951* (2014).

156 '... the worse for drink.' Addison, *Churchill on the Home Front*, p.304.

156 '... nerves and his liver.' Robert Self (ed.), *The Neville Chamberlain Diary Letters* vol.I (2017), p.384.

156 '... cocktails and old brandies.' Chamberlain to Hilda Chamberlain, 9 March 1935, Ibid.

157 '... be worth living', Jenkins, *Churchill*, p.466.

157 '... glasses of port', Denys Blakeway, *The Last Dance: 1935 – the Year of Change* (2015), p.329.

157 '... but very drunk', Blanche Dugdale in Michael J. Cohen, *Churchill and the Jews, 1900–1948* (2013), p.175.

158 '... establish collective security.' HoC, 26 March 1936.

158 '... of these dispensations.' HoC, 14 Apr 1937.

158 '... every possible blunder.' Taylor, *English History*, p.404.

159 '... It's a long way to Tipperary ...' Jenkins, *Churchill*, pp.500–1.

159 '... do it very well,' Taylor, *English History*, p.402.

159 '... the other one', David Cannadine, 'Churchill and the British Monarchy', in Cannadine and Quinault (eds), *Winston Churchill in the Twenty-First Century*, p.104.

159 '... in its closing decade', Soames (ed.), *Speaking For Themselves*, p.426.

159 '... or religion or art.' Herbert Paul (ed.), *Letters of Lord Acton to Mary Gladstone* (1904), p.210.

159 '... guilt and dishonour', G.M. Young (ed.), *Macaulay: Prose and Poetry* (1952), p.108.

160 '... lucid self-expression', Amory (ed.), *The Letters of Evelyn Waugh*, p.621.

160 '... of the genuine artist.' Donat Gallagher (ed.), *A Little Order* (1977), p.108.

160 '... not a work of literature.' Amory (ed.), *The Letters of Evelyn Waugh*, p.627.

160 '... greatest of English writers.' Paul (ed.), *Letters of Lord Acton to Mary Gladstone*, p.210.

161 '... that speaks out of turn', Newsinger, *The Blood Never Dried: A People's History of the British Empire* (2006), p.138.

161 '... Christian, liberal, noble', Norman Rose, *Churchill: The Unruly Giant* (1995), p.192.

161 '... an anti-Jewish verdict.' Isaiah Friedman, *British Pan-Arab Policy, 1915– 1922* (2010), p.202.

162 '... interests of the British Empire.' Gilbert, *Churchill and the Jews*, p.42.

162 '... friction with the Arabs,' Gilbert, vol.IV, p.484.

163 '... dispersed speedily', Ibid., p.544.

163 '... question of Zionism', Ibid., p.552.

163 '... in suspense.' Ibid., p.561.

163 '... a gross injustice', Ibid., p.563.

163 '... of the indigenous Arabs', Ibid., p.584.

164 '... profoundly associated.' HoC, 14 Jun 1921.

164 '... orangeries planted', Gilbert, vol.IV, p.565.

164 '... return to Palestine', Ibid., p.571.

165 '... safeguarding and conciliatory.' Cohen, *Churchill and the Jews*, p.171.

165 '... to roost with Mr Winston Churchill.' Ibid.

165 '... his own race.' *New York Times*, 11 Mar 2007.

166 '... clear out', Michael Makovsky, *Churchill's Promised Land: Zionism and Statecraft* (2007), pp.153–7.

166 '... beaten out of the place.' *Companion* vol.V, p.605.

166 '... were thrown out.' Makovsky, *Churchill's Promised Land*, pp.155–6.

166 '... taken their place.' *Companion* vol.V, pp.614–6.

167 '... his time, not ours,' Mark Twain, *Personal Reflections of Joan of Arc*, (1896), 'Translator's Preface'.

167n '... thinking at the time', Roberts, *Churchill*, p.415.

167n '... profoundly racist than most.' Andrew Roberts, *Eminent Churchillians*, p.211.

168 '... salvaging our people.' Brian J. Horowitz, *Vladimir Jabotinsky's Russian Years, 1900–1925* (2020), p.228.

168 '... versus the claims of starvation', Ibid., p.229.

168 '... allotted the Jews,' *Companion* vol.V, p.721.

168 '... to Chartwell if necessary.' Shmuel Katz, *Lone Wolf: A Biography of Vladimir (Ze'ev) Jabotinsky* (1996), p.1554.

168 '... results were excellent', Ibid.

168 '... as they are portrayed.' WSC, 'Palestine Partition', 23 July 1937, in *Companion* vol.V, pt.3, p.735.

169 '... the Jewish race in Europe!' Reichstag speech, 30 Jan 1941.

Chapter 8, pages 171–95

171 '... behindhand with Marlborough.' Clarke, *Mr Churchill's Profession*, p.185.

171 '... but in his own country,' Mark 6:4.

171 '... no one paid attention.' Fulton Missouri speech, 5 Mar 1946.

171 '... I told you so.' Byron, *Don Juan*, canto 14.

171 '... the wicked to rearm.' WSC, *The Gathering Storm*, p.ix.

172 '... weakness of the virtuous.' Ibid., p.7.

172 '... firing of a single shot.' Fulton Missouri speech, 5 Mar 1946.

173 '... a peculiarly barbaric sort.' A.J.P. Taylor, *The Origins of the Second World War*, 2nd ed. (1963), 'Second Thoughts', p.9.

173 '... in permanent subjugation.' *Pall Mall*, 24 Sep 1925.

173 '... and Germany to be friends.' WSC, *The Gathering Storm*, p.65.

173 '... in a happier age.' WSC, *Strand Magazine*, Nov 1935.

174 '... peace and tolerance.' WSC, *The Times*, 7 Nov 1938.

174 '... blame for EVERYTHING', Florian Huber, *Promise Me You'll Shoot Yourself: The Downfall of Ordinary Germans, 1945* (2019), p.137.

174 '... shameless avowal', Socialist and Anti-Communist Union speech, 17 Feb 1933.

175 '... in brutish mutual extermination,' WSC, *My Early Life*, p.65.

175 '... is likely to occur.' CBS interview, 9 Mar 1932.

176 '... hindering the old?' *Saturday Evening Post*, 15 Feb 1930.

176 '... whom we cannot resemble.' Samuel Johnson, *The Rambler*, no.135.

177 '... our armaments in the air.' HoC, 14 Mar 1933.

177 '... will always get through', HoC, 10 Nov 1932.

177 '... in our aerial defences.' HoC, 7 Feb 1934.

178 '... continuous air attack', HoC, 16 Nov 1937.

178 '... under war conditions', HoC, 28 Nov 1934.

178 '... darker than it was.' WSC, *The Gathering Storm*, p.182.

179 '... on the continental model.' *New Statesman*, 7 Jan 1939.

180 '... shield of the French army.' 3 Nov 1937, in Gilbert, vol.V, p.886.

180 '... their own safety.' HoC, 14 Mar 1933.

180 '... more serviceable moods.' WSC, *English-Speaking Peoples* vol.III, ch.2.

180 '... to be our war Prime Minister.' Baldwin (lost letter) to J.C.C. Davidson 1935, in Gilbert, vol.V, p.687.

180 '... embraced by its proponents', David Aaronovitch, *The Times*, 12 Apr 2019.

181 '... which exist in Europe', Imperial Conference speech, 7 July 1921, in Gilbert, vol.IV, p.897.

181 '... loaded with dynamite', Robert Lansing secret memorandum, 30 Dec 1918.

182 '... will wish to secede.' Walter Lippmann, *US War Aims* (1944), p.174.

183 '... include German Bohemia', *Daily Telegraph*, 5 Mar 1919.

183 '... to Czech rule', Taylor, *The Origins of the Second World War*, p.235.

183 '... lightweight Eden is,' 8 Jan 1936, Gilbert, vol.V, p.696.

184 '... stage by stage.' HoC, 14 Mar 1938.

184 '... advantage of events.' Taylor, *English History*, p .424.

184 '... dictators and demagogues', HoC, 11 Mar 1975.

185 '... Churchill talks sense', John Lukacs, *The Duel: The Eighty-Day Struggle Between Churchill & Hitler* (1990), p.56.

185 '... enslavement of Europe.' 9 May 1938, Addison, *The Unexpected Hero*, p.149.

186 '... party before country,' WSC, *The Gathering Storm*, index s.v. Baldwin.

186 '... enlightened Tories, too.' Anthony Powell, *At Lady Molly's* (1957), p.63.

186 '... hawking your conscience', Labour Party conference 1 Oct 1935.

187 '... have been redressed', *Daily Telegraph*, 23 June 1938.

187 '... we know nothing', radio broadcast, 27 Sept 1938.

187 '... with one another again', Heston Airport speech, 30 Sep 1938.

187 '... peace with honour', Downing Street speech, 30 Sep 1938.

187n '... the Astor family were shot.' Private information.

188 '... as in the olden time.' HoC, 5 Oct 1938.

188 '... in half an hour.' Addison, *The Unexpected Hero*, p.148.

188 '... principle of self-determination.' WSC, *The World Crisis*, quoted by John Simon, HoC, 5 October 1938.

189 '... conditions in their country.' Patricia Meehan, *The Unnecessary War, Whitehall and the German Resistance to Hitler* (1992), pp.1–2.

189 '... she was falling.' Brussels speech, November 1945.

191 '... had ousted them.' WSC, *The Gathering Storm*, ch.16.

192 '... Good man,' Self, *Neville Chamberlain*, p.328.

192 '... bitterly anti-Fascist', Barbara Leaming, *Jack Kennedy: The Education of a Statesman*, p.58.

192 '... so darn sick of it.' Ibid., p.59.

192 '... to fight to the last Englishman', Ibid., p.80.

192 '... unfavourable popular reaction', Lippmann, *US War Aims*, p.24.

193 '... if very Jew,' Richard Breitman and Allan J. Lichtman, *FDR and the Jews*, p.17.

193 '... party was appalling,' Ibid.

193 '... Americans except words,' C.A. MacDonald, *The United States, Britain and Appeasement, 1936–1939* (1981), p.48.

194 '... outsiders and amateurs.' Simon Ball, *The Guardsmen* (2004), p.216.

194 '... What help shall I give?' Guy Burgess 1951, recording broadcast by Channel 4, 17 Jan 2014.

194 '... common consent be his.' Tom Hopkinson, *Picture Post 1938–1950* (1970).

195 '... government than Fascism.' *New Statesman*, 7 Jan 1939.

195 '... of the workers, I presume?' *Evening Standard*, 20 Sep 1939.

Chapter 9, pages 197–219

197 '... we should win this war.' Colville, *The Fringes of Power*, p.128.

198 '... for England, Arthur.' Taylor, *English History*, p.452.

198 '... the right will prevail.' Chamberlain declaration of war, 3 Sep 1939.

199 '... our consciences are at rest.' HoC, 3 Sep 1939.

200 '... wartime afloat', 'First Lord's Minutes', 24 Mar 1940.

200 '... against external misfortunes.' 17 Nov 1939, Gilbert (ed.), *The Churchill War Papers* vol.1 (2008), p.379.

200 '... will write hereafter.' David Reynolds, *In Command of History* (2004), p.112.

200 '... for his broadcasts', Amory (ed.), *The Letters of Evelyn Waugh*, p.131.

201 '... has missed the bus', Conservative Party speech, 4 April 1940.

201 '... will be sunk', HoC, 11 April 1940.

201 '... name of God, go!' HoC, 7 May 1940.

202 '... of what you did last night.' Jenkins, *Churchill*, p.583.

202 '... not to have him as PM.' Taylor, *English History*, p.475.

202 '... I would certainly do so.' WSC, *The Gathering Storm*, p.525.

202 '... ordinary Party antagonisms.' Ibid., p.527.

203 '... for the British Empire.' HoC, 13 May 1940.

203 '... than a decisive weapon', Reynolds, *In Command of History*, ch.8.

203 '... to be a disappointment', WSC, *News of the World*, 24 April 1938.

203 '... should have done.' WSC, *Their Finest Hour*, p.39.

203 '... heavy tidings', HoC, 28 May 1940.

204 '... we shall fight on.' WSC, *Their Finest Hour*, p.88.

204 '... between 14 and 16 May,' Allan Allport, *Britain at Bay: The Epic Story of the Second World War: 1938–1941* (2020), p.254.

204 '... an intellectual victory.' Marc Bloch, *A Strange Defeat 1940* (1999).

205 '... the Constable of France.' WSC, *Their Finest Hour*, p.182.

205 '... but not a war,' BBC broadcast, 18 Jun 1940.

205 '... we shall never surrender.' HoC, 4 Jun 1940.

205 '... he has *les défauts de ses qualités*', Addison, *The Unexpected Hero*, p.123.

206 '... perverted science', HoC, 18 Jun 1940.

207 '... KBO', Gilbert, vol.VI, p.1273.

207 '... what I wanted to believe,' WSC, *My Early Life*, p.115.

208 '... a victorious conclusion.' HoC, 13 May 1940.

208 '... rather than give in.' WSC, *Their Finest Hour*, p.88.

208 '... behind you, Winston.' *Evening Standard*, 14 May 1940.

209 '... half-breed American', Colville, *The Fringes of Power*, p.122.

209 '... king over the water', Ibid.

209 '... island from end to end.' WSC, *Their Finest Hour*, p.88.

209 '... old and cold and weary,' Rupert Brook, 'Peace'.

209 '... fighting has increase.' Julian Grenfell, 'Into Battle'.

210 '... rich in heroes', 'Cato', *Guilty Men* (1940), p.11.

210 '... this year or next', Stephen E. Koss, *The Rise and Fall of the Political Press in Britain: the twentieth century* (1981), p.571.

210 '... a dozen guilty men,' 'Cato', *Guilty Men*, preface.

210 '... hard the road may be.' HoC, 13 May 1940.

211 '... which is all we've got.' WSC to Minister of Food, 21 Mar 1941, in *The Grand Alliance*, appendix C.

211 '... a substitute for victory,' Max Hastings, *Winston's War* (2010), p.116.

211 '... those speeches in 1940,' Clementine in Clarke, *Mr Churchill's Professions*, pp.293–4.

211 '... the issues at stake.' WSC, *Their Finest Hour*, p.231.

211 '... Psalm form,' Gilbert, vol.VI, p.665.

211 '... grave matters to the test,' Bew, *Churchill and Ireland*, p.69.

212 '... very simple: Victory!' Clemenceau, 30 Nov 1917.

212 '... hunger, thirst, battles and death', Garibaldi, 2 July 1849.

212 '... many to so few', HoC, 20 Aug 1940.

212 '... blood upon the ground.' Gilbert, vol.VI, p.420.

212 '... as slaves in ignominy.' Cicero, *Philippics* 3.14.35.

212 '... not for ourselves alone.' radio broadcast, 14 Jul 1940.

212 '... well, alone.' *Evening Standard*, 18 Jun 1940.

214 '... liberation of the old.' HoC, 4 Jun 1940.

214 '... broader lands and better days.' HoC, 20 Aug 1940.

215 '... I have ever been concerned,' WSC, *Their Finest Hour*, p.206.

215 '... solemn stentorian accord.' Ibid., p.211.

215 'Collar the lot', Although there is no precise evidence that Churchill uttered this phrase, it was widely attributed to him at the time, and it certainly sounds like him.

216 '... it was exaggerated.' HoC, 15 Aug 1940.

216 '... horrid little boy', Ben Pimlott, *Hugh Dalton* (1985), p.14.

216 '... Set Europe ablaze!' Jenkins, *Churchill*, p.629.

216 '... a way through.' WSC, *Their Finest Hour*, p.567.

216 '... indiscriminate bombings of London', radio broadcast, 11 Sep 1940.

217 '... out of the question.' Chamberlain diary entry 9 Sep 1940 in David Reynolds, *From World War to Cold War: Churchill, Roosevelt, and the International History of the 1940s* (2006), p.77.

218 '... voice of the whole nation', Addison, *Churchill on the Home Front*, p.359.

219 '... and with clean hearts.' HoC, 12 Nov 1940.

219 '... the other way round.' Gilbert, vol.VI, p.902.

Chapter 10, pages 221–45

221 '... War's greatest picture', *Daily Mail*, 31 Dec 1940.

222 '... like God Almighty', Jenkins, *Churchill*, p.472.

222 '... someone else would pick it up.' Private information.

222 '... I thought then piggish', Walter Thompson, *I Was Churchill's Shadow* (1951), p.17.

222 '... curiously inconsiderate', Colville, *The Fringes of Power*, pp.98–102.

222 '... & watchful Clementine.' Soames (ed.), *Speaking for Themselves*, p.454.

223 '... bed at 1.30 am', Colville, *The Fringes of Power*, p.129.

223 '... period of discussion.' WSC, *The Hinge of Fate*, ch.5.

224 '... men, women and children', HoC, 20 Aug 1940.

224 '... choice in the matter!' Dwight MacDonald, *The Responsibility of Peoples and Other Essays in Political Criticism* (1974), p.27.

224 '... now and England', T.S. Eliot, 'Little Gidding'.

226 '... Italy as an enemy.' *Daily Telegraph*, 13 Apr 1939.

226 '... Naples and Pompeii,' Colville, *The Fringes of Power*, p.123.

226 '... to Greece and Turkey.' Reynolds, *In Command of History*, p.194.

226n '... stopped them at Alamein,' *Sahara*, 1943.

227 '... three or four months,' Warren F. Kimball (ed.), *Churchill and Roosevelt: The Complete Correspondence* vol.I (1984), p.57.

227 '... the situation in Norway,' Will Swift, *The Kennedys Amidst the Gathering Storm: A Thousand Days in London, 1938–1940*, ch.18.

227 '... drunk half of his time', Simon Berthon and Joanna Potts, *Warlords: In The Heart of Conflict 1939–1945*, prologue.

228 '... any foreign wars.' FDR, Boston speech, 30 Oct 1940.

228 '... most unsordid act', HoC, 17 Apr 1940.

228 '... at our sovereignty', John Charmley, 'Churchill and the American Alliance', in Cannadine and Quinault (eds), *Winston Churchill in the Twenty-First Century*, p.150.

229 '... eyes of the British Empire', Richard Aldous, *Reagan and Thatcher: The Difficult Relationship*, p.9.

229 '... safe for democracy,' address to Congress, 2 Apr 1917.

230 '... with some satisfaction' WSC, broadcast, 9 Feb 1941.

230 '... as if in Kipling's "Recessional"', Evelyn Waugh, *Men at Arms*, ch.7.

230 '... Dakar and Greece.' Andrew Roberts, *Masters and Commanders: How Roosevelt, Churchill, Marshall and Alanbrooke Won the War in the West* (2008), p.220.

232 '... that I can foresee.' WSC, broadcast, 9 Feb 1941.

232 '... the whole scene.' WSC, *The Gathering Storm*, p.526.

232 '... and of Lloyd George.' Evelyn Waugh, *Men at Arms*, ch.7.

232 '... Respectable Tendency', Roberts, *Eminent Churchillians*, p.147.

232 '... in complete control.' Ibid.

233 '... in the last war,' Ibid.

233 '... most awful people', John Lukacs, *Blood, Toil, Tears and Sweat*, (2008).

233 '... *and he likes 'em.*' Self, *Chamberlain*, p.432.

233 '... control myself,' Roberts, *Eminent Churchillians*, p.141.

233 '... utterly unfitted for.' Ibid., p.146.

234 '... with reckless abandon,' Brendan Bracken, *ODNB*.

235 '... run by the House of Lords.' Richard Davenport-Hines and Adam Sisman (eds), *One Hundred Letters from Hugh Trevor-Roper* (2014), pp.29–35.

236 '... anyone more dislikable,' A.J.P. Taylor, *Politicians, Socialism and Historians* (1980), p.233.

236 '... wished to murder.' Henry Hardy (ed.), *Isaiah Berlin: Letters 1928–1946* (2004), p.175.

236 'scientist *manqué*', Rhodes James, *Churchill: A Study in Failure 1900–1936* (1990), p.242.

237 '... with Hitler is our foe.' radio broadcast, 22 Jun 1941.

237 '... in the House of Commons.' Colville, *The Fringes of Power*, p.350.

238 '... one of the authors.' Kimball, *Churchill and Roosevelt*.

238 '... you can't bomb me.' 'Blitzkrieg Baby', Fred & Doris Fisher, performed by Una Mae Carlisle, RCA, 1941.

238 '... America out of the war.' Allport, *Britain at Bay*, p.433.

239 '... crime without a name.' radio broadcast, 24 Aug 1941.

239 '... how it has to be.' Nicholas Stargardt, *The German War: A Nation Under Arms, 1939–1945*, ch.6.

240 '... the western democracies.' Peter Stansky (ed.), *Churchill: A Profile* (1973), p.95.

241 '... it in our lifetime.' Gilbert, vol.IV, p.76.

241 '... within the hour.' Mansion House speech, 10 Nov 1941.

241 '... won after all!' WSC, *The Grand Alliance*, p.539.

242 '... Jews around Roosevelt', Max Domarus (ed.), *Hitler, Speeches and Proclamations* vol.4 (1990), p.2543.

244 '... friendship with anyone', Doris Kearns Goodwin, *No Ordinary Time: Franklin and Eleanor Roosevelt: The Home Front in World War II* (1994), p.306.

244 '... ashamed to be its masters.' speech to Congress, 26 Dec.

Chapter 11, pages 247–67

247 '... for the British Empire', HoC, 13 May 1940.

247 '... institutions and our Empire', HoC, 18 Jun 1940.

247 '... the valley of humiliation', Goodwin, *No Ordinary Time*, p.343.

247 '... liquidation of the British Empire.' Mansion House speech, 10 Nov 1942.

247 '... stage of the British Empire,' Toye, *Churchill's Empire*, epigraph.

248 '... gone well for us.' George Orwell, *New Statesman and Nation*, 21 Nov 1942.

248 '... a vague menace', Gilbert, vol.VI, p.1271.

248 '... a decisive character,' Addison, *The Unexpected Hero*, p.142.

249 '... "This is the worst".' Shakespeare, *King Lear*, Act 4, Scene 1.

249 '... our race is involved.' Gilbert, vol.VII, p.54.

249 '... largest capitulation in British history', WSC, *The Hinge of Fate*, p.81.

249 '... I ought to have asked.' Ibid., p.43.

249 '... the Wops of Asia', Manchester & Reid, *The Last Lion* vol.III, ch.3.

249 '... disgrace is another,' Ibid.

250 '... end of the British Empire.' Brendon, *Decline and Fall*, p.428.

250 '... for Winston's sake.' Colville, *The Fringes of Power*, pp.146–7.

250 '... with Winston's speeches', Amory (ed.), *The Letters of Evelyn Waugh*, p.151.

251 '... All too true.' Ibid., p.153.

251 '... full of innocent fun', Ibid., p.154.

251 '... than in England.' Lynne Olson, *Citizens of London: The Americans Who Stood With Britain in Its Darkest, Finest Hour* (2010), ch.1.

252 '... a lonely figure.' Soames, *Clementine Churchill*, ch.23.

252 '... your soldiers won't fight.' Hastings, *Winston's War*, p.225.

252 '... a great general.' HoC, 27 Jan 1942.

252 '... were always slow.' Niall Barr, *Yanks and Limeys: Alliance Warfare in the Second World War* (2016), p.180.

252 '... unit for unit.' Roberts, *Masters and Commanders*, p.354.

253 '... the corpus of the liberating offensive.' WSC, *The Grand Alliance*, ch.34.

253 '... easy in operation.' WSC, *The Hinge of Fate*, Appendix C.

254 '... with the Germans', Roberts, *Masters and Commanders*, p.183.

254 '... to the war effort.' Waugh, *Officers and Gentlemen*.

254 '... great strategic plans.' Roberts, *Eminent Churchillians*, p.63.

254 '... for the rest of the war', WSC, *The Hinge of Fate*, ch.7.

256 '... at the right time', William Stewart, *Admirals of the World: A Biographical Dictionary, 1500 to the Present* (2014), p.228.

257 '... in great form.' Hastings, *Winston's War*, p.269.

257 '... you'd shit a corkscrew.' Private information.

257 '... but not unfruitful', WSC, *The Hinge of Fate*, p.459.

257 '... Panzer divisions in France.' *Evening Standard*, 21 Aug 1942, in Anne Chisholm and Michael Davie, *Beaverbrook: A Life* (1992), p.441.

258 '... rattledom within?' Soames (ed.), *Speaking for Themselves*, p.463.

258 '... weaken his authority,' Jonathan Schneer, *Ministers At War: Winston Churchill and his War Cabinet* (2015), p.166.

258 '... unless I join as Prime Minister', Ibid., p.167.

258 '... offensive action', Ibid., p.168.

258 '... I believe I could do it.' Ibid., p.167.

258 '... to her German enemy.' Ibid., p.168.

259 '... rejoicing as we go.' Ibid., p.173.

260 '... giving up Tobruk', Roberts, *Walking with Destiny*, p.737.

260 '... the reputation of the British army.' WSC, *The Hinge of Fate*, p.343.

260n '... Yes, indeed, jolly funny.'" Personal information.

261 '... afraid of the Germans.' David Roll, *The Hopkins Touch: Harry Hopkins and the Forging of the Alliance to Defeat Hitler* (2013), p.227.

261 '... belly as the snout', Edward C. Keefer (ed.), *Foreign Relations of the United States: Diplomatic Papers* (1961), p.618.

263 '... their Allied counterparts did.' Max Hastings, *New York Review of Books*, 28 May 2020.

263 '... a mystery to me.' Michael Howard, *Captain Professor: A Life in War and Peace* (2006), p.89.

263 '... masters of the African shore,' WSC, *The Hinge of Fate*, p.698.

266 '... its own with Stalingrad.' Ibid.

267 '... the facade of equality', William Waldegrave, *A Different Kind Of Weather: A Memoir* (2015).

267 '... and two cigars.' Manchester and Reid, *The Last Lion* vol.III, p.634.

267 '... to take him about.' Gilbert, vol.VII, pp.329–30.

Chapter 12, pages 269–91

269 '... persecution will be ended.' Gilbert, vol.VII, p.245.

269 '... mass electrical methods' Roberts, *Masters and Commanders*, p.305.

270 '... principal Nazi slaughterhouse', *The Joint Declaration by Members of the United Nations*, 17 Dec 1942.

270 '... about that the better,' Hastings, *Winston's War*, p.301.

271 '... can be very cruel.' Ibid.

272 '... for the purpose of mere terrorism,' HoC, 6 Feb 1940.

272 '... purpose of demoralisation', Taylor, *English History*, p.454.

272 '... weight of the war', Ibid., p.519.

273 '... greatly exaggerated.' Gilbert, vol.VI, p.1205.

273 '... claims too high.' Ibid., pp.1205–6.

273 '... than a human habitation', Max Hastings, *Bomber Command*, (1979) p.147.

274 '... chance of it working.' Richard Overy, *The Bombing War: Europe 1939–1945* (2013), p.324.

274 '... German munitions output', speech to Congress 19 May 1943, in *The New York Times*, 20 May 1943.

275 '... is being liquidated.' British Movietone reel, 12 Aug 1943.

276 '... brutish mutual extermination', WSC, *My Early Life*, p.65.

276 '... taken this too far?' Gilbert, vol.VII, p.437.

276 '... cost Germany the war.' Hastings, *Bomber Command*, p.257.

276 '... the means of victory', WSC, *Their Finest Hour*, ch.23.

277 '... on entering it.' Benn Steil, *The Marshall Plan: Dawn of the Cold War*, ch.3.

277 '... used in other ways', Overy, *The Bombing War*, p.633.

277 '... the other services knew it.' Ibid., p.xxiv.

278 '... against the alcoholism', *ODNB* s.v. Stafford Cripps.

279 '... Burglars Union', Peter Clarke, *The Cripps Version: The Life of Sir Stafford Cripps, 1889–1952* (2002), p.64.

279 '... a post-dated cheque', Ibid., p.305.

279 '... a toy he dislikes.' Gabriel Gorodetsky (ed.), *The Maisky Diaries: Red Ambassador to the Court of St James's 1932–1943* (2015), p.421.

280 '... bitter and bloody.' Colville, *The Fringes of Power*, p.79.

280 '... or aggregate supply', Amartya Sen, *Development* (2001), p.164.

280 '... public distribution system,' Amartya Sen, *Poverty and Famines: An Essay on Entitlement and Deprivation* (1981), p.79.

280 '... that is their due,' Colville, *The Fringes of Power*, p.534.

281 '... with hostility and contempt.' Lionel Knight, *Britain in India, 1858–1947* (2012), p.145.

281 '... starvation is in Europe.' Max Hastings, *All Hell Let Loose* (2012).

281 '... his outlook and Hitler's', Rose, *The Literary Churchill*, p.380.

281 '... with his rebuttals.' Rudyard Kipling, *Something of Myself* (1991 edn), p.73.

282 '... are the Negroes.' George Orwell, *Tribune*, 3 Dec 1943, in *The Complete Works of George Orwell* vol.16, p.12.

282 '... and American Negro Soldiers.' Clive Davis, *Sunday Times*, 18 June 2020.

283 '... he's one of the band.' David Olusoga, *Black and British: A Forgotten History* (2016), p.477.

283 '... troops in this country,' Harold L. Smith, *Britain in the Second World War: A social history* (1996), p.56.

283 '... prove the contrary in 1943.' Giuseppe Di Lampedusa, *The Leopard* (2010 edn), p.171.

284 '... eligible for public office', WSC, *Hinge of Fate*, ch.44.

284 '... future of the world.' Guildhall speech, 30 June 1943, in Winston S. Churchill (ed.), *The Best of Winston Churchill's Speeches: Never Give In!* (2003), p.356.

284 '... foreigners to one another.' Harvard speech, 6 Sept 1943, Ibid., pp.356–8.

285 '... the English-speaking peoples', Roberts, *Walking with Destiny*, p.793–4.

285 '... to the United States', Taylor, *English History*, p.564.

285 '... which I found distasteful', *ODNB* s.v. Harold Macmillan.

285 '... the Emperor Claudius.' Alistair Horne, *Harold Macmillan* vol.I (1989), p.160.

286 '... eternal and perpetual.' HoC, 1 March 1848.

287 '... example, not warning.' Taylor, *English History*, p.573.

287 '... fought somewhere else', Ibid., p.49.

287 '... designed for defensive war.' Michael Howard, *The Times Literary Supplement*, 25 Jun 2008.

287 '... no chance for a *coup de théâtre*.' Rose, *Literary Churchill*, p.40.

287 '... a squalid nuisance', HoC, 6 Dec 1945.

287 '... up the backbone.' Michael Foot, *Aneurin Bevan: A Biography* vol.1 (1973), ch.12.

288 '... start at the bottom.' Michael Howard, *Captain Professor* (2006), p.155.

288 '... a postponement of Overlord', John Kelly, *Saving Stalin: Roosevelt, Churchill, Stalin and the Cost of Allied Victory in Europe*, ch.14.

288 '... strategist of our day', Dwight Macdonald, *Politics Past: Essays in Political Criticism* (1970), p.117.

289 '... democracy and peace.' *Life*, 30 Aug 1948.

289 '... right way home.' John Wheeler-Bennett, *Action This Day* (1967), p.96.

290 '... arguing with the Somme.' John Keegan, *The Face of Battle: A Study of Agincourt, Waterloo and the Somme* (2004), p.280.

291 '... tore the guts out', Gilbert, vol.VII, p.975.

Chapter 13, pages 293–317

293 '... same coach on the bench', Dominick Graham and Shelford Bidwell, *Tug of War: The Battle of Italy 1943–1945* (1986), ch.8.

295 '... strains of intellectual opinion', HoC, 24 May 1944.

296 '... not been fighting the enemy', Ibid.

296 '... form of government?' Richard Langworth (ed.), *Churchill in His Own Words* (2012), p.184.

297 '... are unsurpassed.' HoC, 24 May 1944.

297 '... chapter by chapter,' Colville, *The Fringes of Power*, p.264.

297 '... nothing can displace me,' Clarke, *Mr Churchill's Profession*, p.250.

297 '... if not for the war', HoC, 13 Oct 1943.

297 '... in the National Government', WSC, *The Hinge of Fate*, p.337.

299 '... of their country.' WSC, *The Dawn of Liberation: War Speeches by the Right Hon. Winston S. Churchill* (1947), p.60.

300 '... drunken mood.' Alex Danchev and Daniel Todman (eds), *War Diaries 1939–1945: Field Marshal Lord Alanbrooke* (2001), p.566.

300 '... a very wicked man', Chisolm and Davie, *Beaverbrook* (1972), p.140.

302 '... Acquiesce', Lough, *No More Champagne*, p.302

302 '... able to write a different book', Ibid., p.304.

302 '... an admirable arrangement,' Ibid., p.296.

303 '... would like to see it', Ibid., p.314.

303 '... to ask you for them.' Ibid.

303 '... written by our friend', Ibid., p.309.

304 '... Korda the film rights.' Ibid.

304 '... the present War,' Ibid., p.310.

304 '... as that is not the case', Ibid.

304 '... any kind with them,' Ibid., p.311.

304 '... every one of us is indebted', Ibid., p.312.

305 '... himself, tax-free', Clarke, *Mr Churchill's Profession*, p.272.

305 '... any scenario writer of skill', *Daily Herald*, 16 Nov 1943.

306 '... the fighting men.' Macdonald, *Politics Past*, p.95.

306 '... each other the better.' Patton, *New York Times*, 26 Apr 1944.

306 '... he really likes FDR,' Duff Hart-Davis (ed.), *King's Counsellor: Abdication and War: the Diaries of Sir Alan Lascelles* (2006), p.306.

306 '... Churchill appeases America,' Orwell, 'A Letter from England', *Partisan Review 3*, January 1943, in *The Complete Works of George Orwell* vol.XIV, p.293.

306 '... and beg like Fala', Walter Reid, *Churchill 1940–1945: Under Friendly Fire* (2008), p.144.

307 '... *je vous liquiderai*.' Hart-Davis (ed.), *King's Counsellor*, p.231.

307 '... at the British and Americans?' Gilbert, vol.VII, p.646.

307 '... always choose Roosevelt.' Charles de Gaulle, *War Memoirs: Unity, 1942–1944* (1959), p.253.

307 '... grandeur is re-emerging.' Julian Jackson, *A Certain Idea of France: The Life of Charles de Gaulle* (2018), p.313.

307 '... in the great battle', Ibid.

308 '... *et par lui-même*,' Ibid.

308 '... our Allies won.' Ibid., p.776.

308 '... San Tropez in the centre', Soames (ed.), *Speaking For Themselves*, p.500.

309 '... blunders – of the Germans,' HoC, 28 Sep 1944.

309 '... is thereby assisted.' Gilbert, vol.VII, p.815.

310 '... standards of society', HoC, 24 May 1944.

310 '... naughty document', Gilbert, vol.VII, p.995.

310 '... this is the delicate side,' Soames (ed.), *Speaking for Themselves*, p.506.

310 '... North American region.' Walter Lippmann, *U.S. Foreign Policy*, p.230.

311 '... greatest villains imaginable.' Gilbert, vol.VII, p.1010.

312 '... We disobeyed.' Martin Middlebrook, *The Battle of Hamburg* (1994), p.349.

312 '... German population centres.' Hastings, *Bomber Command*, p.343.

313 '... best of spirits.' Soames (ed.), *Speaking for Themselves*, p.513.

313 '... frankly, terrible', Gladwyn Jebb, *The Memoirs of Lord Gladwyn* (1972), p.153.

313 '... from Poles abroad', Ernest Llewellyn Woodward, *British Foreign Policy in the Second World War* vol.1 (1962), p.499.

314 '... and unusual friend', Soames, *Clementine Churchill*, ch.17.

314 '... so long in the past.' HoC, 17 Nov 1944.

314 '... remaining Holocaust ally.' Edward Luttwak, *The Independent*, 3 Nov 2012.

315 '... has been proved.' WSC, *Triumph and Tragedy*, p.597.

315 '... with a smile' Joseph Lelyveld, *His Final Battle: The Last Months of Franklin Roosevelt* (2016), p.288.

315 '... innocent bystander.' Ibid., p.291.

315 '... going to kill them,' Ibid., p.292.

315 '... fraudulent prospectus.' Kimball (ed.), *Churchill and Roosevelt* vol.II, pp.547–51.

315 '... poor Poland either.' Colville, *The Fringes of Power*, p.527.

316 '... yielding to force or fear', HoC, 27 Feb 1945.

316 '... to go to church,' Colville, *The Fringes of Power*, p.546.

316 '... died in 1945,' Reynolds, *In Command of History*, p.525.

316 '... battle of the whole war', HoC, 28 Sep 1944.

317 '... to please Stalin', Hastings, *Winston's War*, p.350.

317 '... influence from outside,' *New York Times*, 6 Dec 1944.

317 '... as I wooed Roosevelt,' Colville, *The Fringes of Power*, p.587.

317 '... dislikes them immensely.' Mark Garnett, Simon Mabon, Robert Smith, *British Foreign Policy Since 1945* (2017), p.114.

317 '... of the conquerors,' HoC, 13 May 1901.

317 '... except by wars.' Colville, *The Fringes of Power*, p.231.

317 '... new, disgusting year', Ibid., p.521.

Chapter 14, pages 319–38

319 '... No, it is yours.' Gilbert, vol.VII, p.1347.

319 '... optimism of November 1918.' *Manchester Guardian*, 9 May 1945.

319 '... justice and retribution.' Gilbert, vol.VII, p.1344.

320 '... the Marines get all the credit.' MacDonald, *Politics Past*, p.96.

320 '... paid a soldier's debt.' Shakespeare, *Macbeth*, Act 5, Scene 8.

321 '.. begin to understand.' George MacDonald Fraser, *National Review*, 26 Jan 1998.

322 '... disease-ridden country', Max Hastings, *Nemesis: The Battle for Japan, 1944–45* (2008), p.77.

322 '... voting for you,' Ronald Lewin, *Churchill As Warlord* (1982), p.262.

322 '... old bugger's pissed.' Personal information.

322 '... We'll vote Labour.' Howard, *Captain Professor*, p.117.

323 '... of Nazism and fascism.' Mckinstry, *Attlee and Churchill: Allies in War, Adversaries in Peace*, ch.23.

323 '... on all your helmets,' Gilbert, vol.VIII (1988), p.27.

323 '... They don't deserve it.' Addison, *The Unexpected Hero*, p.214.

324 '... much in common,' Andrew Roberts, *A History of the English-Speaking Peoples since 1900*, (2011).

325 '... anti-national propaganda', Paul Bew, *Ireland: The Politics of Emnity 1789–2006* (2007), p.474.

325 '... or Mr de Valera.' *New York Times*, 4 May 1945.

325 '... to their heart's content.' broadcast, 13 May 1945.

325 '... against aggression', broadcast, 16 May 1945.

326 '... long and costly.' Hastings, *Winston's War*, p.465.

326 '... quite impossible.' Danchev and Todman (eds), *Lord Alanbrooke's War Diaries*, p.693.

326 '... humanely directed', broadcast, 4 Jun 1945.

327 '... IF SOCIALISTS WIN' *Daily Express*, 5 Jun 1945.

327 '... not an original joke.' *New Statesman and Nation*, 30 Jun 1945.

328 '... of Lord Beaverbrook.' Attlee broadcast, 5 Jun 1945.

328 '... "I like that man."' Jenkins, *Churchill*, p.796.

329 '... my carriage', Gilbert, vol.VIII, p.109.

329 '... effectively disguised.' Ibid., p.108.

331 '... to hand them over.' Alastair Horne, *Harold Macmillan: 1894–1956* (1989), p.259.

331 '... they were to go to Italy.' Ibid.

331 '... by the other side.' HoC, 24 May 1944.

332 '... as to drown them.' Macdonald, *Politics Past*, p.93.

332 '... I'd kick her in the belly.' Ibid.

332 '... of the Japanese – *in toto*.' Ibid.

332 '... than the war in Europe.' Ibid.

333 '... however impressive.' Gilbert, vol.VII, p.1257.

335 '... dangerous to human life', The MAUD Report, 1941.

336 '... our Army and Navy!' broadcast, 3 Jul 1941.

337 '... against her interest.' broadcast, 15 Aug 1945.

337 '... obtained I this freedom.' Acts 22:28.

338 '... a financial Dunkirk', Taylor, *English History*, p.513.

Chapter 15, pages 341–63

341 '... Best regards – Harry S. Truman.' Wright, *The Iron Curtain*, p.27.

342 '... working-class John Bull', Andrew Adonis, *Ernest Bevin: Labour's Churchill* (2020), epigraph.

342 '... Minister of Disease', Addison, *Churchill On The Home Front*, p.400.

343 '... the poor suffered.' HoC, 28 Mar 1945.

343 '... a National Health Service,' broadcast, 20 March 1942.

343 '... to all citizens', 1945 Conservative Party Manifesto, 'Health'.

343 '... on the brave and true!' Gilbert, vol.VIII, p.181.

344 '... bomb of an Englishman', Ibid., p.183.

344 '... bad statesmanship.' Ibid., p.189.

344 '... day is over,' Reynolds, *In Command of History*, p.11.

344 '... across the Continent.' Fulton Missouri speech, 5 Mar 1946.

344 '... Stettin to Trieste' Karl Marx, *New York Tribune*, 12 Apr 1853.

345 '... would be slaughtered.' Joseph Goebbels, *Das Reich*, 25 Feb 1945.

345 '... against the Red peril.' James Delingpole, *The Spectator*, 16 Nov 2013.

345n '... of modern Soviet society.' Macdonald, *Politics Past*, p.183.

346 '... army has won' speech, 8 Feb 1946.

346 '... RED BID FOR POWER', *Fulton Daily Sun-Gazette*, 6 Mar 1946.

346 '... poisonous', *Chicago Sun*, 6 Mar 1946.

346 '... soon as possible', Addison, *The Unexpected Hero*, p.223.

347 '... Russian Soviet Government', HoC, 27 Feb 1945.

347 '... going to be bolshevised' Colville, *The Fringes of Power*, p.527.

348 '... might be shocked', Gilbert, vol.VII, p.992.

348 '... cannot be otherwise.' Milovan Djilas, *Conversations with Stalin* (1962), p.114.

349 '... you and we espouse.' Fulton speech, 5 Mar 1946.

349 '... painful and thankless task', Cohen, *Churchill and the Jews*, p.60.

349 '... moment to espouse it.' HoC, 1 Aug 1946.

350 '... freezing February day', Soames, *A Daughter's Tale*, p.343.

350 '... after the struggle was over.' HoC, 1 Aug 1946.

350 '... a camp called Treblinka', HoC, 19 May 1943.

351 '... fucking well could', Brendon, *Decline and Fall*, p.484.

351 '... probable results of your action', Norman Rose, *A Senseless, Squalid War': Voices from Palestine, 1890s to 1948* (2014), p.127.

351 '... peace in Palestine', Ibid., p.73.

351 '... Jews in New York.' Ibid., p.125.

352 '... as the away team.' Ben Shephard, *The Long Road Home: The Aftermath of the Second World War* (2011), p.356.

353 '... Jews against the Arabs', Orwell, 'London Letter', *Partisan Review*, Fall 1945, in *Complete Works* vol.17, p.248.

353 '... as the Jews move in,' Labour Party Manifesto 1945.

353 '... probably side with the Arabs.' Orwell, Ibid.

354 '... iron and blood,' Otto von Bismarck, 30 Sep 1862.

354 '... their own religion.' HoC, 26 Jan 1949.

354 '... attention to age ... Implement immediately.' Benny Morris, *1948: A History of the First Arab-Israeli War* (2008), p.290.

357 '... background of our lives.' Gilbert, vol.VIII, p.341.

357 '... chair for gangsters', Manchester and Reid, *The Last Lion* vol.3, p.527.

357 '... unfolded the question', David Reynolds, *The Long Shadow: The Great War and the Twentieth Century* (2013), p.290.

358 '... if we had lost,' Gilbert, vol.VIII, p.285.

358 '... from German domination', Moscow Declaration, Oct 1943.

358 '... want America in Europe.' Max Beloff, 'Churchill and Europe', in Blake and Louis (eds), *Churchill*, p.446.

358 '... United States of Europe.' Zurich speech, 19 Sep 1946.

359 '... "Let Europe arise!"' Ibid.

359 '... the world is going', Raymond Daniell, *New York Times*, 9 Feb 1947.

359 '... to let him alone,' Ibid.

359 '... Do I know you?' James Margach, *The Abuse of Power* (1978).

360 '... embarrassing', Ramsden, *Man of the Century*, p.78.

360 '... that Winston must go.' Ibid.

360 '... will "Hand Over" Soon', *The Evening News*, 15 Mar 1946.

360 '... before completing the work', Daniell, *New York Times*, 9 Feb 1947.

361 '... pro-Zionist leanings.' Gilbert, vol.VIII, p.417.

361 '... pink pansies', Piers Brendon, *Churchill: A Brief Life* (1984), p.202.

362 '... party manager', WSC, *The Gathering Storm*, vol.I, p.26.

362 '... silly old Attlee', McKinstry, *Attlee and Churchill*, introduction.

363 '... not what they once were.' Peter Clarke, *The Last Thousand Days of the British Empire* (2007), ch.12.

363 '... a great nation.' Hugo Young, *This Blessed Plot: Britain and Europe from Churchill to Blair* (1999), p.24.

Chapter 16, pages 365–90

365 '... Duke of Norfolk', Shakespeare, *Henry IV*, Part 2, Act 3, Scene 2.

366 '... a frightful toll.' Addison, *Unexpected Hero*, p.86.

366 '... some of Britain's liabilities,' Ibid., p.130.

366 '... Europe's peace than that.' Ibid., pp.154–5.

367 '... because Marshall's right.' Elliot Roosevelt, *As He Saw It* (1974), p.184.

367 '... conduct of the war', Gilbert, vol.VIII, p.235.

368 '... during their term of office', HoC, 14 Feb 1946.

368 '... confiscate my earnings.' Waugh, 'Fan Mail', *A Little Order*, p.29.

368 '... so what's the use?' Lough, *No More Champagne*, p.319.

369 '... not for money.' Ibid., p.326.

369 '... actually represent me', Reynolds, *In Command of History*, p.60.

369 '... total 1400', Lough, *No More Champagne*, p.339.

370 '... write a book,' Gilbert, vol.II, p.127.

370 '... me and my work.' 'Yugoslavia: The Gale of the World', *Time*, 22 July 1946.

371 '... before the Gestapo,' Gilbert, vol.VI, p.943.

371 '... hate them now,' WSC, *Triumph and Tragedy*, p.545.

371 '... a spiritually great Germany,' Zurich speech, 19 Sep 1946.

371 '... fat but impotent', Tony Judt, *Postwar: A History of Europe Since 1945* (2005), p.275.

372 '... revolt in September 1938', David Reynolds, 'Churchill and the Gathering Storm', in Cannadine and Quinault (eds), *Winston Churchill in the Twenty-First Century*, pp.127–8.

372 '... is apt to "shoot a line".' Ibid.

372 '... to dwell on their efforts for peace.' Ibid.

373 '... "I knocked off about 1500".' Eric Mark obituary, *The Times*, 21 Nov 2020.

373 '... participate in them.' Reynolds, *The Long Shadow*, p.321.

374 '... Churchill's Mein Kampf', *Tribune*, 8 Oct 1948.

374 '... greatness is all around.' *Christian Science Monitor*, 24 Jun 1948.

374 '... the height of the incredible.' *Newark News*, 23 Apr 1950.

374 '... he wrote it himself', *The New Yorker*, 10 Jul 1948.

375 '... White Christmas', Henry Hardy (ed.), *Isaiah Berlin: Letters* vol.1, p.479.

375 '... too brutal', Addison, *The Unexpected Hero*, p.238.

376 '... trusted and loved.' Isaiah Berlin, *The Proper Study of Mankind: An Anthology of Essays* (1998), p.607.

376 '... terribly disappointed', Reynolds, *In Command of History*, p.276.

376 '... The old boy is chiseling on us.' Ibid.

376 '... for its production', private information.

376 '... read him through?' Edmund Burke, *Reflections on the Revolution in France* (2003 edn), p.76.

377 '... from the heart of yourself', Gilbert, vol.VIII, p.393.

377 '... one of the historians.' Reynolds, *In Command of History*, p.38.

377 '... that history myself.' HoC, 23 Jan 1948.

377 '... search for vindication', Reynolds, *In Command of History*, p.504.

377 '... a contribution to history', Maurice Ashley, *Churchill as Historian*, p.159.

377 '... it is my case.' William Deakin paraphrasing WSC, in Gilbert, vol. VIII, p.315.

378 '... vigorous leadership', WSC, *Closing the Ring*, p.457.

379 '... into the darkness', HoC, October 1938.

380 '... called a warmonger,' Addison, *The Unexpected Hero*, p.215.

381 '... path to world peace.' HoC, 14 December 1950.

382 '... can't refuse Winston.' Nigel Nicolson, *Alex: The Life of Field Marshal Earl Alexander of Tunis* (1973), p.302.

382 'On theirs, old cock,' Andrew Roberts, *Hitler and Churchill: Secrets of Leadership*.

383 '... of Prime Minister Winston Churchill', *New York Times*, 1 January 1952.

383 '... the civilian population,' WSC, memorandum to Lord Alexander, 22 August 1952.

383 '... house on fire.' Gilbert, vol.VII, p.664.

384 '... parley at the summit', Edinburgh speech, 15 Feb 1950.

384 '... finger on the trigger?' *Daily Mirror*, 25 Oct 1951.

384 '... a third world war,' Plymouth speech, 23 Oct 1951.

384 '... without victory', Ron Hirschbein, *The United States and Terrorism: An Ironic Perspective* (2015), p.105.

385 '... equipped hospitals.' speech, 16 Apr 1953.

385 '... a puppet State.' HoC, 11 May 1953.

386 '... France give up Indo-China?' Gilbert, vol.VIII, p.861.

386 '... when he's happy.' Lewis Carroll, *Alice's Adventures in Wonderland & Through the Looking-glass* (1993), p.214.

386 '... don't make an army.' Roberts, *Eminent Churchillians*, p.214.

386 '... skelping the kaffirs!' Ibid.

386 '... England White', Addison, *The Unexpected Hero*, p.233.

386 '... the light of Asia', Gilbert, vol.VIII, p.1094.

387 '... just and wise treatment', Toye, *Churchill's Empire*.

387 '... oddly, the Middle East,' HoC, 20 Aug 1940.

387 '... never have emerged."' James, *Churchill and Empire*, p.367.

388 '... but no right,' Colville, *The Fringes of Power*, p.376.

389 '... in international affairs.' Howard, *Captain Professor*.

Chapter 17, pages 393–412

393 '... an old man in a hurry', Jenkins, *Churchill*, p.5.

393 '... can touch the heights', Attlee, 1 Dec 1954.

393 '... to give the roar.' WSC, 1 Dec 1954.

394 '... infinitely derisory.' *Punch*, 3 February 1954.

394 '... modern art', Gilbert, vol.VIII, p.1073.

394 '... gorilla-like', *The New York Times*, 5 Dec 1958.

395 '... never despair.' HoC, 1 Mar 1955.

395 '... Anthony can do it."' Gilbert, vol.VIII, p.1122.

396 '... was situated in the Nile', Henry Pelling, *Churchill's Peacetime Ministry, 1951–55* (1997), p.60.

396 '... Hitler on the Nile', Tony Judt, *Reappraisals: Reflections on the Forgotten Twentieth Century* (2008), p.281.

396 '... before the war', HoC, 2 Aug 1956.

396 '... in a generation', Peter G. Boyle (ed.), *The Eden-Eisenhower Correspondence, 1955–1957* (2005), pp.161–2.

397 '... Israel would attack Egypt', HoC, 20 Dec 1956.

397 '... *vous ai compris*,' Judt, *Postwar*, p.287.

398 '... by academic historians,' Addison, *The Unexpected Hero*, p.240.

399 '... he has ever written,' Ibid.

399 '... utmost simplicity of soul,' Ibid.

399 '... this book be published,' Danchev and Todman (eds), *Lord Alanbrook's War Diaries*, p.xi.

399 '... to their own race', Richard Griffiths, *What Did You Do During The War? The Last Throes of the British Pro-Nazi Right, 1940–45* (2016), pp.35–6.

401 '... the Americans did it.' Gilbert, vol.VII, p.1220.

401 '... next for party axe?' *Private Eye*, 25 Oct 1981.

401 '... Dying Englishman', *Private Eye*, 8 Feb 1963.

402 '... whole tone of the war.' Ronald Bergan, *Beyond the Fringe ... and Beyond: A Critical Biography of Alan Bennett, Peter Cook, Jonathan Miller and Dudley Moore* (1989), p.38.

403 '... You slept too, didn't you!' Thomas Maier, *When Lions Roar*, ch.18.

403 '... missile gap', Senate speech, 14 Aug 1958.

404 '... fire jobs,' Thomas M. Coffey, *Iron Eagle: The Turbulent Life of General Curtis LeMay* (1986), p.111.

404 '... appeasement at Munich', Rose, *The Literary Churchill*, p.445.

404 '... every American move', Robin Renwick, *Fighting With Allies: America and Britain in Peace and War* (1996), p.260.

405 '... the Connecticut valley.' David S. McLellan and David C. Acheson (eds), *Among Friends: Personal Letters of Dean Acheson* (1980), p.238.

406 '... as its military power.' West Point speech, 5 Dec 1962.

406 '... stab in the back', Benjamin Grob-Fitzgibbon, *Continental Drift: Britain and Europe from the End of Empire to the Rise of Euroscepticism* (2016), p.298.

406 '... in dress than in judgement', Ibid.

406 '... to their attention.' Douglas Brinkley (ed.), *Dean Acheson and the Making of U.S. Foreign Policy* (1993), p.35.

406 '... Napoleon, the Kaiser and Hitler', Richard William Johnson, *The Politics of Recession* (1985), p.35.

406 '... found a role.' HoC, 20 Nov 1969.

406 '... in world affairs,' Douglas Brinkley, *Dean Acheson: The Cold War Years, 1953–71* (1992), p.178.

407 '... rich and powerful man.' Soames (ed.), *Speaking for Themselves*, p.604.

407 '*Vive la France!*' Jackson, *A Certain Idea of France*, p.586.

408 '... himself before them.' Ibid., pp.586–7.

408 '... a large part of my life.' WSC speech (read by Randolph S. Churchill), 9 April 1963.

409 '... had it so good', Bedford speech, 20 Jul 1957.

409 '... join Europe', broadcast, 20 Sep 1962.

410 '... interest to have us in.' Peter Hennessy, *Winds of Change: Britain in the Early Sixties* (2020).

410 '... habits and traditions.' press conference, 14 Jan 1963.

410 '... of the same spirit.' Earl of Avon, *The Eden Memoirs* vol.II (1965), p.250.

411 '... wasted years', Labour Manifesto 1964.

411 '... become prime minister in 1963', 'Too Obviously Cleverer', Ferdinand Mount, *London Review of Books*, 8 Sep 2011.

412 '... but we might have been better off.' Ibid.

Chapter 18, pages 415–38

415 '... soldiers and bands.' 'Great Britain: Requiem for Greatness', *Time*, 5 February 1965.

415 '... but labour and sorrow.' Psalm 90.

415 '... then a Great Man,' Roberts, *Walking with Destiny*, p.31.

416 '... at military display.' WSC, *Their Finest Hour*, p.568.

417 '... distinctions should be encouraged,' Ibid.

417 '... Churchill kept living.' Private information.

418 '... his old friend.' Brian Montgomery, *A Field Marshal in the Family* (2010), p.349.

420 '... it was a triumph.' Soames, *Clementine Churchill*, ch.29.

420 '... It seems impossible.' 24 January 1965, in Peter Catterall (ed.), *The Macmillan Diaries* vol.II.

420 '... the end of a nation.' Dominic Sandbrook, *White Heat: A History of Britain in the Swinging Sixties 1964–1970* (2007), p.xv.

420n '... really broke me up', Soames speaking on 'Churchill's Funeral' BBC TV 2015.

421 '... a glowworm.' Gilbert, vol.II, p.249.

421 '... not everyone else would.' Ramsden, *Man of the Century*, p.41.

421 '... Lloyd George's discreditable,' A.J.P. Taylor, *The New York Review of Books*, 3 Jun 1935.

421 '... without being straight', Ibid.

421 '... at any rate unusual', Ibid.

423 '... avoid clinical details.' *The Times*, 23 Apr 1966.

423 '... great historical figure', *The Times*, 25 Apr 1966.

423 '... to get it on paper,' Soames, *Clementine Churchill*, ch.30.

423 '... have the truth.' Moran, *Churchill: The Struggle for Survival*, p.15.

423 '... nor does my mother,' *The Times*, 26 Apr 1966.

423n '... European civilisation', *ODNB* s.v. George Macaulay Trevelyan.

424 '... with their physicians.' *The Times*, 26 Apr 1966.

424 '... he is a Victorian,' Moran, *Churchill: The Struggle for Survival* p.151.

424 '... every hour or two.' Amory (ed.), *The Letters of Evelyn Waugh*, p.191.

425 '... Isn't God a shit!' Philip Eade, *Evelyn Waugh: A Life Revisited* (2017), ch.9.

425 '... at luncheon parties.' Amory (ed.), *The Letters of Evelyn Waugh*, p.248.

425 '... The Press: Randolph v. The People', *Time*, 22 Oct 1956.

425 '... apt and opprobrious,' *Spectator*, 22 Mar 1957.

425 '... and the *People*'s.' Soames (ed.), *Speaking for Themselves*, p.613.

425n '... decent old buffers.', Amory (ed.), *The Letters of Evelyn Waugh*, p.320.

426 '... by my father in 1940.' Martin Gilbert, *In Search of Churchill* (1994), pp.36–7.

426 '... come in first.' *The Times*, 24 Oct 1966.

428 '... by the War Cabinet.' *The Times,* 2 Jan 1969.

429 '... honoured citizen', speech, 9 Apr 1966.

430 '... battalion of the Black Watch,' Martin Woollacott, *After Suez: Adrift in the American Century* (2006), p.109.

430 '... brings only greater threats.' Joseph M. Siracusa, 'The Munich Analogy', *Encyclopedia of American Foreign Policy* vol.2 (2002), p.452.

431 '... Czechoslovakia. Then Poland.' Mike Gravel, *The Pentagon Papers: The Defense Department History of United States Decisionmaking on Vietnam* vol.3, p.737.

431 '... indolence at Munich?' Siracusa, 'The Munich Analogy', *Encyclopedia of American Foreign Policy* vol.2, p.451.

431 '... Munichs win nothing.' Ibid.

431 '... the Munich conference,' Peter Beinart, *The Icarus Syndrome: A History of American Hubris* (2010), p.170.

433 '... the future of mankind', *New York Times*, 20 Apr 1964.

433 '... that is forever England', Rupert Brooke, 'The Soldier'.

433 '... finest hour,' Robert H. Pilpel, *Churchill in America, 1895–1961: An Affectionate Portrait* (1976), p.214.

433 '... rolling green hills', Wright, *The Iron Curtain*, p.52.

433 '... my statue will go,' *The Times*, 2 Nov 1973.

435 '... swept the world.' HoC, 16 Feb 1922.

436 '... so-called special relationship', Edward Heath, *Old World, New Horizons: Britain, the Common Market and the Atlantic Alliance* (1970), p.63.

437 '... large or petty.' Christopher Hitchens, *Blood, Class and Empire: The Enduring Anglo-American Relationship* (1990), p.183.

437 '... before Watergate.' Ibid.

438 '... the "special relationship" is dead', *The Times*, 12 Aug 1974.

438 '... let the family down.' *The Times*, 22 Dec 2007.

Chapter 19, pages 441–63

441 '... where Winston sat', John Campbell, *Margaret Thatcher* vol.2 (2008), p.183.

441 '... goodness and greatness.' Michael Howard, 'The End of Churchillism?', *Foreign Affairs*, Sep/Oct 1993.

441 '... down at Cambridge,' J.K. Stephens, 'Sincere Flattery of R.B'.

444 '... the world's confidence', Charles Moore, *Margaret Thatcher: The Authorized Biography* vol.1, p.53.

445 '... from Russian Communism.' John Campbell, *Margaret Thatcher* vol.1 (2000), p.55.

445 '... great as Churchill.' Piers Brendon, *Eminent Elizabethans: Murdoch, Thatcher, Jagger and Prince Charles* (2013), p.135.

446 '... shared public performances,' Aldous, *Reagan and Thatcher* (2012), p.15.

446 '... the great Winston', Thomas Dixon, *Weeping Britannia: Portrait of a Nation in Tears*.

446 '... problems are always with us.' Luxembourg speech, 18 Oct 1979.

447 '... Churchill and Roosevelt', Aldous, *Reagan and Thatcher*, p.1.

447 '... there's nothing there.' Dominic Sandbrook, *Who Dares Wins: Britain, 1979–1982* (2019), ch.18.

447 '... the world's strongest economy.' Inaugural Address, 20 Jan 1981.

448 '... days were numbered,' Roberts, *Walking with Destiny*, p.763.

448 '... shot without result.' *New York Times*, 1 Apr 1981.

448 '... with other nations.' State of the Union Address, 26 Jan 1982.

448 '... in all countries."' Memorial Day Speech, 31 May 1982.

449 '... in 1937 are here', Podhoretz, *Harper's*, Oct 1977.

449 '... compromise at Munich.' Ibid.

449 '... under any circumstances', Jeane J. Kirkpatrick, *Making War to Keep Peace: Trials and Errors in American Foreign Policy from Kuwait to Baghdad* (2009), p.29.

449 '... must never be liquidated.' Campbell, *Margaret Thatcher* vol.1, pp.53–4.

449 '... to run their course', Churchill, *History of the English-Speaking Peoples* vol.4, ch.19.

450 '... a good European', Nicholas Soames, *Independent*, 22 Jan 2015.

451 '... the relentless flow', *Independent*, 29 May 1993.

451 '... except perhaps Churchill', Campbell, *Margaret Thatcher* vol.2, p.139.

452 '... done so incompetently.' Aldous, *Reagan and Thatcher*, p.107.

452 '... quite unsuccessfully', Ibid., p.119.

452 '... damage Anglo-American relations.' Ibid., p.2.

452 '... we were not out,' Anthony Barnett, *Iron Britannia: Why Parliament Waged its Falklands War* (1982), p.48.

452 '... gigantic and leonine', Ramsden, *Man of the Century*, p.578.

453 '... Great Power.' Michael Blackwell, *Clinging to Grandeur: British Attitudes and Foreign Policy in the Aftermath of the Second World War* (1993), p.12.

453 '... Great *back* into Britain.' Cheltenham speech, 3 Jul 1982.

45 '... their military disasters', Michael Howard, *Captain Professor*.

453 '... old national delusions.' Max Hastings, panegyric at Sir Michael Howard's memorial service, 25 Feb 2020.

453 '... thrives on adversity,' Eric J. Evans, *Thatcher and Thatcherism* (2013), p.99.

453 'backbone', Hugo Young, *One of Us: A Biography of Margaret Thatcher* (1989), p.396.

454 '... than Winston Churchill.' Joint Houses of Congress speech, 20 Feb 1985.

454 '... across the United States,' Howard, *Foreign Affairs*, Sep/Oct 1993.

454 '... keeps on rolling along.' HoC, 20 Aug 1940.

454 '... traditional values', Hitchens, *Blood, Class and Empire*, ch.7.

455 '... ebb and flow of national politics.' *New York Times*, 25 Apr 1981.

455 '... who comes to mind.' speech, 5 Nov 1987.

455 '... Dunkirk and the Blitz', Hitchens, *Blood, Class and Empire*, ch.7.

455 '... might of the enemy.' Harrow speech, 29 October 1941; Rhodes James (ed.), *Churchill Speaks*, p.772.

456 '... is to hate him,' *New York Times,* 24 November 1974.

456 '... use your facilities?' Melvyn Bragg, *Rich: The Life of Richard Burton*.

457 '... no consequence whatsoever?' Moore, *Margaret Thatcher* vol.2, ch.5.

458 '... I'm a chemist', Young, *One of Us*, p.17.

458n '... practise to deceive,' Walter Scott, *Marmion: A Tale of Flodden Field*, Canto VI, verse XVII.

459 '... in some other area!' Moore, *Margaret Thatcher* vol.2, p.709.

459 '... tear down this wall!' West Berlin speech, 12 Jun 1987.

460 '... We can do business.' BBC broadcast, 17 Dec 1984.

460 '... I can do business,' Rose, *The Literary Churchill*, p.261.

460 '... lifelong and unwavering', Andrew Roberts, 'The Genius of Thatcherism Will Endure', *Wall Street Journal*, 8 Apr 2013.

460 '... terrible suffering', Azriel Bermant, *Margaret Thatcher and the Middle East* (2016), p.82.

461 '... to mention the two sergeants', Ibid.

461 '... the vilest gangsters', Gilbert, vol.VIII, p.430.

461 '... Arafat in his Bunker!' Ze'ev Schiff and Ehud Ya'ari, *Israel's Lebanon War* (1985), p.39.

461 '... Churchill leave London?' *New York Times*, 2 Jul 1982.

462 '... no time to go wobbly', Bermant, *Margaret Thatcher and the Middle East*.

462 '... marched right in', speech, 7 Mar 1991.

462 '... president for this crisis.' Christopher Hitchens, 'Churchillian Delusions', *For the Sake of Argument: Essays and Minority Reports*.

Chapter 20, pages 465–88

465 '... Churchill wept.' White House dinner speech, 5 Feb 1998.

466 '... devastated Europe in 1945', Charles Moore, *The Telegraph*, 1 Jun 2009.

466 '... almost worthless', Max Hastings, *The Sunday Times*, 8 Dec 2013.

467 '... sold his soul', David Cannadine, *History in Our Time* (1998), pp.225–7.

467 '... Germans and others', Maurice Cowling, 'The Case Against Going to War', *Finest Hour* (1991), p.70,

467 '... in a Labour victory.' Thomas E. Ricks, *Churchill and Orwell: The Fight for Freedom* (2017), p.209.

468 '... of the empire overseas', Alan Clark, *The Times*, 2 Jan 1993.

468 '... moved to Singapore', Ibid.

468 '... than did Hitler', John Lukacs, *Washington Post*, 22 Aug 1993.

468 '... of our Island life', Gilbert, vol.VI, p.836.

469 '... a senile Victorian.' Gilbert, 'The Rounded Picture', *Finest Hour* (1989), p.65.

469 '... Lovely grub!' Robert Harris, *Sunday Times*, 19 Jun 1994.

469 '... a metal foldback clip', Ibid.

469n '... grateful to my friend Erich Segal for these facts.' Ibid.

470 '... doesn't even drink very much.' Ibid.

472 '... didn't get drafted', Maureen Dowd, *New York Times*, 9 June 1994.

472 '... America in the military.' James Fallows, *The Atlantic*, April 1993.

473 '... the road to perdition,' Jeff Randall, on 'The Reunion', BBC Radio 4, 16 Aug 2020.

475 '... much higher figures', *Independent*, 26 Apr 1995.

475 '... to the nation', Ibid.

475 '... given for free.' Ibid.

475 '... by so many to so few,' *Daily Mirror*, 30 Apr 1995.

476 '... five years to victory.' *Daily Telegraph*, 7 May 2015.

476 '... friendly feelings', Ibid.

477 '... upon our shoulders.' Belfast, 7 Apr 1998.

477 '... of Neville Chamberlain', David Reynolds, *Summits: Six Meetings That Shaped The Twentieth Century* (2010), p.236.

477 '... creative genius.' Tony Blair, *A Journey* (2011), p.59.

477 '... long into the night', Ibid., p.61.

478 '... his virtuous behaviour,' Jason Epstein, *The New York Review of Books*, 21 Apr 1994.

478 '... is another matter.' Blair, *A Journey*, p.61.

478 '... found its soul', Gilbert, vol.VI, p.1043.

479 '... stop him later.' Speech, 22 April 1999.

479 '... to the Iraq debacle', Philippe Sands, *New York Review of Books*, 30 Sep 2010.

479 '... of the free world', Paul Berman, PBS *Frontline* interview, 22 Mar 2003.

479 '... magnetic resonance.' Timothy Garton Ash, *Guardian*, 16 Sep 2004.

479 '... to Adolf Hitler earlier?' speech, 24 Mar 2000.

479 '... twenty-first century begin,' Tony Judt, *New Republic*, 24 Sep 2001.

481 '... Rudy Was Churchill?' *New York Observer*, 24 Sep 2001.

481 '... were bound to win.' Tim Pooley, *Time*, 31 Dec 2001.

481 '... that very moment.' Rudy Giuliani, *Forbes*, 9 Sep 2011.

481 '... in a baseball cap', Celia Sandys, 19 Sep 2007.

481 '... a Giuliani-esque leader,' Ramsden, *Man of the Century*, p.586.

482 '... had to fake it.' *Irish Examiner*, 13 Feb 2002.

482 '... as it was then.' Blair, *A Journey*, p.346.

482 '... the American people.' *Washington Post*, 21 Sep 2001.

482 '... visionary', Blair, *A Journey*, p.367.

483 '... back to Iraq.' *Guardian*, 4 Apr 2004.

483 '... world around us.' Labour Party conference speech, 2 Oct 2001.

483 '... Blair's Finest Hour', *Daily Telegraph*, 3 Oct 2001.

483 '... authoritative', Harold Evans, *New York Times*, 11 Nov 2001.

484 '... It's Mama.' Private information.

484 '... I am Churchill.' David Owen, *In Sickness and in Power: Illness in Heads of Government During the Last 100 Years* (2008), p.276.

484 '... serious and current', Blair foreword, *Iraq's Weapons of Mass Destruction: The Assessment of the British Government Position*, Sep 2002.

485 '... what to do.' HoC, 18 Mar 2003.

485 '... of the English-speaking world.' WSC, *War Speeches* vol.2 (1951), p.69.

485 '... an inescapable presence.' Edward Rothstein, *New York Times*, 29 Mar 2003.

485 '... the modern Middle East,' Winston S. Churchill, *Wall Street Journal*, 10 Mar 2003.

485 '... is at America's side.' *Daily Mail*, 1 Mar 2003.

485 '... Roosevelt and Churchill.' Sir Martin Gilbert obituary, *The Times*, 4 Feb 2015.

485 '... by grandstanding,' Chris Mullin, *A View From The Foothills: The Diaries of Chris Mullin* (2010), p.265.

486 '... as a result.' Andrew Marr, 'Buoyant mood in Downing Street', BBC, 9 Apr 2003.

486 '... Ambassador to the World', *Wall Street Journal*, 4 Jan 2002.

487 '... kind of late, but sorry.' speech to Congress, 17 Jul 2003.

488 '... choice is very hard.' Judt, *London Review of Books*, 25 Mar 2010.

488 '... his English poodle', Dowd, *New York Times*, 9 Dec 2006.

Chapter 21, pages 491–509

491n '... our schools, our churches,' Strom Thurmond obituary, *New York Times*, 27 Jun 2003.

492 '... is short for "Jewish"' David Brooks, *New York Times*, 6 Jan 2004.

493 '... an enemy by essence', David Remnick, *New Yorker*, 25 May 1998.

493 '... to understand the father.' Ibid.

493 '... in three to five years', Jonathan Freedland, *New York Review of Books*, 4 Mar 2015.

493 '... to your own nation.' Netanyahu in *The Economist*, 30 Mar 2019.

493 '... America is America.' Ari Shavit, *New York Times*, 8 May 2018.

493 '... get rid of Rabin,' Roger Cohen, *New York Times*, 4 Dec 2019.

493 '... again under assault.' Gertrude Himmelfarb, *New Republic*, 26 Nov 2001.

494 '... touring the United States.' Lady Bird Johnson, *A White House Diary* (2007), p.327.

494 '... Soviet communism.' Michael Lind, *Spectator*, 24 Apr 2001.

494 '... Can Save Us – Again', Ibid.

494 '... the first neocon.' Jacob Heilbrunn, *New York Times*, 27 Feb 2005.

495 '... can learn, at any time.' Leo Strauss, *Washington Examiner*, 3 Jan 2003.

495 '... riling isolationist opinion', Lind, *Spectator*, 24 April 2001.

496 '... empire in denial', Niall Ferguson, *Guardian*, 2 Jun 2003.

496 '... pith helmets.' Max Boot, *Weekly Standard*, 15 Oct 2001.

496 '... stand on principle', Heilbrunn, *New York Times*, 27 Feb 2005.

496 '... a "closing net of doom."' speech, 4 Feb 2004.

497 '... the right of force."' Dana Milbank, *Washington Post*, 30 Oct 2001.

497 '... came under attack.' Christopher Hitchens, *Love, Poverty and War: Journeys and Essays* (2004), p.7.

497 '... a bodyguard of lies.' Ibid.

498 '... extremely right-wing', Johann Hari, *The New Republic*, 23 Apr 2007.

499 '... worthiness as an ally', Kemper Lecture, 26 Mar 2000.

499 '... paralysed by gentility', Michael E. Kinsley, *Curse of the Giant Muffins And Other Washington Maladies* (1987), p.224.

500 '... noble anti-fascist tradition.' Christopher Hitchens, *Slate*, 27 Feb 2007.

500 '... and wished they had been', Ian Parker, *New Yorker*, 9 Oct 2006.

501 '... clarity and action.' Charles Moore, *Spectator*, 2 Mar 2002.

501 '... against Islamic fundamentalist terrorism,' Roberts, *A History of the English-Speaking Peoples Since 1900*, inside front dust cover.

502 '... Robert and Mathilde Agostinelli', Andrew Roberts, *The Spectator*, 24 Mar 2007.

503 '... he just doesn't get it!' Andrew Rawnsley, *The End of the Party: The Rise and Fall of New Labour*, ch.8.

503 '... before the invasion of Iraq.' Lionel Barber, *Financial Times*, 29 Jun 2012.

504 '... never have emerged', Grob-Fitzgibbon, *Continental Drift*, p.164.

504 '... unconstrained than before.' Stephen Fidler, *Financial Times*, 20 Aug 2007.

504 '... a defeat.' Peter Mansoor on BBC Radio 4, 29 Sep 2010.

504 '... who needed help?' Nicholson Baker, *Human Smoke: The Beginnings of World War II, the End of Civilization* (2009), p.473.

504 '... in their own homelands and cities.' Ibid., p.358.

505 '... the war they had invited', Patrick Buchanan, *Churchill, Hitler and the Unnecessary War: How Britain Lost Its Empire and the West Lost the World* (2008).

505 '... for 200 years.' *Spectator*, 30 Sep 2006.

505 '... dislike of the British empire', *Independent*, 22 Apr 2016.

506 '... peace in our time.' Julian Borger, *Guardian*, 9 Sep 2008.

506 '... invasion of Czechoslovakia', Robert Kagan, *Washington Post*, 11 Aug 2008.

506 '... *un nouveau Munich*?' *Le Monde*, 22 Sep 2009.

506 '... have been avoided.' BBC News, 15 May 2008.

507 '... junior partners in 1940', *Guardian*, 5 Aug 2010.

508 '... We are not Brits in India!' *Daily Telegraph*, 26 Feb 2011.

508 '... Netanyahu, The Churchill Of Our Time', Steve Forbes, *Forbes*, 28 Jan 2015.

Epilogue, pages 511–35

511 '... has been renamed,' George Orwell, *1984* (1961) p.128.

511 '... an exalted character,' WSC, *History of the English-Speaking Peoples* vol.IV, ch.10.

511 '... ideals of the American people,' WSC, *The World Crisis* vol.IV, ch.7.

511 '... have yet to run their course,' WSC, *History of the English-Speaking Peoples* vol.IV, ch.19.

512 '... will *never* be torn down', *Daily Mail*, 13 Jun 2020.

513 '... stood by their Winnie.' Paul Reid, *The Last Lion* vol.III, ch.2.

515 '... David his ten thousands.' 1 Samuel 29:5.

515 '... been such a fervent defender', Boris Johnson, *The Sun*, 22 Apr 2016.

516 '... Winston Churchill will do so.' *New York Times*, 2 Aug 2012.

516 '... the United States ever had.' *Daily Telegraph*, 30 Oct 2013.

517 '... the neo-imperialist gang.' *Guardian*, 18 Jun 2012.

517 '... surely have approved.' Niall Ferguson, *Newsweek*, 3 Dec 2012.

517 '... the magpie society,' Roberts, *Eminent Churchillians*, p.225.

518 '... a delightful book', A.J.P. Taylor, *New York Review of Books*, 3 June 1965.

518 '... intimate and cliquey', Soames, *A Daughter's Tale*, p.132.

519 '... at a golf club bar', Boris Johnson, *The Churchill Factor: How One Man Made History* (2014), p.150.

519 '... the unpasteurised Churchill', Ibid., p.337.

519 '... ocean-going creep', Ibid., p.110.

519 '... carrot-topped Irish fantasist', Ibid., p.33.

519 '... the beanpole-shaped appeaser', Ibid., p.247.

519 '... wonky ... bonkers ... tootling', Ibid., p.38, p.58, p.11.

519 '... the issues at stake', WSC, *Their Finest Hour*, p.231.

520 '... self-aggrandising pot-boiler', Niall Ferguson, *Sunday Times*, 24 Apr 2016.

521 '... European Economic Community.' Richard M. Langworth, *Winston Churchill, Myth and Reality: What He Actually Did and Said* (2017), p.189.

522 '... continent to its fate.' *The Times*, 16 Jun 2016.

522 '... to discover it to be a myth.' *The Times*, 26 Apr 2016.

522 '... My finest hour of the campaign', David Cameron, *For the Record*.

522 '... become Conservative leader.' Dominic Lawson, *Sunday Times*, 3 Nov 2019.

523 '... you should let me know.' *Independent*, 17 Nov 2016.

523 '... something of a joke', Jeremy Shapiro, *The Times*, 11 Oct 2017.

524 '... titanic thespian aspirations', A.A. Gill, *Sunday Times*, 6 Mar 2016.

524 '... rendition of the old sot', A.A. Gill, *Sunday Times*, 6 Nov 2016.

525 '... to go the other,' Charles Moore, *Spectator*, 3 Feb 2018.

525 '... literary purgatory', Richard Toye, *TLS*, 2 Nov 2018.

525 '... Churchill yet written', Richard Aldous, *New York Times,* 13 Nov 2018.

526 '... provocative humour', Roberts, *Walking with Destiny* p.787.

526 '... physical and moral courage.' Andrew Roberts, *Spectator*, 9 Mar 2019.

526 '... has outlived its usefulness', *Financial Times*, 24 Oct 2019.

526 '... figure he is,' Tim Stanley, *Daily Telegraph*, 20 Oct 2019.

526 '... Dear Boris, Hallelujah!' Andrew Roberts, *Daily Telegraph*, 13 Dec 2019.

526 '... Henry V after Agincourt', Taki, *Spectator*, 8 Feb 2020.

527 '... prime ministership of *Boris Johnson*,' private information.

528 '... to show strength.' *Guardian*, 7 Jan 2021.

528 '... trial by combat', Ibid.

529 '... the psyche of activist civilians', Andrew Roberts, *Daily Telegraph*, 9 Jan 2021.

529 '... physical and emotional clone', *The Hill*, 13 Dec 2019.

529 '... BBC? I'm Irish,' *Foreign Policy*, 19 Nov 2020.

530 '... staunch critic of the British Empire', *Daily Mail*, 11 Feb 2011.

530 '... in all our universities.' Ibid.

532 '... real risk', *Daily Telegraph*, 5 Sep 2016.

532 '... battle of Blenheim', Eleventh Duke of Marlborough obituary, *Daily Telegraph*, 16 Oct 2014.

533 '... and not a melodrama.' I.F. Stone in D.D. Guttenplan, *American Radical: The Life and Times of I.F. Stone* (2012), p.476.

535 '... Neville Chamberlain's tomb?' HoC, 12 Nov 1940.

Picture Credits

Integrated illustrations

Prologue
Drawing by Julie Pannett, © National Portrait Gallery, London

Chapter 1
'Can't ye stand like men!' *Saturday Herald*, 18 November 1899

Chapter 2
Book cover *of My African Journey*, 1908

Chapter 3
'English Variety – What will emerge from Churchill's dance of the seven veils? The naked egotist', front page of the German satirial magazine *Ulk*, 28 November 1913

Chapter 4
'Winston's Bag' by David Low, *The Star*, 21 January 1920, © D·d Low/dmg media licensing

Chapter 5
'Our own Mussolini', *Weekly Westminster*, 16 March 1924

Chapter 6
'Nazi movement – local version' by Will Dyson, *Daily Herald*, ·· 1933, © Mirrorpix/Reach Licensing

Chapter 7
'The wood-carvings of M'Bongo M'Bongo: A Streuth··ophet· of Doom?'

Chapter 8
'Calling Mr. Churchill' by Sidney George Strube, *Daily Express*, 6 July 1939, © Mirrorpix/Reach Licensing

Chapter 9
'All behind you, Winston' by David Low, *Evening Standard*, 14 May 1940, © David Low/dmg media licensing

Chapter 10
Japanese photo-montage

Chapter 11
'Westfront Hurricane, Mr. Churchill last night: "We are ready to face it"' by Leslie Gilbert Illingworth, *Daily Mail*, 20 May 1940, © Leslie Gilbert Illingworth/dmg media licensing

Chapter 12
'Himmel! It's That Man Again' by Bert Thomas, *Evening News*, 13 November 1939, © Bert Thomas/dmg media licensing

Chapter 13
Drawing by Oscar Nemon, © the Estate of Oscar Nemon

Chapter 14
'Two Churchills' by David Low, *Evening Standard*, 31 July 1945, © David Low/dmg media licensing

Chapter 15
'Ilton's Finest Hour', American cartoon

Chapter 16
'...man goeth forth unto his work ...', cartoon in *Punch*, © Punch Cartoon Library/TopFoto

Chapter 17
... by Graham Sutherland, © National Portrait Gallery, London

Chapter 18
'... his time plays many parts' by George Strube, *Daily Express*, ... 1953, © Mirrorpix/Reach Licensing

Chapter 19
Cartoon by John Minnion on book jacket of *Iron Britannia* by Anthony Barnett, Allison and Busby, 1982

Chapter 20
Cartoon by Ben Heine, © Ben Heine

Chapter 21
Cartoon by Steve Bell, *Guardian*, 29 October 2006, © Steve Bell

Epilogue
'Go to it' by Sidney George Strube, *Daily Express*, 8 June 1940, © Sidney George Strube/dmg licensing

Plate section

The images in the plate section are © the following organisations and individuals: 1: Time Life Pictures/New York Times Paris Bureau Collection/National Archives/The LIFE Picture Collection via Getty Images • 2: Bettmann via Getty Images • 3: Library of Congress/Corbis/VCG via Getty Images • 4: Granger Historical Picture Archive/Alamy Stock Photo • 5: Fremantle/Alamy Stock Photo • 6: Alex Segre via Getty Images • 7: Prisma Bildagentur/Universal Images Group via Getty Images • 8: Andre Jenny/Alamy Stock Photo • 9: courtesy of Sotheby's • 10: Tolga Akmen/AFP via Getty Images • 11: public domain (sourced via Reagan Presidential Library) • 12: Tim Sloan/Staff via Getty Images • 13: Stephen Simpson/Shutterstock • 14: Bettmann via Getty Images • 15: Allstar Picture Library Ltd/Alamy Stock Photo • 16: Keystone/Stringer via Getty Images • 17: Landmark Media/Alamy Stock Photo • 18 and 19: PA Images/Alamy Stock Photo • 20: Chris Jackson/Staff via Getty Images • 21: MacConnal-Mason Gallery, London • 22: Solo Syndicate • 23: Isabel Infantes/AFP via Getty Images • 24: The Times/News Licensing • 25: Ingram Pinn/Financial Times.

Every effort has been made to trace and contact copyright holders. The publishers will be pleased to correct any mistakes or omissions in future editions.

Index